SMJ

Federal hook/ingredient = 1331 P 326

Diversity 1332

Only named parties need to be diverse - not unnamed

Complete diversity, - $75k<

∴ Class claims cannot be aggregated to meet 75k

Supplemental 1367   1. Do yo have JDX 2. Does 1367b take away

- OG JDX founded solely on diversity, under 1332

- Is it a claim <u>by π</u> against someone made party by Rule 14, 9, 20, or 24? <u>or</u> is it a claim by a person to be joined as a π under rule 19, or intervene as π under rule 24?

- Would supp JDX be inconsistent w requirements of 1332

3. Should the court exercise discretion to determine under 1367(c) - Court's discretion

---

CAFA P 335 / 1332d
336

Only putative class action

Minimal diversity (looks at whole class - Not just Reps)

Aggregate claims to $5m

Removal - P 337

To remand to st court - 339

Narrow exception intended, π has burden of proof

Carolina Academic Press Context and Practice Series

Michael Hunter Schwartz
Series Editor

Administrative Law
Richard Henry Seamon

Advanced Torts
Alex B. Long and Meredith J. Duncan

Antitrust Law
Steven Semeraro

Civil Procedure
Gerald F. Hess, Theresa M. Beiner, and Scott R. Bauries

Civil Procedure for All States
Benjamin V. Madison, III

Complex Litigation
James M. Underwood

Constitutional Law
David Schwartz and Lori Ringhand

A Context and Practice Global Case File:
An Intersex Athlete's Constitutional Challenge,
Hastings v. USATF, IAAF, and IOC
Olivia M. Farrar

A Context and Practice Global Case File:
Thorpe v. Lightfoot, **A Mother's International Hague Petition**
for the Return of Her Child
Olivia M. Farrar

Contracts
Second Edition
Michael Hunter Schwartz and Adrian Walters

Criminal Law
Steven I. Friedland, Catherine Carpenter,
Kami Chavis, and Catherine Arcabascio

Current Issues in Constitutional Litigation
SECOND EDITION
Sarah E. Ricks, with co-author Evelyn M. Tenenbaum

Employment Discrimination
SECOND EDITION
Susan Grover, Sandra F. Sperino, and Jarod S. Gonzalez

Energy Law
Joshua P. Fershee

Evidence
Pavel Wonsowicz

International Business Transactions
Amy Deen Westbrook

International Women's Rights, Equality, and Justice
Christine M. Venter

The Lawyer's Practice
Kris Franklin

Professional Responsibility
Barbara Glesner Fines

Sales
SECOND EDITION
Edith R. Warkentine

Secured Transactions
Edith R. Warkentine and Jerome A. Grossman

Torts
Paula J. Manning

Workers' Compensation Law
SECOND EDITION
Michael C. Duff

Your Brain and Law School
Marybeth Herald

Print ISBN 978-1-61163-901-8
Ebook ISBN 978-1-61163-967-4
LCCN 2016954510

Carolina Academic Press, LLC
700 Kent Street
Durham, North Carolina 27701
Telephone (919) 489-7486
Fax (919) 493-5668
www.cap-press.com

Printed in the United States of America

Contents

of the criminal filings over the same time frame. In 1962, 11.5% of federal civil cases were disposed of by trial. By 2002, that figure had plummeted to 1.8%."

Patricia Lee Refo, Chair Section of Litigation for the American Bar Association, *The Vanishing Trial*, 30 Litigation 2 (Winter 2004).

Finally, the Federal Rules of Civil Procedure have changed drastically during the 20th century, not only with the formal rules changes in 1938 (that liberalized joinder rules) and the class action rules in 1966 (that breathed new life into a somewhat dormant area) but also to courts' attitudes toward more liberalized discovery as well as more aggressive screening of cases through both motions for summary judgment and motions to dismiss for failure to state a cause of action. Lawsuits can be much more expensive to handle now and the juries are arguably less important with more and more cases being resolved by settlement or motion during the pretrial stages. So the identity of the judge becomes arguably more important than ever. This phenomenon (or at least a perception of reality) impacts lawyers' ideas about settlement leverage and, hence, impacts the importance of the choice of forum for the handling of the lawsuit. Lawyers have greater incentive than ever to have a strategic say in who will preside over their lawsuits.

2. Why Study Complex Litigation?

One reason to study complex litigation is because you might be a nerd, and nerds love procedure courses in law school. This is after all, a subject that comes with a book of rules written out in black and white (see Appendix I). But there are much grander reasons to study this subject. The cultural and legal changes that have been witnessed in the United States during the last 75 years, as mentioned in the preceding section, and which continue today, have made the study of complex litigation more important than ever. These changes result in the greater likelihood of both multi-party cases and of multiple related cases being filed involving some or all of the same parties. Good advocates are lawyers who know about the procedural rules available to them, understand how they can play a role in enhancing their clients' chances of gaining litigation leverage, and are accustomed to thinking strategically about invoking those tools. While there are a great many conceptual and philosophical facets to the study of complex litigation, it is ultimately useful as a course designed to enhance your ability to "win" cases for your clients at the pretrial stages.

Principles

"How you handle the pretrial phase of your practice of law will likely dictate how you live your life. If you do not manage the pretrial process, it will manage you. An inability to properly focus on the task at hand limits the ability of an attorney to effectively represent their client, thus creating a maelstrom of activity that does not move the litigation forward. Will you constantly be in a reactive mode bouncing from one situation to the next? Will you be in a disorganized and frenzied state of worry? Will you procrastinate from indecision and suffer from the stress of potentially missing deadlines? Or will you act with the confidence of someone who knows how to prepare a case and actually follow through on that knowledge … taking charge of your case? Practicing law is a demanding profession and being an advocate is the most stressful form of law practice."

Charles Rose & James Underwood, *Fundamental Pretrial Advocacy: A Strategic Guide to Effective Litigation* 6–7 (West 2d ed. 2012).

Familiarity with concepts or tools breeds confidence in their use. Because complex litigation often involves "high stakes" or "bet the company" litigation, mastering the tools of complex litigation allows an advocate to think creatively, take the offensive, and be the true master of the litigation rather than be paralyzed with indecision and fear and merely react to your opponent's moves. Study of the subjects covered in this text—ultimately, along with years of practice implementing these lessons—will help to transform you into a highly effective and sought after advocate. But the process must begin somewhere and a course in complex litigation is designed to help you undertake that journey. Let's begin with a true to life scenario that will help to introduce issues we will uncover in this course. Read the following and keep it in mind as we proceed.

B. Chapter 1 Problem

Internal Memorandum

To: Associate
From: Jim Underwood, Sr. Partner
RE: Lawsuit against insured

Our client, is Mary McFarland (she is insured by our firm's long-time client Southeastern Mutual). She has just been sued and served with the papers. We need to file a timely answer and think about how we want to handle the claims.

She was driving her Chevy Lumina automobile when another driver, Bill Johnson, pulled out of another lane and into her path. Mr. Johnson was driving a Ford Fusion and we have no idea why he did what he did. Mary immediately (and reasonably) attempted to slam on her brakes. The brakes seemed to fail and the two cars ended up colliding, causing massive damage to each vehicle and sending both drivers to the hospital.

Bill, who lives in the adjoining state, has just filed his lawsuit for property damages and personal injuries in state court. (At a minimum we need to consider a possible removal immediately.) Mary obviously needs to consider a possible counterclaim to pursue her own damage claims although she would prefer, obviously, to just bring her own claims in a local court closer to home. Is there any way we can just file her damage claims in a separate case? I am also trying to figure out what to do about the failure of the brakes on her car. Her mechanic looked at the brakes after the accident and said it appears there was a sudden loss of hydraulic pressure in the brakes from a line that was prematurely corroded. Her car is only two years old and should not have had this problem. The mechanic wonders if the manufacturer chose a cheaper material to save money. Anyway, do we file a separate lawsuit against the car maker or should they be brought into the lawsuit with Bill? I'm not sure of our options—it's been a long time since I studied the applicable rules. If we do sue the manufacturer, will Bill be able to add them as co-defendant on his claim against our client Mary?

I've also done some preliminary internet research and have come up with a number of hits involving others claiming their same car also suffered sudden brake failure during an accident. We need to see if anyone has already sued them and, if so, have the cases gone to trial? If so, who won? Further, and thinking real big, does Mary have a possible class action to bring against the manufacturer on behalf of all other owners of this vehicle? Or at least, all others who have been in accidents involving failed brakes? If not a class action, should we consider finding other victims to add as co-parties when we sue the car maker?

The more I sit here dictating this memo the more potential questions I have. But no answers. That's where you need to come in. Think about these matters and come see me first thing tomorrow morning.

And, in general, please do the necessary on this file. Thank you.

C. This Book's Approach to Complex Litigation

1. The Trinity of Complex Litigation Themes

As you work through the materials in this text, three course themes will become obvious. These themes or principles are involved in nearly every issue, doctrine, rule and statute we will explore. The themes are (1) litigant autonomy, (2) system efficiency, and (3) fairness to the parties. In some contexts, all of the themes may push in a common direction and compel a fairly obvious result. More often, however, the themes will be in some tension perhaps with two of the three urging one result or rule and the other theme pushing in the opposite direction. Many of the doctrines and rules in this text can be rationalized by reference to the state of tension among these three principles. A good many others have reached similar conclusions in their study of this field. Consider the following general observations from a noted scholar in the field:

> Aggregation of cases promises savings by eliminating duplication and providing *economies* of scale. Critics of case aggregation, however, argue that the savings are not nearly so clear.
>
> ...
>
> A principal reason often cited for opposing aggregation of claims is individual *litigant autonomy*. This value encompasses both the right of the plaintiff to select the time and forum for asserting his claim and right of all parties to control the strategies for individually developing their cases.
>
> ...

In evaluating case aggregation, perhaps the most compelling concern is whether the lack of individuation so affects the quality of decisionmaking that it denies *fairness* and due process.

Edward F. Sherman, *Aggregate Disposition of Related Cases: The Policy Issues*, 10 Rev. of Litigation 231 (1991). Another scholar has offered a similar thought about the study of complex litigation and the tension and need for balancing among these three priorities:

Managing complex mass tort litigation fairly and efficiently poses a number of intractable procedural problems. The root cause of these problems is the inescapable tension between the interest of individual litigants in preserving *individual control* of claims and *procedural fairness*, on the one hand, and the interest of the judicial system in the *efficient* joinder of related claims, on the other. This tension forces courts to choose among a variety of joinder techniques for balancing these basic interests. The choice is important because our justice system relies almost exclusively on private litigation to compensate mass tort victims.

Roger H. Trangsrud, *Joinder Alternatives in Mass Tort Litigation*, 70 Cornell L. Rev. 779 (1985).

These three course themes will weave throughout this text so there is no need to belabor the point for now. Just keep these in mind as you move forward in your reading. Like Waldo, they are lurking everywhere and give you a nice analytical framework to think about some of the policy issues behind the various rules and doctrines.

2. Substantive Coverage

After this chapter overview, the remainder of this book is broken down into five remaining sections. Our substantive coverage will begin with an exploration of the rules and concepts surrounding Joinder of Claims & Parties in Chapter 2. We will explore the purposes behind the issue and claim preclusion rules of collateral estoppel and res judicata. We will see how they prevent the relitigation of issues and claims and, thus, discourage the splitting up of causes of action into multiple actions and avoid re-examination of the same issue once resolved in a prior case when doing so is deemed fair and basic due process has been assured. We will consider the related Rule 13(a) which defines *compulsory counterclaims* and, in effect, tells a defendant that they are required to assert in a forum they did not choose a claim simply *because it is so related to the plaintiff's claim against them. This rule governs the joinder of claims*—at times compelling the joinder and for unrelated claims merely permitting them to be asserted in the same case. We will then move to the joinder of additional parties—the move beyond the one-on-one scenario. Rule 20 is one of the most utilized procedural rules governing the joinder of parties, permitting but not requiring plaintiffs to join additional co-plaintiffs or to sue multiple defendants in the same case so long as a two-part test is met which assures the joinder is both fair and efficient. In rare instances Rule 19 labels an absent party *necessary* and compels their joinder by the plaintiff whether plaintiff desires their presence or not. We will explore Rule 14 *impleader* that with respect to liability-shifting scenarios that permit a defending party to invite someone else into plaintiff's litigation party. And, finally, we will explore Rule 24 that allows in some instances an outsider to *intervene* in the parties' litigation without invitation. As we explore these joinder concepts, we will practice gaining a strategic understand of these joinder devices and find illustrations of the tension in our three course themes of autonomy, efficiency, and fairness.

In Chapter 3 Forum Battles we will engage in an exploration of rules governing battles between litigants as to the court that will be permitted to adjudicate their dispute. Sometimes there are literally races to the courthouses when the dark clouds of controversy enter into potential litigants' horizons, each one trying to choose a court deemed more convenient or otherwise advantageous for their selfish litigation interests. We will encounter the widely (though not universally) employed *first-to-file* rule but consider the significant exceptions to that rule. Often in these races to the courthouse, we will see courts generally desiring to avoid the inefficiency of redundant lawsuits both moving forward by giving priority to a case based upon the seemingly arbitrary rule premised solely on the timing of the suits' filing but with exceptions premised upon notions of fairness. We will explore these races from multiple perspectives and involving different scenarios. We will also begin to see how important lawyers believe the forum battle is to their attempts to maximize leverage in the lawsuit. We will also consider instances where there may not be a race to the courthouse but the defending party, using either *forum non conveniens* or *§ 1404*, asks the original forum to dismiss or transfer the case to a place that makes more sense—in terms of fairness or efficiency—and thereby trumps the normal presumption favoring the plaintiff's autonomy of picking its own chosen forum. In complex litigation, a major tool used to impact the forum for *pretrial* proceedings is the increasingly important *Multi-District Litigation* statute—§ 1407—that allows a panel of judges to transfer potentially thousands of pending federal cases to one court for all pretrial matters. Another potential tool to prevent a multiplicity of redundant lawsuits—a court injunction stopping another case in its tracks—is limited due to reasons of federalism by the *Anti-Injunction Act* that generally forbids federal courts from enjoining parallel state court proceedings. We will explore the three exceptions to this prohibition. Our final stop on our study of forum battles will focus on the vertical forum choice of a state versus a federal forum by considering the important doctrine of *fraudulent joinder* that allows a federal court to accept diversity removals despite the apparent lack of complete diversity. This chapter will be of paramount interest to future litigators that appreciate how the choice of forum might be the most important decision for litigants in the life of their case.

The second half of the course focuses upon class action practice—the ultimate joinder rule that permits a litigant to try the claims of absent parties and to bind them to the results. Chapter 4 Class Actions: Certification will introduce the prerequisites to class certification. We will begin with Rule 23(a) prerequisites for any possible class action—its hurdles that all who file a putative class action need to transverse before a court can even consider certification. These include the requirement of a well-defined class of which the plaintiff is a party, and the explicit requirements of Rule 23(a) for *numerosity, commonality, typicality*, and *adequacy of representation*—features that must be present in any class action to assure that representative litigation (hardly the norm for a traditional lawsuit) is both fair and efficient. These concepts of fairness and efficiency are critical because representative litigation seriously undermined the normal autonomy of one possessing a claim to decide whether to pursue the claim or not and to be the master of their own lawsuit. We will then transition into Rule 23(b) that sets fourth four categories of permissible class actions. These four categories include some that are mandatory class actions (where notice to class members need not be given and the class member is stuck in the case whether they want their claims adjudicated or not) and permissive class actions where class member are owed notice as well as an opportunity to opt-out of the case. We will see how the 1966 changes to Rule 23 ushered in a golden era of class actions. We will then consider whether that golden era has passed and how the current interpretation of the certification rules impact current practices.

Chapter 5 Managing Class Action touches on a variety of other important class action topics. These issues include variations on the normal civil procedure doctrines such as personal and subject matter jurisdiction, choice of law, and tolling of statutes of limitation. We will discover when and what type of notice is due a class upon certification, what rights class members have to possibly intervene in a class action and take some control over their own destiny, and the process by which class actions are settled. Because few class actions are tried, understanding the unique fiduciary role that a court plays in overseeing settlements will be critical to appreciation of the seemingly bizarre concept of a party's claims being settled without their consent and often over their objections. This is a world very much at odds with our normal view of American justice.

"To me, a lawyer is basically the person that knows the rules of the country. We're all throwing the dice, playing the game, moving our pieces around the board, but if there is a problem the lawyer is the only person who has read the inside of the top of the box."

Jerry Seinfeld

Chapter 6 shifts back to a broader focus over all forms of complex litigation by analyzing the topic of Attorney's Fees. We will briefly consider how fees are assessed as a private matter between client and attorney before shifting to the two scenarios in complex litigation when courts are required to determine and assess attorney's fees. These two scenarios are (a) when there is a fee-shifting statute that departs from the *American Rule* and compels a defendant to pay (as an extra item of damages) the claimant's attorney's fees and (b) when the efforts of one litigant (or their counsel) has bestowed a benefit on another litigant and is considered to have thereby created a *common benefit* where courts will require the beneficiary of those efforts to pay for the services of the attorney. Class actions and multi-district litigation are the two prime examples of the application of this doctrine. In either of these scenarios, courts are required to determine the attorney's fees without the benefit of a governing fee agreement to determine either the method or the amount of fees deemed reasonable. We will see how courts have responded to this unique role they are forced to play and how the very possibility of achieving such a fee is often a primary motivation for many forms of complex litigation.

3. Mechanics of This Book (Sample Final, Chapter Goals, Exercises)

This book, being part of Carolina's *Context and Practice* series, consciously attempts to present materials in a way designed to help students of the law to appreciate why the issues are being discussed and to have a chance to practice their application. Yes it is still a "casebook" and is filled with many edited (sometimes heavily) cases that provide the spine of the book's contents. Reading cases is still a wonderful tool for gaining an understanding of the law because reading of a doctrine or literally reading the text of a rule in a vacuum has extremely limited value and is unlikely to be something you would ever retain. The cases put these rules and doctrines into specific contexts where you can appreciate why they are important and how lawyers use these devices. But this Context and Practice series is designed to go beyond the mere reading of cases.

Therefore, each chapter will begin (after a short introduction to the chapter's general topics) with a *Chapter Problem*. As you are doing the reading, pause and carefully read each such problem and keep it in the back of your mind as you dig into the substance of the chapter. In multiple instances thereafter (in the *Notes and Problems* section following cases) you will be explicitly invited to consider a particular issue raised by that case in the context of the Chapter Problem. Of course, you should keep the general fact pattern of the problem in mind throughout all of the materials and consider application of the materials to that particular problem. Further, at the end of each chapter you will encounter a *Chapter Problem Revisited* which will often invite you to analyze a multitude of the issues studied in that chapter in light of the Chapter Problem. The idea is that, in the "real world," lawyers encounter issues in the context of particular problems raised by their representation of specific clients. Further, studies have shown that people learn lessons better when there is an opportunity for immediate application and practice of those lessons. This also helps to keep the course coverage from become entirely academic.

In addition to the Chapter Problems, and Chapter Problem Revisited sections, you will often see additional *Problems* raised in the Notes and Problems sections of the book. These tend to be very brief opportunities to consider the issues raised in the case and ask whether those principles still apply when you tweak the facts to modify the context somewhat. These problems are designed to help sharpen the edges of your understanding of what might otherwise appear to be mere fuzzy principles discussed in the cases.

Yet another opportunity for you to practice your understanding of the materials comes in the form of *Pulling It All Together Exercises* scattered throughout the book, often at the end of a larger section of material or also near the end of a chapter. These are intended as opportunities for you to actually analyze and write out an answer to a particular question given a relatively small set of facts. They might be similar to a law school short answer or essay question but are intended to be less academic and more related to answering issues likely to arise when a legal practitioner confronts issues of complex litigation.

Finally, at the end of the book in Appendix II you will find a sample Final Exam series of questions presented in three formats: (1) a set of a dozen "short answer" questions, (2) a more traditional law school essay question, and (3) thirty multiple-choice questions. Depending on how you learn best, and what form of final exam your own professor gives, you might find this to be a fruitful way to test your own knowledge of both the macro and micro details of the doctrines and devices covered in this book. Your professor may even post or otherwise make available to you your professor's sample answers to the questions so that you can check your own work as a diagnostic tool.

The book is also designed to be student friendly in other respects. The cases have been carefully chosen to avoid redundancy, to refrain from pursuing mere rabbit trails, and to offer good examples of the relevant contexts for a discussion of the relevant rules and doctrines. They have also undergone extensive editing where feasible to avoid unrelated or unnecessary chatter without doing an injustice to the spirit of the original opinion or to cause you to be misled in any way. The *Notes and Problems* after each case are restrained. The notes are limited to core matters in relation to the issues raised by the cases rather than to provide exhaustive coverage of all issues on all topics. This course is designed, after all, to introduce the world of complex litigation rather than to be your final destination as a practitioner. Important questions about each case are typically raised in the text before the case and immediately after in the Notes and Problems. Further, the text of the book is sprinkled with numerous text boxes containing short *Principles* (often useful or enlightening quotations) and *In Practice* discussions that elaborate on how the rules or doctrine you are covering pertains to the practice of law.

There are two additional features of this book designed to help you get the "big picture." Often near the end of major sections or at the end of chapters this text will contain a feature titled *Upon Further Review*. This is designed to be a big picture re-articulation or summary of what you have just read. I frequently advise students of my courses that they are challenged to both understand the specific rules, doctrines, or claims covered in that course but also to be able to zoom out (like on Google Maps) and find the context and to appreciate larger relationships in the law between one area and another related area. Understanding the law at both levels (the "trees and the forest") allows one to gain much greater depth of understanding. In this same vein, each chapter recommends some additional reading—often some law review article or a section of a larger treatise on the topic—for the student that is interested in *Going Deeper* in their study of the topics raised in that chapter.

Consider the contents of this book ripe for your harvest and throw yourself into all of the book's features—don't just read the cases and show up for class. The interactive format (and even writing style) of the book should encourage you to fully digest the concepts and ultimately to master them.

Upon Further Review

The study of complex litigation is advanced exploration of civil procedure topics that arise in anticipation of, or response to, litigation scenarios involving a multiplicity of parties or potential parties as well as a multiplicity of related or redundant lawsuits. The law of complex litigation is interested in furthering the efficient use of courthouses by litigants, both for ensuring that the system works best for everyone, but also to discourage waste in the litigation process incurred by litigants themselves. On the other hand, our American tradition of litigation and its heavy emphasis on the adversarial process to find truth and resolve disputes has long favored allowing a claimant to exercise great autonomy in deciding when, where, and against whom to bring their lawsuits. These liberties are subject to some limits, particularly when such autonomy threatens the efficiency that our system seeks and needs (at some level) or threatens fundamental fairness concepts. These three principles—autonomy, efficiency, and fairness—are woven throughout the topics in this book, apply in varying ways in each context, and help to explain many of the rules and doctrines that typically involve some delicate balancing of the principles—each of which sounds good in the abstract.

Chapter Problem Revisited

Go back and re-read the facts and issues raised by your senior partner in the Chapter Problem set forth earlier in this chapter. You have a meeting with the senior partner tomorrow morning. From your general recollection of civil procedure and with your copy of the Federal Rules of Civil Procedure nearby (see Appendix 1), prepare a chart outlining the various strategic and legal issues raised in the memorandum and, for each issue, see if you can identify the applicable Rule of Civil Procedure or doctrine that will govern the analysis of that issue.

Plan to spend at least 20 minutes preparing this chart and have it handy when you go to see your Senior Partner tomorrow morning. You may not have answers yet but you will at least be able to demonstrate that you know where to find the answers.

Going Deeper

Additional recommended readings to enhance your understanding of some of the topics in this Chapter include:

- Jay Tidmarsh, *Unattainable Justice: The Form of Complex Litigation and the Limits of Judicial Power*, 60 Geo. Wash. L. Rev. 1683 (1992) (providing an historic and over-arching look for a definition of "complex litigation" and the many ways complex cases present challenges for courts and litigants).

- David Rosenberg, *Class Actions for Mass Torts: Doing Individual Justice by Collective Means*, 62 Ind. L.J. 561 (1987) (provides a good articulation of the goals of courts in balancing the desire to offer fair procedure to protect individuals and their claims while also achieving collective justice, often in the form of a class action).

- Roger H. Trangsrud, *Joinder Alternatives in Mass Tort Litigation*, 70 Cornell L. Rev. 779 (1985) (provides good overview of various procedural alternatives available to balance efficiency versus fairness in the context of multiple claimants with similar cases against a common defendant).

Chapter 2

Joinder of Claims & Parties

Chapter Goals

- Understand the consequences of an issue being resolved in one case for another case.

- Learn the difference between *permissible* parties and *necessary* parties.

- Recognize the options a *defending* party has to expand the scope of the lawsuit by asserting her own claims and bringing in new parties.

- Know when a non-party can join someone else's lawsuit on his own volition and without the original plaintiff's permission.

- Begin to think strategically about these joinder issues.

- Recognize how the themes of autonomy, efficiency, and fairness are balanced in each joinder scenario.

A. Overview: Dealing with Duplicative & Related Litigation

Viewed through the lens of potentially complex litigation, a logical starting point for analysis is with the doctrines and rules that provide the parameters for defining the scope of a particular lawsuit. In this chapter, we will encounter doctrines and rules of civil procedure that serve this function. These rules often answer questions about when and where claims need to be asserted, who a litigant might join in her lawsuit either as a co-plaintiff or an additional defendant, what claims can be asserted in a lawsuit and what claims might have to be asserted in a lawsuit, when a court might trump a litigant's choice of who to sue by demanding the addition of a missing party to the lawsuit, when it is appropriate for a defending party to be permitted to bring others into the case, and when someone left out of the lawsuit is entitled to gain entry to the courthouse to intervene in others' disputes. Viewed at a very macro level, many of these rules and doctrines share a common principle of trying to facilitate, if not encourage or mandate, the joinder of multiple parties to the same lawsuit in order to avoid unnecessary multiplicity of actions—for reasons primarily of efficiency. We will begin with the common law "one bite at the apple" doctrines of res judicata and collateral estoppel. But first, to provide some context, review the Chapter Problem below and consider the possible strategic and legal questions it raises. The remainder of this chapter will provide analytical ammunition to tackle these issues and questions.

B. Chapter 2 Problem

Underwood & Associates, P.A.
Internal Memo

To: Associate
From: Jim Underwood, Sr. Partner
Re: New Case Opportunity: Paula Jones

A potential new client, Paula Jones, came by our offices today and is interested in retaining us. I need your help analyzing the best strategy for organizing this new lawsuit. Below are the basics. I also have attached a relevant newspaper article.

Paula bought a slightly used "Camel" convertible car recently. It's manufactured by an Eastern European automaker named Kazakh Motors. As far as Paula knew this auto was in perfect condition. The local retail dealer (it's a franchise owned separate from the manufacturer) told her it was in great shape, it had low mileage, and had no evidence of any problems. To make a long story short, the brakes failed on her one morning on the interstate here in town. She tried to apply them to avoid another driver who was swerving into her lane of traffic. (She recalls only this other driver's first name, "Ted," and that he did not have any proof of insurance when asked by the police. She thinks there might be more information in the police report about him.) When she applied the brakes nothing happened. She ended up hitting the other car, spinning out of control, and going off of a small bridge. She was hospitalized with some broken bones and has been unable to work while she is undergoing physical therapy every day. The car was wrecked, of course. She has medical and therapy bills over $50,000 already and they continue to be incurred. Between those losses and her lost wages, her economic damages will easily be over $100,000 with additional non-economic damages for pain and suffering.

After her discharge from the hospital, Paula was quite upset. She posted some Facebook messages about what a "crappy car the Camel is" and accused Kazakh of intentionally selling sub-par products into the United States. She says she recently received a letter from Kazakh telling her to "cease and desist from publishing additional false lies that constitute business disparagement."

In a few minutes of online research, I came across the attached newspaper article discussing this phenomenon of brakes going out on this particular model vehicle. There appear to be some other lawsuits against the company, including two jury verdicts on cases alleging design defects on the brakes on the Camel (one verdict was for the plaintiff and another for the defendant).

There is one other loose thread in this tale. Paula purchased the car on a promissory note from the retailer. She was making $300 monthly payments until the time of the accident. She has refused to continue making those payments despite getting a series of late notices from the retailer.

After you review these materials, consider our best options for resolving our client's claims and come see me.

New England Times Herald
Vol. CLXV $1.50

Multi-Million Dollar Jury Verdict Rendered Against Auto Company

Portsmouth—A local Portsmouth jury returned its verdict following a week's long trial in the district court of Potawatomie County yesterday finding the car manufacturer Kazakh Motors liable for $5 million in damages. Edith Bunker had filed the wrongful death suit after her husband's tragic and violent death two years earlier. In that fateful accident, Mr. Bunker's car went through a guardrail and burst into flames when it hit the bottom of a steep ravine. According to police reconstruction reports at the time, Mr. Bunker had apparently attempted to apply his brakes but they did not fully engage. Plaintiff offered proof at trial that a new design in the Camel convertible caused its braking system to sometimes suddenly lose hydraulic fluid without prior warning. Kazakh disputed these findings and suggested the accident was the sole cause of Mr. Bunker's inattention and failure to apply the brakes before hitting the guardrail.

Local lawyer Jackie Chiles represented Ms. Bunker. After the verdict, he said that both he and his client were very pleased with the jury's ability to see through the "outrageous" attempts by Kazakh to "blame the victim" when it was "quite clear that the failure of the braking system on the convertible Camel vehicle was the sole explanation for his untimely death." Mr. Chiles expressed considerable admiration for the jury as he noted that in the only other similar case to be tried against the Camel's braking system, a year previously in another state, that jury had rejected the design defect allegations finding no fault of the car in causing the unrelated crash of another Camel vehicle. Mr. Chiles expressed his belief that the Portsmouth jury "had sent a message that Americans will not tolerate foreign manufacturers' disregard for the safety of Americans." He also noted that there were dozens of reports of other similar Camel accidents in the last twelve months allegedly due to ineffective brakes. Mr. Chiles would not say if he was planning to represent any of those other victims but he did add, "I am always here to stand in the gap representing David against another filthy rich Goliath." Kazakh has said it is considering all of its legal options including an appeal to the state court of appeals.

C. One Bite at the Apple:
Res Judicata and Collateral Estoppel

We begin our journey through the governing body of rules and doctrines that impact, ultimately, issues about the size and contours of a lawsuit, by turning to the "One Bite at the Apple" doctrines. Res judicata and collateral estoppel are doctrines slightly familiar, perhaps, from your first-year course on civil procedure. These, alongside Rule 13

Compulsory Counter Claims, play a large role in the complex litigation arena. The purpose of these doctrines is to promote efficient claims resolution and a sense of finality for litigants in the resolution of particular disputes by mandating that litigants bring all related causes of action at one time and by avoiding unnecessary re-litigation of issues and claims.

Res judicata, or "claim preclusion" bars the re-litigation of the "same claim." Thus, the art of issue spotting you learned in your first year classes is more than simply a skill for exams. For if a lawyer attempts to bring in a second suit causes of action that should have been brought in the initial lawsuit between the same parties, this doctrine will bar those claims. The elements of res judicata are: 1) must be the "same" claim, arising from the same transaction or occurrence; 2) between the same parties; 3) after a "final" judgment (final means at the trial court level); 4) on the "merits." For practical purposes, this means that a claimant must bring all claims that are possibly related in one suit. This holds true whether the claims belong to a plaintiff or a defendant (as a defendant, additional issues regarding compulsory counterclaims are implicated). In many instances where a claimant attempts in a second suit to bring a claim arguably related to a prior lawsuit, the application of res judicata depends primarily on whether it is the "same claim"—whether or not it arises out of the same "transaction or occurrence" as the claim in the prior lawsuit. We will explore this issue in the *Swaida v. Gentiva Health Services* case below.

The related doctrine of *collateral estoppel* or "issue preclusion" prevents the re-litigation of the same issue. This not only avoids the inefficiency of trying the same issue over and over again but avoids as well the seeming embarrassment of multiple juries announcing inconsistent "truths" in their verdicts. The basic rule for collateral estoppel is when: 1) an issue of fact or a mixed issue of fact and law is; 2) actually litigated and determined by; 3) a valid final judgment; and 4) the determination is essential to the judgment, then the determination is conclusive in a subsequent action between the parties, even on an entirely different claim.

Unlike res judicata, collateral estoppel only applies when the same issue was actually litigated and determined in the prior lawsuit. Originally collateral estoppel was only applied when there was mutuality—the same parties in the two lawsuits. And due process still absolutely forbids the application of collateral estoppel against a party who never had the chance to litigate the issue in the prior lawsuit. In other words, every litigant is entitled to at least one bite at the proverbial apple. But if a current litigant previously lost on an issue and that issue comes up in subsequent litigation against a different party, may the prior loss be used against the litigation loser? This issue involves what is termed either offensive or defensive *non-mutual collateral estoppel*. As you will see below, courts no longer hesitate to apply non-mutual collateral estoppel when it is asserted by a new litigant in defense of a claim by the prior litigation loser. But when it is asserted in an offensive manner to establish a claim by a new party against a prior litigation loser, the issue of whether to apply collateral estoppel is more complicated and involves weighing various factors in light of the circumstances. This will be explored further in this section. The two concepts of res judicata and collateral estoppel are easily conflated; thus, it is important to master the differences now.

1. Res Judicata Basics

Swaida v. Gentiva Health Services
238 F. Supp. 2d 325 (D. Mass. 2002)

Keeton, District Judge.

Plaintiff, Cynthia Swaida, was employed by Gentiva (formerly Olsten Health Services) from October 5, 1992 through October 17, 1997. Plaintiff's employment was terminated on October 17, 1997.

Res Judicata, a Latin phrase, literally means, "A thing adjudicated." (Black's Law Dictionary)

On October 17, 2000, Plaintiff filed a civil action pro se in Massachusetts Superior Court, Barnstable County, alleging that Gentiva terminated her in retaliation for her co-operation with a United States Department of Labor investigation. Gentiva removed the action to federal court and filed a motion to dismiss for failure to state claims upon which relief could be granted. The court granted plaintiff additional time to respond to defendant's motion, but plaintiff never filed a response. The court then granted Gentiva's motion to dismiss on March 1, 2001 and the clerk entered the order of dismissal the next day.

Plaintiff filed the current lawsuit pro se on May 10, 2002. Her current suit is based on the same termination at issue in the earlier dismissed suit. She now claims, however, that Gentiva terminated her based on her age, in violation of Mass. Gen. Laws ch. 151B §4 and the Age Discrimination in Employment Act ("ADEA"). Plaintiff also alleges that she received a "Right to Sue Letter" from the Equal Employment Opportunity Commission ("EEOC") in February 2002, before filing her second suit. The parties have made no showing regarding when plaintiff filed her initial charge with the EEOC. Plaintiff appeared pro se in both her lawsuits. She did not retain counsel in this current suit until November of 2002.

Defendant moves, under Fed.R.Civ.P. 12(b)(6), to dismiss this action [because] res judicata precludes this action [as it] arises "from the very *same* employment termination and is brought by the *same* plaintiff against the *same* defendant" as the earlier dismissed suit.

Plaintiff argues that the claims are not sufficiently identical to require the application of res judicata. In addition, plaintiff argues that res judicata cannot be achieved at the expense of fairness to a pro se litigant, and that applying res judicata in this case would be fundamentally unfair. Plaintiff also claims that she met all procedural requirements by filing with the EEOC and filing this action within ninety days of receipt of her right-to-sue letter.

The Merits
A. Plaintiff's claims are barred by res judicata.

Federal law governs the res judicata effect of a previous judgment in a federal court. *Massachusetts School of Law at Andover v. American Bar Association,* 142 F.3d 26, 37 (1st Cir.1998). Under the doctrine of res judicata a final judgment on the merits of an action precludes the parties and their privies "from relitigating issues that were or could have been raised in that action." *Perez v. Volvo Car Corp.,* 247 F.3d 303, 311 (1st Cir.2001) (quoting *Allen v. McCurry,* 449 U.S. 90, 94, 101 S.Ct. 411, 66 L.Ed.2d 308 (1980)). Federal law requires three elements before applying the preclusive effect of res judicata, "(1) a final judgment on the merits in an earlier action; (2) an identity of the cause of action in both the earlier and later suits; and (3) an identity of parties or privies in the two suits." *Havercombe v. Dep't of Educ. of the Commonwealth of Puerto Rico,* 250 F.3d 1, 3 (1st Cir.2001) (quoting *Kale v. Combined Ins. Co. of America,* 924 F.2d 1161, 1166 (1st Cir.1991)). It is undisputed that the third element, identicality of the parties, is met. In the remainder of this opinion, I will focus on the first and second elements.

1. The court's dismissal of plaintiff's first lawsuit resulted in a final judgment on the merits.

On March 1, 2001, the court granted Gentiva's motion, under Fed.R.Civ.P. 12(b)(6), to dismiss for failure to state a claim. According to the Supreme Court of the United States, "the dismissal for failure to state a claim under Federal Rule of Civil Procedure 12(b)(6) is a 'judgment on the merits.'" *Federated Department Stores, Inc. v. Moitie,* 452 U.S. 394, 399 n.3, 101 S.Ct. 2424, 69 L.Ed.2d 103 (1981). A Rule 12(b)(6) dismissal does not need any specific notation that the dismissal was "on the merits." Instead, "this type of dismissal, presumed to be with prejudice unless the order explicitly states otherwise, has a claim preclusive effect" *Andrews-Clarke v. Lucent Techs., Inc.,* 157 F.Supp.2d 93, 99 (D.Mass.2001) (citations omitted). Under federal law, the first judgment against plaintiff was a final judgment on the merits, and in plaintiff's second opposition, plaintiff concedes that this first element is satisfied.

2. Plaintiff's two causes of action are sufficiently identical.

Under the second element, a sufficient showing of identicality between the two suits is required. The First Circuit has "adopted a transactional approach to determine whether causes of action are sufficiently related to support a res judicata defense." *Mass. Sch. of Law,* 142 F.3d at 38. Under this approach, the First Circuit routinely relies on three factors to determine whether the two claims are substantially identical. *In re Iannochino,* 242 F.3d 36, 46 (1st Cir.2001). "First, we look to 'whether the facts are related in time, space, origin or motivation,' second, to 'whether they form a convenient trial unit', and third, to 'whether their treatment as a unit conforms to the parties' expectations.'" *Id.* (quoting *Porn v. Nat'l Grange Mut. Ins. Co.,* 93 F.3d 31, 34 (1st Cir.1996)). After careful evaluation of all three factors, this court determines that a sufficient showing of identicality has been made.

Both suits are based on facts that are almost identical in time, space, origin, and motivation. Plaintiff's first suit involves the same termination as her second suit. Thus, the time of the facts and the origin appear identical. As defendant states, "both of [p]laintiff's actions are based on the same factual underpinnings (i.e., the circumstances leading up to and resulting in the termination of [p]laintiff's employment)." Plaintiff's motivation for both suits is also identical; she was seeking compensation for damages caused by Gentiva's allegedly wrongful termination of plaintiff.

The only difference between the two claims is the label applied. In her first claim, plaintiff alleged that the termination was in retaliation for her cooperation with a United States Department of Labor investigation. In this second claim, plaintiff alleges that the termination was based on her age. According to the First Circuit, if the two claims were sufficiently related, that is, if they were founded upon the same transaction, arose out of the same nucleus of operative facts, and sought redress for essentially the same basic wrong, the two suits advanced the same cause of action notwithstanding any differences in remedies sought or theories of recovery pleaded. *A fortiori*, our focus must not be the theoretical raiment in which the claims are robed, but "whether the underlying facts of both transactions were the same or substantially similar." *Kale v. Combined Ins. Co. of America*, 924 F.2d 1161 (1st Cir.1991) (quoting *Manego v. Orleans Bd. of Trade*, 773 F.2d 1, 6 (1st Cir.1985)). Because these two claims do arise out of the same nucleus of operative facts and seek redress for the same basic wrong (the allegedly wrongful termination) they are founded on the same transaction.

The second factor focuses on what would happen at trial. *Iannochino*, 242 F.3d at 47. For this factor, the court must "determine whether the witnesses or proofs required to prove the factual basis of both claims substantially overlap." *Id.* The witnesses in plaintiff's first and second suit would substantially overlap. Both trials would likely involve the following witnesses: plaintiff's supervisor, plaintiff's colleagues at Gentiva, and Gentiva's decision-makers. Because the witnesses and much of the testimony would be identical, the two claims would have formed a convenient trial unit, a factor that "argues powerfully for claim preclusion." *Mass. Sch. of Law*, 142 F.3d at 38.

In Practice

Though FRCP 18 *permits* a plaintiff to assert multiple causes of action and the doctrine of res judicata sometimes *compels* the joinder of certain claims, other considerations may offer additional practical sources of encouragement for asserting as many plausible claims as possible, such as: (1) uncertainty as to which claims will prove to have merit, (2) making the defense of the case more complicated, (3) possibly impacting the perceived settlement value of the case, and (4) possible expansion of the scope of permissible discovery.

The third factor focuses on the parties' expectations at the time plaintiff filed her first suit for wrongful termination. "When evaluating the parties' expectations, we are guided by the principle that, where 'two claims arose in the same time frame out of similar facts, one would reasonably expect them to be brought together.'" *Iannochino*, 242 F.3d at 48 (quoting *Porn*, 93 F.3d at 37). When examining the third factor, "rather than considering whether [plaintiff] knew of the precise legal contours of [her second] claim, we must instead determine whether [she] knew of the factual basis of that claim." *Id.* at 48–49.

The record establishes that plaintiff was aware of the factual basis of her age discrimination claim when she filed her first suit. Plaintiff filed the first suit on October 17, 2000. The record shows that in November 1998 plaintiff participated in an investigative conference before the MCAD to evaluate plaintiff's claim that she was terminated because of her age. Therefore, almost two years before her first suit, plaintiff was already aware of the factual basis of her claim.

In addition to having knowledge of the factual basis of her claims, plaintiff also must have been able to assert the claims during the pendency of her first suit. Although plaintiff did not have an EEOC right-to-sue letter during her first suit, res judicata still applies to both her [state law] 151B claim and her ADEA claim. As a panel of the First Circuit has stated, "the lack of a right-to-sue letter would not have prevented plaintiff from notifying the court of [her] allegations … and, if need be, asking for a stay until the EEOC issued [her] the letter." *Havercombe,* 250 F.3d at 8. Plaintiff has presented no showing that she was unable to bring her age discrimination claims during the pendency of her first suit. In addition, the record does not establish when she requested the right-to-sue letter, and she makes no showing that she alerted the court to her possible claims or that she requested an accelerated process from the EEOC.

Lastly, unlike Title VII, the ADEA has no requirement that the EEOC issue a right-to-sue letter before the federal suit commences. *Crossman v. Crosson,* 905 F.Supp. 90, 93 n.1 (E.D.N.Y.1995) (citing *Tolliver v. Xerox Corp.,* 918 F.2d 1052, 1057 (2d Cir.1990)). Instead, the ADEA states, "No civil action may be commenced by an individual under this section until 60 days after a charge alleging unlawful discrimination has been filed with the Equal Employment Opportunity Commission." 29 U.S.C. § 626(d). Accordingly, the lack of a right-to-sue letter does not alter the application of res judicata because the plaintiff could have brought the federal age discrimination suit even in the absence of a right-to-sue letter.

3. No equitable exception prevents the preclusion of plaintiff's second suit.

Res judicata precludes plaintiff's current lawsuit because all three required elements are met.

In her opposition, plaintiff argues that "res judicata cannot be justified if it is achieved at the expense of fairness to a pro se litigant." In plaintiff's second opposition, she makes a similar argument, asking this court to look at the equities and apply an exception to res judicata. This court, however cannot create such an exception in this case. According to the Supreme Court,

> the doctrine of res judicata serves vital public interests beyond any individual judge's ad hoc determination of the equities in a particular case. There is simply "no principle of law or equity which sanctions the rejection by a federal court of the salutary principle of res judicata."

Moitie, 452 U.S. 394, 401, 69 L. Ed. 2d 103, 101 S. Ct. 2424 (quoting *Heiser v. Woodruff,* 327 U.S. 726, 733, 90 L. Ed. 970, 66 S. Ct. 853 (1946)). The fact that plaintiff appeared pro se, therefore, is insufficient to create any equitable exception. *Iannochino,* 242 F.3d at 49 ("We reject the suggestion implicit in their argument that parties can ignore facts indicating that they should assert a claim solely because of lack of representation.")

In her first opposition, plaintiff also argues that "there is an over-arching policy concern in favor of deciding cases on their merits rather than on procedural technicalities." Res judicata, however, is more than a mere procedural technicality. The Supreme Court emphasizes that

> [the] doctrine of res judicata is not a mere matter of practice or procedure inherited from a more technical time than ours. It is a rule of fundamental and

substantial justice, of public policy and of private peace which should be cordially regarded and enforced by the courts.

Moitie, 452 U.S. at 401.

Even if this court were to evaluate the equities present in this case, such an evaluation would tip in favor of defendant. To fail to apply res judicata in this case would unfairly prejudice the defendant, requiring it to defend a suit that is at least seven years old and could easily have been brought much earlier.

Because all three elements of res judicata are satisfied, no equitable exception can prevent the preclusive effect of res judicata.

FRCP 18 Joinder of Claims

A party asserting a claim, counterclaim, crossclaim, or third-party claim may join, as independent or alternative claims, as many claims as it has against an opposing party.

Summary

Plaintiff's age discrimination claims under 151B and the ADEA are barred by res judicata because the record shows (1) a final judgment on the merits in an earlier action, (2) an identity of the cause of action in both the earlier and later suits, and (3) an identity of parties in the two suits. No equitable exception can prevent the preclusive effect of res judicata in this case. [In addition to being barred by res judicata, plaintiff's 151B claim was also barred by a three-year statute of limitation.]

Notes and Problems

1. The First Circuit in the foregoing opinion uses a three-prong test to determine the relatedness or "identicality" of the two suits. This approach is not used by all courts; analyze the test to determine its effectiveness. Can you think of a fact pattern where this three-prong test might lead to inappropriate results? Do any of the three tests strike you as superior? Are any redundant?

2. The plaintiff in *Swaida v. Gentiva Health Services* argues that even if the elements of res judicata are present in the case, equity required the court to ignore the preclusive effects and allow the litigation to proceed. The court disagreed with the plaintiff, but what effect would the court's decision have made on the doctrine of res judicata if it had agreed with the plaintiff? Should we have equitable exceptions to the application of preclusion rules?

3. The court in *Swaida v. Gentiva Health Services* declined to apply an equitable exception to the res judicata doctrine. Interestingly, the court went on to state that even if it has applied an equitable exception, equity would still favor the defendant. This is because res judicata is partially driven by a policy to give defendants peace of mind. Imagine a doctor who is sued as a result of a failed medical procedure. The plaintiff sues and claims the procedure disfigured her face. She wins, and the doctor is looking forward to putting this incident behind him. Subsequently she sues the doctor again for the same procedure alleging that the procedure caused her to experience separate emotional distress. Is it fair to the doctor to allow her to bring this claim? At some point, should the doctor be able to have peace of mind that he is through litigating claims related to a particular incident?

4. Rule 18 of the Federal Rules of Civil Procedure ("FRCP") permits a party to join any claims that it has against another party. But joinder of claims under Rule 18 is permissive—that is to say the rule does not require a party to join all its claims against another. This rule, however, has to be read in conjunction with the doctrine of res judicata, which acts as a caveat to Rule 18. If the claims arise out of the same transaction or occurrence, then a party must bring it (despite Rule 18's permissive language) or risk waiving the claim under Res Judicata.

5. Given the claim preclusive effect of res judicata, parties often include an entry of "take nothing" final judgment when settling disputes rather than just having the claimant dismiss the lawsuit. Then, if a party breaches the settlement agreement and sues anyway, the other party has both a release defense (based upon settlement agreement's release language) and a res judicata defense that will bar the claim.

6. *Problems:* Consider whether the claims below are sufficiently related to be required to be brought together in the same lawsuit:

yes

a. Peter wants to sue Dennis for breaching a contract through non-performance of it—Dennis failed to deliver rocking chairs as he promised. Peter also is contemplating a fraud claim against Dennis because he believes Dennis never intended to perform the promise and was merely trying to deceive Dennis into paying for the chairs.

yes

b. Pamela wants to sue Appliances, Inc. in strict products liability for selling her a defectively designed toaster that exploded after a few months' use and caused her burns. She also has a cause of action against Appliances, Inc. for negligently designing such a flawed toaster.

yes

c. Pedro was hit by David in a rear-end collision on the highway. He suffered property damages and sues David for negligently hurting his car. He is also considering suing David for physical injuries he suffered in the accident leading to repeated visits to the chiropractor.

no

but they can under Rule 18

d. Porsche, an office supply retailer, received a shipment of software from Demetrius. She paid for the software but wants to sue for her money back because she now believes it is full of glitches and not in conformity with warranties. On a later shipment, she refuses to pay for the goods upon delivery, and is considering a declaratory judgment claim seeking a declaration that the second shipment was non-conforming and excusing her from any payment obligations.

7. *Chapter Problem:* With regard to Paula's possible lawsuit, if she sues the local retailer on a tort claim for selling her a defective automobile and causing her injuries, must she also consider adding some additional cause of action to relieve her of her contract liabilities to the retailer? If she doesn't include any such contract theories in the tort case, will she face some risk down the line? What about in her possible strict liability suit against Kazakh; must she assert all of her claims for damages in that lawsuit? Because some of her medical bills and physical condition are still evolving, can she assert claims at a later date just for the future losses?

2. Collateral Estoppel: Mutuality and Its Abandonment

For a long time, courts applied collateral estoppel narrowly, limiting its application to issues previously litigated between the same parties. Because both were equally bound by the prior findings, application of the doctrine seemed both fair and efficient. But the mutuality requirement began to erode with the U.S. Supreme Court's decision in *Blonder-Tongue Laboratories, Inc. v. University of Illinois Foundation*, 402 U.S. 313 (1971), when it permitted the doctrine's defensive use. When used defensively, a party defending a claim can hold the claimant to a prior adverse finding from a prior case against another party where the *claimant lost* the same issue. This served efficiency concerns as well as seemed fair because the claimant had already had its full day in court. Further, in many such instances, the claimant might have been permitted procedurally to bring both cases together. Thus, the doctrine's application actually encouraged the claimant to sue both defendants in the same proceeding and avoid piecemeal litigation. Most courts have since embraced defensive non-mutual collateral estoppel.

The thornier issue now involves when it is fair to permit the *offensive* use of non-mutual collateral estoppel. That is, to allow a new claimant to hold a defendant to the defendant's prior litigation loss on an identical issue. The Supreme Court has also authorized this application of res judicata but subject to some important limiting qualifications. *See Parklane Hosiery Co. v. Shore*, 439 U.S. 322 (1979). We will first review the basic application of collateral estoppel as between the "same parties" and then explore its possible non-mutual application in an offensive context.

Freeman v. Lester Coggins Trucking, Inc.

771 F.2d 860 (5th Cir. 1985)

TATE, CIRCUIT JUDGE:

This is a Mississippi diversity action. The plaintiff Freeman sues for the wrongful death of his infant daughter Laura, on behalf of himself and of four other statutory wrongful death beneficiaries (*i.e.*, Laura's mother and her three minor siblings). Freeman appeals from the dismissal of these claims on the ground of collateral estoppel. The district court based its dismissal on the circumstance that—in a previous suit brought by Freeman individually against the present same defendants for his own personal injuries arising from the same accident in which Laura was killed—Freeman's individual suit had been dismissed, upon a jury verdict exculpating the defendants of negligence in the accident.

Principles

"The requirement of mutuality must yield to public policy. To hold otherwise would be to allow repeated litigation of identical questions, expressly adjudicated, and to allow a litigant having lost on a question of fact to re-open and re-try all the old issues each time he can obtain a new adversary...."

Coca-Cola v. Pepsi-Cola Co., 172 A. 260 (Del Super. Ct. 1934).

We affirm the dismissal of Freeman's own wrongful death claim. However, finding no privity between him and the other wrongful death beneficiaries, we reverse the dismissal of the claims of the four other wrongful death beneficiaries, holding further that the doctrine of "virtual representation" does not justify the application of collateral estoppel.

This litigation arises out of a collision in Mississippi between a vehicle driven by Freeman and a truck driven by the defendant Deis in the course of his employment with the co-defendant Lester Coggins Trucking, Inc. As a result of the collision, Freeman and a passenger in his vehicle sustained personal injuries, and two other passengers, including the present decedent Laura, Freeman's infant daughter, were killed. Four suits were filed in federal court for personal injuries or wrongful death, of which for present purposes we need note only the present suit (by Freeman for himself and as representing four other claimants as Laura's wrongful death beneficiaries), and the earlier-tried one by Freeman individually for his own personal injuries. The latter suit was dismissed after an adverse jury verdict that by special interrogatory found the same two defendants free of the same negligence asserted by the present suit.

Based upon this adverse jury finding and the resulting dismissal of Freeman's action for his own personal injuries, the district court granted the defendants' motion for summary judgment grounded on collateral estoppel.

I.

Freeman's suit was dismissed in federal court. Consequently, although both it and the present suit are Mississippi diversity cases, "the doctrines of *res judicata* and collateral estoppel require application of the federal rule when, as in this case, a party seeks to estop a claim from being raised in a diversity action brought in federal court on the basis of an earlier determination made in a federal court sitting pursuant to its diversity jurisdiction." *Stovall v. Price Waterhouse Co.*, 652 F.2d 537, 540 (5th Cir. 1981). Federal law determines the res judicata and collateral effect given a prior decision of a federal tribunal, regardless of the bases of the federal court's jurisdiction. *Id.*

"Federal common law permits the use of collateral estoppel upon the showing of three necessary criteria[.]" *Hicks v. Quaker Oats Company*, 662 F.2d 1158, 1166 (5th Cir. 1981). *See also Holmes v. Jones*, 738 F.2d 711, 713 (5th Cir. 1984). The three criteria are:

(1) that the issue at stake be identical to the one involved in prior litigation;

(2) that the issue has been actually litigated in the prior litigation; and

(3) that the determination of the issue in the prior litigation has been a critical and necessary part of the judgment in that earlier action.

Hicks, supra, 662 F.2d at 1166; *Holmes, supra*, 738 F.2d at 713. All three of these requirements have been satisfied in the present case. The issue here, as in the first case, was based on Deis' negligence. This issue was actually litigated in the first case, and its determination there was a critical and necessary part of the judgment.

"[A] right, question, or fact distinctly put in issue and directly determined as a ground of recovery by a court of competent jurisdiction collaterally estops a party or his privy from relitigating the issue in a subsequent action." *Hardy v. Johns-Manville Sales Corporation*, 681 F.2d 334, 338 (5th Cir. 1982). Freeman was clearly a party to the earlier suit for his own personal injuries. Despite Freeman's contention that the circumstance in the present suit that he is acting in a different capacity (*i.e.*, as wrongful death claimant) somehow makes collateral estoppel unavailable to the defendants, it is plain that in the present suit—as to *his own* claim for wrongful death damages—he is likewise a party suing in his individual capacity to recover damages due him. *See Jones v. Texas Tech University*, 656 F.2d 1137, 1143 (5th Cir. 1981). Since Freeman had a full and fair opportunity in the first action to litigate the issue of Deis' negligence, we conclude that the district court acted properly in ruling that he is collaterally estopped from doing so again, in his individual capacity, in this action.[2]

---

2. Throughout this litigation, the parties have viewed Bobby Freeman's wrongful death claim solely in terms of collateral estoppel. The district court did the same in reviewing and ruling upon

We will therefore affirm the district court's dismissal on collateral estoppel grounds of Freeman's claim for damages due him individually because of Laura's allegedly wrongful death.

II.

A different issue, however, is presented as to whether collateral estoppel should bar the wrongful death claims here asserted on behalf of the mother and siblings of Laura. They were not parties to the first suit by Freeman, brought by him individually for his own personal injuries. Although Freeman himself as plaintiff brings the present action for their injuries in a representative capacity, the issue is whether *their* claims are precluded because of the adverse determination of Freeman's individual claims in the earlier suit.

The ordinary rule is that a party appearing in a representative capacity for others is not bound by the determination of an earlier suit in which he appeared only in an individual capacity. *Sayre v. Crews*, 184 F.2d 723, 724 (5th Cir. 1950) (determination of negligence in individual suit by the father had no preclusive effect in subsequent suit by father brought in representative capacity for his minor daughter); *Smith v. Hood*, 130 U.S. App. D.C. 43, 396 F.2d 692, 693–94 (D.C. Cir. 1968) (no collateral estoppel; earlier determination in mother's individual suit of non-traumatic cause of husband's death does not bar subsequent suit by mother in her representative capacity for her children for their wrongful death damages arising from accident).

Likewise, viewing these present wrongful death claims as asserted on behalf of the mother and siblings of Laura, they would not ordinarily be precluded as barred by the unfavorable judgment in the first suit brought by their husband-father Freeman, for close family relationships are not sufficient by themselves to establish privity with the original suit's party, or to bind a nonparty to that suit by the judgment entered therein. *See Leonhard v. United States*, 633 F.2d 599, 616 (2d Cir. 1980), *cert. denied*, 451 U.S. 908, 101 S. Ct. 1975, 68 L. Ed. 2d 295 (1981); *Smith v. Hood*, 130 U.S. App. D.C. 43, 396 F.2d 692, 693 (D.C.Cir. 1968); *Sayre v. Crews*, 184 F.2d 723, 724 (5th Cir. 1950); 1B Moore's Federal Practice, para. 0.411[11] (1984); 18 Wright, Miller, and Cooper, Federal Practice and Procedure § 4459 (1981). As summarized with respect to the present issue by the cited Wright treatise:

> Each [family member] has an independent cause of action for personal injuries, free from claim preclusion, just as other multiple plaintiffs are presumed to own separate claims. None is bound by issue preclusion in an action for personal injuries, for the same reasons as apply to preclusion among unrelated parties.... Preclusion does not apply between litigation conducted by one family member in a personal capacity and litigation conducted by the same person as a representative of another family member.

Wright, Miller, and Cooper, *supra*, § 4459 at pp. 524–25.

The district court recognized these principles, but it felt that the Fifth Circuit's expanded notion of "virtual representation," *see* 18 Wright, Miller, and Cooper, *supra*, § 4457, permitted application of collateral estoppel to bar the present subsequent suit by the

---

the defendants' motion for summary judgment. This issue might perhaps better be viewed in terms of res judicata, since both suits concerned grounds for relief, though differing, that arose out of conduct complained of in the first action. *See Kilgoar v. Colbert County Board of Education*, 578 F.2d 1033, 1035 (5th Cir. 1978). As explained in the text, however, collateral estoppel bars Freeman's wrongful death claim even if res judicata does not. Consequently, we need not decide here whether res judicata applies.

mother and siblings of Laura. Under this doctrine, "a person may be bound by a [prior] judgment even though not a party if one of the parties to the suit is so closely aligned with his interests as to be his virtual representative." *Aerojet General Corporation v. Askew,* 511 F.2d 710, 719 (5th Cir.), *cert. denied,* 423 U.S. 908, 96 S. Ct. 210, 46 L. Ed. 2d 137 (1975) (local governmental unit's subsequent suit precluded by prior judgment involving state agencies asserting defenses in close relationship to local unit).

In *Southwest Airlines, supra,* we outlined generally the circumstances in which the relationship between the one who is party in the first, and the nonparty thereto sought to be bound or precluded by collateral estoppel in the second suit, may be sufficiently close as to justify preclusion:

> First, a nonparty who has succeeded to a party's interest in property is bound by any prior judgments against that party.... Second, a nonparty who controlled the original suit will be bound by the resulting judgment.... Third, federal courts will bind a nonparty whose interests were represented adequately by a party in the original suit....

Southwest Airlines, supra, 546 F.2d at 95 (citations omitted).

Since the mother and the siblings of the second suit obviously did not succeed in property to any interest of Freeman asserted in the first suit, and obviously did not control the original suit by Freeman, the district court apparently concluded that the interests of the nonparty mother and siblings "were represented adequately" by Freeman in the first suit. However, both from *Southwest Airlines* itself and the succeeding decisions of this circuit, the concept of "adequate representation" does not refer to apparently competent litigation of an issue in a prior suit by a party holding parallel interest; rather, it refers to the concept of virtual representation, by which a nonparty may be bound because the party to the first suit "is so closely aligned with his [the nonparty's] interests as to be his virtual representative," *Aerojet General Corp., supra,* 511 F.2d at 719.

Further, as the jurisprudence of this circuit after *Southwest Airlines* makes plain, for parties to be so "closely aligned," or that the party's representation in the first suit "adequately" represents the non-party's interests in the first suit so as to preclude a nonparty in subsequent litigation, requires more than a showing of parallel interests or, even, a use of the same attorney in both suits.

[Prior decisions in this Circuit demonstrate that for "virtual representation" to exist demands the existence of an express or implied legal relationship in which parties to the first suit are accountable to nonparties who file a subsequent suit raising identical issues. Privity is "not established by the mere fact that persons may be interested in the same question or in proving the same set of facts."]

In *Pollard v. Cockrell,* 578 F.2d 1002 (5th Cir. 1978), we rejected the contention that one group of massage parlor owners were bound by a judgment in a prior lawsuit by another group. As we stated in *Hardy, Pollard* rejected virtual representation "despite nearly identical pleadings filed by the groups and representation by common attorneys." Pertinently to the present case—where the attorney in the present suit for the wrongful death damages of Laura's mother and siblings is the same as the attorney in Freeman's earlier suit for his own personal injuries—we concluded in *Pollard* that, for collateral estoppel purposes, "representation by the same attorneys cannot furnish the requisite alignment of interest." Although *Pollard* involved unrelated plaintiffs who had retained the same attorneys, we perceive no reason why a different principle should here apply because the attorney for the father-husband in his earlier unsuccessful suit happens to be the same attorney who now represents the mother and children in their independent action for wrongful death damages. Nor do we see any principled justification for holding that virtual representation applies because of the identity of attorneys here, whereas it would not if Freeman, on the one hand, and the mother and children, on the other, had retained different attorneys to file suit on their separate and independent causes of action.

III.

We conclude, therefore, that the plaintiff Freeman's present action, insofar as in his capacity representing the wrongful death claims of Laura's mother and siblings, is not barred by the judgment based upon jury determination of non-negligence dismissing the earlier suit brought by Freeman individually to recover only for his own personal injuries sustained in the same accident. The mother and siblings were not parties to the first suit nor were they in privity with Freeman in his first suit, nor—within the contours of the limited exception of this court permitting non-parties to be bound because of their virtual representation in the first suit—were the mother and siblings so closely aligned in legal interest with Freeman as to justify a holding that their interests were adequately represented in the first suit. We are re-enforced in this conclusion because, so far as we can ascertain, no appellate decision has ever applied collateral estoppel in like circumstances, whereas its application has consistently been rejected in the few reported instances in which sought.

An underlying principle is that "it is a violation of due process for a judgment [in a prior suit] to be binding on a litigant who was not a party or a privy and therefore has never had an opportunity to be heard." *Parklane Hosiery Company, Inc. v. Shore*, 439 U.S. 322, 327 n.7, 99 S. Ct. 645, 649 n. 7, 58 L. Ed. 2d 552 (1979). Collateral estoppel, with its purposes of protecting litigants from relitigating identical issues and promoting judicial economy by preventing needless litigation, may indeed be appropriate where the litigant has earlier had a "full and fair opportunity for judicial resolution of the same issue." 439 U.S. at 328, 99 S. Ct. at 650. Nevertheless, "some litigants—those who never appeared in a prior action—may not be collaterally estopped without litigating the issue. They have never had a chance to present their evidence and arguments on the claim. Due process prohibits estopping them despite one or more existing adjudications of the identical issue which stand squarely against their position." *Blonder-Tongue Laboratories, Inc. v. University of Ill. Foundation*, 402 U.S. 313, 329, 91 S. Ct. 1434, 1443, 28 L. Ed. 2d 788 (1971). The price of due process, thus, may include the possibility of conflicting adjudications in order to assure each litigant his or her day in court.

Conclusion

For the foregoing reasons, we AFFIRM the district court's judgment [dismissing] plaintiff Freeman's individual claim for wrongful death damages, but we REVERSE the district court's judgment [dismissing] the claims asserted on behalf of the other wrongful death beneficiaries of Laura Freeman.

Hardy v. Johns-Manville Sales Corp.

681 F.2d 334 (5th Cir. 1982)

GEE, CIRCUIT JUDGE:

This appeal arises out of a diversity action brought by various plaintiffs—insulators, pipefitters, carpenters, and other factory workers—against various manufacturers, sellers, and distributors of asbestos-containing products. The plaintiffs, alleging exposure to the products and consequent disease, assert various causes of action, including negligence, breach of implied warranty, and strict liability. The pleadings in each of the cases are substantially the same. No plaintiff names a particular defendant on a case-by-case basis but, instead, includes several—often as many as twenty asbestos manufacturers—in his individual complaint. The rationale offered for this unusual pleading practice is that, given the long latent period of the diseases in question, it is impossible for plaintiffs to isolate the precise exposure period or to identify the particular manufacturer's product responsible. The trial court accepted this rationale and opted for a theory of enterprise- or industry-wide liability used in, for example, *Sindell v. Abbott Laboratories*, 26 Cal.3d 588, 163 Cal.Rptr. 132, 607 P.2d 924 (1980), cert. denied, 449 U.S. 912, 101 S. Ct. 286, 66 L. Ed. 2d 140 (1980) (on proof that plaintiffs contracted a DES-related cancer and that their mothers took DES during pregnancy, market share apportionment determines a manufacturer's liability unless a given manufacturer exculpates itself by proving that its product could not have caused the injury).

Defendants' interlocutory appeal under 28 U.S.C.§ 1292(b) is directed at the district court's amended omnibus order dated March 13, 1981, which applies collateral estoppel to this mass tort. The omnibus order is, in effect, a partial summary judgment for plaintiffs based on nonmutual offensive collateral estoppel derived from this court's opinion in *Borel v. Fibreboard Paper Products Corp.*, 493 F.2d 1076 (5th Cir. 1973), cert. denied, 419 U.S. 869, 95 S. Ct. 127, 42 L. Ed. 2d 107 (1974) (henceforth *Borel*). *Borel* was a diversity lawsuit in which manufacturers of insulation products containing asbestos were held strictly liable to an insulation worker who developed asbestosis and mesothelioma and ultimately died. The trial court construed *Borel* as establishing as a matter of law and/or of fact that: (1) insulation products containing asbestos as a generic ingredient are "unavoidably unsafe products," (2) asbestos is a competent producing cause of mesothelioma and asbestiosis, (3) no warnings were issued by any asbestos insulation manufacturers prior to 1964, and (4) the "warning standard" was not met by the *Borel* defendants in the period from 1964 through 1969. The sole issue on appeal is the validity of the order on grounds of collateral estoppel or judicial.

In *Flatt v. Johns-Manville Sales Corp.*, 488 F. Supp. 836 (E.D.Tex.1980), the same court outlined the elements of proof for plaintiffs in asbestos-related cases. There the court stated that the plaintiff must prove by a preponderance of the evidence that

1. Defendants manufactured, marketed, sold, distributed, or placed in the stream of commerce products containing asbestos.

2. Products containing asbestos are unreasonably dangerous.

3. Asbestos dust is a competent producing cause of mesothelioma.

4. Decedent was exposed to defendant's products.

5. The exposure was sufficient to be a producing cause of mesothelioma.

6. Decedent contracted mesothelioma.

7. Plaintiffs suffered damages.

Id. at 838, citing Restatement (Second) of Torts § 402A(1) (1965). The parties agree that the effect of the trial court's collateral estoppel order in this case is to foreclose elements 2 and 3 above. Under the terms of the order, the plaintiffs need not prove that the defendants either knew or should have known of the dangerous propensities of their products and therefore should have warned consumers of these dangers, defendants being precluded from showing otherwise. On appeal, the defendants contend that the order violates their rights to due process and to trial by jury. Because we conclude that the trial court abused its discretion in applying collateral estoppel and judicial notice, we reverse.

[The court held that federal collateral estoppel law applied.]

Having determined that federal law of collateral estoppel governs, we next turn to an examination of just what that law is. In *Parklane Hosiery Co. v. Shore*, 439 U.S. 322, 99 S. Ct. 645, 58 L. Ed. 2d 552 (1979), the Supreme Court was asked to determine "whether a party who has had issues of fact adjudicated adversely to it in an equitable action may be collaterally estopped from relitigating the same issues before a jury in a subsequent legal action brought against it by a new party." The Court responded affirmatively, noting offensive collateral estoppel's "dual purpose of protecting litigants from the burden of re-litigating an identical issue with the same party or his privy and of promoting judicial economy by preventing needless litigation." The Court reiterated that mutuality is not necessary to proper invocation of collateral estoppel under federal law, citing *Blonder-Tongue Laboratories, Inc. v. University of Illinois Foundation*, 402 U.S. 313, 91 S. Ct. 1434, 28 L. Ed. 2d 788 (1971), and further held that the use of offensive collateral estoppel does not violate a defendant's seventh amendment right to a jury trial. To avoid problems with the use of the doctrine, the Court adopted a general rule of fairness, stating "that in cases where plaintiff could easily have joined in the earlier action or where ... for other reasons, the application of offensive collateral estoppel would be unfair to a defendant, a trial judge should not allow the use of offensive collateral estoppel."

In the wake of *Parklane*, it is clear that a right, question, or fact distinctly put in issue and directly determined as a ground of recovery by a court of competent jurisdiction collaterally estops a party or his privy from relitigating the issue in a subsequent action. So stated, the doctrine recognizes that a person "cannot be bound by a judgment unless he has had reasonable notice of the claim against him and opportunity to be heard in opposition to that claim. 1B J. Moore, Moore's Federal Practice ¶0.411 at 1252 (2d ed.1982) (henceforth Moore's). The right to a full and fair opportunity to litigate an issue is, of course, protected by the due process clause of the United States Constitution. While *Parklane* made the doctrine of mutuality effectively a dead letter under federal law, the case left undisturbed the requisite of privity, i.e., that collateral estoppel can only be applied against parties who have had a prior "'full and fair' opportunity to litigate their claims." The requirement that a person against whom the conclusive effect of a judgment is invoked must be a party or a privy to the prior judgment retains its full vigor after *Parklane* and has been repeatedly affirmed by our court.

THE NON-*BOREL* DEFENDANTS

[The court held that it was clearly an error for the trial court to apply collateral estoppel against sellers of the product who were not even parties to the *Borel* case. This would clearly violate their due process rights to be heard on the matter.]

THE *BOREL* DEFENDANTS

The propriety of estopping the six defendants in this case who were parties to *Borel* poses more difficult questions. In ascertaining the precise preclusive effect of a prior judgment on a particular issue, we have often referred to the requirements set out, inter alia, in *International Association of Machinists & Aerospace Workers v. Nix*, 512 F.2d 125, 132 (5th Cir. 1975). The party asserting the estoppel must show that: (1) the issue to be concluded is identical to that involved in the prior action; (2) in the prior action the issue was "actually litigated"; and (3) the determination made of the issue in the prior action must have been necessary and essential to the resulting judgment.

As the appellants at times concede in their briefs, "if *Borel* stands for any rule at all, it is that defendants have a duty to warn the users of their products of the long-term dangers attendant upon its use, including the danger of an occupational disease." Indeed, the first sentence in our *Borel* opinion states that that case involved "the scope of an asbestos man-ufacturer's duty to warn industrial insulation workers of dangers associated with the use of asbestos." Our conclusion in *Borel* was grounded in that trial court's jury instructions concerning proximate cause and defective product. Close reading of these instructions convinced our panel in *Borel* that a failure to warn was necessarily implicit in the jury's verdict.

Nonetheless, we must ultimately conclude that the judgment in *Borel* cannot estop even the *Borel* defendants in this case for three interrelated reasons.

First, after review of the issues decided in *Borel*, we conclude that *Borel*, while conclusive as to the general matter of a duty to warn on the part of manufacturers of asbestos-containing insulation products, is ultimately ambiguous as to certain key issues. As the authors of the Restatement (Second) — Judgments § 29, comment g (1982), have noted, collateral estoppel is inappropriate where the prior judgment is ambivalent:

> The circumstances attending the determination of an issue in the first action may indicate that it could reasonably have been resolved otherwise if those cir-cumstances were absent. Resolution of the issue in question may have entailed reference to such matters as the intention, knowledge, or comparative responsibility of the parties in relation to each other.... In these and similar situations, taking the prior determination at face value for purposes of the second action would extend the effects of imperfections in the adjudicative process beyond the limits of the first adjudication, within which they are accepted only because of the practical necessity of achieving finality.

The *Borel* jury decided that Borel, an industrial insulation worker who was exposed to fibers from his employer's insulation products over a 33-year period (from 1936 to 1969), was entitled to have been given fair warning that asbestos dust may lead to asbestosis, mesothelioma, and other cancers. The jury dismissed the argument that the danger was obvious and regarded as conclusive the fact that Borel testified that he did not know that inhaling asbestos dust could cause serious injuries until his doctor so advised him in 1969. The jury necessarily found "that, had adequate warnings been provided, Borel would have chosen to avoid the danger." In *Borel*, the evidence was that the industry as a whole issued no warnings at all concerning its insulation products prior to 1964, that Johns-Manville placed a warnings label on packages of its products in 1964, and that Fibrebaord and Rubberoid placed warnings on their products in 1966.

Given these facts, it is impossible to determine what the *Borel* jury decided about when a duty to warn attached. Did the jury find the defendants liable because their warnings after 1966, when they acknowledged that they knew the dangers of asbestosis, were in-sufficiently explicit as to the grave risks involved? If so, as appellants here point out, the jury may have accepted the state of the art arguments provided by the defendants in *Borel*—i.e., that the defendants were not aware of the danger of asbestosis until the 1960's. Even under this view, there is a second ambiguity: was strict liability grounded on the fact that the warnings issued, while otherwise sufficient, never reached the insulator in the field? If so, perhaps the warnings, while insufficient as to insulation workers like Borel, were sufficient to alert workers further down the production line who may have seen the warnings—such as the carpenters and pipefitters in this case. Alternatively, even if the *Borel* jury decided that failure to warn before 1966 grounded strict liability, did the duty attach in the 1930's when the "hazard of asbestosis as a pneumoconiotic dust was universally accepted," *id.* at 1083, or in 1965, when documentary evidence was presented of the hazard of asbestos insulation products to the installers of these products?

Not all the plaintiffs in this case were exposed to asbestos-containing insulation products over the same 30-year period as plaintiff Borel. Not all plaintiffs here are insulation workers isolated from the warnings issued by some of the defendants in 1964 and 1966. Some of the products may be different from those involved in *Borel*. Our opinion in *Borel*, "limited to determining whether there [was] a conflict in substantial evidence sufficient to create a jury question," did not resolve that as a matter of fact all manufacturers of asbestos-containing insulation products had a duty to warn as of 1936, and all failed to warn adequately after 1964. Although we determined that the jury must have found a violation of the manufacturers' duty to warn, we held only that the jury could have grounded strict liability on the absence of a warning prior to 1964 or "could have concluded that the [post-1964 and post-1966] 'cautions' were not warnings in the sense that they adequately communicated to Borel and other insulation workers knowledge of the dangers to which they were exposed so as to give them a choice of working or not working with a dangerous product." [O]ur opinion in *Borel* merely approved of the various ways the jury could have come to a conclusion concerning strict liability for failure to warn. We did not say that any of the specific alternatives that the jury had before it were necessary or essential to its verdict.

Like stare decisis, collateral estoppel applies only to issues of fact or law necessarily decided by a prior court. Since we cannot say that *Borel* necessarily decided, as a matter of fact, that all manufacturers of asbestos-containing insulation products knew or should have known of the dangers of their particular products at all relevant times, we cannot justify the trial court's collaterally estopping the defendants from presenting evidence as to the state of the art.

Principles

"There is reason for saying that a man shall not lose his cause in consequence of the verdict given in a former proceeding to which he was not a party; but there is no reason whatever for saying that he shall not lose his cause in consequence of the verdict in a proceeding to which he was a party, merely because his adversary was not."

3 Jeremy Bentham, "Rational of Judicial Evidence" 579 (1827)

Even if we are wrong as to the ambiguities of the *Borel* judgment, there is a second, equally important, reason to deny collateral estoppel effect to it: the presence of inconsistent verdicts. In *Parklane Hosiery v. Shore*, 439 U.S. at 330–31, the Court noted that collateral estoppel is improper and "unfair" to a defendant "if the judgment relied upon as a basis for the estoppel is itself inconsistent with one or more previous judgments in favor of the defendant." Not only does issue preclusion in such cases appear arbitrary to a defendant who has had favorable judgments on the same issue, it also undermines the premise that different juries reach equally valid verdicts. One jury's determination should not, merely because it comes later in time, bind another jury's determination of an issue over which there are equally reasonable resolutions of doubt.[13]

---

13. The injustice of applying collateral estoppel in cases involving mass torts is especially obvious. Thus, in *Parklane* the Court cited Prof. Currie's "familiar example": "A railroad collision injures 50 passengers all of whom bring separate actions against the railroad. After the railroad wins the first 25 suits, a plaintiff wins in suit 26. Professor Currie argues that offensive use of collateral estoppel should

The parties inform us that there have been approximately 70 similar asbestos cases thus far tried around the country. Approximately half of these seem to have been decided in favor of the defendants. A court able to say that the approximately 35 suits decided in favor of asbestos manufacturers were all decided on the basis of insufficient exposure on the part of the plaintiff or failure to demonstrate an asbestos-related disease would be clairvoyant. Indeed, the appellants inform us of several products liability cases in which the state of the art question was fully litigated, yet the asbestos manufacturers were found not liable. Although it is usually not possible to say with certainty what these juries based their verdicts on, in at least some of the cases the verdict for the defendant was not based on failure to prove exposure or failure to show an asbestos-related disease. In *Starnes v. Johns-Manville Corp.*, No. 2075-122 (E.D.Tenn.1977), one of the cases cited in *Flatt v. Johns-Manville Sales Corp., supra*, the court's charge to the jury stated that it was "undisputed that as a result of inhaling materials containing asbestos, Mr. Starnes contracted the disease known as asbestosis." The verdict for the defendant in Starnes must mean, that the jury found the insulation products involved in that case not unreasonably dangerous. This court takes judicial notice of these inconsistent or ambiguous verdicts pursuant to Fed.R.Evid. 201(d). We conclude that the court erred in arbitrarily choosing one of these verdicts, that in *Borel*, as the bellwether.

Finally, we conclude that even if the *Borel* verdict had been unambiguous and the sole verdict issued on point, application of collateral estoppel would still be unfair with regard to the *Borel* defendants because it is very doubtful that these defendants could have foreseen that their $68,000 liability to plaintiff Borel would foreshadow multimillion dollar asbestos liability. As noted in *Parklane*, it would be unfair to apply collateral estoppel "if a defendant in the first action is sued for small or nominal damages [since] he may have little incentive to defend vigorously, particularly if future lawsuits are not foreseeable." 439 U.S. at 330. While in absolute terms a judgment for $68,000 hardly appears nominal, the Supreme Court's citation of *Berner v. British Commonwealth Pacific Airlines*, 346 F.2d 532 (2d Cir. 1965), cert. denied, 382 U.S. 983 (1966) (application of collateral estoppel denied where defendant did not appeal an adverse judgment awarding damages of $35,000 and defendant was later sued for over $7 million), suggests that the matter is relative. The reason the district court here applied collateral estoppel is precisely because early cases like *Borel* have opened the floodgates to an enormous, unprecedented volume of asbestos litigation. According to a recent estimate, there are over 3,000 asbestos plaintiffs in the Eastern District of Texas alone and between 7,500 and 10,000 asbestos cases pending in United States District Courts around the country. The omnibus order here involves 58 pending cases, and the many plaintiffs involved in this case are each seeking $2.5 million in damages. Such a staggering potential liability could not have been foreseen by Borel.

[We] sympathize with the district court's efforts to streamline the enormous asbestos caseload it faces. None of what we say here is meant to cast doubt on any possible alternative ways to avoid reinventing the asbestos liability wheel. We hold today only that courts cannot read *Borel* to stand for the proposition that, as matters of fact, asbestos products are unreasonably dangerous or that asbestos as a generic element is in all products a

---

not be applied so as to allow plaintiffs 27 through 50 automatically to recover." 439 U.S. at 331 n.14, 99 S. Ct. at 651 n.14, citing Currie, *Mutuality of Estoppel: Limits of the Bernhard Doctrine*, 9 Stan.L.Rev. 281, 304 (1957).

competent producing cause of cancer. To do otherwise would be to elevate judicial expedience over considerations of justice and fair play.

REVERSED

Notes and Problems

1. In the *Freeman* case, why do you think that the individual plaintiff failed to bring the wrongful death claims in the first lawsuit when he sued for his own injuries? Do you see the distinction in the wrongful death claim between his entitlement to sue and that of the other family members? Also, consider footnote 2 in that opinion. Is the case better understood as a res judicata case or as a collateral estoppel case?

2. In *Hardy*, what do you think is the most compelling reason to deny plaintiff the ability to rely upon offensive non-mutual collateral estoppel? Regarding the inconsistency of prior verdicts in similar cases, lower federal courts have themselves been very inconsistent about how to treat this circumstance. In addition to the reasons given by the court in that case, courts have also invoked two other concerns raised by the Supreme Court in *Parklane Hosiery* to sometimes deny collateral estoppel in a non-mutual offensive setting: (a) a difference in pretrial procedure or trial evidence between the two cases, and (b) the opportunity for the subsequent claimant to have joined in the earlier litigation (referred to as "wait and see" plaintiffs).

3. As you can see, res judicata and collateral estoppel are similar doctrines, and they both have the same essential goal—to produce efficient litigation. But in some ways, both doctrines can claim to be larger than the other. Res judicata can bar the litigation of a matter that has never been litigated before so long as it arises out of the same transaction or occurrence as a previously litigated claim. In that regard, res judicata is broader than collateral estoppel, which requires than an issue is actually litigated before the doctrine can apply. However, collateral estoppel may apply even if no mutuality of parties exists so long as it is fair to use non-mutual collateral estoppel. More importantly, collateral estoppel can be used offensively to force the defendant to lose in future litigation. Res judicata, on the other hand, can only work defensively to preclude a claim.

4. There are many instances where defendants engage in a pattern of conduct that causes injuries to many people. This phenomenon makes offensive non-mutual collateral estoppel a potentially potent weapon to be wielded against such defendants and also a potentially useful device for courts to achieve efficiency. Would it be better for a defendant to litigate all the liability issues directly against multiple claimants in one case rather than to potentially have one adverse verdict used against it in future cases? The feasibility of a case being structured in such a manner will be explored under both Rule 20's joinder provisions and in the class action coverage, later in this text, under Rule 23.

5. *Problems.* Consider whether collateral estoppel should avoid re-litigation of the following issues:

a. Two neighbors have a hard time getting along. Tim gets upset about Florence's holding of loud pool parties in her backyard every weekend. Tim finally sues Florence and obtains a jury verdict finding that Florence's use of her property constitutes a nuisance. A few months later, Florence begins a woodworking business out of her garage. Again, bothered by the constant noise late at night, Tim suits Florence a second time seeking another finding that the continued noise is a nuisance.

b. Julius is accused of murdering his girlfriend. He is tried in criminal court and found not guilty. The parents of the girlfriend, suing on behalf of the decedent, file a survival claim for battery against Julius asserting that his conduct in allegedly murdering their daughter is a tort entitling them to recover damages on her behalf.

c. A popular reality-show star on the current season of the Bachelor television show becomes the subject of much debate when the New York Times publishes an article falsely asserting that he is a convicted pedophile. The Bachelor sues the paper for libel but loses based upon a finding that he was a public figure and that the paper did not have actual malice. The Los Angeles Times also similarly reports on the same matter. He is now suing that paper for libel as well.

d. Petrov sues General Motors contending that the steering mechanism on the 2016 Suburban he purchased was defective causing him to have an accident. The jury in that case rejects the claim finding no defect in the vehicle's design. Susan also purchased the same vehicle and, upon hearing stories of multiple Suburbans having steering problems, sues General Motors for a return of her purchase price based upon the alleged steering defect.

6. *Chapter Problem:* On behalf of Paula Jones, would it be likely that a court would use defendant Kazakh's one recent litigation loss (reported in the newspaper article earlier in this chapter) to preclude Kazakh from re-litigating the issue of the allegedly defective braking system in the Camel automobile? What would Kazakh's best arguments be against invocation of the doctrine? Is it even constitutionally permissible for Paula Jones to invoke this doctrine without having been a party to that prior lawsuit? How should the court rule on the issue of Paula's attempted application of the doctrine of non-mutual offensive collateral estoppel? Finally, can Kazakh use its one prior litigation victory concerning the Camel's braking system to defeat Paula's current claim? How would a court have to rule on such an attempt by Kazakh to plead collateral estoppel in support of a defensive motion for summary judgment?

Pulling It All Together Exercise

Big Bend Developers, Inc. buys a large unit of land and plans to develop the land into a large, upscale subdivision. To appeal to potential homebuyers, Big Bend promises to subject the land to easements in which every owner will have access to multiple common areas in the subdivision. Additionally, Big Bend promises to build a boat marina for owners to use. Bob and Janice buy a house in the subdivision with grand plans to own a boat and use the marina. Big Bend fails to build the marina, and subsequently intends to develop the common areas into more homes. Bob and Janice sue Big Bend seeking declaratory relief stating that they have a right to use the common area free of obstructions and rescission of the contract because Big Bend failed to build the marina. The court grants declaratory relief in favor of Bob and Janice, but does not rescind the contract. Subsequently, Bob and Janice sue Big Bend seeking specific performance of Big Bend's promise to build the marina. They argue that their claim is not barred by res judicata because the issue of whether they were entitled to enforce Big Bend's promise to build the marina was not litigated in the prior suit. You are the judge. How do you rule?

Spend 30 minutes writing your analysis of the foregoing problem. Be sure to explain each of your conclusions.

D. Compulsory Counterclaims

The characterization of counterclaims is important in a few circumstances. If a party files and litigates a counterclaim in the original case, it may not really matter what we characterize it as, so long as an independent basis for federal court subject matter jurisdiction exists for the counterclaim. But if not, the difference between concluding that the counterclaim was compulsory or permissive will determine whether the court has power to hear the counterclaim in that proceeding. Further, if the counterclaim is not brought in response to the plaintiff's original suit but in a later suit by the original defendant, characterization of the claim as a compulsory counterclaim results in its waiver. In the *Plant v. Blazer Financial Servs., Inc.* case below, the court considers various tests for determining whether the counterclaim was compulsory or permissive. Ask yourself why bringing the claim in the same proceeding was so important to the defendant. Following *Plant*, we will encounter the compulsory counterclaim debate in the waiver context in the *Ferrarri* case. As you read these cases, consider whether the context might impact a court's motivation to apply either a broad or a narrow application of Rule 13's commands.

Rule 13. Counterclaim and Crossclaim

(a) **Compulsory Counterclaim.**

    (1) **In General.**

        A pleading must state as a counterclaim any claim that—at the time of its service—the pleader has against an opposing party if the claim:

        (A) arises out of the transaction or occurrence that is the subject matter of the opposing party's claim; and

        (B) does not require adding another party over whom the court cannot acquire jurisdiction

    (2) **Exceptions.** The pleader need not state the claim if:

        (A) when the action was commenced, the claim was the subject of another pending action.

(b) **Permissive Counterclaim.** A pleading may state as a counterclaim against an opposing party any claim that is not compulsory.

Plant v. Blazer Financial Services

598 F.2d 1357 (5th Cir. 1979)

RONEY, J.,

In this truth-in-lending case, we resolve [an] important issue[] to this field of the law. [W]e decide that an action on the underlying debt in default is a compulsory counterclaim that must be asserted in a suit by the debtor on a truth-in-lending cause of action....

Although plaintiff prevailed on her truth-in-lending claim in this case, both her award and the attorney's fees allowed were setoff against the lender defendant's counterclaim on the underlying debt. [P]laintiff attacks the jurisdiction of the court to entertain the counterclaim.

facts

On July 17, 1975 plaintiff Theresa Plant executed a note in favor of defendant Blazer Financial Services, Inc. for $2,520.00 to be paid in monthly installments of $105.00. No payments were made on the note. In March 1976 plaintiff commenced a civil action under § 1640 of the Truth-in-Lending Act, 15 U.S.C.A. § 1601 et seq., for failure to make disclosures required by the Act and by Regulation Z, 12 C.F.R. § 226.1 et seq. (1978), promulgated thereunder. Defendant counterclaimed on the note for the unpaid balance. Based on defendant's failure to disclose a limitation on an after-acquired security interest, the trial court held the disclosure inadequate and awarded plaintiff the statutory penalty of $944.76 and $700.00 in attorney's fees ...

The trial court, however, offset the plaintiff's award and the attorney's fee award against the judgment for defendant on the counterclaim. From this judgment and setoff, plaintiff appeals ... the jurisdiction of the court to entertain the counterclaim.

I. Counterclaim

Plaintiff challenges the trial court's ruling that defendant's counterclaim on the underlying debt was compulsory. The issue is jurisdictional. A permissive counterclaim must have an independent jurisdictional basis [this result was codified by § 1367(a)'s requirement that a supplemental claim must arise from the same constitutional "case or controversy" to be within the court's supplemental jurisdiction], while it is generally accepted that a compulsory counterclaim falls within the [supplemental] jurisdiction of the federal courts even if it would ordinarily be a matter for state court consideration. In the instant case there is no independent basis since neither federal question nor diversity jurisdiction is available for the counterclaim. Consequently, if the counterclaim were to be treated as permissive, defendant's action on the underlying debt would have to be pursued in the state court.

The issue of whether a state debt counterclaim in a truth-in-lending action is compulsory or permissive is one of first impression in this Circuit, [and] has never, to our knowledge, been decided by a court of appeals, and has received diverse treatment from a great number of district courts.

RULE

Rule 13(a), Fed.R.Civ.P., provides that a counterclaim is compulsory if it "arises out of the transaction or occurrence" that is the subject matter of plaintiff's claim. Four tests have been suggested to further define when a claim and counterclaim arise from the same transaction:

1) Are the issues of fact and law raised by the claim and counterclaim largely the same?

2) Would res judicata bar a subsequent suit on defendant's claim absent the compulsory counterclaim rule?

3) Will substantially the same evidence support or refute plaintiff's claim as well as defendant's counterclaim?

4) Is there any logical relation between the claim and the counterclaim?

6 Wright & Miller, Federal Practice and Procedure § 1410 at 42 (1971). An affirmative answer to any of the four questions indicates the counterclaim is compulsory.

The test which has commended itself to most courts, including our own, is the logical relation test. *Revere Copper & Brass, Inc. v. Aetna Casualty & Surety Co.*, 426 F.2d 709, 714 (5th Cir. 1970); 6 Wright & Miller at 48. The logical relation test is a loose standard which permits "a broad realistic interpretation in the interest of avoiding a multiplicity of suits." 3 Moore's Federal Practice P 13.13 at 300. "The hallmark of this approach is its flexibility." 6 Wright & Miller at 46–47.

In *Revere Copper & Brass* this Court added a third tier to the counterclaim analysis by further defining "logical relationship" to exist when the counterclaim arises from the same "aggregate of operative facts" in that the same operative facts serves as the basis of both claims or the aggregate core of facts upon which the claim rests activates additional legal rights, otherwise dormant, in the defendant.

Applying the logical relationship test literally to the counterclaim in this case clearly suggests its compulsory character because a single aggregate of operative facts, the loan transaction, gave rise to both plaintiff's and defendant's claim. Because a tallying of the results from the district courts which have decided this question, however, shows that a greater number have found such a counterclaim merely permissive, we subject the relationship between the claims to further analysis.

The split of opinion on the nature of debt counterclaims in truth-in-lending actions appears to be, in large part, the product of competing policy considerations between the objectives of Rule 13(a) and the policies of the Truth-in-Lending Act, and disagreement over the extent to which federal courts should be involved in state causes of action for debt. While Rule 13(a) is intended to avoid multiple litigation by consolidating all controversies between the parties, several courts and commentators have observed that accepting creditors' debt counterclaims may obstruct achievement of the goals of the Truth-in-Lending Act. Various arguments are made compositely as follows: The purpose of the Act is[:]

> to assure a meaningful disclosure of credit terms so that the consumer will be able to compare more readily the various credit terms available to him and avoid the uninformed use of credit.

15 U.S.C.A. § 1601. This purpose is effectuated by debtors' standing in the role of private attorneys general not merely to redress individual injuries but to enforce federal policy. The success of this private enforcement scheme would be undermined if debtors were faced with counterclaims on debts often exceeding the limits of their potential recovery under the Act. The purpose of the Act would suffer further frustration if federal courts were entangled in the myriad factual and legal questions essential to a decision on the debt claims but unrelated to the truth-in-lending violation. In *Roberts v. National School of Radio & Television Broadcasting*, 374 F. Supp. 1266 (N.D.Ga.1974), the court also noted the incongruity of enlisting the federal court's resources to assist in debt collection by the very target of the legislation which gives the plaintiff its cause of action.

Several other factors have been cited to offset the attractiveness of treating all related disputes in a single action under Rule 13. For example, courts have predicted a flood of debt counterclaims, greatly increasing the federal court workload. Furthermore, permitting debt counterclaims might destroy truth-in-lending class actions by interjecting vast numbers of individual questions. The judicial economy of consolidated litigation might be countered by the delay of having to provide a jury trial for the debt claim though none is available to the truth-in-lending plaintiff. Other courts have suggested that regarding such debt counterclaims as compulsory would infringe on the power of states to adjudicate disputes grounded in state law.

Courts which have concluded debt counterclaims to be permissive have found the nexus between the truth-in-lending violation and debt obligation too abstract or tenuous to regard the claims as logically related. One claim, they reason, involves the violation of federal law designed to deter lender nondisclosure and facilitate credit shopping and the other concerns merely a default on a private duty....

After careful consideration of the factors relied upon in these cases to find counterclaims permissive, we opt for the analysis applied by district courts in Louisiana, Alabama, Texas and Georgia in determining debt counterclaims to be compulsory.

In *Carter v. Public Finance Corp.*, 73 F.R.D. 488 (N.D.Ala.1977), the court concluded that both claims arose from a single loan transaction and that other than proof of default necessary to prove the counterclaim, the evidence in each would overlap. The court rejected the four suggested tests and held that the single transaction of Rule 13(a) encompassed the loan and everything necessarily done in connection with its closing.

The results reached in Carter were found "inescapable" in *George v. Beneficial Finance Co. of Dallas*, 81 F.R.D. 4 (N.D.Tex.1977). Emphasizing the goal of judicial economy furthered by a single presentation of facts, the court observed that "suits on notes will inevitably deal with the circumstance of the execution of the notes and any representation made to 'induce' the borrowing." ...

We add to these arguments the observation that one of the purposes of the compulsory counterclaim rule is to provide complete relief to the defendant who has been brought involuntarily into the federal court. Absent the opportunity to bring a counterclaim, this party could be forced to satisfy the debtor's truth-in-lending claim without any assurance that his claims against the defaulting debtor arising from the same transaction will be taken into account or even that the funds he has been required to pay will still be available should he obtain a state court judgment in excess of the judgment on the truth-in-lending claim. In addition, a determination that the underlying debt was invalid may have a material effect on the amount of damages a debtor could recover on a truth-in-lending claim.

To permit the debtor to recover from the creditor without taking the original loan into account would be a serious departure from the evenhanded treatment afforded both parties under the Act. Truth-in-lending claims can be brought in either state or federal court. To the extent this dual jurisdiction was intended to permit litigation of truth-in-lending claims in actions on the debt, it reflects a purpose that the debt claim and the truth-in-lending claims be handled together. To the extent it was intended to relieve federal courts of any of this litigation, the purpose would be frustrated by providing a sanctuary from the creditor's claims in one jurisdiction but not in the other. State courts would always have jurisdiction of a creditor's counterclaim. Had Congress intended to insulate recovery in truth-in-lending actions in federal court from the counterclaims of creditors, of which it surely was aware, it could have easily done so.

We conclude that the obvious interrelationship of the claims and rights of the parties, coupled with the common factual basis of the claims, demonstrates a logical relationship between the claim and counterclaim under the test of *Revere Copper & Brass*. We affirm the trial court's determination that the debt counterclaim is compulsory.

Ferrari v. E-Rate Consulting Servs.

655 F. Supp. 2d 1194 (M.D. Ala. 2009)

FULLER, C.J.,

INTRODUCTION

This case is presently before the Court on a Motion to Dismiss Pursuant to Rule 12(b)(6), which defendant Jonathan Slaughter filed on February 16, 2009, and a second, materially identical Motion to Dismiss Pursuant to Rule 12(b)(6), which defendant E-

Rate Consulting Services filed the same day (Doc. # 8). After careful consideration of the arguments of the parties and the applicable authorities, the Court finds that the Motions are due to be GRANTED in part and DENIED in part.

FACTUAL AND PROCEDURAL HISTORY

The following facts are taken from the Complaint in this case (the "Federal Complaint") and the Complaint in a related state court case (the "State Complaint"), as they must be for purposes of these Motions. *See Am. United Life Ins. Co. v. Martinez,* 480 F.3d 1043, 1057 (11th Cir.2007); *Davis v. Williams Commc'ns, Inc.,* 258 F.Supp.2d 1348, 1352 (N.D.Ga.2003).

Defendant Jonathan Slaughter ("Slaughter") is a resident of Elmore County, Alabama and the sole owner of Defendant E-Rate Consulting Services ("E-Rate"), an Alabama Limited Liability Company. Plaintiff Shannon Ferrari ("Ferrari") worked for E-Rate for three weeks in the summer of 2007. That brief employment resulted in a lawsuit in state court by E-Rate and Slaughter against Ferrari and the instant case by Ferrari against E-Rate and Slaughter. The details of the two cases follow.

Slaughter and E-Rate commenced an action against Ferrari in the Circuit Court of Montgomery County, Alabama on January 12, 2008. The State Complaint alleges that Ferrari was a problem employee who demanded more money than the salary at which she was hired and regularly complained about her compensation. The State Complaint also alleges that she continued to complain about her compensation upon her termination and demanded that Slaughter and E-Rate pay her a large severance and a continuing monthly income, provide her with health insurance, and provide her a new wardrobe. The State Complaint states that Ferrari threatened that if Slaughter and E-Rate did not pay her she would "make their life difficult" and they "would regret not paying her" as she demanded. The State Complaint alleges that when Slaughter and E-Rate did not meet Ferrari's requests she threatened to make claims and institute suits against them, for, among other things, sexual harassment.

The State Complaint details an incident on January 2, 2008, in which Slaughter approached Ferrari in a local bar to discuss the problems arising from her termination. According to the State Complaint, Ferrari filed a baseless criminal complaint for harassment against Slaughter the day after the incident in the local bar. The State Complaint alleges that the criminal harassment complaint contained false, libelous, and defamatory statements. The State Complaint also details an attempt on January 4, 2008, by Ferrari to interrupt E-Rate's business by calling the Commissioner of Agriculture and Industries, with whom E-Rate works under contract, and sharing with the Commissioner false and defamatory statements.

The State Complaint presents claims arising from these occurrences in three counts: one each for libel and slander, false light, and intentional interference with contractual and/or business relations. Ferrari answered the State Complaint on February 14, 2008.

Ferrari, defendant in the state court action, filed a Complaint in this Court on January 21, 2009. The Federal Complaint named Slaughter and E-Rate, plaintiffs in the state court action, as defendants. The Federal Complaint alleges that Slaughter began sexually harassing Ferrari daily shortly after hiring her. The harassment began, according to the Federal Complaint, when Slaughter offered to put Ferrari on a "full scholarship," which meant an increased salary if she would stay home with her children and move into a house he claimed he owned, and would include a BMW automobile if she would travel with him and be his girlfriend. The Federal Complaint lists other instances of sexual harassment, including overt sexual propositioning of Ferrari by Slaughter, groping, attempts to massage, and regular references to Ferrari's private parts by a nickname Slaughter contrived. Finally, the Federal Complaint alleges that Slaughter took Ferrari on a trip with other males and insisted that she do drugs with them. Ferrari quit her job on July 27, 2007, after this final incident.

According to the Federal Complaint, Ferrari asked Slaughter about certain money that he owed her after her resignation, and Slaughter agreed to pay her a bonus he had promised her and three months severance pay. The Federal Complaint also alleges that Slaughter has continued to attempt to harm Ferrari by telling people he had been having a sexual affair with her. The Federal Complaint also details the altercation at the nightclub detailed in the State Complaint, though this time the allegation is that Slaughter followed Ferrari to the club, grabbed her, pulled her off a bar stool, and told her to leave with him. The Federal Complaint also details the subsequent harassment charge, though it claims the allegations were justified.

Finally, the Federal Complaint alleges that as a result of these happenings, on or about January 10, 2008, Ferrari filed a Charge of Discrimination with the Equal Employment Opportunity Commission ("EEOC"). The Federal Complaint states that Ferrari received a notice of right to sue on or about November 16, 2008.

The Federal Complaint contains five counts, one each for sexual harassment in violation of Title VII, constructive termination, assault and battery under state law, retaliation, and outrage.

DISCUSSION

Defendants argue in their Motions that the compulsory counterclaim rule bars the instant action. They claim that "the very allegations contained in the Plaintiff's complaint at bar are addressed in the State Complaint filed by the E-Rate Consulting and Jonathan Slaughter in the action against the Plaintiff Shannon Ferrari." Hence, Defendants argue, Ferrari's claims are compulsory counterclaims that Ferrari failed to assert in the prior-in-time state case. The federal case must therefore be dismissed, or so the argument goes.

Ferrari disputes Defendants' assertions. First, she claims she was not able to bring her claims as compulsory counterclaims in the state case because her Title VII claims did not mature until she received the right-to-sue letter on or about November 16, 2008, "well into the process of the state court case." Ferrari also claims that she was free to not bring the instant claims in the state court proceeding because they do not arise from the same transaction or occurrence as the state court claims brought by E-rate Consulting Services in state court. Ferrari argues that the Title VII sexual harassment claims are both factually and legally distinct from the libel, slander, false light, and intentional interference with contractual and/or business relations claims against her in state court.

Ferrari's claims are barred if they were compulsory counterclaims that should have been alleged in the state case that names her as a defendant. Alabama law governs the question of whether Ferrari's claims were compulsory counterclaims in the earlier action. *See Montgomery Ward Dev. Corp. v. Juster*, 932 F.2d 1378, 1380 (11th Cir. 1991) ("Whether failure to bring a compulsory counterclaim in a prior state court proceeding bars a diversity action on that claim in a federal district court ... depends upon state law."); *Amey, Inc. v. Gulf Abstract & Title, Inc.*, 758 F.2d 1486, 1509 (11th Cir. 1985) ("when a federal court exercises federal question jurisdiction and is asked to give res judicata effect to a state court judgment, it must apply the "res judicata principles of the law of the state whose decision is set up as a bar to further litigation."). Since the res judicata rules of the State of Alabama control what actions can be brought in federal court when there was prior related state court litigation, Ferrari's claim should be barred here if the same suit would be barred in an Alabama state court.

Alabama's compulsory counterclaim rule tracks Rule 13(a) of the Federal Rules of Civil Procedure, whose purpose is "to prevent multiplicity of actions" by "[resolving] in a single lawsuit ... all disputes arising out of common matters." *S. Constr. Co. v. Pickard,* 371 U.S. 57, 60, 83 S. Ct. 108, 9 L. Ed. 2d 31 (1962). Thus, if such a counterclaim is not brought with the original action, "relitigation of the claim may be barred by the doctrines of res judicata or collateral estoppel by judgment in the event certain issues are determined adversely to the party electing not to assert the claim." *Id.*[1] Alabama Rule of Civil Procedure 13(a) requires that a pleading "state as a counterclaim any claim which at the time of serving the pleading the pleader has against any opposing party, if it arises out of the transaction or occurrence that is the subject matter of the opposing party's claim." The rule has two requirements: (1) that the claims arise from the same transaction or occurrence, and (2) that they be available to the defendant at the time she serves her answer in the first case. The Court takes these requirements up in turn.

A. Same Transaction or Occurrence

A claim can only be a compulsory counterclaim under Alabama Rule 13(a) if it arises from the same transaction or occurrence as the subject of the opposing party's claim. Ala. R. Civ. P. 13(a). Alabama courts have interpreted this provision realistically and broadly to avoid a "wasteful multiplicity of litigation on claims that arose from a single transaction or occurrence." *Grow Group, Inc. v. Indus. Corrosion Control, Inc.,* 601 So. 2d 934, 936 (Ala. 1992). In its efforts to avoid inefficiency, the Alabama Supreme Court has concluded that a "counterclaim is compulsory if there is any logical relation of any sort between the original claim and the counterclaim." *Ex parte Cincinnati Ins. Cos.,* 806 So. 2d 376, 380 (Ala. 2001) (quoting Ala. R. Civ. P. 13(a), Committee Comments on 1973 Adoption of Rule 13, at P 6); *see also Akin v. PAFEC Ltd.,* 991 F.2d 1550, 1561 (11th Cir. 1993). Under the logical-relationship standard, a counterclaim is compulsory if "(1) its trial in the original action would avoid a substantial duplication of effort or (2) the original claim and the counterclaim arose out of the same aggregate core of operative facts." *Ex parte Cincinnati,* 806 So. 2d at 380. To determine whether the claims arise from the same core of operative facts, a court should ask if "the facts taken as a whole serve as the basis for both claims" or whether "the sum total of facts upon which the original claim rests creates legal rights in a party which would otherwise remain dormant." *Id.* (quoting *Ex parte Canal Ins. Co.,* 534 So. 2d 582, 584 (Ala. 1988)). Pursuant to these standards, any

---

1. There is some question about whether failure to assert a claim that is a compulsory counterclaim in a prior-in-time action can operate to bar pursuit of such a claim when the prior-in-time action has not proceeded to judgment. The Alabama Supreme Court has held, however, that when a matter raised in a later-filed case constituted a compulsory counterclaim in a previously filed but still pending case, the compulsory counterclaim rule barred prosecution of the counterclaims and required dismissal of the later-filed action. *Ex parte Canal Ins. Co.,* 534 So. 2d 582, 584–85 (Ala. 1988); *see also Blue Cross and Blue Shield of Ala. v. Hobbs,* 209 F.R.D. 218, 220 (M.D. Ala. 2002) (Albritton, J.) ("Although it is clear that claims asserted in a subsequent action are due to be dismissed when they should have been asserted as compulsory counterclaims in a case which proceeded to judgment, claims may also be dismissed when the prior action is still pending.") (citation omitted).

claims which arose from the same transaction or occurrence and which Ferrari had at the time she filed the Answer in the state case are barred by res judicata.

The claims by Ferrari in the federal case arise from the same transaction or occurrence as the claims against her in the state case. The original claim in the state case and the claims Ferrari makes in this case are logically related because they arose from the same core of operative facts. Indeed, the State and Federal Complaints read like two versions of the same story—one by Ferrari and one by Slaughter and E-Rate—and this is the essence of the same transaction or occurrence test. For example, the first focus of the State Complaint is Ferrari's demands relating to her compensation and alleged threats that she would "make their life difficult" and that Slaughter and E-Rate "would regret not paying her" as she demanded. The Federal Complaint also focuses on issues of compensation, except Ferrari presents her demands for compensation as justified and benign. Another dominant feature of the State Complaint is the encounter between Ferrari and Slaughter in a local nightclub and the subsequent harassment charge. The Federal Complaint also goes into great length about this encounter and ties it to Ferrari's discrimination claims. More generally, the claims in both cases all arise from the three-week employment relationship—they are closely tied in time, the parties are the same in both complaints, and they both depend on the same discrete events. These complaints embody the very multi-jurisdictional he-said, she-said situation the Alabama Supreme Court seeks to eliminate by the compulsory counterclaim rule. *See Grow Group,* 601 So. 2d at 936 (stating that the purpose of the compulsory counterclaim rule is to avoid wasteful and multiplicitous litigation arising from the same transaction or occurrence). Though there are facts in the State Complaint that are not in the Federal Complaint and facts in the Federal Complaint that are not in the state complaint, the facts, taken as a whole, serve as the basis for both claims. *Brooks,* 414 So. 2d at 917. Moreover, because of their close factual relationship and the identity of the parties, the trial of the claims in the Federal Complaint "in the original action would avoid a substantial duplication of effort." *Ex parte Cincinnati,* 806 So. 2d at 380. Therefore, to the extent the claims in the Federal Complaint otherwise meet the requirements for Rule 13(a) to apply, they are barred by the compulsory counterclaim rule in this federal case.

B. Claims Ferrari "Had" at the Time of Serving the Answer

Alabama Rule of Civil Procedure 13(a) requires that a pleading "state as a counterclaim any claim *which at the time of serving the pleading the pleader has against any opposing party,* if it arises out of the transaction or occurrence that is the subject matter of the opposing party's claim." (emphasis added). Thus, to determine whether Ferrari's claims, which arose from the same transaction or occurrence as the claims against her in the state case, are barred by the compulsory counterclaim rule the Court must determine whether Ferrari "had" these claims when she served her Answer in the state case. The Court will address the Title VII claims first and then turn briefly to the state law claims.

Ferrari filed an Answer in the state case on February 14, 2008, and received the right to sue letter from the EEOC on or about November 16, 2008. However, her Title VII claims accrued prior to the date she served the Answer, as the alleged discriminatory acts occurred in the summer of 2007. Thus, the relevant events happened in this order: alleged discrimination and accrual of Title VII claims; EEOC complaint; state suit against victim of alleged discrimination and EEOC complainant; answer in the state case; victim/complainant receives right-to-sue notification; victim/complainant files suit in federal court. Applying Alabama Rule 13, if Ferrari "had" the discrimination claims upon their accrual or upon the filing of her complaint with the EEOC, the claims are barred as non-filed compulsory counterclaims. If, on the other hand, she did not "have" the claims until receipt of the right-to-sue letter, the claims are not barred by the compulsory counterclaim rule. The issue, therefore, is whether a party who has allegedly suffered discrimination and filed a charge of discrimination with the EEOC but has not received a right-to-sue letter must file her discrimination claims as counterclaims in a suit in the courts of the state of Alabama brought against her by her employer, given that the discrimination claims arise from the same transaction or occurrence for purposes of Alabama Rule 13(a) as the claims made against her in the state case. Though there is no Alabama case directly on-point, Alabama Supreme Court precedent makes it clear that such a counterclaim is not compulsory.

Alabama's compulsory counterclaim rule does not require a defendant to file as a compulsory counterclaim a claim that has not yet "matured." *Bedsole v. Goodloe*, 912 So. 2d 508, 517 (Ala. 2005) ("[T]he party need not assert a counterclaim that has not matured at the time he serves his pleading. This is derived from the language in the rule limiting its application to claims the pleader has 'at the time of serving the pleading.' A counterclaim acquired by defendant after he has answered will not be considered compulsory, even if it arises out of the same transaction as does plaintiff's claim.") (quoting *Liberty Mut. Ins. Co. v. Wheelwright Trucking Co.*, 851 So. 2d 466, 484 (Ala. 2002)); *see also Steinberg v. St. Paul Mercury Ins. Co.*, 108 F.R.D. 355, 358 (S.D. Ga. 1985) ("Rule 13(a) applies to counterclaims that have matured at the time the defendant serves his pleadings. Thus, a counterclaim acquired by defendant after he has answered will not be considered compulsory, even if it arises out of the same transaction as does plaintiff's claim. A counterclaim which is likely to arise or is contingent at the time the defendant serves his answer, is not 'matured' for the purposes of Rule 13(a).") (internal citations, quotations, and alterations removed).[2] The Alabama Supreme Court has explained what it means to have a claim: "To be deemed compulsory, the counterclaim must be in actual existence, as distinguished from inchoate or potential existence, at the time the defendant answers the complaint.... Although the counterclaim is likely to arise or is contingent at the time the defendant serves an answer, it has not 'matured' for purposes of [Alabama Rule of Civil Procedure 13(a).]" *Id.* at 517 (citing 27 Fed. Proc., L.Ed. §62.230 (1996)); *see also Steinberg*, 108 F.R.D. at 358 ("Defendant's counterclaim must be completely vested at the time defendant serves his answer for such claim to be matured for the purposes of Rule 13(a).").

It is well settled that before bringing a Title VII suit in federal court, an aggrieved employee must file a charge of discrimination with the EEOC and obtain a right-to-sue letter. *See* 42 U.S.C. §2000e-5(e); *Wilkerson v. Grinnell Corp.*, 270 F.3d 1314, 1317 (11th Cir. 2001) ("Before a potential plaintiff may sue for discrimination under Title VII, she must first exhaust her administrative remedies."); *Forehand v. Florida State Hosp.*, 89 F.3d 1562, 1567 (11th Cir. 1996) ("Before instituting a Title VII action in federal district court, a private plaintiff must file an EEOC complaint against the discriminating party and receive statutory notice from the EEOC of his or her right to sue the respondent named in the charge."); *Pinkard v. Pullman-Standard*, 678 F.2d 1211, 1215 (11th Cir. 1982) ("Before instituting a Title VII action in federal district court, a private plaintiff must file an EEOC complaint against the discriminating party within 180 days of the alleged discrimination and receive statutory notice of the right to sue the respondent named in the charge."). An aggrieved party may obtain a right-to-sue letter after filing a timely EEOC complaint in one of two ways: (1) if, after the expiration of 180 days, the charge has not

---

2. The Alabama Supreme Court has noted that compulsory-counterclaim language from Rule 13(a), Ala. R. Civ. P., is identical to the language of Rule 13(a), Fed. R. Civ. P. *Bedsole*, 912 So. 2d at 517 n.5.

been dismissed and no other action has been taken by the EEOC, the EEOC is required to notify the claimant and that claimant may bring suit in district court within 90 days thereafter; or, (2) the complainant may request a right-to-sue letter before the 180-day period has expired and the EEOC may grant such a request. *Forehand*, 89 F.3d at 1567.

The Title VII claim was not "mature" at the time Ferrari served the Answer. As detailed extensively above, the filing of a charge of discrimination with the EEOC is a condition precedent to bringing a Title VII civil rights action. 42 U.S.C. § 2000e-5(e); *Ex parte Sverdrup Corp.*, 692 So. 2d 833, 835 (Ala. 1996); *see also Pinkard*, 678 F.2d at 1218–19 (right-to-sue letter is a "condition precedent"); *Forehand*, 89 F.3d 1569–70 (holding that a private plaintiff must file a charge of discrimination and obtain a right-to-sue letter prior to commencing an action and that the right-to-sue letter is a "statutory precondition"). Therefore, had Ferrari brought her Title VII claims as compulsory counterclaims in the state case they would have been subject to dismissal. A claim subject to dismissal for failure to satisfy statutory prerequisites is by no means mature. Moreover, once a potential plaintiff files a charge of discrimination with the EEOC, the availability of a justiciable claim is contingent upon failure of the EEOC to obtain voluntary compliance with the law. As the Alabama Supreme Court has noted with approval, the former Fifth Circuit once explained that:

> A charge of discrimination is not filed as a preliminary to a lawsuit. On the contrary, the purpose of a charge of discrimination is to trigger the investigatory and conciliatory procedures of the EEOC. Once the charge has been filed, the Commission carries out its investigatory function and attempts to obtain voluntary compliance with the law. Only if the EEOC fails to achieve voluntary compliance will the matter ever be the subject of court action.

Sverdrup, 692 So. 2d at 836 (quoting *Sanchez v. Std. Brands, Inc.*, 431 F.2d 455, 466 (5th Cir. 1970). It seems plain, then, that Ferrari's claim did not mature when the alleged discrimination occurred or even when she filed a charge of discrimination with the EEOC. Rather, her claim did not mature until she received the right-to-sue letter in November, 2008. A potential plaintiff awaiting a right-to-sue letter has but an inchoate cause of action, contingent upon failure of the EEOC to successfully conciliate the dispute, and which would be subject to dismissal if pressed. *See Bedsole*, 912 So. 2d at 517. Such a claim is not in "actual existence" and is not "mature" under Alabama law. *See id.* Hence, failure to file it does not trigger the compulsory counterclaim rule.

In Practice

The availability of a defendant to assert *any* counterclaim—however unrelated—and the requirement for a defendant to assert all counterclaims transactionally related to the plaintiff's claim, should serve as a warning to any potential plaintiff. Plaintiff's counsel must consider when advising a prospective claimant about not only the merits of her own claim but on the possibility of the defendant taking the offensive tack of filing counterclaims. Counsel must be vigilant about asking would-be plaintiff clients about the potential availability of counterclaims. Sometimes a sleeping dog is better left sleeping.

Although there is no binding Alabama precedent or persuasive Eleventh Circuit precedent directly on point, the Tenth Circuit has addressed this issue in the context of the Americans with Disabilities Act ("ADA") and reached the same conclusion as the Court does here.

In *Stone v. Department of Aviation*, 453 F.3d 1271, (10th Cir. 2006), the Tenth Circuit addressed the question of whether at the time a federal court plaintiff filed his answer in a previously filed state-court action, he had a "matured" ADA claim which he could have asserted against the state-court plaintiff. At the time he filed the answer, however, the federal-court plaintiff had filed his charge of discrimination with the EEOC but had not yet received a right-to-sue letter on his ADA claim. The Tenth Circuit noted, as this Court has, that without the right-to-sue letter, the ADA claim would have been subject to dismissal by the state court. The Tenth Circuit went on to hold that it was "axiomatic that a party does not have a matured claim, sufficient to be deemed a compulsory counterclaim, if that claim is subject to dismissal because all the conditions precedent to asserting it have not yet occurred." Because of its closely analogous facts and careful reasoning, the Court finds this opinion highly persuasive.

For the foregoing reasons, Ferrari's claims pursuant to Title VII, specifically Counts I, II, and IV, were not mature at the time she served the answer in the State Court suit. Therefore, the Motions to Dismiss are due to be denied with respect to these Counts. Counts III and V, for assault and battery and outrage respectively, were mature at the time Ferrari served her answer in the state court suit because they accrued at the time of the injuries—which was before she served the Answer—and there were no bars to bringing those claims immediately upon their accrual. *See Locker v. City of St. Florian*, 989 So. 2d 546, 549 (Ala. Civ. App. 2008) (holding that the claim of a party who alleges he suffered assault and battery and outrage accrued at the time of the injury and that the party was entitled to bring an action for redress of his alleged injuries on the date of that injury). Therefore, the assault and battery and outrage claims (Counts III and V) should have been brought as counterclaims in the state case and are barred by the compulsory counterclaim rule from being litigated in this federal action. The Motions to Dismiss are therefore due to be granted with respect to these Counts.

CONCLUSION

For the foregoing reasons, it is hereby ORDERED that the Motions to Dismiss are GRANTED in part and DENIED in part. The Motions are granted with respect to Counts III and V, which are DISMISSED with prejudice, and denied with respect to the remaining Counts.

Notes and Problems

1. In *Plant v. Blazer Financial Services*, the court discussed the impact that defining the counterclaim as permissive would have on the jurisdiction of the court. Prior to the adoption in 1990 of 28 U.S.C. § 1367—the Supplemental Jurisdiction statute—courts referred to extended notions of subject matter jurisdiction using the phrases ancillary and pendent. It was well accepted that compulsory counterclaims were within federal courts' ancillary jurisdiction but that permissive claims were not and needed their own independent jurisdictional basis in order to be asserted in a federal forum. The Supplemental Jurisdiction Statute has essentially codified most of these ancillary and pendent jurisdiction doctrines.

2. Should a court determine the compulsory nature of a counterclaim by looking to the purpose of the statute underlying the plaintiff's original claim? Why, or why not? If so, how does this fall within any of the several tests courts have defined to determine the compulsory nature of counterclaims?

3. In its classic application, the compulsory counterclaim rule is designed to result in a waiver of the omitted counterclaim when it is filed instead in a subsequent lawsuit

between the original parties. This was the context of the debate in *Ferrari v. E-Rate Consulting Servs.* above. How did the court distinguish between the claims that were found to be barred and other claims permitted to be brought later? Given the underlying purposes behind Rule 13(a), do you agree with the court's decision?

4. *Problems:*

a. Perot is involved in a car accident with Demarcus, each sustaining property damage and Perot also claiming to have been physically injured. Perot sues Demarcus. Must Demarcus assert as a counterclaim in that lawsuit his own claim for property damages?

b. Paul is detained while shopping at Wal-Mart and accused of stealing a television set from the store's receiving dock late at night — Wal-Mart having obtained some video evidence of someone matching his description that night at the loading dock. The district attorney found the evidence inconclusive (no television being found in Paul's car in the parking lot) and refuses to file charges. Paul has now sued Wal-Mart for false imprisonment, asserting Wal-Mart lacked reasonable belief necessary to detain him. Must Wal-Mart assert as a compulsory counterclaim its cause of action for conversion of the television set?

c. Petronus, Inc. enters into a contract to provide marketing services for Wizards, Inc. — a company in the business of selling magic kits. Due to a difference of artistic style regarding the proposed marketing campaign, Petronus' principals "walk off" refusing to provide any additional services until Wizards relents on these differences. Wizards stops making the contractual monthly payments and sues Petronus for anticipatory breach of contract. Must Petronus assert its claim for unpaid sums under the contract in the same lawsuit?

5. *Chapter Problem:* If Paula Jones files a lawsuit against Kazakh for strict products liability seeking damages for her car accident, will Kazakh be *required* to assert its threatened business disparagement claims against Paula as a compulsory counterclaim? Consider each of the tests referenced in the above cases to analyze this issue. Further, even if Kazakh is not required to assert such a counterclaim, would it be *permitted* to do so?

Pulling It All Together Exercise

Will Cosby is sued for sexual battery by a woman who has publicly stated that he covertly gave her drugs to render her unconscious and then proceeded to engage in unconsented sexual relations with her. He is sued in a jurisdiction that is both inconvenient for him and perhaps one that might tend to favor the plaintiff (a local citizen). As counsel for Mr. Cosby, you are considering whether to file a counterclaim against the plaintiff for defamation or to instead file that defamation lawsuit in Mr. Cosby's home state. Do you have any choice in this matter?

Spend 15 minutes writing out your analysis.

Upon Further Review

Both of the preclusion doctrines of res judicata and collateral estoppel serve a shared principle of promoting efficiency by allowing courts to refuse to re-litigate either claims (res judicata) or at least issues (collateral estoppel). The related Rule 13 achieves a similar efficiency by requiring defendants to bring their related counterclaims in the same proceeding rather than holding that claim for a subsequent lawsuit between the same parties. In their simplest application, each doctrine is relatively straightforward and can be applied without much controversy. But sometimes their application requires a bit more head scratching by litigant, lawyer, and judge. It is not always abundantly clear, for example, whether a cause of action clearly involves the litigation of the same "claim"—using the same transaction or occurrence standard. And, in the case of collateral estoppel, it might often be relatively straightforward to identify if the same issue is being re-litigated by the same parties, but with the abandonment of the "mutuality" limitation on issue preclusion, the much tougher issue arises of when a court should permit an offensive invocation of non-mutual collateral estoppel—with the less-than-precise concept of "fairness" as a check on the doctrine's application. Some things are clear; for example, the due process doctrine of "one bite of the apple" gives every litigant at least one attempt at prevailing on a claim or issue before any preclusion doctrine can be applied to them. Further, one of the primary combined impacts of these two cousin doctrines is that they create incentives by existing litigants to expand the scope (and perhaps intensity) of their current litigation efforts for fear that they will be precluded from raising other matters in subsequent proceedings. In this manner, these doctrines arguably create complexity in a current suit by avoiding the prospect of a multiplicity of related suits.

E. Rule 20 Permissive Joinder and Rule 42 Consolidation

Joinder of parties under Rule 20 *permits* multiple plaintiffs to bring a suit together when the relief sought by each of the plaintiffs arises from the same or a series of transactions or occurrences and contain a common question of law or fact. The rule also allows for the joinder of multiple defendants in a similar manner to the joinder of multiple plaintiffs. This joinder can take place in the plaintiff's original complaint (and is thus self-effectuating unless challenged by the defendant) or by subsequent amendment of pleadings pursuant to Rule 15. By permitting the joinder of the claims of multiple plaintiffs or the claims against multiple defendants, Rule 20 promotes the efficiency of the action by allowing multiple parties to litigate the same or similar claims in one proceeding. But it carefully balances this efficiency with notions of both fairness and autonomy as well, perhaps more vividly than any other rule or doctrine we will encounter in this Chapter.

Rule 20. Permissive Joinder of Parties

(a) **Persons Who May Join or Be Joined.**

    (1) **Plaintiffs.** Persons may join in one action as plaintiffs if:

        (A) they assert any right to relief jointly, severally, or in the alternative with respect to or arising out of the same transaction, occurrence, or series of transactions or occurrences; and

(B) any question of law or fact common to all plaintiffs will arise in the action.

(2) **Defendants.** Persons ... may be joined in one action as defendants if:

(A) any right to relief is asserted against them jointly, severally, or in the alternative with respect to or arising out of the same transaction, occurrence, or series of transactions or occurrences; and

(B) any question of law or fact common to all defendants will arise in the action.

While reading *Mosley v. General Motors Corp.* below, pay particular attention to the analysis regarding the common question of law or fact to all parties. Also, ask yourself if the debate concerns the joinder of multiple plaintiffs or defendants. In the three cases to follow — *In re Stand 'n Seal, Merck,* and *Volkswagen* — how do the courts view the "transaction or occurrence" that gave rise to the litigation? Is it the incidents of exposure or the defendants' design and manufacture of the products? How would these two different perspectives impact the analysis? Does one approach make more sense?

Consolidation under Rule 42 provides an avenue for the consolidation or severance of trials when concerns of fairness and efficiency outweigh the concerns of autonomy. Consolidation provides the court an avenue to combine trials when the Rule 20 same transaction or occurrence requirement is not met, but common questions of law or fact exist. The consolidation of the originally separate actions may be in whole or in part. Further, although the joinder of parties may meet the requirements specified by Rule 20, a court may order the severance of trials under Rule 42 "[f]or convenience, to avoid prejudice, or to expedite and economize." Fed. R. Civ. P. 42. While reading through the Rule 20 and Rule 42 cases, think about how the two rules interact and why each still plays a role, though one may disturb the application of the other.

1. Going the Distance: Liberal Application of Rule 20

Mosley v. General Motors Corp.

497 F.2d 1330 (8th Cir. 1974)

Ross, J.,

Nathaniel Mosley and nine other persons joined in bringing this action individually and as class representatives alleging that their rights guaranteed under 42 U.S.C. § 2000e et seq. and 42 U.S.C. § 1981 were denied by General Motors and Local 25, United Automobile, Aerospace and Agriculture Implement Workers of America (Union) by reason of their color and race. Each of the ten named plaintiffs had, prior to the filing of the complaint, filed a charge with the Equal Employment Opportunity Commission (EEOC) asserting the facts underlying these claims. Pursuant thereto, the EEOC made a reasonable cause finding that General Motors, Fisher Body Division and Chevrolet Division, and the Union had engaged in unlawful employment practices in violation of Title VII of the Civil Rights Act of 1964. Accordingly, the charging parties were notified by EEOC of their right to institute a civil action in the appropriate federal district court, pursuant to § 706(e) of Title VII, 42 U.S.C. § 2000e-5(e).

In each of the first eight counts of the twelve-count complaint, eight of the ten plaintiffs alleged that General Motors, Chevrolet Division, had engaged in unlawful employment practices by: "discriminating against Negroes as regards promotions, terms and conditions of employment"; "retaliating against Negro employees who protested actions made unlawful by Title VII of the Act and by discharging some because they protested said unlawful acts"; "failing to hire Negro employees as a class on the basis of race"; "failing to hire females as a class on the basis of sex"; "discharging Negro employees on the basis of race"; and "discriminating against Negroes and females in the granting of relief time." Each additionally charged that the defendant Union had engaged in unlawful employment practices "with respect to the granting of relief time to Negro and female employees" and "by failing to pursue 6a grievances." The remaining two plaintiffs made similar allegations against General Motors, Fisher Body Division. All of the individual plaintiffs requested injunctive relief, back pay, attorneys fees and costs. Counts XI and XII of the complaint were class action counts against the two individual divisions of General Motors. They also sought declaratory and injunctive relief, back pay, attorneys fees and costs.

General Motors moved to strike portions of each count of the twelve-count complaint, to dismiss Counts XI and XII, to make portions of Counts I through XII more definite, to determine the propriety of Counts XI and XII as class actions, to limit the scope of the class purportedly represented, and to determine under which section of Rule 23 Counts XI and XII were maintainable as class actions. The district court ordered that "insofar as the first ten counts are concerned, those ten counts shall be severed into ten separate causes of action," and each plaintiff was directed to bring a separate action based upon his complaint, duly and separately filed. The court also ordered that the class action would not be dismissed, but rather would be left open "to each of the plaintiffs herein, individually or collectively ... to allege a separate cause of action on behalf of any class of persons which such plaintiff or plaintiffs may separately or individually represent."

In reaching this conclusion on joinder, the district court followed the reasoning of *Smith v. North American Rockwell Corp.*, 50 F.R.D. 515 (N.D.Okla.1970), which, in a somewhat analogous situation, found there was no right to relief arising out of the same transaction, occurrence or series of transactions or occurrences, and that there was no question of law or fact common to all plaintiffs sufficient to sustain joinder under Federal Rule of Civil Procedure 20(a). Similarly, the district court here felt that the plaintiffs' joint actions against General Motors and the Union presented a variety of issues having little relationship to one another; that they had only one common problem, i.e. the defendant; and that as pleaded the joint actions were completely unmanageable. Upon entering the order, and upon application of the plaintiffs, the district court found that its decision involved a controlling question of law as to which there is a substantial ground for difference of opinion and that any of the parties might make application for appeal under 28 U.S.C. § 1292(b). We granted the application to permit this interlocutory appeal and for the following reasons we affirm in part and reverse in part.

Rule 20(a) of the Federal Rules of Civil Procedure provides:

> All persons may join in one action as plaintiffs if they assert any right to relief jointly, severally, or in the alternative in respect of or arising out of the same transaction, occurrence, or series of transactions or occurrences and if any question of law or fact common to all these persons will arise in the action.

Additionally, Rule 20(b) and Rule 42(b) vest in the district court the discretion to order separate trials or make such other orders as will prevent delay or prejudice. In this manner, the scope of the civil action is made a matter for the discretion of the district court, and a determination on the question of joinder of parties will be reversed on appeal only upon a showing of abuse of that discretion. *Chicago, R.I. & P.R.R. v. Williams*, 245 F.2d 397, 404 (8th Cir.), cert. denied, 355 U.S. 855, 78 S.Ct. 83, 2 L.Ed.2d 63 (1957). To determine whether the district court's order was proper herein, we must look to the policy and law that have developed around the operation of Rule 20.

The purpose of the rule is to promote trial convenience and expedite the final determination of disputes, thereby preventing multiple lawsuits. 7 C. Wright, Federal Practice and Procedure § 1652 at 265 (1972). Single trials generally tend to lessen the delay, expense and inconvenience to all concerned. Reflecting this policy, the Supreme Court has said:

> Under the Rules, the impulse is toward entertaining the broadest possible scope of action consistent with fairness to the parties; joinder of claims, parties and remedies is strongly encouraged.

United Mine Workers of America v. Gibbs, 383 U.S. 715, 724 (1966).

Permissive joinder is not, however, applicable in all cases. The rule imposes two specific requisites to the joinder of parties: (1) a right to relief must be asserted by, or against, each plaintiff or defendant relating to or arising out of the same transaction or occurrence, or series of transactions or occurrences; and (2) some question of law or fact common to all the parties must arise in the action.

In ascertaining whether a particular factual situation constitutes a single transaction or occurrence for purposes of Rule 20, a case by case approach is generally pursued. 7 C. Wright Federal Practice and Procedure § 1653 at 270 (1972). No hard and fast rules have been established under the rule. However, construction of the terms "transaction or occurrence" as used in the context of Rule 13(a) counterclaims offers some guide to the application of this test. For the purposes of the latter rule, "Transaction" is a word of flexible meaning. It may comprehend a series of many occurrences, depending not so much upon the immediateness of their connection as upon their logical relationship. *Moore v. New York Cotton Exchange*, 270 U.S. 593, 610, 46 S.Ct. 367, 371, 70 L.Ed. 750 (1926). Accordingly, all "logically related" events entitling a person to institute a legal action against another generally are regarded as comprising a transaction or occurrence. 7 C. Wright, Federal Practice and Procedure § 1653 at 270 (1972). The analogous interpretation of the terms as used in Rule 20 would permit all reasonably related claims for relief by or against different parties to be tried in a single proceeding. Absolute identity of all events is unnecessary.

This construction accords with the result reached in *United States v. Mississippi*, of which depended to a large extent upon "question(s) of law or fact common to all of them." the election commissioners, and six voting registrars of the State, charging them with engaging in acts and practices hampering and destroying the right of black citizens of Mississippi to vote. The district court concluded that the complaint improperly attempted to hold the six county registrars jointly liable for what amounted to nothing more than individual torts committed by them separately against separate applicants. In reversing, the Supreme Court said:

> But the complaint charged that the registrars had acted and were continuing to act as part of a state-wide system designed to enforce the registration laws in a way that would inevitably deprive colored people of the right to vote solely because of their color. On such an allegation the joinder of all the registrars as defendants in a single suit is authorized by Rule 20(a) of the Federal Rules of Civil Procedure.... These registrars were alleged to be carrying on activities which

were part of a series of transactions or occurrences, the validity of which depended to a large extent upon "question(s) of law or fact common to all of them."

Id. at 142–143.

Here too, then, the plaintiffs have asserted a right to relief arising out of the same transactions or occurrences. Each of the ten plaintiffs alleged that he had been injured by the same general policy of discrimination on the part of General Motors and the Union. Since a "state-wide system designed to enforce the registration laws in a way that would inevitably deprive colored people of the right to vote" was determined to arise out of the same series of transactions or occurrences, we conclude that a company-wide policy purportedly designed to discriminate against blacks in employment similarly arises out of the same series of transactions or occurrences. Thus the plaintiffs meet the first requisite for joinder under Rule 20(a).

The second requisite necessary to sustain a permissive joinder under the rule is that a question of law or fact common to all the parties will arise in the action. The rule does not require that all questions of law and fact raised by the dispute be common. Yet, neither does it establish any qualitative or quantitative test of commonality. For this reason, cases construing the parallel requirement under Federal Rule of Civil Procedure 23(a) provide a helpful framework for construction of the commonality required by Rule 20. In general, those cases that have focused on Rule 23(a)(2) have given it a permissive application so that common questions have been found to exist in a wide range of context. 7 C. Wright, Federal Practice and Procedure § 1763 at 604 (1972). Specifically, with respect to employment discrimination cases under Title VII, courts have found that the discriminatory character of a defendant's conduct is basic to the class, and the fact that the individual class members may have suffered different effects from the alleged discrimination is immaterial for the purposes of the prerequisite. *Hicks v. Crown Zellerbach Corp.*, 49 F.R.D. 184, 187–188 (E.D.La.1968). *See also Washington v. Lee*, 263 F.Supp. 327, 330 (M.D.Ala.1966), aff'd per curiam, 390 U.S. 333, 88 S.Ct. 994, 19 L.Ed.2d 1212 (1968); *Like v. Carter*, 448 F.2d 798, 802 (8th Cir. 1971), cert. denied, 405 U.S. 1045, 92 S.Ct. 1309, 31 L.Ed.2d 588 (1972). In this vein, one court has said:

> Although the actual effects of a discriminatory policy may thus vary throughout the class, the existence of the discriminatory policy threatens the entire class. And whether the Damoclean threat of a racially discriminatory policy hangs over the racial class is a question of fact common to all the members of the class.

Hall v. Werthan Bag Corp., 251 F.Supp. 184, 186 (M.D.Tenn.1966). *See also Johnson v. Georgia Highway Express, Inc.*, 417 F.2d 1122, 1124 (5th Cir. 1969); *Mack v. General Electric Co.*, 329 F.Supp. 72, 75–76 (E.D.Pa.1971); *Bennett v. Gravelle*, 323 F.Supp. 203, 219 (D.Md.), aff'd, 451 F.2d 1011 (4th Cir. 1971), cert. denied, 407 U.S. 917, 92 S.Ct. 2451, 32 L.Ed.2d 692 (1972).

The right to relief here depends on the ability to demonstrate that each of the plaintiffs was wronged by racially discriminatory policies on the part of the defendants General Motors and the Union. The discriminatory character of the defendants' conduct is thus basic to each plaintiff's recovery. The fact that each plaintiff may have suffered different effects from the alleged discrimination is immaterial for the purposes of determining the common question of law or fact. Thus, we conclude that the second requisite for joinder under Rule 20(a) is also met by the complaint.

For the reasons set forth above, we conclude that the district court abused its discretion in severing the joined actions. The difficulties in ultimately adjudicating damages to the various plaintiffs are not so overwhelming as to require such severance. If appropriate, separate trials may be granted as to any particular issue after the determination of common questions.

The judgment of the district court disallowing joinder of the plaintiffs' individual actions is reversed and remanded with directions to permit the plaintiffs to proceed jointly. That portion of the district court's judgment that withholds determination of the propriety of the purported class until further discovery is affirmed. We consider the application of the appellants for attorneys fees on this appeal to be premature, and they will be denied without prejudice to their right to reassert that claim upon final disposition of the case.

Bridgeport Music, Inc. v. 11CMusic

202 F.R.D. 229 (M.D. Tenn., Nashville Div., July 25, 2001)

CAMPBELL, DISTRICT JUDGE,

I. *Introduction*

P's claims

Plaintiffs, entities engaged in publishing, recording, and distributing music, bring this action against over 770 named publishing companies, copyright administrators, record labels, entertainment companies, copyright clearance companies, and performance rights organizations. Plaintiffs assert a variety of claims arising out of numerous instances of what they describe as the "sampling" of music in which they claim an ownership interest. ["Sampling" refers to the copying of portions of a prior master sound recording onto new sound recordings.] They allege copyright infringement [among other state and common law causes of action]. Due primarily to the number of Defendants, Plaintiffs' complaint is an exceptionally large document. It includes 486 counts, most of which contain multiple claims. It is 901 pages long not including exhibits.

D's claim

Defendants argue that Plaintiffs have violated Rule 20 because Defendants are not properly joined. Defendants move the court to sever Plaintiffs' various claims. For the reasons set forth below, the Court finds that Defendants are misjoined. Accordingly, Defendants' Motions for Severance are GRANTED.

II. *Analysis*

Defendants argue that they are not properly joined. Rule 20(a) provides that:

> all persons ... may be joined in one action as defendants if there is asserted against them jointly, severally, or in the alternative, any right to relief in respect of or arising out of the same transaction, occurrence, or series of transactions or occurrences and if any question of law or fact common to all defendants will arise in the action.

Rule 20(a) is designed to promote judicial economy and trial convenience. *See Mosley v. Gen. Motors Corp.*, 497 F.2d 1330, 1332 (8th Cir. 1974). This accords with the general principle under the Federal Rules of Civil Procedure to allow "the broadest possible scope of action consistent with fairness to the parties." *United Mine Workers of Am. v. Gibbs*, 383 U.S. 715 (1966) ("Joinder of claims, parties and remedies is strongly encouraged.").

Permissive joinder is circumscribed, however, by the dual requirements of a common question and transactional relatedness. The first of these, the common question test, is usually easy to satisfy. *See* 4 James Wm. Moore et al., Moore's Federal Practice, ¶ 20.04 (3d ed. 1999). The transactional test, however, is more forbidding. It requires that, to be joined, parties must assert rights, or have rights asserted against them, that arise from related activities—a transaction or an occurrence or a series thereof. *See, e.g., Michaels*

Bld. Co. v. Ameritrust Co, 848 F.2d 674, 682 (6th Cir. 1982) (finding that a loan made to the plaintiff by one defendant was unrelated to loans made to the plaintiff by other defendants and that joinder was therefore improper); *Demboski v. CSX Transp., Inc.*, 157 F.R.D. 28, 29–30 (S.D. Miss. 1994) (holding that four separate railway accidents involving the same defendant did not constitute a series of occurrences); *Rappaport v. Steven Spielberg, Inc.*, 16 F. Supp.2d 481, 496 (D. N.J. 1998) (severing a plaintiffs' claims against defendants where plaintiff alleged copyright infringement in separate works in different media). This test is easy to articulate, but it is often difficult to apply. Because it does not lend itself to bright-line rules, it generally requires a case by case analysis.

Defendants argue that they are misjoined in this action because Plaintiffs' claims against them do not arise out of the same series of transactions or occurrences. According to Defendants, Plaintiffs' 477 counts of alleged copyright infringement "are really 477 separate lawsuits rolled into one enormous pleading;" each allegedly infringing song represents a separate transaction or occurrence. They suggest that each infringement count brought by Plaintiffs will require a unique set of proof. Defendants also argue that the infringement counts in Plaintiffs' complaint do not present common questions of law or fact. They contend that Plaintiffs are simply relying on the fact that their claims are based on a common legal theory—i.e., copyright infringement.

Plaintiff responds that all of its infringement counts and claims arise out of "the same series of transactions or occurrences." Specifically, Plaintiffs argue 1) that Defendants and the claims against them are intricately interrelated; 2) that Defendants have inflicted the same harm against Plaintiffs; 3) that certain Defendants repeatedly infringed Plaintiffs' copyrights, often in different capacities (e.g., as publisher, administrator, label, or entertainment company); and 4) that a small number of clearance companies, manufacturers, and distributors were involved in most of the allegedly infringing songs giving rise to Plaintiffs' claims. They also contend that the counts in their complaint present common questions of law and fact. According to Plaintiffs, these common questions concern 1) ownership of the allegedly infringed songs; 2) whether copyright material was actually copied; 3) the existence of licenses; and 4) whether copied material is subject to *de minimis* or fair use exceptions. Plaintiffs also anticipate that the parties will rely on expert testimony to prove many of these factual questions and that the same testimony will be applicable to numerous questions.

The Court finds that the musical compositions and/or sound recordings ("songs") giving rise to the counts in Plaintiffs' complaint and the activities leading to the production and distribution of those songs are not a series of transactions or occurrences. Each song and the alleged sampling contained therein represents a discrete occurrence. The fact that certain Defendants were involved in the production, publishing, and distribution of more than one allegedly offending song does not, in itself, cause these songs to be related occurrences in the manner contemplated by Rule 20(a). In this respect, this case is similar to *Demboski*, where the fact that a single railway Defendant was involved in separate train crashes did not create a series of occurrences sufficient to allow joinder of plaintiffs. The Court also finds support in *Rappoport*, which ordered severance based in significant part on the fact that claims against various defendants arose out of separate allegedly infringing works. Furthermore, the Court is not persuaded by Plaintiffs' argument that its infringement counts are properly joined because Plaintiffs suffered the same harm in each instance. According to this logic, a copyright plaintiff could join as defendants any otherwise unrelated parties who independently copy material owned by the plaintiff.

Even if the counts in Plaintiffs' complaint arose from the same series of occurrences, the Court would exercise the discretion afforded it to order a severance to avoid causing unreasonable prejudice and expense to Defendants and to avoid a great inconvenience in the administration of justice. *See* 7 Charles Alan Wright et al., Federal Practice and Procedure § 1652 (3d ed. 2001) ("The court has discretion to deny joinder if it determines that the addition of the party under Rule 20 will not foster the objectives of the rule, but will result in prejudice, expense or delay."). As a practical matter, this case is unmanageable in its current form. Because this Court's courtroom would seat only a small fraction of Defendants and their attorneys, it cannot even hold a hearing on the motions currently pending; it cannot host a management conference; it certainly cannot try all—or even most—of the Plaintiffs' counts together. If joined in one action, hundreds of Defendants will be subjected to an overwhelming onslaught of materials and information unrelated to the specific claims against them—all of which they must pay their attorneys to review.

Holding

The Court therefore finds that Defendants are misjoined to the extent that Plaintiffs have asserted claims against them arising out of separate instances of sampling. Because each allegedly infringing song represents a single occurrence, however, Defendants named in each separate count are properly joined with each other. Thus, the Plaintiffs' 477 copyright infringement counts shall be severed. *See* Rule 21.

Based on the above, it appears that the severed copyright infringement counts should proceed separately as 477 individual cases.

For the reasons described above, Defendants' Motions for Severance are granted.

Notes and Problems

1. The plaintiffs in *Mosley* can be broken down into three groupings: those the defendant failed to hire, current employees, and former employees. How does the presence of these distinct groups in any suit help or hurt the chances a court will find the joinder of the plaintiffs is appropriate under Rule 20? How did the court analyze the differences here while still finding joinder appropriate? If you accept the court's discussion concerning a possible unwritten racially discriminatory policy underlying the plaintiff's claims, what about the plaintiffs who were asserting instead claims for sexual discrimination? Did the court consider them in its analysis?

2. Is *Bridgeport Music* at all inconsistent with *Mosley*? After all, *Mosley* permitted claims involving different parties, arising at different times, with different claimed injuries, and different circumstances to all be brought together as one "transaction or occurrence." Or does *Bridgeport Music* merely represent the reality that some limit must be placed upon the concept of a "transaction or occurrence"? How important were the practical obstacles to a common trial that the court mentions near the end of the opinion to the court's motivation to find that the claims against the various defendants were not sufficiently related?

3. The defendants in *Mosely* wanted the claims by each plaintiff severed, thus requiring the plaintiffs to bring the claims separately. What is the defendant's *motivation* behind this? Why would the defendant desire a less efficient resolution of the claims when that may result in different judgments? If the claimants' claims in *Mosley* were severed, might the defendant still face the application of offensive non-mutual collateral estoppel if it loses the first trial?

4. With respect to the *Bridgeport Music* case, why did the plaintiff's attorney want to combine literally hundreds of copyright claims against numerous defendants in one proceeding? What advantages, if any, might that bring to the plaintiff? Why were each of the defendants so opposed to having to defend themselves in the same lawsuit with other defendants?

5. Rule 20 protects the doctrines of efficiency, fairness, and autonomy. Consider the various components to the rule and articulate how each doctrine is embodied within the rule.

6. Notice that both Rules 20 and 13(a) use the "same transaction or occurrence" standard. Given the different contexts and consequences of each rule, do you see any argument that this standard should be given a more liberal interpretation in one setting than in the other?

7. *Mosley* is often cited as the classic example of liberal application of Rule 20. What motivation is there for courts to construe Rule 20 in such a broad manner?

8. *Problems:* Is the attempted joinder of the multiple parties acceptable under Rule 20 in each scenario below?

a. Jason was beaten up at a Taco Bell restaurant late one evening by another customer, Edna, in the presence of a store clerk who did nothing to intervene or summon assistance. Jason filed a battery claim against Edna and a negligence (premises liability) claim against Taco Bell in one lawsuit.

b. Mary and Bill, a married couple, were on a Sunday afternoon drive, cruising through a green light at an intersection, when their Corvette was struck simultaneously by two cars going through a red light driven, respectively, by Dan and Danielle. The force of the combined impact caused their Corvette to turn over several times, injuring both of them severely. Mary and Bill file one lawsuit against both Dan and Danielle.

c. Maria was the subject of massive gossiping around her high school campus following an incident at the prom during her junior year of high school. She filed a lawsuit against two fellow students who she discovered were each among the gossip mongers, claiming they were liable to her for slander.

d. Chekov was a property owner who hired Bob as a general contractor to remodel his master bathroom. Bob, in turn, hired Sammy as a subcontractor to do the plumbing work inside the shower. After the completion of the project, a leak occurred in the shower while Chekov was on vacation and this resulted in flooding of the house with significant property damage. Chekov files a negligence lawsuit against both Bob and Sammy.

9. *Chapter Problem:* With regard to the possible claims of Paula Jones, how would she benefit from suing both the manufacturer and retailer in the same lawsuit? Would there be any advantages to her from filing separate lawsuits against each of them?

2. Conflicts in Application: What Is a "Transaction or Occurrence" in a Strict Product Liability Context?

Products liability litigation raises a significant issue over which courts have yet to reach uniform agreement. Specifically, in a products case, is the "transaction or occurrence" the accident of each victim or the defendants' conduct in designing, manufacturing and/or drafting warnings for their products? Do you see the argument that, depending upon one's view of the appropriate focal point for the analysis, it might be relatively easy or rather difficult for multiple injured consumers to unite together in bringing products liability claims against common opponents? Consider each of the following three cases involving this general Rule 20 issue. Does one court's approach seem better to you than another?

In re Stand 'N Seal Products Liability Litig.

2009 WL 2224185 (N.D. Ga. 2009)

THRASH, J.,

Background

Facts

This is one of the personal injury cases involving the Stand 'n Seal "Spray-On" Grout Sealer. Stand 'n Seal was a consumer product used to seal ceramic tile grout in kitchens, bathrooms, and similar areas. The purported advantage of Stand 'n Seal was that users could easily stand and spray the sealant onto the grout without the strain of using a brush and manually applying the sealant. The Plaintiffs say that the problems with Stand 'n Seal began when the manufacturer changed its chemical components. Stand 'n Seal was originally manufactured with a fluoropolymer chemical known as Zonyl 225. But from April to May 2005, and again in July 2005, the manufacturer of Stand 'n Seal switched from Zonyl to a different fluoropolymer chemical known as Flexipel S-22WS. The Plaintiffs say that users of Stand 'n Seal immediately began experiencing respiratory problems, such as chemical pneumonitis, from exposure to Stand 'n Seal. By August 31, 2005, Stand 'n Seal with Flexipel was recalled.

P's claims

In this case, the Plaintiffs are seven individuals who purchased and used Stand 'n Seal. They all purchased the product in Georgia. The Plaintiffs assert claims for strict products liability, breach of warranty, and negligence against each of the companies involved in the manufacture, distribution, and sale of Stand 'n Seal with Flexipel. The Defendants now move to sever the claims of each Plaintiff, or in the alternative, order separate trials for each Plaintiff.

I. *Legal Standard*
II.

"Plainly, the central purpose of Rule 20 is to promote trial convenience and expedite the resolution of disputes, thereby eliminating unnecessary lawsuits." *Alexander v. Fulton County,* 207 F.3d 1303, 1323 (11th Cir.2000), *overruled on other grounds by, Manders v. Lee,* 338 F.3d 1304, 1328 n. 52 (11th Cir.2003). Therefore, courts liberally interpret Rule 20. "It may comprehend a series of many occurrences, depending not so much upon the immediateness of their connection as upon their logical relationship." *Id.*

If joinder is improper, then "the court may at any time, on just terms, add or drop a party. The court may also sever any claim against a party." Fed.R.Civ.P. 21. And, even if joinder is proper, "[f]or convenience, to avoid prejudice, or to expedite and economize, the court may order a separate trial of one or more separate issues, claims, crossclaims, counterclaims, or third-party claims." Fed.R.Civ.P. 42(b).

Discussion

The Plaintiffs are properly joined under Rule 20 and separate trials are not necessary. The Plaintiffs each assert a right to relief arising out of the manufacture, distribution, and sale of Stand 'n Seal with Flexipel. Although the Plaintiffs purchased Stand 'n Seal at different times and suffered different injuries, their claims rely on the same core allegation: aerosolized Flexipel is hazardous. This core allegation satisfies the requirement of a series of logically related transactions or occurrences and the requirement of a question of law or fact common to all plaintiffs. *See Abraham v. Volkswagen of Am., Inc.,* 795 F.2d 238, 251 (2d Cir.1986) (allowing joinder where plaintiffs all alleged "the faulty valve stem seal as a single defect"); *Poleon v. General Motors Corp.,* Civ. No.1999-127, 1999 WL 1289473, at *2 (D.Vi. Jan.05, 1999) (allowing joinder where plaintiffs all alleged the "malfunctioning of the brake system and the failure of the air bag system to deploy" as the defect). This core allegation also distinguishes this case from the cases cited by the Defendants. *See Saval v. BL Ltd.,* 710 F.2d 1027, 1031 (4th Cir.1983) (denying joinder where plaintiffs "had not demonstrated that any of the alleged similar problems resulted from a common defect"); *Coughlin v. Rogers,* 130 F.3d 1348, 1350 (9th Cir.1997) (denying joinder where the plaintiffs "do not allege that their claims arise out of a systematic pattern of events").

The Defendants say that, even if joinder is proper, the Court should order separate trials for each Plaintiff. Because the Plaintiffs' claims rely on the same core allegation that aerosolized Flexipel is hazardous, separate trials would require redundant testimony that is not in the interest of judicial economy. There is some risk of jury confusion and prejudice, but that risk is minimized by the straightforward nature of the Plaintiffs' claims and the appropriate use of jury instructions. *See Alexander,* 207 F.3d at 1325 ("[T]he potential for prejudice was minimized because of the core similarities in [p]laintiffs' claims."); *Hanley v. First Investors Corp.,* 151 F.R.D. 76, 80 (E.D.Tex.1993) ("[The jury] will be instructed to keep each plaintiff's claim separate, and to force each plaintiff to prove his or her claim and damages separately."). In addition, a single trial will serve more effectively as a bellwether trial in this multidistrict litigation.

Conclusion

For the reasons set forth above, the Defendants' Motion to Sever Plaintiffs' Claims or, in the Alternative, Motion for Separate Trials ... is DENIED.

SO ORDERED.

McNaughton v. Merck & Co.

2004 U.S. Dist. LEXIS 30287 (S.D. N.Y. 2004)

PRESKA, J.,

Plaintiff, Walter McNaughton, moves for leave to [amend] his complaint by adding 64 additional plaintiffs who have (or their spouses have), like McNaughton, allegedly suffered serious health consequences or death as a result of taking the drug VIOXX.

A motion to amend under Rule 15(a) will not be permitted if it is futile. *See Foman v. Davis,* 371 U.S. 178, 83 S. Ct. 227, 9 L. Ed. 2d 222 (1962); *Ricciardi v. Kone, Inc.,* 215 F.R.D. 455, 456 (E.D.N.Y. 2003). The proper mechanism for joining additional plaintiffs under these circumstances is pursuant to Rule 20, governing permissive joinder, and, therefore the question is whether joinder is proper pursuant to Rule 20. Fed. R. Civ. P. 20. If joinder of the additional 64 plaintiffs is improper under Rule 20, then amending the complaint would be futile and should be denied pursuant to Rule 15(a).

Rule 20(a) states "[a]ll persons may join in one action as plaintiffs if they assert any right to relief jointly, severally, or in the alternative in respect of or arising out of the same transaction, occurrence, or series of transactions or occurrences and if any question of law or fact common to all these persons will arise in the action." Fed. R. Civ. P. 20(a). Therefore, Rule 20(a) has two distinct requirements for the joinder of plaintiffs: (1) a right to relief must be asserted by each plaintiff relating to or arising out of the same transaction or occurrence, and (2) there must be some question of law or fact common to all plaintiffs. *See* 7 C. Wright, A. Miller & M. Kane, *Federal Practice and Procedure* § 1653. In this case, McNaughton submits that, like himself, all of the proposed plaintiffs took VIOXX, they were all improperly warned of the alleged dangers of the drug by defendant, Merck & Co., Inc. ("Merck"), and they all suffered serious medical ills as a result. Yet, although Merck does not dispute that these similarities give rise to common questions of law or fact, Merck contends that these similarities do not satisfy the same transaction or occurrence requirement imposed by Rule 20(a). Upon reviewing the parties' arguments and the relevant caselaw, I agree with Merck that McNaughton has not proffered evidence sufficient to support the contention that he and the 64 potential plaintiffs assert a right to relief arising out of the same transaction or occurrence.

Principles

"The balancing of efficiency versus fairness leads to the conclusion that the substantial claims of mass tort victims deserve an uncompromised due process. Our judicial system should treat the claims of the many victims of a major airplane crash or hotel fire with as much care and sensitivity as it does the claim of the lone victim of the accident. The practice [of joint trials in mass tort cases] involving substantial injuries should cease because it cannot be reconciled with this principle."

Roger H. Trangsrud, *Joinder Alternatives in Mass Tort Litigation*, 70 Cornell L. Rev. 779, 782 (1985).

The mere existence of common questions of law or fact does not satisfy the same transaction or occurrence requirement. *See In re Asbestos II Consol. Pretrial*, Nos. 86 C 1739, 89 C 452, 1989 U.S. Dist. LEXIS 5621, 1989 WL 56181, at *1 (N.D. Ill. May 10, 1989) ("Distinct claims cannot be properly joined under Rule 20 merely because they have common theoretical underpinnings."). In particular, drug liability cases have held that related factual or legal issues, such as a similar injury allegedly caused by the same drug, are insufficient for Rule 20 joinder purposes. In this district, for example, the Honorable Lewis A. Kaplan held that although all of the plaintiffs were exposed to the drug Rezulin, because the plaintiffs "do not allege that they received Rezulin from the same source or that they were exposed to Rezulin for similar periods of time" the same transaction or occurrence requirement of Rule 20(a) was not satisfied. *In re Rezulin Prods. Liab. Litig.*, 168 F. Supp. 2d 136, 145–46 (S.D.N.Y. 2001). Numerous courts in other districts have reached similar conclusions in drug liability cases. *See Graziose v. American Home Prods.*

Corp., 202 F.R.D. 638, 640 (D. Nev. 2001) ("The only concrete similarity among the various Plaintiffs are that they (or their spouse) took a medicine containing PPA ... and they allegedly suffered an injury. This is insufficient to justify joinder. ..."); *Chaney v. Gate Pharms. (In re Diet Drugs Prods. Liab. Litig.)*, No. Civ. A. 98-20478, 1999 U.S. Dist. LEXIS 11414, 1999 WL 554584, at *4 (E.D. Pa. July 16, 1999) ("[T]he claims of plaintiffs who have not purchased or received diet drugs from an identical source, such as a physician, hospital or diet center, did not satisfy the transaction or occurrence requirement."); *In re Orthopedic Bone Screw Prods. Liab. Litig.*, MDL No. 1341, 1995 U.S. Dist. LEXIS 10138, 1995 WL 428683, at *1–2 (E.D. Pa. July 15, 1995) ("[J]oinder based on the belief that the same occurrence or transaction is satisfied by the fact that claimants have the same or similar device of a defendant manufacturer implanted in or about their spine is ... not a proper joinder.").

Unlike the majority of cases, in *In re Norplant Contraceptive Products Liability Litigation*, 168 F.R.D. 579 (E.D. Tex. 1996), the court held that the Rule 20 joinder requirements are met if plaintiffs' claims arise out of the same acts and omissions of defendants. *See also Kemp v. Metabolife Intern., Inc.*, No. Civ. A. 00-3513, 2003 WL 22272186, at *3 (E.D. Pa. Oct. 1, 2003). However, the Norplant decision has not been widely followed and has been criticized by some district courts. *See In re Baycol Prods. Liab. Litig.*, MDL No. 1431, 2002 U.S. Dist. LEXIS 28002, 2002 WL 32155269, at *2 (D. Minn. July 5, 2002). Without citing to the Norplant case in particular, at oral argument on the motion, counsel for McNaughton put forth a similar position and argued that because Merck's conduct in allegedly failing to warn consumers and doctors of the potential harms of VIOXX is common to all 65 of the potential plaintiffs, the requirements of Rule 20 were satisfied. I decline to follow the Norplant case and am persuaded by the interpretation of Rule 20 espoused by Judge Kaplan and others. Accordingly, while Merck's actions certainly give rise to some factual and legal questions relevant to all of the potential plaintiffs, Merck's actions do not satisfy the same transaction or occurrence requirement. *See* 2002 U.S. Dist. LEXIS 28002, at [WL] *2 (holding that the fact that defendant's conduct is common to all plaintiffs' claims is insufficient for Rule 20 purposes.).

The claims asserted by McNaughton and the 64 other potential plaintiffs against Merck are based upon the plaintiffs' ingestion of the drug VIOXX and the injuries they allegedly sustained as a result of that ingestion. The claims are not otherwise related, and joinder under these circumstances would be improper. To group the plaintiffs together primarily for filing convenience does not satisfy the requirements of Rule 20.

Accordingly, because joinder of the additional 64 plaintiffs would be improper under Rule 20, McNaughton's motion to amend his complaint to add an additional 64 plaintiffs, pursuant to Rule 15, is denied.

Abraham v. Volkswagen

795 F.2d 238 (2d Cir. 1986)

WINTER, CIRCUIT JUDGE:

This litigation originated as a class action suit involving alleged defects in the oil systems of Volkswagen Rabbits. The district court dismissed [many of the claimants' claims] on the ground that they did not meet the joinder requirements of Rule 20(a), Fed. R. Civ. P.

We hold that joinder of the [disputed] plaintiffs should have been allowed under Rule 20(a).

BACKGROUND

The 119 plaintiffs are owners of Volkswagen Rabbits, model years 1975–79. They brought a class action lawsuit against the manufacturer, Volkswagen of America ("VWOA") alleging, *inter alia*, breach of the express warranty given in connection with the sale of each car and breach of the implied warranty of merchantability. Their claim, as originally stated, was that the oil system in the 1975–79 Rabbits was defective, causing excessive oil consumption, engine damage and failure, and decreased resale value of the cars. Not all plaintiffs claim to have suffered each form of damage, but all claim to have suffered at least one of the varieties specified. The complaint, as later amended, alleged that the damages claimed resulted from a single defective part, the valve stem seal, which is supposed to prevent oil from leaking into the engine's combustion chamber. The seal allegedly was made of an inferior material that caused it to harden and crack prematurely, which in turn led to oil leakage and the other types of damage claimed.

[The case was originally brought by more than 75 plaintiffs who sought relief individually and as representatives of a proposed class action. For various reasons the trial court concluded that a class action was improper here. Then the court turned its attention to the joinder of the claimants under Rule 20 on their individual claims.]

The court next addressed the second element of the motion to dismiss—the motion to sever all remaining individual claims, and then to dismiss each one for lack of federal jurisdiction. This question turned on whether the $50,000 amount in controversy requirement of Section 2310(d)(3)(B) [of the Magnuson-Moss Act] was satisfied. None of the 75 remaining plaintiffs claimed individual damage of that magnitude. However, individual claims may be aggregated toward satisfaction of the $50,000 requirement if the claims satisfy the requirements for joinder under Rule 20. 15 U.S.C. § 2310(d)(3)(B). *Saval v. BL Ltd.*, 710 F.2d 1027 (4th Cir. 1983). The aggregate damage claims of the 75 remaining plaintiffs did exceed $50,000, but the court concluded that Rule 20 had not been satisfied.

In denying joinder, the district court focused on Paragraph 22 of the First Amended Complaint, which alleged defects in a variety of components in the oil system, such as the oil pan, valve stem seals, and oil warning light. The answers to interrogatories revealed that some of the alleged defects had occurred on some cars but not others, and that some plaintiffs had needed repairs at 20,000 miles while others had not needed them until 80,000 miles. The court concluded that this disparity in timing of problems made the driving and maintenance history of each car vitally important to proof of each individual claim, and thus held that the 75 plaintiffs had not satisfied the "same transaction or occurrence" test of Rule 20. It then dismissed all of the remaining individual claims.

Plaintiffs moved for reconsideration on the joinder issue, and for permission to amend the complaint to clarify the nature of the defect alleged. Permission to amend was granted. The substituted paragraphs of the complaint were designed to make clear that the same defect—the faulty valve stem seal—was alleged to be at fault in every case, and that the differences noted by the court, such as mileage disparities, went only to the amount of damage and not to the basis of liability. The district court was unpersuaded, however, and on June 25, 1985, again dismissed the action "for substantially the reasons set forth" in its earlier decision.

On appeal, the plaintiffs claim that the district court erred in holding that the 75 remaining plaintiffs did not meet the Rule 20 requirement for joinder.

Joinder of Remaining Plaintiffs

The district court declined to permit joinder of the 75 plaintiffs remaining after others had been excluded as not having valid implied or express warranty claims. We believe the refusal to permit joinder was an abuse of discretion.

Rule 20(a) requires that the claims for relief asserted by each plaintiff must lead to or arise out of the same transaction or occurrence or series of transactions or occurrences, and that some question of law or fact common to all parties will arise in the litigation. The district court held that because some of the defects alleged did not occur on all cars and the mileage at which repairs were required varied greatly, the plaintiffs had not satisfied the same transaction or occurrence requirement.

We believe that the amendment to the complaint, alleging the faulty valve stem seal as a single defect that caused the various damages, satisfied the same transaction or occurrence (or series thereof) requirement. All plaintiffs now allege as the basis for their claims the purchase of a Volkswagen Rabbit with a valve stem seal made of defective material that will cause it to harden and break over time. We think that amply satisfies the requirement of a series of logically related transactions. *See* 7 C. Wright and A. Miller, *Federal Practice and Procedure* § 1653 (1972). To hold otherwise would largely read the $50,000 aggregation provision for federal jurisdiction out of the Act. Because it is indisputable that the remaining plaintiffs raise common questions of law and fact, the second requirement of Rule 20(a) is also satisfied.

Notes and Problems

1. The foregoing three cases demonstrate some divergence of views among the federal courts as to how to apply Rule 20's seemingly straightforward prerequisites to products liability litigation. Do you agree with the pro-joinder approach revealed in *Volkswagen* or the anti-joinder approach in *Merck*? Given the purposes behind Rule 20, which way would you rule in each of the two cases? Are their approaches inconsistent or is it just that the factual circumstances are distinguishable?

2. Another court, in *In re Chochos*, similarly dealt with the joinder of multiple defendants under Rule 20, and stated:

> Rule 20(a) ... establishes two separate requirements for joinder and both of them must be satisfied for it to be proper. There must be both a common transaction or occurrence giving rise to the defendants' asserted liability *and* a common question of law or fact. As for what constitutes a common transaction or occurrence, this is determined on a case by case basis. It is a somewhat flexible concept that looks to the logical relationship between the events giving rise to the plaintiff's claims, which is interpreted in such a way as to permit all reasonably related claims for relief against different parties to be brought in a single proceeding. *Mosley v. General Motors Corp.*, 497 F.2d at 1333. Nonetheless, it is not so flexible that courts will permit a single proceeding to be brought against multiple defendants simply because they are all liable to the plaintiff under the same theory or similar causes of action. *In re Nuclear Imaging Systems, Inc.*, 277 B.R. 59, 63 (Bankr.E.D.Pa.2002).

> [Here, the] trustee's claims against the different defendants all have a common theme — each of them was the transferee of a transfer made either to or for the benefit of the debtor's wife, Lonetta (Norkus) Chochos. Count I seeks to recover real estate that the debtor transferred to Mrs. Chochos prior to the petition.

Counts II through VI seek to recover debts he paid on her behalf, both before and after filing bankruptcy. Each count is directed to and seeks judgment against a single defendant for the transfers it received. There is no assertion that any of the defendants are jointly, severally, or alternatively liable as a result of the transfers.

The common theme that runs through the trustee's claims is not sufficient to connect what are otherwise a series of separate transactions or to supply a reason why these independent claims should logically be tied together. *See, Papagiannis v. Pontikis,* 108 F.R.D. 177, 179 (N.D.Ill.1985). If it were, joinder would require nothing more than a prosecution based upon the same cause of action or legal theory, *see, In re Nuclear Imaging Systems, Inc.,* 277 B.R. at 63–64, and would not also involve an assertion of joint, several or alternative liability. *In re M & L Business Machine Co., Inc.,* 132 B.R. 433, 434–35 (Bankr.D.Colo.1991). In saying this, the court recognizes the trustee's arguments that the claims involve common legal and factual issues and the testimony of the same witnesses at trial. Yet, these considerations are only a part of the analysis Rule 20 requires. Proper joinder requires more than the common questions of law or fact that the trustee emphasizes; the plaintiff must also seek to hold the defendants jointly, severally or alternatively liable as a result of the same transaction or occurrence.

In re Chochos, 325 B.R. 780, 785 (Bankr. N.D. Ind. 2005). Given the requirement for more than overlapping issues of fact or law, what else does Rule 20 seek to guarantee beyond efficiency?

3. *Chapter Problem:* The newspaper article from earlier in this Chapter referenced there being other accidents allegedly caused by the Camel's braking system. Attorney Jackie Chiles seems to invite other such claimants to contact him about suing Kazakh. Should you, as counsel for Paula Jones, seek to identify these other accident victims and bring their claims along with Paul's claim in the same lawsuit utilizing Rule 20's liberal joinder provisions? What would be the benefits of doing so? Are there any possible negative repercussions of attempting this joinder? Given the divergent views of Rule 20's application to strict products liability claims illustrated by the above case opinions, how do you think a court would rule on your attempt to join all of these claimants against Kazakh in one proceeding?

Pulling It All Together Exercise

If you were the trial court addressing the propriety of joinder in the following scenarios, how would you rule? *Spend 10 minutes for each scenario below writing out your analysis.*

1. Fifty sports broadcasters, who each work for different television stations, have been released by their stations. The broadcasters believe that they have been discriminated against on the basis of their age. They think the sports television industry has a pattern or practice of age discrimination. They join together and sue all fifty television stations. They assert that the parties are properly joined because they are based on a pattern of age discrimination. Essentially, they argue that the industry has an unofficial policy of firing broadcasters once they get too old.

2. Joe is a current reality star appearing on the Bachelor. Apparently confusing him with another person by the same name, two different newspapers (the

LA Times and the New York Times) each, as a result of separate investigations, independently report that Joe is a convicted pedophile. He files a single defamation lawsuit against both seeking to recover for their false and defamatory statements.

3. Bob owns a snow cone shack ("Bahama Bob's") for which he maintains a business interruption insurance policy. He hires a welder to do some work for him inside the shack and the welder messes up the job, causing a fire that demolishes the premises. He sues the welder for negligence seeking to recover the fair market value of the destroyed shack. He also names as a co-defendant the insurance company that has refused to pay on the policy claiming that Bob was guilty of arson. On that claim, Bob seeks to recover solely the lost profits from the business.

3. At the Intersection of Rules 20 & 42: A Delicate Dance

The following two cases deal with the interplay between Rules 20 and 42. Rule 20, of course, permits claims to be joined that meet the two-part test of a common question arising from one transaction or occurrence. On the other hand, Rule 42 permits a court to join for a common hearing or trial separate claims (that arose from different occurrences) so long as a common question exists among them. And Rule 42 also permits a court to sever claims properly joined under Rule 20. Thus, Rule 42 seems to allow a district court to ignore at least one of Rule 20's prerequisites and permit the court to structure a case—or a trial—how the court desires. Pay close attention to how each case below illustrates an inverse use of the two rules. Also consider, to the extent Rule 42 permits a court to disregard the dual requirements of Rule 20, what practical purpose does Rule 20 serve?

Stanford v. Tennessee Valley
18 F.R.D. 152 (M.D. Tenn. 1955)

MILLER, J.,

The action is before the Court upon the separate motions of defendants, Monsanto Chemical Company and Armour & Company, to dismiss and for alternative relief. The grounds of the motion will be separately discussed.

By an agreed order heretofore entered, the action was dismissed as to the Tennessee Valley Authority, with the result that the complaint, as it is presently framed, seeks to recover damages from the defendants, Monsanto Chemical Company and Armour & Company, jointly and severally, allegedly caused by fluorine gas fumes emitted from the plants of the said defendants located within the vicinity of the plaintiffs' property.

Both defendants move the Court to dismiss the action upon the ground that there is a misjoinder of defendants. It is insisted first, that the defendants, as shown by the averments of the complaint, are not joint tortfeasors, and secondly, that the conditions required by Rule 20 of the Federal Rules of Civil Procedure for a permissive joinder of defendants, are not present.

In the alternative, both defendants, in the event the motions to dismiss are overruled, request the Court to order a severance of the claims, requiring that the plaintiffs' claim against each defendant be tried separately.

It appears to be altogether clear from the Tennessee decisions that the defendants, upon the facts set forth in the complaint, are not joint tortfeasors and that under the Tennessee practice they may not be joined for the purposes of trial. *Swain v. Tennessee Copper Co.*, 111 Tenn. 430, 78 S.W. 93 (1903); *Madison v. Ducktown Sulphur, Copper & Iron Co.*, 113 Tenn. 331, 83 S.W. 658 (1904); *Hale v. City of Knoxville*, 189 Tenn. 491, 226 S.W.2d 265, 15 A.L.R.2d 1283 (1950).

But the right to join the defendants for trial, being procedural rather than substantive in character, is governed by the Federal Rules of Civil Procedure, 28 U.S.C.A., and not by the practice obtaining in the state courts.

Rule 20 of the Federal Rules of Civil Procedure permits all persons to be joined in one action as defendants 'if there is asserted against them jointly, severally, or in the alternative, any right to relief in respect of or arising out of the same transaction, occurrence, or series of transactions or occurrences and if any question of law or fact common to all of them will arise in the action.'

An analysis of the complaint discloses that the defendants' plants are separately owned and operated and that they are located at different distances from the plaintiffs' property. Their activities are separate and distinct from each other although they are engaged in the same general type of business. There is nothing on the face of the complaint from which it could be concluded that the plaintiffs' claims against the two defendants arise out of the same transaction or occurrence, or out of the same series of transactions or occurrences. The transactions are separate as to each defendant. It follows, therefore, that there is a misjoinder of defendants.

Such misjoinder under Rule 21 is not ground for dismissal of the action, but at most would require that the claims be severed and proceeded with separately. On the other hand, Rule 42 authorizes the Court to order a joint hearing or trial of any or all matters in issue in the actions, or to consolidate the actions, if they involve 'a common question of law or fact.'

In the instant case, it would appear from the averments of the complaint that common questions of law and fact are sufficiently involved to meet the requirements of Rule 42. In the first place, there is a question as to whether the plaintiffs have a cause of action for a permanent nuisance or one of a temporary or recurring nature, a mixed question of law and fact common to both defendants. Also, on a strictly factual basis, the actions against both defendants involve the question whether the fluorine gas fumes are capable of producing and in fact did produce the damage or damages described in the complaint. Still another question of fact, at least in large part common to both defendants, is whether there are devices or processes available which could be used in an operation of this kind to eliminate or curtail the damages allegedly caused by the fumes. Stated in broader terms, the issue is whether the condition is one which can be eliminated by human labor and skill or by the expenditure of money. It is conceivable that other issues, common to both parties, may arise after the answers are filed, or after a further development of the case. It results that the necessary conditions are present to authorize the Court to order a joint trial under Rule 42, and the only remaining question is whether the Court should exercise its discretion to that effect.

The apparent contention of the defendants is that they would be prejudiced by a joint trial because of the difficulty in determining the responsibility of each defendant on account of its alleged contribution to the plaintiffs' damage.

Concededly, in cases of this nature, there is the inherent difficulty of segregating and determining the nature and extent of the contribution made by each party to the common nuisance. This difficulty, however, would not be altogether removed if the claims were tried separately. If the claim against one defendant should be separately tried, the jury would still be confronted with the necessity of determining whether the plaintiffs' damage was caused by the defendant before the Court, or whether it was caused by the other defendant not before the Court. There would also exist the necessity of determining the extent that the activities of the defendant on trial contributed to the plaintiffs' damage as contrasted with the activities of the defendant not on trial.

On the other hand, a joint trial has many advantages, including a saving of trial time, as well as a saving of expense not only to the Government but to the parties. Doubtless in a large measure, the trial of both claims will involve the use of the same witnesses and the same evidence. Upon the whole case, the Court feels that the ends of justice will be met by a joint trial of the claims.

The order should accordingly provide that the claims are severed for all purposes and to be proceeded with separately except that they will be tried together before the same jury.

Decision

This will entail the filing of separate complaints against the defendants, and thereafter the filing or entry of separate pleadings, motions, verdicts, judgments, etc. Such an order, as contrasted with a consolidation, will preserve to each defendant the procedural advantages of a separate trial, including the right to peremptory challenges of jurors. Cf. *Signal Mountain Portland Cement Co. v. Brown*, 6 Cir., 141 F.2d 471, 476, 477 (6th Cir. 1944).

An order will be submitted in conformity with this memorandum.

Hall v. E.I. Du Pont/Chance v. Du Pont

345 F. Supp. 353 (E.D.N.Y. 1972)

WEINSTEIN, J.,

These two cases arise out of eighteen separate accidents scattered across the nation in which children were injured by blasting caps. Damages are sought from manufacturers and their trade association, the Institute of Makers of Explosives (I.M.E.). The basic allegation is that the practice of the explosives industry during the 1950's—continuing until 1965—of not placing any warning upon individual blasting caps and of failing to take other safety measures created an unreasonable risk of harm resulting in plaintiffs' injuries.

P's claim

I. THE CHANCE CASE

A. Facts and Proceedings

Thirteen children were allegedly injured by blasting caps in twelve unrelated accidents between 1955 and 1959. The injuries occurred in the states of Alabama, California, Maryland, Montana, Nevada, North Carolina, Tennessee, Texas, Washington and West Virginia. Plaintiffs are citizens of the states in which their injuries occurred. They are now claiming damages against six manufacturers of blasting caps and the I.M.E. on the grounds of negligence, common law conspiracy, assault, and strict liability in tort. In addition, two parents sue for medical expenses. Federal jurisdiction is based on diversity of citizenship. 28 U.S.C. § 1332.

relief sought

While the plaintiffs' injuries occurred at widely varied times and places, the complaint alleges certain features common to them all. Each plaintiff, according to the complaint, "came into possession" of a dynamite blasting cap which was not labeled or marked with a warning of danger, and which could be easily detonated by a child. In each instance an injurious explosion occurred.

commonality of Ps

[The complaint did not establish the manufacturer of the specific blasting caps that caused their injuries, but all the plaintiffs allege that the harm was caused by the lack of a warning label on the blasting caps to prevent the particular injuries that occurred. The allegations include industry practices and an association with actual knowledge of the harms the blasting caps caused children. Defendants moved for dismissal or in the alternative, severance. The court also dealt with the choice of law problem, but requested supplemental briefing on this issue.]

The central question raised by defendants' motion is whether the defendants can be held responsible as a group under any theory of joint liability for injuries arising out of their individual manufacture of blasting caps. Joint tort liability is not limited to a narrow set of relationships and circumstances. It has been imposed in a wide range of situations, requiring varying standards of care, in which defendants cooperate in various degrees, enter into business and property relationships, and undertake to supply goods for public consumption. Developments in negligence and strict tort liability have imposed extensive duties on manufacturers to guard against a broad spectrum of risks with regard to the general population. The reasoning underlying current policy justifies the extension of established doctrines of joint tort liability to the area of industry-wide cooperation in product manufacture and design.

Can Ds be held liable?. <u>yes</u>

[The court denied the Defendants' motion to dismiss finding several possible theories of liability including: enterprise liability, concert of action and through application of § 433B of the Restatement of Torts (Second).]

Joinder, Transfer and Conflict of Laws

To justify permissive joinder of parties, plaintiffs must show both a "common question of law or fact" and a right to relief "arising out of the same transaction or occurrence or series of transactions or occurrences." Fed.R.Civ.P. 20(a). Defendants move for severance

RULE 20

of plaintiffs on the ground that the complaint fails to satisfy either requirement, and for dismissal or transfer of the claims thus severed. 28 U.S.C. § 1404(a). They assert that the substantive law of the ten states will govern liability, and hence the claims present no common question of law.

The question of which state's law will govern which aspects of this case cannot be settled by assertion. In diversity cases, a federal court is bound to apply the choice-of-law principles of the state in which it sits. *Klaxon v. Stentor Electric Mfg. Co.*, 313 U.S. 487, 61 S.Ct. 1020, 85 L.Ed. 1477 (1941). Under New York law, the choice of applicable law in personal injury cases is not determined by the traditional "place of injury" test, but by "the flexible principle that the law to be applied to resolve a particular issue is 'the law of the jurisdiction which, because of its relationship or contact with the occurrence or the parties, has the greatest concern' with the matter in issue and 'the strongest interest' in its resolution." *Long v. Pan American World Airways*, 16 N.Y.2d 337, 341, 266 N.Y.S.2d 513, 515, 213 N.E.2d 796, 798 (1965), quoting *Babcock v. Jackson*, 12 N.Y.2d 473, 481, 484, 240 N.Y.S.2d 743, 749, 751, 191 N.E.2d 279, 282, 285 (1963) (Fuld, J.).

The locus of defendants' joint activity was allegedly at least in part in New York, the location of the I.M.E. Whether proof of this connection would be sufficient to support the application of New York law to some or all of the claims is a complex question involving consideration of New York choice-of-law principles and federal constitutional law. The parties are directed to supply briefs on this issue and on the general question of the law applicable to the different aspects of this case. Prior to a full consideration of the choice-of-law question, this court cannot rule on whether the plaintiffs' claims contain a common question of law. It should be noted, however, that Rule 20(a) requires only "*any* common question of law or fact." Thus the presence of questions of law not common to all the plaintiffs will not, in itself, defeat joinder. *See Music Merchants v. Capitol Records*, 20 F.R.D. 462 (E.D.N.Y.1957); 7 Wright & Miller, Federal Practice and Procedure § 1653 at 274 (1972).

Plaintiffs' claims do contain, moreover, common questions of fact; for example, whether the defendants exercised joint control over the labeling of blasting caps and operated, for purposes of tort liability, as a joint enterprise with respect to such labeling. The presence of these questions satisfies the requirement of Rule 20(a) that "any question of law *or* fact common to all these persons" arise in the action.

Defendants also contend that because the accidents occurred at different times and places, plaintiffs' rights to relief do not arise out of the same transaction or occurrence, or series of transactions or occurrences. There is no rigid rule as to what constitutes "the same transaction or occurrence" for purposes of joinder under Rule 20(a). "[T]he approach must be the general one of whether there are enough ultimate factual concurrences that it would be fair to the parties to require them to defend jointly" against the several claims. *Eastern Fireproofing Co., Inc. v. United States Gypsum Co.*, 160 F.Supp. 580, 581 (D.Mass.1958). Application of this flexible standard presents a certain challenge in this case. It would be neither fair nor convenient to any of the parties nor to the court to determine in this court all the relevant issues of fact involved in each accident. At the same time it would be unfair and burdensome to require each plaintiff to prove the alleged joint activities in ten separate and (to that extent) repetitive actions.

The solution does not lie in wholesale severance, and the cases cited by defendants do not support that result. Rather, fairness to the parties may be maximized by permitting plaintiffs to litigate the issues of joint activity in this court, and then transferring the questions which turn on the particular facts of each accident to the federal districts in which the accidents occurred. *See* 28 U.S.C. § 1404(a), Rules 20(b) and 42(a) and (b), Federal Rules of Civil Procedure. Whether this procedure would entail full separate trials of different issues, or special findings of fact in this court, or other possible procedures, will be decided after consideration of the choice-of-law problem and in consultation with the parties.

II. THE HALL CASE

[Three families (from New York, Ohio, and North Dakota), together sued as defendants two manufacturers of blasting caps (Du Pont and Hercules). Two of the plaintiff families complained of Hercules and the other family complained of Du Pont. No product identification problem existed on these claims yet they attempted to bring them together in a single suit against both manufacturers.]

The central question raised by defendants' motions is whether the amended complaint presents a claim of joint liability against the manufacturers. We hold that the amended complaint in *Hall* does not [present] the joint liability aspects of the case. [Though courts give plaintiffs latitude in naming multiple parties to their case there are "limits on the plaintiff's choice." The "redundant naming of an additional manufacturer results from the happenstance of joinder of claims by unrelated plaintiffs." Plaintiff will not be permitted to burden the court and defendants by an unnecessary and inappropriate joinder of a party having no real interest in the suit. McClintock, Handbook of Principles of Equity, 22 (2d ed. 1948); 3A Moore's Federal Practice ¶ 20.08. This improper joinder justifies dismissal of each family's claims against the manufacturer not accused of producing the cap that injured their child.]

With each plaintiff now having claims against the manufacturer of the injury-causing cap, defendants' motion for severance under Rule 20(a) must be granted. While evidence of joint action may well be relevant in the claims against each manufacturer, proof of such responsibility will not be necessary for recovery on each plaintiff's claims. Recovery in each case will turn on the legal-factual questions of negligence and strict liability, and on evidence about the circumstances of each of the separate accidents. The claims by the three groups of plaintiffs present sufficiently diverse questions of law and fact to require severance. [Using § 1404(a) transfer for convenience, the court then transferred the North Dakota and Ohio plaintiffs' suits to their respective home jurisdictions where those incidents each occurred.]

Notes and Problems

1. The court in *Stanford v. Tennessee Valley Authority* analyzed both the "same transaction or occurrence" element and the "common question of law or fact" element. However, the analysis of the common question of law or fact was done in relation to Rule 42. In finding that the claims met the common question of law or fact element under Rule 42, the court permitted a common trial to occur despite Rule 20 not permitting the joinder of the parties' claims. Did you agree with the court's conclusion regarding Rule 20's test not being met on these facts?

2. *Hall* (in the portion of the opinion referring to the "Chance" case) might arguably be read in one of two ways: (1) that the transaction or occurrence test was not met but that the court was going to use Rule 42 to join together the core liability issues for a common trial, or (2) that the transaction or occurrence test was met for Rule 20 purposes but that the court was going to use Rule 42(b) to sever the claims of the various claimants after the common trial on core liability issues. Which makes most sense? Does it ultimately matter which view the court took?

3. After reading both *Stanford* and *Hall*, it would appear that the purposes of Rule 20 can become muddied if not frustrated altogether. If Rule 20 can be trumped by the use of Rule 42 (by consolidation or severance of parties), why do we have Rule 20? What practical importance might it have? Does Rule 20 at least raise a presumption as to what constitutes a proper litigation unit?

4. *Problems.* Would the following claims be proper candidates for either Rule 42(a) consolidation or Rule 42(b) severance?

a. The Bachelor files two lawsuits in the same district court in Memphis. One is against the New York Times and the other against the Los Angeles Times—each of whom has independently investigated the Bachelor's background and reported in separate stories that he was a convicted pedophile. He has sued each for libel contending that the stories are false and defamatory. The two separate defendants have each filed answers contending that the stories were true.

b. Same scenario as above, except that the Bachelor sued the LA. Times in southern California federal court and sued the N.Y. Times in New York federal court.

5. *Chapter Problem:* If Paula Jones' claims were brought separate from the other accident victims (injured in their separate Camel incidents), would it still be appropriate for a court to order the consolidation of the various lawsuits for a common trial on whether the Camel brakes were defective? What would have to be true about all of these lawsuits for Rule 42's provisions to be applicable? Is that likely to be the case?

Pulling It All Together Exercise

Juda is driving through an intersection when she is broadsided, on both sides of her car, by two different drivers—Dan and Darla, who have each run a red light. The combined force of the collisions causes Juda's car to spin out of control until she hits a telephone pole by the side of the street causing great damage to her car and personal injuries. She has come to you for legal representation. You are considering structuring your lawsuit(s). Can you sue both Dan and Darla in one suit under Rule 20? Consider the court's opinion in the foregoing *Stanford* case in articulating your answer.

Spend 10 minutes writing your analysis of this problem.

F. Rule 19 Compulsory Joinder

Rule 19, compulsory joinder applies in exceptional scenarios where fundamental concerns over fairness demand that the plaintiff join some missing party or parties or else face possible dismissal of the entire action. The focus is upon three possible areas of concern: 1) whether the plaintiff can get complete relief through the suit against those that are currently joined (protects the plaintiff); 2) will the missing parties suffer harm from the court not requiring joinder (protects the missing party); 3) by not including the missing parties, would the defendant be subject to multiple inconsistent judgments (protects the defendant). Keep these considerations in mind while reading the cases below.

Although a large purpose of Rule 19 is to protect the existing and the missing parties — seemingly noble purposes — consider whether defendants' attempted invocation of the rule is always motivated by such lofty concerns. See how this works in *Temple v. Synthes Corp.* and in *Eldredge v. Carpenters 46 Northern Calif. Counties JACT.* If there are good reasons why it would make more sense to compel joinder of missing parties, why are courts so stingy about its application? If Rule 19 is inapplicable in each of those two contexts, when should it apply?

Rule 19. Required Joinder of Parties

(a) Persons Required to Be Joined if Feasible.

   (1) **Required Party.**

      A person who is subject to service of process and whose joinder will not deprive the court of subject-matter jurisdiction must be joined as a party if:

      (A) in that person's absence, the court cannot accord complete relief among existing parties; or

      (B) that person claims an interest relating to the subject of the action and is so situated that disposing of the action in the person's absence may:

         (i) as a practical matter impair or impede the person's ability to protect the interest; or

         (ii) leave an existing party subject to a substantial risk of incurring double, multiple, or otherwise inconsistent obligations because of the interest.

Temple v. Synthes Corporation, Ltd.

498 U.S. 5 (1990)

PER CURIAM.

facts

Petitioner Temple, a Mississippi resident, underwent surgery in October 1986 in which a "plate and screw device" was implanted in his lower spine. The device was manufactured by respondent Synthes Corp., Ltd. (U. S. A.) (Synthes), a Pennsylvania corporation. Dr. S. Henry LaRocca performed the surgery at St. Charles General Hospital in New Orleans, Louisiana. Following surgery, the device's screws broke off inside Temple's back.

Temple filed suit against Synthes in the United States District Court for the Eastern District of Louisiana. The suit, which rested on diversity jurisdiction, alleged defective design and manufacture of the device. At the same time, Temple filed a state administrative proceeding against Dr. LaRocca and the hospital for malpractice and negligence. At the conclusion of the administrative proceeding, Temple filed suit against the doctor and the hospital in Louisiana state court.

Relief sought

Synthes did not attempt to bring the doctor and the hospital into the federal action by means of a third-party complaint, as provided in Federal Rule of Civil Procedure 14(a). Instead, Synthes filed a motion to dismiss Temple's federal suit for failure to join necessary parties pursuant to Federal Rule of Civil Procedure 19. Following a hearing, the District

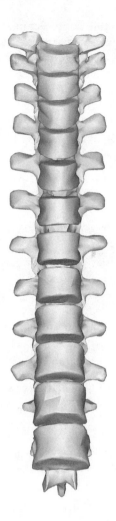

Court ordered Temple to join the doctor and the hospital as defendants within 20 days or risk dismissal of the lawsuit. According to the court, the most significant reason for requiring joinder was the interest of judicial economy. The court relied on this Court's decision in *Provident Tradesmens Bank & Trust Co. v. Patterson*, 390 U.S. 102, 19 L. Ed. 2d 936, 88 S. Ct. 733 (1968), wherein we recognized that one focus of Rule 19 is "the interest of the courts and the public in complete, consistent, and efficient settlement of controversies." When Temple failed to join the doctor and the hospital, the court dismissed the suit with prejudice.

Temple appealed, and the United States Court of Appeals for the Fifth Circuit affirmed. [*Appellate Reasoning*] The court deemed it "obviously prejudicial to the defendants to have the separate litigations being carried on," because Synthes' defense might be that the plate was not defective but that the doctor and the hospital were negligent, while the doctor and the hospital, on the other hand, might claim that they were not negligent but that the plate was defective. The Court of Appeals found that the claims overlapped and that the District Court therefore had not abused its discretion in ordering joinder under Rule 19. A petition for rehearing was denied.

pis claim

In his petition for certiorari to this Court, Temple contends that it was error to label joint tortfeasors as indispensable parties under Rule 19(b) and to dismiss the lawsuit with prejudice for failure to join those parties. We agree. Synthes does not deny that it, the doctor, and the hospital are potential joint tortfeasors. It has long been the rule that it is not necessary for all joint tortfeasors to be named as defendants in a single lawsuit. Nothing in the 1966 revision of Rule 19 changed that principle. The Advisory Committee Notes to Rule 19(a) explicitly state that "a tortfeasor with the usual 'joint-and-several' liability is merely a permissive party to an action against another with like liability." There is nothing in Louisiana tort law to the contrary.

The opinion in *Provident Bank, supra*, does speak of the public interest in limiting multiple litigation, but that case is not controlling here.... [That case did not involve any alleged joint tortfeasors].

Here, no inquiry under Rule 19(b) is necessary, because the threshold requirements of Rule 19(a) have not been satisfied. As potential joint tortfeasors with Synthes, Dr. LaRocca and the hospital were merely permissive parties. The Court of Appeals erred by failing to hold that the District Court abused its discretion in ordering them joined as defendants and in dismissing the action when Temple failed to comply with the court's order. For these reasons, we grant the petition for certiorari, reverse the judgment of the Court of Appeals for the Fifth Circuit, and remand for further proceedings consistent with this opinion.

Eldredge v. Carpenters 46 JATC

662 F.2d 534 (9th Cir. 1981)

FLETCHER, CIRCUIT JUDGE:

This is an appeal from the district court's order dismissing the action for failure to join indispensable parties. Fed.R.Civ.P. 19. We reverse and remand.

I
FACTS

relief sought

The facts underlying this suit are recounted in great detail in the district court opinion, 440 F.Supp. at 510–14, and need only be summarized here. Plaintiffs Eldredge and Mazur brought suit under Title VII, 42 U.S.C. § 2000e-2, against the Carpenters 46 Northern California Counties Joint Apprenticeship and Training Committee (JATC), alleging sex discrimination in the operation of JATC's apprenticeship program. Plaintiffs brought the suit as a class action, but the district court has not yet considered the question of class certification.

Defendant JATC is a joint labor-management committee established under an agreement that provides for a trust fund contributed to by the parties to the master collective bargaining agreements in the Northern California construction industry. JATC is composed of equal numbers of labor and management representatives, and acts as a board of trustees for the administration of the Carpenters Apprenticeship and Training Trust Fund for Northern California. It is responsible for establishing, supporting, and maintaining programs to educate and train journeymen and apprentices in all classifications covered by any collective bargaining agreement that requires employer contributions to the trust fund. 440 F.Supp. at 510–11.

pis claim

Plaintiffs allege that the process by which JATC selects applicants to its apprenticeship training program discriminates against women. Although JATC has employed other selection procedures in the past, see *id*. at 511–12, it presently relies on what is known as the "unrestricted hunting license" system. Under this system, an individual must first convince an employer to hire him or her as a beginning apprentice. JATC then places the individual's name on its applicant register. *Id*. at 512. The applicant enters into an apprenticeship agreement with JATC and is dispatched through the union hiring hall. *Id*. An individual needs no prior training to become an apprentice; all that is required is that he or she be 17 years of age and have a high school diploma or its equivalent. *Id*. at 511.

The master collective bargaining agreements under which JATC operates require employers to hire one apprentice for every five journeymen employed. The apprenticeship is a four-year program. Employers are under no obligation to hire beginning as opposed to experienced apprentices. *Id*. at 519. In May of 1976, only thirteen of JATC's 3220 registered apprentices were women. *Id*. at 514.

The essence of plaintiffs' complaint is that, by relying on the unrestricted hunting license system to recruit apprentices, JATC has adopted an entrance requirement for its program which is known to have a discriminatory effect on women. Plaintiffs argue that JATC knows that individual employers do not hire women under the unrestricted hunting license system, and that JATC's use of this system is therefore illegal under Title VII. The district court assumed for the purposes of its rule 19 analysis that plaintiffs had stated a claim on which relief could be granted. 440 F.Supp. at 518 (citing *Crockett v. Green*, 388 F.Supp. 912 (E.D.Wis.1975), aff'd, 534 F.2d 715 (7th Cir. 1976)).

The district court held that the 4500 employers and 60 union locals covered by the master labor agreement, or adequate representatives of their interests, were indispensable to the litigation under the standards imposed by rule 19(b). It ordered them joined within 60 days. 440 F.Supp. at 527. Plaintiffs were granted extensions of time in which to explore the possibilities for joinder, see, 83 F.R.D. 136, 20 Fair Empl.Prac.Cas. at 898–99, but joinder of all 4500 employers proved impossible. The plaintiffs then sought to join the Northern California Homebuilders' Conference (NCHBC) to represent the absent employers' interests. The court held this inadequate and dismissed the case. *Id*. at 900, 83 F.R.D. 136. We conclude that the employers are not necessary parties under rule 19(a) and thus cannot be indispensable parties under rule 19(b). We reverse.

II
ANALYSIS

Rule 19 requires two separate inquiries. First, are there persons who should be joined, either because their own interests or the interests of the parties might be harmed by their absence? Such persons, referred to as "necessary parties," must be joined if feasible. Fed.R.Civ.P. 19(a). Second, if parties determined to be necessary under rule 19(a) cannot be joined, should the action in "equity and good conscience" be dismissed? Only if the court determines that the action should be dismissed is the absent party labelled "indispensable." Fed.R.Civ.P. 19(b); see *English v. Seaboard Coast Line Railroad*, 465 F.2d 43, 48 (5th Cir. 1972).

The nature of the rule 19 inquiry is described at some length in *Provident Tradesmens Bank & Trust Co. v. Patterson*, 390 U.S. 102, 88 S.Ct. 733, 19 L.Ed.2d 936 (1968). The inquiry should focus on the practical effects of joinder and nonjoinder. *Id*. at 116 n.12, 88 S.Ct. at 741 n.12; *Schutten v. Shell Oil Co*., 421 F.2d 869, 874 (5th Cir. 1970).

Rule 19(a) describes two categories of persons who should be joined if feasible. If the absent employers fall into either of these two categories, they are "necessary parties."

The first category comprises those persons in whose absence "complete relief cannot be accorded among those already parties." Fed.R.Civ.P. 19(a)(1). This portion of the rule is concerned only with "relief as between the persons already parties, not as between a party and the absent person whose joinder is sought." 3A Moore's Federal Practice P 19.07-1(1), at 19–128 (2d ed. 1980); accord, *Morgan Guaranty Trust Co. v. Martin*, 466 F.2d 593, 598 (7th Cir. 1972). The district court concluded that the absent employers could frustrate any relief granted against JATC, and that complete relief would therefore not be possible unless the employers were made parties. The court reasoned that the employers could defeat any order against JATC by refusing to hire any apprentices, by hiring only unregistered, nonunion apprentices, or by rejecting all female apprentices dispatched to them. 440 F.Supp. at 519–20. We believe that the district court misapprehended the legal inquiry required by rule 19(a)(1).

If JATC's activities violate Title VII, a question not yet decided, then the court has both the power and the duty to enjoin those activities. The possibility that such an injunction may induce employers to avoid JATC's services, or ultimately to disband the training and referral system altogether, should not defeat the present action against JATC. JATC may not avoid its own liability for practices illegal under Title VII by relying on the employers' possible future conduct that might frustrate the remedial purposes of any court-ordered changes in the apprenticeship program. See, e.g., *United States v. Sheet Metal Workers Local 36*, 416 F.2d 123, 132 & n.16 (8th Cir. 1969) (enjoining union from continuing discriminatory referral practices, even though those practices were required by collective bargaining agreement with absent employers).

The district court appears to assume that the employers would discriminate against women because of their sex, and that they would refuse to hire women training in the apprentice program. There is no evidence to this effect in the record. On the contrary, the employers have previously participated, apparently successfully, in a state-mandated affirmative action program designed to increase the number of minority apprentices. See 440 F.Supp. at 511–12.

While it might be desirable to join all 4500 employers in order to eradicate sex discrimination in the industry, we conclude that relief on plaintiffs' claims against JATC as an entity could be afforded by an injunction against JATC alone. Both sides agree that JATC has the power under the trust fund agreement to structure its apprenticeship program in any way it sees fit. 440 F.Supp. at 510–11. It is quite possible that a court-ordered restructuring of the program could effectively increase the participation of women in the apprenticeship program. See, e.g., *EEOC v. Local 638, Sheet Metal Workers' Union*, 565 F.2d 31, 34–35 (2d Cir. 1977).

The second inquiry required by rule 19(a) concerns prejudice, either to the absent persons or to those already parties. Rule 19(a)(2)(i) provides that a person should be joined if he claims an interest relating to the subject of the action, and the disposition of the action may "as a practical matter impair or impede his ability to protect that interest."

The district court held that the employers should be joined since they have a right to select their own employees, a substantial interest that they have a right to protect. We disagree. The trust fund agreement grants full authority to JATC to structure the apprenticeship program and to select the apprentices. We conclude that the employers have by contract ceded to JATC whatever legally protectable interest they may have had in selecting apprentices to be trained. On the other hand, without the joinder of the employers, any court order that may be entered to enjoin JATC to institute programs cannot go beyond the authority granted JATC under the trust fund agreement. The absent employers are thus assured that an injunction against JATC will not trench on any rights reserved to the employers under the agreement. We must conclude that the employers' ability to protect whatever interest in employee selection they retain will not be "impaired or impeded" if they are not made parties. They are therefore not necessary parties under rule 19(a)(2)(i).

The district court was understandably concerned that the absent employers might have interests that would be unrepresented in the present suit. Although we have concluded that their interests are not the sort that would make the employers necessary under rule 19, on remand it is possible that some employers, or the NCHBC, may move to intervene. The district court may then consider whether to permit intervention under Fed.R.Civ.P. 24. See e.g., *United States v. Allegheny-Ludlum Industries, Inc.*, 517 F.2d 826, 846 (5th Cir. 1975), cert. denied, 425 U.S. 944, 96 S.Ct. 1684, 48 L.Ed.2d 187 (1976).

We hold that the trial court erred in dismissing the case for non-joinder of necessary parties. We REVERSE and REMAND for further proceedings.

Notes and Problems

1. What argument for prejudice did the defendant make in *Temple*? Do you buy that argument? What other options did the defendant have rather than seek dismissal based upon Rule 19? Consider Rule 14 third party practice, which we will discuss next in this chapter, which provides:

> A defending party may, as third-party plaintiff, serve a summons and complaint on a nonparty who is or may be liable to it for all or part of the claim against it. But the third-party plaintiff must, by motion, obtain the court's leave if it files the third-party complaint more than 10 days after serving its original answer.

Fed. R. Civ. P. 14. What role could this rule have provided in *Temple*? In particular, what effect does this rule's presence have on the prejudice the defendant must suffer for a party to be a necessary party under Rule 19? What do you think the defendant's actual motive was in *Temple* for filing the Rule 19 motion?

2. How did the court in *Eldredge* find the plaintiffs would receive complete relief without the joinder of all of the employers? Is the defendant's strategy in using Rule 19 the same in *Temple* and *Eldredge*? Also, would the various employers be considered proper parties joined under Rule 20 if the plaintiff had sought to join them initially?

3. Using the three questions appearing in the text at the beginning of this section, analyze whether the hospital and doctors were required parties under Rule 19. What affect would this decision have had on cases involving joint tortfeasors if the court had affirmed the decision of the district court?

4. In both *Temple* and *Eldredge*—where Rule 19 was found inapplicable to force joinder—did good reasons exist to include the missing parties in the case? Would that be both logical and efficient? If so, what does the inapplicability of Rule 19 in these situations tell us about Rule 19's focus? What else does it say about the principle of litigant autonomy?

5. Rule 19 is often used out of a motivation by a defendant to compel an order of dismissal (using 19(b)) rather than a desire to look out for the interests of the plaintiff or missing parties. Therefore, it is invoked by defendants more often than it should actually apply to compel an order of forced joinder. When Rule 19 actually applies, often it is when the parties and the so-called absent but necessary parties are joined through joint interests in either property or contracts rights.

6. In *Ass'n of Co-op. Members, Inc. v. Farmland Indus., Inc.*, 684 F.2d 1134, 1143 (5th Cir. 1982), the court examined the application of Rule 19 to a missing party. The court ultimately determined that the missing party was a necessary party under Rule 19 stating:

> The licensor of a trademark is usually treated as a necessary or indispensable party in an infringement action by its licensee. Sound reasons support this rule.
>
> The licensor of a trademark that is the subject of an infringement action by a licensee falls squarely within the language and policy of this rule. As owner of the mark, the licensor has a legally protected interest in the subject matter of the action. A judgment for the alleged infringer, whether based on a finding that the licensed mark is not a valid trademark or that the defendant's mark does not infringe it, may prejudice the licensor's rights in his own mark. A judgment for the plaintiff-licensee could result in double obligations for the defendant, should the licensor subsequently sue on his own.

Ass'n of Co-op. Members, Inc. v. Farmland Indus., Inc., 684 F.2d 1134, 1143 (5th Cir. 1982) (citations omitted).

7. *Chapter Problem:* One possible way for Paula Jones to structure her lawsuit is to go after the smaller retailer. Under the common law of Torts, even an otherwise "innocent retailer" can often be found strictly liable as a seller of a defective product despite having played no role in the design of the challenged product. Common law often recognizes, however, the right of such an innocent retailer to later sue the original manufacturer for indemnification for any liability incurred in the original lawsuit by the retailer. Given this state of the law, if Paula were to omit Kazakh from the original lawsuit, how would the court rule if the retailer filed a Rule 19 motion insisting on either the joinder of Kazakh or the dismissal of the case if, for example, Kazakh was beyond the personal jurisdiction of the court? What is the best argument for Kazakh being considered a necessary party?

Pulling It All Together Exercise

Utilize the language and underlying concerns of Rule 19 to frame your analysis in each of the following two scenarios:

1. Bob/Plaintiff enters into a contract for the sale of land from Sam (Husband) and Samantha (Wife) in a community property state. When they refuse to convey the land, what should the court's reaction be if Bob sues only Sam seeking specific performance?

2. Jackson sues Goliath Bank seeking an injunction forcing Goliath to issue certain shares of common stock to him. Goliath refuses to issue the stock because the stock certificates are in a different person's name (Eric). Jackson alleges that he and Eric jointly purchased shares of the bank's stock. Jackson had requested Eric to direct the bank to issue the shares in a manner that reflected Jackson's 50% ownership but Eric apparently did not relay this information to the bank. Thus, the bank does not believe that Jackson is entitled to any portion of the stock. The bank is concerned about its potential liability to Eric if it is forced to issue the stock certificates to Jackson as requested by this lawsuit. Should rule 19 supply a remedy to the bank's concern?

Spend 15 minutes writing your analysis to each of the two foregoing scenarios.

G. Rule 14 Impleader

Rule 14, when it applies, permits a defending party (either a defendant or a plaintiff in response to a counterclaim) to add to the complexity of a lawsuit by naming additional parties on a claim by the defending party. Unlike Rule 20's fairly broad grant of a joinder right limited only by notions of a "transaction or occurrence," rule 14 is far more limited. Consider why this might be so, taking into account our familiar themes of plaintiff autonomy, efficiency, and fairness to the litigants. You will find a delicate balancing of these three principles in the operation of Rule 14. The following Rule 14 cases provide a good glimpse of the essentials of Rule 14 practice and procedure. As you read these next two cases, you will discover that Rule 14's joinder test is significantly narrower than the test for permissive joinder we have covered under Rule 20. Ask yourself why that is.

Rule 14. Third-Party Practice

(a) When a Defending Party May Bring in a Third Party.

    (1) Timing of the Summons and Complaint.

        A defending party may, as third-party plaintiff, serve a summons and complaint on a nonparty who is or may be liable to it for all or part of the claim against it. But the third-party plaintiff must, by motion, obtain the court's leave if it files the third-party complaint more than 10 days after serving its original answer.

Price v. CTB, Inc.

168 F. Supp. 2d 1299 (M.D. Ala. 2001)

Ira DeMent, J.,

MEMORANDUM OPINION AND ORDER

Before the court is Third Party Defendant Illinois Tool Work, Inc.'s ("ITW") Motion to Dismiss. After careful consideration of the arguments of counsel, the relevant law, and the record as a whole, the court finds that ITW's Motion to Dismiss is due to be denied.

I. BACKGROUND

[Price, a chicken farmer, hired Latco, a building contractor, to build a new chicken house. Alleging that the structure was defective, Price sued CTB, which equips poultry houses, and Latco as the original defendants in the underlying action concerning the quality of the workmanship in constructing chicken houses for various Alabama farmers. The causes of action against Latco included breach of the construction contract, fraudulent misrepresentation of the caliber of materials to be used, and negligence and wantonness in the construction. Latco moved to file a Third Party Complaint against ITW on February 21, 2001, approximately six months after the case had been removed to the Middle District of Alabama.... In the Third Party Complaint, Latco alleged that ITW, a nail manufacturer, defectively designed the nails used in the construction of the chicken houses. The specific causes of action include breach of warranty, violation of the Alabama Extended Manufacturer's Liability Doctrine, and common law indemnity. ITW argued that it was improperly impleaded under Rule 14 of the Federal Rules of Civil Procedure, or, alternatively, that the Third Party Complaint was barred by the equitable doctrine of laches.]

II. DISCUSSION

RULE
14

Under Rule 14(a), a defendant may assert a claim against anyone not a party to the original action if that third party's liability is in some way dependent upon the outcome of the original action. There is a limitation on this general statement, however. Even though it may arise out of the same general set of facts as the main claim, a third party claim will not be permitted when it is based upon a separate and independent claim. Rather, the third party liability must in some way be derivative of the original claim; a third party may be impleaded only when the original defendant is trying to pass all or part of the liability onto that third party.

Principles

"The heart of impleader is the requirement that the claim supporting it be based on secondary or derivative liability. That is, the third-party plaintiff must seek reimbursement from the third-party defendant for all or part of the former's liability to plaintiff. It is not enough that the impleader claim arose out of the same transaction or occurrence as the original plaintiff's claim; the impleader must, in addition, be contingent or derivative.

"The answer [to whether impleader is proper] is not supplied by Rule 14, which merely provides the procedure by which such a duty is asserted as an impleader claim. Instead, the answer must be found in the applicable substantive law."

Note, *Developments in the Law: Multiparty Litigation in the Federal Courts*, 71 Harv. L. Rev. 874, 906 (1958).

Latco argues that ITW is the prototypical third party defendant under Rule 14. It asserts that ITW can be found liable for the warranty surrounding its products if Latco is first found liable for faulty construction. Furthermore, insists Latco, this derivative liability merely involves a shift in the overall responsibility of the allegedly defective chicken houses. ITW contends, however, that because Rule 14 is merely a procedural rule, the propriety of its application depends upon the existence of a right to indemnity under the substantive law. ITW accurately states the law in this regard, but its conclusion that there is no viable substantive claim under Alabama law is incorrect.

Conceding that Alabama does not recognize a right to contribution among joint tortfeasors, Latco directs the court's attention to the concept of implied contractual indemnity. Under this doctrine, Alabama courts recognize that a manufacturer of a product has impliedly agreed to indemnify the seller when 1) the seller is without fault, 2) the manufacturer is responsible, and 3) the seller has been required to pay a monetary judgment. Under Latco's theory, should it be found liable for its construction of the chicken houses, it can demonstrate that the true fault lies with the nail guns and the nails manufactured by ITW.

Alabama caselaw, not to mention the parties' briefs, is especially sparse with respect to the contours of the doctrine of implied indemnity. However, Illinois courts have applied the doctrine in similar cases, and the court finds no reason to believe that Alabama courts would interpret the common law principles in a different manner. Indeed, the reasoning of the Supreme Court of Illinois in an almost identical case compels the court to find that impleader is proper here. In *Maxfield*, an individual brought suit against a contractor alleging that the latter had constructed the roof of the plaintiff's home in a "poor and shoddy manner." The contractor, in turn, filed a third party complaint against the manufacturer and the seller of the roof trusses, alleging that their defective nature entitled the contractor to indemnification.

The court finds that Alabama law provides Latco a cause of action under common law indemnity against ITW.

It must be noted, however, that, under Alabama law, the doctrine permits recovery only when the party to be indemnified is "without fault." Whether, in fact, such a factual scenario will be proven at trial is irrelevant for present purposes. The only issue before the court is whether there exists a legal basis to implead ITW, not whether ITW is, in fact, liable to Latco. Since Rule 14 permits Latco to implead any party who "may be liable," Fed. R. Civ. P. 14(a), it follows that the court must permit development of the factual record so the extent of that liability may be determined.

Furthermore, since Latco has established a basis upon which it may properly implead ITW, the court need not address the applicability of Rule 14 to the other claims in Latco's Third Party Complaint. It is well established that a properly impleaded claim may serve as an anchor for separate and independent claims under Rule 18(a). In short, the court finds that Latco has properly impleaded ITW under Rule 14(a).

III. ORDER

Accordingly, it is CONSIDERED and ORDERED that ITW's Motion to Dismiss be and the same is hereby DENIED.

Tiesler v. Martin Paint Stores, Inc.
76 F.R.D. 640 (E.D. Pa. 1977)

McGLYNN, JR., JUDGE.

This is an action for personal injuries resulting from an explosion of a can of denatured alcohol which showered the minor plaintiff with burning liquid. Plaintiff seeks damages from Martin Paint Stores (Martin) for allegedly failing to comply with the rules and orders of the Consumer Product Safety Commission (CPSC) in labeling and packaging the alcohol, which failure proximately caused the minor plaintiff's injuries. In addition plaintiffs allege Martin's breach of implied warranty, negligence and liability under § 402A, Restatement of Torts [strict products liability].

Jurisdiction in this case is based on 15 U.S.C. § 2072 which confers power on the United States district courts to hear suits for damages by persons injured by reason of any knowing violations of the rules or orders of the CPSC. The additional claims against Martin are properly before the court by the doctrine of pendent jurisdiction. The parties to the litigation are residents of Pennsylvania and the accident took place there. Plaintiffs' original complaint alleged that minor Joseph Keller was also responsible for the accident but the complaint was amended and Keller dropped as a defendant when this court granted a motion to dismiss him, since a plaintiff may not bring in as a party someone over whom the court does not have independent jurisdiction. Subsequently the defendant Martin, pursuant to Rule 14, impleaded Joseph Keller as a third-party defendant claiming that his negligent use of the product was the proximate cause of the plaintiff's injuries.

Presently before the court is a motion to dismiss the third-party complaint because it is not related to the allegations against the original defendants and is based on ordinary negligence principles. For the reasons set forth below, the court finds that the third-party defendant, Joseph Keller, was properly joined as a party to this action and thus the motion to dismiss the third-party complaint is denied.

Whether Joseph Keller may be impleaded is controlled by the language of Rule 14(a) which provides that a defendant may implead a person not a party to the action "who is or may be liable to him for all or part of the plaintiff's claim against him." The use of the word "claim" in Rule 14(a) avoids the narrow concepts of "cause of action" and instead employs the idea of the claim as a group of operative facts giving occasion for judicial action. The purpose of rule 14 is to effectively dispose of the entire related litigation in the suit which is properly before the court and, for jurisdictional purposes, such a claim is ancillary to the main action so the inclusion of a third-party claim is justified though it does not of itself meet the diversity test or raise a federal question.

In seeking to have the third-party complaint dismissed, the movant relies on the rule that an entirely separate and independent claim cannot be maintained against a third party under Rule 14, even though it does arise out of the same general set of facts as the main claim. Impleader is proper and the claim not separate or independent if the third party's liability is in some way derivative of the outcome of the main claim in that the defendant seeks to hold the third party secondarily liable to him or to pass on to the third party all or part of the liability asserted against the defendant. It is immaterial that the liability of the third party is not identical to or rests on a different theory than that underlying plaintiff's claim.

Thus, it is not permissible to bring in a person as a third-party defendant simply because he is or may be liable to the plaintiff. Third party practice is permitted only where the defendant can show that if he is found liable to plaintiff, the third party will be liable to him. However, the Rule is not limited to situations in which the third-party defendant would automatically be liable for all or part of plaintiff's claim. Rather, the complaint should be allowed to stand, even if recovery is not certain, if under some construction of facts which might be adduced at trial, recovery would be possible.

The Rule creates no substantive rights and does not enlarge, abridge or modify the substantive rights of any litigant. But the impleader rule does require that the defendant have a substantive basis for his claim against the third party. The defendant in the present case claims that the third party is a joint tortfeasor and is jointly or severally liable in tort for the same accident and injury to the plaintiff. The right of contribution among joint tortfeasors is one of substantive law and since the parties to the action are residents of Pennsylvania and the accident occurred here, it is Pennsylvania law which governs. The Pennsylvania Statute provides for contribution among joint tortfeasors and it may well be that as the facts are developed, the case in so far as it involves general tort and negligence principles, would be one for contribution under the statute. Martin may substantively claim that if it is found to have been negligent, the third-party defendant, Joseph Keller, is or may be found to be liable to him. Therefore, the motion to dismiss the third party complaint is denied.

Notes and Problems

1. The *Price* and *Tiesler* courts recognized the limitation on joinder under Rule 14. Not only must the defendant have a claim against the party the defendant desires to bring

in under Rule 14, but the claim it holds must owe its very "life" to the outcome of the claim filed against the defendant. How does the breadth of the Rule 14 joinder rule compare to Rule 20—which rather than links joinder to a derivative nature of the claim, merely provides that it arise out of the same transaction or occurrence? How is this difference in their scope explained by reference to principles of efficiency, fairness, and autonomy? Consider who is seeking the joinder of the third-party defendant under Rule 14 versus who is seeking to join the additional party in a Rule 20 scenario.

2. One court has described the noble purpose of Rule 14 as "to avoid circuity of action and to dispose of the entire subject matter arising from one set of facts in one action." *LASA Per L'Industria Del Marmo Societa Per Azioni v. Alexander*, 414 F.2d 143, 146 (6th Cir. 1969). Given that salutary objective, why not take the issue of joinder out of the hands of the litigants and instead consider the third-party defendant a "necessary" party under Rule 19?

3. Do you see why, although Rule 14 governs the propriety of impleader practice, ultimately the question of whether Rule 14 is being involved correctly turns on state substantive law? What was the nature of the dispute in the *Price* and the *Tiesler* cases as to whether joinder was permitted? Why did each court reject the objections to joinder of the third-party defendants?

4. Notice the way Rule 18 complements Rule 14 (near the end of the *Price* opinion), permitting a defendant/third-party plaintiff to assert any *additional* claims—whether related at all or not—against the third-party defendant once the anchor derivative claim is asserted. *See* Rule 18(a); *Schwab v. Erie Lackawanna R.R.*, 438 F.2d 62 (3d Cir. 1971). Once a party is properly impleaded (given the limited scope of the Rule 14 right) does it make sense to permit additional unrelated claims to be added against that party? What principle is thus served?

5. *Problem:* A landowner sues the 16-year-old teenager, Dennis, who lives next door alleging that Dennis was responsible for throwing a brick through the landowner's front window one night. Dennis denies that he had anything to do with the broken window. He seeks to implead another who he claims is the real culprit. Would Rule 14 impleader be appropriate here? Consider the following observation in analyzing your response: "[W]hen a third party's conduct furnishes a complete defense against the defendant's liability [to the original plaintiff], the defendant may raise that conduct defensively in the answer but may not use it as a foundation for impleader." Jack H. Friedenthal, Mary K. Kane & Arthur R. Miller, *Civil Procedure* § 6.9, at 382 (4th ed. 2005).

6. *Chapter Problem:* If Paula filed suit solely against the auto retailer from whom she purchased the vehicle, would that party be entitled to join the manufacturer under Rule 14? Further, if Paula sued both the retailer and the manufacturer in one suit on strict liability claims, could they properly implead the other driver who swerved in front of her? Consider whether that makes a more logical litigation unit for trial.

Pulling It All Together Exercise

Sherman is suing Barron on a breach of warranty/contract theory after the in-ground swimming pool that Barron built in Sherman's back yard began leaking soon after construction was completed on it. Sherman has alleged that the problems arose from either faulty workmanship by Barron or due to Barron's use of inferior gunite concrete on the walls of the pool. Sherman is seeking either the cost to repair the pool or the cost to replace the entire pool. Barron has filed an answer denying any wrongdoing on its part or the use of any inferior materials. Barron then filed a motion under Rule 14 to implead RockHard, Inc., its supplier of gunite concrete. Barron claims that it overpaid for a shipment of gunite, including gunite used in the building of Sherman's pool, and seeking reimbursement.

Take 10 minutes to write a short response on behalf of the plaintiff, Sherman, opposing the requested joinder.

Spend 10 minutes writing out your analysis of the propriety of the Rule 14 impleader here.

H. Rule 24 Intervention

It seems odd to say that someone would ever want to volunteer herself as a defendant in a lawsuit; however, this is often the gist of an intervenor's motion to join an existing lawsuit. Rule 24 may be used to intervene as either a plaintiff or defendant; however, both cases below will illustrate the request of a party to intervene as a defendant within an existing suit. When a potential party has: 1) a recognized interest; 2) that would be impaired without their presence in the suit; and 3) the current parties do not adequately represent the interest the party seeks to present to the court, they *must* be permitted to "intervene" within the suit. Though a party does not meet the requirements of Rule 24(a), the court *may* still allow the intervention under Rule 24(b) when the party meets the requirements of permissive intervention.

Planned Parenthood v. CCA

558 F.2d 861 (8th Cir. 1977)

GIBSON, Chief Judge.

The plaintiff, Planned Parenthood of Minnesota, Inc. (Planned Parenthood), has operated a comprehensive family planning clinic in St. Paul, Minnesota, since 1932. In January 1976, it decided to offer first trimester abortion services to its patients in conjunction with its other activities. To accommodate its expanded activities Planned Parenthood in March of 1976 finalized its plan to purchase a building at 1965 Ford Parkway in St. Paul to house its administrative offices, training facilities, research center and a medical clinic for furnishing family planning services including first trimester abortions. The prospective establishment of the abortion clinic met a hostile reception from a number of the residents of the area involved. In response to public protests, the St. Paul City Council temporarily frustrated the construction and operation of the abortion clinic by enacting an ordinance which imposed a six-month moratorium on the construction of "separate abortion facilities and other like facilities within the City of St. Paul" pending a study to determine whether special zoning restrictions should be imposed on such facilities. Planned Parenthood filed the present action challenging the constitutionality of the ordinance and seeking injunctive and monetary relief. The District Court, perceiving serious questions as to the constitutionality of the City Council's action, issued a preliminary injunction against the enforcement of the ordinance. On this appeal, we review the propriety of his disposition of certain pretrial motions.

Planned Parenthood instituted the present action against the City of St. Paul, all City Council members and the Mayor, City Attorney, City Architect and Supervisor of Inspectors of St. Paul. Planned Parenthood sought a declaratory judgment that the moratorium ordinance was unconstitutional and an injunction against its enforcement. The complaint also requested $25,000 compensatory damages, $20,000 punitive damages and attorney's fees from the Mayor of St. Paul and the five council members voting in favor of the ordinance.

Soon after the complaint was filed, a motion to intervene was filed by the Citizens for Community Action, a neighborhood association expressing an interest in preserving property values and assuring that abortion facilities do not adversely affect the health, welfare and safety of citizens in St. Paul. Joining in the motion to intervene were two couples residing in the vicinity of the proposed clinic.

In a pretrial memorandum opinion, the District Court ruled on the motion to intervene and the request for a preliminary injunction. The court overruled the motion to intervene, concluding that the applicants for intervention had failed to establish their right to intervene under Fed. R. Civ. P. 24(a)(2). The applicants were also denied permissive intervention under Fed. R. Civ. P. 24(b). In regard to the request for a preliminary injunction, ... the preliminary injunction was issued.

An application for intervention was filed by the Citizens for Community Action, a neighborhood association comprised of St. Paul citizens, taxpayers and homeowners. The professed purpose of the association is to preserve property values and insure that abortion facilities do not affect the health, welfare and safety of citizens. The application for intervention was joined by two couples, Donald and Mary Ann Lennon and Norman and Kathleen Vernig, who own property in the vicinity of the proposed Ford Parkway abortion facility. The Lennons and Vernigs wish to intervene to assure that their property values are not adversely affected by the creation of an abortion clinic in their neighborhood. The District Court refused to allow the applicants to intervene as of right under Fed. R. Civ. P. 24(a)(2) or to intervene permissibly under Fed. R. Civ. P. 24(b).

Upon filing a timely application for intervention as of right under Rule 24(a)(2),[1] the applicant is entitled to intervene if he satisfies the following tripartite test:

1) That he has [a] recognized interest in the subject matter of the primary litigation,

2) That his interest might be impaired by the disposition of the suit, and

3) That his interest is not adequately protected by the existing parties.

Edmondson v. Nebraska, 383 F.2d 123, 126 (8th Cir. 1967).

In regard to the first requirement, the interest identified must be more than peripheral or insubstantial; the applicant must assert a "significantly protectable interest." *Donaldson v. United States*, 400 U.S. 517, 531, 27 L. Ed. 2d 580, 91 S. Ct. 534 (1971). Here, the St. Paul City Council has enacted an ordinance imposing a moratorium on the construction of abortion clinics pending a study to determine whether all abortion clinics should be subjected to special zoning requirements. The applicants for intervention are vigorously defending this ordinance, arguing that such a measure is necessary to preserve their property values.[2] "Interests in property are the most elementary type of right that Rule 24(a) is designed to protect." *Diaz v. Southern Drilling Corp.*, 427 F.2d 1118, 1124 (5th Cir. 1970). This litigation, which will establish the validity or invalidity of the ordinance, necessarily bears directly on the property interests the applicants seek to preserve. We conclude that the applicants have a significantly protectable interest in the subject matter of this litigation.

As required by Rule 24(a)(2), the applicants' ability to protect their interest may be impaired or impeded by the disposition of this case. If defendants remain enjoined from enforcing the ordinance, Planned Parenthood can lawfully establish an abortion facility at the Ford Parkway site. A judicial declaration that municipalities can not impose moratoriums on the construction of abortion clinics or, in a broader context, can not subject first trimester abortion clinics to special zoning requirements would have an inhibitive effect on the assertion of applicants' claims. In order to prevent what they view as an incipient erosion of their property values, the applicants must participate in this litigation, and be given the opportunity to present their views to the court in their endeavor to uphold the ordinance as a legitimate and constitutional exercise of municipal power. *See Atlantis Development Corp. v. United States*, 379 F.2d 818, 828–29 (5th Cir. 1967).

Finally, in order to intervene under Rule 24(a)(2), the applicants must carry the "minimal" burden of showing that their interests are not adequately protected by the existing parties. *Trbovich v. United Mine Workers*, 404 U.S. 528, 538 n.10, 30 L. Ed. 2d 686, 92 S. Ct. 630 (1972); *see Edmondson v. Nebraska, supra* at 127. The District Court concluded that the applicants are adequately represented by defendants, with whom they seek to align themselves. We disagree.

Concededly, both the applicants and defendants are interested in upholding the constitutionality of the ordinance. However, their respective interests, while not adverse, are disparate. Defendants are accused of invidiously discriminating against Planned Parenthood in particular and abortion clinics in general. Allegations of bad faith have been directed

---

1. The application for intervention in this case was filed on July 12, 1976, twelve days after the filing of the complaint. Defendants concede that the motion was timely filed and we agree.

2. The applicants' contention that the creation of an abortion clinic will lower their property values is not unsubstantiated. The record contains the testimony of a real estate expert who stated that an abortion clinic would lower residential and commercial property values in the immediate area.

against the defendants. Many of the defendants are seeking to avoid personal liability for allegedly infringing upon Planned Parenthood's constitutional rights. At trial, defendants will argue that the adoption of the ordinance was neither arbitrary nor discriminatory. They will seek to prove that the ordinance is consistent with the City's developing comprehensive zoning plan and existing principles of land use regulation.

The applicants, however, are concerned only with their own property values; they are exposed to no risk of personal liability and are defending no charges of discrimination or bad faith. As stated in *Joseph Skillken and Co. v. City of Toledo*, 528 F.2d 867, 876 (6th Cir. 1975), *vacated on other grounds*, 429 U.S. 1068, 97 S. Ct. 800, 50 L. Ed. 2d 786 (1977):

> The municipal defendants had enough to do to defend themselves against the charges leveled against them by the plaintiffs. They do not have the same interest in protecting the values of the homeowners' properties as do the homeowners themselves.

In the present case, the City Council is divided on the issue of whether the moratorium ordinance is proper or advisable. The ordinance was passed by a 5 to 2 vote; thus, a switch of two votes could completely change the attitude of the City Council and the municipality in regard to the issues presented in this litigation. The protection of the interests of the individual property owners rests primarily in the hands of a few individual council members, most of whom are threatened with personal liability for their discrete actions in voting favorably on the challenged ordinance. The record shows that the defendants have presented little evidence to show how the operation of an abortion clinic would affect applicants' important property interests.

We, therefore, conclude that the applicants to intervene have presented sufficient evidence to show that defendants are not adequate representatives of the applicants' interests.

Based on the foregoing discussion, the District Court erred in refusing to allow the applicants to intervene under Rule 24(a)(2).

Atlantic Refinishing & Restor., Inc. v. Travelers

272 F.R.D. 26 (D. D.C. 2010)

Urbina, J.

I. INTRODUCTION

This matter is before the court on the motion of Desbuild, Inc. ("the petitioner"), to intervene as a defendant. The petitioner was selected as the general contractor for the government-funded restoration of a historical building in Washington, D.C. The plaintiff, one of the petitioner's subcontractors on this project, claims that it did not receive full compensation under its contract and is suing the petitioner's surety, Travelers Casualty and Surety Company of America ("Travelers"). Because the petitioner has shown it has a right to intervene under Federal Rule of Civil Procedure 24, the court grants the petitioner's motion.

II. FACTUAL & PROCEDURAL BACKGROUND

The petitioner entered into a contract with the General Services Administration ("GSA") to act as the prime contractor for the exterior masonry repair, repainting and cleaning of the historic Sydney Yates Building in Washington, D.C. The petitioner and the plaintiff subsequently entered into a subcontract whereby the plaintiff, in exchange for payment, would provide certain materials and services for the project. The petitioner asserts that the subcontract also included a mandatory arbitration clause.

On September 18, 2009, and again on September 29, 2009, the GSA terminated the petitioner's contract for cause. While working as a subcontractor, the plaintiff sent the petitioner invoices totaling $197,344.25. The plaintiff alleges that to date, $97,281.25 remains unpaid.

As the prime contractor, the petitioner was required to issue a bond for the benefit of its subcontractors and suppliers ("payment bond"). The bond named the petitioner as the principal and the defendant as the surety. According to the petitioner, the defendant and the petitioner entered into a surety agreement whereby the defendant could seek indemnification from the petitioner for a judgment entered against it due to the petitioner's actions.

The plaintiff commenced this action on April 30, 2010, naming Travelers as the sole defendant. The plaintiff claims that that the petitioner refuses to remit the remainder of the payment which it is entitled to and is therefore demanding payment from the defendant, who the plaintiff maintains, is liable to the plaintiff for such costs. On July 19, 2010, the petitioner filed the present motion to intervene as a defendant. *See generally* Petr's Mot. With this motion now ripe for adjudication, the court turns to the applicable legal standard and the parties' arguments.

III. ANALYSIS
A. Legal Standard for a Motion to Intervene

Federal Rule of Civil Procedure 24 sets forth the requirements for intervention as of right and permissive intervention. Fed. R. Civ. P. 24; *Fund for Animals, Inc. v. Norton,* 322 F.3d 728, 731 (D.C.Cir.2003). First, Rule 24(a) provides for intervention as of right, stating that:

[u]pon timely application anyone shall be permitted to intervene in an action …
when a statute of the United States confers an unconditional right to intervene;
or … when the applicant claims an interest relating to the property or transaction
which is the subject of the action and the applicant is so situated that the disposition
of the action may as a practical matter impair or impede the applicant's ability
to protect that interest, unless the applicant's interest is adequately represented
by existing parties.

Rule

Id. As paraphrased by this Circuit, the rule indicates that an applicant's right to intervene
depends on "(1) the timeliness of the motion; (2) whether the applicant claims an interest
relating to the property or transaction which is the subject of the action; (3) whether the
applicant is so situated that the disposition of the action may as a practical matter impair
or impede the applicant's ability to protect that interest; and (4) whether the applicant's
interest is adequately represented by existing parties." In addition, an applicant must
demonstrate that it has standing. *Jones,* 348 F.3d at 1017–18; *Fund for Animals,* 322 F.3d at
731–32.

B. The Court Grants the Petitioner's Motion to Intervene

The petitioner asserts that it should be permitted to intervene as a matter of right.
More specifically, the petitioner contends that as the principal of the payment bond, its
interests are directly implicated by this action because the defendant will seek
indemnification from it if judgment is awarded for the plaintiff. The petitioner further
asserts that without being permitted to intervene, "its ability to directly protect its financial
interests and avoid the possibility of judgment against it will be materially impaired or
impeded." Lastly, the petitioner argues that its interests are not adequately represented
by the defendant because the petitioner "seeks to enforce the binding arbitration provision
in the [s]ubcontract," a defense which the defendant has not exerted.

The plaintiff responds that the petitioner lacks the requisite interest to intervene in
this matter, and that any interest the petitioner has will be adequately protected by the
defendant. The plaintiff argues that the petitioner has no interest in the current litigation
because its purported interest is contingent on both the court entering judgment in favor
of the plaintiff and the defendant enforcing its indemnity agreement against the petitioner.
The plaintiff further maintains that the petitioner's interests are adequately protected by
the defendant because it is common practice for a bond principal to "end[] up in control
of the defense of the surety," and because the parties have the same counsel.

Under Rule 24, the petitioner is entitled to intervene if it can demonstrate that it has
satisfied all of the requirements: timeliness, interest, impairment of interest, and adequacy
of representation. First, it is undisputed that the petitioner's motion, which was filed
before the scheduling of an initial status hearing in this matter, is timely. Additionally,
the petitioner, as the principal of the payment bond, has a clear interest in this litigation
because if a judgment is granted against the defendant, the defendant is likely to seek indemnification from the petitioner, pursuant to their surety agreement.[3] *United States ex
rel. MPA Constr., Inc. v. XL Specialty Ins. Co.,* 349 F.Supp.2d 934, 937 (D.Md.2004) (holding
that a petitioner seeking to intervene in a suit between its subcontractor and surety "clearly

---

3. The plaintiff relies solely on *Indep. Petrochemical Corp. v. Aetna Cas. & Sur. Co.,* 105 F.R.D. 106
(D.D.C.1985) to argue that the petitioner's contingent liability here does not create the sort of interest
required for intervention as a matter of right. In stark contrast to the *Indep. Petrochemical Corp.* case,
the petitioner's interest is not triggered by a judgment in a wholly different case, but is instead directly
and currently implicated in this case. Stated otherwise, the petitioner is interested *right now* in avoiding
a determination in this proceeding of its liability to the plaintiff for the amount in question.

has a 'direct and substantial interest' in the transaction because [the surety], if held liable, will turn to [the petitioner] for indemnification").

Next, the court considers whether allowing this action to proceed without the petitioner would impair its ability to protect its interest. "In determining whether a movant's interests will be impaired by an action, the courts in this circuit look to the 'practical consequences' to movant of denying intervention." *Schoenborn v. Wash. Metro. Area Transit Auth.*, 247 F.R.D. 5, 7 (D.D.C.2007) (quoting *Am. Horse Prot. Ass'n, Inc. v. Veneman*, 200 F.R.D. 153, 158 (D.D.C.2001)). Here, if the petitioner was not allowed to intervene, it could nonetheless be forced to indemnify the defendant for the debt claimed by the plaintiff without an opportunity to legally dispute its liability. Thus, the practical consequence of denying intervention would be to deprive the petitioner of an opportunity to raise arguments and defenses before the adjudication of its own liability to the plaintiff. It is also insufficient that the petitioner may have additional recourse in the future if it were to defend against an indemnification claim by the defendant. *See id.* (observing that intervention was not improper solely because the petitioner had the opportunity to later challenge the award in a suit for breach of fiduciary duty). Accordingly, the petitioner's ability to protect its interest would be impeded without intervention.

Lastly, the petitioner must demonstrate the inadequacy of the defendant's representation in order to intervene as of right. Prior to Rule 24's inadequacy of representation requirement, it was clear that "a contractor which [had] agreed to indemnify its surety on a bond [could] intervene as a party defendant as of right in suit on that bond against the surety." *XL Specialty Ins. Co.*, 349 F.Supp.2d at 937 (noting that the Second and Fifth Circuits had created a per se right of intervention for a principal of a bond (citing *United States ex rel. Foster Wheeler Corp. v. American Sur. Co.*, 142 F.2d 726, 728 (2d Cir.1944); *Revere Copper & Brass, Inc. v. Aetna Cas. & Sur. Co.*, 426 F.2d 709, 716 (5th Cir.1970))). Under Rule 24, however, courts now presume that the principal is adequately represented by its surety because they both have the "same ultimate objective," *i.e.*, to avoid liability on the payment bond. *See* 6 Fed. Prac. 3 § 24.03 (noting that a presumption of adequate representative exists if both the movant and the existing party have the same ultimate objective); *XL Specialty Ins. Co.*, 349 F.Supp.2d at 937 (observing that a per se right for principals "appears to conflict with Rule 24(a)(2)" because the surety is required to provide a good faith defense for the principal). The petitioner may, however, rebut the presumption of adequacy by showing the existence of "special circumstances" that make the representation inadequate. *Id.; Schoenborn*, 247 F.R.D. at 9. For instance, the petitioner may rebut the presumption by demonstrating that he intends to raise claims or arguments that would not otherwise be raised. *See Jones*, 348 F.3d at 1019–20 (noting that "an existing party who is ... unwilling to raise claims or arguments that would benefit the putative intervenor may qualify as an inadequate representative in some cases").

The court is persuaded that special circumstances exist here due to the petitioner's intention to enforce the subcontract's arbitration clause.[4] The petitioner has been candid about its intention, if allowed to intervene, to move this court to require the plaintiff to arbitrate this suit as purportedly required by their subcontract. Petr's Mot., Ex. 1. Notably, the defendant has not advanced this defense, despite putting forth thirteen

---

4. [The plaintiff argued that because the petitioner and defendant share counsel, the petitioner is then already adequately represented by the defendant's current counsel. However, the court stated that because counsel would not be required to represent the petitioner's interest if the petitioner was not a party to the suit, this is not determinative, and since the petitioner has defenses that were not established by the current defendant, it is reasonable to find a lack of adequate representation.]

other affirmative defenses in its answer. *See generally* Answer. The petitioner should not be forced to rely on the defendant to raise defenses in a case where its own liability is at stake. Because the petitioner has demonstrated that special circumstances exist which make the defendant's representation of the petitioner's interests inadequate, the court grants its motion to intervene.

IV. CONCLUSION

For the foregoing reasons, the court grants petitioner's motion to intervene. An Order consistent with this Memorandum Opinion is separately and contemporaneously issued this 21st day of December, 2010.

Notes and Problems

1. How do Rules 19 and 24 compare? Notice some very similar overlapping language in the two rules. Does this mean that they should be interpreted the same? Consider the consequences in each setting of a decision by the court that the language of the rule applies. With that in mind, should one rule be interpreted more broadly than the other? Or, asked another way, in each of the two cases above, should the proposed intervenor have been considered appropriately a Rule 19 necessary party? Would either court have been likely to dismiss the litigation in the absence of the missing party?

2. The City Council in *Planned Parenthood* was likely interested in litigating the zoning restrictions and not protecting property values, thus, allowing for the intervention of Citizens for Community Action. On the merits of the debate, various courts have reached different conclusions. As one author has framed this debate:

> In abortion clinic zoning cases thus far, none have proved a causal relationship between the operation of an abortion clinic and an undesirable community effect. The prohibition then would lack a rational basis and may be a violation of substantive due process or equal protection. Local governments have tried to use zoning, nevertheless, as a tool to effectuate sentiment against abortion. Courts faced with these cases are reluctant to allow community values against a fundamental right to influence land use. Since the abortion decision is protected by the right of privacy, the right should be beyond the reach of the police power without a compelling governmental interest.

Undesirable Uses, 23 Urb. L. Ann. 467, 478 (1982).

3. If the intervenor in *Planned Parenthood* were simply a pro-life group that wanted to intervene in order to argue on behalf of the zoning restrictions, would intervention make sense? What would be the problem with allowing such groups to intervene in such suits? Consider *Keith v. Daley*, 764 F.2d 1265 (7th Cir. 1985), in which the court rejected intervention by the Illinois Pro-Life Coalition (IPC) as follows:

> In an America whose freedom is secured by its ever vigilant guard on the openness of its "marketplace of ideas," IPC is encouraged to thrive, and to speak, lobby, promote, and persuade, so that its principles may become, if it is the will of the majority, the law of the land. Such a priceless right to free expression, however, does not also suggest that IPC has a right to intervene in every lawsuit involving abortion rights, or to forever defend statutes it helped to enact. Rule 24(a) precludes a conception of lawsuits, even "public law" suits, as necessary forums for such public policy debates.

Is *Keith v. Daley* sufficiently distinguishable from *Planned Parenthood* to explain the different results?

4. The plaintiff in *Atlantic Refinishing & Restoration, Inc.* claimed that the petitioner (party seeking intervention) did not meet the requirements of intervention as of right because the petitioner was being represented by the same counsel as the current defendant. How did the court analyze this situation? How much weight should be given to the use of the same counsel under adequate representation?

5. In *Atlantic*, the court found the petitioner's interest would be impaired because if the court found in favor of the plaintiff the petitioner would be required to indemnify the defendant. Why would the petitioner's interest not have a chance to be litigated?

6. If a party does not meet the requirements of intervention as of right, why should they be able to intervene in a suit permissively? It would seem this trumps the original parties' autonomy by allowing this permissive intervention. *See, e.g., Zimmerman v. Bell*, 101 F.R.D. 329, 330 (D. Md. 1984) (allowing the limited permissive intervention of a party that did not meet the inadequate representation element of intervention as of right because the claims asserted by the party were identical to those before the court).

7. How do you think efficiency of the court factors into a court's consideration of a Rule 24 petition to intervene? *See Venegas v. Skaggs*, 867 F.2d 527, 531 (9th Cir. 1989) *aff'd sub nom. Venegas v. Mitchell*, 495 U.S. 82, 110 S. Ct. 1679, 109 L. Ed. 2d 74 (1990) (holding "judicial economy is a relevant consideration in deciding a motion for permissive intervention.").

8. *Problem.* If another organization seeks intervention, after the court permits the intervention of Citizens for Community Action, in order to protect property values in the city, would this intervention request also have to be granted?

9. *Chapter Problem.* As counsel for Paula, you might identify another case already filed by a different accident victim against Kazakh making the same allegation of defective brakes that you intend to make. Imagine that case is getting close to trial. As you are earning a contingency fee, the prospect of a quick trial is enticing. If you file a motion to intervene in that other lawsuit on behalf of Paula, should the court grant the motion? Can it grant the motion? Consider all of the language of Rule 24 and its principles in formulating your responses.

Pulling It All Together Exercise

A group of plaintiffs in Arkansas during the height of the civil rights era brings a suit against a group of adjacent public school districts seeking consolidation because the schools are not desegregated yet. A teachers' organization representing teachers that are employed by the school districts seeks to intervene. It is concerned that the terms in the contracts of the teachers regarding salary, hours, and term and conditions of employment will not be honored by a newly consolidated school district. Can it intervene? Would your answer change if the individual teachers were trying to intervene instead of the teachers' organization?

Spend 15 minutes writing out your analysis of this problem.

Upon Further Review

The various joinder rules we have covered accomplish different purposes though each involves some balancing of the concepts of fairness, autonomy, and efficiency. There are rules of *voluntary* joinder—Rule 18 that permits a plaintiff to bring multiple claims in one proceeding; Rule 20 that permits a plaintiff to either join to their suit other co-plaintiffs and/or to sue multiple defendants in the same proceeding; Rule 14 that permits a defending party to join non-parties in an attempt to shift some or all of their potential litigation loss to another by way of a claim for contribution or indemnity; and Rule 24 that permits a non-party to knock on the courthouse door asking for a seat at the litigation table. Rule 20 never compels a plaintiff to join additional co-parties or opposing parties and also applies limits (due to concerns over unfairness or inefficiencies) to joinder of parties on unrelated claims. Rule 14 never requires a defending party to seek their claim for contribution or indemnification in the same proceeding as the main claim but, because such efforts to shift a litigation loss are so inextricably tied to the primary claims, Rule 14 permits the expansion of the litigation party beyond the plaintiff's original guest list. Rule 24 puts significant limits on a non-party's ability to crash another's lawsuit—to have a right to intervene one must show more than just a related litigation interest, one must show that their own significant interests are in jeopardy as a practical matter. This promotes the limited autonomy of the original plaintiff to decide the general contours of their lawsuit. By contrast, the primary involuntary joinder provision embodied by Rule 19 sometimes compels a plaintiff to add an additional co-plaintiff or defendant to the lawsuit. Such a "necessary" non-party is often one who could have easily sought intervention in the lawsuit herself under Rule 24 had they been so inclined. But even if the non-party fails to seek intervention and the plaintiff is opposed, a court may compel a plaintiff to join a non-party out of concerns for fairness to that non-party who may be negatively impacted in their absence. Viewed in such a manner, each of these fundamental joinder rules reflects a careful balancing of the interests of litigant autonomy, fairness and efficiency.

Chapter Problem Revisited

Now that we have examined both doctrines and rules of civil procedure that govern the analysis of both claim and party joinder, reconsider the possible lawsuit that Paula has against the retailer and manufacturer of the Camel automobile. As counsel for Paula, advise your senior partner at the firm on how to best structure the lawsuit, including consideration of the breadth of the lawsuit, which parties you should join (and the feasibility of such joinder), whether you can link Paula's claim with the claims of other accident victims, the possibility of relying upon (or being precluded by) the verdicts in other litigation over the same Camel, whether any necessary parties must be joined, and consideration for whether the possible claims of the retailer and manufacturer against your client belong in the same case.

Spend 30 minutes writing out your recommendation to the senior partner on these matters.

Going Deeper

Additional recommended readings to enhance your understanding of some of the topics in this Chapter include:

- Jack Ratliff, *Offensive Collateral Estoppel and the Option Effect*, 67 Tex. L. Rev. 63 (1988) (discussing implications of the Supreme Court decision in

Parklane Hosiery regarding the fairness of non-mutual offensive collateral estoppel).

- Roger H. Trangsrud, *Joinder Alternatives in Mass Tort Litigation*, 70 Cornell L. Rev. 779 (1985) (provides good overview of various procedural alternatives available to balance efficiency versus fairness in the context of multiple claimants with similar cases against a common defendant).

Chapter 3

Forum Battles

Chapter Goals

- Appreciate the importance of choosing forum.

- Know the basic rules of priority that federal and state courts use when there is duplicative litigation in two courts simultaneously.

- Understand the exceptions to these default rules of priority.

- Appreciate the different federalism concerns when the dueling courts are at both the state and federal levels.

- Know the options available as a defendant to get a court to dismiss or transfer due to convenience.

- Become familiar with unique federal option of consolidating many cases together in one place under the MDL statute.

- With respect to the *vertical* forum battle, master the analytical models used by federal courts to decipher when *fraudulent joinder* has occurred, as a means to remove a case to federal court.

A. Overview

Lawyers believe that their forum choice for their dispute makes a difference. As one seasoned trial lawyer and legal scholar opined in legislative testimony, "[e]very trial lawyer ... would agree that [where] the case is to be tried, is without question one of the most significant factors, perhaps the most significant factor, in the outcome of the case."[1] As the cases in this Chapter illustrate, lawyers will engage in sometimes dramatic procedural battles, each trying to gain some leverage through perceived advantage in the identity of the court or judge who will decide their case.

---

1. William D. Underwood, *Reconsidering Derivative-Venue in Cases Involving Multiple Parties and Multiple Claims*, 56 Baylor L. Rev. 579, 581 n.1 (2004) (quoting Professor Louis Muldrow in testimony before the Texas Legislature in the context of possible venue reform legislation). *See also* Note, *Forum Shopping Reconsidered*, 103 Harv. L. Rev. 1677, 1686 (1990) (remarking on the reality that our legal system produces decisions that are premised largely upon the politics of the forum court rather than upon logic alone).

That lawyers believe the forum can make a difference should not be surprising. After all, what teenager has not considered the same strategy when deciding whether to take their request for a curfew extension to mom or dad?

These forum battles can manifest in the form of literal litigant races to the courthouse of their choice, trying to file before the other side does so in a different locale. When this happens, courts have to decide between (a) allowing both of the redundant cases to proceed toward judgment—with the first to final judgment presumably rendering the latter case moot—with all of the inefficiencies involved in dueling litigation over the same subjects, or (b) one case being stayed or put on hold through some injunction entered by the other court. In the first section we will explore this scenario and find what general *rule of priority* courts frequently employ, and the exceptions to those general rules.

We will then move to the use of *motions to transfer venue* under 28 U.S.C. § 1404 or for dismissal under the common law doctrine of *forum non conveniens* in situations where the original case is filed in a most inconvenient forum. Courts have to engage in careful balancing in such instances between honoring the traditional autonomy of the plaintiff's chosen forum and the efficiency (and possible fairness) of mandating that the case proceed in another forum that makes more sense. How to balance these dual desires will be an important point of observation.

Another modern tool available in federal courts (and some states) in scenarios where multiple related (though not necessarily redundant) cases are pending permits pretrial consolidation of cases for efficient handling of discovery and pretrial motion practice. The federal tool is embodied by the Multidistrict Litigation Act, 28 U.S.C. § 1407. We will explore this statutory remedy and discover the incredibly broad power under this statute for federal courts to transfer literally thousands of cases to a particular court for pretrial consolidation (using Rule 42(a) upon receipt of the cases).

One thought that might occur in situations involving dueling litigation between federal and state forums is, "why doesn't a federal court simply enjoin any unnecessary state court cases involving the same subject?" The answer is the federal *Anti-Injunction Act*, 28 U.S.C. § 2283, that generally bars a federal court from enjoining a state court proceeding. There are, however, some important exceptions to this statutory prohibition which we will identify and attempt to understand.

Finally, this Chapter will unearth another scenario involved in forum battles—the jurisdictional poison-pill practice of some plaintiffs to construct a lawsuit to make it suitable only for state courts by naming non-diverse defendants on questionable state-law claims solely to defeat federal court diversity removal by defendants. This practice raises the court-created doctrine of *fraudulent joinder* which, when applicable, permits the federal court to exercise subject matter jurisdiction by disregarding the presence in the suit of the diversity-destroying party. Different federal circuits have employed different analytical frameworks for this doctrine and we will briefly explore those.

As you read these cases, ask yourself how important these forum battles are to the lawyers and litigants. But first, again to offer context for these lessons, review the scenario outlined in the Chapter Problem that follows on the next few pages.

B. Chapter 3 Problem

Messages

To: Jim Underwood
Date: April 1
Time: 9:30 a.m.

From: Mr. Charles Client
Of: Petroleum Energy Res.

Phoned:
Needs Appt.:
Please call:
URGENT:

Message: Very upset to receive service summons and complaint today from the people we were supposed to be suing! Thinks we've been "out-lawyered"! Wondering if needs to hire new counsel for case. Fix this problem!

Plainview Daily Herald

"We shoot straight!"

April 1

Daily Business Briefs
Local energy group faces suit by oil & gas services firm

Plainview — West Texas oil field producer Petroleum Energy Resources, Inc. (PERI) was named a defendant in federal court in Dallas in a lawsuit filed yesterday by oil-servicing company Bresser Industries, Inc. Bresser alleges that it provided oil field stimulation services to PERI over a number of years, faithfully abiding by the terms of its contracts with PERI. Bresser further alleges that, because PERI's wells were not producing as well as originally forecast by PERI's petroleum geologists that PERI made "unfounded allegations of shorting in Bresser's performance of frack jobs on hundreds of wells in west Texas." To clear its good name, Bresser was forced to file the lawsuit in Dallas, Texas — Bresser's headquarters. PERI has thus far declined comment on the lawsuit other than to say "we are exploring all of our legal options."

Underwood & Associates, P.A.
Internal Memo

From: Jim Underwood, Sr. Partner
To: Firm Managing Partner
Re: Unhappy Client

We have a problem on our hands and I need your quick advice. I'm attaching the small newspaper report on the case filed yesterday against our client — Petroleum Resources, Inc. (PERI). PERI's chief executive officer, Charles Client, is threatening to terminate our firm because he feels we've been "out-lawyered."

Charles came to us a few months ago with a story that could only happen in the oil patch. PERI drills and produces thousands of oil wells in west Texas and other places. Due to the nature of the underlying geology, to be truly cost-effective most of the wells in this formation require some stimulation services — "hydraulic fracking." This involves injecting fluids and "proppant" (often sand) into the wellbore at very high pressures to create and then maintain fissures in the rock. These cracks (supported by the sand) become oil superhighways that permit the well to produce much greater quantities of oil and to extend their lifetimes significantly. This additional oil goes right to the bottom line and can make a marginal well highly valuable. Anyway, PERI hired a Dallas-based national oil well servicing company — Bresser Industries — to fracture hundreds of wells for PERI over the last few years. Turns out Bresser may have been "shorting" PERI on the sand for each job in order to reduce its own expenses and to make the frack jobs more profitable. If this is true, it appears to be a good claim for common law fraud and (because interstate mail was used for invoicing) might involve a federal question claim under the RICO statutes.

We were hired to investigate and prosecute any civil claims against Bresser and others. We interviewed some former employees of Bresser and it looks like the claims might be legit — and worth millions due to the loss of production on hundreds of wells. Plus punitive damages! But rather than haul off and file suit, we decided to approach Bresser about a quiet settlement. We drafted a complaint to file in west Texas (where we can go to trial quick and get a local jury) and prepared written discovery. But we didn't file it yet. We told Bresser we'd like a voluntary informal exchange of discovery and then settlement talks. They liked this approach — nobody wants bad press these days — and quickly agreed. They even said they'd "toll" the statute of limitations so we had no need to run to the courthouse until we saw if we could get this thing settled. Things proceeded along these lines for the last few weeks — they began to send us some documents for the frack jobs and we discussed their employees we'd like to interview. But then Charles called my office first thing this morning irate. Bresser went ahead and sued us first in Dallas federal court!

Need your wise counsel on this one boss. Wondering what our options are in response. Do we just litigate in Dallas? Move to dismiss or transfer that case? File our own case; and if so, where? State or federal court? Can we ask our chosen court to enjoin their lawsuit? Not sure which case would move forward if we each filed separate cases. Anyway, I could use your help thinking through this puzzle quickly.

C. Priority of Redundant Cases & Stay Orders

Parties often believe a particular venue is more favorable than another. Thus, when a party finds itself haled into an unfavorable jurisdiction, the party will often file a comparable or identical suit in a more favorable jurisdiction in hopes of having the rules involving duplicative litigation held in their favor. Preserving judicial economy is essential to the courts. Therefore, when parties file multiple, identical or analogous suits, courts have rules which protect judicial economy by deciding which suit will continue forward. This process often involves motions to stay a pending case. However, these rules differ depending on the jurisdictions in which the parties file the duplicative litigation. Thus, careful attention to the differences between the cases below is necessary to understand how duplicative litigation will be handled.

1. Two Competing Federal Actions

a. The General Rule and Its Exceptions

When the two equivalent suits are each filed in federal court, the general rule is that the *first suit filed* will continue forward. This is an easy-to-implement rule; it simply involves looking at the two complaints to find the date/time filed. It is a race-to-file situation. However, there are exceptions to this straightforward rule which courts may use to determine the fairness of the first-to-file rule. First, there is a forum shopping exception. This requires blatant and inequitable forum shopping, mostly determined by the eye of the beholder, rather than just the typical desire to have a venue that is most logical and favorable to a litigant. There is also an exception that some courts have recognized in customer patent infringement cases. This exception deals with the primary-versus-secondary infringer situation. If the indirect infringer is in the first suit, and the direct infringer is brought in the second, the second suit should continue forward. Finally, an exception exists when the second forum makes so much more sense than the first suit given the convenience of the litigants and witnesses that courts find the temptation to disregard the plaintiff's success in filing first too great to resist. Consider the general rule and the application of these possible exceptions in the cases that follow.

"The race is not always to the swift, nor the battle to the strong, but that's the way to bet."

Damon Runyon

William Gluckin & Co. v. International Playtex Corp.
407 F.2d 177 (2nd Cir. 1969)

Moore, J.,

International Playtex Corporation (Playtex) appeals from an order entered in the District Court for the Southern District of New York granting a preliminary injunction which restrains Playtex from further prosecuting a patent infringement suit pending in the United States District Court for the Northern District of Georgia until final disposition of the instant case. The underlying suit here in the Southern District of New York was brought by William Gluckin & Co. (Gluckin) against Playtex for a declaration of patent invalidity and/or non-infringement.

Involved here are two patent infringement suits and the question is which takes priority over the other. The first-commenced action was instituted by the patent holder against the customer of an allegedly infringing manufacturer in the Northern District of Georgia.

The second action is a declaratory judgment suit against the patent holder in the Southern District of New York. ②

On April 25, 1968, Playtex brought a patent infringement action against F.W. Woolworth & Co. (Woolworth), alleging in its complaint that Woolworth was selling a brassiere which infringed a patent which it owned. The action was instituted in the Northern District of Georgia ostensibly because Woolworth was selling the allegedly infringing brassiere at its store in Gainesville, Georgia. Playtex, a Delaware corporation, has three of its five manufacturing plants located in Georgia. Its principal place of business is in New York. Woolworth is a New York corporation, with its principal place of business there, and operates retail stores throughout the nation.

The manufacturer of the challenged brassiere sold by Woolworth is Gluckin, a New York corporation with its principal place of business in New York City. It is not licensed to do business in Georgia and, apparently, not subject to suit there. On May 28, 1968, after Playtex had filed its Georgia action, Gluckin brought a declaratory judgment action for patent invalidity and non-infringement against Playtex in the Southern District of New York.

On July 2, 1968, a preliminary injunction was issued by Judge Motley restraining Playtex from further prosecuting the Georgia suit. Judge Motley held that since the first filed suit was against a customer rather than against Gluckin itself and since New York was the most convenient forum for resolving the questions of patent validity and infringement, special circumstances existed which justified giving priority to the second-filed suit.

The general rule in this Circuit is that, as a principle of sound judicial administration, the first suit should have priority, "absent the showing of balance of convenience in favor of the second action," *Remington Products Corp. v. American Aerovap, Inc.*, 192 F.2d 872, 873 (2d Cir. 1951), *Mattel, Inc. v. Louis Marx & Co.*, 353 F.2d 421, 423 (2d Cir. 1965), petition for cert. dismissed, 384 U.S. 948, 86 S.Ct. 1475, 16 L.Ed.2d 546 (1966), or unless there are special circumstances which justify giving priority to the second. *Joseph Bancroft & Sons Co. v. Spunize Co. of America*, 268 F.2d 522 (2d Cir. 1959). In deciding between competing jurisdictions, it has often been stated that the balancing of convenience should be left to the sound discretion of the district courts. *Mattel*, supra, 353 F.2d at 423, 424; *Kerotest Mfg. Co. v. C-O Two Fire Equipment Co.*, 342 U.S. 180, 183, 72 S.Ct. 219, 96 L.Ed. 200 (1951).

In *Mattel, supra*, two situations were posed which are said to constitute special circumstances justifying a departure from the "first-filed" rule of priority. *Id.*, 353 F.2d at 424. The first example is the so-called "customer action" where the first-filed suit is against a customer of the alleged infringer while the second suit involves the infringer himself. *Delamere Company v. Taylor-Bell Company*, 199 F.Supp. 55 (S.D.N.Y.1961).

The second example is where forum shopping alone motivated the choice of the situs for the first suit. *Rayco Mfg. Co. v. Chicopee Mfg. Co.*, 148 F.Supp. 588 (S.D.N.Y.1957). This, however, is not applicable to the present case because Judge Motley made no specific finding of forum shopping, nor is one inferable because the reasons Playtex asserts justifying the choice of a Georgia forum are not wholly frivolous. *Compare Rayco Mfg. Co., supra.*

Judge Motley, relying on the "customer suit" exception to the first-filed rule mentioned in the *Mattel* case, granted the preliminary injunction. Playtex insists, however, that there is no reason why the first suit should be enjoined simply [because] the defendant happens to be a customer rather than a manufacturer. Section 271 of Title 35 declares manufacturing, using or selling infringing products actionable. Each act is identified as an act of infringement and each is proscribed. 35 U.S.C. § 281. Since Woolworth allegedly has itself "sold thousands of dollars of the infringing merchandise" and is "an infringer of the patent in suit every bit as much as the manufacturer of the infringing article" (Playtex Brief, p. 25), Playtex argues that it has the statutory right as a patentee to sue an infringing seller. *See Sundstrand Corp. v. American Brake Shoe Co.*, 315 F.2d 273, 276 (7th Cir. 1963).

Playtex asserts, therefore, that before the first-filed suit can be enjoined, there must be a finding of harassment, *Kerotest*, supra, 342 U.S. at 185, 72 S.Ct. 219, probable harassment, *see Sundstrand, supra*, 315 F.2d at 276, or forum shopping, *Delamere Company*, supra; *Helene Curtis Industries, Inc. v. Sales Affiliates, Inc.*, 105 F.Supp. 886 (S.D.N.Y.1952), aff'd, 199 F.2d 732 (2d Cir. 1952); *Telephonics Corporation v. Lindly & Company*, 192 F.Supp. 407 (E.D.N.Y.1960), aff'd 291 F.2d 445 (2d Cir. 1961); *United States Time Corporation v. Hamilton Watch Co.*, 327 F.2d 338 (2d Cir. 1964). Moreover, to rely on a "natural theatre" test as the District Court did, 294 F.Supp. 876 (S.D.N.Y. July 2, 1968), is said to be making an application of forum non conveniens which is not sanctioned by the statute.

In response Gluckin argues that the manufacturer of allegedly infringing goods is the real party in interest in the event his customer is charged with infringement of patents and this principle lies at the basis of judicial restraint on customer actions. *Kessler v. Eldred*, 206 U.S. 285, 27 S.Ct. 611, 51 L.Ed. 1065 (1907). Under the direction of the Supreme Court in *Kerotest*, where it was stated[:]

> Wise judicial administration, giving regard to conservation of judicial resources and comprehensive disposition of litigation, does not counsel rigid mechanical solution of such problems. The factors relevant to wise administration here are equitable in nature. Necessarily, an ample degree of discretion, appropriate for disciplined and experienced judges, must be left to the lower courts. Lower courts have properly exercised a broad degree of discretion in implementing this basic doctrine.

An inflexible approach to suits of this type is [certainly] to be avoided. Although the so-called "customer suit" exception to the first-filed rule appears to be in conflict with a flexible approach, as Playtex contends, we nonetheless feel that the issuance of the preliminary injunction in this case was not an abuse of discretion.

This Court, in *Mattel*, stated:

> We believe it to be a sound rule that the issues should be tried in the district where suit is first brought unless there are other factors of substance which support the exercise of the court's discretion that the balance of convenience is in favor of proceeding first in another district.

Judge Motley found that there were factors of substance indicating that the balance of convenience supported priority for the second-filed suit. The Court noted that (1) since Woolworth is simply a customer of Gluckin and upon whom Woolworth must rely exclusively, the primary party is really Gluckin; (2) the Woolworth employee who has the most knowledge concerning the allegedly infringing item is the Woolworth buyer in New York City; (3) no one connected with Woolworth in Gainesville where the first suit was filed, has any knowledge concerning the patent in suit; (4) the allegedly infringing manufacturer Gluckin is a New York corporation with its main offices in New York City; (5)

[margin annotation:] Reasons for NY

Gluckin is not licensed to do business in Georgia; (6) the package in which the article is sold by Woolworth is designed, made and supplied by Gluckin, as are all the promotional materials; (7) arrangements for the purchase of the article were negotiated in New York City; (8) Gluckin's manufacturing plants are located in Pennsylvania and its design facility in New York City; (9) it sells and distributes its products to customers nationwide; (10) Playtex, though a Delaware corporation, has its main office and principal place of business in New York City and its design centers in New Jersey; (11) its marketing and purchasing activities are located in New York; (12) the alleged inventor of the Playtex brassiere at issue resides in New Jersey; (13) Playtex's records relating to the invention are in New York City and Georgia; and (14) witnesses who have knowledge of the patent reside in and about New York City.

In Practice

One way for parties in business relationships to avoid the phenomenon of racing to a courthouse to fix the forum in the event of a dispute is to agree in their governing contract to a *mandatory forum selection clause*. This can not only avoid uncertainty over the appropriate court to take their future disputes, but can perhaps avoid a "trigger happy" litigant from racing to court at all when informal discussions in a less antagonistic environment might yield an easier and inexpensive business resolution.

Reasons for GA

The reasons for which Playtex chose Gainesville, Georgia, as the place of suit are assertedly (1) because of the location of three of its five plants in that State, (2) because the alleged infringement took place there, and (3) because of the possibility of an earlier trial date in the Northern District of Georgia. It also claims that some of its employees in its Georgia plants will be important witnesses in the action there and that their unique knowledge of the manufacturing process is important to that infringement suit. Playtex contends further that it brought suit in Georgia because of the economic interest in defendant and its employees in Georgia in preserving the substantial volume of business of defendant's patented product.

Judge Motley found Playtex's reasons for bringing suit against Woolworth in Georgia "not very persuasive."

The "whole of the war and all the parties to it" are in the Southern District of New York. *Kerotest*, supra, 342 U.S. at 183, 72 S.Ct. at 221. Woolworth, the defendant in the Georgia action, has consented to be made a party here and is amenable to process here as well. All the litigants involved have offices and principal places of business in New York City. Most of the witnesses whose testimony is relevant reside in the New York City area. Woolworth must look to Gluckin to supply evidence in its defense in the Georgia action. All counsel are from New York and the convenience of the major witnesses would unquestionably be better served by a New York venue.

Balancing the convenience of the parties and witnesses and with due regard to the weight given to the initial forum, a judgment that the Georgia suit should be restrained in order that the New York suit may proceed does not appear to be at all unreasonable.

The decision below is affirmed.

NFLPA (Tom Brady) v. NFL

Civ. No. 15-3168 (D. Minn. July 30, 2015)

This matter is before the Court *sua sponte*.

"Sua sponte" in Latin means "of one's own will," and refers to a court's action taken
on its own volition rather than in response to a request or motion from a litigant.

This action arises out of a July 28, 2015 arbitration award (the "Award") issued by
Roger Goodell, Commissioner of Respondent National Football League (the "NFL"). The
Award sustained a four-game suspension imposed on New England Patriots quarterback
Tom Brady as a result of his purported involvement in what has become known colloquially
as "deflate-gate." Brady's union, Petitioner National Football League Players Association
(the "Union"), commenced this action on July 29, 2015, seeking vacatur of the Award on
a host of grounds, primarily that it fails to draw its essence from the parties' collective-
bargaining agreement (CBA).

This Court, however, perceives no reason for this action to proceed in Minnesota. On
the same day the Award was issued, Respondent National Football League Management

Council (the "Council"), the exclusive bargaining representative of the NFL, commenced an action against the Union in the United States District Court for the Southern District of New York seeking to confirm the Award. *See Nat'l Football League Mgmt. Council v. Nat'l Football League Players Assoc.*, No. 15 Civ. 5916 (filed July 28, 2015) (the "New York Action"). The New York Action alleges the converse of the claims here: the Award was "in full accord with the parties' CBA and draws its essence from the parties' agreement" and, hence, is binding on Brady and the Union. In this Court's view, therefore, the New York Action triggers application of the first-filed rule.

Under that rule, the court "initially seized of a controversy" generally "should be the one to decide the case." *Orthmann v. Apple River Campground, Inc.*, 765 F.2d 119, 121 (8th Cir. 1985). The rule recognizes the comity between coequal federal courts and promotes the efficient use of judicial resources by authorizing a later-filed, substantially similar action's transfer, stay or dismissal in deference to an earlier case. *Orthmann*, 765 F.2d at 121; *Johnson Bros. Liquor Co. v. Bacardi U.S.A., Inc.*, 830 F. Supp. 2d 697, 711 (D. Minn. 2011). The Court enjoys ample discretion in determining whether to apply the rule; it "is not intended to be rigid, mechanical, or inflexible, but [rather is] to be applied in a manner best serving the interests of justice." *Nw. Airlines, Inc. v. Am. Airlines, Inc.*, 989 F.2d 1002, 1005 (8th Cir. 1993). Nevertheless, "[t]he prevailing standard is that in the absence of compelling circumstances, the first-filed rule should apply." *Id.*; *accord, e.g.*, *S. Mills, Inc. v. Nunes*, 586 F. App'x 702, 705 (11th Cir. 2014) (*per curiam*) ("[W]here two actions involving overlapping issues and parties are pending in two federal courts, there is a strong presumption across the federal circuits that favors the forum of the first-filed suit under the first-filed rule.").

The Court appreciates no "compelling circumstances" undermining application of the first-filed rule to transfer this action from Minnesota to New York, where the first action was filed. Indeed, the Court sees little reason for this action to have been commenced in Minnesota *at all*. Brady plays for a team in Massachusetts; the Union is headquartered in Washington, D.C.; the NFL is headquartered in New York; the arbitration proceedings took place in New York; and the award was issued in New York. In the undersigned's view, therefore, it makes eminent sense the NFL would have commenced its action seeking confirmation of the award in the Southern District of New York. Why the instant action was filed here, however, is far less clear.[1]

Moreover, this case and the New York Action are "substantially duplicative." *Ritchie Capital Mgmt., L.L.C. v. Jeffries*, 653 F.3d 755, 763 n.3 (8th Cir. 2011). The parties overlap

---

1. The Court strongly suspects the Union filed in Minnesota because it has obtained favorable rulings from this Court in the past on behalf of its members. *See, e.g.*, *Nat'l Football League Players Assoc. v. Nat'l Football League*, Civ. No. 14-4990 (D. Minn. Feb. 26, 2015) (Doty, J.), *appeal docketed*, No. 15-1438 (8th Cir. Feb. 27, 2015); *Brady v. Nat'l Football League*, 779 F. Supp. 2d 992 (D. Minn. 2011) (Nelson, J.), *rev'd*, 644 F.3d 661 (8th Cir. 2011). Indeed, the Union makes only a fleeting attempt to justify venuing this action in Minnesota, noting in two sentences of its 160-paragraph Petition that legal issues raised in the underlying arbitration "were directly related to" legal issues addressed in the action disposed of by Judge Doty in February (concerning Minnesota Vikings running back Adrian Peterson). However, the Court fails to appreciate how legal issues resolved in *Peterson* justify bringing this action here when it enjoys no other connection to Minnesota. Indeed, carried to its logical conclusion, accepting the Union's premise would mean that a court that had decided, for example, a large corporation had engaged in racial discrimination would be the appropriate venue for every future racial-discrimination case against that corporation, no matter where the employee was located or where the alleged discrimination had occurred. Venue simply cannot be predicated on such a thin reed. *See also* 28 U.S.C. § 1391.

in the two cases and the issues are mere flip-sides of the same coin: the Union argues here that the Award should be vacated for failing to draw its essence from the parties' CBA, while the New York Action alleges the precise opposite and asserts the Award draws its essence from the CBA and should be confirmed. Moreover, any claim that the Award cannot stand may be raised by the Union in the New York Action. Simply put, the cases are part and parcel of the same whole and should be heard together in the most appropriate forum: the Southern District of New York, where the arbitration occurred, the Award issued, and the first action concerning the Award was commenced. *See, e.g.*, *S. Mills*, 586 F. App'x at 706 (court should not "fragment a case about a single arbitration award into two suits" by permitting simultaneous actions to confirm and vacate arbitration award); *see also* 9 U.S.C. §§ 9, 10 (petitions to confirm or vacate arbitration awards generally should be brought "in and for the district where the award was made").

Based on the foregoing, and all the files, records, and proceedings herein, the Court concludes the first-filed rule militates in favor of transferring this action to the Southern District of New York. Accordingly, IT IS ORDERED that this action (and its companion miscellaneous case, No. 15-mc-59, in which the Union's papers were initially filed under seal) is TRANSFERRED to the United States District Court for the Southern District of New York. The Clerk of the Court is directed to take all steps necessary to effectuate this transfer in an expeditious fashion.

Notes and Problems

1. What is the general rule of priority applied among federal courts in cases of redundant litigation? Does this rule make any sense or is it just arbitrary? Does it have any advantages over other possible default rules of priority?

2. Which of the exceptions to the general rule does the court apply in *Gluckin*? Does it seem like the use of the exceptions rather than the general *first-to-file rule* was appropriate in that case?

3. In *Gluckin*, why do you think the primary infringer was not brought in the first suit? How does that affect the court's view on the value of the first-filed suit? Should this exception exist, or is it better to have a bright-line rule without the cloudiness exceptions bring to the application of the rule?

4. Also in *Gluckin*, how else might the parties have handled the filing of multiple similar actions? Could the primary infringer have intervened in the suit? Could the named defendant have instead made a Rule 19 motion? Recall from the prior chapter's discussion of Rule 19 necessary parties, that one concern is with non-parties who might as a practical matter be impacted by the court's decision in their absence. If the plaintiff in the first action filed in Georgia prevails against the retailer and obtains an injunction against that retailer selling the infringing product, what is the practical impact of that decision on the manufacturer of the infringing product? Strategically, why do you believe the alleged infringers chose the route they did by bringing their own redundant case in New York rather than addressing their concerns with the Georgia federal court? How would you rule on each of the various approaches if you were the court?

5. In the more recent dispute involving Tom Brady, notice the speed by which the race to the courthouse occurred and, perhaps even more impressively, the quick action by the Minnesota federal court to divest itself of the action through transfer. The underlying arbitration award was on July 28, the NFL filed its action the same day, Tom Brady filed his lawsuit against the NFL (in response to the NFL's lawsuit) on July 29th, and the

Minnesota court raised and resolved the priority issue on July 30th — a whirlwind of legal action in 48 hours. Regardless of whether you agree with the court's decision not to adjudicate the case on the merits, this is an incredible display of prompt action by the federal court. Why do you think the court was so motivated to raise the priority issue itself and to rule on it without even awaiting briefing by the parties?

6. In the Tom Brady dispute, why was the court unpersuaded by Brady's arguments that the first-to-file rule should be disregarded? Is there any downside to such rigid adherence to this arguably arbitrary rule of priority? Did Brady's counsel get out-lawyered? As an aside, observe from the Tom Brady lawsuit that just winning the race to the courthouse doesn't ensure victory on the merits. The New York federal district judge ultimately ruled on the merits in favor of Tom Brady. On the other hand, the Second Circuit Court of Appeals reversed that decision and reinstated the NFL's punishment against Brady. (So, perhaps ironically, the race to the courthouse appears to have been more important at the appellate level than the trial court level.)

7. *Chapter Problem.* Counsel for PERI lost the race to the courthouse apparently because counsel did not realize there was a race; rather PERI believed that the parties were proceeding with some informal alternative dispute resolution mechanism with the goal of both parties avoiding judicial resolution of their legal issues. In light of the two foregoing cases, if PERI proceeds by filing its own federal court lawsuit in west Texas, which case do you believe should proceed? Consider both the general rule and its exceptions as applied to the circumstances in this Problem.

b. Should the First-to-File Rule Still Apply When the Same Party Has Filed Both Cases?

In the *Semmes Motors* case that follows, a plaintiff having first filed its lawsuit in New Jersey federal court changed its mind and then filed the same lawsuit in a federal court in New York. Logically, the original action might have made more sense had it been filed in New York. But having filed two actions, now pending before two different federal courts, should New York court still apply the first-to-file rule? Or would it make more sense to permit the plaintiff the autonomy to decide which of its own cases should move forward? Pay close attention to why the court believes this situation does not warrant a different rule of law. Also consider the plaintiff's true motivation for filing the second suit.

Semmes Motors, Inc. v. Ford Motor Co.

429 F.2d 1197 (2d Cir. 1970)

FRIENDLY, J.,

This heated controversy is predicated both on diverse citizenship and on the Federal Dealer Act, 15 U.S.C. §§ 1221–1225. We affirm, with a modification stated in section IV of this opinion, the temporary injunction issued by Judge Ryan as being within the discretion afforded him, but order that further proceedings be stayed pending termination of the New Jersey litigation.

I.

Commencing with the 1965 vehicles, introduced by Ford in the fall of 1964, the manufacturer has made its warranty directly to the retail purchaser as well as to the dealer. When a purchaser of a Ford car finds a defect which he claims to be within the warranty, he returns the car to the dealer who repairs it and submits a Warranty Refund Claim to Ford. The company reimburses the dealer for replacement parts at cost plus a profit and for labor in an amount determined by multiplying the installation time specified in a Ford schedule by the dealer's then approved labor rate. Dealers have complained that deterioration in quality control at the factory, difficulty in securing skilled repairmen, and other elements have made this policy burdensome; Ford has been concerned over the submission of inflated and even wholly false refund claims.

It will suffice to state the facts and the proceedings below in rather summary form: Although there had been a considerable history of dissatisfaction by Ford with Semmes' warranty refund claims, the kick-off for the present fight was an apparently routine letter, dated July 25, 1969, from S. J. Obringer, Ford's New York District Sales Manager, to Semmes. This announced that in accordance with Company policy, Ford auditors would call on him, would "examine warranty claims and their related dealership records, inspect repaired units and may possibly contact customers for whom you have performed warranty work." It continued that the auditors would bring to Semmes' attention "any opportunities they find for improving warranty administration at your dealership," that the audit findings would be discussed with him, and that claims determined to have been improper might be charged back.

The audit was conducted from August 4 through 28; its results were embodied in a report submitted to Semmes on September 18. Not stating the number of claims examined or the period covered, the report found that 253 claims submitted by Semmes for refund, with a price tag of $10,440, were defective. The most serious were 86 claims, aggregating $4,691, where the auditors found that work for which reimbursement had been obtained had not been performed at all. Fifty of these were determined by visual inspection of vehicles that had come in during the audit, presumably for some other cause; the inspectors reported that 87% "of the inspectable units checked had work not performed." The other 36 claims were ascertained in the course of questioning "during telephone contacts made in the form of an owner satisfaction survey." Despite these seemingly serious findings, the auditors' recommendations were rather bland: Semmes should consider appointing a shop foreman, and there should be better control of the return of defective parts, of the recording of mechanics' time, and of the status of repairs in the shop.

The auditors' insistence on contacting customers led the Alliance and Semmes to file, on August 22, 1969, a complaint in a New Jersey state court, later removed by Ford to the District Court for New Jersey, seeking an injunction against such contacts. However, no application for interlocutory relief was then made.[5] [Ford considered filing counterclaims against Semmes for false and fraudulent refund claims and termination of the Semmes dealership. Ford continued inspections through contact with the owners of the vehicles for which the refund claims were submitted.] These inspections began on September 22 and by October 7 had included 105 vehicles; Ford asserts that in 70% of these, repairs claimed by Semmes had not been performed.

On the afternoon of October 7, Ford's New York counsel informed Scott that plaintiffs' New York attorneys had advised them of an intention to file in the Southern District of New York an action on behalf of Semmes and the Alliance substantially identical to the New Jersey action and to seek a temporary restraining order similar to that which had been there refused, Ford countered by moving on October 8 in the New Jersey action to

---

5. On September 24 Judge Coolahan, in the District Court for New Jersey, declined to issue a temporary restraining order with respect to Ford's investigation.

dismiss Alliance's claim and filing an answer and counterclaim with respect to Semmes. On the same day Judge Ryan, in the Southern District of New York, declined to issue a temporary restraining order against customer contacts pending a hearing on a temporary injunction on October 14.

Meanwhile Scott had been discussing termination of Semmes' dealership with Ford officials in Dearborn. On October 8, a termination notice was signed by the Secretary of Ford and sent to the New York District Sales Office. The next morning Scott cleared this with L.A. Iacocca, Ford's Executive Vice President, and service was made that afternoon. As a result, plaintiffs sought and obtained leave to amend their complaint and their request for a temporary injunction in the Southern District to include the termination of Semmes' dealership.

On November 5, Judge Ryan issued an opinion in which he denied the motion for a stay of the New York action, limited Ford's contacts with Semmes' customers although not to the extent sought by Semmes, and temporarily enjoined termination of the dealership. An injunction order was entered on December 15. On the same day, Ford moved, with elaborate affidavits and exhibits, to vacate the injunction and again to stay proceedings during the pendency of the New Jersey suit.

II.

We must deal at the outset with Ford's contention that the court erred in refusing to stay the New York action until the earlier New Jersey suit had been determined. Since the action was equitable in nature, the denial of the stay would not itself be appealable under 28 U.S.C. § 1292(a)(1) as the denial of an injunction. *City of Morgantown v. Royal Ins. Co., Ltd.*, 337 U.S. 254, 69 S.Ct. 1067, 93 L.Ed. 1347 (1949); *Baltimore Contractors, Inc. v. Bodinger*, 348 U.S. 176, 75 S.Ct. 249, 99 L.Ed. 233 (1955); 6 Moore, Federal Practice ¶ 54.07 n. 19 (1966 and 1969 supplement). But when, as here, the district court has granted a temporary injunction so that the court of appeals has unquestioned jurisdiction of the cause, it would be absurd to require the court to close its eyes to another interlocutory order which, though not itself appealable, might infect the entire proceeding with error and thus require reversal after large expenditure of judicial and professional time. *Deckert v. Independence Shares Corp.*, 311 U.S. 282, 286–287, 61 S.Ct. 229, 85 L.Ed. 189 (1940); *Barber-Greene Co. v. Blaw-Knox Co.*, 239 F.2d 774, 776 (6 Cir. 1957); *National Equipment Rental, Ltd. v. Fowler*, 287 F.2d 43, 45 (2 Cir. 1961); 6 Moore Federal Practice P54.08(1).

When the New York complaint was filed, it was in effect a duplicate of that in New Jersey, although the scope of the New Jersey action had been enlarged by Ford's counterclaim to recover warranty refunds allegedly obtained by Semmes through fraud. Later the New York action was broadened to include Semmes' claim to enjoin termination of the dealership. However, F.R.Civ.P. 13(a) required Semmes to file as a counterclaim in the New Jersey action any claim it had against Ford "at the time of serving the pleading," if the claim arose "out of the transaction or occurrence that is the subject matter of the opposing party's claim." Here "the pleading" was the reply, which was required, F.R.Civ.P. 7(a), to be filed within 20 days after October 8, the very day when Semmes' claim of unlawful termination came into being. This clearly "arose out of the same transaction or occurrence" as Ford's counterclaim, under the broad view expressed in the leading case of *Moore v. New York Cotton Exchange*, 270 U.S. 593, 610, (1926). The New Jersey court therefore should be deemed seized of this claim as well.

Given this situation, there is no doubt that the New Jersey court could properly have enjoined prosecution of the New York action if Ford had sought this, and might even have been bound to do so. *Food Fair Stores, Inc. v. Square Deal Mkt. Co.*, 88 U.S.App.D.C. 176, 187 F.2d 219 (1951). Instead Ford addressed its argument to the New York court. But we can see no reason why the end result should be different when the party seeking to preserve the primacy of the first court moves the second court to stay its hand rather than asking the first court to enjoin prosecution of the second case. Whatever the procedure, the first suit should have priority, "absent the showing of balance of convenience in favor of the second action," *Remington Products Corp. v. American Aerovap, Inc.*, 192 F.2d 872, 873 (2 Cir. 1951). *See Mattel, Inc. v. Louis Marx & Co.*, 353 F.2d 421, 424 (2 Cir. 1965), where we not only reversed an injunction against prosecution of the first action in New Jersey but ordered a stay of the later action in New York.

We recognize that the instant case differs from the more usual situation where, at least in substance, the plaintiff in the first court is the defendant in the second and vice versa. In such instances the plaintiff in the first court is vigorously pressing his desire to proceed in an appropriate forum of his choice and objecting to the defendant's thwarting this by a later suit elsewhere. *See, e.g., National Equip.*, supra; *Mattel, Inc.*, supra; *Gluckin & Co. v. International Playtex Corp.*, 407 F.2d 177 (2 Cir. 1969). Here the same party is plaintiff in both actions, prefers to press the second, and has stipulated to discontinue the first if defendant will consent.[2] While Ford's fears of parallel litigation in two courts could be stilled if it were willing to consent to plaintiffs' discontinuing the New Jersey action, and Ford has no vested right to be proceeded against in the New Jersey rather than the New York federal court, these factors alone are insufficient grounds for departing from the general rule that in the absence of sound reasons the second action should give way to the first.

To begin with, any exception for cases where the same party is plaintiff in both actions would entail the danger that plaintiffs may engage in forum shopping or, more accurately, judge shopping. When they see a storm brewing in the first court, they may try to weigh anchor and set sail for the hopefully more favorable waters of another district. The sequence of events here affords some indication that Semmes might have been attempting to do just that. The defendant is then put to the Hobson's choice of either going along with this ploy by agreeing to dismissal of the first action if the plaintiff is willing or having to defend two lawsuits at the same time. If he makes the latter election, as is his right, not only the parties but the courts pay a heavy price. "Courts already heavily burdened with litigation with which they must of necessity deal should not be called upon to duplicate each other's work in cases involving the same issues and the same parties," *Crosley Corp. v. Hazeltine Corp.*, 122 F.2d at 930. Hence, even when the same party is plaintiff in both actions, the instances where the second court should go forward despite the protests of a party to the first action where full justice can be done, should be rare indeed.

We find no considerations sufficient to justify an exception to the general rule in this case. It is true that if we were free to look at the situation in a vacuum, New York is a more logical forum than New Jersey. The cause of action "arose" here, Semmes relies in part on a New York statute, and witnesses from Scarsdale and from Ford's New York office would find it more convenient to come to Foley Square than to Newark. However, these factors must be weighed in the setting created by Semmes' having initiated litigation in New Jersey and the likelihood that failure to stay the New York action will result in litigation in two courts—a danger the judge recognized when he made his "denial of the stay subject

---

2. Because of Ford's counterclaim the New Jersey court could not dismiss the entire action on plaintiffs' motion even if it were more disposed to do so than it seems to be. F.R.Civ.P. 41(a)(2). Although the purpose of this provision was doubtless to prevent a plaintiff's escaping from a counterclaim and that possibility is here precluded by the New York action, the language of the Rule is unqualified.

to further developments in the two actions and further order of the Court." We thus see little force in his observation that the New Jersey action had been pending only a short time; the potential of future waste and conflict exists nonetheless unless Ford consents to dismissal. With respect to the elements favoring New York, the inconvenience to witnesses is exceedingly slight, as Judge Coolahan pointed out in denying a motion by the plaintiffs to transfer the New Jersey action to New York, and the Scarsdale and New York City witnesses are subject to subpoena for a trial in Newark, F.R.Civ.P. 45(e). Insofar as Semmes relies on the Federal Dealer Act, 15 U.S.C. § 1222, a New Jersey federal court is as well equipped to decide the issues as one in New York. *See Clayton v. Warlick*, 232 F.2d 699 (4 Cir. 1956). So far as the New York statute is concerned, see fn. 13, infra, it can scarcely be doubted that a dealer's purposeful submission of false warranty refund claims would constitute "cause" for termination to the extent that this is consistent with the governing contract. Interpretation of that may pose some problems, as we shall see, but the Ford Sales Agreement provides that it is "to be construed in accordance with the laws of Michigan" — a provision to which we assume both New York and New Jersey would give effect. A.L.I. Restatement of Conflict of Laws 2d § 332a, Tent. Draft. No. 6 (1960). A New Jersey district judge can determine that as well — or badly — as one in New York. None of the factors relied on for giving priority to the second suit comes near the examples given in *Mattel*, supra, 353 F.2d at 424 n. 4. Although a district judge has considerable latitude in these matters, *Kerotest Mfg. Co. v. C-O-Two Fire Equip. Co.*, 342 U.S. 180, 183–184, 72 S.Ct. 219, 96 L.Ed. 200 (1952), we hold that the court below went beyond the allowable bounds of discretion when it refused to grant Ford's motion for a stay and that a stay should be entered, provided that within fifteen days of the issuance of the mandate, Ford stipulates that Semmes, within twenty days thereafter, may file a reply and counterclaim (or, if Semmes prefers, an amended complaint) in the New Jersey action in respect to the termination of the dealership.

Whether the temporary injunction entered by the district court should be set aside is quite another matter. The issues presented by Semmes' motion for a temporary injunction were difficult and complex, and a great deal of time and energy has been spent by Judge Ryan in deciding them and by us in reviewing his action. We see no reason for further expenditure of judicial time on this interlocutory issue when the important thing is to get on with the final hearing. The proper solution is rather to let the temporary injunction stand until the New Jersey action is decided on the merits. In so holding we assume that the New Jersey court will require Semmes to proceed speedily to trial; if that should not occur, the stay should not prevent Ford from asking that the temporary injunction be dissolved.

This disposition will relieve Ford of its present dilemma of having either to yield to Semmes' forum shopping or to litigate in two courts simultaneously, and the courts from the consequent unnecessary burdens. [The court went on to uphold the temporary injunction as properly ordered.]

Notes and Problems

1. How does *Semmes Motors, Inc. v. Ford Motor, Co.* differ from *Gluckin*? Does this lead to different results? Should it? Why should a plaintiff's choice of forum (autonomy) not prevail in situations such as what was seen in *Semmes*? Notice that the court seems to concede that the second filed suit might be the more logical and convenient location for the lawsuit to proceed. Are you surprised by the court's decision to stick to the first-to-file rule?

2. In these scenarios involving dueling mirror-image litigation among federal courts, the parties can take the issue of priority to either court for resolution. Would it make

more sense to generally present the issue to one or the other? In *Twin City Ins. Co. v. Key Energy Services, Inc.*, the Southern District of Texas, Houston Division, provides the following analogous discussion on which court should rule on issues regarding the most appropriate court to resolve a dispute:

> Twin City next contends that the court should look "to the considerations that govern transfer of venue for forum non conveniens under 28 U.S.C. § 1404(a)" to determine whether compelling circumstances justifying departure from the first-to-file rule are present in this case. The court declines to do so in this case.
>
> Currently pending before the Western District of Texas in the Midland Action is Twin City's Opposed Motion to Stay or Transfer Venue. In that motion Twin City asserts that the Midland Action should be transferred to the Southern District of Texas pursuant to 28 U.S.C. § 1404(a). Therefore, in order to rule on that motion, Judge Junell will have to evaluate the same considerations that Twin City is asking this court to evaluate. A primary purpose of the first-to-file rule is "to avoid rulings which may trench upon the authority of sister courts...." *West Gulf Maritime*, 751 F.2d at 729. If this court were to evaluate the § 1404(a) factors, i.e., make a determination as to whether "the convenience of parties and witnesses" and "the interest of justice" favors venue in Houston, 28 U.S.C. § 1404(a), this court would find itself doing exactly what the first-to-file rule is designed to avoid.
>
> Moreover, the Fifth Circuit explained in *Sutter Corp.* — decided seven years after *Igloo Products* — that "the 'first-to-file rule' not only determines which court may decide the merits of substantially similar cases, but also establishes which court may decide whether the second suit filed must be dismissed, stayed or *transferred* and consolidated." *Sutter Corp.*, 125 F.3d at 920 (emphasis added). Thus, the Fifth Circuit made clear that it is the first-filed court, not this court, that should make the § 1404(a) determination.

Twin City Ins. Co. v. Key Energy Services, Inc., CIV A H-09-0352, 2009 WL 1544255 (S.D. Tex. June 2, 2009). Thus, at least according to some lower federal courts, so long as the first-to-file rule applies, allowing the second court to even determine the issue of priority might result in inconsistencies between the two courts. As you will notice in this section, however, litigants often go to either of the two courts with their priority dispute (including in the *Semmes Motors* case above).

3. *Problems.*

a. Pat files a lawsuit against Dawson in South Carolina federal court. A few weeks thereafter, Pat advises Dawson that she has changed her mind about the original forum choice and plans to voluntarily dismiss the case and file the case instead in Tennessee federal court. What, if anything, can Dawson do to try to prevent the case from being resolved in Tennessee?

b. Francis is hurt in an accident in her hometown of St. Louis. Francis sends a pre-suit settlement demand to the out-of-state driver, Dave (from Oklahoma), for a certain sum to cover Francis' property damage and personal injuries. Dave ignores the letter and instead files his own claim against Francis in Oklahoma federal court for the property damages to his car arising out of the same accident. Must Francis assert her claims as a compulsory counterclaim in Oklahoma or may she proceed with her own lawsuit against Dave in Missouri federal court? If she files her own suit, which court should have priority? Is it even redundant litigation?

2. Dueling Courts of Different States

State courts are hardly strangers to filings of duplicative, repetitive litigation. The same or similar suits are filed in different states or different areas of the same state for several reasons. These reasons can be strategic based upon a myriad of circumstances (e.g., a preference for geographic locale, differences among judges, differences among procedures or size of litigation dockets between courts, etc.) and often manifest in terms of attempts to be the first in the door with a filed suit—the race to filing. When two of the same or similar actions are filed in two different state courts, the same general *first-to-file* rule we first saw in the prior section is often applied, though arguably with a little greater discretion. State courts cite comity among the courts (both courts in the same state and out-of-state courts) as the primary motivation for the rule. However, every rule has exceptions. These exceptions are largely based on which court provides the best or most complete location for the adjudication of the suit. Thus, a commonly recited exception to the first-to-file rule in this context is when the second action provides the plaintiff the opportunity to obtain complete relief, but the first does not (consider the possible inability to join a Rule 19 necessary party).

Another commonly debated exception might apply if the first-filed suit is considered an *improper anticipatory suit*. Application of this second exception is often dependent upon the particular factual circumstances of the race to the courthouse. The more a court feels as though the race was unfairly waged, the more likely it is to depart from the first-to-file rule. Thus, just as federal courts acknowledge that bad faith "forum shopping" might justify a departure from the first-to-file rule applied by federal courts, state courts likewise acknowledge that sometimes application of the general rule is unfair and promotes gamesmanship and "sharp practices." Knowledge of the application of these exceptions can play a vital role in your argument for or against a particular forum when faced with duplicative litigation in state courts. The *Big East Conference v. West Virginia University* case below discusses both the general rule and some of these exceptions.

Big East Conference v. West Virginia University

(State of RI and Providence Plantations, Providence SC. Superior Court 2011)
C.A. No. PB 11-6391

Silverstein, J.

Before this Court is Defendant West Virginia University's (Defendant or WVU) Motion to Dismiss pursuant to Super R. Civ. P. 12(b)(2) and 12(b)(5). Defendant moves this court to dismiss Plaintiff the Big East Conference's (Plaintiff or Big East) Complaint for lack of personal jurisdiction and insufficient service of process. Alternatively, Defendant moves the Court to dismiss or stay Plaintiff's Complaint under principles of comity or the doctrine of forum non conveniens.

WVU is a state university with a main campus located in Morgantown, West Virginia. The university was created by West Virginia statute and is overseen by a Board of Governors. *See* W. Va. Code § 18-11-1. The WVU Board of Governors "shall be a corporation, and as such may contract and be contracted with, sue and be sued…." W. Va. Code § 18-11-1.

The Big East is a District of Columbia not-for-profit corporation headquartered in Providence, Rhode Island with the purpose of sponsoring, supervising, and regulating men's and women's intercollegiate athletics in twenty-four sports, including football and basketball. Members of the Big East include WVU, Providence College, and fifteen other schools across the eastern United States. The Big East and its members collaborate to create schedules and negotiate and participate in marketing and broadcast arrangements for athletics. The Big East is governed by Bylaws, with which WVU agreed to comply as a condition of membership in the Conference. WVU has been a member of the Big East conference since 1991.

The Bylaws contain provisions through which a member school may withdraw from the conference. These provisions were adopted unanimously by the member schools, including WVU. The withdrawing member loses all rights in the assets and revenues of the conference upon the effective date of withdrawal; but, immediately upon notice of withdrawal, revenue is credited towards any amounts owed by the member to the conference, and the member is automatically removed from committee membership and other positions within the conference. In the event that a member school does not comply with the requirements for withdrawal, the Bylaws state that non-compliance would cause irreparable harm to the conference, and the Big East is entitled to seek and obtain injunctive relief as well as attorney's fees and costs.

On October 28, 2011, WVU announced publicly that it planned to leave the Big East for the Big 12 Conference. WVU also sent notice to the commissioner of the Big East stating that WVU intended to withdraw from the conference effective June 30, 2012.

On October 31, 2011, WVU filed an action (the West Virginia case) against the Big East in the Circuit Court of Monongalia County, West Virginia, seeking declaratory judgment and permanent injunctive relief and claiming breach of contract. The very next day, WVU filed an Amended Complaint expounding upon its allegations. In the West Virginia case, WVU alleges that the Big East breached its contractual and fiduciary duties to WVU by allegedly failing to maintain the Big East as a viable collegiate football conference. WVU seeks, first and foremost, a declaration that the Bylaws are null and void between WVU and the Big East, that the Big East has accepted WVU's proposal to withdrawal from the conference, or that the Big East has waived the withdrawal provisions of the Bylaws. Further, WVU seeks damages resulting from the Big East's alleged breaches of the Bylaws and an Order permanently enjoining the Big East from enforcing the withdrawal provisions in the Bylaws against WVU.

The Big East Filed its action on November 4, just four days after WVU filed the West Virginia case and within a week of WVU's announcement it would be withdrawing from the conference. In the case at bar, the Big East is claiming breach of contract against WVU and is seeking specific performance, an injunction prohibiting WVU from withdrawing without complying with the Bylaws, damages, and attorney's fees and costs. On or about November 15, 2011 a summons and a copy of the complaint in this matter were delivered by certified mail, return receipt requested, to the president of WVU, James P. Clements.

The West Virginia court has recently entered a scheduling order, with a trial date initially set for June 25, 2012, five days prior to WVU's intended departure from the Big East.

Comity — First to File

As [a] ground for dismissal, WVU asserts that this Court should dismiss the Big East's Complaint in favor of the first-filed action in West Virginia on the basis of comity. According to WVU, the first-to-file rule dictates that the Court should stay or dismiss

* anticipatory lawsuit

this action, allowing the West Virginia case to proceed on its own. The Big East contends, however, that the West Virginia case was an anticipatory lawsuit, and this Court is not compelled to defer to the earlier-filed action.

There is an established rule in Rhode Island with respect to two actions in two courts within this state that "principles of comity shall control and the court whose jurisdiction in first invoked should resolve the issues presented to it." *Barone v. O'Connell*, 785 A.2d 534, 535 (R.I. 2001); *Lippman v. Kay*, 415 A.2d 728, 741 (R.I. 1980) (applying first to file rule with two courts of same state with concurrent jurisdiction); *Welsh v. Personnel Bd. Of Pawtucket*, 101 R.I. 187, 191 (1996) (same). However, there is very limited law in Rhode Island applying the first to file rule as between a case filed in a court in our state and another case filed in a court of a sister state.

This Court has acknowledged in the past a general rule of judicial discretion that a court may stay or dismiss proceedings when there is a prior case pending in another court of competent jurisdiction involving the same issues and the same parties. (citations omitted). This rule, as stated by this court, is "not a mechanical or inflexible rule." (citations omitted). Another Superior Court case held that "the pendency of an action in another state, even though filed prior to the action pending in Rhode Island is not a ground to abate the action in Rhode Island."

The general rule as between cases in two different states is that "[a] state may entertain an action even though an action on the same claim is pending in another state." Restatement (Second) *Conflict of Laws* § 86 (1971). In particular, the Restatement explains:

> Where there is a substantial likelihood the plaintiff will not be able to obtain complete relief in the first action, such as where it is unlikely to result in final judgment on the merits because of a procedural defect or where the exemption laws of the first state would preclude full satisfaction of plaintiff's claim ... the second action will be permitted to continue.

The Rhode Island Supreme Court, in considering abatement of one of two civil actions commenced in Rhode Island courts, employed an analogous rule. The *Pistauro* court explained that "if for any reason a prior pending action is so defective that there can be no recovery therein, or no such effectual recovery or relief as is sought and obtainable in the second action, the prior action is not ground for abating the subsequent one."

Our federal courts have agreed that "[t]he preference for the first-filed action is not a per se rule, but rather a policy governed by equitable considerations." "While the first-filed rule may ordinarily be a prudent one it is so only because it is sometimes more important that there be a rule than that the rule be particularly sound." *Nortek*, 36 F. Supp. 2d at 70. Undeniably, there are special circumstances that justify retaining the second or later-filed case. *See Feinstein*, 304 F. Supp. 2d at 283. Special circumstances must reflect a "balance of convenience" in favor of maintaining the second action. *Nortek*, 36 F. Supp. 2d at 70. The circumstances to consider include blatant forum shopping. *Id.*

When the first-filed case "is the result of a preemptive 'race to the courthouse,' a court may allow a later-filed case to proceed in place of the first-filed action." *Feinstein*, 304 F. Supp. 2d at 283 (citing *Cianbro Corp. v. Curran-Lavoie, Inc.*, 814 F.2d 7, 11 (1st Cir. 1987)). A "court may decline to follow the first-to-file rule and dismiss a declaratory judgment action if that action was filed for the purpose of anticipating a trial of the same issues in a court of coordinate jurisdiction." Where the first-filing party primarily sought a declaration of rights—even though it included the claims for fraud and duress—and the party filed in response to a demand, the first-filed action constituted an improper race to the courthouse, or an anticipatory suit. In determining if a lawsuit is anticipatory, courts have considered factors such as the notice to the plaintiff in the earlier-filed suit, the amount of time between the filing of the two suits, and the nature of the first suit. A declaratory judgment action including other courts that are "not independent claims but are intertwined" with the declaratory judgment claim may be considered an anticipatory lawsuit.

It is apparent that before applying the first-to-file rule as a matter of judicial discretion, the Court should consider whether the plaintiff of the second action could obtain complete relief in the first-filed case and whether the first-filed case was an improperly anticipatory lawsuit. As mentioned previously, this Court is not convinced the Big East would be afforded complete relief in the first-filed action in West Virginia.

Furthermore, the facts before this Court indicate that WVU's first-field lawsuit in West Virginia state court qualifies as an anticipatory action. In fact, that very complaint filed by WVU indicates that it expects the Big East will seek to enforce the Bylaws. The facts indicate that on October 28, 2011 the Commissioner of the Big East, John Marinatto, emailed the president of WVU, Jim Clements, stating that WVU had not sent a proper withdrawal notice, could not withdraw from the conference until June 30, 2014, and "[s]hould [WVU] refuse to abide by the Bylaws, the Conference reserves all of its rights to pursue appropriate recourse, including but not limited to the rights referenced in Article 11.02(b) of the Bylaws." Three days later, on October 31, 2011, WVU filed the West Virginia case, seeking declaratory judgment and permanent injunctive relief while also claiming breach of contract. Just four days later, the Big East filed the instant matter in this Court.

Admittedly on notice that the Big East would pursue remedies to enforce the terms of the Bylaws, WVU filed action in its home court. WVU's action is primarily an action for declaratory judgment. As in *Sutton*, where the party seeking to enforce the agreement was made a defendant in a declaratory judgment action, here the Big East seeks to enforce its Bylaws and would be the proper plaintiff in such an action.

This court is not required to defer based on principles of comity to a case filed four days prior. WVU, aware that the Big East may bring legal action, brought its own anticipatory action in West Virginia just days prior to the Big East's. This Court in its discretion denies WVU's motion to dismiss based on the first-to-file rule.

Notes and Problems

1. Do you agree with the court in the foregoing case that West Virginia's actions in anticipating the lawsuit from the Big East and quickly filing its own action was improper? If a litigant is threatened with litigation, must they simply take a passive stance waiting for a lawsuit to be filed sometime against them? If so, what is the purpose behind courts entertaining declaratory judgments by a litigant seeking the court's help in declaring parties' respective rights and obligations? What if the defendant is a corporation required to make public annual reports of its finances, including contingent liabilities? Must it simply list threatened lawsuits as contingent liabilities on its books (thus arguably reducing its perceived value) indefinitely?

2. Notice that the Rhode Island court above cites to both state and federal cases for the proposition that the first-to-file rule is discretionary and that improper races to the courthouse can trigger an exception to this rule. There is a rich body of caselaw involving

such scenarios, where a would-be defendant threatened with litigation runs to a nearby courthouse seeking to establish a more favorable forum to have the lawsuit resolved. Courts have gone both directions under slightly different circumstances. Part of these different results may arise from courts' different views on whether a race to the courthouse is improper. Other explanations for the difference might involve factors such as the time that has elapsed between the threat and the filing of the lawsuit or between the lapse of time in which the two cases are filed. In this regard, compare along with the *Big East* decision *Northwest Airlines v. American Airlines*, 989 F.2d 1002, 1006 (8th Cir. 1993) (court adhered to first-to-file rule when the threatened party waited six weeks after receiving demand letter before it filed its lawsuit seeking a declaration of non-liability with the court also noting that the threatened party's hiring practices were being chilled because of the lingering threats of litigation between the competitor companies), with *AmSouth Bank v. Dale*, 386 F.3d 763, 788–80 (6th Cir. 2004) (disregarding first-to-file rule after extensive review of case law where threatened company agreed to tolling agreement while parties pursued settlement discussions and then filed declaratory judgment suit against claimant). In sum, courts will consider the totality of the circumstances in considering if "compelling circumstances" exist that justify departure from the general first-to-file rule. A litigant with a possible claim for or against her needs to consider how to posture herself to be able to obtain a favorable forum and make it stick.

3. *Chapter Problem.* In light of the above discussion of the *Big East* case, make your best argument that PERI should be allowed to proceed with its own lawsuit in west Texas rather than have the first-to-file rule applied. How compelling is this argument?

3. A Federal Court vs. State Court

a. Departure from First-to-File

When the same or similar actions are filed before a combination of federal and state courts, the analysis changes — at least from the vantage point of the federal court. In addition to concerns over wise judicial administration, federal courts must consider issues of comity, federalism, and retaining their adjudicative power in instances where Congress has asked them to preside. The U.S. Supreme Court has admonished lower federal courts to be reluctant about refusing to adjudicate cases over which Congress has granted them jurisdictional power. As a result of this different attitude (and given the Anti-Injunction Act's general bar on a federal court enjoining a state court's proceeding despite duplicative litigation being involved),[3] one consequence is the very distinct possibility of both a federal and state court moving forward to resolve the same claim. In such a scenario, of course, whichever court first reaches a final judgment should then become res judicata in the other pending case, yet a serious inefficiency has occurred and perhaps other pre-trial inconsistent rulings have been handed down. In other words, federalism here comes at a price. The following cases introduce and apply in varying detail the abstention doctrine derived from the *Colorado River Water Conservation Dist. v. United States* case. Compare it to the rules of priority we encountered in the prior section. Is one approach better than the other?

---

3. The Anti-Injunction Act will be covered in greater detail later in this Chapter.

Life-Link International, Inc. v. Lalla

902 F.2d 1493 (10th Cir. 1990)

PER CURIAM.

Plaintiff, Life-Link International, Inc., appeals from an order of the district court dismissing this action with prejudice by virtue of duplicative proceedings pending in state court. We reverse the district court's order.

In February 1988, defendant Ozzie Lalla commenced an action in a Colorado state court against plaintiff for collection of a debt. Plaintiff counterclaimed for trademark infringement under 15 U.S.C. § 1114; false designation of origin under 15 U.S.C. § 1125(a); common law unfair competition, trademark infringement, and injury to business reputation; deceptive trade practices under Colo.Rev.Stat. § 6-1-105; and breach of contract.

In June 1988, plaintiff commenced this action in federal district court against defendants Ozzie Lalla and Nena Lalla. Nena Lalla is not a party in the state court action. Plaintiff alleged the same claims in this action as it raised in its state court counterclaim. Plaintiff also moved the state court to stay all proceedings, including discovery, pending completion of the federal action. In September 1988, the state court granted that motion. Defendants subsequently moved to dismiss the federal suit on the ground that plaintiff waived its right to invoke the jurisdiction of the federal court by asserting counterclaims in the state court action rather than removing that action to federal court. The district court granted defendants' motion, dismissing with prejudice. On appeal, plaintiff argues that the district court erred in dismissing its suit and further argues that even if this ruling was correct, dismissal with prejudice was error. Defendant argues only that the district court was correct in dismissing the case, agreeing that dismissal should have been without prejudice. We agree with plaintiff that the district court should not have dismissed this suit.

The district court dismissed this action on the ground asserted by defendants, citing *Paris v. Affleck,* 431 F.Supp. 878 (M.D.Fla.1977). But *Paris* was a removal case regarding whether claims could be concurrently litigated in two federal courts and, thus, is inapplicable to this case of concurrent litigation as between a state and a federal court. *See Colorado River Water Conservation Dist. v. United States,* 424 U.S. 800, 817, 96 S.Ct. 1236, 1246, 47 L.Ed.2d 483 (1976). And the Supreme Court has stated that "[t]his Court never has intimated acceptance of [the] view that the decision of a party to spurn removal and bring a separate suit in federal court invariably warrants the stay or dismissal of the suit under the *Colorado River* doctrine." *Gulfstream Aerospace Corp. v. Mayacamas Corp.,* 485 U.S. 271, 290, 108 S.Ct. 1133, 1144, 99 L.Ed.2d 296 (1988). Therefore, we must hold that the district court erred in dismissing this action solely on the grounds of waiver. So concluding, ordinarily we would remand to the district court with directions to apply the appropriate standard, since "the decision whether to defer to the state courts is necessarily left to the discretion of the district court in the first instance ... [and] such discretion must be exercised under the relevant standard." *Moses H. Cone Memorial Hosp. v. Mercury Constr. Corp.,* 460 U.S. 1, 19, 103 S.Ct. 927, 938, 74 L.Ed.2d 765 (1983). But we believe it would be an abuse of discretion to defer to the state court under the circumstances of this case.

A federal court may decline concurrent jurisdiction under the doctrine of abstention. The Supreme Court has identified three "exceptional circumstances" in which abstention is appropriate: (1) "a federal constitutional issue ... might be mooted or presented in a different posture by a state court determination of pertinent state law;" (2) the case presents "difficult questions of state law bearing on policy problems of substantial public import whose importance transcends the result in the case then at bar" or "exercise of federal review of the question in a case … would be disruptive of state efforts to establish a coherent policy with respect to a matter of substantial public concern;" or (3) "absent bad faith, harassment, or a patently invalid state statute, federal jurisdiction has been invoked for the purpose of restraining state criminal proceedings, state nuisance proceedings antecedent to a criminal prosecution … directed at obtaining the closure of places exhibiting obscene films, or collection of state taxes." *Colorado River,* 424 U.S. at 813–16, 96 S.Ct. at 1244–46 (citations omitted). As is evident from the dearth of discussion in the briefs, abstention cannot even arguably be justified here under any of these criteria. Nonetheless, our inquiry cannot stop here:

> Although this case falls within none of the abstention categories, there are principles unrelated to considerations of proper constitutional adjudication and regard for federal-state relations which govern in situations involving the contemporaneous exercise of concurrent jurisdictions. These principles rest on considerations of "[w]ise judicial administration, giving regard to conservation of judicial resources and comprehensive disposition of litigation."

Colorado River, 424 U.S. at 817, 96 S.Ct. at 1246 (quoting *Kerotest Mfg. Co. v. C-O-Two Fire Equip. Co.,* 342 U.S. 180, 183, 72 S.Ct. 219, 221, 96 L.Ed. 200 (1952)). Even so, we must keep in mind that "the circumstances permitting the dismissal of a federal suit due to the presence of a concurrent state proceeding for reasons of wise judicial administration are considerably more limited than the circumstances appropriate for abstention." *Id.* at 818, 96 S.Ct. at 1246. We must "ascertain whether there exist 'exceptional' circumstances, the 'clearest of justifications,' that can suffice under *Colorado River* to justify the *surrender* of … jurisdiction," *Cone,* 460 U.S. at 25–26, 103 S.Ct. at 942 (emphasis in original), "with the balance heavily weighted in favor of the exercise of jurisdiction," *id.* at 16, 103 S.Ct. at 937.

In Practice

These rules of priority *only apply to duplicative or parallel proceedings*, not to simply related cases. As courts have found, determining whether different proceedings are parallel involves asking whether they "arise out of the same facts" and involve essentially the same factual and legal issues between the same parties. *See, e.g., Interstate Material Corp. v. Chicago,* 847 F.2d 1285, 1288 (7th Cir. 1988) (in context of *Colorado River* abstention doctrine's application); *Zemsky v. New York,* 821 F.2d 148 (2d Cir. 1987) (refusing to consider cases duplicative when the parties were not identical because a stay of one case would not necessarily end piecemeal adjudication); *Fru-Con Construction Corp. v. Controlled Air, Inc.,* 574 F.3d 527, 535 (8th Cir. 2009) ("a substantial similarity must exist between [the two cases] which similarity occurs when there is a substantial likelihood that [one] proceeding will fully dispose of the claims presented [in the other]").

The Supreme Court has announced several factors that guide our analysis: (a) which court first assumed jurisdiction over any property; (b) the inconvenience of the federal forum; (c) the desirability of avoiding piecemeal litigation; and (d) the order in which concurrent jurisdiction was obtained. *Colorado River,* 424 U.S. at 818, 96 S.Ct. at 1246. We must also consider the adequacy of the state court proceedings to protect the parties' rights, *see Cone,* 460 U.S. at 28, 103 S.Ct. at 943, whether issues of federal law are presented, *id.* at 23–26, 103 S.Ct. at 941–42, and whether the attempt to invoke federal jurisdiction was done in bad faith, *id.* at 17 n. 20, 103 S.Ct. at 937 n. 20.

Neither court has jurisdiction over any property, and defendants concede that both forums are equally convenient. The state court action was commenced first. However, "priority should not be measured exclusively by which complaint was filed first, but rather in terms of how much progress has been made in the two actions." *Cone,* 460 U.S. at 21, 103 S.Ct. at 940. The only additional progress in the state court action appears to be some informal discovery, some formal discovery requests, and a scheduling conference at which the judge stayed the proceedings pending the outcome of this suit. So both actions seem to be at a standstill with no significant progress achieved. The case presents issues of both state and federal law. "Although in some rare circumstances the presence of state-law issues may weigh in favor of ... surrender, the presence of federal-law issues must always be a major consideration weighing against surrender." *Id.* at 26, 103 S.Ct. at 942. Defendants speculate that Nena Lalla was not joined in the state proceedings as justification for plaintiff's forum shopping. Appellee's Brief at 2. But plaintiff argues it might not be able to join Nena Lalla in state court because of improper venue, and therefore, piecemeal litigation and inadequate protection of its rights may result if a federal forum is unavailable. In view of the fact that the state court action has been stayed, there could be no piecemeal litigation or inadequate forum problems if the federal suit is continued.

Federal courts have a "virtually unflagging obligation ... to exercise the jurisdiction given them," *Colorado River,* 424 U.S. at 817, 96 S.Ct. at 1246, therefore, "[o]nly the clearest of justifications will warrant dismissal," *id.* at 819, 96 S.Ct. at 1247. Here, no factor clearly warrants dismissal, and several factors favor retention. Therefore, the district court should accept jurisdiction and hear this case on the merits. *Accord American Bankers Ins. Co. v. First State Ins. Co.,* 891 F.2d 882, 885–86 (11th Cir.1990); *Evanston Ins. Co. v. Jimco, Inc.,* 844 F.2d 1185, 1189–93 (5th Cir.1988); *Noonan South, Inc. v. County of Volusia,* 841 F.2d 380, 382–83 (11th Cir.1988).

The judgment of the United States District Court for the District of Colorado is REVERSED, and the case is REMANDED for further proceedings in accordance with this opinion.

Stewart v. W. Heritage Ins. Co.

438 F.3d 488 (5th Cir. 2006)

BENAVIDES, J.,

The parties ask this Court to determine whether the district court correctly stayed this lawsuit pending the outcome of a related state court proceeding. We hold that the lower court erred, and therefore REVERSE and REMAND.

FACTUAL AND PROCEDURAL BACKGROUND

The present case concerns a previous lawsuit in Mississippi state court. The plaintiffs in that suit claimed that Boardwalk Lounge, Inc. was responsible for the wrongful death of one of its patrons, Ryan Yates. Susie Pierce Stewart ("Appellee") is Boardwalk's sole shareholder, officer, and registered agent. Boardwalk was insured by Western Heritage Insurance Company ("Appellant"), who claims to have denied any obligation to defend or indemnify Boardwalk. No one defended the lawsuit and the plaintiffs took a default judgment of $1.4 million. Shortly thereafter, Boardwalk and the Appellee filed for bankruptcy.

On October 23, 2003, the Appellee filed this lawsuit alleging breach of insurance contract and bad faith in the United States District Court for the Southern District of

Mississippi. The case proceeded in federal court with the entry of a case management order followed by a motion for summary judgment filed by the Appellant. The discovery deadline expired in October 2004, and the court set a trial date of February 14, 2005.

Meanwhile, on July 6, 2004, the trustee for Boardwalk filed suit in the Circuit Court of Hinds County, Mississippi. The complaint named the Appellant, the Appellee, Phillip Dunn (an insurance agent), and others who were later dismissed from the suit. The state complaint mirrors the federal suit except that it also includes claims against the Appellee and Appellant for breach of fiduciary duty and claims against Dunn. The Appellant removed the case on grounds of improper joinder. The trustee moved to remand.

Following the commencement of the trustee's suit, the Appellee filed two separate motions to voluntarily dismiss this action. The Appellant opposed both. The Appellee also moved to join Dunn as a party. Additionally, the Appellant filed a motion to join Boardwalk's trustee as a necessary party to this case. The magistrate judge granted that motion and ordered the Appellee to serve the trustee with process. The trustee, however, has never been joined and is not a party to this action.[2] The court set a hearing on all pending motions and a pretrial conference for early February 2005. At the hearing, the court stayed the case pending a ruling on the remand motion in the trustee's suit. The two cases were before different judges.

On March 22, 2005, the trustee's suit was remanded on the grounds that Dunn had been properly joined. On March 31, 2005, the court in this case, acting *sua sponte*, entered an order that "terminated" all pending motions and stayed the case pending the resolution of the trustee's suit in Mississippi state court. The Appellant appeals that order.

DISCUSSION

We review a district court's decision to stay a case pending the outcome of parallel proceedings in state court for abuse of discretion. *Kelly Inv., Inc. v. Continental Common Corp.*, 315 F.3d 494, 497 (5th Cir. 2002). If the decision rests on an interpretation of law, our review is *de novo. Id.*

Principles

Some observers have been critical of the *Colorado River Abstention Doctrine*, referring to it as an "unwieldy six-factor balancing test" which is often difficult for lower courts to apply and encourages unnecessary duplication of efforts by state and federal courts. *See e.g.,* James C. Rehnquist, *Taking Comity Seriously: How to Neutralize the Abstention Doctrine*, 46 Stan. L. Rev. 1049, 1095 (1994).

A district court's decision to enter a permanent stay is governed by *Colorado River Water Conservation District v. United States*, 424 U.S. 800, 813, 96 S. Ct. 1236, 47 L. Ed. 2d 483 (1976). *Colorado River* applies when suits are parallel, having the same parties and the same issues. *Diamond Offshore Co. v. A&B Builders, Inc.*, 302 F.3d 531, 540 (5th Cir. 2002).[3] Under *Colorado River*, a district court may abstain from a case only under "exceptional circumstances." *Colorado River*, 424 U.S. at 813 (describing abstention as "an

---

2. The Appellee states that it never had an opportunity to join the trustee because the district court stayed the case.

3. If the suits are not parallel, the federal court must exercise jurisdiction. *Republicbank Dallas, N.A. v. McIntosh*, 828 F.2d 1120, 1121 (5th Cir. 1987).

extraordinary and narrow exception to the duty of a District Court to adjudicate a controversy properly before it").

In deciding whether "exceptional circumstances" exist, the Supreme Court identified six relevant factors:

> 1) assumption by either court of jurisdiction over a res, 2) relative inconvenience of the forums, 3) avoidance of piecemeal litigation, 4) the order in which jurisdiction was obtained by the concurrent forums, 5) to what extent federal law provides the rules of decision on the merits, and 6) the adequacy of the state proceedings in protecting the rights of the party invoking federal jurisdiction.

We do not apply these factors mechanically, but carefully balance them "with the balance heavily weighted in favor of the exercise of jurisdiction." *Moses H. Cone Mem'l Hosp. v. Mercury Constr. Corp.*, 460 U.S. 1, 16, 103 S. Ct. 927, 74 L. Ed. 2d 765 (1983). The balancing is done on a case-by-case basis.

The district court did not apply the *Colorado River* test when it stayed this case. Therefore, we review the factors for the first time on appeal. We assume, but do not decide, that the cases are parallel.

A. *Res* at Issue

Neither the state nor federal court has assumed jurisdiction over any *res* in this case. We have rejected the contention that the absence of this factor is "a neutral item, of no weight in the scales." *Evanston Ins. Co. v. Jimco, Inc.*, 844 F.2d 1185, 1191 (5th Cir. 1988). This factor supports exercising federal jurisdiction.

B. Inconvenience Between Forums

When courts are in the same geographic location, the inconvenience factor weighs against abstention. *Id.* at 738. Both the state and federal courthouses hearing these two cases are located in Jackson, Mississippi. This factor, therefore, supports exercising federal jurisdiction.

C. Avoidance of Piecemeal Litigation

The pendency of an action in state court does not bar a federal court from considering the same matter. *Bank One, N.A.*, 288 F.3d at 185. While duplicative litigation is permitted, *Colorado River* prevents "*piecemeal* litigation, and the concomitant danger of inconsistent rulings with respect to a piece of property." *Black Sea Inv. v. United Heritage Corp.*, 204 F.3d 647, 650–51. Again, no property is at issue in this case. The potential, however, does exist for some piecemeal litigating as the state court is the only forum hearing the breach of fiduciary duty claims and claims against Dunn. For the remaining issues, a plea of *res judicata* after the completion of one suit could eliminate the problem of inconsistent judgments. *Kelly Inv.*, 315 F.3d at 498. Nonetheless, as the litigation presently exists, the third factor favors abstention.[5]

D. The Order in Which Jurisdiction Was Obtained

The inquiry under this factor is "how much progress has been made in the two actions." *Murphy*, 168 F.3d at 738. The federal lawsuit progressed through an entire case management order, had a summary judgment motion pending at the time of the stay, and a trial date. With regard to the state proceeding, it is undisputed that no trial date exists, and the

---

5. While the current captions suggest that different parties exist, the record is clear that the magistrate intended to have the trustee joined and the Appellee is attempting to join Dunn. These efforts and the ability of the trustee to file a cross-claim could moot these piecemeal characteristics.

record suggests that little, if any, discovery has taken place. We have suggested that this factor only favors abstention when the federal case has not proceeded past the filing of the complaint. *Id.* Here, the case has clearly progressed further. For that reason, this factor favors federal jurisdiction.

E. The Extent Federal Law Governs the Case

"The presence of state law issues weighs in favor of surrender only in rare circumstances." *Black Sea Inv.*, 204 F.3d at 651 (reversing stay in case where state law governed). This case involves only issues of state law as it is being heard by the court under its diversity jurisdiction. Nonetheless, the Appellee has failed to show that "rare circumstances" exist. Therefore, this factor is "at most neutral." *Id.*

F. Adequacy of State Proceedings

The sixth factor is either a neutral factor or one that weighs against abstention. *Id.* The Appellant does not argue that the state court would not adequately adjudicate the case. Under *Black Sea*, therefore, this is a neutral factor.

CONCLUSION

With the exception of the factor considering "piecemeal litigation," all of the *Colorado River* factors weigh against abstention or remain neutral. Given that we must balance these in favor of the exercise of jurisdiction, abstention in this case is inappropriate. The facts do not overcome the "extraordinary and narrow exception" to the "virtually unflagging obligation of the federal courts to exercise the jurisdiction given them." *Colorado River*, 424 U.S. at 814, 817. Because abstention is prohibited by *Colorado River*, we need not address the Appellant's argument that the federal and state cases are not parallel.

For the reasons above, the district court abused its discretion in staying this case. Therefore, we REVERSE and REMAND for proceedings consistent with this opinion.

Notes and Problems

1. Does it seem fair or practical to allow a defendant to essentially choose the forum, something a plaintiff is generally entitled to do, by allowing the filing of multiple suits and a race to judgment?

2. After reading the *Life-Link* and *Stewart* cases, how would you compare the *Colorado River Abstention* doctrine with the first-filed rule we first saw earlier in this section? Why in the federal vs. state context does a different analytical format apply? Do you prefer one or the other? The reality is that under the *Colorado River* abstention doctrine, lower federal courts have not frequently abstained from hearing cases filed in their courts notwithstanding the fact that essentially identical suits were pending in state courts at the same time. When this occurs, unless the state court decides to stay its own hand (as the state court had done in *Life-Link*), there is nothing to stop the litigants from each pushing their own chosen case forward in a race to final judgment.

3. Does it appear that the principles of efficiency and fairness play any role when it comes to federal versus state duplicative suits? What role does the initial race to the courthouse play in this federal vs. state context? What role does the nature of the underlying causes of action play? Should this be a more important consideration given the principle of federalism? When a case is pending in the same city but different courts, why do you suppose the lawyers and litigants might care so much about which case takes priority?

4. The *Life-Link v. Lalla* court mentions other abstention doctrines (those described as inapplicable in the *Colorado River* quote). These doctrines also permit federal courts

to refuse to exercise jurisdiction granted by Congress under different circumstances unique to the duplicative proceeding phenomenon discussed here. *See, e.g., Younger v. Harris*, 401 U.S. 37 (1971) (concerned with federal courts' interference with ongoing state court criminal proceedings or state civil proceedings where the state had a strong interest in the lawsuit); *Burford v. Sun Oil Co.*, 319 U.S. 315 (1943) (federal court should avoid ruling on difficult questions of state law when the adequate state court review is still available and when federal review might be disruptive of state efforts to establish their own clear policy on important matters); *Railroad Comm'n v. Pullman*, 312 U.S. 496 (1941) (federal court should avoid resolving unsettled issues of state law in the context of federal constitutional issues when one interpretation of state law might avoid the thornier federal constitutional issue).

5. *Chapter Problem.* In response to the Dallas federal court lawsuit filed by Bresser against PERI, if PERI responds by filing its own case for fraud in state court against Bresser (presumably closer to home in west Texas), should the first-filed Dallas court proceed to hear the case or abstain under the *Colorado River* doctrine?

b. Federal Declaratory Judgment Act: A Different Standard?

The foregoing rules seem relatively straightforward, at least in terms of the general approaches in each of the various contexts covered above. But one remaining wrinkle remains. Decades prior to the U.S. Supreme Court's decision in the *Colorado River* case, it had handed down a decision regarding the federal declaratory judgment tool. In *Brillhart* a federal declaratory judgment action was pending at the same time as a state court lawsuit involving the same issues and parties. Despite the absence of "exceptional situations" as contemplated in *Colorado River*, the Supreme Court declared that a federal trial court has great discretion to decide whether to entertain a declaratory judgment suit at all and that dismissal of it might well be warranted as unnecessary when a parallel state court proceeding was also underway. The following more recent U.S. Supreme Court case answered the question—when parallel state and federal court cases are pending and the federal action is filed under the Declaratory Judgment Act, does *Colorado River* govern or *Brillhart*?

Wilton v. Seven Falls Co.

515 U.S. 277 (1995)

JUSTICE O'CONNOR delivered the opinion of the Court.

This case asks whether the discretionary standard set forth in *Brillhart v Excess Ins. Co. of America*, 316 U.S. 491 (1942) or the "exceptional circumstances" test developed in *Colorado River Water Conservation Dist. v. U.S.*, 424 U.S. 800 (1976), governs a district court's decision to stay a declaratory judgment action during the pendency of parallel state court proceedings, and under what standard of review a court of appeals should evaluate the district court's decision to do so.

ISSUE

In early 1992, a dispute between respondents (the Hill Group) and other parties over the ownership and operation of oil and gas properties in Winkler County, Texas, appeared likely to culminate in litigation. The Hill Group asked petitioners (London Underwriters) to provide them with coverage under several commercial liability insurance policies. London Underwriters refused to defend or indemnify the Hill Group in a letter dated July 31, 1992. In September 1992, after a 3-week trial, a Winkler County jury entered a verdict in excess of $100 million against the Hill Group on various state law claims.

The Hill Group gave London Underwriters notice of the verdict in late November 1992. On December 9, 1992, London Underwriters filed suit in the United States District Court for the Southern District of Texas, basing jurisdiction upon diversity of citizenship under 28 U.S.C. § 1332. London Underwriters sought a declaration under the Declaratory Judgment Act, 28 U.S.C. § 2201(a) (1988 ed., Supp. V), that their policies did not cover the Hill Group's liability for the Winkler County judgment. After negotiations with the Hill Group's counsel, London Underwriters voluntarily dismissed the action on January 22, 1993. London Underwriters did so, however, upon the express condition that the Hill Group give London Underwriters two weeks' notice if they decided to bring suit on the policy.

On February 23, 1993, the Hill Group notified London Underwriters of their intention to file such a suit in Travis County, Texas. London Underwriters refiled their declaratory judgment action in the Southern District of Texas on February 24, 1993. As promised, the Hill Group initiated an action against London Underwriters on March 26, 1993, in state court in Travis County. The Hill Group's codefendants in the Winkler County litigation joined in this suit and asserted claims against certain Texas insurers, thus rendering the parties nondiverse and the suit non-removable.

On the same day that the Hill Group filed their Travis County action, they moved to dismiss or, in the alternative, to stay London Underwriters' federal declaratory judgment action. After receiving submissions from the parties on the issue, the District Court entered a stay on June 30, 1993. The District Court observed that the state lawsuit pending in Travis County encompassed the same coverage issues raised in the declaratory judgment action and determined that a stay was warranted in order to avoid piecemeal litigation and to bar London Underwriters' attempts at forum shopping. London Underwriters filed a timely appeal.

The United States Court of Appeals for the Fifth Circuit affirmed. Noting that under Circuit precedent, "[a] district court has broad discretion to grant (or decline to grant) declaratory judgment," the Court of Appeals did not require application of the test articulated in *Colorado River* under which district courts must point to "exceptional circumstances" to justify staying or dismissing federal proceedings. Citing the interests in avoiding duplicative proceedings and forum shopping, the Court of Appeals reviewed the District Court's decision for abuse of discretion, and found none.

We granted certiorari to resolve Circuit conflicts concerning the standard governing a district court's decision to stay a declaratory judgment action in favor of parallel state litigation. We now affirm.

Over 50 years ago, in *Brillhart v. Exess Ins. Co. of America*, 316 U.S. 491 (1942), this Court addressed circumstances virtually identical to those present in the case before us today. An insurer, anticipating a coercive suit, sought a declaration in federal court of non-liability on an insurance policy. The District Court dismissed the action in favor of pending state garnishment proceedings, to which the insurer had been added as a defendant. The Court of Appeals reversed, finding an abuse of discretion, and ordered the District Court to proceed to the merits. Reversing the Court of Appeals and remanding to the District Court, this Court held that, "although the District Court had jurisdiction of the suit under the Federal Declaratory Judgments Act, it was under no compulsion to exercise that jurisdiction." The Court explained that "ordinarily it would be uneconomical as well as vexatious for a federal court to proceed in a declaratory judgment suit where another suit is pending in a state court presenting the same issues, not governed by federal law, between the same parties." The question for a district court presented with a suit under the Declaratory Judgment Act, the Court found, is "whether the questions in controversy between the parties to the federal suit, and which are not foreclosed under the applicable substantive law, can better be settled in the proceeding pending in the state court."

Brillhart makes clear that district courts possess discretion in determining whether and when to entertain an action under the Declaratory Judgment Act, even when the suit otherwise satisfies subject matter jurisdictional prerequisites. Although *Brillhart* did not set out an exclusive list of factors governing the district court's exercise of this discretion, it did provide some useful guidance in that regard. The Court indicated, for example, that in deciding whether to enter a stay, a district court should examine "the scope of the pending state court proceeding and the nature of defenses open there." This inquiry, in turn, entails consideration of "whether the claims of all parties in interest can satisfactorily be adjudicated in that proceeding, whether necessary parties have been joined, whether such parties are amenable to process in that proceeding, etc." Other cases, the Court noted, might shed light on additional factors governing a district court's decision to stay or to dismiss a declaratory judgment action at the outset. But *Brillhart* indicated that, at least where another suit involving the same parties and presenting opportunity for ventilation of the same state law issues is pending in state court, a district court might be indulging in "gratuitous interference," if it permitted the federal declaratory action to proceed.

Brillhart, without more, clearly supports the District Court's decision in this case. (That the court here stayed, rather than dismissed, the action is of little moment in this regard, because the state court's decision will bind the parties under principles of res judicata.) Nonetheless, London Underwriters argue, and several Courts of Appeals have agreed, that intervening case law has supplanted *Brillhart*'s notions of broad discretion with a test under which district courts may stay or dismiss actions properly within their jurisdiction only in "exceptional circumstances." In London Underwriters' view, recent cases have established that a district court must point to a compelling reason—which, they say, is lacking here—in order to stay a declaratory judgment action in favor of pending state proceedings. To evaluate this argument, it is necessary to examine three cases handed down several decades after *Brillhart.*

In *Colorado River Water Conservation Dist. v. United States,* 424 U.S. 800 (1976), the Government brought an action in Federal District Court under 28 U.S.C. §1345 seeking a declaration of its water rights, the appointment of a water master, and an order enjoining all uses and diversions of water by other parties. The District Court dismissed the action in deference to ongoing state proceedings. The Court of Appeals reversed, on the ground that the District Court had jurisdiction over the Government's suit and that abstention was inappropriate. This Court reversed again. Without discussing *Brillhart,* the Court began with the premise that federal courts have a "virtually unflagging obligation" to exercise the jurisdiction conferred on them by Congress. The Court determined, however, that a district court could nonetheless abstain from the assumption of jurisdiction over a suit in "exceptional" circumstances, and it found such exceptional circumstances on the facts of the case. Specifically, the Court deemed dispositive a clear federal policy against piecemeal adjudication of water rights; the existence of an elaborate state scheme for resolution of such claims; the absence of any proceedings in the District Court, other than the filing of the complaint, prior to the motion to dismiss; the extensive nature of the suit; the 300-mile distance between the District Court and the situs of the water district at issue; and the prior participation of the Federal Government in related state proceedings.

In *Moses H. Cone Memorial Hospital v. Mercury Constr. Corp.,* 460 U.S. 1 (1983), this Court rejected any argument that *Brillhart* might have application beyond the context of declaratory judgments. In *Moses H. Cone,* the Court established that the *Colorado River* "exceptional circumstances" test, rather than the more permissive *Brillhart* analysis, governs a district court's decision to stay a suit to compel arbitration under § 4 of the Arbitration Act in favor of pending state litigation. [Outside of the invocation of the federal Declaratory Judgment Act context,] "[a]bdication of the obligation to decide cases," the Court reasoned, "'can be justified ... only in the exceptional circumstance where the order to the parties to repair to the State court would clearly serve an important countervailing interest.'" As it had in *Colorado River,* the Court articulated nonexclusive factors relevant to the existence of such exceptional circumstances, including the assumption by either court of jurisdiction over a res, the relative convenience of the fora, avoidance of piecemeal litigation, the order in which jurisdiction was obtained by the concurrent fora, whether and to what extent federal law provides the rules of decision on the merits, and the adequacy of state proceedings. Evaluating each of these factors, the Court concluded that the District Court's stay of federal proceedings was, under the circumstances, inappropriate.

Relying on post-*Brillhart* developments, London Underwriters contend that the *Brillhart* regime, under which district courts have substantial latitude in deciding whether to stay or to dismiss a declaratory judgment suit in light of pending state proceedings (and need not point to "exceptional circumstances" to justify their actions), is an outmoded relic of another era. We disagree. Neither *Colorado River,* which upheld the dismissal of federal proceedings, nor *Moses H. Cone,* which did not, dealt with actions brought under the Declaratory Judgment Act, 28 U.S.C. § 2201(a) (1988 ed., Supp. V). Distinct features of the Declaratory Judgment Act, we believe, justify a standard vesting district courts with greater discretion in declaratory judgment actions than that permitted under the "exceptional circumstances" test of *Colorado River* and *Moses H. Cone.* No subsequent case, in our view, has called into question the application of the *Brillhart* standard to the *Brillhart* facts.

Since its inception, the Declaratory Judgment Act has been understood to confer on federal courts unique and substantial discretion in deciding whether to declare the rights of litigants. On its face, the statute provides that a court "*may* declare the rights and other legal relations of any interested party seeking such declaration," 28 U.S.C. § 2201(a) (1988 ed., Supp. V) (emphasis added). *See generally* E. Borchard, Declaratory Judgments 312–314 (2d ed. 1941); Borchard, *Discretion to Refuse Jurisdiction of Actions for Declaratory Judgments,* 26 Minn. L. Rev. 677 (1942). The statute's textual commitment to discretion, and the breadth of leeway we have always understood it to suggest, distinguish the declaratory judgment context from other areas of the law in which concepts of discretion surface. We have repeatedly characterized the Declaratory Judgment Act as "an enabling Act, which confers a discretion on the courts rather than an absolute right upon the litigant." *Public Serv. Comm'n of Utah v. Wycoff Co.,* 344 U.S. 237, 241 (1952); *Cardinal Chemical Co. v. Morton Int'l, Inc.* 508 U.S. 83, 95 n. 17 (1993). When all is said and done, we have concluded, "the propriety of declaratory relief in a particular case will depend upon a circumspect sense of its fitness informed by the teachings and experience concerning the functions and extent of federal judicial power." *Wycoff* at 243.

Acknowledging, as they must, the unique breadth of this discretion to decline to enter a declaratory judgment, London Underwriters nonetheless contend that, after *Colorado River* and *Moses H. Cone,* district courts lack discretion to decline to hear a declaratory judgment suit at the outset. See Brief for Petitioners 22 ("District courts *must* hear declaratory judgment cases absent exceptional circumstances; district courts *may* decline to enter the requested relief following a full trial on the merits, if no beneficial purpose is thereby served or if equity otherwise counsels"). We are not persuaded by this distinction. London Underwriters' argument depends on the untenable proposition that a district court, knowing at the commencement of litigation that it will exercise its broad statutory discretion to decline declaratory relief, must nonetheless go through the futile exercise of hearing a case on the merits first. Nothing in the language of the Declaratory Judgment Act recommends London Underwriters' reading, and we are unwilling to impute to Congress an intention to require such a wasteful expenditure of judicial resources. If a district court, in the sound exercise of its judgment, determines after a complaint is filed that a declaratory judgment will serve no useful purpose, it cannot be incumbent upon that court to proceed to the merits before staying or dismissing the action.

We agree, for all practical purposes, with Professor Borchard, who observed half a century ago that "there is … nothing automatic or obligatory about the assumption of 'jurisdiction' by a federal court" to hear a declaratory judgment action. Borchard, Declaratory Judgments, at 313. By the Declaratory Judgment Act, Congress sought to place a remedial arrow in the district court's quiver; it created an opportunity, rather than a duty, to grant a new form of relief to qualifying litigants. Consistent with the nonobligatory nature of the remedy, a district court is authorized, in the sound exercise of its discretion, to stay or to dismiss an action seeking a declaratory judgment before trial or after all arguments have drawn to a close.[2] In the declaratory judgment context, the normal principle that federal courts should adjudicate claims within their jurisdiction yields to considerations of practicality and wise judicial administration.

As Judge Friendly observed, the Declaratory Judgment Act "does not speak," on its face, to the question whether discretion to entertain declaratory judgment actions is vested in district courts alone or in the entire judicial system. The Court of Appeals reviewed the District Court's decision to stay London Underwriters' action for abuse of discretion, and found none. London Underwriters urge us to follow those other Courts of Appeals that review decisions to grant (or to refrain from granting) declaratory relief *de novo*. We decline this invitation. We believe it more consistent with the statute to vest district courts with discretion in the first instance, because facts bearing on the usefulness of the declaratory judgment remedy, and the fitness of the case for resolution, are peculiarly within their grasp. While it may be true that sound administration of the Declaratory Judgment Act calls for the exercise of "judicial discretion, hardened by experience into rule," Borchard, Declaratory Judgments, at 293, proper application of the abuse of discretion standard on appellate review can, we think, provide appropriate guidance to district courts. In this regard, we reject London Underwriters' suggestion that review for abuse of discretion "is tantamount to no review" at all.

In sum, we conclude that *Brillhart* governs this declaratory judgment action and that district courts' decisions about the propriety of hearing declaratory judgment actions, which are necessarily bound up with their decisions about the propriety of granting declaratory relief, should be reviewed for abuse of discretion. We do not attempt at this time to delineate the outer boundaries of that discretion in other cases, for example, cases raising issues of federal law or cases in which there are no parallel state proceedings. Like the Court of Appeals, we conclude only that the District Court acted within its bounds in staying this action for declaratory relief where parallel proceedings, presenting

---

2. We note that where the basis for declining to proceed is the pendency of a state proceeding, a stay will often be the preferable course, because it assures that the federal action can proceed without risk of a time bar if the state case, for any reason, fails to resolve the matter in controversy. See, *e.g.,* P. Bator, D. Meltzer, P. Mishkin, & D. Shapiro, Hart and Wechsler's The Federal Courts and the Federal System 1451, n. 9 (3d ed. 1988).

opportunity for ventilation of the same state law issues, were underway in state court. The judgment of the Court of Appeals for the Fifth Circuit is *Affirmed.*

Notes and Problems

1. Did you agree with the Supreme Court's decision that *Colorado River* has no application in the context of the *Wilton* case? Given that ruling, if a would-be defendant anticipates and wins a race to the courthouse to fix the forum by asserting a declaratory judgment lawsuit, would the actual claimant (who threatened litigation in the first place) be better off to file their own parallel lawsuit in a state or a federal court? Or does it matter? If threatened with litigation, and to avoid the *Wilton* holding above, would it be advantageous for the threatened defendant to assert an affirmative claim for relief in the first-filed federal forum rather than just a declaratory judgment action?

2. One other parallel case context we have not considered is how a court in the United States should react to a parallel judicial proceeding between the same parties in a foreign court. There has been no consistent approach yet to this phenomenon. For a good discussion of this situation and the possible answers, see Jocelyn H. Bush, *To Abstain or Not to Abstain: A New Framework for Application of the Abstention Doctrine in International Parallel Proceedings*, 58 American L. Rev. 128, 129–30 (2008) ("At present, federal courts, due to a lack of Supreme Court guidance and no relevant statutory authority, do not uniformly apply one analysis to determine the outcome of such a motion. The lack of uniformity has made the issue of international parallel litigation one of the most unsettled areas of law involving federal jurisdiction in the United States.").

3. An interesting wrinkle to the *Wilton* holding arises when the federal lawsuit includes not just a defensive declaratory judgment request but also contains an additional affirmative or "coercive" claim for relief. Some circuits have held that, whether *Wilton/Brillhart* or *Colorado River* applies might depend upon the extent to which the affirmative claim is "independent" of the declaratory judgment claim. *See Government Employees Ins. v. Dizol*, 133 F.3d 1220, 1226 n. 6 (9th Cir. 1998) (court needs to inquire whether there are "claims in the case that exist independent of any request for purely declaratory relief, that is, claims that would continue to exist if the request for declaration simply dropped from the case"); *R.R. Street & Co., Inc. v. Vulcan Materials Co.* 569 F.3d 711 (7th Cir. 2009) (adopting the 9th Circuit's "independent claim" test and finding that the *Wilton* analysis was inappropriate and that under the *Colorado River* doctrine the district court's dismissal of the federal action was erroneous).

4. *Chapter Problem*. PERI responds to the would-be defendant Bresser's federal declaratory judgment lawsuit in the Dallas action by filing its own state court lawsuit as a mirror image to the first case. Under the guidance from the *Wilton* case above, how should the Dallas federal court respond if PERI moves to dismiss the federal case? Does it matter if the Bresser lawsuit includes, in addition to the count seeking a declaration of non-liability to PERI, a claim for business disparagement based upon PERI's now public accusations of misconduct by Bresser? On the other hand, if Bresser simultaneously files a motion to stay in the west Texas state court, how will that court likely rule?

Upon Further Review

Parties frequently will attempt to beat another party to the courthouse with their lawsuit, in order to attempt to fix the best forum to resolve their dispute. Courts generally are not excited about the inefficiencies that result with such a multiplicity of duplicative claims — claims that generally arise out of the same transaction or occurrence with roughly the same parties and mirror images of one another. The beauty of the *first-to-file* rule is its simplicity and ease of application. It also rewards the litigant that showed the most initiative and discourages dilatory delay in filing lawsuits. On the other hand, like many other general rules, considerations of fairness sometimes dictate a departure from its strict application. When most of the witnesses and parties and sources of proof are found in a different venue, these overwhelming convenience factors sometimes justify such a departure. Or when the court is uneasy with the first rush to the courthouse — perhaps by a threatened party who misled the other into believing they were going to settle the case — it might depart from the rule. Also, sometimes issues of federalism convince federal courts that the federal principle of adjudicating claims given to them by Congress override a mirror-image case pending in a state court.

D. Transfer of Venue and *Forum Non Conveniens*

Another way for a litigant to challenge the plaintiff's chosen forum (aside from trying to win a race to a different courthouse) is to ask the originally chosen forum to consider *transferring* the case to a more "convenient" forum. Obviously doing so would overrule the autonomy normally given to the plaintiff to choose (within jurisdictional and venue limits) their own preferred forum. How to weigh these considerations of autonomy and fairness highlight the contours of the 28 U.S.C. § 1404(a) inquiry. This analysis involves consideration of various public and private interest factors while giving appropriate weight to the plaintiff's original choice. The following two cases illustrate the typical analysis. The first case, *Ginsey*, focuses more upon public factors that favor transfer and the second case, *Volkswagen*, engages in a much more thorough consideration of many public and private interest factors in ruling on the requested transfers.

28 U.S.C. § 1404(a)

"For the convenience of parties and witnesses, in the interest of justice, a district court may transfer any civil action to any other district or division where it might have been brought or to any district or division to which all parties have consented."

1. § 1404(a) Public Interest Factors

Ginsey Industries, Inc. v. I.T.K. Plastics, Inc.

545 F. Supp. 78 (E.D. Pa. 1982)

POLLAK, J.,

Plaintiff, Ginsey Industries, is a Pennsylvania corporation with its principal place of business in Bellmahr, New Jersey, and defendant, I.T.K. Plastics, is a Massachusetts

facts

corporation with its principal place of business in Salem, Massachusetts. In the fall of 1981, plaintiff purchased vinyl plastic sheeting manufactured by defendant. After receiving shipment of the plastic, Ginsey determined that the plastic was not, in its view, fit for the purpose for which it was sold. Ginsey then filed this action to recover the payment it made to I.T.K. as well as consequential damages. This matter is now before the court on defendant's motion to dismiss for lack of personal jurisdiction or, in the alternative, for transfer to the District of Massachusetts.

I.T.K. first contends that its limited contact with this forum is insufficient to bring it within the reach of Pennsylvania's long-arm statute, 42 Pa.C.S.A. § 5301 et seq., or to satisfy the due process standards set forth in *International Shoe Co. v. Washington*, 326 U.S. 310, 316, 66 S.Ct. 154, 158, 90 L.Ed. 95 (1945). Alternatively, I.T.K. argues that transfer to the District of Massachusetts is warranted since a civil action involving the same parties and the same plastic products is currently pending there. In response, plaintiff has not come forward with any specific evidence to support this court's exercise of in personam jurisdiction over I.T.K. but has instead urged that if transfer is considered appropriate this case should be transferred to the District of New Jersey rather than the District of Massachusetts.

On the basis of the record as it now stands, it seems clear that I.T.K.'s connection with Pennsylvania is so tenuous that this court lacks a proper basis to exercise in personam jurisdiction. Perhaps further discovery might reveal some basis for linking I.T.K. to that forum but plaintiff has not sought to pursue this possibility. However, rather than simply dismissing plaintiff's complaint at this point, the better approach, in my view, would be to transfer this matter to a more appropriate forum. See *United States v. Berkowitz*, 328 F.2d 358, 361 (3d Cir.), cert. denied, 379 U.S. 821, 85 S.Ct. 42, 13 L.Ed.2d 32 (1964); *Shong Ching Lau v. Change*, 415 F.Supp. 627, 632 (E.D.Pa.1976).[4]

In considering a motion to transfer, a court must first determine that the transferee district is a district where the action "might have been brought." 28 U.S.C. § 1404(a); *Hoffman v. Blaski*, 363 U.S. 335, 80 S.Ct. 1084, 4 L.Ed.2d 1254 (1960). This criterion, however, does not provide any clear guidance in determining which of the two proposed transferee districts—New Jersey or Massachusetts—is more appropriate since both appear to be districts where plaintiff's claim could have been brought. Both courts clearly have jurisdiction over the subject matter of this case under 28 U.S.C. § 1332 by virtue of the diversity of citizenship of the parties, and both courts may properly exercise in personam jurisdiction over I.T.K. because of I.T.K.'s contacts with New Jersey and its residence in Massachusetts. Venue would also be proper in both districts under 28 U.S.C. § 1391(a).

I turn therefore to the more difficult question whether the balance of convenience weighs decisively in favor of one of the proposed districts. It is well-settled that "unless the balance is strongly in favor of the defendant, the plaintiff's choice of forum should rarely be disturbed." *Gulf Oil Corp. v. Gilbert*, 330 U.S. 501, 508, 67 S.Ct. 839, 843, 91 L.Ed. 1055 (1947). *See Shutte v. Armco Steel Corp.*, 431 F.2d 22, 25 (3d Cir. 1970). Therefore, since the District of New Jersey is clearly plaintiff's preferred alternative forum, that preference must be accorded substantial weight.

---

4. In *Goldlawr, Inc. v. Heiman*, 369 U.S. 463, 82 S.Ct. 913, 8 L.Ed.2d 39 (1962), the Court, over Justice Harlan's dissent, construed 28 U.S.C. § 1406(a) to authorize a district court to transfer to a proper district a case filed in a district where venue is improper, notwithstanding that the transferor court lacks in personam jurisdiction. In *United States v. Berkowitz, supra*, our Court of Appeals extended the *Goldlawr* rationale to § 1404(a).

On the opposing scale, as defendant properly suggests, must be placed the interest in efficient judicial administration which might be advanced by transfer to the District of Massachusetts where an action involving the same parties is pending. By permitting two related cases which are filed initially in different districts to be consolidated, transfer plainly helps avoid needless duplication of effort. For as Justice Black remarked in *Continental Grain Co. v. Barge FBL-585*, 364 U.S. 19, 26, 80 S.Ct. 1470, 1474, 4 L.Ed.2d 1540 (1960): "To permit a situation in which two cases involving precisely the same issues are simultaneously pending in different District Courts leads to the wastefulness of time, energy and money that § 1404(a) was designed to prevent." *See also Celanese Corp. v. Federal Energy Admin.*, 410 F.Supp. 571, 575–77 (D.D.C.1976); *Thomas v. United States Lines, Inc.*, 371 F.Supp. 429, 432–33 (E.D.Pa.1974).

This consideration, of course, loses some of its force where the two pending actions do not stem from precisely the same transaction. A comparison of the complaints filed in Massachusetts and in this action reveals that the actions involve distinct, albeit related, transactions: the Massachusetts allegations speak of an August, 1981 purchase of vinyl plastic valued at $14,000 which Ginsey allegedly failed to pay for; whereas the Pennsylvania claims describe an October or November, 1981 transaction involving a $30,000 payment by Ginsey for vinyl plastic which was rejected as defective. Nevertheless, it would appear that significant economies of time and effort can be achieved if these actions were consolidated in a single district. The essential questions of liability in both actions concern the fitness of I.T.K.'s vinyl products for the commercial purposes Ginsey sought to pursue. The witnesses who will testify about I.T.K.'s product and about Ginsey's reasons for purchasing that product are likely to be the same in both cases. To be sure, consolidation of these actions in the District of Massachusetts imposes a burden on Ginsey. But transfer to that district would, in my judgment, promote efficient judicial administration to such an extent that plaintiff's preference for New Jersey is outweighed. And consolidation ultimately benefits both parties since it is clearly more convenient to conduct related litigation in a single district rather than in two separate forums.

Accordingly, I will order that this matter be transferred to the District of Massachusetts.

2. § 1404(a) Private Interest Factors

In re Volkswagen of America, Inc.

545 F.3d 304 (5th Cir. 2008)

JOLLY, J.,

The overarching question before the *en banc* Court is whether a writ of mandamus should issue directing the transfer of this case from the Marshall Division of the Eastern District of Texas—which has no connection to the parties, the witnesses, or the facts of this case—to the Dallas Division of the Northern District of Texas—which has extensive connections to the parties, the witnesses, and the facts of this case. We grant the petition and direct the district court to transfer this case to the Dallas Division.

I.

On the morning of May 21, 2005, a Volkswagen Golf automobile traveling on a freeway in Dallas, Texas, was struck from behind and propelled rear-first into a flat-bed trailer parked on the shoulder of the freeway. Ruth Singleton was driving the Volkswagen Golf. Richard Singleton was a passenger. And Mariana Singleton, Richard and Ruth Singleton's

facts

seven-year-old granddaughter, was also a passenger. Richard Singleton was seriously injured in the accident. Mariana Singleton was also seriously injured in the accident, and she later died as a result of her injuries.

Richard Singleton, Ruth Singleton, and Amy Singleton (Mariana's mother) filed suit against Volkswagen AG and Volkswagen of America, Inc., in the Marshall Division of the Eastern District of Texas, alleging that design defects in the Volkswagen Golf caused Richard's injuries and Mariana's death.

In response to the Singletons' suit, Volkswagen filed a third-party complaint against the driver of the automobile that struck the Singletons, alleging that the Singletons had the ability to sue him but did not and that his negligence was the only proximate cause of the damages.

Pursuant to 28 U.S.C. §1404(a), Volkswagen moved to transfer venue to the Dallas Division. Volkswagen asserted that a transfer was warranted as the Volkswagen Golf was purchased in Dallas County, Texas; the accident occurred on a freeway in Dallas, Texas; Dallas residents witnessed the accident; Dallas police and paramedics responded and took action; a Dallas doctor performed the autopsy; the third-party defendant lives in Dallas County, Texas; none of the plaintiffs live in the Marshall Division; no known party or non-party witness lives in the Marshall Division; no known source of proof is located in the Marshall Division; and none of the facts giving rise to this suit occurred in the Marshall Division. These facts are undisputed.

The district court denied Volkswagen's transfer motion. Volkswagen then filed a motion for reconsideration, arguing that the district court gave inordinate weight to the plaintiffs' choice of venue and, to state Volkswagen's arguments generally, that the district court failed meaningfully to weigh the venue transfer factors. The district court also denied Volkswagen's motion for reconsideration, and for the same reasons presented in its denial of Volkswagen's transfer motion.

Volkswagen then petitioned this Court for a writ of mandamus. In a *per curiam* opinion, a divided panel of this Court denied the petition and declined to issue a writ. The panel majority held that the district court did not clearly abuse its discretion in denying Volkswagen's transfer motion. Judge Garza wrote a dissenting opinion and in it noted that "[t]he only connection between this case and the Eastern District of Texas is plaintiffs' choice to file there; *all* other factors relevant to transfer of venue weigh overwhelmingly in favor of the Northern District of Texas." (Garza, J., dissenting).

Volkswagen then filed a petition for rehearing *en banc*. The original panel interpreted the petition for rehearing *en banc* as a petition for panel rehearing, granted it, withdrew its decision, and directed the Clerk's Office to schedule the petition for oral argument. A second panel of this Court then heard oral argument on the issues raised for review. The second panel granted Volkswagen's petition and issued a writ directing the district court to transfer this case to the Dallas Division. The Singletons then filed a petition for rehearing *en banc*, which the Court granted. *In re Volkswagen of Am., Inc.*, 517 F.3d 785 (5th Cir. 2008).

II.

Because some suggestion is made that mandamus is an inappropriate means to test the district court's discretion in ruling on venue transfers, we will first turn our attention to this subject. [The court held that mandamus was an appropriate tool to test a district court's abuse of discretion in ruling on transfer orders. It is considered an exceptional appellate tool and is only appropriate where the district court has engaged in an "usurpation of power or a clear abuse of discretion."]

Admittedly, the distinction between an abuse of discretion and a clear abuse of discretion cannot be sharply defined for all cases. As a general matter, a court's exercise of its discretion is not unbounded; that is, a court must exercise its discretion within the bounds set by relevant statutes and relevant, binding precedents. "A district court abuses its discretion if it: (1) relies on clearly erroneous factual findings; (2) relies on erroneous conclusions of law; or (3) misapplies the law to the facts." *McClure v. Ashcroft*, 335 F.3d 404, 408 (5th Cir. 2003) (citation omitted). On mandamus review, we review for these types of errors, but we only will grant mandamus relief when such errors produce a patently erroneous result.

III.

There can be no question but that the district courts have "broad discretion in deciding whether to order a transfer." *Balawajder v. Scott*, 160 F.3d 1066, 1067 (5th Cir. 1998) (quoting *Caldwell v. Palmetto State Sav. Bank*, 811 F.2d 916, 919 (5th Cir. 1987)). But this discretion has limitations imposed by the text of § 1404(a) and by the precedents of the Supreme Court and of this Court that interpret and apply the text of § 1404(a). But— and we stress—in no case will we replace a district court's exercise of discretion with our own; we review only for clear abuses of discretion that produce patently erroneous results. We therefore turn to examine the district court's exercise of its discretion in denying Volkswagen's transfer motion.

The preliminary question under § 1404(a) is whether a civil action "might have been brought" in the destination venue. Volkswagen seeks to transfer this case to the Dallas Division of the Northern District of Texas. All agree that this civil action originally could have been filed in the Dallas Division. *See* 28 U.S.C. § 1391.

Beyond this preliminary and undisputed question, the parties sharply disagree. The first disputed issue is whether the district court erred by giving inordinate weight to the plaintiffs' choice of venue. We have noted earlier that there is nothing that ties this case to the Marshall Division except plaintiffs' choice of venue. It has indeed been suggested that this statutorily granted choice is inviolable. A principal disputed question, then, is what role does a plaintiff's choice of venue have in the venue transfer analysis? We now turn to address this question.

When no special, restrictive venue statute applies, the general venue statute, 28 U.S.C. § 1391, controls a plaintiff's choice of venue. Under § 1391(a)(1), a diversity action may be brought in "a judicial district where any defendant resides, if all defendants reside in the same State." Under § 1391(c), when a suit is filed in a multi-district state, like Texas, a corporation is "deemed to reside in any district in that State within which its contacts would be sufficient to subject it to personal jurisdiction if that district were a separate State." Because large corporations, like Volkswagen, often have sufficient contacts to satisfy the requirement of § 1391(c) for most, if not all, federal venues, the general venue statute "has the effect of nearly eliminating venue restrictions in suits against corporations." 14D Wright, Miller & Cooper, *Federal Practice & Procedure* § 3802 (3d ed. 2007) (noting also that, because of the liberal, general venue statute, "many venue disputes now are litigated as motions to transfer venue under Section 1404 of Title 28").

Congress, however, has tempered the effects of this general venue statute by enacting the venue transfer statute, 28 U.S.C. § 1404. The underlying premise of § 1404(a) is that courts should prevent plaintiffs from abusing their privilege under § 1391 by subjecting defendants to venues that are inconvenient under the terms of § 1404(a). *See Norwood v. Kirkpatrick*, 349 U.S. 29, 75 S. Ct. 544, 99 L. Ed. 789 (1955); *cf. Gulf Oil Corp. v. Gilbert,*

330 U.S. 501, 507, 67 S. Ct. 839, 91 L. Ed. 1055 (1947) ("[The general venue] statutes are drawn with a necessary generality and usually give a plaintiff a choice of courts.... But the open door may admit those who seek not simply justice but perhaps justice blended with some harassment."). Thus, while a plaintiff has the privilege of filing his claims in any judicial division appropriate under the general venue statute, § 1404(a) tempers the effects of the exercise of this privilege.

With this understanding of the competing statutory interests, we turn to the legal precedents. We first turn to *Gilbert* because of its historic and precedential importance to § 1404(a), even today.

In 1947, in *Gilbert*, the Supreme Court firmly established in the federal courts the common-law doctrine of *forum non conveniens*. *See Piper Aircraft Co. v. Reyno*, 454 U.S. 235, 248, 102 S. Ct. 252, 70 L. Ed. 2d 419 (1981) (noting that "the doctrine of *forum non conveniens* was not fully crystallized" until *Gilbert*). The essence of the *forum non conveniens* doctrine is that a court may decline jurisdiction and may actually dismiss a case, even when the case is properly before the court, if the case more conveniently could be tried in another forum. *Gilbert*, 330 U.S. at 507.

Shortly after the *Gilbert* decision, in 1948, the venue transfer statute became effective. The essential difference between the *forum non conveniens* doctrine and § 1404(a) is that under § 1404(a) a court does not have authority to dismiss the case; the remedy under the statute is simply a transfer of the case within the federal system to another federal venue more convenient to the parties, the witnesses, and the trial of the case. Thus, as the Supreme Court has said, "Congress, by the term 'for the convenience of parties and witnesses, in the interest of justice,' intended to permit courts to grant transfers upon a lesser showing of inconvenience." *Norwood*, 349 U.S. at 32.[8]

That § 1404(a) venue transfers may be granted "upon a lesser showing of inconvenience" than *forum non conveniens* dismissals, however, does not imply "that the relevant factors [from the *forum non conveniens* context] have changed or that the plaintiff's choice of [venue] is not to be considered." *Id.*[9] But it does imply that the burden that a moving party must meet to justify a venue transfer is less demanding than that a moving party must meet to warrant a *forum non conveniens* dismissal. And we have recognized as much, noting that the "heavy *burden* traditionally imposed upon defendants by the *forum non conveniens* doctrine — dismissal permitted only in favor of a substantially more convenient

---

8. The district courts are permitted to grant transfers upon a lesser showing of inconvenience under § 1404(a) because § 1404(a) venue transfers do not have the serious consequences of *forum non conveniens* dismissals. *See Norwood*, 349 U.S. at 31 ("'The *forum non conveniens* doctrine is quite different from Section 1404(a). That doctrine involves the dismissal of a case because the forum chosen by the plaintiff is so completely inappropriate and inconvenient that it is better to stop the litigation in the place where brought and let it start all over again somewhere else. It is quite naturally subject to careful limitation for it not only denies the plaintiff the generally accorded privilege of bringing an action where he chooses, but makes it possible for him to lose out completely, through the running of the statute of limitations in the forum finally deemed appropriate. Section 1404(a) avoids this latter danger.'" (quoting *All States Freight v. Modarelli*, 196 F.2d 1010, 1011 (3d Cir. 1952))); *Van Dusen v. Barrack*, 376 U.S. 612, 639, 84 S. Ct. 805, 11 L. Ed. 2d 945 (1964) (holding that a "change of venue under § 1404(a) generally should be, with respect to state law, but a change of courtrooms"); *Ferens v. John Deere Co.*, 494 U.S. 516, 519, 110 S. Ct. 1274, 108 L. Ed. 2d 443 (1990) (applying the *Van Dusen* rule when a plaintiff moves for transfer).

9. Indeed, we have adopted the *Gilbert* factors, which were enunciated in *Gilbert* for determining the *forum non conveniens* question, for determining the § 1404(a) venue transfer question. *See Humble Oil & Ref. Co. v. Bell Marine Serv., Inc.*, 321 F.2d 53, 56 (5th Cir. 1963).

alternative—was dropped in the § 1404(a) context. In order to obtain a new federal [venue], the statute requires only that the transfer be '[f]or the convenience of the parties, in the interest of justice.'" *Veba-Chemie A.G. v. M/V Getafix,* 711 F.2d 1243, 1247 (5th Cir. 1983) (emphasis and first alteration added); *see Piper Aircraft,* 454 U.S. at 254 (noting the "relaxed standards for transfer"). Thus, the district court, in requiring Volkswagen to show that the § 1404(a) factors must substantially outweigh the plaintiffs' choice of venue, erred by applying the stricter *forum non conveniens* dismissal standard and thus giving inordinate weight to the plaintiffs' choice of venue.

IV.

We thus turn to examine the showing that Volkswagen made under § 1404(a) and the district court's response.

As noted above, we have adopted the private and public interest factors first enunciated in *Gulf Oil Corp. v Gilbert,* 330 U.S. 501, 67 S. Ct. 839, 91 L. Ed. 1055 (1947), a *forum non conveniens* case, as appropriate for the determination of whether a § 1404(a) venue transfer is for the convenience of parties and witnesses and in the interest of justice.

The private interest factors are: "(1) the relative ease of access to sources of proof; (2) the availability of compulsory process to secure the attendance of witnesses; (3) the cost of attendance for willing witnesses; and (4) all other practical problems that make trial of a case easy, expeditious and inexpensive." *In re Volkswagen AG,* 371 F.3d 201, 203 (5th Cir. 2004) [hereinafter *In re Volkswagen I*] (citing *Piper Aircraft,* 454 U.S. at 241 n.6). The public interest factors are: "(1) the administrative difficulties flowing from court congestion; (2) the local interest in having localized interests decided at home; (3) the familiarity of the forum with the law that will govern the case; and (4) the avoidance of unnecessary problems of conflict of laws [or in] the application of foreign law." *Id.*

Although the *Gilbert* factors are appropriate for most transfer cases, they are not necessarily exhaustive or exclusive. Moreover, we have noted that "none ... can be said to be of dispositive weight." *Action Indus., Inc. v. U.S. Fid. & Guar. Corp.,* 358 F.3d 337, 340 (5th Cir. 2004).

Before the district court, Volkswagen asserted that a transfer was warranted because: (1) the relative ease of access to sources of proof favors transfer as all of the documents and physical evidence relating to the accident are located in the Dallas Division, as is the collision site; (2) the availability of compulsory process favors transfer as the Marshall Division does not have absolute subpoena power over the non-party witnesses; (3) the cost of attendance for willing witnesses factor favors transfer as the Dallas Division is more convenient for all relevant witnesses; and (4) the local interest in having localized interests decided at home favors transfer as the Volkswagen Golf was purchased in Dallas County, Texas; the accident occurred on a freeway in Dallas, Texas; Dallas residents witnessed the accident; Dallas police and paramedics responded and took action; a Dallas doctor performed the autopsy; the third-party defendant lives in Dallas County, Texas; none of the plaintiffs live in the Marshall Division; no known party or non-party witness lives in the Marshall Division; no known source of proof is located in the Marshall Division; and none of the facts giving rise to this suit occurred in the Marshall Division.

Applying the *Gilbert* factors, however, the district court concluded that: (1) the relative ease of access to sources of proof is neutral because of advances in copying technology and information storage; (2) the availability of compulsory process is neutral because, despite its lack of absolute subpoena power, the district court could deny any motion to quash and ultimately compel the attendance of third-party witnesses found in Texas; (3)

the cost of attendance for willing witnesses is neutral because Volkswagen did not designate "key" witnesses and because, given the proximity of Dallas to the Marshall Division, the cost of having witnesses attend a trial in Marshall would be minimal; and (4) the local interest in having localized interests decided at home factor is neutral because, although the accident occurred in Dallas, Texas, the citizens of Marshall, Texas, "would be interested to know whether there are defective products offered for sale in close proximity to the Marshall Division." Based on this analysis, the district court concluded that Volkswagen "has not satisfied its burden of showing that the balance of convenience and justice weighs in favor of transfer."

We consider first the private interest factor concerning the relative ease of access to sources of proof. Here, the district court's approach reads the sources of proof requirement out of the § 1404(a) analysis, and this despite the fact that this Court has recently reiterated that the sources of proof requirement is a meaningful factor in the analysis. That access to some sources of proof presents a lesser inconvenience now than it might have absent recent developments does not render this factor superfluous. All of the documents and physical evidence relating to the accident are located in the Dallas Division, as is the collision site. Thus, the district court erred in applying this factor because it does weigh in favor of transfer.

The second private interest factor is the availability of compulsory process to secure the attendance of witnesses. As in *In re Volkswagen I*, the non-party witnesses located in the city where the collision occurred "are outside the Eastern District's subpoena power for deposition under Fed. R. Civ. P. 45(c)(3)(A)(ii)," and any "trial subpoenas for these witnesses to travel more than 100 miles would be subject to motions to quash under Fed. R. Civ. P. 45(c)(3)." *Id.* at 205 n.4. Moreover, a proper venue that does enjoy *absolute* subpoena power for both depositions and trial—the Dallas Division—is available. As we noted above, the venue transfer analysis is concerned with convenience, and that a district court can deny any motions to quash does not address concerns regarding the convenience of parties and witnesses. Thus, the district court erred in applying this factor because it also weighs in favor of transfer.

The third private interest factor is the cost of attendance for willing witnesses. Volkswagen has submitted a list of potential witnesses that included the third-party defendant, accident witnesses, accident investigators, treating medical personnel, and the medical examiner— all of whom reside in Dallas County or in the Dallas area. Volkswagen also has submitted two affidavits, one from an accident witness and the other from the accident investigator, that stated that traveling to the Marshall Division would be inconvenient. Volkswagen also asserts that the testimony of these witnesses, including an accident witness and an accident investigator, is critical to determining causation and liability in this case.

In *In re Volkswagen I* we set a 100-mile threshold as follows: "When the distance between an existing venue for trial of a matter and a proposed venue under § 1404(a) is more than 100 miles, the factor of inconvenience to witnesses increases in direct relationship to the additional distance to be traveled." 371 F.3d at 204–05. We said, further, that it is an "obvious conclusion" that it is more convenient for witnesses to testify at home and that "[a]dditional distance means additional travel time; additional travel time increases the probability for meal and lodging expenses; and additional travel time with overnight stays increases the time which these fact witnesses must be away from their regular employment." *Id.* at 205. The district court disregarded our precedent relating to the 100-mile rule. As to the witnesses identified by Volkswagen, it is apparent that it would be more convenient for them if this case is tried in the Dallas Division, as the Marshall Division is 155 miles from Dallas. Witnesses not only suffer monetary costs, but also the personal costs associated with being away from work, family, and community. Moreover, the plaintiffs, Richard

Singleton and Ruth Singleton, also currently reside in the Dallas Division (Amy Singleton resides in Kansas). The Singletons have not argued that a trial in the Dallas Division would be inconvenient to them; they actually have conceded that the Dallas Division would be a convenient venue. The district court erred in applying this factor as it also weighs in favor of transfer.

The only contested public interest factor is the local interest in having localized interests decided at home. Here, the district court's reasoning again disregarded our precedent in *In re Volkswagen I*. There, under virtually indistinguishable facts, we held that this factor weighed heavily in favor of transfer. Here again, this factor weighs heavily in favor of transfer: the accident occurred in the Dallas Division, the witnesses to the accident live and are employed in the Dallas Division, Dallas police and paramedics responded and took action, the Volkswagen Golf was purchased in Dallas County, the wreckage and all other evidence are located in Dallas County, two of the three plaintiffs live in the Dallas Division (the third lives in Kansas), not one of the plaintiffs has ever lived in the Marshall Division, and the third-party defendant lives in the Dallas Division. In short, there is no relevant factual connection to the Marshall Division.

Furthermore, the district court's provided rationale — that the citizens of Marshall have an interest in this product liability case because the product is available in Marshall, and that for this reason jury duty would be no burden — stretches logic in a manner that eviscerates the public interest that this factor attempts to capture. The district court's provided rationale could apply virtually to any judicial district or division in the United States; it leaves no room for consideration of those actually affected — directly and indirectly — by the controversies and events giving rise to a case. That the residents of the Marshall Division "would be interested to know" whether a defective product is available does not imply that they have an interest — that is, a stake — in the resolution of this controversy. Indeed, they do not, as they are not in any relevant way connected to the events that gave rise to this suit. In contrast, the residents of the Dallas Division have extensive connections with the events that gave rise to this suit. Thus, the district court erred in applying this factor as it also weighs in favor of transfer.[13]

The reader will remember that we began our discussion by addressing the three requirements set out by the Supreme Court in *Cheney* for the issuance of the writ of mandamus. Up until this point, all of our discussion has focused upon the second requirement: that the right to mandamus is clear and indisputable. The remaining question as to this second requirement is whether the errors we have noted warrant mandamus relief; that is, whether the district court clearly abused its discretion in denying Volkswagen's transfer motion. The errors of the district court — applying the stricter *forum non conveniens* dismissal standard, misconstruing the weight of the plaintiffs' choice of venue, treating choice of venue as a § 1404(a) factor, misapplying the *Gilbert* factors, disregarding the specific precedents of this Court in *In re Volkswagen I*, and glossing over the fact that not a single relevant factor favors the Singletons' chosen venue — were extraordinary errors. Indeed, "[t]he only connection between this case and the Eastern District of Texas is plaintiffs' choice to file there." *In re Volkswagen of Am., Inc.*, 223 F. App'x 305, 307 (5th Cir. 2007) (Garza, J., dissenting).

In the light of the above, we hold that the district court's errors resulted in a patently erroneous result. Thus, Volkswagen's right to issuance of the writ is clear and indisputable.

---

13. Moreover, the facts do not favor the logic presented. The record indicates that the Volkswagen Golf was purchased from a location in the Dallas Division, and that Marshall, Texas, has no Volkswagen dealership.

[The court further held that petitioner had no other adequate remedy because it would not be able to show, after a trial and judgment in Marshall, that it would have won the case had it been tried in Dallas instead. Seeking mandamus is thus not a mere substitute for an appeal on the denied transfer.]

Thus, for the reasons assigned above, we grant Volkswagen's petition for a writ of mandamus. The Clerk of this Court shall therefore issue a writ of mandamus directing the district court to transfer this case to the United States District Court for the Northern District of Texas, Dallas Division.

KING, CIRCUIT JUDGE, with whom DAVIS, WIENER, BENAVIDES, STEWART, DENNIS, and PRADO, CIRCUIT JUDGES, join, dissenting:

In order to grant mandamus here, the majority proceeds by plucking the standard "clear abuse of discretion" out of the narrow context provided by the Supreme Court's mandamus precedent and then confecting a case—not the case presented to the district court—to satisfy its new standard. I respectfully dissent.

It is important to describe the case actually presented to the district court. The majority notes briefly that this is a products liability case, but its entire opinion proceeds as if this were simply a case in which the victims of a Dallas traffic accident were suing the driver of the offending car. That is not this case. The Singletons' Volkswagen Golf was indeed hit on its left rear panel by Colin Little, spun around, and slid rear-first into a flat-bed trailer parked by the side of the road. Emergency personnel found an unconscious Richard Singleton in his fully reclined passenger seat with Mariana Singleton (who was seated directly behind him) trapped underneath. Mariana later died from the head trauma she received from the seat, and Richard was left paraplegic. The Singletons sued Volkswagen, alleging that the seat adjustment mechanism of Richard's seat was defectively designed, resulting in a collapse of the seat during the accident. Thus, the case before the district court is first and foremost a products liability, design defect case that will depend heavily on expert testimony from both the plaintiffs and Volkswagen. No claim is made by Volkswagen that any of its experts is Dallas-based, and whether this case is tried in Marshall or Dallas will make little, if any, difference—Volkswagen will be able to get its experts (from Germany or elsewhere) to trial regardless. The Dallas connections with the original accident become relevant if there is a finding of a design defect and the court turns to the third party action by Volkswagen against Colin Little, raising issues of causation and damages. Pretrial discovery and the trial itself will have to address those issues, but they are not the only, or even the primary, focus of this case. Finally, Little, the other party to the accident, has explicitly stated that the Eastern District is not an inconvenient forum for him of discretion.

I now turn to the majority's take on the four § 1404(a) factors. The majority would have us believe that since this case involves only a Dallas traffic accident, Dallas is the only convenient location for the Singletons' suit. But, while the convenience inquiry may begin with listing this case's Dallas connections, it does not end there. First for the Dallas documents: the district court's reasoning, where it "note[d] that this factor has become less significant" and concluded that "[a]ny documents or evidence can be easily transported to Marshall," hardly "reads the sources of proof requirement out of the" transfer analysis. Instead, the district court considered the reality that the Northern and Eastern Districts have required ECF (electronic case filing) for a long time and that all the courtrooms are electronic. This means that the documents will be converted to electronic form, and whether they are displayed on monitors in Dallas or Marshall makes no difference to their availability. Secondly, the court's subpoena power runs throughout the state, and an experienced district court can properly discount the likelihood of an avalanche of motions to quash. The majority's novel notion of "absolute subpoena power" results in only the most marginal of convenience gains, if any. Thirdly, the Dallas witnesses will not likely be inconvenienced because (as Volkswagen recognizes) discovery will be, in all likelihood, conducted in Dallas. Additionally, witnesses necessary to establish damages for Mariana's wrongful death—her teachers, neighbors, and friends—all reside in the Eastern District (where the Singletons resided at the time of the accident). And the majority's "100-mile rule" is no proxy for considering the realistic costs and inconvenience for witnesses that will attend the trial, particularly in a state as expansive as Texas. As for the two non-party fact witnesses who submitted identical affidavits asserting inconvenience, if the case goes to trial and if they end up testifying (two very big "ifs," the district court was no doubt aware), the court could reasonably conclude that traveling 150 miles, or two hours on a four-lane interstate (I-20), each way is only minimally inconvenient.

And finally, with regard to the local interest factor, the majority's assertion that Eastern District residents "are not in any relevant way connected to the events that gave rise to this suit" overstates the case and glosses over the fact that this is a products liability suit. A Dallas traffic accident may have triggered the events that revealed a possibly defective product, but that does not change the nature of this suit. Drivers in the Eastern District could be connected to the actual issues in this case as they may be interested to learn of a possibly defective product that they may be driving or that is on their roads. Thus, the majority's "careful review" under the § 1404(a) transfer factors is both erroneous as to its method and misleading as to the facts.

[The dissent went on to argue further that the use of the extraordinary writ of mandamus to provide appellate review of a non-appealable pretrial order was inappropriate.]

Notes and Problems

1. In the *Ginsey* case, why did the court not simply apply the first-to-file rule to avoid the problem of duplicative proceedings? Did parallel litigation exist or just similar, related cases? How many disputed transactions were involved and would the final judgment in one case be res judicata over the other? Despite these differences, was it desirable to consider transfer to a district where consolidation under Rule 42(a) might be possible?

2. When the *Ginsey* court decided to transfer the action, why did the plaintiff not get the second desired forum? Should the plaintiff's (second) choice of forum weigh heavier than the defendant's suggested forum? Why or why not? Come back to this question after you read the *DeMelo* case in the next section on *forum non conveniens*.

3. In terms of their case planning, how did counsel for the plaintiff in *Ginsey* make it easier for the defendant to obtain a transfer of the case to the defendant's preferred forum? What if instead of filing suit in the plaintiff's state of incorporation, the plaintiff had chosen to file suit where it was actually based and where the products were shipped? Would the same result have happened?

4. Notice also the interplay potentially between issues of personal jurisdiction (which focuses in its minimum contacts analysis upon where the relevant activities that gave rise to the case took place) and at least some of the inquiry concerning § 1404 transfer (which focuses upon where the witnesses to the events reside and the connection between the forum and the lawsuit). Given this overlapping inquiry, many defendants in filing Rule 12(b)(2) objections to personal jurisdiction will, in the alternative, also file § 1404(a) motions to transfer venue.

5. The *Ginsey* court found no personal jurisdiction, but instead of dismissing based on this holding, the court transferred to a more favorable venue. Why could the court do this if it found there was no jurisdiction? *Goldlawr, Inc. v. Heiman* held:

> The language of § 1406(a) is amply broad enough to authorize the transfer of cases, however wrong the plaintiff may have been in filing his case as to venue, whether the court in which it was filed had personal jurisdiction over the defendants or not. The section is thus in accord with the general purpose which has prompted many of the procedural changes of the past few years—that of removing whatever obstacles may impede an expeditious and orderly adjudication of cases and controversies on their merits.

369 U.S. 463, 466–67 (1962). Who benefits from the transfer rather than dismissal? Why would the court consider this alternative a better option than simply dismissing the case? The *Heiman* Court further explained:

> If by reason of the uncertainties of proper venue a mistake is made, Congress, by the enactment of § 1406(a), recognized that "the interest of justice" may require that the complaint not be dismissed but rather that it be transferred in order that the plaintiff not be penalized by what the late Judge Parker aptly characterized as "time-consuming and justice-defeating technicalities."

Heiman, 369 U.S. at 467. Why did Judge Parker characterize dismissal actions based on a lack of personal jurisdiction as "time-consuming and justice-defeating technicalities"?

6. Note that the *Volkswagen* opinion was issued after an *en banc* hearing before the entire Fifth Circuit Court of Appeals, with ten judges signing the majority opinion and seven judges dissenting. Normal appeals are not permitted from a trial court's decision to grant or deny a § 1404(a) motion to transfer venue—its simply not a final judgment. With the particular standard of review for issuance of the extraordinary writ requiring a clear abuse of discretion, could one argue that such standard per se could not have been met when the court itself is internally divided on whether the trial court erred? The dissent essentially makes this argument, suggesting that the majority ignored the proper standard of review. In any event, the important point to note from this is how great the discretion is given to district judges applying the various public and private interest factors under § 1404(a). Not only is the analysis itself fairly subjective but the mostly unreviewable nature of the decision typically insulates that decision from practical review in almost all cases.

7. *Chapter Problem.* In the federal lawsuit filed by Bresser against PERI in Dallas federal court (the Northern District of Texas), how might PERI invoke § 1404(a) to its potential advantage in avoiding a Dallas forum for its lawsuit? (Note, PERI is located in the Western District of Texas.)

3. *Forum Non Conveniens*

De Melo v. Lederle Laboratories
801 F.2d 1058 (8th Cir. 1986)

GIBSON, J.,

Cleonilde Nunes de Melo, a citizen of Brazil, appeals the judgment of the district court dismissing her products liability claims against Lederle Laboratories on grounds of *forum non conveniens*. De Melo argues on appeal that the district court abused its discretion in concluding that Brazil was an adequate alternative forum for this litigation, and that on balance, this litigation would be more convenient for the parties and the available fora if tried in Brazil. We affirm.

Lederle Laboratories, a division of American Cyanamid Corporation, developed, tested, patented, and manufactured the drug Myambutol. American Cyanamid is a Maine corporation with headquarters in New Jersey; Lederle is a New York corporation, and maintains its main laboratories, where Myambutol was developed and manufactured, in New York. Both American Cyanamid and Lederle are licensed to do business in Minnesota. American Cyanamid also licenses the foreign manufacture of Myambutol. Under a licensing agreement, Myambutol is manufactured, marketed and distributed in Brazil by a Brazilian corporation, Cyanamid Quimica de Brasil (CQB), a wholly-owned subsidiary of American Cyanamid.

facts

De Melo, a school teacher in her forties, was treated in Brazil for pulmonary tuberculosis. In 1976, in the course of that treatment, de Melo's Brazilian physicians prescribed Myambutol. After a few months of ingesting the drug, de Melo developed optic atrophy, and became permanently blind. The package insert to Myambutol manufactured by CQB, containing information about the appropriate uses and hazards of the product, is a Portuguese translation of an English version prepared by Lederle for domestic distribution. In 1976, the English-language package insert warned of possible permanent vision loss; the Portuguese version, however, warned only of temporary vision loss. In late 1975, Lederle sent a circular to foreign manufacturers of the drug, including CQB, advising that the package insert be amended to include a statement that repeated ingestion of the drug could cause irreversible reduced visual acuity.

De Melo filed suit in federal district court in Minnesota, seeking recovery under theories of strict liability, negligence, failure to warn, breach of express and implied warranties, and fraudulent concealment. The thrust of de Melo's claims is that Lederle had complete control over the manufacture, packaging, and labeling of Myambutol produced and distributed by CQB; that Lederle knew or should have known that Myambutol causes permanent, not temporary, loss of vision; and that it intentionally or negligently failed to provide the appropriate warnings with Brazilian manufactured Myambutol.

Lederle moved to dismiss the action on the ground of *forum non conveniens,* suggesting that Brazil was the more appropriate forum. The district court, applying the balancing test set forth by the Supreme Court in *Gulf Oil Corp. v. Gilbert,* 330 U.S. 501, 67 S.Ct. 839, 91 L.Ed. 1055 (1947), granted the motion contingent upon Lederle's acceptance of four conditions: first, Lederle consent to suit and accept service of process in Brazil in any civil action brought by de Melo on her claim; second, Lederle agree to make available any documents or witnesses within its control necessary for the fair adjudication of any such claim; third, Lederle consent to pay any judgment rendered against it by a Brazilian court in any such action; and fourth, Lederle agree to waive any statute of limitations defense which did not exist at the time de Melo filed the present action.

The district court first found that Brazil presented an adequate alternative forum to resolve this dispute. The court noted that Lederle had consented to jurisdiction and service of process in Brazil, and found, based upon letters from Brazilian attorneys submitted by Lederle, that de Melo's claims stated a cause of action under Brazilian law. The court also rejected de Melo's argument that the lack of contingency fee arrangements in Brazil, delays in civil courts, and absence of punitive damages or recovery for pain and suffering, made meaningful recovery so unlikely as to render Brazil an inadequate forum for this litigation. The court found that de Melo had recourse to legal assistance through contingency fee arrangements or indigent legal services, and would therefore be able to prosecute her suit. It also concluded, based on the Supreme Court's decision in *Piper Aircraft Co. v. Reyno,* 454 U.S. 235, 102 S.Ct. 252, 70 L.Ed.2d 419 (1981), that the limitations on damages did not render the forum inadequate.

The district court next found that the balance of private interests favored litigation in Brazil. While the court acknowledged that evidence relating to the adequacy of the warnings is located predominantly in the United States, it concluded that litigation in this country would leave Lederle without access to compulsory process to secure evidence in Brazil relating to the manufacture and distribution of Myambutol in Brazil and the circumstances surrounding de Melo's treatment. The converse problem would not exist in Brazil, the court noted, because judgment was conditioned on Lederle's agreement to supply all relevant witnesses and documents in Brazil. The court also noted that suit in the United States would prevent Lederle from impleading potential third party defendants, such as de Melo's physicians or CQB, and thereby prevent resolution of all claims in one trial.

Finally, the district court found that the public interest factors weighed in favor of Lederle. Relying on similar district court cases, the court concluded that Brazil had the strongest interest in regulating a drug that was manufactured, distributed, and ingested in that country, and that had harmed one of its citizens. The court noted, moreover, that under Minnesota choice of law rules, Brazilian law would govern the litigation. The district court, thus, concluded that its lack of familiarity with Brazilian law and that country's greater interest in resolving a "local" controversy both strongly suggested that Brazil was the appropriate forum.

De Melo argues that the district court abused its discretion in dismissing this action on the basis of *forum non conveniens.* She contends that Brazil is not an adequate alternative forum for tort litigation of this kind because recovery is severely limited, because she is without the financial ability to maintain the suit absent a contingency fee arrangement, which she contends is rare in Brazil, and because the legal system in Brazil generally is "archaic." She further argues that the district court erred in concluding that the balance of private and public interests weighed in favor of a Brazilian forum.

A.

Under the doctrine of *forum non conveniens,* federal district courts have inherent power to resist the imposition of jurisdiction even where authorized by statute if "the litigation can more appropriately be conducted in a foreign tribunal." *Gulf Oil Corp. v. Gilbert,* 330 U.S. at 504, 67 S.Ct. at 840 (quoting *Canada Malting Co. v. Paterson Steamships, Ltd.,* 285 U.S. 413, 422–23, 52 S.Ct. 413, 415, 76 L.Ed. 837 (1932)).

B.

The doctrine of *forum non conveniens* "presupposes at least two forums in which the defendant is amenable to process." *Gilbert,* 330 U.S. at 506–07, 67 S.Ct. at 842. Thus, "[a]t the outset of any *forum non conveniens* inquiry, the court must determine whether there exists an alternative forum." *Piper Aircraft,* 454 U.S. at 254 n. 22, 102 S.Ct. at 265 n. 22. This requirement is satisfied, ordinarily, if the defendant is amenable to process in the alternative jurisdiction, *id.; Gilbert,* 330 U.S. at 506–07, 67 S.Ct. at 842. Here, the district court ensured this by conditioning dismissal on Lederle's concession to jurisdiction and service of process in Brazil. However, "in rare circumstances," the remedy provided in the alternative forum may be "so clearly inadequate or unsatisfactory that it is no remedy at all." *Piper Aircraft,* 454 U.S. at 254, 102 S.Ct. at 265. In such cases, the alternative forum is not adequate, for "dismissal would not be in the interests of justice." *Id.*

De Melo contends that the unavailability under Brazilian law of punitive damages and recovery for pain and suffering suggests that any recovery she may obtain in Brazil will be grossly inadequate to compensate her for her injuries and deter future misconduct by multinational corporations like the defendant. Moreover, she argues, she is financially unable to prosecute this suit absent some form of contingency arrangement, which, she claims, is rare in Brazil. Thus, the possibility of recovery, however minor, is even more remote.

We do not believe that the district court abused its discretion in finding that Brazil is an adequate alternative forum for this litigation. First, the Supreme Court explicitly held in *Piper Aircraft* that, ordinarily, the fact that the alternative forum's substantive law is decidedly less favorable to the plaintiff should not be given substantial weight in *forum non conveniens* determinations. 454 U.S. at 247, 102 S.Ct. at 261. Where the alternative forum offers a remedy for the plaintiff's claims, and there is no danger that she will be treated unfairly, the foreign forum is adequate. *Id.* at 255, 102 S.Ct. at 265. Affidavits from Brazilian attorneys make clear that de Melo's claims state a cause of action under Brazilian law and that she has a direct action against CQB, Lederle's subsidiary. Furthermore, under Brazilian law, de Melo may recover lost wages, indirect losses, and twice the amount of her medical expenses. These damages, whatever they amount to in this case, are not so paltry as to render the available remedy illusory.

The affidavits also establish that contingency fee arrangements are not uncommon, and free legal assistance is available. Although Brazil may be a less favorable forum for de Melo, we cannot conclude that it is inadequate. *Cf. De Oliveira v. Delta Marine Drilling Co.,* 707 F.2d 843, 846–47 (5th Cir.1983) (no evidence Brazil is inadequate forum); *Vaz Borralho v. Keydril Co.,* 696 F.2d 379, 392–94 (5th Cir.1983) (same); *Santamauro v. Taito do Brasil Industria E Comercia Ltda.,* 587 F.Supp. 1312, 1316 (E.D.La.1984) (same).

C.

The second phase of the *forum non conveniens* inquiry requires the district court to balance the private interest factors, which affect the convenience of the litigants, and the public interest factors, which affect the convenience of the forum. *Piper Aircraft,* 454 U.S. at 241, 102 S.Ct. at 258; *Pain v. United Technologies Corp.,* 637 F.2d 775, 782 (D.C.Cir.1980), *cert. denied,* 454 U.S. 1128, 102 S.Ct. 980, 71 L.Ed.2d 116 (1981). This balance reflects the central purpose of the *forum non conveniens* inquiry: to ensure that the trial is held at a convenient situs.[4]

The factors which bear on the private interest of the litigants include:

> [T]he relative ease of access to sources of proof; availability of compulsory process for attendance of unwilling, and the cost of obtaining attendance of willing, witnesses; possibility of view of premises, if view would be appropriate to the action; and all other practical problems that make trial of a case easy, expeditious and inexpensive. There may also be questions to the enforceability of

---

4. There is ordinarily a strong presumption that a plaintiff's choice of forum will not be disturbed, absent a clear indication that it would be unnecessarily burdensome for the defendant or the court. The district court properly acknowledged, however, that the plaintiff's choice is entitled to substantially less deference when the plaintiff is foreign. In such a case, the assumption underlying the presumption, that the plaintiff has chosen the forum for her convenience, is less reasonable. It is thus more likely that the forum was chosen to take advantage of favorable law or harass the defendant, both of which suggest that dismissal for *forum non conveniens* is warranted.

a judgment if one is obtained. The court will weigh relative advantages and obstacles to fair trial.

Gilbert, 330 U.S. at 508, 67 S.Ct. at 801. We cannot conclude that the district court erred in finding that the private interest factors weighed in favor of Lederle. De Melo properly points out that ease of access to a substantial body of the relevant evidence favors a domestic forum. Most, if not all, of the evidence relating to the development, testing, and manufacture of Myambutol—and thus the adequacy of warnings accompanying domestically produced Myambutol—presumably is located in New York or New Jersey. Moreover, she points out, litigation in Brazil will require cumbersome translation into Portuguese of all documents located in the United States. *Cf. Friends For All Chidren, Inc. v. Lockheed Aircraft Corp.,* 717 F.2d 602, 608 (D.C.Cir.1983) (burden of translating documents into foreign languages for foreign fora is consideration "not easily ignored").

Countervailing considerations, however, indicate that the balance of private interests was properly struck in favor of a Brazilian forum. First, de Melo's argument only accounts for the location of evidence directly relevant to her failure to warn theory, which she obviously views as her most potent claim. Evidence that Lederle is likely to consider relevant to its defense, such as evidence of CQB's manufacture, distribution, advertisement, and labelling of Myambutol, is in Brazil. Additionally, all the evidence relating to de Melo's illness, course of treatment (by approximately ten physicians), ingestion of Myambutol and injuries—evidence necessary regardless of the theory of recovery—is in Brazil. It is clear, therefore, that a substantial amount of testimonial and documentary evidence will be found in Brazil. And, in light of Lederle's evidentiary needs in Brazil, it is apparent that the translation problem will be oppressive regardless of the forum.

It is of considerable importance, moreover, that litigation in the United States would deprive Lederle of compulsory process to much of the evidence located in Brazil, including the circumstances surrounding de Melo's course of treatment before and after ingesting Myambutol. The district court avoided the converse problem—that de Melo would be without compulsory process to secure evidence in this country if the litigation were held in Brazil—by conditioning dismissal on its agreement to make available in the Brazilian courts all relevant witnesses and evidence located in the United States. *Cf. Piper Aircraft,* 454 U.S. at 257 n. 25, 102 S.Ct. at 267 n. 25 (approving use of conditional dismissals to ensure plaintiff access to sources of proof). Although litigation in this country would afford de Melo greater access to sources of proof relevant to *her* theory, it would box out Lederle from access to concededly important evidence upon which its defense may well rest. *See Pain,* 637 F.2d at 787–88 (relying on *Dahl v. United Technologies Corp.,* 632 F.2d 1027, 1030 (3d Cir.1980)). "Thus, so long as trial were to be conducted in the United States, the inability of both parties to obtain the full panoply of relevant evidence would greatly hinder fair resolution of the dispute." *Id.* at 788; *see also Piper Aircraft,* 454 U.S. at 258, 102 S.Ct. at 267 (witnesses beyond domestic compulsory process a factor in favor of *forum non conveniens* dismissal); *Lockheed Aircraft Corp.,* 717 F.2d at 608 (same).

A second private interest strongly favoring dismissal is Lederle's inability to implead potential third-party defendants in domestic litigation. Lederle has indicated that it is likely to implead de Melo's physicians, the pharmacy from which she purchased the drug, and employees of CQB. De Melo correctly notes that Lederle could maintain a suit for indemnity or contribution against potential third-party defendants in Brazil were it found liable in an action here. However, as the Supreme Court noted in *Piper Aircraft* in response to a similar argument, "[i]t would be far more convenient to resolve all claims in one trial. Finding that trial in the plaintiff's chosen forum would be burdensome [to the defendant] is sufficient to support dismissal on grounds of *forum non conveniens.*" 454 U.S. at 259. Therefore, from the standpoint of the convenience of the parties, we believe that the district court reasonably concluded that the litigation was more appropriate in Brazil.

We also believe that the district court's balancing of the public interest factors was reasonable. The public interest factors, which bear on the convenience of the forum, include:

> The administrative difficulties flowing from court congestion; the "local interest in having localized controversies decided at home"; the interest in having the trial of a diversity case in a forum that is at home with the law that must govern the action; the avoidance of unnecessary problems in conflict of laws, or in the application of foreign law; and the unfairness of burdening citizens in an unrelated forum with jury duty.

Piper Aircraft, 454 U.S. at 241 n. 6, 102 S.Ct. at 258 n. 6 (quoting *Gilbert,* 330 U.S. at 509, 67 S.Ct. at 843). The parties' factual allegations make it clear that neither forum can lay exclusive claim to a "local interest" precisely because this is not an entirely "localized controversy." *See Gilbert,* 330 U.S. at 509, 67 S.Ct. at 843. It is abundantly clear that the forum de Melo has chosen, Minnesota, has no peculiar local interest in this dispute. Further, insofar as there may be a general national interest in resolving this controversy in a domestic forum, we do not believe it is significant in light of Brazil's interests. *See Dowling v. Richardson-Merrell, Inc.,* 727 F.2d 608, 615 (6th Cir.1984), *aff'g* 545 F.Supp. 1130 (S.D.Ohio 1982); *Pain,* 637 F.2d at 792–93; *cf. Piper Aircraft,* 454 U.S. at 260, 102 S.Ct. at 268 (plaintiff's argument that "American citizens have an interest in ensuring that American manufacturers are deterred from producing defective products" is insufficient because any additional deterrence gained from domestic forum over particular foreign forum "is likely to be insignificant").

The crux of this suit concerns the safety of drugs distributed in Brazil: it involves a Brazilian woman who ingested a drug manufactured, distributed, and labelled in Brazil, pursuant to a course of treatment prescribed by Brazilian physicians, purchased from a pharmacy in Brazil, which resulted in an injury and subsequent treatment in Brazil. It would seem that Brazil has a paramount interest in regulating the quality and distribution of drugs through Brazilian products liability law. *See Dowling,* 727 F.2d at 615 (states where suit brought and where defendant corporation headquartered "have a minimal interest in the safety of products which are manufactured, regulated and sold abroad by foreign entities, even though the development and testing occurred in this country."); *Harrison v. Wyeth Laboratories,* 510 F.Supp. 1, 4 (E.D.Pa.1980), *aff'd mem.,* 676 F.2d 685 (3rd Cir.1982) (question as to safety of drugs marketed in foreign country, even if all production and marketing decisions made in defendant's headquarters in United States, is properly the concern of the foreign country). *See also Pain,* 637 F.2d at 793; *Dahl,* 632 F.2d at 1032. Thus, the "local interest in having local controversies decided at home," *Gilbert,* 330 U.S. at 509, 67 S.Ct. at 843, favors litigation in Brazil.

Additionally, the striking fact that this litigation lacks any significant contact with the particular forum chosen by de Melo suggests that it is inappropriate to burden that community with the "enormous commitment of judicial time and resources that would inevitably be required if the case were to be tried there."[6] *Piper Aircraft,* 454 U.S. at 261,

---

6. Minnesota apparently was chosen as a forum because de Melo's attorney, the father of a Peace Corps worker de Melo met in Brazil, lives in Minnesota.

454 U.S. at 268. The only states that have any material connection to this litigation are New York and New Jersey. There simply is no justification for adding to the local docket in Minnesota or imposing jury duty on Minnesota residents on a matter which affects the forum and its residents in such a minimal fashion. *Cf. Pain,* 637 F.2d at 792 (district court properly held that community in plaintiff's chosen forum should not be burdened by dispute which had no significant relationship or contacts with forum).

Finally, the district court held that, under Minnesota conflict of law rules, Brazilian law would likely govern the litigation. This conclusion, particularly in light of the other public factors favoring a foreign forum, strongly supports dismissal for *forum non conveniens. Piper Aircraft,* 454 U.S. at 260 n. 29, 102 S.Ct. at 268 n. 29. There is, as the Court stated in *Gilbert,* a strong interest in resolving a dispute "in a forum that is at home with the law that must govern the action." 330 U.S. at 509, 67 S.Ct. at 843. Our review of these factors leads us to conclude that the district court's balancing of the private and public factors was reasonable.

The judgment of the district court is therefore affirmed.

Notes and Problems

1. In *DeMelo,* which of the general *forum non conveniens* factors does the court weigh more heavily than others? Did the court come to the correct result? How does the court's appellate standard of review affect this analysis and reasoning? How important are the conditions the defendant agreed to in the lower court's dismissal based on *forum non conveniens*?

2. What role does, and should, DeMelo's citizenship (as the appealing party) play in the *forum non conveniens* analysis? The defendants argued that they would be unable to implead third-party defendants. How would a Rule 19 analysis, aside from the *forum non conveniens* question, affect DeMelo's desire to continue litigation in the United States?

3. Given the court's analysis of the various considerations in *DeMelo* can you identify two "red flags" that, when present, seem to offer an extremely compelling case for grant of a *forum non conveniens* motion? They were both present in the circumstances of that case.

4. *Chapter Problem.* Could PERI make a good argument for the Dallas federal court to dismiss the case brought by Bresser using the *forum non conveniens* doctrine? If PERI attempted to move for dismissal on this ground, how should the court rule? Would a better alternative course of action exist for PERI to try to move the case out of Dallas?

Upon Further Review

Practice under both § 1404(a) and the doctrine of *forum non conveniens* are seen as exceptional tools to be used sparingly because of the general presumption that a plaintiff's chosen forum is convenient to the plaintiff and that the plaintiff's autonomy should be honored. This idea of autonomy for the plaintiff is a long-adhered to principle recognizing that plaintiffs should generally get to be the masters of their lawsuits, within limits. Each doctrine, however, recognizes that when consideration of private interests (witnesses, parties, sources of proof, etc.) and public interest factors (local interest in the controversy, speed with which the courts can get to the disputes, applicable substantive laws, etc.) weigh heavily in favor of an alternative forum that would have been appropriate in the first instance, then transfer (§ 1404) or dismissal (*forum non conveniens*) is the most fair way to resolve the forum battle. Of course, when a plaintiff has either not filed in a logical forum (no relationship to the case) or in the plaintiff's own home (and thus the presumption of convenience to the plaintiff is no longer tenable), then such a plaintiff increases the odds of losing their chosen forum.

E. Multidistrict Litigation: 28 U.S.C § 1407

There are many times when several hundred or even thousands of related cases are pending in multiple federal forums. See, for example, the *In re Diet Drugs* case we will read later in this chapter regarding the Anti-Injunction Act. That's exactly the scenario the manufacturer in that case faced following the recall of its diet pills from the market. Many products liability suits are, in a way, "duplicative" of other suits filed around the country. They usually involve different plaintiffs but target the same defendant(s) and often involve similar if not identical issues regarding alleged product defects. While joinder of some of those claims in one case might be possible (though we saw different courts react differently under Rule 20's "transaction or occurrence" prerequisite for joinder), most of the plaintiffs in such cases want to file and pursue their own claims in their own close-to-home chosen forums. And Rule 42(a) consolidation cannot work when the cases are filed in different districts. And while the issues in the cases may overlap considerably, getting courts to avoid re-litigation of those issues through the device of offensive non-mutual collateral estoppel is also unreliable and infrequently invoked when the circumstances of the cases might vary or create an argument that issue preclusion would be unfair. Finally, as we saw earlier in this chapter, a home-filing plaintiff's choice of forum will be given considerable deference when a defendant attempts transfer through § 1404. Thus, absent some other procedural device to promote aggregation of such suits, massive inefficiencies can result in litigating over and over again similar if not identical claims against a common defendant by various federal courts.

28 U.S.C. § 1407(a)

When *civil actions* involving one or more *common questions of fact* are pending in *different districts*, such actions may be transferred to any district for coordinated or consolidated pretrial proceedings. Such transfers shall be made by the *judicial panel* on multidistrict litigation authorized by this section upon its determination that transfers for such proceedings will be for the *convenience* of parties and witnesses and will promote the *just and efficient* conduct of such actions. Each action so transferred *shall be remanded by the panel at or before the conclusion of such pretrial proceedings* to the district from which it was transferred unless it shall have been previously terminated: Provided, however, that the panel may separate any claim, cross-claim, counter-claim, or third-party claim and remand any of such claims before the remainder of the action is remanded.

To promote efficiency and economy, however, the Multidistrict Litigation (MDL) Statute was passed in 1968 to provide a potential solution for this multiplicity of related cases. The MDL statute permits the transfer of cases from one district to another for consolidated pretrial treatment, when (a) there are more than one federal cases pending in different districts, (b) that have any significant common questions of fact, when (c) it would serve the convenience of witnesses and parties and (d) promote the just and efficient resolution of the cases. The MDL Statute permits a federal court to transfer all cases that have "one or more common questions of fact" where it would be convenient and efficient to have all pre-trial matters handled in one court.

Principles

According to one former member of the Judicial Panel for Multidistrict Litigation (a group of seven federal judges appointed by the U.S. Supreme Court) the Panel's deliberations consider:

> only two issues in resolving transfer motions under § 1407 in new dockets. First, the Panel considers whether common questions of fact among several pending civil actions exist such that centralization of those actions in a single district will further the convenience of the parties and witnesses and promote the just and efficient conduct of the actions. Second, the Panel considers which federal district and judge are best situated to handle the transferred matters. In deciding those issues, the Panel exercises its considerable and largely unfettered discretion within the unique circumstances that each motion presents. In fact, appeal from a Panel ruling seldom occurs and is available only by petition for a writ of mandamus or prohibition.

> [T]he Panel considers that eliminating duplicate discovery in similar cases, avoiding conflicting judicial rulings, and conserving valuable judicial resources are sound reasons for centralizing pretrial proceedings. Every transfer decision has the potential to prejudice a particular party or claim among the many. In difficult cases, the Panel will weight the likely benefits of centralization against the possibility of such resulting unfairness. The Panel's purpose is to benefit the judicial system and the litigants as a whole, not any particular party.

John G. Heybur II, *A View From the Panel: Part of the Solution*, 82 Tulane L. Rev. 2225 (2008).

One significant limitation on the power of the transferee MDL judge is that, upon completion of the pretrial activities, the judge *must* "remand" the case back to the original forum chosen by the plaintiff for trial. On the other hand, since the overwhelming percentage of cases are resolved without any trial (by settlement or grant of a dispositive motion), one can seriously question the significance on the limitation of MDL treatment to pretrial matters.

Whether the litigants or counsel involved in a particular case desires the purported efficiency benefits of MDL consolidation varies greatly by the case, the circumstances surrounding it, and the preferences of experienced counsel. Arguably everyone benefits from efficient pretrial handling, but not all are interested in gaining efficiency. Further, the general efficiency gains may be experienced more by a common, target defendant than other litigants who are only involved in a single case among the hundreds (or more) being transferred and consolidated. Further, because MDL cases may be numerous, an MDL transferee judge is unlikely to want to hear from every plaintiff counsel on every pretrial motion. It is common practice, therefore, for the court to require a small group of plaintiffs' counsel to make all of the pretrial decisions, take depositions, and make arguments at hearings for the benefit of the remaining counsel. This *litigation steering committee* approach gives enormous power to the few counsel chosen to serve on it and effectively takes almost all decisionmaking power away from many other plaintiffs' counsel. So one's perspective might vary widely on the desirability of the high-minded statute. (We will also see how an MDL court handles the allocation of attorney's fees in such instances in Chapter 6 Attorney's Fees.)

The following three cases involve decisions by the Judicial Panel on Multidistrict Litigation concerning whether to grant transfer of various cases to a particular judge for consolidated pretrial proceedings pursuant to the MDL statute and, if so, where to send the cases. Consider as you read the first few cases the reasons why various litigants either seek or oppose the MDL treatment. As you will see in the final case, though the statute limits the MDL court to ruling on pretrial issues only, the definition of "pretrial" is quite broad.

1. Whether and Where to Consolidate

In re Shoulder Pain Pump Chondrolysis Products Liability Litigation

571 F. Supp. 2d 1367 (Judicial Panel on Multidistrict Litigation 2008)

John G. Heyburn, II, Chairman.

Before the entire Panel: Plaintiffs in two actions pending in the District of Oregon and one action pending in the District of Minnesota have moved, pursuant to 28 U.S.C. § 1407, to centralize this litigation in the District of Oregon. This litigation currently consists of thirteen actions: six pending in the District of Oregon and one each in the Northern District of Alabama, the District of Colorado, the Southern District of Indiana, the Eastern District of Kentucky, the District of Minnesota, the Eastern District of New York, and the District of Utah, as listed on Schedule A.

Supporting centralization in the District of Oregon are plaintiffs in two other District of Oregon actions, a Northern District of Alabama action, a District of Colorado action, a Southern District of Indiana action, an Eastern District of Kentucky action, an Eastern District of New York action, and a District of Utah action, as well as plaintiffs in four potential tag-along actions pending in the District of Colorado, the Northern District of Florida, the Eastern District of New York, and the Western District of Virginia, respectively. Plaintiffs in the actions pending in the Northern District of Alabama, the Southern District of Indiana, the Eastern District of New York, and the District of Utah advocate selection of their respective districts as transferee district, in the alternative. Responding defendants all oppose centralization. To the extent that they express a preference, most of these defendants support selection of either the Eastern District of Kentucky or the Northern District of Illinois as transferee district, if the Panel orders centralization over their objections.

On the basis of the papers filed and hearing session held, we are not persuaded that Section 1407 centralization would serve the convenience of the parties and witnesses or further the just and efficient conduct of this litigation at the present time. Although these personal injury actions have some commonality as to whether shoulder pain pumps and/

or the anesthetic drugs used in those pumps cause glenohumeral chondrolysis, an indeterminate number of different pain pumps made by different manufacturers are at issue, as are different anesthetic drugs made by different pharmaceutical companies. Moreover, not all of the thirteen constituent actions involve pharmaceutical company defendants, and many defendants are sued only in a minority of those actions. The proponents of centralization have not convinced us that the efficiencies that might be gained by centralization would not be overwhelmed by the multiple individualized issues (including ones of liability and causation) that these actions appear to present. The parties can avail themselves of alternatives to Section 1407 transfer to minimize whatever possibilities there might be of duplicative discovery and/or inconsistent pretrial rulings. *See, e.g., In re Eli Lilly and Co. (Cephalexin Monohydrate) Patent Litigation,* 446 F.Supp. 242, 244 (J.P.M.L.1978); *see also* Manual for Complex Litigation, Fourth, § 20.14 (2004).

IT IS THEREFORE ORDERED that the motion, pursuant to 28 U.S.C. § 1407, for centralization of these thirteen actions is denied.

In re DePuy Orthopaedics Pinnacle Hip Implant Litigation

787 F. Supp. 2d 1358 (Judicial Panel on Multidistrict Litigation 2011)

JOHN G. HEYBURN, II, CHAIRMAN,

Pursuant to 28 U.S.C. § 1407, plaintiff in a Central District of California action (*Falvey*) moves for centralized pretrial proceedings of all actions involving metal-on-metal configurations of Pinnacle Acetabular Cup System hip implants in the Central District of California or the Southern District of Texas. Defendants [DePuy Orthopedics and Johnson & Johnson] support centralization of all actions involving all configurations of Pinnacle Acetabular Cup System hip implants in the Northern District of Texas, the Southern District of Iowa, or the Southern District of Texas.

Plaintiffs' motion includes three actions: two in the Central District of California and one in the Western District of Washington. The Panel has been notified of 54 additional related actions, several of which were filed before the most recently filed action on the motion.

Plaintiffs in the Eastern District of Louisiana *Santorelli* potential tag-along action oppose inclusion of their action in any centralized proceeding. In their briefing, all other responding plaintiffs in various actions or potential tag-along actions support centralization in one or more of the following districts: the Northern District of Alabama, the Northern District of California, the Southern District of Florida, the Western District of Louisiana, the District of Minnesota, the Northern District of Mississippi, the District of New Jersey, the Northern District of New York, the Southern District of New York, the District of Rhode Island, the Eastern District of Pennsylvania, and the Western District of Washington. At oral argument, numerous plaintiffs stated that they also support selection of the Southern District of Texas as the transferee district.

On the basis of the papers filed and the hearing session held, we find that these three actions involve common questions of fact, and that centralization under Section 1407 will serve the convenience of the parties and witnesses and promote the just and efficient conduct of the litigation. The actions share factual questions as to whether DePuy's Pinnacle Acetabular Cup System, a device used in hip replacement surgery, was defectively designed and/or manufactured, and whether defendants failed to provide adequate warnings concerning the device. Centralization under Section 1407 will eliminate duplicative discovery, prevent inconsistent pretrial rulings on discovery and other issues, and conserve the resources of the parties, their counsel and the judiciary.

Several plaintiffs request that the centralized proceedings be limited to solely the metal-on-metal configuration of the DePuy Pinnacle Acetabular Cup System and that the litigation be renamed accordingly. Defendants assert that all configurations of the Pinnacle Acetabular Cup System should be included within the litigation. At this early stage of the litigation, we will not limit the scope of this MDL docket. The transferee judge can further refine the issues and closely scrutinize the arguments of the parties regarding the inclusion of metal-on-metal and other configurations. If he decides to include all configurations, then the transferee judge can employ any number of pretrial techniques — such as establishing separate discovery or motion tracks — to efficiently manage this litigation. It may be that some claims or actions (such as, perhaps, claims or actions involving Pinnacle Acetabular Cup System hip implants in configurations other than the metal-on-metal configuration) can be remanded to their transferor districts in advance of the other centralized actions. But we are unwilling, on the basis of the record before us, to make such a determination at this time. *See In re: Kugel Mesh Hernia Patch Prods. Liab. Litig.*, 493 F. Supp. 2d 1371, 1373 (J.P.M.L. 2007). Should the transferee judge deem remand of any claims or actions appropriate (or, relatedly, the subsequent exclusion of similar types of claims or actions from the centralized proceedings), then he may accomplish this by filing a suggestion of remand to the Panel. *See* Rule 10.1. We are confident in the transferee judge's ability to streamline pretrial proceedings in all actions, while concomitantly directing the appropriate resolution of all claims.

Plaintiffs in the Eastern District of Louisiana *Santorelli* potential tag-along action appeared at oral argument to stress that their action should not be included in any centralized litigation, given the health conditions of plaintiffs and the likelihood of expeditious resolution in the Eastern District of Louisiana. Because this action is a potential tag-along action, plaintiffs' arguments are premature, and we decline to grant plaintiffs' request at this time. The proper approach is for plaintiffs to present their arguments by moving to vacate if we issue an order conditionally transferring their action to the MDL. *See* Rule 7.1. Or plaintiffs may request that the transferee judge remand their action to the transferor court. *See* Rule 10.1.

We conclude that the Northern District of Texas is an appropriate transferee district for centralized pretrial proceedings in this litigation. These cases involve a medical device that was marketed and sold throughout the nation. The Northern District of Texas represents a geographically central and accessible district that enjoys favorable docket conditions. Judge James E. Kinkeade, who presides over a potential tag-along action (*Shirilla*) pending in this district, has the caseload conditions conducive to handling this litigation, and we are confident that he will steer this litigation on a prudent course.

IT IS THEREFORE ORDERED that, pursuant to 28 U.S.C. § 1407, the [three] actions are transferred to the Northern District of Texas and, with the consent of that court, assigned to the Honorable James E. Kinkeade for coordinated or consolidated pretrial proceedings.

In re Aviation Products Liability Litigation

347 F. Supp. 1401 (Judicial Panel on Multidistrict Litigation 1972)

The cases comprising this products liability litigation can be segregated into two broad categories. One category consists of actions by corporate plaintiffs asserting claims for damages allegedly caused by defects in the design, manufacture and installation of a gas turbine helicopter engine produced by the Allison Division of General Motors Corporation. The other category consists of actions asserting claims for personal injuries sustained when a helicopter powered by the same type engine crashed because of an alleged in-flight engine failure.

Plaintiffs in twelve actions pending in seven different districts moved the Panel to transfer these cases (hereinafter referred to as the Schedule A cases) to a single district for coordinated or consolidated pretrial proceedings. The Panel issued an order to show cause why eight apparently related cases (hereinafter referred to as the Schedule B cases) should not also be considered for transfer pursuant to 28 U.S.C. § 1407. On the basis of the papers filed and the hearing held, we find that all of the Schedule A cases and some of the Schedule B cases will clearly benefit from transfer to a single district for coordinated or consolidated pretrial proceedings.

I. Schedule A Cases
A. Background

Plaintiffs in the Schedule A cases are represented by the same lead counsel. Each plaintiff is a corporate owner or operator of a commercial helicopter powered by a gas turbine engine designed and manufactured by the Detroit Diesel Allison Division of General Motors Corporation (hereinafter Allison). Each action concerns the design, manufacture and installation of the helicopter engine, known as the Allison 250-C18. Allegations concerning the design and manufacture of the helicopter frame are common to some of the cases, as are charges of improper performance of overhaul, modification and repair service.

The claims for damages in each of the cases are similar: (1) damages to helicopters and to plaintiff's business as a result of crashes or emergency landings caused by premature failures and malfunctions of the helicopter's engine during flight; (2) damages to plaintiff's business as a result of down time required to make engine modifications and repairs specified by the Federal Aviation Agency and Allison.

B. Arguments of the Parties

Movants urge that the existence of common questions of fact makes transfer to a single district for coordinated or consolidated pretrial proceedings necessary in order to promote the just and efficient conduct of the litigation and to avoid duplicitous discovery and unnecessary inconvenience to the parties and witnesses. Movants contend that the issue of fact central to each lawsuit is the airworthiness of the Allison 250-C18 engine, including its design, development, manufacture and installation. It is asserted that although the specific defects alleged in each separate case may not be identical they are all interwoven so as to cover the engine's general condition and airworthiness. It is also asserted that discovery common to all cases will concern the extent to which Allison controlled and directed the installation of the engine by the helicopter manufacturers and each incident of engine overhaul modification and repair performed by its authorized distributors.

Allison agrees that consolidation of the Schedule A cases for coordinated pretrial proceedings is necessary, but urges that transfer of the Lametti action be denied because discovery is near completion. Allison also points out that transfer of the Freeman action is unnecessary because that case settled shortly after trial began.

All other defendants oppose transfer of any of the cases in which they are named. Although these defendants generally admit that certain common issues of fact are alleged, they argue that these issues are outnumbered by separate and distinct factual issues peculiar to each case. They assert that since the helicopters were operated in different environments under varying atmospheric conditions, both of which affect the performance of the aircraft and the engine, a substantial amount of local discovery concerning each mishap is necessary and will not be common.

These defendants contend that transfer will restrict their efforts to complete local discovery and will require them to participate in discovery not useful to them. They also contend that an important factor weighing against the desirability of transfer under Section 1407 is the lack of a single district with jurisdiction over all defendants, which precludes any real possibility of a common trial on liability.

C. The Question of Transfer

It is clear from the legislative history of Section 1407 that multidistrict products liability litigation was envisioned as susceptible to effective treatment under Section 1407. There is no dispute that two of the three statutory requirements to transfer exist in this litigation: these are civil actions involving one or more common questions of fact which are pending in more than one district. The opposition to transfer, however, strongly urges that the issues of fact are not so common that the convenience of the parties and witnesses and the just and efficient conduct of the litigation will be promoted by transfer under Section 1407. We do not agree.

Each action against Allison will require discovery concerning the design, manufacture and installation of the Allison 250-C18 engine. Even though different component parts are involved in different cases, discovery common to all cases will concern engineers responsible for the overall design and development of the engine. And plaintiffs may also be interested in deposing the company officials who relied on those engineers. Furthermore, if it is true, as plaintiffs assert, that Allison controlled the installation of the engines by the airframe manufacturers and dictated the specifications regarding overhaul, modification and repair to the authorized distributors, discovery on these issues will likely be common.

We are convinced that transfer of the Schedule A cases to a single district for coordinated or consolidated pretrial proceedings is necessary. For the convenience of the parties and witnesses it is highly desirable that witnesses relevant to the common issues be deposed but once. And only through a coordinated pretrial discovery program, tailored to fit the discovery needs of each party and supervised by a single judge, can overlapping and duplicitous discovery be avoided and the just and efficient conduct of the litigation assured.

The Manual for Complex and Multidistrict Litigation specifically resolves defendants' concern that transfer will involve them in unwanted discovery:

> [E]xpenses of counsel in attending depositions on oral interrogatories can be avoided by entry of an order providing an opportunity for a delayed examination by parties who cannot afford to attend all depositions or believe the depositions will not affect their interests....

Under this order a party with limited means or who in good faith believes the deposition is of no interest to him may without risk, decide not to be represented by counsel at the deposition in question. He may read a copy of the transcript of the initial examination and then decide whether he wishes to request a delayed examination on the ground that his interests were inadequately protected at the initial examination. *Manual* Part I, §2.31 (1970).

Furthermore, defendants' argument regarding the unavailability of a single district with jurisdiction over all parties is misdirected. Transfer of civil actions pursuant to 28

U.S.C. §1407 is for pretrial purposes only and the fact that all parties are not amenable to suit in a particular district does not prevent transfer to that district for pretrial proceedings where the prerequisites of Section 1407 are otherwise satisfied. *In re Kauffman Mutual Fund Actions*, 337 F.Supp. 1337, 1339 (J.P.M.L.1972). Succinctly, venue is not a criterion in deciding the propriety of transfer under Section 1407. *In re Hotel Telephone Charge Antitrust Litigation* 341 F.Supp. 771 (J.P.M.L. Mar. 30, 1972).

D. Choice of Transferee Forum

The Southern District of Indiana is the most appropriate transferee forum. Allison is the one party involved in all of the transferred cases and the majority of the common discovery will focus on it. Its plant and offices are located in Indianapolis and all its documents and necessary witnesses are there. Also, the transferred cases are fairly well-scattered throughout the country and Indianapolis provides a convenient geographical center for the litigation.

Judge Morell E. Sharp of the Western District of Washington has conducted a complete discovery program in the now-settled Freeman action. His familiarity with the issues and discovery involved in this litigation will enable him to expedite the consolidated pretrial proceedings. Pursuant to 28 U.S.C. §292(c), Judge Sharp has been designated to sit as a district judge in the Southern District of Indiana and this litigation will be assigned to him for pretrial proceedings.

II. Schedule B cases
A. Cases Transferred

With respect to each action included in the Panel's show cause order, we have examined the complaint, read the briefs filed and heard oral argument. On the basis of our reasoning concerning the Schedule A cases, we conclude that, for the convenience of all parties and witnesses and the just and efficient conduct of the litigation, the following Schedule B cases should be transferred to the Southern District of Indiana for coordinated or consolidated pretrial proceedings.

1. Arizona Helicopters, Inc. v. General Motors Corp. et al., District of Arizona, Civil Action No. Civ.-70-323-PHX

The allegations of plaintiff's complaint closely parallel those made by plaintiffs in the Schedule A cases. Plaintiff, owner of a helicopter powered by an Allison 250-C18 engine, alleges that as a result of engine failures it suffered damage to the aircraft, a loss of revenue due to inability to use the aircraft and additional pecuniary losses. It is alleged that these in-flight failures were a result of defects in the design, material, construction or workmanship (or some combination thereof) regarding the engine and its component parts.

In Practice

Criticisms of the MDL statute in operation have included the following:

> The first problem is endemic to all devices that seek to affect a plaintiff's forum choice: MDL transfer violates the plaintiffs' adversarial ability to control the litigation. Moreover ... the Panel considers only the overall benefits and costs of aggregation; transfer is appropriate even when it imposes excessive costs on certain individuals. Indeed ... the person most benefitted ... is the defendant, who otherwise would have to engage in the same discovery again and again. Thus, an MDL transfer portends a shift in power from the

plaintiff, who can use an inconvenient forum against a defendant, to the defendant, who can now use an inconvenient transferee forum against a plaintiff.

Some of those changes favor plaintiffs and others favor defendants; whichever occurs in a particular case, the aggregation of cases in an MDL proceeding cannot be viewed as an outcome-neutral event.

Jay Tidmarsh & Roger H. Transgrud, *Complex Litigation: Problems in Advanced Civil Procedure* 37–38 (Foundation Press 2002).

All parties to this action oppose transfer. They claim that discovery is substantially complete, except for a few depositions scheduled to be taken in Indianapolis. Although the case had been scheduled for trial on July 11, 1972, we are advised by counsel that the trial date has been continued for approximately six months. In light of this development and to avoid the possibility of duplicitous discovery and unnecessary inconvenience to the Indianapolis witnesses, we think it best to order this case transferred to the Southern District of Indiana for the completion of pretrial discovery. Certainly if this is the only remaining discovery needed, Judge Sharp can devise a program to accommodate these parties and the action may be considered for remand to the District of Arizona.

2. Sabine Offshore Services, Inc. v. General Motors Corp. Eastern District of Texas, Civil Action No. 7647

Plaintiff claims that it is entitled to recover damages for two separate helicopter crashes caused by in-flight engine failures. Both the plaintiff and defendant oppose transfer on the ground that this action does not present questions of fact common to the other cases. We do not agree. Plaintiff alleges that the helicopter's engine, an Allison 250-C18, was defective either in "workmanship, design or material at the time the helicopter's engine manufactured by defendant was delivered to plaintiff." Thus, as far as plaintiff's discovery is concerned, there definitely are areas in which questions of fact exist common to the transferred cases. We believe that both parties will benefit from participation in the consolidated pretrial proceedings before Judge Sharp. Once the common discovery is completed, of course, the action may be considered for remand to the Eastern District of Texas.

3. Ranger et al. v. General Motors Corp. et al., District of Arizona, Civil Action No. Civ.-72-42-PCT

This action, originally filed in state court and subsequently removed to federal court, consists of two claims. The first is a wrongful death claim brought by the personal representative of the estate of a pilot fatally injured in a helicopter crash; the second claim is brought by the corporate owner of two helicopters that were involved in several crashes, one of which resulted in the fatality complained of in the first claim.

A comparison of the second claim with the complaint filed in *Elling Halvorsen, Inc., et al. v. Textron, Inc., et al.*, District of Arizona, Civil Action No. Civ.71-58 PHX (a Schedule A case), reveals that similar allegations are made in that action involving the same parties and concerning the same helicopters and mishaps. Furthermore, counsel representing the corporate plaintiffs in the second claim also serve as lead counsel for the Schedule A plaintiffs. It is therefore clear that the second claim of the Marvel Ranger action should be consolidated with the other cases for the coordinated pretrial proceedings in the Southern District of Indiana and it is so ordered.

Although plaintiffs in the first claim have no objection to transfer of the second claim for coordinated or consolidated pretrial proceedings, they argue that their claim does not present questions of fact sufficiently common to the other actions to warrant transfer at this time. We agree. Section 1407(a) authorizes the Panel to "separate any claim" from the transferred action and to remand that claim to the transferor district. *See, e. g., In re Hotel Telephone Charge Antitrust Litigation, supra; In re Penn Central Securities Litigation,* 325 F.Supp. 309 (J.P.M.L.1971). We therefore remand the first claim of the Marvel Ranger action to the District of Arizona, but without prejudice to later application for transfer should the parties find that discovery will duplicate discovery in the transferee district.

B. Cases Not Transferred

We have considered each of the remaining Schedule B cases on its own merits and have concluded that none of them present sufficient common questions of fact to warrant transfer to the Southern District of Indiana at this time.

1. Richard W. Black v. Fairchild Industries, Inc., et al.,
District of New Jersey, Civil Action No. 63-72 and
John W. Thumann et al. v. Fairchild Industries, Inc., et al.,
District of Maryland, Civil Action No. 72-433M

Both cases are personal injury actions arising out of the crash of a helicopter en route from Baltimore Friendship Airport to Washington National Airport. Although plaintiffs allege that the crash resulted from a failure of the helicopter's engine, an Allison 250-C18, the complaints do not set forth any specific engine defect and we cannot conclude that discovery will involve issues of fact common to the transferred cases. Transfer is therefore denied without prejudice to later application if it is found during the course of pretrial that discovery will duplicate discovery in the transferee forum.

2. Mrs. Doyle R. Avant, Jr., et al. v. Fairchild-Hiller Corp. et al.,
Southern District of Texas, Civil Action No. 70-V-1 and
Barbara G. Hall et al. v. Fairchild-Hiller Corp., et al.,
Southern District of Texas, Civil Action No. 70-V-2

These cases are wrongful death actions arising from the crash of a helicopter near Goliad, Texas. Transfer is opposed on the ground that discovery is complete and that trial is set for August 14, 1972. It is asserted that any discovery that remains does not involve questions of fact common to the transferred litigation. Transfer of these actions is therefore denied without prejudice to the right of a party to seek reconsideration at a later time.

3. Petroleum Helicopters, Inc. v. The Southwest Airmotive Co. et al.,
Western District of Louisiana, Civil Action No. 16224.

Plaintiff asserts claims for damages allegedly caused by defendant's negligence in servicing plaintiff's helicopter. Discovery only involves the maintenance and service performed by the defendant and the circumstances surrounding the forced landings. Since it appears that no questions of fact exist common to the transferred cases, transfer is denied, but without prejudice to later application if the parties deem it necessary to expand their discovery to encompass the discovery in the consolidated actions.

It is therefore ordered that the actions listed on the attached revised Schedule A be, and the same hereby are, transferred pursuant to 28 U.S.C. § 1407 to the Southern District of Indiana and, with the consent of that court, assigned to the Honorable Morell E. Sharp, sitting by designation, for coordinated or consolidated pretrial proceedings.

It is further ordered that, pursuant to 28 U.S.C. § 1407, the action *Marvel Ranger et al. v. General Motors Corp. et al.*, D. Arizona, Civil Action No. 72-42-Pct-WEC, be, and the same hereby is, transferred to the Southern District of Indiana for coordinated or consolidated pretrial proceedings and that the First Claim of that action be, and the same hereby is, separated and remanded to the District of Arizona for further proceedings.

It is further ordered that transfer of the actions listed on the attached revised Schedule B be, and the same hereby is, denied without prejudice to later application of the parties involved.

Notes and Problems

1. Compare and contrast the three foregoing cases on the question of whether § 1407 transfer and consolidation was appropriate. Why did the panel give the various different rulings in each of the three cases? Can you distinguish, factually, the scenarios presented to the Judicial Panel? Given that, when does it appear most likely for the Panel to order consolidation and when is it less likely?

2. Consider the motivations in each of the three cases for parties to urge consolidated treatment and for parties to oppose such treatment. Looking at each case, explain the positions of the parties given their identities and the circumstances of the case. Strategic use of devices like the MDL statute are often employed by good advocates to advance their clients' interests.

3. Notice that in the *In re Aviation Products Liability Litigation* case, all of the Schedule A cases were filed in various courts by the same plaintiffs' counsel. If counsel for those plaintiffs wanted the cases consolidated, why did counsel file them separately to begin with? Is it possible the plaintiffs' counsel wants the benefit of both separate and consolidated handling? Could that block of cases have all been filed together initially?

4. When similar cases are later filed after a motion to transfer has been filed or decided, these other cases may *tag along* with the others for resolution without request by the parties. In many instances, the panel initially creates the MDL case through transfer of a small number of cases and then many more "tag along" cases end up being transferred thereafter for inclusion in the MDL proceeding.

5. In *In re Aviation Products Liability Litigation*, Allison opposed the transfer of two cases. Why? If transfer for consolidated proceedings is deemed more efficient, should this not benefit all of the litigants? Why would some parties oppose such treatment?

6. Also in *In re Aviation Products*, the panel stated that there was not a single location where venue and jurisdiction existed but that this was irrelevant to the transfer motion. How can this be true? Was a great portion of your Civil Procedure class just rendered moot? Consider the implications and limitations of a decision by the panel to grant a transfer motion in light of the due process concerns over personal jurisdiction. On the other hand, how would an opposite view of the necessity of personal jurisdiction and proper venue in an MDL transfer impact the power of the Judicial Panel to effectuate the MDL statute's purposes?

7. Notice in the *In re Aviation Products* case where the Judicial Panel chose to transfer all of the cases—to the primary defendant's home. It was not only centrally located, but because that defendant was named in every case being transferred, it became the geographic

common denominator with witnesses and other sources of proof conveniently located. Wouldn't that often be the case, that a target defendant's home would make a lot of sense to receive all of the cases? If so, do you see this additional reason why defendants might often be very positively inclined to urge § 1407 treatment? Such a defendant can persuasively argue, for pretrial purposes anyway, to remove the forum choice of all of the plaintiffs and to substitute its own home court.

8. *Chapter Problem.* Assume that counsel for PERI discovers the following pending litigation against Bresser:

a. A one-year old dispute between Bresser and one of its suppliers of chemicals. The chemical supplier said that Bresser was contractually obligated to take a certain quantity of chemicals (used in fracking) but only took and paid for half of that quantity. Discovery is ongoing in the federal court case filed in Alabama.

b. Royalty owners for another oil & gas producer filed a putative class action against Bresser claiming that Bresser "botched" numerous fracking jobs for that producer and that, as a result, their royalty payments were less than they should have been. The case was only filed a month ago in federal court in Oklahoma and the only activity was the filing of the complaint and answer and the scheduling of a scheduling conference. The complaint does not specify exactly how the fracking was allegedly done incorrectly.

c. A state court fraud claim was filed three months ago against Bresser by another oil & gas producer who alleged that Bresser breached a contract with the plaintiff by "failing to supply the promised quantities of proppant material" on dozens of fracking jobs in the state of Colorado. Bresser removed that case to federal court but the plaintiff has since filed a motion to remand arguing that the removal was untimely. No decision on the motion to remand has occurred.

d. In Houston state court, a small, independent oil & gas producer has also sued Bresser claiming common law fraud for "shorting" it on the delivery of sand used in a single frack job. That case is set for trial in three months in state court.

Given the foregoing cases, would it make sense for PERI to seek § 1407 MDL transfer and consolidation? Are the statutory requirements likely met? If so, *where* can PERI best advocate the cases all be sent?

2. Powers of Transferee Court: "What Is Pretrial?"

Once cases are transferred to, and consolidated in, particular courts, the transferee judges wield great power over the pretrial activities of the litigants and parties. The court will typically play a very active role in devising and overseeing a discovery plan, will entertain sometimes a great number of pretrial motions on discovery disputes, winnow down the claims, and rule on motions for summary judgment. Further, it is not uncommon for transferee courts to rule on motions for class certification (covered in the next Chapter) and preside over settlement conferences. The reality is that only a small percentage of cases sent to a court for MDL treatment are ever remanded back for trial because so few cases are tried in federal courts nowadays. But even for those cases "remanded" to the original courts for trial, the MDL court's pretrial rulings can still be felt. Consider in the following case the federal transferee judge's view on the scope of its pretrial jurisdiction under the MDL statute.

In re Factor VIII or IX Concentrate
Blood Products Litigation

169 F.R.D. 632 (N.D. Ill. 1996)

GRADY, J.

MEMORANDUM OPINION AND ORDER

The broad question addressed in this opinion is whether a transferee court in multidistrict litigation under 28 U.S.C. § 1407 has the authority to limit the number of common-issue expert witnesses at trials which will take place after remand to the transferor districts. If the answer to that question is in the affirmative, then the second question is what the limit should be in this particular litigation.

Background of the Litigation

Plaintiffs in these consolidated cases are persons suffering from hemophilia, a hereditary disease in which the protein that causes blood clotting is missing. The principal treatment for the disease is the intravenous injection of the missing protein, derived from the plasma of blood donors. Four of the defendants are pharmaceutical companies which collect and process the plasma to derive "factor concentrates," which are then sold for use by hemophiliacs. The manufacturing process for deriving the finished factor concentrate from blood plasma is known as "fractionating," and the four defendants involved in the present dispute are known as "fractionators." Together, they produce all or virtually all of the factor concentrates used in the United States.

In the early 1980s, some hemophiliacs using the defendants' factor concentrates began to show symptoms of a disease later identified as Acquired Immune Deficiency Syndrome ("AIDS"). As is now known, this disease is transmitted by the Human Immunodeficiency Virus ("HIV"). Plaintiffs allege that they were infected with the virus as a result of injecting the defendants' factor concentrates derived from donors who were themselves infected. Plaintiffs allege a variety of negligent acts and omissions on the part of the fractionator defendants, principally the failure to sterilize their products to eliminate the possibility of viral infection (viral inactivation), failure to screen plasma donors so as to eliminate classes of persons, such as intravenous drug users, who presented a high risk of viral infectivity, failure to engage in "surrogate testing" of donors to determine whether they had viral infections (such as hepatitis) suggesting the possibility of other, undetectable viruses as well, failure to warn users of their products of the danger of infection once they knew or reasonably should have known that the newly observed symptoms were caused by a disease that was viral and blood-borne, and failure to withdraw their products from the market when the danger of infection became known.

Defendants have a variety of defenses to plaintiffs' negligence allegations. Among the more important are that the virus in question was unknown and unforeseeable during any period of time defendants were not taking the precautions plaintiffs claim they should have been taking and that, as soon as the presence of a new virus became apparent, they did all they reasonably could have done to eliminate it from their products. With regard to each of the measures plaintiffs allege should have been undertaken earlier, defendants respond with specific reasons as to why it was not feasible to do so. For instance, heat treatment of the concentrates, the method of viral inactivation plaintiffs claim should have been used, was not, in defendants' view, a procedure that was technologically effective or even legally permissible for them to use until most of the plaintiffs had already been infected with the virus. Defendants contend that they began the effective heat treatment of their products as soon as they were able to do so.

A number of lawsuits based upon diversity of citizenship were filed against the fractionators in various federal districts by infected hemophiliacs, their spouses, guardians, and personal representatives. On December 7, 1993, the Judicial Panel on Multidistrict Litigation transferred the then pending federal cases to this court for consolidated pretrial proceedings pursuant to 28 U.S.C. § 1407. The total number of cases now pending, including tag-a-longs, is approximately 192. Another 300 similar cases are pending in various state courts. A Steering Committee appointed by the court, chosen from among the attorneys who represent plaintiffs in individual cases, has been conducting the litigation on behalf of all plaintiffs.

Prior to the MDL consolidation, thirteen cases were tried to verdict in state and federal courts. Twelve verdicts were for defendants and the lone plaintiffs' victory was reversed on appeal. No cases have been tried subsequent to the MDL consolidation.

The practical issue now pending before this court is *how much* discovery remains to be completed before the cases are ready for remand, and that brings us back to the questions posed in the opening paragraph of this opinion.

How the Questions Arose

Until the present dispute arose, discovery had proceeded relatively smoothly, with no more than the usual number of questions requiring decision by the court. We were under the impression that both sides had the same view of what we are doing: conducting the discovery that is common to all of the transferred cases and which is necessary to prepare them for trial. This obviously includes taking whatever depositions are necessary to acquaint the parties with the testimony of the common-issue witnesses who are likely to appear at each trial. For example, each side must depose the expert witnesses the other side is going to present on the question of what was known about blood-borne viruses, and how to prevent their transmission through blood products, in the late 1970s and early 1980s.

To establish the procedures that would govern the conduct of the litigation in this court, we entered a Case Management Order on May 5, 1994. The order was largely a result of cooperative effort. Much of it consists of agreed submissions by the parties, adopted *verbatim* by the court.

[Pursuant to this Case Management Order,] Plaintiffs designated seventeen experts, and all but three of their discovery depositions have been completed.

The present dispute arises from the fact that the fractionator defendants have designated a total of 137 common-issue expert witnesses. Plaintiffs have objected to this number as excessive and have requested an order limiting the defendants to a reasonable number. They suggest twenty-six as a maximum.

Defendants concede that they do not intend to call 137 witnesses in any particular trial, but contend that, for reasons discussed below, they nonetheless need to designate this number as possible trial witnesses. Defendants suggest that plaintiffs should choose which of the witnesses they wish to depose during the MDL proceeding. If defendants choose at any particular trial to present common-issue experts whom plaintiffs have not deposed, the solution, say the defendants, will be for plaintiffs to depose the witnesses at that time. Defendants are making no commitment that any of the 137 witnesses plaintiffs might select for depositions in the MDL would be called at any trial, and they have carefully avoided giving any indication of who the actual trial witnesses are likely to be. Thus, plaintiffs would proceed at their own risk and could well waste their time and resources deposing witnesses who will not be called at trial. In short, if defendants have their way, they reserve the right to render any expert witness depositions taken by the plaintiffs in the MDL a complete waste of time.

Defendants make a number of arguments as to why 137 is a reasonable number of witnesses, but they also advance the basic argument that this court, as transferee court under § 1407, lacks the authority to limit the number of their trial witnesses in any event:

> The role of an MDL Court is to oversee "coordinated or consolidated pretrial proceedings." 28 U.S.C. § 1407. This role does not include the determination of issues related only to trial.

Defendant Fractionators' Memorandum of Law in Opposition to Plaintiffs' Motion to Limit Expert Testimony, at 8. Orders that pertain to the trial of a case, say the defendants, can be made only by the "trial judge," meaning the transferor judges to whom the cases will be remanded upon completion of the MDL discovery.

The Authority of a Transferee Court

Defendants fundamentally misconceive the nature of multidistrict litigation and "the role of an MDL court." The source of their confusion is their failure to understand, or at least to acknowledge, the relationship between the "pretrial proceedings" referred to in § 1407 and the trial itself. The pretrial and the trial are not, as defendants imply, two unrelated phases of the case. Rather, they are part of a continuum that results in resolution of the case, and the relationship between them is intimate. "Pretrial" proceedings are conducted to prepare for trial. A judge who has no power to impose limits as to what will happen at trial is obviously a judge who has little ability to manage pretrial proceedings in a meaningful way, since there would be no assurance that the judge's efforts are directed toward what is likely to happen at trial. That it is essential for the "pretrial" judge to have the authority to enter orders that will be binding as to the conduct of the trial is recognized by Rule 16(c)(4), (13), (14) and (15), of the Federal Rules of Civil Procedure, which gives the judge conducting pretrial conferences authority to enter a variety of orders that will shape the conduct of the trial, including authority to limit the number of expert witnesses and to establish time limits for presenting evidence at trial. Rule 16 conferences are not necessarily conducted by the same district judge who will ultimately try the case; and some district judges routinely refer Rule 16 conferences to magistrate judges who, in the absence of consent by the parties, would not even be authorized to try the case.

A transferee judge in a multidistrict proceeding is one to whom the Judicial Panel on Multidistrict Litigation has transferred a number of different cases pending in different districts "involving one or more common questions of fact" because the Panel has determined that such a transfer "will be for the convenience of parties and witnesses and will promote the just and efficient conduct of such actions." 28 U.S.C. § 1407(a). The purpose of the transfer is "for coordinated or consolidated pretrial proceedings." Unless the transferee judge has the authority to enter pretrial orders that will govern the conduct of the trial, there would be little prospect that the "coordinated or consolidated pretrial proceedings" contemplated by the statute would "promote the just and efficient conduct of such actions." If the transfer is to serve the legislative purpose of § 1407, the transferee judge must have the same authority that any pretrial judge has to enter orders that will ensure the relevance of the pretrial proceedings to the conduct of any trial that occurs after remand to the transferor court. Rule 16 applies to multidistrict proceedings the same as it applies to individual cases, and the transferee court may exercise the authority granted under Rule 16(c)(4) to limit the number of expert witnesses to be called at trial.

The answer to the first question posed in the introduction to this opinion, then, is that the MDL transferee judge is, by force of the statute itself, in charge of the consolidated cases for all purposes consistent with the objectives of § 1407 and of necessity has the authority to limit the number of common-issue trial witnesses. If an additional basis for that authority is desired, Rule 16 of the Federal Rules of Civil Procedure provides it.

It is true, of course, that no pretrial judge, one managing an individual case as well as one managing consolidated pretrial proceedings in a multidistrict litigation, can anticipate everything that might happen up to the point of trial. Obviously, pretrial orders containing limitations that are overtaken by events are subject to adjustment by the judge who will try the case. For instance, a designated expert witness whose deposition has been taken may die before trial, necessitating the designation of a substitute witness and another deposition before trial. But the need for such adjustments is exceptional, not routine. Normally, witness limitations work well. This is especially true in the case of expert witnesses, who often are highly paid and, short of death, likely to be available for trial. Pretrial proceedings have to be conducted on the assumption that the needs of the trial can be fairly anticipated by the pretrial judge. Any other approach would render pretrial proceedings pointless.

This is not to suggest that in the absence of unforeseen developments the transferor judges in this litigation are bound by what this court does. The extent to which any transferor judge might see fit to vary what we do here is a matter of his or her own good judgment. We would expect any error on our part to be corrected before the case went to trial. This is not a matter of trying to tie the hands of the trial judge. It is a matter of defining what this court's authority is to enter orders that will bind the parties at trial to the extent the trial judge sees fit to enforce them. (It is also a matter of determining whether the transferor court can, as a matter of law, safely adhere to the orders of the transferee judge should he or she find it otherwise appropriate to do so.) But it is obvious that the objectives of § 1407 can best be achieved when a departure from the transferee judge's pretrial orders is the exception rather than the rule, and it is this court's impression that such departures are in fact exceptional.

Holding that we do have the authority, as the transferee court, to enter an order limiting the number of common-issue expert witnesses the fractionator defendants will be permitted to call at trial, so that we can determine what depositions need to be taken, we turn now to the question of what that number should be. [Judge Grady determined that the defendants could only, collectively, designate 24 common-issue expert witnesses for possible trial witnesses.]

Notes and Problems

1. In the *In re Factor VIII or IX Concentrate Blood Products Liability Litigation* case, the court ruled that as an MDL judge, he was permitted to enter an order requiring a party to designate a smaller number of experts for trial. Although this order affects trial proceedings, the court held the MDL judge has this power. If the MDL court cannot try the case, and if the MDL court does not have to have jurisdiction, why should it be able to make these decisions? If the MDL court could not make this ruling, would it have much power at all?

2. Given the decision by Judge Grady in the case above, and using that logic, how would you define "pretrial" as used in § 1407? In other words, at what point and for what

type of motion would it be inappropriate for the MDL judge to issue a binding ruling on the parties?

3. While MDL judges clearly can rule on Rule 12(b)(6) motions to dismiss for failure to state a claim, discovery motions, sanctions motions, motions under Rule 56 for summary judgment, motions for Rule 23 class certification, and a myriad of other pretrial issues, the U.S. Supreme Court has declared that one thing that MDL judges cannot do is grant a § 1404(a) motion to transfer venue (for the trial) to themselves. The reason is because § 1407 is quite clear that, after the pretrial activities in a given case have been completed, the MDL judge "shall remand" the case to its original forum for trial. Granting a § 1404(a) motion to transfer the trial of a case to the MDL judge would be done in contravention of § 1407's mandate for remand. *See Lexecon Inc. v. Milberg Weiss Bershad Hynes & Lerach*, 523 U.S. 26 (1998). In that case, the MDL judge granted defendant's motion to transfer venue over the plaintiff's objections. Of course, where all of the litigants to a case agree to such a transfer, there would be nobody to challenge the court granting an *agreed* motion for transfer of venue. *See In re Carbon Dioxide Indus. Antitrust Litig.*, 229 F.3d 1321, 1325 (11th Cir.). Further, an MDL judge is certainly capable of trying any cases that were initially filed in that same court. Therefore, it is not uncommon for MDL judges to end up presiding over at least some of the MDL cases that remain after the pretrial phase. Sometimes having such a trial can even serve as a *bellwether* case, useful for providing guidance to counsel on all remaining cases as to case evaluation to inform ongoing settlement talks.

F. Anti-Injunction Act: 28 U.S.C. § 2283

The Anti-Injunction Act generally bars federal courts from enjoining a pending state court suit. The issue is often triggered when multiple identical or similar suits are filed in state and federal court. In situations such as these, it is natural to find the potential for duplicative litigation to be wasteful and unnecessary. However, the statute prohibits a federal court from prohibiting a state court from proceeding with an action pending before the state court even if, for example, the federal court case was the first to be filed. The purpose of this bar is to promote comity and deference to state court adjudication— a concept consistent with federalism. Even if it seems wasteful to permit an unnecessary state court action from proceeding, the thought is that the rules of preclusion we studied in Chapter 1 (res judicata and collateral estoppel) will ultimately be applied after final judgment in one case to bring to cessation the continued wastefulness and possibility of inconsistent judgments that might otherwise ensue.

The statute does not prohibit all injunctions against pending state court actions; rather, it provides three exceptions. Although the Act would typically otherwise apply in these circumstances, these exceptions permit a federal court to enjoin a pending state court suit when the injunction is 1) necessary in aid of federal jurisdiction; 2) necessary to promote or effectuate a federal court's judgments; or 3) when an express statutory exception applies. The extent of these exceptions is detailed in the cases below. Nevertheless, keep in mind, simply because an exception applies does not mean an injunction can automatically be issued. Parties seeking an injunction must still meet the necessary elements for equitable relief. As you read the opinions below, notice how a litigant's tools, such as injunctions, removal, and MDL consolidation, permit "lawsuits [to sometimes be] turned into procedural entanglements." *In re Diet Drugs*, 282 F.3d 220, 232 (3d Cir. 2002). Pay close attention to how the attorneys in the cases below proceed with these tools and the arguments made in support of their uses.

1. Basic Application of Anti-Injunction Act

Standard Microsystems v. Texas Instruments
916 F.2d 58 (2d Cir. 1990)

LEVAL, J.,

This appeal seeks to enforce the Anti-Injunction Act, 28 U.S.C. § 2283. In a patent-licensing dispute, the district judge enjoined the defendant-appellant from prosecuting a suit which it had instituted against plaintiff-appellee in the Texas state courts. Because we hold that this order violated the terms of the Act, the injunction is vacated.

Anti-Injunction Act

A court of the United States may not grant an injunction to stay proceedings in a State court except as expressly authorized by Act of Congress, or where necessary in aid of its jurisdiction, or to protect or effectuate its judgments.

28 U.S.C. § 2283.

The dispute arises out of a patent cross-licensing agreement between Standard Microsystems Corp. ("SMC"), the plaintiff-appellee, and Texas Instruments, Inc., ("TI"), the defendant-appellant, dated October 1, 1976 (the "Agreement"). The Agreement grants to each party the right to make royalty-free use of semiconductor technology owned by the other. It apparently also contains provisions requiring the parties to keep the agreement confidential, and prohibiting the assignment of rights under the Agreement.

TI has licensed certain Japanese and Korean companies to exploit TI's "Kilby patents," which are part of the cross-licensed technology. SMC now proposes to transfer its rights under the Agreement to make royalty-free use of the same TI technology. It proposes to offer these rights to Japanese and Korean entities. TI apparently advised SMC that it would consider such a sale, and disclosure by SMC in preparation for such a sale, as a violation of the Agreement.

On Friday, January 19, 1990, SMC filed this action against TI in the Eastern District of New York. The complaint alleges violations of federal antitrust and securities statutes and breach of contract, and further seeks declaratory relief that SMC's actions do not breach its Agreement. Simultaneously with the filing of the suit, SMC obtained a temporary restraining order signed by Judge Joseph McLaughlin. The order restrained TI from terminating its License Agreement dated October 1, 1976, with plaintiff or revoking any of plaintiff's rights under that Agreement. Judge McLaughlin's order included an Order to Show Cause setting a hearing before Judge Leonard Wexler, the assigned judge, on SMC's application for a preliminary injunction to be held on Monday, January 22, 1990.

At 8:00 a.m. on Monday morning, January 22, TI filed suit in the Texas state court against SMC. The suit seeks to bar SMC from making disclosures in violation of the Agreement and to bar SMC from interfering with TI's license negotiations in Japan.

On January 22, Judge Wexler continued the TRO and adjourned the preliminary injunction hearing to Friday, January 26.

On January 26, counsel for SMC advised Judge Wexler that SMC "would like [the court] to enjoin TI along the same lines as the temporary restraining order, to begin with. We would also like, Your honor, ... to enjoin TI from specifically proceeding in the [Texas] State Court action or any other action with respect to the same contract issues...."

Judge Wexler proceeded to make the following order:

> Until there is a determination, Mr. Cooper [TI's counsel], I'm directing you, your firm, your client, anyone connected with you are stayed from doing anything in Texas or in relationship to that action that has previously been filed. Cease and desist immediately.

That is the order from which TI appeals.[5]

Discussion

TI contends that Judge Wexler's order violates the Anti-Injunction Act, 28 U.S.C. §2283. The Act provides:

> A court of the United States may not grant an injunction to stay proceedings in a State court except as expressly authorized by Act of Congress, or where necessary in aid of its jurisdiction, or to protect or effectuate its judgments.

Its purpose is, *inter alia,* to avoid intergovernmental friction that may result from a federal injunction staying state court proceedings. The Supreme Court has construed the Act to forbid a federal court from enjoining a party from prosecuting a state court action unless one of the three exceptions stated in the statute obtains. The three excepted circumstances are (i) the express provisions of another act of Congress authorizing such an order; (ii) necessity in aid of the federal court's jurisdiction and (iii) the need to protect or effectuate the federal court's judgments. *Atlantic Coast Line R.R. Co. v. Brotherhood of Locomotive Engineers,* 398 U.S. 281, 287–88, 90 S.Ct. 1739, 1743–44, 26 L.Ed.2d 234 (1970).

None of the three statutory exceptions is here pertinent.

A number of circumstances may justify a finding that the exceptions govern. Where the federal court's jurisdiction is *in rem* and the state court action may effectively deprive the federal court of the opportunity to adjudicate as to the *res,* the exception for necessity "in aid of jurisdiction" may be appropriate. *Compare Kline v. Burke Construction Co.,* 260 U.S. 226, 230, 43 S.Ct. 79, 81, 67 L.Ed. 226 (1922) (declining to uphold federal court injunction against state court proceedings where contract obligations were in dispute, rather than rights relating to a *res*); *Heyman v. Kline,* 456 F.2d 123 (2d Cir.), *cert. denied,* 409 U.S. 847, 93 S.Ct. 53, 34 L.Ed.2d 88 (1972) (Act bars federal court injunction issued in *in personam* proceeding involving employment contract); *Vernitron Corp. v. Benjamin,* 440 F.2d 105 (2d Cir.), *cert. denied,* 402 U.S. 987, 91 S.Ct. 1664, 29 L.Ed.2d 154 (1971) (reversing issuance of injunction justified only by the possibility of collateral estoppel in parallel securities litigations); *with Penn General Casualty Co. v. Pennsylvania ex rel. Schnader,* 294 U.S. 189,

---

5. In a written order issued on March 1, 1990, Judge Wexler summarized his earlier order as follows:

> Further, as indicated on the record on January 26, 1990, this Court directed Texas Instruments, its agents and its attorneys, from taking any steps in relation to an action which it instituted on the same issue in Texas state court on the morning of January 22, 1990, shortly before or during the hearing then proceeding in this court.

55 S.Ct. 386, 79 L.Ed. 850 (1935) (affirming injunction against state court proceedings to protect court's ability to control and dispose of property in liquidation proceeding). Analogous circumstances may be found where a federal court is on the verge of settling a complex matter, and state court proceedings may undermine its ability to achieve that objective, *see In re Baldwin-United Corp.,* 770 F.2d 328, 337 (2d Cir. 1985) (upholding injunction against state court actions to protect ability of federal court to manage and to settle multidistrict class action proceeding which was far advanced and in which court had extensive involvement). Or, where a federal court has made conclusive rulings and their effect may be undermined by threatened relitigation in state courts, the exception may be appropriate. *See, e.g., Necchi Sewing Machine Sales Corp. v. Carl,* 260 F.Supp. 665, 669 (S.D.N.Y.1966) (enjoining state court from hearing claims when federal court had found those claims to be properly heard only before an arbitrator).

The suits at issue here are *in personam* actions, brought on successive business days in two different courts, disputing the interpretation of a contract. The existence of the state court action does not in any way impair the jurisdiction of the federal court or its ability to render justice. It is well-settled that such circumstances as these do not justify invocation of the exceptions of the Anti-Injunction Act. *See Vendo Co. v. Lektro-Vend Corp.,* 433 U.S. 623, 642, 97 S.Ct. 2881, 2893, 53 L.Ed.2d 1009 (1977) (reversing injunction of state court proceedings which, like federal court action, involved dispute arising out of covenant not to compete; "[w]e have never viewed parallel *in personam* actions as interfering with the jurisdiction of either court"); *Kline v. Burke Construction Co.,* 260 U.S. at 230, 43 S.Ct. at 81; *Vernitron Corp. v. Benjamin,* 440 F.2d at 108; *Heyman v. Kline,* 456 F.2d at 131–32.

Each court is free to proceed in its own way and in its own time, without reference to the proceedings in the other court. Whenever a judgment is rendered in one of the courts and pleaded in the other, the effect of that judgment is to be determined by application of the principles of *res judicata.*

SMC argues that, nonetheless, Judge Wexler's injunction must be affirmed because it falls within two additional judicially created exceptions to the Act. First, the Act has been held inapplicable to federal injunctions issued prior to the institution of the state court action. *Dombrowski v. Pfister,* 380 U.S. 479, 484 n. 2, 85 S.Ct. 1116, 1119 n. 2, 14 L.Ed.2d 22 (1965); *In re Baldwin-United Corp.,* 770 F.2d 328, 335 (2d Cir. 1985). This exception is based both on policy and the explicit terms of the act. Where no state court proceeding exists, there is less danger that a federal court injunction barring the institution of such a proceeding will cause affront to state authority. Furthermore, the Act bars grant of "an injunction to stay *proceedings* in a State court," 28 U.S.C. §2283 (emph. added), which seems to refer literally to existing proceedings, rather than contemplated proceedings.

SMC contends this case falls within the *Dombrowski* exception because Judge McLaughlin's TRO predated the institution of the Texas action. The contention is frivolous. Although it is true that the TRO predated the Texas action, the TRO did not forbid TI from starting a separate action. The TRO restrained TI only "from terminating [SMC's] License Agreement ... or revoking ... [SMC's] rights under that Agreement." There is no factual basis for SMC's argument that TI's Texas court action was instituted in violation of a federal injunction barring such suit. No order was issued against TI's maintenance of its state court action until January 26, four days after TI started the action.

Second, SMC contends that, notwithstanding the Act, a state court action may be enjoined if a motion to bar the state court action was made before the state court action was started. This argument depends on an exception to the Act created by judicial decision in the Seventh Circuit, *Barancik v. Investors Funding Corp.,* 489 F.2d 933 (7th Cir. 1973), and followed in the First and Eighth Circuits, *see National City Lines, Inc., v. LLC Corp.,* 687 F.2d 1122, 1127–28 (8th Cir. 1982) (following *Barancik*); *Hyde Park Partners, L.P. v. Connolly,* 839 F.2d 837 (1st Cir.1988), but rejected in the Sixth, *see Roth v. Bank of the Commonwealth,* 583 F.2d 527 (6th Cir.1978) (criticizing reasoning of *Barancik*), *cert. dismissed,* 442 U.S. 925, 99 S.Ct. 2852, 61 L.Ed.2d 292 (1979). This circuit has never considered the issue.

In *Barancik,* defendants filed an action in state court while plaintiff's preliminary injunction motion was pending in federal court seeking to bar defendants from commencing a separate legal action. The federal district judge enjoined prosecution of the state court action. The Seventh Circuit affirmed, noting that if the federal judge had immediately decided the motion, the injunction would have preceded the filing of the state court action and therefore, under *Dombrowski,* would not have violated the Anti-Injunction Act. The court found anomalous the possibility that the federal court's authority to rule on a pending motion could be terminated by the action of one of the litigants and concluded that the Anti-Injunction Act did not prohibit a stay of state court proceedings if the state court proceeding was commenced *after* filing of a motion seeking to enjoin it.

We have considerable doubt whether the *Barancik* rule should be adopted in this circuit. We do not find its reasoning compelling. The *Barancik* court found it "unseemly" that a court's power to rule could be defeated by the quicker action of a litigant. 489 F.2d at 937. But it is axiomatic that one is not disabled from acting merely because an adverse litigant has *applied* for an order to bar such action. A party that has not been enjoined is ordinarily free to act, notwithstanding the pendency of applications to enjoin the action. In many circumstances litigants may lawfully moot an application by acting before the court has ruled. To enjoin conduct requires a judge's order, not merely an application for a judge's order. Where speed is needed, the rules of procedure provide for temporary restraining orders, even without notice, to prevent irreparable harm. *See* Fed.R.Civ.Pro. Rule 65. However anomalous it may seem that a party can moot an issue by acting more rapidly than the court, it is far more anomalous and dangerous that a mere application for injunctive relief be deemed equivalent to a court's order issuing an injunction.

The *Barancik* rule, furthermore, creates a still more serious anomaly. Under *Barancik,* merely by filing an application for relief, a party nullifies an Act of Congress. In passing the Anti-Injunction Act, Congress meant to avoid friction in the relationship between federal courts and state courts. The *Barancik* rule places the power in the hands of the plaintiff unilaterally to nullify the effectiveness of an Act of Congress and to create exactly the kind of federal-state conflict that Congress sought to prevent. *Compare Hicks v. Miranda,* 422 U.S. 332, 348–50, 95 S.Ct. 2281, 2291–92, 45 L.Ed.2d 223 (1975).

We need not decide whether the *Barancik* rule will be followed in this circuit because, in any event, it does not apply to these facts.

At the time of TI's commencement of the Texas action, there was no application before the federal court to bar it from doing so. The Order to Show Cause sought a preliminary injunction barring TI from

    a. coercing SMC's compliance in TI's interpretation of the License Agreement;

    b. interfering with SMC's dealings ...;

    c. attempting to monopolize ... through the coercive acts alleged herein; and

    d. terminating the License Agreement and ... revoking any of SMC's rights thereunder ...

SMC's counsel reaches beyond the limits of ingenuity to contrive an argument that the Order to Show Cause applied for an injunction to bar the filing of a parallel action. The argument is to the effect that the application to enjoin TI's "attempt[s] to monopolize ... through the coercive acts alleged herein," especially when combined with the concluding prayer for such "other and different relief as [the court] deems proper and just," incorporates by reference the allegation in the complaint of threats of "sham litigation." Taking all this together, SMC contends its application should be construed as having sought an injunction barring institution of the "sham" Texas action. The argument is more convoluted than convincing. In fact, there was no application before the court to bar TI from starting a lawsuit. Thus, even if we were to adopt the reasoning of *Barancik,* it would not apply to this case.

The district court's order enjoining TI from further prosecuting its action in the Texas state court was issued in violation of the Anti-Injunction Act. Accordingly the order is vacated.

Notes and Problems

1. Explain the nature of the procedural dispute between the litigants in the *Standard Microsystems* case. Why was the second case filed when and where it was? Why did the *Standard Microsystems* court not accept the *Barancik* exception? Why didn't this exception apply here? Did the original plaintiff's attorney arguably make a strategic error in how the case was handled early?

2. What would have been Standard Microsystems' other options in lieu of seeking a federal injunction of a state court? Would these options work in this case? For example, could Standard Microsystems have filed any motions with the state court in Texas asking it to refrain from going forward? In light of the court's ruling above, what should the litigants attempt to do next if they are concerned about litigating on two fronts?

3. The *Standard Microsystems* court did not accept the argument that the Anti-Injunction Act failed to apply because the TRO in question enjoined the firm, clients, and others, but not the court. If the court accepted this argument, would the Anti-Injunction Act effectively bar injunctions as Congress intended?

4. The first statutory exception to the AIA exists when Congress has expressly permitted an injunction against a state court proceeding to be entered by a federal court. This is an extremely narrow exception and is typically limited to the bankruptcy or interpleader contexts. Despite the seemingly clear language of the AIA in describing this exception, the Supreme Court has actually held that the test is whether an "Act of Congress, clearly requiring a federal right or remedy enforceable in a federal court of equity, could be given its intended scope only by the stay of a state court proceeding." *Mitchum v. Foster,* 407 U.S. 225 (1972). Thus, for this first exception to apply, Congress does not actually have to reference § 2283 in the other statute. *See also Pennzoil v. Texaco,* 481 U.S. 1 (1987) (Section 1983 is an exception to the Anti-Injunction Act). Perhaps the largest exception, and the one most hotly debated, is the final exception that permits a federal court to enjoin state court proceedings when "necessary in aid of the [federal] court's jurisdiction." The next case below, *In re Diet Drugs,* tackles the contours of this exception. Read that case carefully, noting in particular the procedural lengths to which the various combatants took to gain a perceived forum advantage.

5. *Problem.* During the pendency of a federal court action, plaintiff overhears defense counsel refer to drafting a state court complaint to attempt to "take this dispute to another

court." The plaintiff files a motion with the federal court to enjoin the defendant from filing a duplicative lawsuit in any other court. The federal court schedules a hearing on the requested injunctive relief for the following Monday. On the Friday before, defendant goes ahead and files the state court action raising the same issues as those pending before the federal court. On Monday the federal court grants the plaintiff's motion and enters an order "prohibiting defendant from filing any duplicative cases or continuing to prosecute any duplicative cases in any other court." Would § 2283 render this injunctive relief void if defendant appealed from its issuance?

2. "Necessary in Aid of Court's Jurisdiction" Exception

The following case is somewhat lengthy but full of great learning material. Read the case closely noting the incredible efforts undertaken by two competing set of counsel to try to fix the forum that would control the litigation. On the one hand, there was a national class action (that arose out of MDL treatment) on the cusp of settlement pending in Philadelphia federal court. On the other, there were determined putative class counsel in a Texas-sized subset class that was trying to control its own destiny and carve itself out of the national case. Once the courts became involved, what ensued was a war between an aggressive Texas state court and a federal court trying to protect its own turf. Whether the federal court erred in entering orders disregarding the actions of the Texas state court became the primary issue on appeal. The court's opinion below does a terrific job explaining the scope of the final exception to the Anti-Injunction Act's prohibitions—the "necessary in aid of jurisdiction" language from the statute. If you are a procedural nerd, or a lawyer wanting to sharpen her blade for possible sharp practices, enjoy the following scenario.

In re Diet Drugs P.L. Litigation
282 F.3d 220 (3d Cir. 2001)

SCIRICA, J.,

In this matter involving competing mass tort class actions in federal and state courts, we address an interlocutory appeal in a complex multidistrict federal class action comprising six million members from an order enjoining a mass opt out of a state class. We will affirm.

I.

The underlying case involves two drugs, both appetite suppressants, fenfluramine—marketed as "Pondimin"—and dexfenfluramine—marketed as "Redux." Both drugs were in great demand between 1995 and 1997. In July 1997, the United States Food and Drug Administration issued a public health advisory alert. On September 15, 1997, American Home Products removed both drugs from the market. Subsequent clinical studies support the view the drugs may cause valvular heart damage.

facts

Following the FDA's issuance of the public health warning, several lawsuits were filed. The number of lawsuits increased exponentially after American Home Products withdrew the diet drugs from the market. Approximately eighteen thousand individual lawsuits and over one hundred putative class actions were filed in federal and state courts around the country. American Home Products removed many of the state cases to federal courts,

approx. 18,000 indv. suits + 100+ punitive class actions

increasing the number of federal cases. In December 1997, the Judicial Panel for Multidistrict Litigation transferred all the federal actions to Judge Louis Bechtle in the United States District Court for the Eastern District of Pennsylvania, creating Multidistrict Litigation 1203 ("MDL 1203").

In April 1999, American Home Products began "global" settlement talks with plaintiffs in the federal action together with several plaintiffs in similar state class actions. The parties reached a tentative settlement agreement for a nationwide class in November 1999. Known as the "*Brown* class," the proposed class included all persons in the United States, as well as their representatives and dependents, who had ingested either or both of the diet drugs. The global settlement contemplated different kinds of relief, including medical care, medical screening, payments for injury, and refunds of the drugs' purchase price.

[The settlement separated short and long-time users to determine the amount the defendant would pay each class member.]

The District Court entered an order on November 23, 1999, conditionally certifying a nationwide settlement class and, concurrently, preliminarily approving the settlement. To opt out, a class member was to "sign and submit written notice to the Claims Administrator[s] with a copy to American Home Products, clearly manifesting the Class Member's intent to opt out of the Settlement." The opt-out period extended until March 23, 2000. The court scheduled a fairness hearing for May 1, 2000 on class certification and final settlement approval. On August 28, 2000, the District Court entered a final order certifying the class and approving the settlement.

In July 1997 — after the FDA warning, but before American Home Products withdrew the drugs from the market — appellants filed a putative class action in Texas state court, *Gonzalez et al. v. Medeva Pharmaceuticals, Inc.,* et al. The *Gonzalez* case was one of the first cases filed and preceded the creation of MDL 1203 by several months. The proposed *Gonzalez* class, including all Texas purchasers of the two diet drugs, was a subset of what would become the *Brown* class. The *Gonzalez* action was limited insofar as it sought actual purchase-price recovery only, together with treble damages under the Texas Deceptive Trade Practices Act-Consumer Protection Act ("DTPA"), Tex. Bus. & Comm.Code, § 17.41 *et seq.*

The *Gonzalez* complaint did not allege a federal cause of action and the named parties were not diverse. Nonetheless, in January 1998, American Home Products removed the case to federal court shortly after MDL 1203 was created, contending federal diversity jurisdiction obtained. American Home Products asserted Medeva Pharmaceuticals, a non-diverse defendant, was fraudulently joined for the purpose of defeating diversity jurisdiction. Soon after removal to the United States District Court for the Southern District of Texas, the *Gonzalez* case was transferred to the Eastern District of Pennsylvania as a part of MDL 1203.

Shortly thereafter, the *Gonzalez* plaintiffs moved to remand the case back to Texas state court, contending Medeva Pharmaceuticals was a proper defendant. The *Gonzalez* plaintiffs also argued the amount-in-controversy requirement was not met, as purchase-price recovery would only amount to a few hundred or, perhaps, a few thousand dollars per plaintiff. Furthermore, they argued they would not be seeking statutory attorneys' fees under the Texas DTPA. As noted, on November 23, 1999, Judge Bechtle granted conditional certification of the *Brown* class and preliminary approval of the settlement. On February 15, 2000 — during the MDL 1203 opt-out period — the District Court granted the *Gonzalez* plaintiffs' motion for remand, finding that Medeva Pharmaceuticals was a proper defendant.

One month later, on March 14, 2000, the *Gonzalez* plaintiffs filed a new complaint, their "Fifth Amended Class Action Petition," in the District Court of Hidalgo County, Texas. They dropped their class claims against Medeva Pharmaceuticals and claimed entitlement to statutory attorneys' fees. Accordingly, American Home Products contends, the barriers to federal diversity jurisdiction were removed.

Less than a week later, on March 20, 2000, the Hidalgo County court held a hearing on certification of the *Gonzalez* class. On March 22, it certified the class, defined as "all persons who purchased dexfenfluramine (Redux) and/or fenfluramine (Pondimin) in Texas, who are solely seeking the recovery of the amounts to acquire same, as well as any statutory trebling which may result from the claims asserted under the Texas Deceptive Trade Practices Consumer Protection Act." The certification of the *Gonzalez* class occurred eight days before the end of the opt-out period for the *Brown* settlement. At this time, most members of the *Gonzalez* class were also members of the *Brown* class, except for those who had individually opted out.

On March 22, the same day as the entry of the Texas class certification order, the *Gonzalez* plaintiffs acted to erase this overlap, by moving, in Hidalgo County, for a court order opting out all of the unnamed members of the *Gonzalez* class from the *Brown* class. The Texas court scheduled a hearing for 9:00 a.m. the next morning. In response, American Home Products sought a temporary restraining order in the District Court for the Eastern District of Pennsylvania, the MDL court, seeking to prevent the *Gonzalez* class from implementing a mass opt out.

On March 23, hearings were held in both courts on their respective motions. In Texas, the Hidalgo County court held its hearing and the same day entered an order partially opting out the *Gonzalez* class from MDL 1203. The District Court for the Eastern District of Pennsylvania also issued an order that day, granting American Home Products' motion and entering a temporary restraining order directed against the relief sought at the Texas hearing. The federal order denied the effect of the sought-for opt out and ordered *Gonzalez* class counsel to refrain from pursuing the opt out. It was to remain in effect for ten days. A hearing was scheduled for March 29 "on whether to make the injunction permanent." The District Court's order was dated, "March 23, 2000 at 11:55 A.M." For what it is worth, the Hidalgo County court would later issue an order "clarifying" that its opt-out order had been issued before 11:55 Eastern Time.

The Texas opt-out order purported to opt out the *Gonzalez* class from MDL 1203 only partially:

> [I]t is … ORDERED, ADJUDGED AND DECREED that the unnamed members of the certified class in this case be [sic] are hereby opted-out of the proposed settlement in MDL 1203, solely to the effect that their purchase price recovery claims, and potential DTPA trebling of same, will be pursued in this case, accordingly, any and all of their other claims, including but not limited to, claims for medical screening, medical monitoring, personal injury, mental anguish and/or punitive damages are not effected [sic] by this order.

Gonzalez v. Medeva Pharm., Inc., No. 4223-97B, at 3 (Tex.Dist.Ct. Mar. 23, 2000). The Texas court also ordered "that Class counsel shall take all other steps necessary, if any, to opt-out the entire certified class in this case from the proposed settlement in MDL 1203 to the extent, and only to the extent, set forth in the preceding paragraph." *Id.*

On March 28, American Home Products took further legal action. First, it filed a second notice of removal to the United States District Court for the Southern District of Texas, contending diversity jurisdiction obtained at that time. It also filed—together with lead counsel for the *Brown* class—a motion for a permanent injunction and declaration with respect to the Hidalgo County court's attempt to opt out the unnamed Texas plaintiffs.

On March 29, the District Court held a hearing on American Home Products's motion for a permanent injunction and declaration. One of the *Gonzalez* class's attorney's, John W. MacPete, was admitted *pro hac vice* for the purpose of opposing the motion. At the hearing, Judge Bechtle announced his intention to enter the permanent order sought by American Home Products and *Brown* class counsel, stating the order of the Hidalgo County court would "interfere with this Court's jurisdiction and the administration of this case, as well as the right and obligation of this court to bring this proceeding to a final judgment." On April 6, 2000, the District Court issued a written order, PTO 12270—the subject of this appeal.

On April 26, 2000, the *Gonzalez* plaintiffs moved to remand *Gonzalez* back to state court a second time. That court declined to rule on the motion, referring it instead to Judge Bechtle, assuming *Gonzalez* would be referred to his court as part of MDL 1203. On May 12, the MDL panel transferred *Gonzalez* to the Eastern District of Pennsylvania. American Home Products contends the *Gonzalez* plaintiffs made no attempt, following transfer, to seek resolution of the remand motion by Judge Bechtle in the Eastern District of Pennsylvania. In any event, no action has been taken directly on the *Gonzalez* matter in federal court since its transfer in May 2000.

The day after they filed their motion to remand, the *Gonzalez* plaintiffs filed a notice of appeal of PTO 1227. Both American Home Products and *Brown* class representatives are appellees.

On August 28, 2000, Judge Bechtle issued a final order certifying the *Brown* class and approving the settlement. The *Gonzalez* case was, at that time, one of the cases consolidated under—and settled as part of—MDL 1203. Judge Bechtle also issued, concurrently, a blanket injunction against commencement or prosecution of parallel actions in other courts.

Appellants [principal] challenge [to] PTO 1227 address[es] whether the District Court overstepped the limitations on its power with respect to state court actions. Appellants contend the District Court's order violates the limitations on federal courts enjoining state court proceedings under the Anti-Injunction Act.

III.

Appellants' central arguments—those based on the Anti-Injunction Act, address constraints on the District Court's authority to limit state court actions and their effects.

This case illustrates the remarkable extent to which lawsuits can be turned into procedural entanglements. One view of this may be that the actions taken here represent nothing more than astute lawyering. Another is that the legal jockeying employed by both sides exhibits a proclivity to attempt to manipulate the rules for immediate tactical advantage—a use at odds with the purposes of these rules, and one dissonant with the equitable nature of class action proceedings.

Rather than enter this tenebrous world of procedural machinations, we think it preferable to address the *Gonzalez* plaintiffs' main arguments. As we discuss, the District Court's order was an appropriate exercise of its authority regardless of the status of the Texas opt-out order.

IV.
a. Anti-Injunction Act/All Writs Act.

The District Court issued PTO 1227 under the All Writs Act, which provides "all courts established by Act of Congress may issue all writs necessary or appropriate in aid of their respective jurisdictions and agreeable to the usages and principles of law." 28 U.S.C. §1651. The power granted by the All Writs Act is limited by the Anti-Injunction Act, 28 U.S.C. §2283, which prohibits, with certain specified exceptions, injunctions by federal courts that have the effect of staying a state court proceeding. Appellants contend the District Court's order was prohibited by the Anti-Injunction Act. American Home Products and the *Brown* plaintiffs claim the injunction falls under one of the Act's exceptions. We hold the District Court's order was not barred by the Anti-Injunction Act and was a valid exercise of its power under the All Writs Act.

Holding

The Anti-Injunction Act prohibits most injunctions "to stay proceedings in a State court." 28 U.S.C. §2283.[6] Insofar as PTO 1227 enjoined *Gonzalez* class counsel, and those working in concert, from pursuing the opt out contemplated by the Texas opt-out order, it operated to stay the proceedings in the Hidalgo County court, if only indirectly. An order directed at the parties and their representatives, but not at the court itself, does not remove it from the scope of the Anti-Injunction Act. "It is settled that the prohibition of §2283 cannot be evaded by addressing the order to the parties...." *Atl. Coast Line R.R. Co. v. Bhd. of Locomotive Eng'rs,* 398 U.S. 281, 287, 90 S.Ct. 1739, 26 L.Ed.2d 234 (1970). Therefore, to the extent PTO 1227 had the effect of staying the Hidalgo County court's proceedings, it was prohibited by the Anti-Injunction Act, unless it fell within one of the Act's exceptions.

By its terms, the Anti-Injunction Act allows such injunctions "as expressly authorized by Act of Congress, or where necessary in aid of its jurisdiction, or to protect or effectuate its judgments." 28 U.S.C. §2283. None of the parties suggests the injunction was expressly authorized by an act of Congress, or the injunction was aimed at protecting or effectuating a judgment of the District Court.[7] Accordingly, the injunction evades the Act's restrictions only if it was "necessary in aid of its jurisdiction."

The exceptions in the Anti-Injunction Act are to be construed narrowly. "Any doubts as to the propriety of a federal injunction against state court proceedings should be resolved in favor of permitting the state courts to proceed in an orderly fashion to finally determine the controversy." *Atl. Coast,* 398 U.S. at 297, 90 S.Ct. 1739. These "exceptions are narrow and are not to be enlarged by loose statutory construction." *Chick Kam Choo,* 486 U.S. at 146, 108 S.Ct. 1684 (citation and alterations omitted); *Prudential,* 261 F.3d at 364.

In *Atlantic Coast,* the Court emphasized an order directed at a state court proceeding must be *necessary* in aid of jurisdiction—"it is not enough that the requested injunction is related to that jurisdiction." 398 U.S. at 295, 90 S.Ct. 1739. Acknowledging the language is nonetheless broad, the Court elaborated: an injunction is necessary in aid of a court's jurisdiction only if "some federal injunctive relief may be necessary to prevent a state

---

6. The Anti-Injunction Act does "not preclude injunctions against the institution of state court proceedings, but only bar[s] stays of suits already instituted." *Dombrowski v. Pfister,* 380 U.S. 479, 484 n. 2, 85 S.Ct. 1116, 14 L.Ed.2d 22 (1965).

7. The exception allowing injunctions necessary "to protect or effectuate ... judgments" applies only where a preclusive judgment has been made. "The exception 'is founded in the well-recognized concepts of res judicata and collateral estoppel.'" "'[A]n essential prerequisite for applying the relitigation exception is that the claims or issues which the federal injunction insulates from litigation in the state proceedings [must] actually have been decided by the federal court.'" *In re Prudential Ins. Co. of Am. Sales Practice Litig.,* 261 F.3d 355, 364 (3d Cir.2001) (quoting *Chick Kam Choo v. Exxon Corp.,* 486 U.S. 140, 147–48, 108 S.Ct. 1684, 100 L.Ed.2d 127 (1988) (alterations in original)).

court from so interfering with a federal court's consideration or disposition of a case as to seriously impair the federal court's flexibility and authority to decide that case." *Id.*

Without more, it may not be sufficient that prior resolution of a state court action will deprive a federal court of the opportunity to resolve the merits of a parallel action in federal court. "The traditional notion is that *in personam* actions in federal and state court may proceed concurrently, without interference from either court, and there is no evidence that the exception to § 2283 was intended to alter this balance." *Vendo Co. v. Lektro-Vend Corp.,* 433 U.S. 623, 642, 97 S.Ct. 2881, 53 L.Ed.2d 1009 (1977) (plurality opinion). In ordinary actions in personam, "[e]ach court is free to proceed in its own way and in its own time, without reference to the proceedings in the other court. Whenever a judgment is rendered in one of the courts and pleaded in the other, the effect of that judgment is to be determined by the application of the principle of *res judicata* by the court in which the action is still pending...." *Kline v. Burke Constr. Co.,* 260 U.S. 226, 230, 43 S.Ct. 79, 67 L.Ed. 226 (1922). Therefore, it may not be sufficient that state actions risk some measure of inconvenience or duplicative litigation. *In re Baldwin-United Corp.,* 770 F.2d 328, 337 (2d Cir.1985). An injunction may issue, however, where "the state court action threatens to frustrate proceedings and disrupt the orderly resolution of the federal litigation." *Winkler v. Eli Lilly & Co.,* 101 F.3d 1196, 1202 (7th Cir.1996). In other words, the state action must not simply threaten to reach judgment first, it must interfere with the federal court's own path to judgment.

Several factors are relevant to determine whether sufficient interference is threatened to justify an injunction otherwise prohibited by the Anti-Injunction Act. We turn first to the nature of the federal action.

We have recognized another category of federal cases for which state court actions present a special threat to the jurisdiction of the federal court. Under an appropriate set of facts, a federal court entertaining complex litigation, especially when it involves a substantial class of persons from multiple states, or represents a consolidation of cases from multiple districts, may appropriately enjoin state court proceedings in order to protect its jurisdiction. *Carlough v. Amchem Prods., Inc.,* 10 F.3d 189, 202–04 (3d Cir.1993). *Carlough* involved a nationwide class of plaintiffs and several defendants—primarily manufacturers of asbestos-related products—and third-party defendants—primarily insurance providers. We found the complexity of the case to be a substantial factor in justifying the injunction imposed. *Id.* at 202–03.

Implicit in *Carlough* is the recognition that maintaining "the federal court's flexibility and authority to decide" such complex nationwide cases makes special demands on the court that may justify an injunction otherwise prohibited by the Anti-Injunction Act. Several other courts have concurred.[8] *See, e.g., Hanlon v. Chrysler Corp.,* 150 F.3d 1011

---

8. In several cases, courts have analogized complex litigation cases to actions in rem. As one court reasoned, "the district court had before it a class action proceeding so far advanced that it was the virtual equivalent of a res over which the district judge required full control." *Baldwin-United,* 770 F.2d at 337; *see also Wesch,* 6 F.3d at 1470; *Battle* 877 F.2d at 882 ("[I]t makes sense to consider this case, involving years of litigation and mountains of paperwork, as similar to a res to be administered."). The in rem analogy may help to bring into focus what makes these cases stand apart. In cases in rem, "the jurisdiction over the same res necessarily impairs, and may defeat, the linejurisdiction of the federal court already attached." *Kline,* 260 U.S. at 229, 43 S.Ct. 79. Similarly, where complex cases are sufficiently developed, mere exercise of parallel jurisdiction by the state court may present enough of a threat to the jurisdiction of the federal court to justify issuance of an injunction. *See Baldwin-United,* 770 F.2d at 337 (noting such cases, like cases in rem, are ones in which "it is intolerable to have conflicting orders from different courts") (quoting 17 Charles Alan Wright, Arthur R. Miller & Edward H. Cooper, *Federal Practice and Procedure,* § 4225, at 105 n. 8 (Supp.1985)). What is ultimately important, in any event, is that in both kinds of cases state actions over the same subject matter ftline

(9th Cir.1998); *Winkler,* 101 F.3d at 1203 ("[T]he Anti-Injunction Act does not bar courts with jurisdiction over complex multidistrict litigation from issuing injunctions to protect the integrity of their rulings."); *Wesch v. Folsom,* 6 F.3d 1465, 1470 (11th Cir.1993); *Battle v. Liberty Nat'l Life Ins. Co.,* 877 F.2d 877, 882 (11th Cir.1989); *Baldwin-United,* 770 F.2d at 337–38; *In re Corrugated Container Antitrust Litig.,* 659 F.2d 1332, 1334–35 (5th Cir. Unit A 1981) (approving injunction in a "complicated antitrust action [that] has required a great deal of the district court's time and has necessitated that it maintain a flexible approach in resolving the various claims of the many parties."); *In re Columbia/HCA Healthcare Corp. Billing Practices Litig.,* 93 F.Supp.2d 876 (M.D.Tenn.2000); *In re Lease Oil Antitrust Litig. No. II,* 48 F.Supp.2d 699, 704 (S.D.Tex.1998); *Harris v. Wells,* 764 F.Supp. 743 (D.Conn.1991); *In re Asbestos Sch. Litig.,* No. 83-0268, 1991 WL 61156 (E.D.Pa. Apr.16, 1991), *aff'd mem.,* 950 F.2d 723 (3d Cir.1991); *In re Joint E. & S. Dist. Asbestos Litig.,* 134 F.R.D. 32 (E.D.N.Y & S.D.N.Y 1990).

This is not to say that class actions are, by virtue of that categorization alone, exempt from the general rule that in personam cases must be permitted to proceed in parallel. *See In re Glenn W. Turner Enters. Litig.,* 521 F.2d 775, 780 (3d Cir.1975). That a state court may resolve an issue first (which may operate as res judicata), is not by itself a sufficient threat to the federal court's jurisdiction that justifies an injunction, unless the proceedings in state courts threaten to "frustrate proceedings and disrupt the orderly resolution of the federal litigation." *Winkler,* 101 F.3d at 1202. Still, while the potentially preclusive effects of the state action may not themselves justify an injunction, they might do so indirectly. If, for example, the possibility of an earlier state court judgment is disruptive to settlement negotiations in federal court, the existence of the state court action might sufficiently interfere with the federal court's flexibility to justify an injunction.

The threat to the federal court's jurisdiction posed by parallel state actions is particularly significant where there are conditional class certifications and impending settlements in federal actions. *Carlough,* 10 F.3d at 203. Many—though not all—of the cases permitting injunctions in complex litigation cases involve injunctions issued as the parties approached settlement. *E.g., Carlough; Baldwin United,* 770 F.2d at 337; *Corrugated Container,* 659 F.2d at 1335; *Asbestos Sch. Litig.,* 1991 WL 61156, at *3; *Joint E. & S. Dist. Asbestos Litig.,* 134 F.R.D. at 36–37. *But see Winkler,* 101 F.3d at 1202 (protecting effect of discovery ruling); *Harris,* 764 F.Supp. at 745–46 (same). Complex cases in the later stages—where, for instance, settlement negotiations are underway—embody an enormous amount of time and expenditure of resources. It is in the nature of complex litigation that the parties often seek complicated, comprehensive settlements to resolve as many claims as possible in one proceeding. These cases are especially vulnerable to parallel state actions that may "frustrate the district court's efforts to craft a settlement in the multi-district litigation before it," *Carlough,* 10 F.3d at 203 (quoting *Baldwin-United,* 770 F.2d at 337), thereby destroying the ability to achieve the benefits of consolidation. In complex cases where certification or settlement has received conditional approval, or perhaps even where settlement is pending, the challenges facing the overseeing court are such that it is likely that almost any parallel litigation in other fora presents a genuine threat to the jurisdiction of the federal court.

This case amply highlights these concerns. MDL 1203 represented the consolidation of over two thousand cases that had been filed in or removed to federal court. The *Brown*

---

have the potential to "so interfer[e] with a federal court's consideration or disposition of a case as to seriously impair the federal court's flexibility and authority to decide the case." *Atl. Coast,* 398 U.S. at 295, 90 S.Ct. 1739.

class finally certified comprised six million members. The District Court entered well over one thousand orders in the case. This massive consolidation enabled the possibility of a global resolution that promised to minimize the various difficulties associated with duplicative and competing lawsuits. The central events in this dispute occurred after two years of exhaustive work by the parties and the District Court, and after a conditional class certification and preliminary settlement had been negotiated and approved by the District Court. There can be no doubt that keeping this enormously complicated settlement process on track required careful management by the District Court. Any state court action that might interfere with the District Court's oversight of the settlement at that time, given the careful balancing it embodied, was a serious threat to the District Court's ability to manage the final stages of this complex litigation. Duplicative and competing actions were substantially more likely to "frustrate proceedings and disrupt the orderly resolution" of this dispute at the time PTO 1227 was issued than they would be in ordinary actions in personam. *Winkler*, 101 F.3d at 1202. This is especially true where, as here, the litigants in state court have the ability to tailor their state actions to the terms of the pending federal settlement.

Determining the applicability of the *Carlough* rule also requires assessment of the character of the state court action, for we must assess the level of interference with the federal action actually threatened by the state court proceeding. In *Carlough*, our approval of the injunction was supported by the direct threat to the federal action the state court action represented. After the district court had provisionally certified the *Carlough* class, and after a preliminary settlement had been negotiated and presented to the court, a parallel action was filed in West Virginia. As here, the plaintiffs in that case — *Gore v. Amchem Products, Inc.* — sought an order of the state court opting out the members of the West Virginia class from the federal class. 10 F.3d at 196. They also sought a declaration that *Carlough* would not be binding on the members of the West Virginia class. *Id.* at 195–96.

We viewed the filing of the West Virginia action as an intentional "preemptive strike" against the federal action. *Id.* at 203. The purpose of the West Virginia filing was "to challenge the propriety of the federal class action." *Id.* We found "it difficult to imagine a more detrimental effect upon the district court's ability to effectuate the settlement of this complex and far-reaching matter then would occur if the West Virginia state court was permitted to make a determination regarding the validity of the federal settlement." *Id.* at 204.

Also significant in *Carlough* was the threat posed by the attempt to secure a mass opt out. We noted that permitting a state court to issue such an order "would be disruptive to the district court's ongoing settlement management and would jeopardize the settlement's fruition." *Id.* Additionally, we noted the confusion that would likely result among West Virginia residents as to their status in the "dueling lawsuits." *Id.* All of this amounted to direct interference with the district court's ability to manage the federal action effectively.

The interference that would have been caused by the Hidalgo County court's order implicates the same concerns that animated our decision in *Carlough*. The Texas court's order directly affected the identity of the parties to MDL 1203 and did so contrary to a previous District Court order. It sought to "declare what the federal court should and should not do with respect to the federal settlement." *GM Trucks II*, 134 F.3d at 145. Furthermore, as in *Carlough*, the Texas order would have created confusion among those who were members of both the federal and the state classes. It would be difficult to discern which, if any, action one was a party to, especially since the Texas order was entered during, and shortly before the end of, the MDL 1203 opt-out period.

Attempting to distinguish their case from *Carlough*, appellants contend their action cannot be characterized as a preemptive strike against the federal action because the Gonzalez action was filed before the creation of MDL 1203. *Cf. GM Trucks II*, 134 F.3d at 145 (distinguishing the state court action there at issue as not falling under this characterization). Yet we do not believe a state court action must necessarily be a preemptive strike before meriting the *Carlough* exception. The test, as always, is whether the state court proceeding "so interfer[es] with a federal court's consideration or disposition of a case as to seriously impair the federal court's flexibility and authority to decide that case." *Atl. Coast*, 398 U.S. at 295, 90 S.Ct. 1739. Of course, where a state court proceeding amounts to an attack on a federal action, we are more likely to find significant interference. We are also less likely to find that comity demands deference to the state court action. But there are any number of factors that may play a role, and we do not understand either *Carlough* or *GM Trucks II* to hold that this element is necessary, in all cases, for application of the exception.

In any event, appellants' attempt to distinguish *Carlough* on this ground fails. While the relative timing of the filing of the actions makes clear that *Gonzalez* was not *filed* as a preemptive strike on MDL 1203, there is no doubt the motion requesting the Texas court to opt *Gonzalez* class members out of the *Brown* class was a preemptive strike. The District Court found it necessary to enjoin only the part of the action that directly—and by design—interfered with the federal action.

Because an injunction must be *necessary* in aid of jurisdiction to fall under this application to the Anti-Injunction Act, it is important to carefully tailor such injunctions to meet the needs of the case. Notably, the relief we approved in *Carlough* was substantially broader than the relief granted by the District Court here. The federal order in *Carlough* enjoined the West Virginia plaintiffs, as well as their attorneys and representatives, from pursuing the *Gore* action or initiating similar litigation in any other forum. 10 F.3d at 196. The injunction in *Carlough* effectively stayed the entire parallel state action, not only the attempted opt out, or other portions directed squarely at the federal action. Here, by contrast, the District Court's order enjoined only the pursuit of the attempted mass opt out-the part of *Gonzalez* that unquestionably interfered with the management of MDL 1203. It did not prevent the *Gonzalez* plaintiffs from individually opting out. Furthermore, the injunction was not directed at a proceeding in which plaintiffs had merely requested relief that threatened to interfere with the federal action, it was directed at a proceeding in which the state court had actually granted such a request, making the interference substantially more manifest. Under these circumstances, we find the District Court's injunction to be well within its "sound discretion." *Carlough*, 10 F.3d at 204.

The propriety of an injunction directed at the Texas order is also consistent with considerations of federalism and comity. The Texas plaintiffs who wished to opt out of the *Brown* class were given an adequate opportunity to individually opt out of the federal action, a factor we found significant in *Carlough*, 10 F.3d at 203–04. As such, Texas residents retained the option to commence lawsuits in the forum of their choice. *Id.* at 203. Furthermore, the injunction only prevented application of a particular order that was directed squarely at the federal action. *Cf. Baldwin-United*, 770 F.2d at 337 ("To the extent that the impending state court suits were vexatious and harassing, our interest in preserving federalism and comity with the state courts is not significantly disturbed by the issuance of injunctive relief."). It did not so much interfere with the state court proceeding as prevent state court interference with the federal proceeding. Failing to act on the Hidalgo County order threatened to "create the very 'needless friction between state and federal courts' which the Anti-Injunction Act was designed to prevent." *Winkler,* 101 F.3d at 1203 (quoting *Okla. Packing Co.,* 309 U.S. at 9, 60 S.Ct. 215). "While the Anti-Injunction Act is designed to avoid disharmony between federal and state systems, the exception in § 2283 reflects congressional recognition that injunctions may sometimes be necessary in order to avoid that disharmony." *Amalgamated Sugar Co. v. NL Indus., Inc.,* 825 F.2d 634, 639 (2d Cir.1987).

The District Court's order clearly falls under the "necessary in aid of its jurisdiction" exception to the Anti-Injunction Act. The complexity of this multidistrict class action in its mature stages — with a provisionally certified class and preliminarily approved settlement — entailed that the District Court required flexibility to bring the case to judgment. The nature of the Texas order was such that the required flexibility and eventual resolution were directly threatened. Finally, the principle embodied in the Anti-Injunction Act that federal courts maintain respect for state court proceedings is not undermined by the issuance of the injunction.

Our holding that PTO 1227 was necessary in aid of the District Court's jurisdiction for purposes of the Anti-Injunction Act necessarily implies it was authorized under the All Writs Act as well. For the All Writs Act grants federal courts the authority to issue all writs "necessary or appropriate in aid" of a court's jurisdiction. 28 U.S.C. § 1651(a). Accordingly, the District Court was empowered to issue PTO 1227 under the All Writs Act, and was not prevented from doing so by the Anti-Injunction Act.

V.

For the foregoing reasons, we will affirm the order issued by the District Court.

Notes and Problems

1. Historically, the "necessary in aid of a federal court's jurisdiction" exception to the Anti-Injunction Act was applied only to *in rem* proceedings. If the exceptions are supposed to be narrowly construed, why did the court find an exception for a class action not based on *in rem* jurisdiction?

2. What exactly was the state court doing in the *Gonzalez* case that interfered with federal jurisdiction in *In re Diet Drugs*? Why does this federal court injunction not "step on the toes" of the state court? After this case, how broad is this third statutory exception? Is that breadth proper? Do you see the tension between the salutary purposes behind the Anti-Injunction Act and the effective and efficient operations of our federal court system?

3. Notice the defendant's invocation of the doctrine of fraudulent joinder to justify the attempted removal of the case from state to federal court. This doctrine is discussed in the next section that follows.

4. *Chapter Problem.* If PERI decides to file its case in state court, would it be appropriate for the Dallas federal court (where Bresser first filed its suit) to enjoin PERI's prosecution of the suit, in order to avoid the inefficiencies in having the two courts move forward simultaneously?

Pulling It All Together Exercise

Sarah and Jenny have been in a business relationship for some time when they begin to have disputes over some of their transactions. Sarah files a state court case against Jenny for breach of contract. Jenny believes that the contract Sarah is attempting to enforce is part of an unlawful antitrust conspiracy involving Sarah's business. So in addition to filing an answer to Sarah's state court suit asserting among other things that the contract is unenforceable under the federal antitrust laws, Jenny also files her own federal lawsuit asserting an antitrust violation against Sarah. The federal court declines to abstain, citing the *Colorado River* doctrine (covered earlier in this chapter) and instead issues an injunction to stop the state court from adjudicating the merits of the lawsuit before it because the federal court believes that a federal court should be the primary source of authority regarding the interpretation of that federal statute.

Is this injunction permitted under §2283? Would it make more sense to have the federal court rule on the interpretation of the federal antitrust statute?

Spend 15 minutes writing your analysis of the questions raised above. Be sure to explain your conclusions.

G. Fraudulent Joinder: Vertical Forum Shopping

Fraudulent joinder is a doctrine that permits federal courts to essentially ignore the inclusion in a lawsuit of a nondiverse (typically local) party who would otherwise destroy federal diversity jurisdiction when the district court concludes that the party's joinder is a sham. It is an important court-created exception to the Supreme Court's declaration in *Strawbridge v. Curtis* that the general diversity statute, 28 U.S.C. §1332, demands complete diversity of citizenship between plaintiff(s) and defendant(s). This doctrine has an enormous impact on the determination of which state law claims receive a federal forum and, despite its long roots in our legal system, is still the subject of controversy among the federal circuit courts of appeal as to the correct analytical standard governing its application. Consider the following two approaches.

In Practice

Empirical research has confirmed what most trial lawyers have intuited—when a defendant is successful in depriving the state-court plaintiff of their original forum through removal, the plaintiff's win rate is reduced dramatically. *See* Kevin M. Clermont & Theodore Eisenberg, *Do Case Outcomes Really Reveal Anything About the Legal System? Win Rates and Removal Jurisdiction*, 83 Cornell L. Rev. 581, 599 (1998). As one researcher concluded, "a plaintiff's ability to avoid removal [from state to federal court] could mean the difference between winning and losing." Allyson Singer Breeden, *Federal Removal Jurisdiction and Its Effect on Plaintiff Win-Rates*, Res Gestae at 26 (Sept. 2002).

1. The 12(b)(6) Standard

Boyer v. Snap-On Tools Corp.

913 F.2d 108 (3d Cir. 1990)

SLOVITER, J.,

This is an appeal by a former dealer of Snap-on Tools Corporation of the district court's grant of summary judgment for defendants Snap-on and two of its employees. We must consider at the outset whether there was subject matter jurisdiction on the basis of diversity of citizenship and whether the district court erred in denying the plaintiffs' motion to remand.

I. *Procedural Background and Facts*

facts

Appellant James Boyer and Snap-on Tools Corporation, a corporation which sells automotive hand tools to a nationwide network of dealers for resale to auto mechanics, entered into a Dealership Agreement (Agreement) in July, 1985. In meetings leading to the signing of the agreement, Boyer met with appellee Kenneth Baldwin, a branch manager at Snap-on, and Keith Kaiser, a Snap-on field manager. Boyer invested more than $40,000 in his dealership, had an inventory of more than $29,000 worth of Snap-on tools, and mortgaged his home in order to borrow money to invest in the dealership. By early 1988, the dealership proved unprofitable for Boyer and Snap-on, and Boyer was orally advised by Snap-on personnel at a January 14, 1988 meeting that he would be terminated.

term. agreement

The Snap-on Agreement provided that on termination of a dealership "with the consent of the Company, the Dealer may sell to the Company at the price paid by the Dealer any of the Products which have been purchased by the Dealer and which remain in its possession in new, saleable condition." In accordance with this provision, Boyer participated in a two-day inventory and turn-in of his tools at the Snap-on branch office in Harrisburg on February 11 and 12, 1988. On the first day, Baldwin presented Boyer with a Termination Agreement that included a release clause which specified, *inter alia*, that "both parties to this Agreement freely waive any and all claims they may have against each other arising out of the Dealership terminated by this Agreement."

threats

Boyer averred in an affidavit and testified on deposition that he was told by a Snap-on employee, Michael Brown, on the first day of the inventory turn-in that if he did not sign the termination agreement (which contained the above release), Snap-on would not pay Boyer for the turned-in tools or other funds allegedly owed by Snap-on to Boyer, that Brown repeated this the second day of the tool turn-in, and that Boyer signed the Agreement later that day based on Brown's representations, because he believed that he would otherwise lose his home and car. Boyer testified that he consulted with his wife, but not an attorney, between the first and second days of the tool turn-in.

The Boyers, residents of Pennsylvania, filed this complaint on December 13, 1988 in the Court of Common Pleas of Lebanon County, Pennsylvania, against Snap-on, a Delaware Corporation with its principal place of business in Wisconsin, and Baldwin and Kaiser, both residents of Pennsylvania. The complaint alleged fraud and deceit, fraudulent conspiracy, interference with contract, wrongful termination of dealership, violation of Pennsylvania Unfair Trade Practices and Consumer Protection Law, and intentional infliction of emotional distress.

claim

In his detailed 47-page complaint, Boyer alleges five broad aspects of defendants' fraud and misrepresentations. First, Boyer contends that Snap-on through its written materials and through oral statements of Kaiser misrepresented the profitability of the dealership and the risk of failure during the period of time leading up to the signing of the Agreement. Second, he contends that they fraudulently misrepresented the number of customers in Boyer's territory in an inaccurate survey. Third, he alleges that both Kaiser and Baldwin misrepresented the amount of initial capital needed to begin a dealership and that his dealership was bound to fail because he was undercapitalized.

Fourth, Boyer alleges that while he was a dealer Snap-on engaged in a fraudulent scheme through its "Promotional Tools Program" which involved a mandatory shipment of tools selected by Snap-on, initially represented to be $200 to $300 weekly but which increased by 1987 to $1,112 per week. Because he did not fulfill all of the requirements of that program, he was penalized by being barred from placing orders for his customers during 56 weeks of his dealership. Finally, Boyer alleges wrongful termination of his dealership. In addition to fraud, the complaint alleges breach of contract and warranties against Snap-on.

The defendants filed a removal petition on January 9, 1989. Although on the face of the complaint there was no federal question or complete diversity of citizenship because the Boyers and the individual defendants were Pennsylvania citizens, the removal petition alleged that Baldwin and Kaiser were "fraudulently and improperly joined" because the complaint does not state a cause of action against the individual defendants, because these defendants were alleged to have acted only in the interests of Snap-on and were therefore privileged under Pennsylvania law, and because Boyer signed a release against the individual defendants.

The Boyers filed a motion to remand under 28 U.S.C. §1447(c). The district court, without expressly holding that Baldwin and Kaiser were sham defendants, denied the motion to remand on the ground that the "in-state defendants would prevail in a motion for summary judgment ... by reason of the release in the termination agreement."

The defendants thereafter moved for summary judgment, primarily relying on the release clause in the Termination Agreement. The Boyers opposed the motion, arguing that the release was procured through fraud, economic duress, or in violation of Snap-on's fiduciary duty; that the release covered claims of which the Boyers were unaware; that at the time the Boyers signed the release they were unaware of the alleged fraudulent practices, which they first learned of in July 1988, when they saw an NBC television news story and a Forbes Magazine article detailing Snap-on's practices; and that [plaintiff Boyer's wife,] who did not sign the release, had an independent action against the defendants.

The district court granted the motion for summary judgment. The court rejected Boyer's claim of economic duress and fraud in the procurement of the release, and held that the release was broad enough to cover undiscovered fraud. The Boyers filed a timely appeal.

II. *Discussion*

[W]e do not reach the propriety of the district court's grant of summary judgment unless we are satisfied that the district court had subject matter jurisdiction. That, in turn, is dependent upon its decision to disregard the presence of the two individual defendants whose citizenship would destroy diversity.

As a general proposition, plaintiffs have the option of naming those parties whom they choose to sue, subject only to the rules of joinder of necessary parties. While the plaintiffs' decision in this regard may have repercussions for purposes of diversity jurisdiction, there is no reason for a court to interfere with this inevitable consequence of a plaintiff's election unless the plaintiff had impermissibly manufactured diversity or used an unacceptable device to defeat diversity.

Principles

"[T]he basis for [attorneys'] position is not that they love the state courts less but that they love the choice of forum more."

Charles Alan Wright, *Restructuring Federal Jurisdiction: The American Law Institute Proposals*, 26 Wash. & Lee L. Rev. 185, 207 (1969).

There are substantially more cases dealing with a plaintiff's attempt to manufacture diversity than to destroy it. The first Judiciary Act of 1789, 1 Stat. 73, sought to restrain manufactured diversity jurisdiction and a more general effort to avoid collusively created diversity was enacted in 1875. *See* Pub. L. No. 61-7031, 36 Stat. 1098. The current version of that statute, codified at 28 U.S.C. § 1359, requires the federal court to dismiss or remand a suit in which any party, by assignment or otherwise, has been improperly or collusively joined to invoke federal diversity jurisdiction.

invoke vs. avoid fed. jurisdiction

As the commentary in the highly regarded *ALI Study of the Division of Jurisdiction between State and Federal Courts* (1969) notes, "there is ... a qualitative difference between a device designed to invoke federal jurisdiction and one designed to avoid it. In the former instance, the already overburdened federal courts are being asked to adjudicate a case that, in the absence of the device, would fall outside their statutory, and perhaps their constitutional, competence. In the latter, if the device succeeds, a case depending on state law merely remains in the state court." Of course, we recognize, as did the ALI Reporter, that "so long as federal diversity jurisdiction exists ... the need for its assertion may well be greatest when the plaintiff tries hardest to defeat it." However, that concern cannot defeat plaintiff's right to retain as defendants those parties properly joined, even if the consequence is that defendants must litigate in state court.

Defendants removed Boyer's action from state court pursuant to 28 U.S.C. § 1441. Plaintiffs' motion to remand was filed pursuant to 28 U.S.C. § 1447(c) which provides, in relevant part, that "if at any time before final judgment it appears that the district court lacks subject matter jurisdiction, the case shall be remanded." 28 U.S.C. § 1447(c) (1988). The removal statutes "are to be strictly construed against removal and all doubts should be resolved in favor of remand." *Steel Valley Auth. v. Union Switch and Signal Div.*, 809 F.2d 1006, 1010 (3d Cir. 1987). Because a party who urges jurisdiction on a federal court bears the burden of proving that jurisdiction exists, a removing party who charges that a plaintiff has fraudulently joined a party to destroy diversity of jurisdiction has a "heavy burden of persuasion." *Steel Valley*, 809 F.2d at 1010, 1012 n. 6.

This court has recently stated that joinder is fraudulent "where there is no reasonable basis in fact or colorable ground supporting the claim against the joined defendant, or no real intention in good faith to prosecute the action against the defendant or seek a joint judgment." *Abels*, 770 F.2d at 32. A district court must resolve all contested issues of substantive fact in favor of the plaintiff and must resolve any uncertainties as to the current state of controlling substantive law in favor of the plaintiff. "If there is even a possibility that a state court would find that the complaint states a cause of action against any one of the resident defendants, the federal court must find that joinder was proper and remand the case to state court." *Coker v. Amoco Oil Co.*, 709 F.2d 1433, 1440–41 (11th Cir. 1983).

Turning to this case, we note first that there is no suggestion by defendants that plaintiffs have falsely alleged their Pennsylvania citizenship or that of Baldwin and Kaiser. In other words, this is not a situation where "there has been outright fraud in the plaintiff's pleadings of jurisdictional facts." *B., Inc.*, 663 F.2d at 549; *see Green v. Amerada Hess Corp.*, 707 F.2d 201, 205 (5th Cir. 1983), *cert. denied*, 464 U.S. 1039 (1984).

Second, this is not a case where the action against the individual defendants is defective as a matter of law. *See* 1A *Moore's Federal Practice* para. 0.161[2] at 274 ("The joinder may be fraudulent if the plaintiff fails to state a cause of action against the resident defendant, and the failure is obvious according to the settled rules of the state."). Under Pennsylvania law there is a cause of action against employees whose fraud and misrepresentations contributed to plaintiff's damages, even if these actions were taken in the course of their employment. *See Loeffler v. McShane*, 372 Pa. Super. 442, 446–47, 539 A.2d 876, 878 (1988) (quoting *Wicks v. Milzoco Builders, Inc.*, 503 Pa. 614, 621, 470 A.2d 86, 90 (1983)) ("officer of a corporation who takes part in the commission of a tort by the corporation is personally liable therefor"); *see also Village at Camelback Property Owners' Ass'n. v. Carr*, 371 Pa. Super. 452, 462–63, 538 A.2d 528, 533–34 (1988), *aff'd*, 524 Pa. 330, 572 A.2d 1 (1990); *Moy v. Schreiber Deed Sec. Co.*, 370 Pa. Super. 97, 101–03, 535 A.2d 1168, 1170–72 (1988); *Shonberger v. Oswell*, 365 Pa. Super. 481, 530 A.2d 112 (1987). Thus, there is no basis to analogize this case to *Tedder v. F.M.C. Corp.*, 590 F.2d 115 (5th Cir. 1979) (per curiam), cited by defendants, where the court held that joinder of non-diverse fellow employees could be disregarded because there was no reasonable basis under which plaintiffs could avoid the state's broad grant of immunity conferred on fellow employees.

Defendants argue that the court may pierce the pleadings to determine whether there has been a fraudulent joinder. Assuming some piercing is appropriate to decide whether plaintiffs have asserted a "colorable" ground supporting the claim against the joined defendant, that inquiry is far different from the summary judgment type inquiry made by the district court here. The limited piercing of the allegations to discover fraudulent joinder is illustrated by *Smoot v. Chicago, Rock Island & Pac. R.R. Co.*, 378 F.2d 879 (10th Cir. 1967), where the non-diverse employee of defendant railroad had uncontestedly discontinued his employment with the railroad 15 months before the accident in question. *See also Lobato v. Pay Less Drug Store, Inc.*, 261 F.2d 406 (10th Cir. 1958) (absence of allegations that individual non-diverse defendants participated in tortious acts alleged).

In this case, we need not decide the extent of permissible inquiry into the validity of the release of Boyer's claims against Baldwin and Kaiser, the non-diverse defendants, because that issue, which the district court stated "is likely to be dispositive of plaintiffs' claims against Baldwin and Kaiser," is equally applicable to Snap-on. In fact, ultimately, that is what the district court decided when it granted summary judgment. Thus, the district court, in the guise of deciding whether the joinder was fraudulent, stepped from the threshold jurisdictional issue into a decision on the merits. As the Supreme Court held in *Chesapeake & Ohio Ry. v. Cockrell*, 232 U.S. 146 (1914), this it may not do.

Because *Cockrell* is directly applicable, the underlying facts and the procedural posture are significant. The administrator of an estate, who was a Kentucky citizen, sued a Virginia railroad company and its engineer and fireman, who were citizens of Kentucky, for negligently causing the death of the intestate. The defendants removed the case to federal court on the ground that the charges of negligence against the employees were fraudulently made, thereby vesting the federal court with jurisdiction over the diverse parties, the railroad and administrator. The Supreme Court, after noting first that under Kentucky law employees were jointly liable with the employer for negligent acts committed by the employees, held that removal was improper.

The railroad had sought removal on the ground that the charges of negligence against the employees were false and untrue and made for the sole and fraudulent purpose of affording a basis for the fraudulent joinder. The Court stated that while this contention "may have disclosed an absence of good faith on the part of the plaintiff in bringing the action at all ... it did not show a fraudulent joinder of the engineer and fireman." *Id.* at 153. The Court continued:

> As no negligent act or omission *personal to the railway company* was charged, and its liability, like that of the two employees, was, in effect, predicated upon the alleged negligence of the latter, *the showing manifestly went to the merits of the action as an entirety and not to the joinder*; that is to say, it indicated that the plaintiff's case was ill founded as to all the defendants.... As [the two employees] admittedly were in charge of the movement of the train and their negligence was apparently the principal matter in dispute, the plaintiff had the same right, under the laws of Kentucky, to insist upon their presence as real defendants as upon that of the railway company.

Id. (emphasis added).

Although Snap-on seeks to distinguish *Cockrell* on the ground that the Boyers asserted certain allegations against Snap-on which were not asserted against the non-diverse employees, we find *Cockrell* indistinguishable because the dispositive defense, that based on the release, was raised by all three defendants. Similarly, the Boyers' arguments that the release was invalid involve identical legal and factual issues applicable to the individual defendants and Snap-on. Informed by *Cockrell*, we hold that where there are colorable claims or defenses asserted against or by diverse and non-diverse defendants alike, the court may not find that the non-diverse parties were fraudulently joined based on its view of the merits of those claims or defenses. Instead, that is a merits determination which must be made by the state court.

III. *Conclusion*

For the reasons set forth above, we will vacate the entry of summary judgment entered against the plaintiffs because the district court was without jurisdiction; we will reverse the district court's order denying the plaintiffs' motion to remand; and we will remand to that court with directions to remand this case to the state court.

2. The Motion for Summary Judgment Standard

Travis v. Irby

326 F.3d 644 (5th Cir. 2003)

Davis, J.,

We deny the Defendants' motion for rehearing. In response to their petition for panel rehearing, we substitute the following opinion in place of the opinion as originally issued:

Plaintiff Mary Travis appeals the district court's denial of her Motion to Remand after the defendants removed this case from the Circuit Court of Holmes County, Mississippi, and the district court's dismissal of her claims on summary judgment. Based on our finding that the non-diverse defendant, Arthur Irby, was not fraudulently joined, we vacate and remand.

I.

Michael Travis was killed on May 16, 1997, when his car was struck by a train at the Mileston railroad crossing on Epps Road in Holmes County, Mississippi. Illinois Central Railroad Company ("Illinois Central") owned the train and engineer Arthur Irby operated the train at the time of the fatal accident.

facts

Plaintiff originally filed this action in the Circuit Court of Holmes County against Illinois Central, Irby and John Does 1 through 10, identified only as agents, servants, employees or representatives of Illinois Central. Plaintiff Mary Travis is an adult resident of Madison County, Mississippi, and is the natural mother of Michael Travis, deceased. Defendant Illinois Central is an Illinois corporation registered to do business in the State of Mississippi. Defendant Irby is an adult resident of Leake County, Mississippi.

In her First Amended Complaint filed on December 9, 1997, plaintiff alleged that the defendants, collectively, were negligent for

> failing to make a proper and timely application of the brakes of the train, failing to keep a proper and reasonable lookout, failing to properly train the crew of the train, failing to adopt and enforce adequate policies and procedures relating to train operating under similar circumstances, failing to take proper precautions under the circumstances existing, failing to properly mark, warn of, and restrict access to its crossing under dangerous circumstances, and under circumstances where Defendants knew or should have known that such crossing was unreasonably dangerous, and any such other acts or omissions of negligence which will be shown at a trial of this matter.

P's initial allegations

Discovery did not proceed smoothly in state court. After considerable procedural wrangling and a Motion to Compel, on September 25, 1998, the plaintiff supplemented answers to certain interrogatories. The defendants, contending that those responses established that Defendant Irby was fraudulently joined, removed the action to federal court on October 2, 1998. The district court agreed, dismissed Defendant Irby and the John Doe defendants, and denied a Motion to Remand.

After additional discovery, the defendants filed a Motion for Summary Judgment seeking dismissal of plaintiff's remaining claims against Illinois Central. The district court granted this motion on March 16, 2001, dismissing the case. Plaintiff timely appealed.

II.

The decisive issue in this case is whether the district court erred in denying plaintiff's Motion to Remand based on fraudulent joinder of Defendant Irby.[2] Fraudulent joinder can be established in two ways: (1) actual fraud in the pleading of jurisdictional facts, or (2) inability of the plaintiff to establish a cause of action against the non-diverse party in state court. *Griggs v. State Farm Lloyds*, 181 F.3d 694, 698 (5th Cir. 1999). The defendants do not dispute that Irby is a Mississippi resident. Accordingly, we focus on the second test.

test

---

2. Plaintiffs also allege that the Notice of Removal was not timely based on both the one-year time limit and the 30-day time limit in 28 U.S.C. § 1446. Because we find that the Defendants were not entitled to removal on a theory of fraudulent joinder, we need not decide whether their Notice of Removal was timely under either schedule.

Neither our circuit nor other circuits have been clear in describing the fraudulent joinder standard. The test has been stated by this court in various terms, even within the same opinion. For example, the *Griggs* opinion states,

> To establish that a non-diverse defendant has been fraudulently joined to defeat diversity, the removing party must prove ... that there is *absolutely no possibility* that the plaintiff will be able to establish a cause of action against the non-diverse defendant in state court.

181 F.3d at 699 (emphasis added). The *Griggs* opinion later restates that test as follows —

> Stated differently, we must determine whether there is *any reasonable basis* for predicting that [the plaintiff] might be able to establish [the non-diverse defendant's] liability on the pleaded claims in state court.

181 F.3d at 699 (emphasis added; again citing *Burden*, and *Cavallini*.) Similarly, in summing up federal law, *Moore's Federal Practice* states at one point: "To establish fraudulent joinder, a party must demonstrate ... the *absence of any possibility* that the opposing party has stated a claim under state law". 16 Moore's Federal Practice § 107.14[2][c][iv][A] (emphasis added). It then comments: "The ultimate question is whether there is arguably a *reasonable basis* for predicting that state law might impose liability on the facts involved." *Id.* (emphasis added.) Although these tests appear dissimilar, "absolutely no possibility" vs. "reasonable basis," we must assume that they are meant to be equivalent because each is presented as a restatement of the other.

> Describing the chaos among the circuits, one scholar observed, "A circuit split has developed, with several courts recognizing only one of the categories of fraudulent joinder. The Fourth, Fifth, and Tenth Circuits follow the 'pierce the pleadings' approach, in which the court examines the entire state court record to determine if the plaintiff might possibly prove a cause of action. The Third and Eleventh Circuits follow the 'pleadings only' approach ... [and the remainder] are split internally."
>
> John B. Oakley, *Prospectus for the American Law Institute's Federal Judicial Code Revision Project*, 31 U.C. Davis L. Rev. 855, 1011 (1998).

Any argument that a gap exists between the "no possibility" and "reasonable basis" of recovery language was recently narrowed, if not closed. *Badon v. R J R Nabisco, Inc.* held:

> Plaintiffs appear to argue that *any mere theoretical possibility* of recovery under local law — no matter how remote or fanciful — suffices to preclude removal. We reject this contention. As cited authorities reflect, there must at least be arguably a *reasonable basis* for predicting that state law would allow recovery in order to preclude a finding of fraudulent joinder.

236 F.3d 282, 286 n.4 (5th Cir. 2000) (first emphasis in original). *Great Plains Trust Co. v. Morgan Stanley Dean Witter & Co.* confirmed this point:

> The court determines whether that party has *any possibility of recovery* against the party whose joinder is questioned. If there is arguably a *reasonable basis* for predicting that the state law might impose liability on the facts involved, then there is no fraudulent joinder. This *possibility, however, must be reasonable*, not merely theoretical.

313 F.3d 305, 312 (5th Cir. 2002) (emphasis added; internal citation and quotations omitted; citing *Badon*).

Our cases have also noted the similarity of the test for fraudulent joinder and the test for a Rule 12(b)(6) motion alleging failure to state a claim. For instance, *Great Plains Trust* states that the Rule 12(b)(6) standard is: "The court should not dismiss the claim unless the plaintiff would not be entitled to relief under *any set of facts or any possible theory* that he could prove consistent with the allegations in the complaint". *Id.* at 313. It states the fraudulent joinder standard as: "After all disputed questions of fact and all ambiguities in the controlling state law are resolved in favor of the nonremoving party, the court determines whether that party has *any possibility of recovery* against the party whose joinder is questioned." *Id.* at 312. This language appears adopted from the Rule 12(b)(6) standard under which "the central issue is whether, in the light most favorable to the plaintiff, the complaint states a *valid claim for relief*".

Of course, although the fraudulent joinder and Rule 12(b)(6) standards appear similar, the scope of the inquiry is different. For Rule 12(b)(6) motions, a district court may only consider the allegations in the complaint and any attachments. *E.g., Great Plains Trust*, 313 F.3d at 313. For fraudulent joinder, the district court may, as it did in this case, "pierce the pleadings" and consider summary judgment-type evidence in the record, but must also take into account all unchallenged factual allegations, including those alleged in the complaint, in the light most favorable to the plaintiff. *Carriere*, 893 F.2d at 100; *Griggs*, 181 F.3d at 699–702. Any contested issues of fact and any ambiguities of state law must be resolved in Travis's favor. *Griggs*, 181 F.3d at 699. The burden of persuasion on those who claim fraudulent joinder is a heavy one. *B, Inc.*, 663 F.2d at 549.

As all parties acknowledge, Travis clearly stated a claim against Irby. Under Mississippi law, Irby owed a duty to exercise reasonable care to avoid injuring Michael Travis at the railroad crossing. *New Orleans & N.R. Co. v. Lewis*, 214 Miss. 163, 58 So. 2d 486, 490 (1952). Irby can be held personally responsible for negligent acts committed within the scope of his employment for Illinois Central. *Harrison v. Illinois C. R. Co.*, 219 Miss. 401, 69 So. 2d 218, 222 (1954). Plaintiff Travis alleges facts in her complaint attributable to defendant Irby that constitute negligence, including failing to make a proper and timely application of the brakes of the train, failing to keep a proper and reasonable lookout, and failing to take proper precautions under the circumstances existing at the time of the accident.

The bases for the defendants' opposition to the Motion to Remand were the responses Travis made in her Second Supplemental Response to interrogatories posed by the defendants. One of the interrogatories read:

> You have alleged in paragraph 12 of the Complaint that Engineer Irby "failed to keep a proper and reasonable lookout." With respect to this allegation, please state:
>
> a. List all facts indicating that Irby failed to keep a proper and reasonable lookout and state the name and address of all witnesses having discoverable knowledge supporting your answer.

Plaintiff's supplemental response was as follows:

> Plaintiff does not possess the facts supporting said allegations at this time nor has a determination been made as to who may be called to provide expert witness testimony, at such time a determination is made, Plaintiff will promptly supplement this request in accordance with M.R.C.P.

A similar response was made in answer to an interrogatory regarding plaintiff's allegation of failure to take proper precautions under the circumstances. Also, in response to an interrogatory regarding plaintiff's allegations that defendant failed to brake timely, the plaintiff responded that she did not know the location of the locomotive when the brakes were applied. The district court found that "while Plaintiff clearly seeks the chance to engage in further discovery, she has failed to present any evidence in support of a claim against Defendant Irby. She fails to provide even cursory evidence which gives the Court reason to believe that there is a potential that Irby may be found liable." This led the district court to find that Irby was fraudulently joined. The court therefore denied the Motion to Remand.

We conclude that the district court relied too heavily on the interrogatory responses noted above without considering them in the context of the entire record, the status of discovery, and without resolving all ambiguities in Travis' favor. The district court agreed with the defendant that Travis' second supplemental interrogatory responses should be treated as admissions that she had no factual basis or evidence in support of her claims against Defendant Irby. We disagree with that conclusion. Travis' supplemental answers did not withdraw her earlier responses. Plaintiff responded earlier that expert testimony was required to fully respond and provided lists of eyewitnesses from whose testimony the plaintiff expected to establish facts to support her allegations against Irby. The defendants did not point to any evidence that would negate Irby's fault as alleged in the complaint. Under these circumstances, the defendants have not negated the possibility that Irby could be held liable to Travis on the claims alleged.

Principles

"Fraudulent joinder has significant impact on the determination of which state law claims receive a federal forum, yet it has been largely ignored by the academic community, even while the federal circuits are enmeshed in a seemingly intractable and fruitless search for an analytical Rosetta stone—the proper standard to apply to the doctrine.

"The time is ripe for the Supreme Court to abandon … the convoluted proxies created by the federal courts to administer the unnecessary fraudulent joinder doctrine.

"A better paradigm would hold that any pretrial dismissal by a state court of a claim against a local defendant can create complete diversity needed for removal. This change would involve the state courts in the adjudication of pure state claims—those involving state law and nondiverse litigants—while permitting diversity jurisdiction where the only viable claims involve diverse litigants."

James M. Underwood, *From Proxy to Principle: Fraudulent Joinder Reconsidered*, 69 Albany L. Rev. 1013 (2006).

Also, a review of the events leading up to those responses reveals that they were made at defendants' suggestion to account for the gaps in discovery at the time the interrogatory responses were due. After considerable discussion between the attorneys about discovery, defendants filed a Motion to Compel on the ground that plaintiff's interrogatory responses were inadequate. The transcript of the hearing on that motion reflects that the plaintiff informed the court that she could not answer many questions because of the status of discovery at the time. The defendants had been successful in avoiding depositions of Irby and other railroad representatives, claiming that until they received satisfactory and fully responsive answers to their interrogatories, depositions were inappropriate. Also, the parties had not deposed witnesses to the accident or developed expert testimony necessary to establish appropriate railroad safety procedures and any breaches thereof. The defendants argued that plaintiff could answer their interrogatories by responding that they "don't know at this time ... but our investigation is continuing." The defendants argued that these answers could then be supplemented when experts were retained and as information was received. As to one interrogatory, the defendant's counsel stated that "If he doesn't know, it's not going to throw him out of Court to say, in response to the interrogatory, 'We do not know at this time of any such violations.' He could then easily supplement if his expert comes back and they want to claim some violations in the future." Plaintiff's supplemental responses to the interrogatories relied on by the district court appear to be directly responsive to those comments. Placed in context, they should not form the basis for barring remand to the plaintiff's chosen forum.

It is also clear from the record, as the district court acknowledged, that discovery was continuing. The district court acknowledged that both sides had engaged in dilatory tactics and found that "neither Plaintiff nor Defendants have presented any substantive evidence regarding Defendant Irby. Defendants merely point to Plaintiff's lack of evidence, while Plaintiff apparently clings to the need for further discovery." In this circumstance, in which the defendant has the burden of establishing fraudulent joinder and the plaintiff can clearly state a claim upon which relief can be granted as to the non-diverse defendant, the lack of substantive evidence as to the non-diverse defendant does not support a conclusion that he was fraudulently joined. In order to establish that Irby was fraudulently joined, the defendant must put forward evidence that would negate a possibility of liability on the part of Irby. As the defendants cannot do so, simply pointing to the plaintiff's lack of evidence at this stage of the case is insufficient to show that there is no possibility for Travis to establish Irby's liability at trial.

Under these circumstances, the district court erred in concluding that Travis had no possibility of establishing Irby's liability for negligence because Illinois Central failed to meet its burden of establishing that the non-diverse defendant was fraudulently joined. Accordingly, the Motion to Remand should have been granted.

III.

For reasons stated above, we vacate the district court's judgment and remand this case to the district court with instructions to remand this case to the Circuit Court of Holmes County, Mississippi.

VACATED and REMANDED.

Notes and Problems

1. What is the real significance of the debate between which analytical model to use for application of the fraudulent joinder doctrine? Is one more effective than the other? If you were a plaintiff, which analytical standard would you prefer be applied to consideration of any allegation of fraudulent joinder?

2. Before defense counsel reflexively, and perhaps aggressively, attempts removal of a case to federal court through invocation of the fraudulent joinder rule, it might be a good idea to think soberly about the costs of doing so:

> Defense counsel should carefully advise clients of the potential costs and benefits of removing a case to federal court prior to doing so. The pros and cons will, of

course, vary depending upon the circumstances. The most obvious disadvantage of removal is the reality that fighting fraudulent joinder requires reasonable preparation and, as a consequence, can substantially raise litigation costs. The process easily can be as expensive or more so than preparing a motion for summary judgment, and efforts will probably fail under the "no possibility" standard. Apparently erroneous decisions by the district court, moreover, are final because remand orders are generally not reviewable by appeal or writ of mandamus. Even worse, there is the possibility that the corporate client will have to pay opposing counsel's attorneys' fees under 28 U.S.C. §1447(c) in the even the district court determines that the removal was improvident. Finally, accusing the plaintiff and opposing counsel of fraudulent joinder can precipitate animosity, compromise settlement negotiations and raise litigation costs even further.

Jay S. Blumenkopf, *Fighting Fraudulent Joinder: Proving the Impossible and Preserving Your Corporate Client's Right to a Federal Forum*, 24 Am. J. Trial Advoc. 297, 310–11 (2000).

3. The name "fraudulent" joinder is a misnomer, as the Supreme Court has long held that a removing party need not prove fraud or deceit by the plaintiff in naming the non-diverse party. *See Mecom v. Fitzsimmons Drilling Co.*, 284 U.S. 183, 189 (1931) (referring to the "principle that in a removal proceeding the motive of the plaintiff in joining defendants is immaterial" so long as there is a basis in the law and facts for the claim to be asserted); *Smallwood v. Illinois Central R.R. Co.*, 385 F.3d 568, 571 n. 1 (5th Cir. 2004) (en banc) ("We adopt the term 'improper joinder' as being more consistent with the statutory language than the term 'fraudulent joinder,' which has been used in the past. Although there is no substantive difference between the two terms, 'improper joinder' is preferred.") Nevertheless, most federal courts still refer to this doctrine by its original name.

4. Under the umbrella of fraudulent or improper joinder there are a few other related varieties of the doctrine that permits courts to ignore the diversity-destroying party's presence in the suit. One is the situation where the plaintiff actually does misstate the facts concerning the citizenship of a party in order to create the false impression that diversity is lacking. There is also another related doctrine where the non-diverse party can be ignored because, pursuant to Rule 20, they were not properly joined with the primary, diverse defendant. *See, e.g., John S. Clark Co., Inc. v. Travelers Insurance Co. of Ill.*, 359 F. Supp. 2d 429 (M.D. N.C. 2004) ("Procedural misjoinder of parties is a relatively new concept that has emerged from the Eleventh Circuit and appears to be part of the doctrine of fraudulent joinder."); *Tapscott v. MS Dealer Serv. Corp.*, 77 F.3d 1353, 1359–60 (11th Cir. 1996) (misjoinder due to procedural irregularity may be just as fraudulent as joinder of a claim against a defendant that the plaintiff has no claim against). These other two varieties of improper joinder are relatively rare and not the focus of this text.

5. In terms of the timing for asserting fraudulent joinder, the removal statute, 28 U.S.C. §1446, requires the filing of a notice of removal within 30 days after service on a defendant of a document (typically the complaint) showing federal court jurisdiction exists. If the original complaint does not demonstrate the removability of the case, defendant can attempt removal later (still within the 30-day window) but a diversity based removal must be attempted within one year after the lawsuit's filing "unless the district court finds that the plaintiff has acted in bad faith in order to prevent a defendant from removing the action." 28 U.S.C. §1446(c)(1). Thus, it is conceivable that an attempted removal based upon fraudulent joinder might be entertained now even after one year. In the past, the statute made no express exception for a diversity removal after one year though some federal courts found an equitable basis might exist for considering such an otherwise

untimely removal when bad faith existed. This one-year limit on diversity removals (even when fraudulent joinder was invoked), explains why the plaintiff in the Texas state court *Gonzalez* case (discussed in length in the *In re Diet Drugs* case explored earlier in this Chapter under the Anti-Injunction Act) dropped the diversity-destroying local defendant and even increased the claimed amount in controversy after one year had passed. Even under the newly revised § 1446, a defendant is better spotting fraudulent joinder and attempting removal as soon as possible. Doing so is actually required by the general 30-day window for removals (once the case becomes removable) and avoids the requirement of demonstrating bad faith so long as the attempted removal occurs within the first year of the case's life.

6. The reason that federal courts are placed in a position of having to guess as to the possible validity of the disputed state law claim against the non-diverse defendants is because of the so-called *voluntary/involuntary rule.* Under this rule, in terms of determining the complete diversity of the parties under the general diversity statute, federal courts have held that they must disregard any involuntary dismissal of a party. If a plaintiff voluntarily dismisses or "nonsuits" a defendant, then that defendant's citizenship no longer counts in the analysis. But a state court grant of summary judgment in favor of a defendant does nothing to alter the requirement that federal courts continue to consider the diversity of the now-dismissed defendant. *Insinga v. La Bella*, 845 F.2d 249, 253–54 (11th Cir. 1988) ("If a resident defendant was dismissed from the case by the voluntary act of the plaintiff, the case became removable, but if the dismissal was the result of either the defendant's or the court's action against the wish of the plaintiff, the case could not be removed."). The idea behind this court-created rule is the supposed "obvious principle ... [that] the plaintiff may by the allegations of his complaint determine the status with respect to the removability of the case." *Great Northern Railway Co. v. Alexander*, 246 U.S. 276, 282 (1918). Not all agree that this rationale makes any sense. *See Jenkins v. Nat'l Union Fire Ins.*, 650 F. Supp. 609, 614 (N.D. Ga. 1986) (rule is "baseless," "antiquated," and "absurd"); James M. Underwood, *From Proxy to Principle: Fraudulent Joinder Reconsidered*, 69 Albany L. Rev. 1013, 1094–1098) (suggesting an abandonment of the voluntary/involuntary rule as well as the doctrine of fraudulent joinder as unnecessary encroachments on federalism). As a result of this rule, however, federal courts are forced to ask themselves whether a "possible claim" exists rather than just waiting on a state court to do so for them.

7. *Problem.* Practice utilizing the 12(b)(6) and the summary judgment analytical models for considering claims of fraudulent joinder with respect to the following scenario. Plaintiff files a cause of action for malpractice against Defendant Doctor three years after so-called "botched penile implant surgery." The applicable statute of limitations requires such claims to be brought within 2 years of the date of the alleged malpractice. Plaintiff's complaint does not reference the date of the surgery. Defendant raises the issue of limitations in its answer as an affirmative defense, reciting the dates of the surgery and the filing of the plaintiff's complaint. May this case be properly removed under the fraudulent joinder doctrine?

8. *Chapter Problem.* In response to Bresser's federal suit in Dallas, PERI files its own state court complaint against Bresser Industries in west Texas. It is concerned, however, that Bresser (being a non-Texas company) will immediately remove the case to federal court and then invoke the federal court's "first-to-file" rule to have the case transferred to the Northern District of Texas (where the Dallas federal action is pending) for consolidation. To try to defeat the complete diversity requirement from being met, PERI also asserts a claim against a Texas supplier of sand, Gritty, Inc., which supplied the sand

to Bresser used on all Bresser fracking jobs in Texas. PERI alleges a common law "conspiracy" between Gritty and Bresser for the illegal purpose of defrauding customers. In response to written discovery in state court from Bresser as to the evidence supporting this conspiracy count, PERI honestly concedes "PERI is not currently aware of any evidence supporting this allegation but asserts it solely upon information and belief. PERI will supplement this answer if we discover any supporting evidence."

Upon Further Review

Litigants and their counsel care passionately about having their lawsuits resolved in front of the most convenient and favorable forum possible. Doing so may not guarantee success but, at a minimum, it increases the perception of an advantage and so increases their settlement leverage. And, short of settlement, doing so puts them in the best position to win at trial. Counsel are careful to strategize about where to file a claim and, having made the selection so carefully, will fight hard to preserve such forum from the attacks of the defendant. Likewise, defendants will fight to deprive a plaintiff of their preferred forum, either with an anticipatory filing of their own claim or by attacking the plaintiff's original filing. The tools discussed in this chapter are used by lawyers to engage in these battles, and your familiarity with them will best position you to be the best advocate for your clients in the future. When it comes to dueling litigation, a point of initial reference is the *first-to-file* rule, used by both federal and state courts at least generally and subject to exceptions where the first suit is considered to involve bad faith forum shopping (e.g., the possible improper use of the federal declaratory judgment statute) or where the balance of convenience swings wildly against the plaintiff's initial chosen forum. But the *Colorado River Abstention Doctrine* presents a federal departure from the presumptive first-to-file doctrine when the dueling cases are in the federal/state context. Even when filing an alternative suit is not feasible for the party losing the race to the courthouse, other options exist for a more direct assault on the plaintiff's forum choice— either a *§ 1404(a)* request to transfer for convenience or, when applicable, a motion for dismissal under the doctrine of *forum non conveniens*—both utilizing the same list of public and private considerations. When multiple related cases have already been filed or removed to federal court, *§ 1407* might present another way to move the case to a different forum, even if only for pretrial purposes. Finally, lawyers need to be mindful that sometimes the forum fight exists at the vertical level, with defendants attempting to remove what appear to be un-removable cases under the doctrine of *fraudulent joinder*. Familiarity with these devices is critically important for effective advocates.

Chapter Problem Revisited

In light of the various doctrines, rules, and statutes we have covered in this chapter, ask yourself as counsel for PERI what is, tactically, the best response it should make to the new federal lawsuit filed against it by Bresser in Dallas. Recall that the client's goal is to have its claims adjudicated with as much speed as possible and at home in front of a local jury sympathetic to a local business being defrauded by a big city company lacking west Texas values (not part of the Northern District of Texas where the Dallas case is pending). Do you just proceed to file your own case and, if so, would it better to do so in state or federal court? Should an injunction be sought against the original lawsuit's continued prosecution? If you do file your own suit now, what will Bresser do in response and how do you anticipate that and best position PERI to win the forum battle? Can other devices such as *forum non conveniens*, § 1404 or § 1407 help in any way?

Spend 30 minutes writing out your recommended course of action to your partners.

Going Deeper

Additional recommended readings to enhance your understanding of some of the topics in this Chapter include:

- Michael Cicero, *First-to-File and Choice of Forum Roots Run Too Deep for Micron*, 2009 Emerging Issues 3917 (2009) (exploring historical roots of first-to-file rule and its modern applications in patent disputes).

- Richard L. Marcus, *Cure-All for an Era of Dispersed Litigation? Toward a Maximalist Use of the Multi-District Litigation Panel's Transfer Power*, 82 Tul. L. Rev. 2245 (2008) (surveying the panel's attitudes toward aggressive use of 28 U.S.C. § 1407's powers to consolidate related cases).

- Daniel A. Richards, *An Analysis of the Judicial Panel on Multidistrict Litigation's Selection of Transferee District and Judge*, 78 Fordham L. Rev. 311 (2009) (discussing considerations panel uses in making the "most difficult decision the Panel faces").

- James M. Underwood, *From Proxy to Principle: Fraudulent Joinder Reconsidered*, 69 Albany L. Rev. 1013 (2007).

Chapter 4

Class Actions: Certification

Chapter Goals

- Appreciate the concept of representative litigation and how that comports with due process.
- Appreciate the unique ethical issues involved in allowing a stranger to represent another in pursuing a claim without any agreement.
- Become familiar with the four prerequisites for certification of any class action contained in Rule 23(a).
- Recognize the four major categories of approved class actions contemplated by Rule 23(b).
- Discover the qualitative differences between certifying a mandatory non-opt-out class action under Rule 23(b)(1)–(2) and a damages class action under Rule 23(b)(3).
- Understand the unique role played by class counsel with duties owed primarily toward the entire class.
- Recognize how the themes of autonomy, efficiency, and fairness are balanced in class actions.

A. Overview

It is possible to regard class actions as simply another procedural rule of joinder that permits large numbers of claimants to have claims that bear some relationship to one another represented in a joint attempt at vindicating their claims together. Rather than all attempting to join pursuant to Rule 20 (with its same "transaction or occurrence" limitation), in a class action one (or more) claimants file suit both individually and on behalf of the missing class action members. Viewing Rule 20 as simply another joinder device, however, would vastly understate the importance of the device and the far-reaching implications for its use, particularly in the last few decades.

1. Historical Perspective

Prior to the 1966 amendments to Rule 23, class action practice in America was fairly limited. In the roughly quarter-century since the adoption of the Federal Rules of Civil

Procedure in 1938, the rules governing class actions were rarely invoked. The language in them was obscure and lawyers seemed disinclined to navigate their murky waters. There were examples of some "true" class actions where multiple claimants seeking "joint or common" vindication of their rights could join together. There were also "hybrid" class actions where the right was several, rather than joint, but the lawsuit sought the adjudication of claims affecting specific property. Of far more interest, though not utilized greatly, was the "spurious" class action whereby the plaintiff sought to vindicate several claims not only on the plaintiff's own behalf but also on behalf of a class of missing claimants with claims raising common questions of law or fact. But in order to bind the missing members of the spurious class, the missing members had to affirmatively "opt in" to the case. It almost resembled more of a group intervention than anything resembling a modern day class action. And because inertia is the most powerful force in the universe, spurious class actions did not happen frequently. Nevertheless, the spurious class action would become the genesis for something much grander with the advent of the 1966 rewrite of Rule 23.

Referring to the historical "spurious" class action, one treatise has opined that "when [such a suit was brought] it was merely an invitation to joinder—an invitation to become a fellow traveler in the litigation, which might or might not be accepted."

3B J. Moore, *Federal Practice* ¶ 23.10[1] (2d ed.).

At about the same time that the Rules Advisory Committee was re-working other joinder rules in an effort to maximize the productivity of the federal courts by permitting, if not encouraging, joinder of multiple claims and claimants in singular proceedings, the substantive law was changing in America. America in the 1960s was experiencing massive change, including the dawn of the Civil Rights Movement, Title VII employment rights, increased recognition of toxic-tort claims, and beginning with Justice Traynor's historic opinion in 1963 in *Greenman v. Yuba Power Products, Inc.*, 377 P.2d 897 (Cal. 1963), courts quickly were recognizing for the first time liability of product sellers for defective goods even without a traditional showing of fault. All of these movements coalesced in the re-working of what is now Rule 23 and the subsequent meteoric rise of class action practice in these and other areas of the law.

2. Modern Practice

In 1966, the Federal Rules of Civil Procedure were amended into more or less the present format. These amendments replaced the prior opaque classifications with functional tests related to the underlying policies behind modern class action treatment. The revisions concerning class actions were designed to be consistent with furthering these two disparate but laudatory aims:

> The entire reconstruction of the rule bespoke an intention to promote more vigorously than before the dual missions of the class-action device: (1) to reduce units of litigation by bringing under one umbrella what might otherwise be many separate but duplicating actions; [and] (2) even at the expense of increasing litigation, to provide means of vindicating the rights of groups of people who individually would be without effective strength to bring their opponents into court at all.

Benjamin Kaplan, *A Prefatory Note*, 10 Boston College Ind. & Com. L. Rev. 497 (1969). On the one hand, the reformers sought to reduce the number of related lawsuits pending in various courts by permitting one court, in a class action, to resolve all of the claims together. This could be particularly helpful by having a single forum facilitate the increasing numbers of civil rights and employment rights claims being asserted. Yet at the same time, the group sought to make the filing of negative-value claims possible. These are generally consumer claims for small individual amounts where consumers were unlikely to assert a traditional lawsuit because it would cost more to pursue the case than the amounts sought to be obtained as damages. Due to the economies of scale, corporations involved in wrongdoing impacting thousands or millions of consumers could avoid justice and continue the reap the benefits of their misconduct. But if the claims could be aggregated in a class action, suddenly the economics made the pursuit of such a case — still small at the per capita level but quite large taken together — lucrative enough to entice class representatives and counsel to bring the case to court.

Principles

"Damage class actions have significant capacity to achieve public goals: to compensate those who have been wrongly injured, to deter wrongful behavior, and to provide individuals with a sense that justice has prevailed. But what drives damage class actions is private gain: the opportunity they offer lawyers to secure large fees.... These financial incentives produce significant opportunities for lawyers to make mischief, to misuse public and private resources for litigation that does not serve a useful purpose. How to respond to this dilemma is the central question for public policy."

Deborah R. Hensler, *Class Action Dilemmas: Pursuing Public Goals for Private Gain* 6–7 (2000).

Under the modern rules, every class action — in order to be certified as such — needs to satisfy each of Rule 23(a)'s general prerequisites and then to fit into one of the categories or cubby holes of a permitted class under Rule 23(b). The enumerated prerequisites for certification of any class include (1) a sufficient number of class members involved, (2) a common question of law or fact binding the claims, (3) that the class representative bringing the suit have claims typical of the other class members, and (4) that the representative be an adequate representative of the absent class members. In essence, these prerequisites are designed to ensure some base level of efficiency before certification can be seriously entertained (the *numerosity* and *commonality* requirements) while having sufficient attributes of fairness (*typicality* and *adequacy of representation*) to make representative litigation palatable to our sense of justice and concerns for the due process rights of the class members. Beyond these enumerated requirements, Rule 23 has been interpreted to assure adequate definition be given to the class so that the courts can determine who is, or is not, a member.

Just because the prerequisites for certification are present, the plaintiff seeking certification must also demonstrate how the case falls into either 23(b)(1), (2) or (3) — the functional varieties of modern class actions. Rule 23(b)(1) deals with situations (similar to Rule 19 necessary parties) where a class member might be harmed without certification or a defendant might be harmed without certification. Rule 23(b)(2) applies to instances where the defendant has misbehaved in a way that supports entry of a judgment for declaratory or injunctive relief for the benefit of the entire class. Rather than have different courts consider possibly overlapping, duplicative, or inconsistent forms of equitable relief, it can all be done at once by one court. Rule 23(b)(3) is the modern re-invention of the old "spurious" class action; these classes involve claims for damages that have common questions of law or fact where great efficiency is to be achieved. But unlike the old mostly ineffective "spurious" class action, a modern 23(b)(3) damages class binds all members who fit the class definition who have not affirmatively "opted out" of the case.

Principles

"[I]t is the business community that has been the source of the lion's share of criticism of class actions over the years."

Deborah R. Hensler, *Class Action Dilemmas: Pursuing Public Goals for Private Gain* 53 (2000).

"Class actions are 'just another milking of the system by professionals, in this case lawyers.'"

Martha Neil, *New Route for Class Actions*, A.B.A. J., July 2003, at 48, 50 (quoting Lawrence W. Schonbrun).

The popularity (and notoriety) of modern class action practice has risen and fallen in the ensuing decades since 1966. While class actions are much more commonplace today than in 1966, there has also been great hostility and criticism, at times, directed at class action practice. Alleged abuses have caused some courts to be rather stingy regarding application of Rule 23's standards. Some of these alleged abuses led to revisions in 2003 to some provisions within Rule 23, though the changes have hardly been revolutionary. Finally, the Class Action Fairness Act passed in 2005 following several decades of debate over the possible unfairness of certain magnet state courts being too liberal with class certification standards and approvals of questionable class action settlements that generated handsome fees for class counsel and coupons of questionable value for class members. Criticisms of class actions came, of course, from corporate interests (the U.S. Chamber of Commerce among the harshest of critics) but also from some consumer advocates.

Whatever one's perspective is on whether class actions are good for the country, no one would deny that the class action device is powerful—capable of being an effective instrument for good, or wreaking incredible havoc. After reading the Chapter Problem below to gain some continuing context for our coverage, this Chapter will begin with a glimpse into at least one illustration of some of the judicial hostility toward the modern class action.

B. Chapter 4 Problem

Underwood & Associates, P.A.
Internal Memo

To: Associate
From: Jim Underwood, Sr. Partner
Re: New Class Action Lawsuit Against Client

Our firm's long-standing local client, Taco Muy Grande ("TMG"), has just received service of an alleged class action. I need your help to analyze the viability of this being certified as a class action and, going forward, with the general defense of this case. Please look at the attached excerpt from the pleadings that TMG just emailed to me this morning.

Please do the necessary.

In the District Court
McClennan County
Civil Division

MERRI CHANCE, on her own behalf and on behalf of all others similarly situated,	§ § § § §	
Plaintiff	§ §	
v.	§ §	No. 16:6185
TACO MUY GRANDE, INC. & John Does 1–10,	§ § §	
Defendants.	§	

Plaintiff's Class Action Complaint

Plaintiff, on her own and on behalf of all others similarly situated, complains as follows:

1. Plaintiff, a citizen of Texas, has purchased numerous products containing corn (e.g. taco shells, nacho chips, etc.) at various Taco Muy Grande restaurants, owned and operated by defendant Taco Muy Grande, Inc. ("TMG"), a corporation headquartered in McClennan County, Texas and incorporated in Delaware.

2. Plaintiff purchased and consumed the corn products of TMG based upon the express and implied warranties that they were fit to eat and safe for human consumption.

3. Recent reports have indicated that TMG's products have, for some time, been found to contain trace levels of AstroLink—a variety of corn intended solely for animal feed and which the FDA has never approved as safe for human consumption.

4. TMG's products are thus unfit and defective and unreasonably dangerous.

5. On behalf of herself and the nationwide class, Plaintiff seeks injunctive relief to prohibit TMG's continued sales of contaminated corn products, actual damages (economic losses as well as for personal injuries for any class member who became ill), and punitive damages. Actual damages are estimated to be in excess of $25 million.

6. Plaintiff requests that she be designated a class representative on behalf of the following class: "All persons in the United States who have been affected, or feel that they might be affected, by the purchase or consumption of contaminated food sold by defendant TMG at any time after the period of two years before the filing of this lawsuit."

7. Plaintiff would show that the class consists of hundreds of thousands, if not millions, of consumers dispersed across the United States (as defendant operates restaurants across the country), that they each have claims against defendant TMG based upon the common issue of whether the defendant's food was improperly contaminated with corn not approved by the FDA for human consumption and thus unlawful under federal regulations, that the plaintiff's claims are typical of the class in that plaintiff has likewise purchased and eaten contaminated food sold by TMG, and that plaintiff would be an adequate class representative because she was motivated to file this lawsuit and seeks redress against TMG similar to the remainder of the class.

8. This class would be properly certified under Rule 23(b)(1), (2) and (3) because (1) TMG's assets are limited and, due to the large number of sales of contaminated products, there are limits to TMG's assets relative to the size of the claims nationwide, (2) plaintiff seeks an injunction to stop defendant from continuing to sell contaminated food in its restaurants and (3) all of the class claims involve many common questions of law and fact concerning the contamination of the products, whether this contamination violated FDA regulations, whether the selling of food that the FDA determines is unfit violates express and implied warranties and constitutes a product defect, and what are the appropriate remedies to the class, these common questions predominate over any individual question of damages and class treatment is the superior method for resolving the claims of such a large number of victims particularly since many claimants' claims are too small to be litigated effectively on their own.

Respectfully Submitted.

C. Ethics of Representative Litigation

We begin with one judge's criticism of some aspects of the class device—some of which we have already raised in the Overview. As you read this case, ask yourself how valid are the objections of this judge? Are there counterpoints to the criticisms raised in *Kline*?

Kline v. Coldwell Banker & Co.

508 F.2d 226 (9th Cir. 1974)

[A married couple sued on behalf of themselves and a class of approximately 400,000 sellers of residential real estate in L.A. County alleging a conspiracy by local realtors to fix an artificially high commission rate (6%). The named defendants include 32 named realtors who were sued individually and on behalf of a proposed defendant class of 2,000 local realtors. The district court certified the 23(b)(3) damages class and the Ninth Circuit reversed on the ground that plaintiff's proposed reliance on a Los Angeles Realty Board's commission schedule was insufficient to possibly establish any price-fixing conspiracy through any generalized proof and, accordingly, that there were not adequate common questions of law or fact to justify certification. The concurring opinion follows.]

Principles

"The romantic class action narrative—perpetuated by the plaintiffs' bar, judicial opinions, and academic adherents—has its counterpart in a darker narrative about class litigation advanced by corporate defendants, skeptical courts, and assorted defense-side interest groups. The defense-side narrative, of course, renders a bleaker portrait of class litigation...

"Thus, class action commentators have suggested that not all class members are helpless victims in need of assistance in asserting their rights, contending that such sweeping generalizations amount to a form of unattractive paternalism. In addition, class action critics contend that in many cases, class members may not even know that they have been harmed, may not care about minor injuries, and may be entirely disinterested in pursuing litigation. In this version of the narrative, class counsel are often portrayed as stirring up litigation; impermissibly soliciting clients in order to pursue the attorney's own class action agenda, ideological cause, or (more cynically) out-sized legal fees; or pursuing a combination of these aims."

Linda S. Mullenix, *Ending Class Actions as We Know Them: Rethinking the American Class Action*, 64 Emory L.J. 399, 413–14 (2014).

DUNIWAY, J., concurring.

I concur in the judgment, but for somewhat different reasons.

I cannot believe that Rule 23, as amended, was intended or should be construed to authorize the kind of judicial juggernaut that plaintiffs and their counsel seek to create here. The plaintiffs Kline have been designated as the representatives of an estimated 400,000 sellers of real property in Los Angeles County, sellers of residential dwellings containing up to twelve units. The Klines sold one residence, in 1970, for $42,500. They paid a commission to one broker, Lelah Pierson, of 6%, or $2,550. She is a named defendant. Their theory of damages is that, but for the charged conspiracy, the commission would have been less, but they do not tell us how much less. If we assume that the broker would have done her work for nothing, an obviously improper assumption, their maximum damages would be $2,550, which, trebled, would be $7,650. Realistically, this is a grossly exaggerated figure. Yet the plaintiffs seek to parlay their claim into a lawsuit on behalf of 400,000 sellers, not one of whom, so far as we are advised, except the Sherman plaintiffs, has indicated the slightest interest in suing anyone. The Shermans, too, made but one sale. They paid a 6% commission of $2,700, which was divided between two brokers, neither of whom is named as a defendant. The plaintiffs, by this device, seek to recover from Ms. Pierson, among 2,000 others, $750,000,000 in damages, plus attorneys' fees and costs.

Principles

"The reports of aggregate litigation's death are greatly exaggerated....

"[M]y experience with lawyers who typically represent clients on the left side of the 'v,' of both the public interests and entrepreneurial stripe, is that many of them are incredibly inventive, talented, and tenacious—some might call them stubborn. After all, it was these risk-assumptive personalities who, in a sense, 'created' the modern class (and mass) action; gave it wide-angle application; and nurtured its growth into a major, constantly evolving, and sophisticated procedural vehicle, sometimes embracing the concept of the private attorney general along the way. I doubt they will flee this field of litigation. And so I hope it will be talented, committed lawyers—both social action and entrepreneurial—who will find ways to preserve and resuscitate aggregate litigation even if new modalities for doing so must be created and the present ones reformulated and modified. As a gifted plaintiffs' lawyer friend of mine is fond of saying: 'We know how to find the back doors.'"

Arthur R. Miller, *The Preservation and Rejuvenation of Aggregate Litigation: A Systematic Imperative*, 64 Emory L.J. 293, 306 (2014).

The named defendants are 32 real estate brokers and five associations of real estate brokers. They have been designated as representatives of a class of 2,000 brokers. Only one of the "representative" defendants, Ms. Pierson, ever dealt with the "representative" plaintiffs Kline.

At oral argument, plaintiffs explained how easy it will be for them to identify the members of the respective classes. First, they propose, under the aegis of the court, to compel the defendant associations to furnish them with lists showing the name and address of every broker who was a member of any of them at any time during the four-year period preceding the filing of this action. These brokers, estimated at 2,000, will be the class of represented defendants. Next, plaintiffs propose, under the aegis of the court, to compel each of these 2,000 brokers to search his files and supply the name and address of every person who, during the same period, paid the broker a commission on a sale of residential property containing twelve units or less. These persons, estimated at 400,000, will be the class of represented plaintiffs. Plaintiffs do not tell us at whose expense all this is to be done.

Next, notice will be sent to each of the 400,000 represented plaintiffs. I would expect that the Rule 23 notice to each "represented" plaintiff, as prepared by plaintiffs' counsel, would give him a brief description of the nature of the case, and then would tell him

(Rule 23(c)(2)(A)) that he can "opt out," but would also tell him that, if he does not opt out, he will incur no financial obligation, while, if the suit is won, he will share in the loot. I wonder if this is proper. Why shouldn't a "represented" plaintiff be told that if he elects to participate in the alleged bonanza, he may, by so electing, subject himself to liability for his share of the costs of suit if the bonanza is not forthcoming? Why should the court offer him a free ride in a case in which the defendants' costs, if they win, may be very large, and will probably not be collectible from the named plaintiffs? Why shouldn't what I have said also apply to plaintiffs' attorneys' fees, unless there is an ironclad agreement by the attorneys that they will collect no fees from anyone if the suit is lost? Rule 23(c)(2)(B) states that the notice shall advise each member of the class that "the judgment, whether favorable or not, will include all members who do not request exclusion." In most cases, one of the incidents of an adverse judgment is liability for costs. No doubt it will be said that the potential liability for costs might cause many represented plaintiffs to opt out. If so, what is so wrong about that? It may also be said that the potential liability is meaningless. How would defendants collect? However, there may be a possible alternative. The real bonanza in a case like this, if it is won, will go to counsel. Perhaps the class action order could be conditioned upon an agreement by counsel that they will pay all costs of all defendants if the suit is lost!

Notice will also go to each of the 2,000 represented defendants. Here I note a peculiarity of Rule 23 that none of the parties has mentioned. Rule 23(c)(2)(A) requires that the notice to each member of the class must advise him that "the court will exclude him from the class if he so requests by a specified date." I have read and re-read the rule and I can find nothing in it to indicate that this provision is not just as applicable to members of a "class" of defendants as it is to members of a "class" of plaintiffs. The notice, therefore, must tell the represented defendant that he can opt out. What member of a class of defendants who is in his right mind, and who is told that, if he does not elect to be excluded, he may be liable for $750,000,000 plus very large attorneys' fees and costs, will fail to opt out? It seems more than probable that the court, having gone to the trouble and expense of learning the name and address of each potential broker defendant and of devising a proper notice and having it sent out, will wind up with no "class" of defendants, but only those who are named as defendants and are served with process in the ordinary way.

I venture to suggest that none of the class action features of this case was dreamed up by the named plaintiffs, but that all of them are the brain children of their attorneys. In California, barratry is a crime (Cal. Pen. C. § 158). The Rules of Professional Conduct of the State Bar, authorized by Cal. Bus. and Prof. Code § 6076, provide (Rule 2 § a): "a member of the State Bar shall not solicit professional employment by advertisement or otherwise." Does solicitation cease to be solicitation when done under the aegis of a judge? If so, what has become of the centuries old policy of the law against stirring up litigation? Did the Supreme Court, when it adopted Rule 23, as amended, intend to abrogate that policy for a case like this? I am loath to believe that it did. I also have grave doubt whether such a change in the law, if intended, can properly be called a matter of procedure. In other words, I doubt that the Supreme Court has power, by a procedural rule, to abrogate the policy to which I have referred, assuming that that is what the Court intended.

Principles

"There seems to be a bit of schizophrenia in the world of class actions. On the one hand, corporate defendants hate them; on the other, they love them. When a class complaint is filed against a corporate defendant, it will do all it can to prevent class certification, otherwise known as a nuclear bomb the plaintiff seeks to hang over its head. But, when it suits their needs, corporate defendants may try to achieve a global peace by negotiating a class settlement with the plaintiff class's attorneys."

Georgene Vairo, *Is the Class Action Really Dead? Is that Good or Bad for Class Members?*, 64 Emory L.J. 476, 478 (2014).

Perhaps more important is the practical effect of such a suit as this. The burden that it can impose on the court—discovery, pre-trial, notice to the classes, etc., and on a jury, if one is ever empanelled, is staggering. It is inconceivable to me that such a case can ever be tried, unless the court is willing to deprive each defendant of his undoubted right to have his claimed liability proved, not by presumptions or assumptions, but by facts, with the burden of proof upon the plaintiff or plaintiffs, and to offer evidence in his defense. The same applies, if he is found liable, to proof of the damage of each "plaintiff." I doubt that plaintiffs' counsel expect the immense and unmanageable case that they seek to create to be tried. What they seek to create will become (whether they intend this result or not) an overwhelmingly costly and potent engine for the compulsion of settlements, whether just or unjust. Most, though by no means all, real estate brokers are small business men. They cannot afford even to participate in such an action as this, much less to defend it effectively. I suspect, for example, that this is true of Ms. Pierson. It is almost inevitable, if the judge's order is permitted to stand, and even if all potential defendants opt out, that many of the named defendants will settle for whatever amount they can bargain for, and without regard as to whether they are really liable or not, with a good chunk of the money going to plaintiffs' lawyers.

I do not say that the Rule 23(b)(3) class action is always unethical and improperly coercive. Doubtless there are circumstances in which it is the only viable means of obtaining relief for classes of truly and actively aggrieved plaintiffs. But courts should not be in the business of encouraging the creation of lawsuits like this one.

I join in the judgment of reversal.

Notes and Problems

1. In reading Judge Duniway's last paragraph of his concurrence, why do you think he says that "courts should not be in the business of encouraging the creation of lawsuits like this one"? What becomes of the judge's views if one pauses and, hypothetically, assumes that there really was a price-fixing conspiracy by the defendant real estate brokers. Does this view of the merits impact the legitimacy of these criticisms?

2. Would the filing of 400,000 separate lawsuits make discovery less cumbersome for the defendants in that case? Can defendants ever benefit from the Rule 23 class treatment of what would otherwise be numerous other lawsuits? Is the class device inherently pro-plaintiff or pro-defendant?

3. *Kline* represents a *negative value* class action—where the cost of pursuing an individual claim on its own would outweigh any potential recovery by the claimant. If the claims cannot be brought together as a class action, what do you think happens to the underlying claims?

4. *Chapter Problem.* Which of the judge's criticisms from the *Kline* case would have equal application to the new class action lawsuit filed by Ms. Chance against TMG? Though

we have not yet gone into the particulars of Rule 23, given the opinion from *Kline*, would you be more or less inclined to certify the contaminated corn case than the real estate commission dispute? Why?

Pulling It All Together Exercise

From the *Kline* opinion above, make a chart showing each of the judge's criticisms of class treatment of that dispute. In another column, try to think of a possible counter-argument that another judge inclined to affirm a certification decision might raise in support of the class. Going through your chart, consider which arguments should prevail. Does the answer change depending upon whether you are talking in general or just focusing upon the *Kline* dispute?

Spend 15 minutes preparing your table of arguments and counter-arguments.

Rule 23. Class Actions

(a) **Prerequisites.**

One or more members of a class may sue or be sued as representative parties on behalf of all members only if:

(1) the class is so numerous that joinder of all members is impracticable,

(2) there are questions of law or fact common to the class,

(3) the claims or defenses of the representative parties are typical of the claims or defenses of the class; and

(4) the representative parties will fairly and adequately protect the interests of the class.

D. Class Prerequisites

As discussed previously, there are specific prerequisites to class certification. Most of these are set forth in Rule 23(a). However, courts have also found that Rule 23 implicitly required any certified class to have a definition capable of demonstrating the identities of the class members sought to be represented. The current Rule 23(c)(1)(B) now explicitly calls for any certification order to "define the class and the claims, issues, or defenses, and must appoint class counsel under Rule 23(g)." Rule 23(a) then provides the essential character traits for a proper class, usually referred to as *numerosity, commonality, typicality, and adequacy of representation*. Remember that these prerequisites are designed to provide some minimal assurances that allowing the case to proceed as a class action will be both efficient and fair.

1. Defining the Class

The class must be defined in a manner that provides the current court and future courts the ability to determine whether a person is or was within the class. Although this does not appear to be a problem in the abstract, there are many times when a plaintiff would prefer to define a class on a basis that would not provide an immediate answer to the question of whether a person was or is currently is within the defined class. In these situations, the court has to consider whether the definition prevents certification. In *Simer v. Rios*, the court struggles with the definition of a class reliant on the mental state of its members. While reading the case, determine why and when problems with the definition of a class can come up. Are there some instances when a tightly constructed definition is less important?

Simer v. Rios

661 F.2d 655 (7th Cir. 1981)

HARLINGTON WOOD, JR., CIRCUIT JUDGE.

This case raises many issues concerning the legality and eventual vacating of a settlement agreement entered into by the plaintiffs and the Community Services Administration (CSA).

I.

Suit was initiated on September 24, 1979 by eight individuals and Gray Panthers of Chicago, an unincorporated non-profit organization, as a class action. The complaint alleged several claims against CSA for its administration of the Crisis Intervention Program (CIP).

CIP was a program funded [by the federal government] and was designed "to enable low income individuals and families, including the elderly ... to participate in the energy conservation programs designed to lessen the impact of the high cost of energy ... and to reduce ... energy consumption."

One aspect of this program provided cash assistance for fuel and utility bills to qualified individuals. The pertinent regulations adopted by CSA conditioned the grant of assistance payments upon the production of a shut-off notice from a utility company. Plaintiffs' complaint alleged that this regulation violated EECSP which provided that "(e)ligibility for any of the programs authorized under this section shall not be based solely on delinquency in payment of fuel bills." 42 U.S.C. § 2809(a)(5).

[A proposed settlement and class certification were presented to the district court for review. On appeal, a foundational issue was whether the case was certifiable as a class action under Rule 23(b)(3) as damages were being sought as the primary remedy.]

Initially we note that our review of the district court's denial of class certification is limited. We can reverse this determination only if the district court's decision denying certification was an abuse of discretion.

The parties, as did the district court, focus on the concept of "manageability" of a class action and whether the issue of each individual plaintiff's state of mind makes the class action unmanageable. We agree that the issue of "state of mind" does make this case difficult to manage as a class action. However, we also conclude that the class action fails for other reasons.

It is axiomatic that for a class action to be certified a "class" must exist. *De Bremaecker v. Short*, 433 F.2d 733, 734 (5th Cir. 1970); 3B Moore's Federal Practice, ¶ 23.04(1) at 23–111 (3d ed. 1980). In the present case serious problems existed in defining and identifying the members of the class. As noted above, the complaint defined the class as those individuals eligible for CIP assistance but who were denied assistance or who were discouraged from applying because of the existence of the invalid regulation promulgated by CSA.

In Practice

One court has opined that crafting a class definition is "more of an art than a science" and that issues with the definition "can and often should be solved by refining the class definition rather than by flatly denying class certification on that basis."

Messner v. Northshore Univ. HealthSystem, 669 F.3d 802, 825 (7th Cir. 2012).

Cases have recognized the difficulty of identifying class members whose membership in the class depends on each individual's state of mind. *De Bremaecker*, 433 F.2d at 734; *Chaffee v. Johnson*, 229 F.Supp. 445, 448 (S.D.Miss.1964), aff'd on other grounds, 352 F.2d 514 (5th Cir. 1965), cert. denied, 384 U.S. 956, 86 S.Ct. 1582, 16 L.Ed.2d 553 (1966); *Capaci v. Katz & Besthoff, Inc.*, 72 F.R.D. 71, 78 (E.D.La.1976). In *De Bremaecker* a class action was filed on behalf of all state residents active in the peace movement who had been harassed or intimidated as well as those who feared harassment or intimidation in the exercise of their constitutional rights. The court held that this did not satisfy the requirement of an adequately defined and clearly ascertainable class. It could not be concluded that all state residents were "chilled" in such a manner and therefore there was no way to identify those individuals affected by defendant's policies. See also *Chaffee*, 229 F.Supp. at 448 (class described as all persons working to end race discrimination and encouraging blacks to exercise rights held too vague because depends on each individual's state of mind); cf. *Simon v. Merrill Lynch, Pierce, Fenner and Smith, Inc.*, 482 F.2d 880, 882 (5th Cir. 1973) (differences in misrepresentations alleged as well as degrees of reliance thereon made class suit inappropriate).

Problems similar to those in *De Bremaecker* exist in the present case. The first problem is to identify those individuals who qualify for CIP assistance. This by no means is an easy or inexpensive task. Cf. *Ihrke v. Northern States Power Company*, 459 F.2d 566, 572 (8th Cir.), vacated as moot, 409 U.S. 815, 93 S.Ct. 66, 34 L.Ed.2d 72 (1972) (denied class certification because of vagueness of class which included all persons who because of poverty are unable to pay for utility service). After completing this task, the court and parties would have to proceed with the Sisyphean task of identifying those individuals who not only qualified for CIP assistance, but also knew of the existence of the regulation and were discouraged from applying for assistance because of the shut-off notice requirement. Such an attempt to identify those individuals who were "chilled" would be a burden on the court and require a large expenditure of valuable court time.

Identification of the class serves at least two obvious purposes in the context of certification. First, it alerts the court and parties to the burdens that such a process might entail. In this way the court can decide whether the class device simply would be an inefficient way of trying the lawsuit for the parties as well as for its own congested docket. Second, identifying the class insures that those actually harmed by defendants' wrongful conduct will be the recipients of the relief eventually provided.

The district court was well aware of problems in identifying the class. At the hearing on January 4, 1980 the district court stated:

District court's considerations

How are we going to find out which persons were chilled from applying because of knowledge of this shutoff notice requirement? How are we going to gather the facts on which persons, other than your named plaintiffs, were turned down on that account in the region? We could spend the 15 million dollars gathering the facts in this case. I say that facetiously, but by the time we gather them, it will be another year down the road and then we would be in the '81 program before we decided who was actually entitled to any money. Is it worth it?

These statements make it evident that the district court, as well as the parties, were aware of the problems attendant to identifying the members of the class. The district court believed that it would require a great deal of its own time as well as a large amount of money to accomplish this task. In light of these circumstances this certainly was a proper factor for the district court to consider in denying class certification.

[The court also found that other Rule 23(b)(3)-specific requirements were not satisfied in this case and, for these additional reasons, certification was improper.]

Notes and Problems

1. What problem did the court have with the definition of the class in *Simer*? With that in mind, how could the class counsel have re-defined the class to avoid this issue? What motivation would counsel have for defining the class in the way chosen?

2. Why does the court in *Simer* indicate that it has to know who would be a member of the class? Can you think of a scenario where it might be acceptable, even necessary, to define a class in a way that might not currently reveal all of its members?

3. Consider the following class definition: "All former employees of Defendant who were wrongfully terminated between the years of 2000–2010 on account of their race." What becomes of the class, after certification, if after a trial on the merits the jury concludes that defendant discriminated against nobody? Referring back to the class definition in light of the jury verdict, can you argue that the adverse verdict is binding on nobody? Some courts have objected to so-called *fail safe* class definitions that, taken literally, only include as class members those who are entitled to prevail. In the context of such a class definition, upon a defense verdict, one court suggested it "could not enter judgment against [someone] because [they] would no longer fit within the class definition. This type of class definition is called a 'fail safe' class because the class definition precludes the possibility of an adverse judgment against class members; the class members either win or are not in the class." *Genenbacher v. Century-Tel Fiber Co.*, 244 F.R.D. 485 (C.D. Ill. 2007). Other courts have found such objections to be more academic and, therefore, overlooked such hyper-literal readings of the class definition. *See, e.g., Mullen v. Treasure Chest Casino*, 186 F.3d 620 (5th Cir. 1999) (rejecting arguments against fail safe class that defined class in terms of those whose illnesses were caused by defendants' wrongdoing); *Forbush v. JC Penney Co.*, 994 F.2d 1101, 1105 (5th Cir. 1993) (rejecting defendant's contention that class definition was "hopelessly circular" because membership in class was defined by those who suffered improper reduction in benefits, the court holding that such readings of class definitions "would preclude certification of just about any class of persons alleging injury from a particular action.").

4. The class definition might also be problematic when its terms includes claimants who are not currently in the class but will be in the future. Is it proper to define a class to include future class members? In an antitrust case challenging the merger between the old ABA and the NBA, plaintiff defined the class to include "all presently active players,

those who were active at the time the action was originally commenced, and future players in the NBA" in seeking injunctive, declaratory relief and damages. Defendants objected to the inclusion of future NBA players arguing that might include any of "hundreds of thousands" of high school players around the country. The court did not accept this objection indicating that the proposed class was "neither amorphous, nor imprecise; at the present time there are three hundred and sixty-five class members ... [and this court can] determine at any time whether a particular individual is a member of the class." *Robertson v. NBA*, 389 F. Supp. 867 (S.D.N.Y. 1975).

5. How important the specificity of the class definition needs to be seems to depend in large part on the nature of the proposed class action and the remedy being sought in the case. This is very logical because, as we will see in the next chapter, Rule 23(b)(3) classes demand individual notice to class members while Rule 23(b)(1)–(2) classes generally require no notice be given to class members. If the court needs to approve a method for providing the required notice in a Rule 23(b)(3) case, the court will need to be able to identify the class members covered by the definition. Further, if the object of the case is to obtain a monetary award to be disbursed to individual class members, this will only be feasible if the identities and whereabouts of the class members can be determined. On the other hand, if the claim is merely for injunctive relief in a Rule 23(b)(2) case, the court need not order any notice to the class and the injunctive relief will be implemented with reference solely to the defendant. In such a case, other then a generalized concern for knowing who is bound by the results of litigation, a court's ability to state who is in the class is much less important. And the claim or issue preclusion concern would only arise in a subsequent case where one who fit the description as a class member attempts to file the same type of claim against the same defendant—at that point the court could make a determination as to whether that current litigant's claim would be barred by preclusion.

6. *Problems.* Consider the appropriateness of the following class definitions in light of the foregoing discussion.

a. "All female employees of Defendant X Corp. who have been subjected to unwanted sexual advances at the workplace and suffered retaliation when they complained to superiors."

b. "Victims of Defendants' illegal and monopolistic price-fixing conspiracy."

c. "Current and Former employees of Defendant who during the previous four years before the filing of this complaint were passed over for promotions."

d. "All customers of Defendant that purchased the allegedly defective Model X514C product and were in an accident when the unit failed during its use."

7. *Chapter Problem.* Is the proposed class definition in the Merri Chance v. TMG case problematic? If you are counsel for the target defendant, what arguments might you make concern the definition? Would such objections likely be upheld? If so, what would be an alternative definition Ms. Chance might consider?

2. Numerosity

A court may only certify a class action if the number of litigants is so large that traditional joinder is impracticable. In other words, only when the efficiency of a class action outweighs the normal preference for traditional litigation will this prerequisite be satisfied. In terms of satisfying this requirement, is it feasible for the courts to simply declare a certain minimum number needed to show sufficient numerosity in the class? Consider this question as you read the following case.

Board of Education Township v. Climatemp

1980 U.S. Dist. LEXIS 11092 (E.D. Ill. 1981)

LEIGHTON, J.

[This is a] treble damage antitrust action alleging bid-rigging and allocation of jobs by sheet metal construction companies in the Chicago area. [A consolidated suit was previously filed with this court naming 50 enterprises and individuals as defendants. Several months thereafter] the Attorney General of the State of Illinois and the State's Attorney of Cook County, Illinois filed a similar action on behalf of the State of Illinois, the Chicago Board of Education, and Cook County, against substantially the same defendants, known as *State of Illinois, et al. v. Climatemp, Inc., et al.*, No. 79 C 4898. The allegations in both complaints substantially track those contained in the indictment in *United States v. Climatemp, Inc., et al.*, No. 78 CR 388 (N.D. Ill. 1978).

[In both cases, plaintiffs allege] that since 1963, defendants have supplied a substantial portion of the sheet metal construction and services performed in the Chicago metropolitan area, and they engaged in a combination and conspiracy in unreasonable restraint of trade in violation of Section 1 of the Sherman Act, 15 U.S.C. § 1, consisting of a continuing agreement and concert of action to: exchange information concerning sheet metal projects, allocate among themselves sheet metal projects, agree on amounts of low bids, and submit noncompetitive, collusive, rigged, and complementary bids, or when necessary, refrain from bidding on sheet metal projects.

[Plaintiffs also allege that] the furnishing and installation of sheet metal services and supplies is a specialized field of business which is engaged in by a limited group of companies. The sheet metal phase of construction includes installation of duct work which conveys heating, cooling, and ventilating air to various rooms in buildings, as well as installation of other sheet metal supplies. These supplies and services are purchased by customers on a direct basis, through negotiations, or through solicitation of competitive bids. On public projects, the sheet metal phase of construction is usually awarded through the solicitation of competitive bids from sheet metal contractors.

It is further alleged by plaintiffs in No. 79 C 4898 that their suit is properly maintainable as a class action, brought on behalf of:

> all public entities of the State of Illinois in the Chicago area supported by public revenues that have purchased sheet metal supplies and services directly, or indirectly pursuant to cost plus contracts, from defendants during the period alleged in the Complaint (1963–1976) and have sustained damages as a result of the combination and conspiracy in violation of Section 1 of the Sherman Act....

Defendants in No. 79 C 4898 filed a motion to strike class action allegations made by the State of Illinois [which is now before the court for resolution].

Preliminarily, it is noted that the motion before the court in the State of Illinois case is one to strike class action allegations rather than one for certification of an alleged class, in accordance with this court's indication at a pretrial conference held June 10, 1980 that it would entertain such a motion. Although the Attorney General claims that such a motion is improper technically and procedurally, motions to strike are a reflection of the court's inherent power to prune pleadings in order to expedite the administration of justice and to prevent abuse of its process. This procedure is useful in bringing into focus issues the resolution of which governs the broader question of whether a class action is maintainable, and a number of courts in this circuit have employed it.

Defendants claim that the class action procedure should be used only when it is clearly superior to other available methods for fair and efficient adjudication of the particular controversy, and that procedures other than a class action are available to plaintiff which would be far superior to a class action. Alternatives pressed by defendants include permissive joinder under Rule 20 (e.g., *In Re Anthracite Coal Antitrust Litigation*, 78 F.R.D. 709, 715 (M.D. Pa. 1978)), permitting intervention under Rule 24 (e.g., *City and County of Denver v. American Oil Company*, 53 F.R.D. 620, 638 (D.C. Colo. 1971)), or allowing the named plaintiffs to proceed individually (e.g., *United States Dental Institute v. American Association of Orthodontists*, 1977-2 TRADE CASES, ¶ 61,557 at p. 72,218 (N.D. Ill. 1977)). The defendants point out that the number of political subdivisions with potential claims is not so numerous as to make joinder impracticable, and note that after two years of grand jury proceedings, the government's initial voluntary bill of particulars identified only 80 projects subject to the alleged conspiracy, and that 79 of the projects were for the three plaintiffs — 16 for Cook County, 55 for Chicago Board of Education, and 8 for State of Illinois. According to defendants, several practical considerations would best be served by liberal joinder or intervention, including immediate identification of actual claimants, limitation of the litigation to those political subdivisions with actual claims, and rapid ascertainment of the amount of individual and aggregated claims, thus permitting early determination of whether resolution through settlement is feasible. Finally, defendants argue that their suggestions would serve to eliminate time-consuming and costly class action discovery while preserving the benefits of a class action proceeding at less time and expense.

Plaintiffs, represented by the Attorney General, contend that a class action procedure is the only means of insuring that the potential claimants will be able to successfully vindicate their rights, and that defendants' suggestions conflict with the express purpose of Rule 23, Fed. R. Civ. P., which has been said to be to prevent a multiplicity of actions and to permit small claimants individually lacking means to prosecute to vindicate their rights. Manual for Complex Litigation (1979) at 23. [Finally], defendants requested that further discovery be permitted to determine the number of potential claimants. This request was effectively granted by this court's order of September 11, 1980 which required the parties to provide the court with information regarding the extent of sheet metal services and supplies provided to governmental entities during 1973–76.

Pursuant to that order, the Attorney General mailed letters to 919 governmental entities located in Cook, DuPage, Lake and Will Counties on October 17. An additional 37 letters were mailed to entities inadvertently omitted from the first mailing. As of November 20, the Attorney General had received approximately 50 responses. In addition, the Attorney General began contacting non-responding entities by telephone. Of the 125 calls that were made, 11 entities indicated that they had made purchases; another 10 indicated that they did not know and would check their records. Despite the Attorney General's extensive efforts, approximately 700 entities had not responded by December 10, 1980, the due date for the information. In summary, the Attorney General's efforts disclosed the following. Fifty-six governmental purchasers of sheet metal supplies and services were identified, 20 of which were grade school districts, 15 of which were high school districts, 10 of which were public colleges, and 1 of which were local governmental units.

Similarly, the defendants conducted investigations of their own and provided the following information, which categorized approximately 404 projects into plaintiff-oriented categories. Thus, projects for plaintiff State of Illinois were broken down into the following sub-entities: Capital Development Board, State Colleges and Universities other than the University of Illinois, Illinois Building Association, Illinois Building Authority, and University of Illinois. Projects for plaintiff City of Chicago were categorized according to the following subentities: Chicago Transit Authority, Public Building Commission, City Colleges, Chicago Park District, and Chicago Board of Education, and so on. The total of public entities, both as main entities and subentities, was calculated to be 135. These figures were apparently obtained from the defendants' own records.

The issue before this court is whether the numerosity requirement of Rule 23, Fed. R. Civ. P., is satisfied by the circumstances presented. This court finds that it is not, and consequently, grants the motion to strike class action allegations in No. 79 C 4898.

Rule 23(a) of the Federal Rules of Civil Procedure specifies that numerosity, typicality, adequacy of representation, and commonality be present as prerequisites to maintenance of a class action. The party seeking to represent an alleged class carries the burden of demonstrating that these elements have been satisfied. Plaintiffs have failed to show that the first element, that of numerosity, is satisfied. At best, figures compiled as described above indicate that 135 public sub-entities may have been victims of the alleged antitrust actions. The Attorney General was able to unearth only 56 governmental purchasers of sheet metal services and supplies. While it is reasonable to assume that continued discovery may disclose additional purchasers, this court finds that the number of entities potentially victimized is not so numerous that intervention or joinder of plaintiffs is impractical.

The question of what constitutes impracticability depends on the facts of a given case, and no arbitrary rules concerning satisfaction of numerosity have been imposed by the courts. Wright & Miller, Federal Practice and Procedure: Civil § 1762 (1972). While joinder has been held to be impracticable with as few as 40 members of a class in *Swanson v. American Consumer Indus., Inc.*, 415 F.2d 1326, 1333 n. 9 (7th Cir. 1969), class actions have not been maintainable with as many as 350 potential members. *State of Utah v. American Pipe & Constr. Co.*, 49 F.R.D. 17 (C.D. Calif. 1969). There, the state of Utah filed an antitrust action against certain concrete and steel pipe manufacturing companies and sought to represent a class described as those "public bodies and agencies of state and local government in the State of Utah who are end users of pipe acquired from the defendants, coconspirators and others." Although plaintiffs alleged that its class was so numerous that joinder of all 800 listed potential members was impracticable, the court refused to accept that all public bodies had claims against the defendants. From prior experience, the court concluded that the number of public entities injured by the alleged antitrust conspiracy was more reasonably estimated to be 350, and that joinder of them was not impracticable. The court found that a class action would not achieve economies of time, effort, and expenses or promote any more uniformity of decision than would joinder; to the contrary, joinder and intervention would permit actual determination of actual plaintiffs and damages suffered in a simpler fashion than a class action would permit. *State of Utah v. American Pipe and Constr. Co.*, 49 F.R.D. at 21. See *Minersville Coal Co. v. Anthracite Export Assoc.*, 55 F.R.D. 426 (M.D. Penn. 1971), where the court found, in an antitrust case alleging violations of the Sherman and Clayton Acts, that a class numbering 330 plaintiffs was not so numerous that joinder of all members was impractical.

There is no "magic number" which automatically determines whether or not the numerosity requirement is met. Other factors are to be considered as well. *Ewh v. Monarch Wine Co., Inc.*, 73 F.R.D. 131 (E.D.N.Y. 1977). For example, the geographical location of the potential plaintiffs is a major factor to be considered in determining whether joinder is impractical. *Demarco v. Edens*, 390 F. 2d 836 (2nd Cir. 1968). In the case at bar, potential plaintiffs have been limited by the allegations contained in the complaint to those located in the Chicago metropolitan area, a limitation which lends itself readily to the procedure of joinder or intervention. For the foregoing reasons, this court concludes that the State of Illinois case is not maintainable as a class action, and that allegations to the contrary must be stricken.

So ordered.

Notes and Problems

1. As a review of the prior section on class definitions, practice your understanding of that material by critiquing the proposed class definition in the foregoing case. Do you see any difficulties understanding who might be included within the class? Will the court be in a position to know who is going to be bound by the decision? Is the proposed class defined according to objective criteria? Given the context of this case, should the proposed class definition be a problem or not?

2. Should there be a "magic number" that determines in every case whether the Rule 23(a)(1) requirement of numerosity is satisfied? What would be the downside to this approach? Many courts state a presumption of numerosity being satisfied when the class exceeds 40 and that numerosity is presumed to be not satisfied when it is less than 20. *See Celano v. Marriott International, Inc.*, 242 F.R.D. 544, 549 (N.D. Cal. 2007). Did the court in *Simer* agree with such presumptions?

3. When Rule 23(a)(1) refers to a class so large that joinder would be "impractical," does that refer to some implicit limit on how many people can be joined under Rule 20? In Chapter 2, did we discover any such limits? If not, what does this phrase mean?

4. The fact that Rule 23(a)(1) precludes class certification in cases where traditional joinder of the class members is feasible reflects a certain values-based determination concerning traditional litigation versus representative, aggregate litigation. What are those values? Do you agree with such a view?

5. How does the geographic distribution of a proposed class factor into the analysis of numerosity? How did that impact the court's decision in the foregoing case? Does this make sense?

6. Can you imagine any instance where, as a practical matter, courts might show greater leniency toward entertaining a class action with smaller numbers of claimants? What about situations where class claimants might be hesitant to file a case in their own name or wary of joining another class member in doing so, per Rule 20? *See, e.g., Mullen v. Treasure Chest Casino*, 186 F.3d 620 (5th Cir. 1999) (noting that some current employees might be reluctant to sue their employer individually); *J.D. v. Nagin*, 255 F.R.D. 406 (E.D. La. 2009) (challenge to conditions at juvenile correction facility with a maximum occupancy of 30 residents at time, court observing that the constantly revolving population at the facility rendered joinder impractical).

7. *Chapter Problem.* Would it appear that the numerosity requirement of Rule 23(a)(1) is satisfied in the putative class action being brought by Merri Chance? Explain your reasoning.

3. Commonality

Rule 23(a)(2) contains the relatively simple-sounding requirement that all class actions involve "questions of law or fact common to the class." We have previously encountered the "common question of law or fact" requirement of Rule 20 which embodies the concern for efficiency when traditional joinder is being employed. Rule 23(a)(2)'s commonality requirement shares this concern for making class action treatment only available when it serves the principle of efficiency. And for many years, courts were often swift in finding commonality a fairly easy requirement to satisfy. As one court confessed, "the commonality standard is quite low." *Oplchenski v. Parfums Givenchy, Inc.*, 254 F.R.D. 489 (N.D. Ill. 2008). In the following case, however, the U.S. Supreme Court reminded lower courts not to overlook commonality in their zeal to certify class actions.

Wal-Mart Stores, Inc. v. Dukes (Part A)
564 U.S. 338 (2011)

SCALIA, J.,

I

[handwritten: 1 1/2 million plaintiffs]

We are presented with one of the most expansive class actions ever. The District Court and the Court of Appeals approved the certification of a class comprising about one and a half million plaintiffs, current and former female employees of petitioner Wal-Mart who allege that the discretion exercised by their local supervisors over pay and promotion matters violates Title VII by discriminating against women. In addition to injunctive and declaratory relief, the plaintiffs seek an award of backpay. We consider whether the certification of the plaintiff class was consistent with Federal Rules of Civil Procedure 23(a) and (b)(2). [This excerpt focuses exclusively on Rule 23(a). Part II, later in our materials, will contain the excerpt regarding Rule 23(b)(2).]

A.

Petitioner Wal-Mart is the Nation's largest private employer. It operates four types of retail stores throughout the country: Discount Stores, Supercenters, Neighborhood Markets, and Sam's Clubs. Those stores are divided into seven nationwide divisions, which in turn comprise 41 regions of 80 to 85 stores apiece. Each store has between 40 and 53 separate departments and 80 to 500 staff positions. In all, Wal-Mart operates approximately 3,400 stores and employs more than one million people.

[handwritten: walmart's promotional + raise criteria]

Pay and promotion decisions at Wal-Mart are generally committed to local managers' broad discretion, which is exercised "in a largely subjective manner." 222 F.R.D. 137, 145 (ND Cal. 2004). Local store managers may increase the wages of hourly employees (within limits) with only limited corporate oversight. As for salaried employees, such as store managers and their deputies, higher corporate authorities have discretion to set their pay within pre-established ranges.

Promotions work in a similar fashion. Wal-Mart permits store managers to apply their own subjective criteria when selecting candidates as "support managers," which is the first step on the path to management. Admission to Wal-Mart's management training program, however, does require that a candidate meet certain objective criteria, including an above-average performance rating, at least one year's tenure in the applicant's current position, and a willingness to relocate. But except for those requirements, regional and district managers have discretion to use their own judgment when selecting candidates for management training. Promotion to higher office—e.g., assistant manager, co-manager, or store manager—is similarly at the discretion of the employee's superiors after prescribed objective factors are satisfied.

B

The named plaintiffs in this lawsuit, representing the 1.5 million members of the certified class, are three current or former Wal-Mart employees who allege that the company discriminated against them on the basis of their sex by denying them equal pay or promotions, in violation of Title VII of the Civil Rights Act of 1964, 78 Stat. 253, as amended, 42 U.S.C. § 2000e-1 *et seq.*

Betty Dukes began working at a Pittsburgh, California, Wal-Mart in 1994. She started as a cashier, but later sought and received a promotion to customer service manager. After a series of disciplinary violations, however, Dukes was demoted back to cashier and then to greeter. Dukes concedes she violated company policy, but contends that the disciplinary actions were in fact retaliation for invoking internal complaint procedures and that male employees have not been disciplined for similar infractions. Dukes also claims two male greeters in the Pittsburgh store are paid more than she is.   *P1*

Christine Kwapnoski has worked at Sam's Club stores in Missouri and California for most of her adult life. She has held a number of positions, including a supervisory position. She claims that a male manager yelled at her frequently and screamed at female employees, but not at men. The manager in question "told her to 'doll up,' to wear some makeup, and to dress a little better."   *P2*

The final named plaintiff, Edith Arana, worked at a Wal-Mart store in Duarte, California, from 1995 to 2001. In 2000, she approached the store manager on more than one occasion about management training, but was brushed off. Arana concluded she was being denied opportunity for advancement because of her sex. She initiated internal complaint procedures, whereupon she was told to apply directly to the district manager if she thought her store manager was being unfair. Arana, however, decided against that and never applied for management training again. In 2001, she was fired for failure to comply with Wal-Mart's timekeeping policy.   *P3*

These plaintiffs, respondents here, do not allege that Wal-Mart has any express corporate policy against the advancement of women. Rather, they claim that their local managers' discretion over pay and promotions is exercised disproportionately in favor of men, leading to an unlawful disparate impact on female employees. And, respondents say, because Wal-Mart is aware of this effect, its refusal to cabin its managers' authority amounts to disparate treatment. Their complaint seeks injunctive and declaratory relief, punitive damages, and backpay. It does not ask for compensatory damages.

Importantly for our purposes, respondents claim that the discrimination to which they have been subjected is common to *all* Wal-Mart's female employees. The basic theory of their case is that a strong and uniform "corporate culture" permits bias against women to infect, perhaps subconsciously, the discretionary decisionmaking of each one of Wal-Mart's thousands of managers—thereby making every woman at the company the victim of one common discriminatory practice. Respondents therefore wish to litigate the Title VII claims of all female employees at Wal-Mart's stores in a nationwide class action.

want all female employees represented in the class

C

[R]espondents moved the District Court to certify a plaintiff class consisting of "'[a]ll women employed at any Wal-Mart domestic retail store at any time since December 26,

1998, who have been or may be subjected to Wal-Mart's challenged pay and management track promotions policies and practices.'" As evidence that there were indeed "questions of law or fact common to" all the women of Wal-Mart, as Rule 23(a)(2) requires, respondents relied chiefly on three forms of proof: statistical evidence about pay and promotion disparities between men and women at the company, anecdotal reports of discrimination from about 120 of Wal-Mart's female employees, and the testimony of a sociologist, Dr. William Bielby, who conducted a "social framework analysis" of Wal-Mart's "culture" and personnel practices, and concluded that the company was "vulnerable" to gender discrimination.

Required proof

Wal-Mart unsuccessfully moved to strike much of this evidence. It also offered its own countervailing statistical and other proof in an effort to defeat Rule 23(a)'s requirements of commonality, typicality, and adequate representation. Wal-Mart further contended that respondents' monetary claims for backpay could not be certified under Rule 23(b)(2). With one limitation not relevant here, the District Court granted respondents' motion and certified their proposed class.

D

A divided en banc Court of Appeals substantially affirmed the District Court's certification order. The majority concluded that respondents' evidence of commonality was sufficient to "raise the common question whether Wal-Mart's female employees nationwide were subjected to a single set of corporate policies (not merely a number of independent discriminatory acts) that may have worked to unlawfully discriminate against them in violation of Title VII."

We granted certiorari.

II

The class action is "an exception to the usual rule that litigation is conducted by and on behalf of the individual named parties only." *Califano* v. *Yamasaki*, 442 U.S. 682 (1979). In order to justify a departure from that rule, "a class representative must be part of the class and 'possess the same interest and suffer the same injury' as the class members." *East Tex. Motor Freight System, Inc.* v. *Rodriguez*, 431 U.S. 395, 403, 97 S. Ct. 1891, 52 L. Ed. 2d 453 (1977) (quoting *Schlesinger* v. *Reservists Comm. to Stop the War*, 418 U.S. 208, 216, 94 S. Ct. 2925, 41 L. Ed. 2d 706 (1974)). Rule 23(a) ensures that the named plaintiffs are appropriate representatives of the class whose claims they wish to litigate. The Rule's four requirements—numerosity, commonality, typicality, and adequate representation—"effectively 'limit the class claims to those fairly encompassed by the named plaintiff's claims.'" *General Telephone Co. of Southwest* v. *Falcon*, 457 U.S. 147, 156, 102 S. Ct. 2364, 72 L. Ed. 2d 740 (1982) (quoting *General Telephone Co. of Northwest* v. *EEOC*, 446 U.S. 318, 330, 100 S. Ct. 1698, 64 L. Ed. 2d 319 (1980)).

Key factor

The crux of this case is commonality—the rule requiring a plaintiff to show that "there are questions of law or fact common to the class." Rule 23(a)(2).[5] That language is easy

---

5. We have previously stated in this context that "[t]he commonality and typicality requirements of Rule 23(a) tend to merge. Both serve as guideposts for determining whether under the particular circumstances maintenance of a class action is economical and whether the named plaintiff's claim and the class claims are so interrelated that the interests of the class members will be fairly and adequately protected in their absence. Those requirements therefore also tend to merge with the adequacy-of-representation requirement, although the latter requirement also raises concerns about the competency of class counsel and conflicts of interest." *General Telephone Co. of Southwest* v. *Falcon*, 457 U.S. 147, 157–158, n. 13, 102 S. Ct. 2364, 72 L. Ed. 2d 740 (1982). In light of our disposition

to misread, since "[a]ny competently crafted class complaint literally raises common 'questions.'" Nagareda, *Class Certification in the Age of Aggregate Proof*, 84 N.Y.U. L. Rev. 97, 131–132 (2009). For example: Do all of us plaintiffs indeed work for Wal-Mart? Do our managers have discretion over pay? Is that an unlawful employment practice? What remedies should we get? Reciting these questions is not sufficient to obtain class certification. Commonality requires the plaintiff to demonstrate that the class members "have suffered the same injury," *Falcon, supra,* at 157, 102 S. Ct. 2364, 72 L. Ed. 2d 740. This does not mean merely that they have all suffered a violation of the same provision of law. Title VII, for example, can be violated in many ways—by intentional discrimination, or by hiring and promotion criteria that result in disparate impact, and by the use of these practices on the part of many different superiors in a single company. Quite obviously, the mere claim by employees of the same company that they have suffered a Title VII injury, or even a disparate-impact Title VII injury, gives no cause to believe that all their claims can productively be litigated at once. Their claims must depend upon a common contention—for example, the assertion of discriminatory bias on the part of the same supervisor. That common contention, moreover, must be of such a nature that it is capable of classwide resolution—which means that determination of its truth or falsity will resolve an issue that is central to the validity of each one of the claims in one stroke.

> "What matters to class certification … is not the raising of common 'questions'—even in droves—but, rather the capacity of a classwide proceeding to generate common *answers* apt to drive the resolution of the litigation. Dissimilarities within the proposed class are what have the potential to impede the generation of common answers." Nagareda, *supra,* at 132.

Rule 23 does not set forth a mere pleading standard. A party seeking class certification must affirmatively demonstrate his compliance with the Rule—that is, he must be prepared to prove that there are in fact sufficiently numerous parties, common questions of law or fact, etc. We recognized in *Falcon* that "sometimes it may be necessary for the court to probe behind the pleadings before coming to rest on the certification question," 457 U.S., at 160, 102 S. Ct. 2364, 72 L. Ed. 2d 740, and that certification is proper only if "the trial court is satisfied, after a rigorous analysis, that the prerequisites of Rule 23(a) have been satisfied," *id.,* at 161, 102 S. Ct. 2364, 72 L. Ed. 2d 740; see *id.,* at 160, 102 S. Ct. 2364, 72 L. Ed. 2d 740 ("[A]ctual, not presumed, conformance with Rule 23(a) remains … indispensable"). Frequently that "rigorous analysis" will entail some overlap with the merits of the plaintiff's underlying claim. That cannot be helped.

In this case, proof of commonality necessarily overlaps with respondents' merits contention that Wal-Mart engages in a pattern or practice of discrimination. That is so because, in resolving an individual's Title VII claim, the crux of the inquiry is "the reason for a particular employment decision," *Cooper* v. *Federal Reserve Bank of Richmond,* 467 U.S. 867, 876, 104 S. Ct. 2794, 81 L. Ed. 2d 718 (1984). Here respondents wish to sue about literally millions of employment decisions at once. Without some glue holding the alleged *reasons* for all those decisions together, it will be impossible to say that examination of all the class members' claims for relief will produce a common answer to the crucial question *why was I disfavored.*

This Court's opinion in *Falcon* describes how the commonality issue must be approached. There an employee who claimed that he was deliberately denied a promotion on account

---

of the commonality question, however, it is unnecessary to resolve whether respondents have satisfied the typicality and adequate-representation requirements of Rule 23(a).

of race obtained certification of a class comprising all employees wrongfully denied promotions and all applicants wrongfully denied jobs. We rejected that composite class for lack of commonality and typicality, explaining:

> "Conceptually, there is a wide gap between (a) an individual's claim that he has been denied a promotion [or higher pay] on discriminatory grounds, and his otherwise unsupported allegation that the company has a policy of discrimination, and (b) the existence of a class of persons who have suffered the same injury as that individual, such that the individual's claim and the class claim will share common questions of law or fact and that the individual's claim will be typical of the class claims." *Id.*, at 157–158, 102 S. Ct. 2364, 72 L. Ed. 2d 740.

Falcon suggested two ways in which that conceptual gap might be bridged. First, if the employer "used a biased testing procedure to evaluate both applicants for employment and incumbent employees, a class action on behalf of every applicant or employee who might have been prejudiced by the test clearly would satisfy the commonality and typicality requirements of Rule 23(a)." *Id.*, at 159, n. 15, 102 S. Ct. 2364, 72 L. Ed. 2d 740. Second, "[s]ignificant proof that an employer operated under a general policy of discrimination conceivably could justify a class of both applicants and employees if the discrimination manifested itself in hiring and promotion practices in the same general fashion, such as through entirely subjective decisionmaking processes." *Ibid*. We think that statement precisely describes respondents' burden in this case. The first manner of bridging the gap obviously has no application here; Wal-Mart has no testing procedure or other companywide evaluation method that can be charged with bias. The whole point of permitting discretionary decisionmaking is to avoid evaluating employees under a common standard.

In Practice

"Though [*Wal-Mart*] itself was an employment-discrimination class action, the Court's decision, authored by [the late] Justice Antonin Scalia, will likely affect class-certification decisions in other contexts as well, although the full extent to which it will do so remains an open question."

ABA Section of Litigation, *The Effects of Wal-Mart v. Dukes on Class Certification*: http://apps.americanbar.org/litigation/committees/securities/email/winter2012/winter2012-wal-mart-dukes-initial-effects-securities-fraud-class-certification.html (accessed June 1, 2016).

The second manner of bridging the gap requires "significant proof" that Wal-Mart "operated under a general policy of discrimination." That is entirely absent here. Wal-Mart's announced policy forbids sex discrimination, and as the District Court recognized the company imposes penalties for denials of equal employment opportunity. The only evidence of a "general policy of discrimination" respondents produced was the testimony of Dr. William Bielby, their sociological expert. Relying on "social framework" analysis, Bielby testified that Wal-Mart has a "strong corporate culture," that makes it "'vulnerable'" to "gender bias." *Id.*, at 152. He could not, however, "determine with any specificity how regularly stereotypes play a meaningful role in employment decisions at Wal-Mart. At his deposition ... Dr. Bielby conceded that he could not calculate whether 0.5 percent or 95 percent of the employment decisions at Wal-Mart might be determined by stereotyped thinking." 222 F.R.D. 189, 192 (ND Cal. 2004). The parties dispute whether Bielby's testimony even met the standards for the admission of expert testimony under Federal Rule of Evidence 702 and our *Daubert* case, see *Daubert* v. *Merrell Dow Pharmaceuticals, Inc.*, 509 U.S. 579, 113 S. Ct. 2786, 125 L. Ed. 2d 469 (1993). The District Court concluded that *Daubert* did not apply to expert testimony at the certification stage of class-action proceedings. 222 F.R.D., at 191. We doubt that is so, but even if properly considered, Bielby's testimony does nothing to advance respondents' case. "[W]hether 0.5 percent or 95 percent of the employment decisions at Wal-Mart might be determined by stereotyped thinking" is the essential question on which respondents' theory of commonality depends. If Bielby admittedly has no answer to that question, we can safely disregard what he has to say. It is worlds away from "significant proof" that Wal-Mart "operated under a general policy of discrimination."

The only corporate policy that the plaintiffs' evidence convincingly establishes is Wal-Mart's "policy" of allowing discretion by local supervisors over employment matters. On its face, of course, that is just the opposite of a uniform employment practice that would provide the commonality needed for a class action; it is a policy against having uniform employment practices. It is also a very common and presumptively reasonable way of doing business—one that we have said "should itself raise no inference of discriminatory conduct," *Watson* v. *Fort Worth Bank & Trust*, 487 U.S. 977, 990, 108 S. Ct. 2777, 101 L. Ed. 2d 827 (1988).

To be sure, we have recognized that, "in appropriate cases," giving discretion to lower-level supervisors can be the basis of Title VII liability under a disparate-impact theory—since "an employer's undisciplined system of subjective decisionmaking [can have] precisely the same effects as a system pervaded by impermissible intentional discrimination." *Id.*, at 990–991, 108 S. Ct. 2777, 101 L. Ed. 2d 827. But the recognition that this type of Title VII claim "can" exist does not lead to the conclusion that every employee in a company using a system of discretion has such a claim in common. To the contrary, left to their own devices most managers in any corporation—and surely most managers in a corporation that forbids sex discrimination—would select sex-neutral, performance-based criteria for hiring and promotion that produce no actionable disparity at all. Others may choose to reward various attributes that produce disparate impact—such as scores on general aptitude tests or educational achievements, see *Griggs* v. *Duke Power Co.*, 401 U.S. 424, 431–432, 91 S. Ct. 849, 28 L. Ed. 2d 158 (1971). And still other managers may be guilty of intentional discrimination that produces a sex-based disparity. In such a company, demonstrating the invalidity of one manager's use of discretion will do nothing to demonstrate the invalidity of another's. A party seeking to certify a nationwide class will be unable to show that all the employees' Title VII claims will in fact depend on the answers to common questions.

Respondents have not identified a common mode of exercising discretion that pervades the entire company—aside from their reliance on Dr. Bielby's social frameworks analysis that we have rejected. In a company of Wal-Mart's size and geographical scope, it is quite unbelievable that all managers would exercise their discretion in a common way without some common direction.

The dissent misunderstands the nature of the foregoing analysis. We quite agree that for purposes of Rule 23(a)(2) "'[e]ven a single [common] question'" will do. We consider dissimilarities not in order to determine (as Rule 23(b)(3) requires) whether common questions predominate, but in order to determine (as Rule 23(a)(2) requires) whether there is "[e]ven a single [common] question." And there is not here. Because respondents provide no convincing proof of a companywide discriminatory pay and promotion policy, we have concluded that they have not established the existence of any common question.

[handwritten margin note: No common question]

In sum, we agree with Chief Judge Kozinski that the members of the class:

> "held a multitude of different jobs, at different levels of Wal-Mart's hierarchy, for variable lengths of time, in 3,400 stores, sprinkled across 50 states, with a kaleidoscope of supervisors (male and female), subject to a variety of regional policies that all differed.... Some thrived while others did poorly. They have little in common but their sex and this lawsuit." 603 F.3d, at 652 (dissenting opinion).

Notes and Problems

1. The *Wal-Mart v. Dukes* decision from the 2010 was highly anticipated, both for interpretational guidance of specific Rule 23 issues (in terms of whether Rule 23(a)(2) would be given more teeth and the scope of the Rule 23(b)(2) hybrid class action—discussed later in this chapter) and, more generally, for an indication as to the Supreme Court's general temperament regarding class actions. The decision was not good for advocates of expansive use of Rule 23 as a tool in aggregate litigation. Just how bad it was for those advocates is still a matter of some debate among scholars.

2. Despite the fact that for many years, federal courts had treated the Rule 23(a)(2) commonality requirement as almost a formality, in *Wal-Mart*, the Court signaled that it was a prerequisite that could be used to weed out many proposed class actions. In sum, the Court held that the commonality prerequisite meant more than just asserting a list of hypothetical or academic issues (e.g., are all the class members really women?) "even in droves," but rather of demonstrating that the claims of all of the class members raise issues of significance, the answer to which will drive the adjudication of all of the claims of the class members in a meaningful way. Applying this new understanding of the commonality requirement to the facts in *Wal-Mart*, what seemed to be the fundamental problem with the putative class action? Asked another way, if the certified class had gone to trial and a jury found that one particular class member had been terminated based upon her sex by the manager of her store, in what way would this finding have been important to the claim by another class member allegedly mistreated at a different store, in a different place, by a different manager? Could the class counsel—with hindsight, at least—have framed the issues in the case in a different way to try to avoid tripping over the commonality hurdle?

3. Is it possible that the Supreme Court in *Wal-Mart* was slipping into de-certifying the class on the basis of not Rule 23 but disbelief in the merits of the underlying contention that the class members were mistreated on account of their sex? The Supreme Court even acknowledged that the issue of commonality had some "overlap with the merits of the plaintiff's underlying claim." And the Court ended with its observation that the class representatives "provide no convincing proof of a companywide discriminatory pay and promotion policy." Is this an appropriate reason to refuse to allow the trial court to adjudicate the merits of the claim on a classwide basis?

4. As we continue to work our way through Rule 23's prerequisites, it is worth pausing to consider the reality that many proposed class actions include "subclasses." Rule 23(c)(5) permits courts to divide up a class into various subclasses when doing so helps with the manageability of the class actions. Perhaps different subclasses suffered injuries in different ways or have claims that might be subject to different substantive law, or might be subject to certain affirmative defenses. In such cases, the court can come up with a custom tailored plan to adjudicate each subclass in an appropriate manner. But even when

subclasses are being utilized, the courts have been clear that each subclass needs to independently demonstrate that it would be the proper subject for certification under Rule 23(a)–(b)'s requirements. *See, e.g., Betts v. Reliable Collection Agency, Ltd.*, 659 F.2d 1000 (9th Cir. 1981).

5. You will recall in Chapter 2 Joinder of Claims & Parties the fairly lenient application of Rule 20 to the widespread allegations of race and sex allegations in *Mosley v. General Motors*. Remember that Rule 20 requires for joinder of parties that their claims arise out of the same transaction or occurrence as well as raise "common questions of law or fact," this latter requirement mirroring the commonality requirement of Rule 23(a)(2). There are some similarities between the contentions of the claimants in *Wal-Mart* and *Mosley*. To the extent *Wal-Mart* found the current and former employees' claims of discrimination did not raise sufficient common questions, does this implicitly overrule the decision in *Mosley* that the employees' claims did raise common questions?

6. *Problems.* Consider whether the following proposed class actions would meet the Supreme Court's understanding of the Rule 23(a)(2) commonality requirement after *Wal-Mart*:

a. Claimants all used a spray-on grout sealer to seal grout in their bathrooms and now claim different forms of respiratory ailments. They contend the sealant was defective in its design by utilizing chemicals that could cause respiratory illness.

b. Claimants all were consumers of an auto manufacturer. They were each allegedly involved in different accidents where their vehicles turned over and they claim to have suffered different manifestations of head, neck, or spinal injuries.

c. Claimants are law students of every accredited law school in America and claim they were defrauded by their respective schools into believing that they would have a legal job within 9 months of graduating, but failed to secure such a job.

7. *Chapter Problem.* With respect to the allegations in the Merri Chance putative class action, do the class members' claims meet the threshold requirement of having questions of law or fact common to the class? If this is unclear, as counsel for the target defendant TMG, what additional discovery would you be interested in obtaining in order to attack the certification of the proposed class on commonality grounds?

4. Typicality

Rule 23(a)(3) requires for certification that the "claims ... of the representative parties are typical of the claims ... of the class." This prerequisite is designed to help ensure that when the class representative pursues their own individual claim, they will necessarily be advancing the ball on behalf of the class as well because of the substantial overlap between the claims. Unlike the Rule 23(a)(1)–(2) requirements of numerosity and commonality—which consider the claims of the entire class as a whole—the last two prerequisites in Rule 23(a)(3)–(4) focus on the traits of the class representative and the extent to which the representative's claim is similar enough to the rest of the class to ensure fair representation. While many courts view the various requirements of Rule 23(a)(1)–(4) as somewhat overlapping, they do each require court's separate attention. Notice how in the following case, some factual differences between the proposed class representative's claims and the claims of other class members negatively impact a finding of both commonality and typicality.

In re American Medical Systems, Inc.

75 F.3d 1069 (6th Cir. 1996)

Suhrheinrich, J.,

Petitioners American Medical Systems ("AMS") and Pfizer, Inc., defendants below, both seek a writ of mandamus directing the district court to vacate orders conditionally certifying a class in a products liability suit involving penile prostheses. [O]n the extraordinary facts of this case we find that the district judge's disregard of class action procedures was of such severity and frequency so as to warrant its issuance here.

Since 1973, AMS, a wholly-owned subsidiary of Pfizer, has manufactured and marketed penile prostheses, which are used to treat impotence. The plaintiffs, respondents in this proceeding, all use or have used AMS' products.

Plaintiff Paul Vorhis was implanted with an AMS penile prosthesis on April 25, 1989. It failed to function in January of 1993, and Vorhis had the prosthesis replaced with an AMS 700 Ultrex prosthesis in May 1993. This second prosthesis caused him pain and discomfort, and plaintiff had it removed in August of 1993 and replaced with a third AMS prosthesis, with which he is presently satisfied. Vorhis filed this action against defendant AMS in the Southern District of Ohio on December 5, 1994, individually and on behalf of others similarly situated who suffered damages as a result of the implantation of penile prostheses manufactured by AMS. The complaint alleges strict product liability, negligence, breach of implied and express warranties, fraud and punitive damages, and seeks a declaratory judgment for medical monitoring.

On December 29, 1994, Vorhis filed a motion for class certification.

At the class certification hearing, AMS challenged Vorhis' suitability as a class representative on several grounds. First, AMS pointed out that Vorhis had a history of psychiatric problems, for which he received total and permanent disability benefits from the State of Ohio. AMS introduced reports prepared by Vorhis' psychiatrist and psychologist showing that Vorhis suffered from memory loss, impaired concentration, and a lack of common sense, all factors which AMS maintained would interfere with plaintiff's ability to make rational decisions on behalf of other members of the purported class. AMS also contended that Vorhis was an unsuitable representative because his need for the prosthesis stemmed from a unique condition, Peyronie's disease, or curvature of the penis. Third, AMS argued that because Vorhis had a problem with only one of the ten types of prostheses AMS manufactured, he could not represent those who had problems with the other kinds of devices. [Plaintiff later added three additional class representatives.]

Without any further discovery, briefing, or argument, the district judge issued an order of class certification on March 16, 1995. The judge found that all the prerequisites of Fed. R. Civ. P. 23(a) had been met, and that the class was maintainable under Fed. R. Civ. P. 23(b)(3) because common questions of law or fact predominated. As to "numerosity," the court [found that there were 15,000 to 120,000 class members and that 23(a)(1) was easily satisfied.] Regarding "commonality," the judge stated: "As persons who have undergone implantation of Defendants' inflatable penile prostheses [plaintiffs] appear to have a common right to assert a claim against Defendants." For the third requirement of subsection (a), "typicality," the judge held:

> The proposed representatives of the class assert claims that are typical of the class in that all plaintiffs allege injury from the American Medical Systems, Inc./Pfizer, Inc. inflatable penile prostheses manufactured and distributed by Defendants.

These claims are similar enough to those of the class that the representatives will adequately represent such class. *General Telephone v. Falcon*, 457 U.S. 147, 157, 72 L. Ed. 2d 740, 102 S. Ct. 2364 (1982).

[Finding the remaining requirements of Rule 23(a) and (b)(3) met, the district judge] certified the class as:

> All persons residing in the United States, who have had inflatable penile prostheses developed, manufactured and/or sold by Defendant American Medical Systems, Inc. and/or Defendant Pfizer, Inc. implanted in their bodies.

In the notice attached to the class, the district judge named Vorhis as one of the parties that was bringing the class action lawsuit on behalf of all members of the class.

The Supreme Court has required district courts to conduct a "rigorous analysis" into whether the prerequisites of Rule 23 are met before certifying a class. *General Tel. Co. v. Falcon*, 457 U.S. 147, 161 (1982). The trial court has broad discretion in deciding whether to certify a class, but that discretion must be exercised within the framework of Rule 23. *Gulf Oil Co. v. Bernard*, 452 U.S. 89, 100, 68 L. Ed. 2d 693, 101 S. Ct. 2193 (1981); *Cross v. National Trust Life Ins. Co.*, 553 F.2d 1026, 1029 (6th Cir. 1977) ("district court has broad discretion in determining whether a particular case may proceed as a class action so long as it applies the criteria of Rule 23 correctly"); *Boggs v. Divested Atomic Corp.*, 141 F.R.D. 58, 62–63 (S.D. Ohio 1991) (same). *See generally* In re NLO, Inc., 5 F.3d 154, 157 (6th Cir. 1993) (district court's inherent power to manage docket must be exercised in manner that is in harmony with the Federal Rules of Civil Procedure).

A class is not maintainable as a class action by virtue of its designation as such in the pleadings. *Cash v. Swifton Land Corp.*, 434 F.2d 569, 571 (6th Cir. 1970). Although a hearing prior to the class determination is not always required, "it may be necessary for the court to probe behind the pleadings before coming to rest on the certification question." *Falcon*, 457 U.S. at 160. This court has stated that:

> Mere repetition of the language of Rule 23(a) is not sufficient. There must be an adequate statement of the basic facts to indicate that each requirement of the rule is fulfilled. Maintainability may be determined by the court on the basis of the pleadings, if sufficient facts are set forth, but ordinarily the determination should be predicated on more information than the pleadings will provide.... The parties should be afforded an opportunity to present evidence on the maintainability of the class action.

Weathers v. Peters Realty Corp., 499 F.2d 1197, 1200 (6th Cir. 1974) (citation omitted).

The party seeking the class certification bears the burden of proof. *See Falcon*, 457 U.S. at 161; *Senter v. General Motors Corp.*, 532 F.2d 511, 522 (6th Cir.), *cert. denied*, 429 U.S. 870, 50 L. Ed. 2d 150, 97 S. Ct. 182 (1976). Subsection (a) of Rule 23 contains four prerequisites which must *all* be met before a class can be certified. Once those conditions are satisfied, the party seeking certification must also demonstrate that it falls within at least *one* of the subcategories of Rule 23(b). We shall examine each of these factors individually.

1.   *prerequisite #1*

The first subdivision of Rule 23(a)(1) requires that the class be "so numerous that joinder of all members is impracticable." "The reason for [the impracticability] requirement is obvious. Only when joinder is impracticable is there a need for a class action device." 1 Herbert B. Newberg & Alba Conte, Newberg on Class Actions, § 3.01, at 3–4 (3d ed.

1992). There is no strict numerical test for determining impracticability of joinder. *Senter*, 532 F.2d at 523 n.24 (and citations therein). Rather, "the numerosity requirement requires examination of the specific facts of each case and imposes no absolute limitations." *General Tel. Co. v. EEOC*, 446 U.S. 318, 330, 64 L. Ed. 2d 319, 100 S. Ct. 1698 (1980). When class size reaches substantial proportions, however, the impracticability requirement is usually satisfied by the numbers alone. 1 Newberg, *supra*, § 3.05, at 3-26.

In the original complaint, Vorhis alleged that although he was unable to state the exact size of the class, "members of the class number at least in the thousands." The first amended complaint modified that estimate to "over 150,000." The district judge's finding of a class of 15,000 to 120,000 persons may not be unreasonable, especially since AMS has been producing penile prostheses for over twenty years, and has the largest share of the penile implant market. *See Senter*, 532 F.2d at 523 (district judge may consider reasonable inferences drawn from facts before him at early stage in proceedings in determining whether class is sufficiently numerous to make joinder impracticable). Defendant, moreover, does not contest this factor. Although the district judge made no findings but merely rubberstamped the plaintiffs' assertions that such potential class members truly exist, we do not hold that this factor is not established because petitioners do not contest it.

prerequisite #2   2.

Rule 23(a)(2) requires that for certification there must be "questions of law or fact common to the class." The commonality requirement is interdependent with the impracticability of joinder requirement, and the "tests together form the underlying conceptual basis supporting class actions." 1 Newberg, *supra*, § 3.10, at 3-47. As the Supreme Court described in *Falcon*:

> The class-action was designed as "an exception to the usual rule that litigation is conducted by and on behalf of the individual named parties only." *Califano v. Yamasaki*, 442 U.S. 682, 700–01, 99 S. Ct. 2545, 2557–2558, 61 L. Ed. 2d 176. Class relief "is 'peculiarly appropriate' when the 'issues involved are common to the class as a whole' and when they 'turn on questions of law applicable in the same manner to each member of the class.'" *Id.* at 701, 99 S. Ct. at 2557. For in such cases, "the class-action device saves the resources of both the courts and the parties by permitting an issue potentially affecting every [class member] to be litigated in an economical fashion under Rule 23."

Ibid. 457 U.S. at 155. The commonality test "is qualitative rather than quantitative, that is, there need be only a single issue common to all members of the class." 1 Newberg, supra, § 3.10, at 3-50. *See also Sterling v. Velsicol Chem. Corp.*, 855 F.2d 1188, 1197 (6th Cir. 1988) ("mere fact that questions peculiar to each individual member of the class remain after the common questions of the defendant's liability have been resolved does not dictate the conclusion that a class action is impermissible"). But, as we shall see, there is an important check on this requirement under Rule 23(b)(3).

Plaintiffs' complaint and class certification motion simply allege in general terms that there are common issues without identifying any particular defect common to all plaintiffs. Yet AMS introduced uncontradicted evidence that since 1973 AMS has produced at least ten different models, and that these models have been modified over the years. Plaintiffs' claims of strict liability, fraudulent misrepresentation to both the FDA and the medical community, negligent testing, design and manufacture, and failure to warn will differ depending upon the model and the year it was issued.

Proofs as to strict liability, negligence, failure to warn, breach of express and implied warranties will also vary from plaintiff to plaintiff because complications with an AMS device may be due to a variety of factors, including surgical error, improper use of the device, anatomical incompatibility, infection, device malfunction, or psychological problems. Furthermore, each plaintiff's urologist would also be required to testify to determine what oral and written statements were made to the physician, and what he in turn told the patient, as well as to issues of reliance, causation and damages.

The amended complaint reflects that the plaintiffs received different models and have different complaints regarding each of those models. In the absence of more specific allegations and/or proof of commonality of any factual or legal claims, plaintiffs have failed to meet their burden of proof on Rule 23(a)(2).

This failure of proof highlights the error of the district judge. Despite evidence in the record presented by the nonmoving party that at least ten different models existed, testimony from a urologist that there is no "common cause" of prostheses malfunction, and conclusory allegations by the party with the burden of proof on certification, we find not even the hint of any serious consideration by the judge of commonality. Moreover, although not dispositive, it is noteworthy that a Judicial Panel on Multidistrict Litigation denied consolidation of all federal AMS penile prostheses case pursuant to 28 U.S.C. § 1407, concluding that "the degree of factual commonality among the actions in this litigation [does not] rise[] to a level that warrants Section 1407 transfer." *In re Penile Implants Prod. Liab. Litig.*, MDL No. 1020 (J.P.M.L. Sept. 30, 1994). The district judge was made aware of this ruling, and still did not give the question of commonality any discernible degree of scrutiny.

3.   Prerequisite #3

Rule 23(a)(3) requires that "claims or defenses of the representative parties [be] typical of the claims or defenses of the class." Typicality determines whether a sufficient relationship exists between the injury to the named

> plaintiff and the conduct affecting the class, so that the court may properly attribute a collective nature to the challenged conduct. In other words, when such a relationship is shown, a plaintiff's injury arises from or is directly related to a wrong to a class, and that wrong includes the wrong to the plaintiff. Thus, a plaintiff's claim is typical if it arises from the same event or practice or course of conduct that gives rise to the claims of other class members, and if his or her claims are based on the same legal theory.

1 Newberg, *supra*, § 3-13, at 3-76 (footnote omitted). *See also General Tel. Co. v. EEOC*, 446 U.S. at 330 ("typicality requirement is said to limit the class claims to those fairly encompassed by the named plaintiffs' claims"); *Senter*, 532 F.2d at 525 n.31 ("to be typical, a representative's claim need not always involve the same facts or law, provided there is a common element of fact or law"). A necessary consequence of the typicality requirement is that the representative's interests will be aligned with those of the represented group, and in pursuing his own claims, the named plaintiff will also advance the interests of the class members. 1 Newberg, *supra*, § 3.13, at 3-75. Vorhis' specific/unique experience

Vorhis' claim relates to a previous AMS penile prosthesis which, several years after insertion, allegedly could not be inflated due to a possible leak in the input tube of a CX device. This in turn may have been caused by rear-tip extender surgery Vorhis had in 1990, in an attempt to increase penile length that was lost through surgery to correct a curvature of his penis. Based on what little we have to go on, it is hard to imagine that Vorhis' claim is typical of the class certified in this case.

Because the district judge issued its amended order of certification before discovery of the plaintiffs other than Vorhis, we have less information about them. However, we know from the amended complaint that each plaintiff used a different model, and each experienced a distinct difficulty. York claims that his 700 inflatable penile prosthesis fails to fully inflate. Kennedy alleges that his Ultrex inflatable penile prosthesis malfunctioned because the cylinders and pump leaked. Finally, Gordy maintains that his Hydroflex failed, and that his current implant, the Dynaflex prosthesis, inflates on one side only. These allegations fail to establish a claim typical to each other, let alone a class.

Once again, it should have been obvious to the district judge that it needed to "probe behind the pleadings" before concluding that the typicality requirement was met. *See Falcon*, 457 U.S. at 160. Instead, the district judge gave no serious consideration to this factor, but simply mimicked the language of the rule. This was error. *Id.* at 158–59 (reversing certification for failure of proof on typicality element, holding that it was error for district court to presume that respondent's claim was typical of other claims against petitioner).

[The court found additional problems with the adequacy of representation requirement of Rule 23(a)(4) as well as certification under Rule 23(b)(3).]

Under the various formulations of the writ, we conclude that petitioners have met their heavy burden. For all the foregoing reasons, the petitions for writ of mandamus are GRANTED, and the district judge is directed to decertify the plaintiff class.

Notes and Problems

1. The test applied by the court above asked about the extent to which the class representative claimed the same injury from the same theory of misconduct on the part of the defendant as that suffered by the rest of the class members. If so, the court can be comforted with the "collective nature" of the case to rightfully assume that the class members' claims will be fairly and vigorously prosecuted on their behalf. As you will see in the next section, this concern with fair representation results in the typicality requirement overlapping with the final requirement of Rule 23(a) for "adequate representation." Each, however, requires separate consideration from the court in considering certification. One court offered this useful explanation of the typicality inquiry:

> The typicality requirement goes to the heart of a representative party's ability to represent a class, particularly as it tends to merge with the commonality and adequacy-of-representation requirements. The representative party's interest in prosecuting his own case must simultaneously tend to advance the interests of the absent class members.

Deiter v. Microsoft Corp., 436 F.3d 461, 466 (4th Cir. 2006). Thus, while all courts agree that the representative's claim need not be "identical" with that of each other class member, the greater the variation, the more hesitation a court will have in finding that Rule 23(a)(3) has been satisfied.

2. Given the applicable legal standard for Rule 23(a)(3)'s requisite showing for typicality, what was wrong with the proposed class action in the *American Medical Systems* case? Could the case have been brought instead by the class representatives on behalf of a smaller class and thereby met the typicality requirement?

3. *Problems.* Consider whether sufficient typicality would likely exist in the following scenarios between the class representative and the remainder of the class:

> a. Plaintiff is a former employee of Defendant Zerox, Inc. He was also a union official and complained to Zerox about their mistreatment of African-American em-

ployees working in several scattered company warehouses in terms of the conditions of their jobs. He was fired by Zerox allegedly in retaliation for voicing such complaints to management of Zerox. He now seeks to sue individually (for his wrongful termination) and on behalf of a class of all other African-American employees of Zerox who work at these particular warehouse locations.

b. Plaintiff is the owner of a restaurant located along the Gulf Coast. He complains about the activities of the oil company, Slicks Incorporated, whose drilling activities allegedly caused a massive oil spill, contaminating area waters and harming fisherman, restaurant owners, charter boat owners, and other area businesses.

c. Plaintiff owns a late-model automobile made by Nexxus. Recent reports indicated that the vehicle might engage in sudden acceleration. Numerous accidents involving alleged sudden acceleration of this same model auto have been reported. Even though Nexxus has issued a voluntary recall to apply a fix to the problem, Plaintiff contends the fair market value of her auto has permanently been reduced regardless of the recall. She seeks to sue on behalf of herself and all others who own such autos or have been involved in sudden acceleration accidents.

4. *Chapter Problem.* Given the scope of the proposed class in the putative Merri Chance class action against TMG, do you see any problems with her ability to satisfy the typicality standard for the entire class? Would a smaller class action avoid this problem?

5. Adequacy

Finally, Rule 23(a)(4) demands that any proposed class representative "will fairly and adequately protect the interests of the class." As should be fairly obvious, the reason for this requirement is to help ensure that the representative litigation will be conducted in a fair manner on behalf of the absent class members. After all, nobody wants to have their cause of action brought by an incompetent representative. As the seminal case of *Hansberry* illustrates, this adequacy requirement inquires into not only the proposed representative's competence but their loyalty to the absent class member as well. Further, as demonstrated below, adequacy of representation is both a requirement of Rule 23 as well as the Due Process Clause. Understanding and appreciating this particular certification hurdle is, therefore, fundamental to an understanding of the very nature of a class action. After *Hansberry*, we will see in the *West Publishing* case that not all conflicts between a class representative and the class members are inherent. Some may be created by the conduct of class counsel.

a. Inherently Conflicting Interests

Hansberry v. Lee
311 U.S. 32 (1940)

STONE, J.,

The question is whether the Supreme Court of Illinois, by its adjudication that petitioners in this case are bound by a judgment rendered in an earlier litigation to which they were not parties, has deprived them of the due process of law guaranteed by the Fourteenth Amendment.

[The Hansberrys, who were African-American, bought and moved into a Chicago home in an area covered by a racially restrictive covenant. In reaction, owners of neighboring homes sued in an Illinois state court to void the sale to the Hansberrys. The Hansberrys defended on the ground that the covenant never became effective because it wasn't signed by 95% of the homeowners in the area (about 500 homes), as required by its own terms. The trial court found that only 54% of the landowners had signed the agreement. Nevertheless, the trial court voided the sale to the Hansberrys and ordered them to move out because it found they were bound by a decision that the covenant was valid from a prior class action, *Burke v. Kleiman*. In that earlier suit to enforce the covenant in another Illinois state court, a local property owner's association filed suit against Kleiman, a white property owner who rented to an African-American, and Hall, his black tenant. That suit was brought on "behalf of all" landowners in the area and alleged that the covenant had been signed by 95% of the owners. In that case, the defendants had (improvidently it seems) stipulated that the requisite number of signatures had been obtained and defended instead on grounds of changed conditions. The court in that earlier suit rejected that defense and held the agreement enforceable on behalf of the class of landowners.

In *Hansberry*, the trial court found that it could not reopen the issue concerning the number of signatures approving of the covenant because *Burke* had been a class action and was binding on the Hansberrys' grantor, and therefore was binding on the Hansberrys in the present litigation. The Illinois Supreme Court affirmed this decision against the Hansberrys.]

State courts are free to attach such descriptive labels to litigations before them as they may choose and to attribute to them such consequences as they think appropriate under state constitutions and laws, subject only to the requirements of the Constitution of the United States. But when the judgment of a state court, ascribing to the judgment of another court the binding force and effect of res judicata, is challenged for want of due process it becomes the duty of this Court to examine the course of procedure in both litigations to ascertain whether the litigant whose rights have thus been adjudicated has been afforded such notice and opportunity to be heard as are requisite to the due process which the Constitution prescribes.

It is a principle of general application in Anglo-American jurisprudence that one is not bound by a judgment in personam in a litigation in which he is not designated as a party or to which he has not been made a party by service of process. *Pennoyer v. Neff*, 95 U.S. 714; 1 Freeman on Judgments (5th ed.), § 407. A judgment rendered in such circumstances is not entitled to the full faith and credit which the Constitution and statute of the United States prescribe and judicial action enforcing it against the person or property of the absent party is not that due process which the Fifth and Fourteenth Amendments require.

To these general rules there is a recognized exception that, to an extent not precisely defined by judicial opinion, the judgment in a "class" or "representative" suit, to which some members of the class are parties, may bind members of the class or those represented who were not made parties to it.

It is familiar doctrine of the federal courts that members of a class not present as parties to the litigation may be bound by the judgment where they are in fact adequately represented by parties who are present, or where they actually participate in the conduct of the litigation in which members of the class are present as parties.

In all such cases, so far as it can be said that the members of the class who are present are, by generally recognized rules of law, entitled to stand in judgment for those who are not, we may assume for present purposes that such procedure affords a protection to the parties who are represented, though absent, which would satisfy the requirements of due process and full faith and credit. Nor do we find it necessary for the decision of this case to say that, when the only circumstance defining the class is that the determination of the rights of its members turns upon a single issue of fact or law, a state could not constitutionally adopt a procedure whereby some of the members of the class could stand in judgment for all, provided that the procedure were so devised and applied as to insure that those present are of the same class as those absent and that the litigation is so conducted as to insure the full and fair consideration of the common issue. We decide only that the procedure and the course of litigation sustained here by the plea of res judicata do not satisfy these requirements.

The restrictive agreement did not purport to create a joint obligation or liability. If valid and effective its promises were the several obligations of the signers and those claiming under them. The promises ran severally to every other signer. It is plain that in such circumstances all those alleged to be bound by the agreement would not constitute a single class in any litigation brought to enforce it. Those who sought to secure its benefits by enforcing it could not be said to be in the same class with or represent those whose interest was in resisting performance, for the agreement by its terms imposes obligations and confers rights on the owner of each plot of land who signs it. If those who thus seek to secure the benefits of the agreement were rightly regarded by the state Supreme Court as constituting a class, it is evident that those signers or their successors who are interested in challenging the validity of the agreement and resisting its performance are not of the same class in the sense that their interests are identical so that any group who had elected to enforce rights conferred by the agreement could be said to be acting in the interest of any others who were free to deny its obligation.

Because of the dual and potentially conflicting interests of those who are putative parties to the agreement in compelling or resisting its performance, it is impossible to say, solely because they are parties to it, that any two of them are of the same class. Nor without more, and with the due regard for the protection of the rights of absent parties which due process exacts, can some be permitted to stand in judgment for all.

It is one thing to say that some members of a class may represent other members in a litigation where the sole and common interest of the class in the litigation, is either to assert a common right or to challenge an asserted obligation. It is quite another to hold that all those who are free alternatively either to assert rights or to challenge them are of a single class, so that any group, merely because it is of the class so constituted, may be deemed adequately to represent any others of the class in litigating their interests in either alternative. Such a selection of representatives for purposes of litigation, whose substantial interests are not necessarily or even probably the same as those whom they are deemed to represent, does not afford that protection to absent parties which due process requires. The doctrine of representation of absent parties in a class suit has not hitherto been thought to go so far.

The plaintiffs in the *Burke* case sought to compel performance of the agreement in behalf of themselves and all others similarly situated. They did not designate the defendants in the suit as a class or seek any injunction or other relief against others than the named defendants, and the decree which was entered did not purport to bind others. In seeking to enforce the agreement the plaintiffs in that suit were not representing the petitioners here whose substantial interest is in resisting performance. The defendants in the first suit were not treated by the pleadings or decree as representing others or as foreclosing by their defense the rights of others; and, even though nominal defendants, it does not appear that their interest in defeating the contract outweighed their interest in establishing its validity. For a court in this situation to ascribe to either the plaintiffs or defendants the performance of such functions on behalf of petitioners here, is to attribute to them a power that it cannot be said that they had assumed to exercise, and a responsibility which, in view of their dual interests it does not appear that they could rightly discharge.

Reversed.

b. Manufactured Adequacy Problems

Rodriguez v. West Publishing Corp.

563 F.3d 948 (9th Cir. 2009)

RYMER, J.,

West Publishing Corp. and Kaplan, Inc. entered a settlement agreement in an antitrust class action brought by those who purchased a BAR/BRI course between August 1, 1997 and July 31, 2006. (BAR/BRI is a subsidiary of West that provides preparation courses for state bar exams.) [Plaintiffs claimed West—which purchased Kaplan—violated the antitrust laws by entering into a deal in 1997 to limit competition in providing bar-prep courses. This deal led Kaplan not to enter into the field which allegedly gave West a monopoly at the time. Some of the disputed conduct of West included offering first-year students a non-refundable option for the BAR/BRI course, offering free access to Westlaw to students enrolling in the course, and advertising BAR/BRI on Westlaw constantly. The suit originally sought up to $1,000 for each of the estimated 300,000 student class members, plus injunctive relief. The district court certified a class of all who purchased BAR/BRI from August 1997 until the 2009 certification. Thereafter, the parties negotiated a settlement by which defendants agreed to create a $49 million settlement fun from which class members could recover up to 30% of their purchase price. Defendants also agree to modify their business arrangements and conduct. Class members were given notice of the settlement, which notice advised the class that class counsel intended to seek incentive awards of $25,000 to four of the class representatives and $75,000 for three others.]

The district court approved the settlement, and several class members who object (Objectors) appeal. Their principal objection relates to incentive agreements that were entered into at the onset of litigation between class counsel and five named plaintiffs who became class representatives. [The incentive awards were not initially revealed to either the class or the court. As it turns out, class counsel had entered into retainer agreements with five of the class representatives making a commitment to apply for incentive awards according to a schedule: if the settlement were $500,000 or greater, counsel would seek an award of $10,00 for each of them; if it were $1.5 million or more, counsel would seek a $25,000 award; and if it were $10 million or more, counsel would seek a $75,000 incentive award. Even though the $49 million settlement entitled these five representatives to $75,000 awards, two of the five agreed to lower their request to $25,000. Two other class representatives had no advance incentive agreement but class counsel sought an award of $25,000 for each of them. Various class members objected to the settlement, primarily based upon these previously undisclosed incentive award agreements, and appealed when the district court overruled their objections, approved the settlement, and award fees to class counsel as well.]

Much of the appeal turns on the presence—and nondisclosure to the class—of the incentive agreements. In particular, Objectors assert that the Settlement Notice offends due process because it omitted material information about the agreements, and that the settlement itself should have been rejected because the incentive agreements prevented the class representatives from providing adequate representation. Relatedly, Objectors contend that they benefitted the class by successfully opposing the incentive awards and should be allowed attorney's fees for the effort. Conversely, they question the attorney's fee award to class counsel as California law precludes the recovery of fees for conflicting representation.

Incentive *awards* are fairly typical in class action cases. *See* 4 William B. Rubenstein et al., *Newberg on Class Actions* § 11:38 (4th ed. 2008); Theodore Eisenberg & Geoffrey P. Miller, *Incentive Awards to Class Action Plaintiffs: An Empirical Study*, 53 U.C.L.A. L. Rev. 1303 (2006) (finding twenty-eight percent of settled class actions between 1993 and 2002 included an incentive award to class representatives). Such awards are discretionary, *see In re Mego Fin. Corp. Sec. Litig.*, 213 F.3d 454, 463 (9th Cir. 2000), and are intended to compensate class representatives for work done on behalf of the class, to make up for financial or reputational risk undertaken in bringing the action, and, sometimes, to recognize their willingness to act as a private attorney general. Awards are generally sought after a settlement or verdict has been achieved.

The incentive *agreements* entered into as part of the initial retention of counsel in this case, however, are quite different. Although they only bound counsel to apply for an award, thus leaving the decision whether actually to make one to the district judge, these agreements tied the promised request to the ultimate recovery and in so doing, put class counsel and the contracting class representatives into a conflict position from day one.

The arrangement was not disclosed when it should have been and where it was plainly relevant, at the class certification stage. Had it been, the district court would certainly have considered its effect in determining whether the conflicted plaintiffs—Rodriguez, Frailich, Nesci, Brazeal, and Gintz—could adequately represent the class. The conflict might have been waived, or otherwise contained, but the point is that uncovering conflicts of interest between the named parties and the class they seek to represent is a critical purpose of the adequacy inquiry.

In fact, the incentive agreements came to the fore when Objectors pounced on them in opposing class counsel's motion for incentive awards to the class representatives. This happened after preliminary approval of the settlement. In that context the district court held that the agreements were inappropriate and contrary to public policy for a number of reasons: they obligate class counsel to request an arbitrary award not reflective of the amount of work done, or the risks undertaken, or the time spent on the litigation; they create at least the appearance of impropriety; they violate the California Rules of Professional Conduct prohibiting fee-sharing with clients and among lawyers; and they encourage figure head cases and bounty payments by potential class counsel. The court found it particularly problematic that the incentive agreements correlated the incentive request solely to the settlement or litigated recovery, as the effect was to make the contracting class representatives' interests actually different from the class's interests in settling a case instead of trying it to verdict, seeking injunctive relief, and insisting on compensation greater than $10 million. It further observed that the parties' failure to disclose their agreement to the court, and to the class, violated the contracting representatives' fiduciary duties to the class and duty of candor to the court.

We agree. By tying their compensation—in advance—to a sliding scale based on the amount recovered, the incentive agreements disjoined the contingency financial interests of the contracting representatives from the class. As the district court observed, once the threshold cash settlement was met, the agreements created a disincentive to go to trial; going to trial would put their $75,000 at risk in return for only a marginal individual gain even if the verdict were significantly greater than the settlement. The agreements also gave the contracting representatives an interest in a monetary settlement, as distinguished from other remedies, that set them apart from other members of the class. Further, agreements of this sort infect the class action environment with the troubling appearance of shopping plaintiffships. If allowed, ex ante incentive agreements could tempt potential plaintiffs to sell their lawsuits to attorneys who are the highest bidders, and vice-versa. In addition, these agreements implicate California ethics rules that prohibit representation of clients with conflicting interests. *See Image Tech. Serv., Inc. v. Eastman Kodak Co.*, 136 F.3d 1354, 1358 (9th Cir. 1998) (noting that "[s]imultaneous representation of clients with conflicting interests (and without informed written consent) is an automatic ethics violation in California"); *Flatt v. Superior Court*, 9 Cal. 4th 275, 36 Cal. Rptr. 2d 537, 885 P.2d 950, 955 (Cal. 1994).

Although we have not previously encountered incentive *agreements*, we expressed concern about similar problems with incentive *awards* in *Staton v. Boeing Co.*, 327 F.3d 938 (9th Cir. 2003). There, we declined to approve a settlement agreement where the awards request indicated that the class representatives were "more concerned with maximizing [their own] incentives than with judging the adequacy of the settlement as it applies to class members at large." *See Staton*, 327 F.3d at 977–78. We explained that excess incentive awards may put the class representative in a conflict with the class and present a "considerable danger of individuals bringing cases as class actions principally to increase their own leverage to attain a remunerative settlement for themselves and then trading on that leverage in the course of negotiations." *Id.* at 976–77. The danger is exacerbated if the named plaintiffs have an advance guarantee that a request for a relatively large incentive award will be made that is untethered to any service or value they will provide to the class.

In Practice

"An empirical study published in 2006 suggests that incentive awards are granted in only about a quarter of class suits, and that the average award per class representative is roughly $16,000, with the median award per class representative being closer to $4,000."

Anna K. Wooster, *Propriety of Incentive Awards or Incentive Agreements in Class Actions*, 60 A.L.R. 6th 295.

In sum, we disapprove of the incentive agreements entered into between the named plaintiffs and class counsel in this case. They created an unacceptable disconnect between the interests of the contracting representatives and class counsel, on the one hand, and members of the class on the other. We expect those interests to be congruent. *See Molski v. Gleich*, 318 F.3d 937, 955 (9th Cir. 2003) (noting that adequate representation consists of an "absence of antagonism" and a "sharing of interests between representatives and absentees").They also gave rise to a disturbing appearance of impropriety. And failing to disclose the incentive arrangements in connection with class certification compounded these problems by depriving the court, and the class, of the safeguard of informed judicial consideration of the adequacy of class representation.

This said, we do not believe the district court was required to reject the settlement for inadequate representation. Only five of the seven class representatives had an incentive agreement. Brewer and Rimson did not. "[T]he adequacy-of-representation requirement is satisfied as long as one of the class representatives is an adequate class representative." *Local Joint Executive Bd. of Culinary/Bartender Trust Fund v. Las Vegas Sands, Inc.*, 244 F.3d 1152, 1162 n.2 (9th Cir. 2001); 7A Charles A. Wright et al., *Federal Practice and Procedure* § 1765, at 326 (2005) ("[I]f there is more than one named representative, it is not necessary that all the representatives meet the Rule 23(a)(4) standard; as long as one of the representatives is adequate, the requirement will be met."). There is no evidence or contention that these two had any other conflict with the class.

Objectors submit only that Brewer and Rimson should have told the district court about the incentive agreements. Even assuming these two knew about the incentive agreements and understood the implications, this did not create a conflict of interest or otherwise interfere with their ability or motivation to represent the class. Other factors indicate that the class was adequately represented: Judge Weinstein, who mediated the settlement, attested that the negotiations were conducted at arm's length; there was no evidence of collusion; and the settlement fund far exceeded the ten million dollar trigger for the contracting class representatives' incentive agreements.

Accordingly, we conclude that the presence of conflicted representatives was harmless. Similarly, the adequacy requirement for class counsel is satisfied. Fed. R. Civ. P. 23(a)(4), (g)(4). Judge Weinstein, who oversaw the settlement negotiations, believed that "[e]ach side aggressively advocated their positions," class counsel "ha[d] as their primary goal achieving the maximum substantive relief that they could," and agreement "was arrived at through arm's length negotiations by counsel who were skilled and knowledgeable about the facts and law of this case."

Having upheld approval of the settlement agreement, we must consider the award of attorney's fees to class counsel. This brings us back to the incentive agreements. [The court decided to remand to the district court the issue of whether, under California ethics laws, class counsel should forfeit their entire fee due to their ethical violations.]

Therefore, we affirm approval of the settlement. We reverse and remand the award of attorney's fees to class counsel for consideration of the effect, if any, of the incentive agreements on entitlement to fees. We also reverse and remand the denial of fees to Objectors' counsel for a determination of a reasonable amount given their contribution to the denial of the requests for incentive awards.

Notes and Problems

1. As *Hansberry* makes clear, without an adequate class representative pursuing the absent litigant's cause of action, there is no due process being given to that litigant. Without due process, the absent class member is not bound by the results of the class adjudication and may engage in a collateral attack of it. Thus, even if the Rules' drafters decided to delete Rule 23(a)(4), it seems unlikely to change the outcome in a case such as *Hansberry*. With respect to the *Hansberry* decision, given the divergent interests of the residents in the affected residential community, do you understand why no one representative could be an adequate representative for all of the homeowners subject to the restrictive covenants?

2. Could the problems with adequacy of representation in *Hansberry* possibly have been solved had the original class action lawsuit been a bilateral class action — that is both a plaintiff class and a defendant class (as in the *Kline* case at the beginning of this chapter)?

If so, how would the plaintiff and defendant classes be defined—by reference to race? Do you see why even those of the same race might have held divergent views regarding the desirability of such clauses, either philosophically or financially? For an interesting historical perspective on the dynamics of this particular litigation, see Stephen Yeazell, *From Medieval Group Litigation to the Modern Class Action* 233–36 (1987). If a class definition by race would not be feasible, could the plaintiff class be defined as "all those homeowners who are in favor of the enforceability of the restrictive covenant" and the defendant class defined as "all those homeowners who are against the enforcement of the restrictive covenant"? Would this present a problem with a state-of-mind definition? To that end, consider whether the court would need to know whether a particular resident was a plaintiff or defendant in order to bind that resident to the final judgment in the original case.

3. In the *West Publishing* decision, consider which was worse in terms of destroying adequacy of representation—the existence of the various incentive agreements or the failure of class counsel to disclose such agreements to the court prior to certification? Given the finding of inadequacy, how did the appellate court nevertheless affirm the settlement of the class action? From this, can you gather how many class representatives it takes in order to find adequate representation for a class under Rule 23(a)(4)?

4. Notice at the end of its opinion, the appellate court in *West Publishing* remanded the case to the district court to determine, despite the ultimate affirmance of the approval of the class settlement, whether class counsel should lose all or a portion of its legal fees due to the misconduct in shielding the facts from the district court regarding the incentive fee agreements. Upon remand, the trial court held that due to the primary class counsel's "ethical violations" that "gave rise to a conflict of interest that tainted [their] representation" the proper remedy was "automatic forfeiture" of the entirety of their attorney's fees. 2010 U.S. Dist. LEXIS 24155 (C.D. Cal. 2010). Appreciation for legal principles, and adherence to the law's tenets, can have a direct impact on counsel's pocketbook. We will separately consider other requirements for courts' awards of attorneys fees in complex litigation in a subsequent chapter.

c. Other Adequacy Prerequisites

While conflicting loyalties present a profound problem with finding adequacy of representation, others have raised other possible bases for disqualification of a proposed class representative. Try to appreciate the potential tension between the due process concerns of ensuring that an absent class member's claims are appropriately being prosecuted on her behalf with the reality that too high of an adequacy bar may practically preclude class actions being brought, with the result that the absent class members' claims are not adjudicated at all. Might the push for perfection in a class representative destroy the potential good offered by class treatment? Consider the objections raised by the defendant in the following case. Also, ask yourself whether it is odd for a defendant to be raising concerns that a class representative will not do a good enough job suing the defendant.

Peil v. National Semiconductor Corp.
86 F.R.D. 357 (E.D. Pa. 1980)

HANNUM, J.,

Before the Court is the motion of the plaintiff pursuant to F.R.Civ.P. 23(c)(1) for an order determining that the Complaint involved in this litigation and commenced on behalf of similarly situated persons should proceed as a class action. The class that the plaintiff proposes to represent would be defined as consisting of all persons or entities who purchased the common stock of the defendant National Semiconductor Corporation (hereinafter "NSC") during the period between approximately July 1, 1976 to March 1, 1977 and who sustained damages thereby, whether by selling such securities at reduced prices, continuing to hold them at reduced market values, or otherwise.

The essence of the plaintiff's Complaint alleges that the defendants Charles E. Sporck (hereinafter "Sporck") and Peter J. Sprague (hereinafter "Sprague"), President and Chairman of the Board of NSC, respectively, engaged in a conspiratorial course of conduct to artificially inflate the value of NSC stock in order to permit Sporck and Sprague to dispose of their privately owned shares at the inflated value. The plaintiff contends that the defendants Sporck and Sprague actively misrepresented and failed to disclose facts that hindered potential and actual investors from gaining an accurate portrayal of the financial condition of NSC and that as a result many investors sustained losses when the market finally reflected the actual value of the stock. The plaintiff seeks to represent the class in rectifying this alleged securities violation because on October 1, 1976, he purchased 500 shares of NSC common stock at $35.75 per share and subsequently sold these same shares on February 3, 1977, at the price of $19.50 per share, a loss of $16.25 per share.

The Complaint instituting this litigation was filed on December 13, 1977, several months after the plaintiff had sold his shares of NSC common stock.

Class Action Certification.

The applicability and utility of the class action device to cases involving the securities laws has been cogently recognized on a number of occasions. The nature of the securities laws is complex and litigation therein concerned expensive. Without the class action device, many actionable wrongs would go uncorrected and persons affected thereby un-recompensed. In essence, the class action device is a bona fide method for redressing violations of the securities laws and for compelling compliance with their mandates. Accordingly, "the interests of justice require that in a doubtful case, … any error, if there is to be one, should be committed in favor of allowing the class action." *Esplin v. Hirschi*, 402 F.2d 94, 101 (10th Cir. 1968).

[The court found that the other prerequisites for certification found in Rule 23(a)(1)–(3) were satisfied in this case.]

Adequate Representation. The fourth enumerated requirement of F.R.Civ.P. 23(a) provides that the "representative parties will fairly and adequately protect the interests of the class." In an effort to define this somewhat vague standard for representation, the Third Circuit has adopted the following rule to which a plaintiff must demonstrate his compliance:

> (1) they have no interests which are antagonistic to other members of the class, and (2) their attorney is capable of prosecuting the instant claim with some degree of expertise.

Wetzel v. Liberty Mutual Insurance Co., 508 F.2d 239, 247 (3d Cir. 1975); *Dorfman v. First Boston Corp.*, 62 F.R.D. 466 (E.D.Pa.1973).

The defendants apparently recognize the applicability of the rule articulated in Wetzel but offer a third requirement for adoption; that the plaintiff have first-hand knowledge of the facts giving rise to the cause of action. Essentially, the defendants contend that the plaintiff's counsel, Richard D. Greenfield, Esquire, is the real party in interest but for his lack of standing because he has unearthed the facts and unraveled the complexities attendant to their application to the securities laws. Reliance for this advancement is upon the decision rendered in *In re Goldchip Funding Co.*, 61 F.R.D. 592, 594–95 (M.D.Pa.1974):

> In my view, facts regarding the personal qualities of the representatives themselves are relevant, indeed necessary, in determining whether "the representative parties will fairly and adequately protect the interests of the class." ... A proper representative can offer more to the prosecution of a class action than mere fulfillment of the procedural requirements of Rule 23. He can, for example, offer his personal knowledge of the factual circumstances, and aid in rendering decisions on practical and nonlegal problems which arise during the course of litigation. An attorney who prosecutes a class action with unfettered discretion becomes, in fact, a representative of the class. This is an unacceptable situation because of the possible conflicts of interest involved....

See also *Levine v. Berg,* 79 F.R.D. 95 (S.D.N.Y.1978).

In Practice

According to the Manual for Complex Litigation (Fourth), "[s]ome discovery may be necessary [at the pre-certification stage] when the facts relevant to any of the certification requirements are disputed ... Courts often bifurcate discovery between certification issues and those related to the merits of the allegations. [However,] there is not always a bright line between the two."

Manual for Complex Litigation, Fourth, § 21.14.

The *Wetzel* rule, as it presently obtains, implicitly recognizes that a class representative need not be the best of all possible representatives but rather one that will pursue a resolution of the controversy with the requisite vigor and in the interest of the class. What is "requisite" is determined by considering the nature of the litigation and the factual and legal basis underlying it; necessarily a case-by-case analysis. To require a person unschooled in the realm of our complex and abstract securities laws to have first-hand knowledge of facts cloaked in an alleged conspiratorial silence and which present themselves as a wrongdoing that may be actionable would render the class action device an impotent tool. In order to responsibly allege and later adequately prove the accusations contained in the plaintiff's Complaint, the plaintiff's counsel must have engaged in and will engage in extensive investigation and discovery conducted with a working knowledge of the securities laws.

The Court is cognizant of the fact that by it not requiring the class representation to have the degree of first-hand knowledge of the factual basis of this litigation suggested by the defendants, that counsel may proceed without various restraints. The Court *In re Goldchip Funding Co., supra,* expressed a similar concern in its ruling to the effect that such unbridled discretion of counsel may render him a class representative rather than its counsel, thereby creating a conflict of interest. The Court is unmoved by this assertion. Aside from the normal degree of flexibility enjoyed by counsel when presenting a client's case, the Court may intervene, if appropriate, pursuant to its inherent power to protect the class members. Moreover, much influence and control is exercised by the Court by the fact that it controls the fee award to the plaintiff's counsel should the plaintiff prevail. In essence, the Court recognizes the existence of its inherent powers to control the actions of the plaintiff's counsel in the event that a conflict of interest appears. Otherwise, counsel for both parties may exercise the discretion they deserve and enjoy when presenting their respective clients' positions.

Ruling in accordance with the numerous cases that expressly reject the *In re Goldchip Funding Co., supra*, precedent and declining to adopt the defendant's proposed third requirement to the *Wetzel* rule, the Court turns to the two existing requirements: (1) the representative has no antagonistic interests and (2) his counsel has the requisite expertise to prosecute the action. It is not disputed that the plaintiff carries no interest that could conceivably be considered antagonistic to the common interests of the class he seeks to represent. Accordingly, the Court deems this requirement satisfied. In addition, the second requirement is not contested and is therefore deemed satisfied. The plaintiff's counsel's ability to prosecute similar actions with a sufficient degree of expertise has been noted on at least one prior occasion. *Simon v. Westinghouse Electric Corp.*, 73 F.R.D. 480, 24 F.R.Serv.2d 1078 (E.D.Pa.1977). The Court is of the opinion, and so rules, that the plaintiff is an adequate class representative pursuant to the requirements of F.R.Civ.P. 23(a)(4).[7]

ORDER

AND NOW, this 21st day of March, 1980, the plaintiff's motion is GRANTED and the class is certified as follows:

> All persons other than the defendants herein who purchased NSC common stock during the period of July 9, 1976 to January 28, 1977, and sustained damages thereby, whether by selling such securities at reduced prices, continuing to hold them at reduced market values, or otherwise.

Notes and Problems

1. *Peil* is representative of a large number of securities fraud class actions. If ever a large dispute gave courts an incentive to certify a class, it might well be in the securities fraud arena. Consider the alternative to class certification — thousands (potentially) of separate lawsuits filed in different courts all seeking to adjudicate the same or very similar contentions. Or, without certification, a multitude of injured small-amount investors might have their claims go without vindication due to their negative value claims and wrongdoers would be able to reap their profits from their misconduct and have every incentive to continue to cheat the investing public. Eventually public belief in the fairness of the stock markets would erode and all investors would suffer. For this reason, many courts are inclined to certify class actions in this context even in otherwise close cases. As one court (quoted in *Peil*) candidly observed, "the interests of justice require that in a doubtful case … any error, if there is to be one, should be committed in favor of allowing the class action." *Esplin v. Hirschi*, 402 F.2d 94, 101 (10th Cir. 1968). Since 1995, some aspects of securities class actions are governed by the Private Securities Litigation Reform Act which, among other things, modifies the Rule 23(a)(4) standards for adequacy by creating a presumption that the aggrieved shareholder with the largest financial stake in the outcome of the litigation (for the class) should be the class representative. *Berger v. Compaq Computer Corp.*, 257 F.3d 475, 483 (5th Cir. 2001) (PSLRA raises the adequacy requirement requiring that

---

7. When determining the adequacy of potential class representatives, courts must consider personal qualities such as vigor, tenaciousness and willingness to make a financial commitment. *See Sharp v. Reybold Homes, Inc.*, 24 F.R.Serv.2d 1111 (E.D.Pa.1977); *Cohen v. Uniroyal, Inc.*, 77 F.R.D. 685 (E.D.Pa.1977). In the present case the plaintiff has actively pursued his case on behalf of himself and potential class members as well as stated his willingness to make the financial commitment attendant to class notification and other aspects of a class action.

"securities class actions be managed by active, able class representatives who are informed and can demonstrate that they are directing the litigation.").

2. The court in *Peil* reaffirms the *Wetzel* rule which only enumerates two requirements for demonstrating adherence with Rule 23(a)(4)—(1) absence of any antagonism between the class representative and the remainder of the class, and (2) capable class counsel. Notwithstanding this brief list, however, even the *Peil* court goes a little further by also considering whether the proposed representative will "pursue a resolution of the controversy with the requisite vigor and in the interest of the class." The court, however, expressly rejects any additional requirement that the class representative have personal knowledge of the key facts and an understanding of the legal theories upon which the case is founded. Other courts have agreed with *Peil* that only minimal competence is necessary, in general, to qualify as a class representative. *See, e.g., Black v. Rhone-Poulenc, Inc.*, 173 F.R.D. 156 (S.D.W.Va. 1996) ("While some of the representative Plaintiffs demonstrated less than a complete understanding of their responsibilities and of the technical legal issues, that alone does not bar certification."). As another court stated, "as long as the plaintiffs, as class representatives, know something about the case, even though they are not knowledgeable of the complaint's specific allegations, the class should be certified." *Lerner v. Haimsohn*, 126 F.R.D. 64, 67 (D. Colo. 1989). Do you see how such a requirement, if it were to be adopted by courts, would make it often difficult to find a suitable class representative in complex business litigation or esoteric strict products liability cases premised upon intricate engineering flaws in a product? Why is the court so comfortable allowing an unknowledgeable and unsophisticated plaintiff to serve as a check on the powers of class counsel? Who else will help "guard the henhouse"?

3. Some observers have opined that, due to the relatively low hurdles placed before proposed class representatives, the reality is that class actions are often completely premised on the whims of class counsel spotting the claims and asserting the claims without any real client driving any portion of the process. For this reason, these observers have suggested that counsel be permitted to file class actions without any real class representative using fictional "John Doe" names instead. *See, e.g., Decorative Figureheads: Eliminating Class Representatives in Class Actions*, 42 Hasting L.J. 165 (1990). Can you think why courts (and the Rules drafters) might be disinclined to adopt such a novel method for bringing class actions?

4. Notwithstanding the general rejection of a requirement that a class representative have personal knowledge of all relevant facts and demonstrate insightful understanding of the nuances of the causes of action, courts have been open to rejecting proposed representatives having a variety of other flaws, such as:

a. Courts sometimes consider the financial resources of a proposed representative to fund litigation (and their willingness to do so) though most courts are satisfied so long as class counsel be in a position to fund the case appropriately. *Compare Weber v. Goodman*, 9 F. Supp. 2d 163 (E.D.N.Y. 1998) (rejecting certification), *with Rand v. Monsanto*, 926 F.2d 596, 599 (7th Cir. 1991) (reversing district court denial of certification, stating that a "conscientious plaintiff is likely to be willing to make some financial commitment to the case. But no person need be willing to stake his entire fortune for the benefit of strangers. Class actions can be frightfully expensive. No (sane) person would pay the entire cost of a securities class action in exchange for a maximum benefit of $1,135. None would even put up $25,000 or even $2,500 against a hope of recovering $1,135."), *and Rand v. Monsanto*, 926 F.2d 596 (7th Cir. 1991) (class representative not required to underwrite costs of litigation and class counsel are appropriate for this purpose).

b. Courts have sometimes been concerned with the appearance of a "professional" class representative for fear that if the case were to go before a jury, this might taint the jury's view of the case's merits. *Compare In re Gibson Greetings Securities Litigation*, 159 F.R.D. 499 (S.D. Ohio) (denying certification when class representative had filed 182 class actions), *with Murray v. GMAC Mortgage Corp.*, 434 F.3d 948 (7th Cir. 2006) (reversing denial of certification despite class representative having filed 50 other suits).

c. Courts are often bothered by the lack of an arms-length relationship between the class representative and class counsel. *See, e.g., London v. Wal-Mart Stores, Inc.*, 340 F.3d 1246 (11th Cir. 2003) (representative was lifelong friend of class counsel and court believed he might put the lawyer's interests ahead of the class); *Malchman v. Davis*, 706 F.2d 426 (2d Cir. 1983) (representative was sister of class counsel's chauffeur); *Lewis v. Goldsmith*, 95 F.R.D. 15 (D.N.J. 1982) (representative was uncle of class counsel).

d. Class representatives that have a demonstrated lack of credibility have been found to be inadequate representatives. *See, e.g., Kaplan v. Pomerantz*, 132 F.R.D. 504 (N.D. Ill. 1990) (court decertified class action after plaintiff class representative found to have given dishonest answers in his deposition); *but cf. Biben v. Card*, [1985–86] Fed. Sec. L. Rep. (CCH) ¶ 92,462 (W.D. Mo. 1986) (variances in memory of class representative during deposition do not impair his adequacy).

5. Some courts have held that, if a case is otherwise appropriate for certification but lacks an adequate class representative, it is error for the district court to fail to allow class counsel time to find another class representative before denying certification. *Birmingham Steel Corp. v. Tennessee Valley Authority*, 353 F.3d 1331 (11th Cir. 2003).

6. *Problem.* Jonathon is a resident of a state hospital that houses and treats patients with significant mental disabilities. He, of course, also has a mental disability. He has filed a class action lawsuit challenging the conditions of the facility in which he resides. Defendant contends that his mental disability will interfere with his ability to comprehend the litigation and to counsel with the class lawyer and that, therefore, he is not an adequate representative. How should the court rule?

7. *Chapter Problem.* Consider that you are an associate counsel at the defense law firm hired to represent TMG and to resist the certification efforts of class claimant Merri Chance. You are asked to prepare an outline of possible questions to ask of Ms. Chance during her deposition regarding certification matters. Specifically, you are asked to draft a bullet-point list of deposition topics that you believe might shed some light on whether Ms. Chance is an adequate class representative. On each topic, be prepared to explain why the topic might give rise to the discovery of relevant information regarding her adequacy.

Pulling It All Together Exercise

Elmer is the senior class student body president at Union High School. He is upset that the administration has placed an across-the-board ban on student signs and posters at school athletic contests after one student held up a sign saying "Fight Corrupt School Officials!" This sign was an oblique reference to a rumor going around the school at the time that the Union High principal was using school funds designated for purchasing textbooks to fund a trip for himself and other school officials to the Cayman Islands for an education conference. It turns out the rumor was false. The school decided that it was better to have no signs at school sporting events than to risk libel occurring. Through counsel, Elmer has filed a putative class action in federal court claiming that the school's conduct violates the First Amendment rights of the student body by choosing an overly restrictive means in backlash to a single, isolated instance of misconduct by one student. Elmer has proposed a class of "all current and future students at Union High School who have attempted, or desired, to utilize signs at sporting events but not been allowed due to the implementation of the unconstitutional policy of Union High School." Plaintiff seeks a declaration that the school's policy violates the First Amendment and an injunction preventing enforcement of the current policy, as well as recovery of attorney's fees incurred in the lawsuit. He also seeks recovery of compensatory damages for any student who has suffered depression due to the loss of their rights. Union High School has approximately 800 students. When asked in a deposition if he ever was refused entry into any Union High sporting event, he stated "No, I have not bothered to attempt to bring a sign into any such game but, as student body president, I feel it is my job to assert the rights of the student body. Also, I have great empathy for my fellow students who have suffered under this totalitarian regime." The school president testified in his deposition that the policy was content neutral and that "only a handful of students have been turned away at the gates with signs. And, by the way, those signs had hateful messages on them. One was aimed at taunting the visiting team's cheerleaders. That team mascot is the Goats. The sign said the cheerleaders looked liked goats. It was inappropriate. Even those were permitted re-entry as soon as they left their signs in their cars. Nobody has complained to me about this policy except for Elmer, who seems intent to make a mountain out of a mole hill."

Spend 20 minutes analyzing the issues that would arise in attempting to show the prerequisites for certification under Rule 23(a). Would this case likely be certified or not?

Upon Further Review

Before any court can consider certification of a class action, certain prerequisites must be certified. Implicit within the prerequisites for class certification are that the class be definable and class members ascertainable, at least sufficient for the court to carry out its obligations to provide notice of certification (if applicable) and to implement the remedy sought by the class upon entry of judgment. Beyond this, the enumerated requirements in Rule 23(a) essentially serve to ensure that sufficient minimal efficiency gains would be realized by classwide treatment of the controversy to overcome the general preference for traditional one-on-one litigation. So Rule 23(a) demands that the class have sufficient *numerosity* of membership and that the class claims give rise to a *commonality* of fact or legal issues. Beyond this basic notion of efficiency, the prerequisites in Rule 23(a)(3)–(4) also are designed to foster a sense that the class representative can be trusted to litigate the claims of the absent class members on their behalf. This seems to be the case when the class member has suffered a similar injury as the alleged class and is asserting a common legal theory of recovery against the defendant (*typicality*) and that he is free of conflicts of interest and shows a requisite minimal vigor and competence (*adequacy*). When these foundational requirements are satisfied, the court can at least contemplate a possible class action, assuming the case meets one of the models found in Rule 23(b).

E. Different Types of Classes

Even after clearing the Rule 23(a) hurdles, class counsel's efforts to obtain certification are not yet complete. Courts have made abundantly clear that a class is not guaranteed simply by checking off the Rule 23(a) boxes. *Lowery v. Circuit City Stores, Inc.*, 158 F.3d 742, 757–58 (4th Cir. 1998). Rather, class counsel must also demonstrate that the proposed class is appropriate under one of the provisions in Rule 23(b). Remember that prior to 1966, the class certification standards set forth in the Federal Rules were opaque descriptions that were difficult to grasp. The 1966 re-write of the rules was intended, in part, to remove the cloud of obscurity and to provide easier-to-comprehend descriptions of the sorts of class actions that were considered appropriate by the drafters of modern Rule 23. We will consider each of these types of class actions in order of their delineation in Rule 23(b). As you read through these following cases in the remainder of the chapter, ask yourself whether the drafts succeeded in making the current categories fairly straightforward.

Rule 23(b)(1)

A class action may be maintained if Rule 23(a) is satisfied and if:

(1) prosecuting separate actions by or against individual class members would create a risk of:

    (A) inconsistent or varying adjudications with respect to individual class members that would establish incompatible standards of conduct for the party opposing the class; or

    (B) adjudications with respect to individual class members that, as a practical matter, would be dispositive of the interests of the other members not parties to the individual adjudications or would substantially impair or impede their ability to protect their interests.

---

1. Rule 23(b)(1) Classes

a. Rule 23(b)(1)(A): Incompatible Standards Classes

In general, Rule 23(b)(1) serves as a class action parallel to Rule 19 necessary parties. Just as Rule 19 concerns, in part, whether litigation in the absence of someone might infringe upon concerns for fairness for either the missing party or the defendant, Rule 23(b)(1) contemplates certification when fairness dictates that class treatment is the best way to ensure the fair treatment of the named defendant or the missing class members. Rule 23(b)(1) is delineated by subparts (A) and (B). Subpart (A) covers situations where, in the absence of a class action, the defendant would face the risk of "inconsistent or varying adjudications with respect to individual class members that would establish incompatible standards of conduct" for the defendant. When the class seeks *declarative or injunctive* relief in order to establish a binding legal standard for the defendant, this language seems potentially applicable. After all, what if multiple courts enter mutually exclusive injunctive relief directed at the same defendant? Having numerous potential injunctive relief lawsuits adjudicated instead under the auspices of one court as a class action avoids this potential scenario of requiring defendant to serve two masters. But may numerous related suits for *monetary damages* offer a similar effect on a defendant? After all, if there are inconsistent results of such lawsuits, what clear standard has been communicated to the defendant? The following state law case permits certification in such a situation. But as you will see in the court's discussion below, federal courts have now consistently ruled otherwise under the federal version of Rule 23(b)(1)(A). Which offers the right answer — the federal rule or the "better Texas rule"?

When is mandatory class cert. permitted?

Morgan v. Deere Credit

889 S.W.2d 360 (Tex. App. — Houston [14th Dist.] 1994)

ROBERTSON, J.,

This interlocutory appeal is from the certification of a mandatory class under Rule 42(b) of the Texas Rules of Civil Procedure.

Principles

Rule 23(b)(1) addresses situations where individual litigation might have a seriously unfair impact on other potential plaintiffs or on the defendant (some see this as Rule 19 mandatory joinder for cases where there are too many parties to actually join).

The underlying suit concerns the claims of Texas residents who entered financing agreements with Deere to purchase boats or recreational vehicles ("RV's"). About 15,000 Texas residents purchased Deere's RV's and boats between February 1988 and December 1991 and financed them through Deere. In its standardized loan contract forms, Deere failed to use the statutorily required typographic style on its choice of law clauses. See Tex. Bus. & Com. Code Ann. 35.53 (Vernon Supp. 1994) Each contract stated the law of Iowa, Deere's home state, governed the transaction, but the clause was not printed in boldface type. Upon discovering this omission, in January 1992 Deere sent "cure" letters to over 10,000 Texas residents who had obtained financing through these contracts, informing them that their contracts may not have complied with Texas law. Deere gave them the option to ratify the Iowa choice of law provision. Many of these consumers with whom Deere had contracted began [threatening] claims that Texas law applies and the contracts violate the Texas Consumer Credit Code. See Tex. Rev. Civ. Stat. Ann. art. 5069-1.02–8.06 (Vernon 1987 & Supp. 1994). The residents alleged Deere violated Texas usury laws, which require certain lenders to be licensed and regulated by the Texas Consumer Credit Commissioner. Without the license, lenders are prohibited from charging interest rates of more than 10 percent, as Deere did in making these loans. In addition to the common law and statutory usury causes of action, some of the residents also alleged Deere violated the Texas Deceptive Trade Practices Act. The residents named in this suit [sued Deere and its affiliated corporations] attempting to avoid their contractual obligations and recover penalties from Deere.

[The trial court granted a motion for certification of a mandatory class defined as follows:]

"All persons who, on or after February 19, 1988 and prior to December, 1991, and while he or she was a Texas resident, entered into an agreement with John

Deere Company for financing the purchase of a boat or recreational vehicle, primarily for personal, family or household use."

At the time of the hearing, the class was composed of approximately 550 members. There is no dispute on appeal that the four prerequisites for class certification under rule 42(a) have been met. The issues in this case instead center on the trial court's determination of the category of class to be maintained under rule (42)(b).

Our rule 42(b)(1)(A), [is] the identical counterpart to federal Rules 23(b)(1)(A). [This rule provides]:

> **(b) Class Actions Maintainable.** An action may be maintained as a class action if the prerequisites of subdivision (a) are satisfied, and in addition:
>
> (1) the prosecution of separate actions by or against individual members of the class would create a risk of
>
> (A) inconsistent or varying adjudications with respect to individual members of the class which would establish incompatible standards of conduct for the party opposing the class.

At the certification stage, class proponents generally are not required to make an extensive evidentiary showing in support of a motion for class certification. *Life Ins. Co. of the Southwest v. Brister*, 722 S.W.2d 764, 773 (Tex. App.—Fort Worth 1986, no writ). Under Rule 42(c)(1), like its federal counterpart, the trial court may alter, amend, or withdraw class certification at any time before final judgment. *Salvaggio v. Houston I.S.D.*, 709 S.W.2d 306, 309–310 (Tex. App.—Houston [14th Dist.] 1986, writ dism'd). Thus, when a trial court makes a determination of class status at an early stage of the proceeding before supporting facts are fully developed, it should favor maintenance of a class action. *Clements v. League of United Latin American Citizens (LULAC)*, 800 S.W.2d 948, 952 (Tex. App.—Corpus Christi 1990, no writ).

[Another of the nearly identical lawsuits filed out of this dispute—the "Durrett" case— was originally filed in Texas state court but later removed to federal court. In that case, the federal court determined that the case could not be certified under Rule 23(b)(1)(A), as follows]:

> It is clear that Rule 23(b)(1)(A) does not apply to the facts at issue because adjudications in actions other than this action would not subject a party to the danger of inconsistent adjudications in which compliance with one judgment would constitute noncompliance with another.

150 F.R.D. at 560.

[Although Texas' version of Rule 23(b) is identical to the federal rule,] those rules that are identical sometimes have been applied differently by Texas courts.

In support of these differing standards, [movants cited] *Adams v. Reagan*, 791 S.W.2d 284 (Tex. App.—Fort Worth 1990, no writ). In that investors' suit against former officers and directors of a financial investment company, the court held that "the better Texas rule" would be to certify a class action "where to fail to certify would result in inconsistent or varying results." *Id.* at 292–93. The court in Adams certified a mandatory class under rule 42(b)(1)(A) even though appellees sought money damages, rejecting the federal court interpretation that there is no risk of inconsistency where a defendant is liable for damages to one plaintiff but not to another. *Id.* at 292, citing *McBirney v. Autrey*, 106 F.R.D. 240, 245 (N.D. Tex. 1985). The finding in *McBirney* that the federal counterpart to our rule 42(b)(1)(A) is applicable only where judgments in separate suits would "trap the party opposing the class in the inescapable legal quagmire of not being able to comply with one such judgment without violating the terms of another" was disavowed by *Adams*. 106 F.R.D. at 245. The *Adams* court emphasized that class certification where there were between 800 and 1100 potential class members was preferable to individual suits where uniformity of results would be unlikely. Similarly, the trial court here, in its discretion, found that under these facts, a mandatory class is a superior method of litigating these claims. While we may disagree with the holding and reasoning in *Adams*, we find the trial court did not abuse its discretion in basing its decision on these guiding principles.

Appellants point to the United States Supreme Court's pronouncement that due process requires permitting a plaintiff to opt out of a class in a suit for money damages. The Court stated:

> If the forum State wishes to bind an absent plaintiff concerning a claim for money damages or similar relief at law, it must provide minimal procedural due process protection. The plaintiff must receive notice plus an opportunity to be heard and participate in the litigation, whether in person or through counsel. The notice must be the best practicable, "reasonably calculated under the circumstances, to apprise interested parties of the pendency of the action and afford them an opportunity to present their objections." The notice should describe the action and the plaintiffs' rights in it. Additionally, we hold that due process requires at a minimum that an absent plaintiff be provided with an opportunity to remove himself from the class by executing and returning an "opt out" or "request for exclusion" form to the court.

Phillips Petroleum Co. v. Shutts, 472 U.S. 797, 811–12, 105 S. Ct. 2965, 2974, 86 L. Ed. 2d 628 (1985) (discussing opt out procedure in Kansas class action statute). We find *Shutts* inapplicable to these facts. The due process issue considered there was whether "the 'opt out' notice to absent class members ... was insufficient to bind class members who were not residents of Kansas or who did not possess 'minimum contacts' with Kansas." 472 U.S. at 803, 105 S. Ct. at 2969. The holding appellants rely upon relates to the due process rights of absent class members, meaning class members over whom the Kansas court did not have personal jurisdiction. In this case, all class members are by definition Texas residents.

[A]ppellants contend the trial court abused its discretion in certifying a class by erroneously finding a risk of "inconsistent and varying adjudications." The trial court found certification proper under rule 42(b)(1)(A) to prevent inconsistent adjudications. Appellants argue the rule requires more; it requires that these adjudications result in incompatible standards of conduct. They contend mandatory certification is improper in a suit for money damages, relying on *McBirney v. Autrey*, 106 F.R.D. 240 (N.D. Tex. 1985). *Adams* rejected *McBirney* and found a "better Texas rule" allowing mandatory certification when judicial economy so requires. We find no abuse of discretion in the trial court following this reasoning in applying rule 42(b)(1)(A).

There is no dispute that the claims of each of the class members involve identical issues of fact and law. The contractual language made the basis of this suit is identical in each financing agreement. The claims and defenses are virtually the same. Without mandatory certification, Deere may have to defend the identical suit numerous times. When the repeated litigation of common issues would be grossly inefficient, generate exorbitant costs or waste judicial resources, Texas law allows mandatory class certification. See *Adams*, 791 S.W.2d at 292–3.

Notes and Problems

1. The idea behind Rule 23(b)(1)(A) — the "incompatible standards" class action — is to protect the defendant from the unfairness of being subjected to inconsistent demands from courts in the form of declaratory or injunctive relief. The test used by federal courts is whether the possible conflicting forms of relief might cause a defendant, acting in accordance with one potential judgment, to put itself in contempt of court with another court that issued different requirements for the defendant. By contrast, the above court following the "better Texas rule" cites "judicial economy" as the excuse for certifying under 23(b)(1)(A) merely because it would avoid multiple courts separately ruling on similar monetary damage claims against the defendant. While there certainly would be a possibility of different courts reaching different results, is that the sort of inconsistency that raises fundamental fairness as grounds for certification? And observe the court's recognition that certification under Rule 23(b)(1)(A) comes without individual notice and rights to opt out of litigation (traditionally afforded in Rule 23(b)(3) damage class actions). Do you see any potential mischief involved in applying mandatory non-opt-out treatment to individual damage claims?

2. In rejecting an argument for Rule 23(b)(1)(A) certification in a case where only claims for damages were involved, one federal court disavowed the interpretation given to this rule by the foregoing Texas court, explaining:

> The advisory committee notes make it clear that the situation in which a party is faced with inconsistent results requiring it to pay some class members but not others is covered by Rule 23(b)(3) and not Rule 23(b)(1). See Advisory Committee Note of 1966 to Rule 23(b)(3). The risk of "incompatible standard of conduct" which Rule 23(b)(1)(A) was designed to protect against involves situations where the non-class party does not know, because of inconsistent ajudications, whether or not it is legally permissible for it to pursue a certain course of conduct. Thus, Rule 23(b)(1)(A) is designed to protect against the nonclass party's [defendant's] being placed in a stalemated or conflicted position and is applicable only to actions in which there is not only a risk of inconsistent adjudications but also where the nonclass party could be sued for different and incompatible affirmative relief.

Employers Insurance of Wausau v. FDIC, 112 F.R.D. 52, 54 (E.D. Tenn. 1986). Despite the clarity of this admonition, there have been some federal court decisions consistent with the minority "better Texas rule" — even outside of the Lone Star State. *See, e.g., Hernandez v. Motor Vessel Skyward*, 61 F.R.D. 558 (S.D. Fla. 1973) (certifying under Rule 23(b)(1)(A) personal injury damage case by passengers who became ill while on a cruise ship from contaminated food, the court finding certification proper to avoid "defendants [being otherwise] taken to task by one passenger after another until a judgment against the defendants was obtained" and referring to this process as a waste of "needless judicial time and energy.").

3. When we turn to Rule 23(b)(2) injunctive relief claims you will discover the overlap between Rule 23(b)(1)(A) incompatible standards class actions and Rule 23(b)(2) injunctive relief classes. Because both are mandatory, non-notice, and non-opt out types of class actions, the distinction between (b)(1) and (b)(2) is more academic than practically important.

b. Rule 23(b)(1)(B): Limited Fund Classes

By contrast with Rule 23(b)(1)(A), Rule 23(b)(1)(B)'s primary concern is with the fairness of absent class members who, in the absence of certification, might "as a practical matter" be prejudiced by their absence in the litigation. By far the most important scenario where this occurs is with the *limited fund* scenario — where due to a finite pot at the end of the litigation rainbow, the first to judgment get full relief while the stragglers find the pot empty. As the Supreme Court will discuss, there was historical precedent for the modern Rule 23(b)(1)(B) limited fund scenario that had certain character traits present. When these are found, certification under Rule 23(b)(1)(B) seems clear. But sometimes enterprising class counsel might attempt to take a Rule 23(b)(3) damages case and squeeze it into the limited fund cubby hole for particular strategic advantage. Whether such efforts will be successful depends on issues of fairness that help to clarify the limits of the mandatory Rule 23(b)(1)(B) limited fund class action.

Ortiz v. Fibreboard Corp.

527 U.S. 815 (1999)

SOUTER J.,

This case turns on the conditions for certifying a mandatory settlement class on a limited fund theory under Federal Rule of Civil Procedure 23(b)(1)(B). We hold that applicants for contested certification on this rationale must show that the fund is limited by more than the agreement of the parties, and has been allocated to claimants belonging within the class by a process addressing any conflicting interests of class members.

I.

[T]his case is a class action prompted by the elephantine mass of asbestos cases, and [illustrates] how this litigation defies customary judicial administration and calls for national legislation. In 1967, one of the first actions for personal asbestos injury was filed in the United States District Court for the Eastern District of Texas against a group of asbestos manufacturers. In the 1970's and 1980's, plaintiffs' lawyers throughout the country, particularly in East Texas, honed the litigation of asbestos claims to the point of almost mechanical regularity, improving the forensic identification of diseases caused by asbestos, refining theories of liability, and often settling large inventories of cases. See D. Hensler, W. Felstiner, M. Selvin, & P. Ebener, Asbestos in the Courts: The Challenge of Mass Toxic Torts vii (1985); McGovern, *Resolving Mature Mass Tort Litigation*, 69 B.U. L. Rev. 659, 660–661 (1989).

Respondent Fibreboard Corporation was a defendant in the 1967 action. Although it was primarily a timber company, from the 1920's through 1971 the company manufactured a variety of products containing asbestos, mainly for high-temperature industrial applications. As the tide of asbestos litigation rose, Fibreboard found itself litigating on two fronts. On one, plaintiffs were filing a stream of personal injury claims against it, swelling throughout the 1980's and 1990's to thousands of new claims for compensatory damages each year. On the second front, Fibreboard was battling for funds to pay its tort claimants. From May, 1957, through March, 1959, respondent Continental Casualty Company had provided Fibreboard with a comprehensive general liability policy with limits of $1 million per occurrence, $500,000 per claim, and no aggregate limit. Fibreboard also claimed that respondent Pacific Indemnity Company had insured it from 1956 to 1957 under a similar policy. Beginning in 1979, Fibreboard was locked in coverage litigation with Continental and Pacific in a California state trial court, which in 1990 held Continental and Pacific responsible for indemnification as to any claim by a claimant exposed to Fibreboard asbestos products prior to their policies' respective expiration dates. The decree also required the insurers to pay the full cost of defense for each claim covered. The insurance companies appealed.

With asbestos case filings continuing unabated, and its secure insurance assets almost depleted, Fibreboard in 1988 began a practice of "structured settlement," paying plaintiffs 40 percent of the settlement figure up front with the balance contingent upon a successful resolution of the coverage dispute. By 1991, however, the pace of filings forced Fibreboard to start settling cases entirely with the assignments of its rights against Continental, with no initial payment. To reflect the risk that Continental might prevail in the coverage dispute, these assignment agreements generally carried a figure about twice the nominal amount of earlier settlements. Continental challenged Fibreboard's right to make unilateral assignments, but in 1992 a California state court ruled for Fibreboard in that dispute.

Meanwhile, in the aftermath of a 1990 Federal Judicial Center conference on the asbestos litigation crisis, Fibreboard approached a group of leading asbestos plaintiffs' lawyers, offering to discuss a "global settlement" of its asbestos personal-injury liability. Early negotiations bore relatively little fruit, save for the December 1992 settlement by assignment of a significant inventory of pending claims. This settlement brought Fibreboard's deferred settlement obligations to more than $1.2 billion, all contingent upon victory over Continental on the scope of coverage and the validity of the settlement assignments.

In February 1993, after Continental had lost on both issues at the trial level, and thus faced the possibility of practically unbounded liability, it too joined the global settlement negotiations. Because Continental conditioned its part in any settlement on a guarantee of "total peace," ensuring no unknown future liabilities, talks focused on the feasibility of a mandatory class action, one binding all potential plaintiffs and giving none of them any choice to opt out of the certified class. Negotiations continued throughout the spring and summer of 1993, but the difficulty of settling both actually pending and potential future claims simultaneously led to an agreement in early August to segregate and settle an inventory of some 45,000 pending claims, being substantially all those filed by one of the plaintiffs' firms negotiating the global settlement. The settlement amounts per claim were higher than average, with one-half due on closing and the remainder contingent upon either a global settlement or Fibreboard's success in the coverage litigation. This agreement provided the model for settling inventory claims of other firms.

With the insurance companies' appeal of the consolidated coverage case set to be heard on August 27, the negotiating parties faced a motivating deadline, and about midnight before the argument, in a coffee shop in Tyler, Texas, the negotiators finally agreed upon $1.535 billion as the key term of a "Global Settlement Agreement." $1.525 billion of this sum would come from Continental and Pacific, in the proportion established by the California trial court in the coverage case, while Fibreboard would contribute $10 million, all but $500,000 of it from other insurance proceeds.

On September 9, 1993, as agreed, a group of named plaintiffs filed an action in the United States District Court for the Eastern District of Texas, seeking certification for settlement purposes of a mandatory class comprising three groups: all persons with personal injury claims against Fibreboard for asbestos exposure who had not yet brought suit or settled their claims before the previous August 27; those who had dismissed such a claim but retained the right to bring a future action against Fibreboard; and "past, present and future spouses, parents, children, and other relatives" of class members exposed to Fibreboard asbestos. The class did not include claimants with actions presently pending

certified group [handwritten marginal note]

against Fibreboard or claimants "who filed and, for cash payment or some other negotiated value, dismissed claims against Fibreboard, and whose only retained right is to sue Fibreboard upon development of an asbestos-related malignancy." The complaint pleaded personal injury claims against Fibreboard, and, as justification for class certification, relied on the shared necessity of ensuring insurance funds sufficient for compensation.

[The district court granted class certification, and enjoined commencement of further separate litigation against Fibreboard by class members.]

As finally negotiated, the Global Settlement Agreement provided that in exchange for full releases from class members, Fibreboard, Continental, and Pacific would establish a trust to process and pay class members' asbestos personal injury and death claims. Claimants seeking compensation would be required to try to settle with the trust. If initial settlement attempts failed, claimants would have to proceed to mediation, arbitration, and a mandatory settlement conference. Only after exhausting that process could claimants go to court against the trust, subject to a limit of $500,000 per claim, with punitive damages and pre-judgment interest barred.

After an extensive campaign to give notice of the pending settlement to potential class members, the District Court allowed groups of objectors, including petitioners here, to intervene. After an 8-day fairness hearing, the District Court certified the class and approved the settlement as "fair, adequate, and reasonable," under Rule 23(e). Satisfied that the requirements of Rule 23(a) *were* met, the District Court certified the class under Rule 23(b)(1)(B), citing the risk that Fibreboard might lose or fare poorly on appeal of the coverage case or lose the assignment-settlement dispute, leaving it without funds to pay all claims. *Id*. at 526. The "allowance of individual adjudications by class members," the District Court concluded, "would have destroyed the opportunity to compromise the insurance coverage dispute by creating the settlement fund, and would have exposed the class members to the very risks that the settlement addresses." *Id*. at 527. In response to intervenors' objections that the absence of a "limited fund" precluded certification under Rule 23(b)(1)(B), the District Court ruled that although the subdivision is not so restricted, if it were, this case would qualify. It found both the "disputed insurance asset liquidated by the $ 1.535 billion Global Settlement," and, alternatively, "the sum of the value of Fibreboard plus the value of its insurance coverage," as measured by the insurance funds' settlement value, to be relevant "limited funds."

On appeal, the Fifth Circuit affirmed both as to class certification and adequacy of settlement. Agreeing with the District Court's application of Rule 23(a), the Court of Appeals found that there was commonality in class members' shared interest in securing and equitably distributing maximum possible settlement funds, and that the representative plaintiffs were sufficiently typical both in sharing that interest and in basing their claims on the same legal and remedial theories that absent class members might raise. The Fifth Circuit also thought that there were no conflicts of interest sufficiently serious to undermine the adequacy of class counsel's representation. As to Rule 23(b)(1)(B), the Court approved the class certification on a "limited fund" rationale based on the threat to "the ability of other members of the class to receive full payment for their injuries from Fibreboard's limited assets." The Court of Appeals cited expert testimony that Fibreboard faced enormous potential liabilities and defense costs that would likely equal or exceed the amount of damages paid out, and concluded that even combining Fibreboard's value of some $235 million with the [$1.5 billion provided by the settlement trust] the company would be unable to pay all valid claims against it within five to nine years.

We granted certiorari and now reverse.

II.

The nub of this case is the certification of the class under Rule 23(b)(1)(B) on a limited fund rationale.

Although representative suits have been recognized in various forms since the earliest days of English law, class actions as we recognize them today developed as an exception to the formal rigidity of the necessary parties rule in equity, as well as from the bill of peace, an equitable device for combining multiple suits, see Z. Chafee, Some Problems of Equity 161–167, 200–203 (1950). The necessary parties rule in equity mandated that "all persons materially interested, either as plaintiffs or defendants in the subject matter of the bill ought to be made parties to the suit, however numerous they may be." *West v. Randall*, 29 F. Cas. 718, 721 (No. 17,424) (CC RI) (1820) (Story, J.). But because that rule would at times unfairly deny recovery to the party before the court, equity developed exceptions, among them one to cover situations "where the parties are very numerous, and the court perceives, that it will be almost impossible to bring them all before the court; or where the question is of general interest, and a few may sue for the benefit of the whole; or where the parties form a part of a voluntary association for public or private purposes, and may be fairly supposed to represent the rights and interests of the whole...." *Id.* at 722; see J. Story, Commentaries on Equity Pleadings § 97 (J. Gould 10th rev. ed. 1892); F. Calvert, A Treatise upon the Law Respecting Parties to Suits in Equity 17–29 (1837) (hereinafter Calvert, Parties to Suits in Equity). From these roots, modern class action practice emerged in the 1966 revision of Rule 23. In drafting Rule 23(b), the Advisory Committee sought to catalogue in "functional" terms "those recurrent life patterns which call for mass litigation through representative parties." Kaplan, *A Prefatory Note*, 10 B.C. Ind. & Com. L. Rev. 497 (1969).

Rule 23(b)(1)(B) speaks from "a vantage point within the class, [from which the Advisory Committee] spied out situations where lawsuits conducted with individual members of the class would have the practical if not technical effect of concluding the interests of the other members as well, or of impairing the ability of the others to protect their own interests." Kaplan, *Continuing Work of the Civil Committee: 1966 Amendments of the Federal Rules of Civil Procedure (I)*, 81 Harv. L. Rev. 356, 388 (1967) (hereinafter Kaplan, *Continuing Work*). Thus, the subdivision (read with subdivision (c)(2)) provides for certification of a class whose members have no right to withdraw, when "the prosecution of separate actions ... would create a risk" of "adjudications with respect to individual members of the class which would as a practical matter be dispositive of the interests of the other members not parties to the adjudications or substantially impair or impede their ability to protect their interests." Fed. Rule Civ. Proc. 23(b)(1)(B).

One recurring type of such suits was the limited fund class action, aggregating "claims ... made by numerous persons against a fund insufficient to satisfy all claims." Adv. Comm. Notes 697; cf. Newberg § 4.09, at 4-33 ("Classic" limited fund class actions "include claimants to trust assets, a bank account, insurance proceeds, company assets in a liquidation sale, proceeds of a ship sale in a maritime accident suit, and others").

The cases forming this pedigree of the limited fund class action as understood by the drafters of Rule 23 have a number of common characteristics, despite the variety of circumstances from which they arose. The points of resemblance are not necessarily the points of contention resolved in the particular cases, but they show what the Advisory Committee must have assumed would be at least a sufficient set of conditions to justify binding absent members of a class under Rule 23(b)(1)(B), from which no one has the right to secede.

The first and most distinctive characteristic is that the totals of the aggregated liquidated claims and the fund available for satisfying them, set definitely at their maximums, demonstrate the inadequacy of the fund to pay all the claims. The concept driving this type of suit was insufficiency, which alone justified the limit on an early feast to avoid a later famine. The equity of the limitation is its necessity.

Second, the whole of the inadequate fund was to be devoted to the overwhelming claims. See, *e.g.*, *Dickinson*, 197 F.2d at 979–980 (rejecting a challenge by holder of funds to the court's disposition of the entire fund); see also *United States* v. *Butterworth-Judson Corp.*, 269 U.S. 504, 513, 70 L. Ed. 380, 46 S. Ct. 179 (1926) ("Here, the fund being less than the debts, the creditors are entitled to have all of it distributed among them according to their rights and priorities"). It went without saying that the defendant or estate or constructive trustee with the inadequate assets had no opportunity to benefit himself or claimants of lower priority by holding back on the amount distributed to the class. The limited fund cases thus ensured that the class as a whole was given the best deal; they did not give a defendant a better deal than *seriatim* litigation would have produced.

Third, the claimants identified by a common theory of recovery were treated equitably among themselves. The cases assume that the class will comprise everyone who might state a claim on a single or repeated set of facts, invoking a common theory of recovery, to be satisfied from the limited fund as the source of payment. Once the represented classes were so identified, there was no question of omitting anyone whose claim shared the common theory of liability and would contribute to the calculated shortfall of recovery. Once all similar claims were brought directly or by representation before the court, these antecedents of the mandatory class action presented straightforward models of equitable treatment, with the simple equity of a pro rata distribution providing the required fairness.

In sum, mandatory class treatment through representative actions on a limited fund theory was justified with reference to a "fund" with a definitely ascertained limit, all of which would be distributed to satisfy all those with liquidated claims based on a common theory of liability, by an equitable, pro rata distribution.

III.

The Advisory Committee, and presumably the Congress in approving subdivision (b)(1)(B), must have assumed that an action with these characteristics would satisfy the limited fund rationale cognizable under that subdivision. The question remains how far the same characteristics are necessary for limited fund treatment. While we cannot settle all the details of a subdivision (b)(1)(B) limited fund here (and so cannot decide the ultimate question whether settlements of multitudes of related tort actions are amenable to mandatory class treatment), there are good reasons to treat these characteristics as presumptively necessary, and not merely sufficient, to satisfy the limited fund rationale for a mandatory action. At the least, the burden of justification rests on the proponent of any departure from the traditional norm.

It is true, of course, that the text of Rule 23(b)(1)(B) is on its face open to a more lenient limited fund concept, just as it covers more historical antecedents than the limited fund. But the greater the leniency in departing from the historical limited fund model, the greater the likelihood of abuse in ways that will be apparent when we apply the limited fund criteria to the case before us. The prudent course, therefore, is to presume that when subdivision (b)(1)(B) was devised to cover limited fund actions, the object was to stay close to the historical model. As will be seen, this limiting construction finds support in the Advisory Committee's expressions of understanding, minimizes potential conflict with the Rules Enabling Act, and avoids serious constitutional concerns raised by the mandatory class resolution of individual legal claims, especially where a case seeks to resolve future liability in a settlement-only action.

To begin with, the Advisory Committee looked cautiously at the potential for creativity under Rule 23(b)(1)(B), at least in comparison with Rule 23(b)(3). Although the committee crafted all three subdivision of the Rule in general, practical terms, without the formalism that had bedeviled the original Rule 23, the Committee was consciously retrospective with intent to codify pre-Rule categories under Rule 23(b)(1), not forward-looking as it was in anticipating innovations under Rule 23(b)(3).

Consistent with its backward look under subdivision (b)(1), as commentators have pointed out, it is clear that the Advisory Committee did not contemplate that the mandatory class action codified in subdivision (b)(1)(B) would be used to aggregate unliquidated tort claims on a limited fund rationale. While the Advisory Committee focused much attention on the amenability of Rule 23(b)(3) to such cases, the Committee's debates are silent about resolving tort claims under a mandatory limited fund rationale *under* Rule 23(b)(1)(B). It is simply implausible that the Advisory Committee, so concerned about the potential difficulties posed by dealing with mass tort cases under Rule 23(b)(3), with its provisions for notice and the right to opt out, see Rule 23(c)(2), would have uncritically assumed that mandatory versions of such class actions, lacking such protections, could be certified under Rule 23(b)(1)(B). We do not, it is true, decide the ultimate question whether Rule 23(b)(1)(B) may ever be used to aggregate individual tort claims, but we do recognize that the Committee would have thought such an application of the Rule surprising, and take this as a good reason to limit any surprise by presuming that the Rule's historical antecedents identify requirements.

The inherent tension between representative suits and the day-in-court ideal is only magnified if applied to damages claims gathered in a mandatory class. Unlike Rule 23(b)(3) class members, objectors to the collectivism of a mandatory subdivision (b)(1)(B) action have no inherent right to abstain. The legal rights of absent class members (which in a class like this one would include claimants who by definition may be unidentifiable when the class is certified) are resolved regardless either of their consent, or, in a class with objectors, their express wish to the contrary. And in settlement-only class actions the procedural protections built into the Rule to protect the rights of absent class members during litigation are never invoked in an adversarial setting.

IV

The record on which the District Court rested its certification of the class for the purpose of the global settlement did not support the essential premises of mandatory limited fund actions. It failed to demonstrate that the fund was limited except by the agreement of the parties, and it showed exclusions from the class and allocations of assets at odds with the concept of limited fund treatment and the structural protections of Rule 23(a).

A.

The defect of certification going to the most characteristic feature of a limited fund action was the uncritical adoption by both the District Court and the Court of Appeals of figures agreed upon by the parties in defining the limits of the fund and demonstrating its inadequacy. When a district court, as here, certifies for class action settlement only, the moment of certification requires "heightened attention," to the justifications for binding the class members. This is so because certification of a mandatory settlement class, however provisional technically, effectively concludes the proceeding save for the final fairness hearing.

We have already alluded to the difficulties facing limited fund treatment of huge numbers of actions for unliquidated damages arising from mass torts, the first such hurdle being a computation of the total claims. It is simply not a matter of adding up the liquidated amounts, as in the models of limited fund actions. Although we might assume *arguendo* that prior judicial experience with asbestos claims would allow a court to make a sufficiently reliable determination of the probable total, the District Court here apparently thought otherwise, concluding that "there is no way to predict Fibreboard's future asbestos liability with any certainty." 162 F.R.D. at 528. Nothing turns on this conclusion, however, since there was no adequate demonstration of the second element required for limited fund treatment, the upper limit of the fund itself, without which no showing of insufficiency is possible.

In Practice

"Over the objection of several commentators, courts have generally refused to use the limited fund class action unless it is virtually certain that the assets of the defendant and his insurance coverage will prove inadequate to satisfy the claims of all those the mass tort allegedly injured."

Roger H. Trangsrud, *Joinder Alternatives in Mass Tort Litigation*, 70 Cornell L. Rev. 779, 784 (1985).

The "fund" in this case comprised both the general assets of Fibreboard and the insurance assets provided by the two policies. As to Fibreboard's assets exclusive of the contested insurance, the District Court and the Fifth Circuit concluded that Fibreboard had a then-current sale value of $235 million that could be devoted to the limited fund. While that estimate may have been conservative, at least the District Court heard evidence and made an independent finding at some point in the proceedings. The same, however, cannot be said for the value of the disputed insurance.

The insurance assets would obviously be "limited" in the traditional sense if the total of demonstrable claims would render the insurers insolvent, or if the policies provided aggregate limits falling short of that total; calculation might be difficult, but the way to demonstrate the limit would be clear. Neither possibility is presented in this case, however. Instead, any limit of the insurance asset here had to be a product of potentially unlimited policy coverage discounted by the risk that Fibreboard would ultimately lose the coverage dispute litigation. This sense of limit as a value discounted by risk is of course a step removed from the historical model, but even on the assumption that it would suffice for limited fund treatment, there was no adequate finding of fact to support its application here. Instead of undertaking an independent evaluation of potential insurance funds, the District Court (and, later, the Court of Appeals), simply accepted the [$1.5 billion] Settlement Agreement figure as representing the maximum amount the insurance companies could be required to pay tort victims.

Settlement value is not always acceptable, however. One may take a settlement amount as good evidence of the maximum available if one can assume that parties of equal knowledge and negotiating skill agreed upon the figure through arms-length bargaining, unhindered by any considerations tugging against the interests of the parties ostensibly represented in the negotiation. But no such assumption may be indulged in this case, or probably in any class action settlement with the potential for gigantic fees. In this case, certainly, any assumption that plaintiffs' counsel could be of a mind to do their simple best in bargaining for the benefit of the settlement class is patently at odds with the fact that at least some of the same lawyers representing plaintiffs and the class had also negotiated the separate settlement of 45,000 pending claims, 90 F.3d at 969–970, 971, the full payment of which was contingent on a successful global settlement agreement or the successful resolution of the insurance coverage dispute. Class counsel thus had great incentive to reach any agreement in the global settlement negotiations that they thought might survive a Rule 23(e) fairness hearing, rather than the best possible arrangement for the substantially unidentified global settlement class. The resulting incentive to favor the known plaintiffs in the earlier settlement was, indeed, an egregious example of the conflict noted in *Amchem* resulting from divergent interests of the presently injured and future claimants.

We do not, of course, know exactly what an independent valuation of the limit of the insurance assets would have shown. It might have revealed that even on the assumption that Fibreboard's coverage claim was sound, there would be insufficient assets to pay claims, considered with reference to their probable timing; if Fibreboard's own assets would not have been enough to pay the insurance shortfall plus any claims in excess of policy limits, the projected insolvency of the insurers and Fibreboard would have indicated a truly limited fund. (Nothing in the record, however, suggests that this would have been a supportable finding.) Or an independent valuation might have revealed assets of insufficient value to pay all projected claims if the assets were discounted by the prospects that the insurers would win the coverage cases. Or the Court's independent valuation might have shown, discount or no discount, the probability of enough assets to pay all projected claims, precluding certification of any mandatory class on a limited fund rationale. Throughout this litigation the courts have accepted the assumption that the third possibility was out of the question, and they may have been right. But objecting and unidentified class members alike are entitled to have the issue settled by specific evidentiary findings independent of the agreement of defendants and conflicted class counsel.

B.

The explanation of need for independent determination of the fund has necessarily anticipated our application of the requirement of equity among members of the class. There are two issues, the inclusiveness of the class and the fairness of distributions to those within it. On each, this certification for settlement fell short.

The definition of the class excludes myriad claimants with causes of action, or foreseeable causes of action, arising from exposure to Fibreboard asbestos. While the class includes those with present claims never filed, present claims withdrawn without prejudice, and future claimants, it fails to include those who had previously settled with Fibreboard while retaining the right to sue again "upon development of an asbestos related malignancy," plaintiffs with claims pending against Fibreboard at the time of the initial announcement of the Global Settlement Agreement, and the plaintiffs in the "inventory" claims settled as a supposedly necessary step in reaching the global settlement, see 90 F.3d at 971. The number of those outside the class who settled with a reservation of rights may be uncertain, but there is no such uncertainty about the significance of the settlement's exclusion of the 45,000 inventory plaintiffs and the plaintiffs in the unsettled present cases, estimated by the Guardian Ad Litem at more than 53,000 as of August 27, 1993. It is a fair question how far a natural class may be depleted by prior dispositions of claims and still qualify as a mandatory limited fund class, but there can be no question that such a mandatory settlement class will not qualify when in the very negotiations aimed at a class settlement, class counsel agree to exclude what could turn out to be as much as a third of the claimants that negotiators thought might eventually be involved, a substantial number of whom class counsel represent.

Might such class exclusions be forgiven if it were shown that the class members with present claims and the outsiders ended up with comparable benefits? The question is academic here. On the record before us, we cannot speculate on how the unsettled claims would fare if the Global Settlement were approved. As for the settled inventory claims, their plaintiffs appeared to have obtained better terms than the class members. They received an immediate payment of 50 percent of a settlement higher than the historical average, and would get the remainder if the global settlement were sustained (or the coverage litigation resolved, as it turned out to be); the class members, by contrast, would be assured of a 3-year payout for claims settled, whereas the unsettled faced a prospect of mediation followed by arbitration as prior conditions of instituting suit, which would even then be subject to a recovery limit, a slower payout and the limitations of the trust's spendthrift protection.

On the second element of equity within the class, the fairness of the distribution of the fund among class members, the settlement certification is likewise deficient. Fair treatment in the older cases was characteristically assured by straightforward pro rata distribution of the limited fund. While equity in such a simple sense is unattainable in a settlement covering present claims not specifically proven and claims not even due to arise, if at all, until some future time, at the least such a settlement must seek equity by providing for procedures to resolve the difficult issues of treating such differently situated claimants with fairness as among themselves.

First, it is obvious after *Amchem* that a class divided between holders of present and future claims (some of the latter involving no physical injury and to claimants not yet born) requires division into homogeneous subclasses under Rule 23(c)(4)(B), with separate representation to eliminate conflicting interests of counsel.

Second, the class included those exposed to Fibreboard's asbestos products both before and after 1959. The date is significant, for that year saw the expiration of Fibreboard's insurance policy with Continental, the one which provided the bulk of the insurance funds for the settlement. Pre-1959 claimants accordingly had more valuable claims than post-1959 claimants, see 90 F.3d at 1012–1013 (Smith, J., dissenting), the consequence being a second instance of disparate interests within the certified class. While at some point there must be an end to reclassification with separate counsel, these two instances of conflict are well within the requirement of structural protection recognized in *Amchem*.

C.

A third contested feature of this settlement certification that departs markedly from the limited fund antecedents is the ultimate provision for a fund smaller than the assets understood by the Court of Appeals to be available for payment of the mandatory class members' claims; most notably, Fibreboard was allowed to retain virtually its entire net worth. Given our treatment of the two preceding deficiencies of the certification, there is of course no need to decide whether this feature of the agreement would alone be fatal to the Global Settlement Agreement. To ignore it entirely, however, would be so misleading that we have decided simply to identify the issue it raises, without purporting to resolve it at this time.

Fibreboard listed its supposed entire net worth as a component of the total (and allegedly inadequate) assets available for claimants, but subsequently retained all but $500,000 of that equity for itself. On the face of it, the arrangement seems irreconcilable with the justification of necessity in denying any opportunity for withdrawal of class members whose jury trial rights will be compromised, whose damages will be capped, and whose payments will be delayed. With Fibreboard retaining nearly all its net worth, it hardly appears that such a regime is the best that can be provided for class members. Given the nature of a limited fund and the need to apply its criteria at the certification stage, it is not enough for a District Court to say that it "need not ensure that a defendant designate a particular source of its assets to satisfy the class' claims; [but only that] the amount recovered by the class [be] fair." 162 F.R.D. at 527.

V.

In sum, the applicability of Rule 23(b)(1)(B) to a fund and plan purporting to liquidate actual and potential tort claims is subject to question, and its purported application in this case was in any event improper. The Advisory Committee did not envision mandatory class actions in cases like this one, and both the Rules Enabling Act and the policy of avoiding serious constitutional issues counsel against leniency in recognizing mandatory limited fund actions in circumstances markedly different from the traditional paradigm. Assuming arguendo that a mandatory, limited fund rationale could under some circumstances be applied to a settlement class of tort claimants, it would be essential that the fund be shown to be limited independently of the agreement of the parties to the action, and equally essential under Rule 23(a) and (b)(1)(B) that the class include all those with claims unsatisfied at the time of the settlement negotiations, with intraclass conflicts addressed by recognizing independently represented subclasses. In this case, the limit of the fund was determined by treating the settlement agreement as dispositive, an error magnified by the representation of class members by counsel also representing excluded plaintiffs, whose settlements would be funded fully upon settlement of the class action on any terms that could survive final fairness review. Those separate settlements, together with other exclusions from the claimant class, precluded adequate structural protection by subclass treatment, which was not even afforded to the conflicting elements within the class as certified.

The judgment of the Court of Appeals, accordingly, is reversed, and the case is remanded for further proceedings consistent with this opinion.

It is so ordered.

Notes and Problems

1. According to the Supreme Court in *Ortiz*, what are the three traditional character traits of a true limited class scenario? How were these three traits absent from the proposed settlement and certification in *Ortiz*? Why is the absence of these factors important?

2. Was the settlement reached in *Ortiz* necessarily a bad deal for the class members? Would they actually be better off instead of reaping the positives from the proposed settlement to stand in a rather long queue each waiting for their own turn to litigate their personal injury claims against the defendants? Does the court offer any assurance that there will be funds available at that point to satisfy any class member claims? What happens if, on appeal to the California Supreme Court, the pro-defendant insurance coverage opinions are reversed and the insurance coverage for the class members' claims is extinguished? Given that uncertainty, should the Supreme Court have affirmed the certification and settlement instead of reading Rule 23(b)(1)(B) in a rather narrow and ancient manner? Justices Breyer and Stevens dissented from the majority opinion in *Ortiz*, arguing that "Rule 23 itself does not require modern courts to trace every contour of ancient case law with literal exactness" and that "[t]here is no doubt that the settlement made far more money available to satisfy asbestos claims than was likely to occur in its absence."

3. A few years before *Ortiz*, beginning with the Fifth Circuit's decision in *Castano* (covered later in this Chapter), federal courts had begun looking askance at the certification

of nationwide personal injury mass tort claims under Rule 23(b)(3). One way to view the attempted Rule 23(b)(1)(B) certification in *Ortiz* was as a creative attempt by class counsel to avoid the problems with certification under the more obvious Rule 23(b)(3) track. Beyond this, why else were the parties all interested in certifying the *Ortiz* case under Rule 23(b)(1) rather than (b)(3)? What did defendants seek so desperately?

4. The Court in *Ortiz* makes reference to another U.S. Supreme Court decision involving the certification of an asbestos class action—*Amchem Products, Inc v. Windsor*, 521 U.S. 591 (1997), decided just two years before. *Amchem* was a personal injury case involving class members exposed to asbestos. The parties agreed to a settlement and presented the case to the court for both certification (under Rule 23(b)(3)) and approval of the settlement (under Rule 23(e)) at the same time. The district court's decision to certify the enormous case under Rule 23(b)(3) was seen as necessary due to a litigation crisis involving asbestos claims. The Third Circuit, in affirming the certification, held that special more lenient certification criteria should be applied to the case because the certification decision came at the same time as the settlement of the case. Yet the Supreme Court, for the most part, rejected this idea. The Court did agree that issues of "manageability" of such a case (a Rule 23(b)(3) criteria for certification) might be moot—because there would be no trial if the case were settling. But otherwise the Court held that the normal certification standards apply with *at least* as much vigor: "But other specifications of the rule—those designed to protect absentees by blocking unwarranted or overbroad class definitions—demand undiluted, even heightened, attention in the settlement context. Such attention is of vital importance, for a court asked to certify a settlement class will lack the opportunity, present when a case is litigated, to adjust the class, informed by the proceedings as they unfold." After *Amchem*, therefore, the mere fact that the certification decision may happen at the same time as a settlement has been reached does not absolve the district courts of their duties to carefully apply the same rigorous analysis of Rule 23(a)–(b)'s criteria. *See, e.g., Walker v. Liggett Group*, 175 F.R.D. 226 (S.D. W. Va. 1997) ("*Amchem* decimated the notion of some circuits that Rule 23 requisites were relaxed in the settlement context.").

5. *Problem.* A statewide lottery offers a $10 million pot to the person holding the ticket matching all 6 numbers correctly. According to the lottery officials, only one winning ticket was issued with those numbers. But through some technical computer glitch, lottery ticket counters had accidently issued 1,000 of the same, identical winning tickets to various lottery ticket buyers throughout the state. The way the lottery is run in that state, with each lottery, the commission empties its coffers of all sums remaining after the winning tickets are redeemed to various state educational programs. This means that the lottery commission does not hold additional funds beyond those held for disbursement of any current lottery drawing. As a result of the computer glitch, the lottery commission faces possible claims of not $10 million but $10 billion. It is true that the lottery commission is a state agency, but the state does not have an extra $10 billion in its current budget year set aside to cover lottery glitches. If a winning ticket holder files a class action under Rule 23(b)(1)(B), should it be certified?

In re Simon II Litigation

407 F.3d 125 (2d Cir. 2005)

OAKES, J.,

Defendant-appellant tobacco companies appeal from the order of the United States District Court for the Eastern District of New York, Jack B. Weinstein, Judge, which certified a nationwide non-opt-out class of smokers seeking only punitive damages under state law for defendants' alleged fraudulent denial and concealment of the health risks posed by cigarettes. Having granted permission to appeal pursuant to Federal Rule of Civil Procedure 23(f), we must decide whether the district court properly certified this class under Rule 23(b)(1)(B).

Defendant-appellants challenge the propriety of certifying this action as a limited fund class action pursuant to a "limited punishment" theory. The theory postulates that a constitutional limit on the total punitive damages that may be imposed for a course of fraudulent conduct effectively limits the total fund available for punitive awards.

We hold that the order certifying this punitive damages class must be vacated because there is no evidence by which the district court could ascertain the limits of either the fund or the aggregate value of punitive claims against it, such that the postulated fund could be deemed inadequate to pay all legitimate claims, and thus plaintiffs have failed to satisfy one of the presumptively necessary conditions for limited fund treatment under *Ortiz v. Fibreboard Corp.*, 527 U.S. 815 (1999).

Based on our holding, we vacate the district court's certification order and remand for further proceedings.

I.

FACTS AND PROCEDURAL HISTORY

The district court certified the class proposed by the Third Amended Consolidated Class Action Complaint and an accompanying motion for class certification, both filed on July 26, 2002. The district court's September 19, 2002, order and the supplemental memorandum and order of October 22, 2002, are published together at *In re Simon II Litigation*, 211 F.R.D. 86, 96, 101 (E.D.N.Y. 2002), and will be referred to collectively as the "Certification Order."

Plaintiffs sought certification to determine defendants' fraudulent course of conduct and total punitive damages liability to a class consisting of those who suffered from, or had died from, diseases caused by smoking. Plaintiffs did not seek a class-wide determination or allocation of compensatory damages or seek certification of subclasses. The certification followed extensive briefing and argument, not to mention numerous iterations of both the complaint and the proposed class.

[handwritten margin note: P1f claim]

An abbreviated history of the course of the litigation is outlined below.

The industry conspiracy prompting this litigation is described briefly in the allegations of the Third Amended Complaint and in considerable detail in the Certification Order. See 211 F.R.D. at 114–26. We will simply excerpt a relevant portion of the district court's description of the allegations:

> Plaintiffs allege, and can provide supporting evidence, that, beginning with a clandestine meeting in December 1953 at the Plaza Hotel in New York City among the presidents of Philip Morris, R.J. Reynolds, American Tobacco, Brown & Williamson, Lorillard and U.S. Tobacco, tobacco companies embarked on a systematic, half-century long scheme to ... : (a) stop competing with each other in making or developing less harmful cigarettes; (b) continue knowingly and willfully to engage in misrepresentations and deceptive acts by, among other things, denying knowledge that cigarettes caused disease and death and agreeing not to disseminate harmful information showing the destructive effects of nicotine and tobacco consumption; (c) shut down research efforts and suppress medical in-

[handwritten margin note: Background of P1f claim]

formation that appeared to be adverse to the Tobacco Companies' position that tobacco was not harmful; (d) not compete with respect to making any claims relating to the relative health-superiority of specific tobacco products; and (e) to confuse the public about, and otherwise distort, whatever accurate information about the harmful effects of their products became known despite their "[efforts to conceal such information]."

On July 26, 2002, Plaintiffs filed the Third Amended Complaint and an accompanying amended and renewed motion for class certification, which precipitated the Certification Order at issue here. Plaintiffs sought certification of a single class of smokers suffering from various diseases which the medical community attributes to smoking, including 20-pack-year smokers with lung cancer, for the sole purpose of determining defendants' total liability for punitive damages.

Upon considering the class proposed by plaintiffs' Third Amended Complaint and the motion for certification, the district court certified a punitive damages non-opt-out class pursuant to Rule 23(b)(1)(B). The class definition included current and former smokers of defendants' cigarettes who are U.S. residents, or who resided in the U.S. at time of death, and were first diagnosed between April 9, 1993, and the date of dissemination of class notice, with one or more of the following diseases: lung cancer, laryngeal cancer, lip cancer, tongue cancer, mouth cancer, esophageal cancer, kidney cancer, pancreatic cancer, bladder cancer, ischemic heart disease, cerebrovascular heart disease, aortic aneurysm, peripheral vascular disease, emphysema, chronic bronchitis, or chronic obstructive pulmonary disease.

The district court determined that the class action would proceed in three stages. In the first stage, a jury would make "a class-wide determination of liability and estimated total value of national undifferentiated compensatory harm to all members of the class." *Id.* at 100. The sum of compensatory harm would "not be awarded but will serve as a predicate in determining non-opt-out class punitive damages." *Id.* The same jury would determine compensatory awards, if any, for individual class representatives, although the class itself did not seek compensatory damages. In the second stage, the same jury would determine whether defendants engaged in conduct that warrants punitive damages. *Id.* In the third stage, the same jury would determine the amount of punitive damages for the class and decide how to allocate damages on a disease-by-disease basis. The court would then distribute sums to the class on a pro-rata basis by disease to class members who submit appropriate proof. The order specified that the jury would apply New York law according to conflicts of laws principles, and reiterated that the court was not presented with and did not rule upon a compensatory class.

II.
DISCUSSION

We note that this case raises issues of first impression insofar as this Circuit has never squarely passed on the validity of certifying a mandatory, stand-alone punitive damages class on the proposed "limited punishment" theory.

Prerequisites for a Class Action under Rule 23(a)

The district court found that the proposed class satisfied the Rule 23(a) requirements of numerosity, commonality, typicality, and adequacy of representation. Appellants do not contest these particular findings. Rather, they direct their arguments to the district court's conclusion that this class action could be maintained under Rule 23(b)(1)(B).

Standards for Maintaining a Class Action under Rule 23(b)(1)

In addition to showing that the class action prerequisites set out in Rule 23(a) have been met, a plaintiff must show that a class action is maintainable under either Rule 23(b)(1), (2) or (3).

Plaintiffs in this case sought certification under Rule 23(b)(1)(B),[6] for which the relevant inquiry is whether separate actions by individual members of the class create a risk that individual adjudications would as a practical matter dispose of other class members' interests in punitive damages or substantially impair or impede their ability to protect their interests.

Suits under Rule 23(b)(1) are often referred to as "mandatory" class actions because they are not subject to the Rule 23(c) provision for notice to absent class members or the opportunity for potential class members to opt out of membership as a matter of right. See *Ortiz v. Fibreboard Corp.*, 527 U.S. 815, 833 n. 13, 144 L. Ed. 2d 715, 119 S. Ct. 2295 (1999). The Advisory Committee's Note for the 1966 Amendment of Rule 23 explains that "the vice of an individual action would lie in the fact that the other members of the class, thus practically concluded, would have had no representation in the lawsuit." The Committee Note cites by way of illustration several suits pre-dating the amendment that had warranted class treatment, including a suit by policyholders against a fraternal benefit association to attack the financial reorganization of the society, a suit by shareholders to compel declaration of a dividend or to compel proper recognition and handling of redemption and preemption rights, and an action charging a breach of trust by an indenture trustee or fiduciary, affecting a class of security holders or beneficiaries and requiring an accounting or other measure to restore the subject of the trust.

Regarding the subset of these cases involving a limited fund, the Committee's Note remarks:

> In various situations an adjudication as to one or more members of the class will necessarily or probably have an adverse practical effect on the interests of other members who should therefore be represented in the lawsuit. This is plainly the case when claims are made by numerous persons against a fund insufficient to satisfy all claims. A class action by or against representative members to settle the validity of the claims as a whole, or in groups, followed by separate proof of the amount of each valid claim and proportionate distribution of the fund, meets the problem.

Limited Fund Class Action Based on the "Limited Punishment" Theory.

The district court, in certifying the punitive damages class under Rule 23(b)(1)(B), cited recent scholarship and court decisions that "have concluded that the theory of limited punishment supports a punitive damages class action." 211 F.R.D. at 184. "Under this theory," the district court stated, "the limited fund involved would be the constitutional cap on punitive damages, set forth in *BMW v. Gore* [517 U.S. 559, 134 L. Ed. 2d 809, 116 S. Ct. 1589 (1996)] and related cases."

The premise for this theory is that there is a constitutional due process limitation on the total amount of punitive damages that may be assessed against a defendant for the same offending conduct. Whether the limitation operates to prejudice the respective

---

6. Plaintiffs did not move for certification under Rule 23(b)(1)(A), although the Third Amended Complaint invokes Clause (A) and asserts that separate punitive awards "would establish incompatible standards of conduct for Defendants." We express no opinion regarding whether the circumstances here could satisfy Clause (A)'s requirements. "Courts are still struggling to develop guidelines governing the scope of Rule 23(b)(1)(A)." Herbert B. Newberg & Alba Conte, 2 *Newberg on Class Actions* § 4:4 (4th ed. 2005).

parties, it seems, turns on two contrary assumptions. For the potential plaintiff, piecemeal individual actions or successive class actions for punitive damages would operate to his disadvantage if punitive awards in earlier-filed suits subtract from the constitutional total and thereby reduce or preclude punitive damages for future claimants. This proposition assumes that courts identify and successfully enforce the postulated total limit, and that plaintiffs have an interest in a ratable portion of the permissible damages. For defendants, piecemeal individual or successive class actions would pose a threat of excessive punishment in violation of their due process rights if successive juries assess awards that exceed the limit of what is necessary for deterrence and retribution. This proposition, to the contrary, assumes that early suits exhaust or exceed the constitutional limit and successive trial or appellate courts fail to enforce it by either reducing or barring awards. It is not clear whether the theory supposes that successive individual awards, which considered alone may be constitutionally permissible if they are reasonable and proportionate to the given plaintiff's harm and bear a sufficient nexus to that harm, may reach a point where the goals of punitive damages have been served, and successive victims of the same tortious course of conduct by the tortfeasor should be unable to recover punitive damages.

The notion of a constitutional cap on total allowable aggregate punitive damages awards, or on the number of times punitive awards can be made, has never been squarely articulated by the Supreme Court, but is said to derive from its precedents regarding punitive damages. In the Supreme Court's most recent punitive damages decision, *State Farm Mut. Auto. Ins. Co. v. Campbell*, 538 U.S. 408, 155 L. Ed. 2d 585, 123 S. Ct. 1513 (2003), Justice Kennedy, writing for the majority, reiterated what the Court's precedents had made clear: "While States possess discretion over the imposition of punitive damages, it is well established that there are procedural and substantive constitutional limitations on these awards. The Due Process Clause of the Fourteenth Amendment prohibits the imposition of grossly excessive or arbitrary punishments on a tortfeasor." *Id.* at 416 The Court pointed to concerns voiced in earlier cases: "To the extent an award is grossly excessive, it furthers no legitimate purpose and constitutes an arbitrary deprivation of property." *State Farm*, 538 U.S. at 417 (quoting Justice O'Connor's dissent in *Haslip*, 499 U.S. at 42 (1991)).

Despite the long-recognized possibility that defendants may be subjected to large aggregate sums of punitive damages if large numbers of victims succeed in their individual punitive damages claims, see, e.g., *Roginsky v. Richardson-Merrell, Inc.*, 378 F.2d 832, 839 (2d Cir. 1967) (Friendly, J.) ("We have the gravest difficulty in perceiving how claims for punitive damages in such a multiplicity of actions throughout the nation can be so administered as to avoid overkill."), the United States Supreme Court has not addressed whether successive individual or class action punitive awards, each passing constitutional muster under the relevant precedents, could reach a level beyond which punitive damages may no longer be awarded.

The Traditional "Limited Fund" Class Action Under Ortiz v. Fibreboard Corp.

This brings us to appellants' chief argument — that class certification under Rule 23(b)(1)(B) is precluded by the Supreme Court's decision in *Ortiz v. Fibreboard Corp.*, 527 U.S. 815, because the proposed class plaintiffs have failed to demonstrate what the Supreme Court identified as the "presumptively necessary" conditions for certification in limited fund cases. Although *Ortiz* considered a set of circumstances quite unlike those in the instant case when it reviewed the certification of a Rule 23(b)(1)(B) mandatory settlement class on a limited fund theory, it identified, in the historical antecedents to Rule 23, the characteristic conditions that justified binding absent class members. It summarized those characteristics as "a 'fund' with a definitely ascertained limit, all of which would be distributed to satisfy all those with liquidated claims based on a common theory of liability, by an equitable, pro rata distribution." Given the presumptive necessity of these characteristics, "the burden of justification rests on the proponent of any departure from the traditional norm."

While neither the Rule itself, nor the Advisory Notes accompanying it, purports to delineate the outer limits of the Rule's application in the particular subset of "limited fund" cases, the Supreme Court in *Ortiz* has read the "limited fund" case as being moored to the Rule's historical antecedents, describing the classic actions as involving, for instance, "claimants to trust assets, a bank account, insurance proceeds, company assets in a liquidation sale, proceeds of a ship sale in a maritime accident suit, and others." *Id.* at 834 (quoting Herbert B. Newberg & Alba Conte, 1 *Newberg on Class Actions* § 4.09, at 4-33 (3d ed. 1992)). In these cases, "equity required absent parties to be represented, joinder being impractical, where individual claims to be satisfied from the one asset would, as a practical matter, prejudice the rights of absent claimants against a fund inadequate to pay them all." *Id.* at 836.

The proposed fund in this case, the constitutional "cap" on punitive damages for the given class's claims, is a theoretical one, unlike any of those in the cases cited in Ortiz, where the fund was either an existing res or the total of defendants' assets available to satisfy claims. The fund here is—in essence—postulated, and for that reason it is not easily susceptible to proof, definition, or even estimation, by any precise figure. It is therefore fundamentally unlike the classic limited funds of the historical antecedents of Rule 23.

Not only is the upper limit of the proposed fund difficult to ascertain, but the record in this case does not evince a likelihood that any given number of punitive awards to individual claimants would be constitutionally excessive, either individually or in the aggregate, and thus overwhelm the available fund.

Without evidence indicating either the upper limit or the insufficiency of the posited fund, class plaintiffs cannot demonstrate that individual plaintiffs would be prejudiced if left to pursue separate actions without having their interests represented in this suit, as Rule 23(b)(1)(B) would require.

CONCLUSION

The proposed class having failed to satisfy the threshold requirements for certification set forth in Ortiz and Rule 23(b)(1)(B), we must vacate the district court's certification order and remand for further proceedings.

Notes and Problems

1. One can view *In re Simon II* as a very creative attempt by class counsel to obtain certification of a case that would struggle being certified under Rule 23(b)(3)—as we will see in the *Castano* case in the next section. Why did the court reject certification under the limited fund theory posited by class counsel in *In re Simon II*? Was this decision sound in your estimation?

2. Others have suggested that the presence of a punitive damage claim might be a circumstances favoring certification under either Rule 23(b)(1) or Rule 23(b)(3), but courts have been slow to embrace such applications of the rules. *See, e.g.,* James M. Underwood, *Road to Nowhere or Jurisprudential U-Turn? The Intersection of Punitive Damage Class Actions and the Due Process Clause*, 66 Wash. & Lee L. Rev. 763 (2009) ("[R]ather than portend the death of the punitive damage class action, the recent Supreme Court

jurisprudence creates powerful new arguments in favor of the aggregate model of punitive damage adjudication that offers a route back toward the viable use of class actions in mass tort scenarios."); Richard L. Marcus & Edward F. Sherman, *Complex Litigation* 316 (Thomson West 2004) (citing various examples of courts certifying punitive damage class actions based upon the notion of a potential limit to the constitutional level of punitive damages a company should face from one mass tort-causing instance).

3. *Problem.* What would the U.S. Supreme Court have to hold regarding a constitutional limit on punitive damages in order to make certification under a limited fund theory plausible in a case involving punitive damage liability such as *In re Simon II*?

4. *Chapter Problem.* Is there any good argument for class certification in the Merri Chance case against TMG based upon either a limited fund theory or an incompatible standards theory? Is there any additional information you would need to form an opinion?

2. Rule 23(b)(2) Classes

Rule 23(b)(2) has remarkably simpler language than Rule 23(b)(1)(A)–(B) studied above. It permits certification when the defendant has "acted or refused to act on grounds generally applicable to the class, so that final injunctive relief or ... declaratory relief is appropriate" to the class. Sometimes referred to as the *equitable relief class action* or the *injunctive relief class action* this subsection is arguably unnecessary. As seen earlier with the "incompatible standards" class under 23(b)(1)(A), cases where the class members might seek mandatory injunctive relief against a common defendant already potentially qualify for certification under that section if the defendant might face possibly conflicting affirmative injunctive relief. The history behind Rule 23(b)(2) emphasizes that the drafters merely wanted to ensure that class actions would be available to remedy civil rights violations. Indeed, the Civil Rights Act of 1964 was still in its infancy when the 1966 amendments to Rule 23 were passed and the Rule 23(b)(2) class action was conceived. Thus, many putative class actions seeking purely injunctive or declarative relief could be certified under both Rule 23(b)(1)(A) and 23(b)(2). Because both contemplate non-notice, mandatory class actions, the decision to certify under either of those two sections does not seem to matter. The interesting interpretational dilemma regarding Rule 23(b)(2) concerns its possible application in cases where in addition to the equitable relief of injunction or declaration of rights, the putative class seeks monetary damages. Is this hybrid relief possible? Courts have focused upon one passage in the rule's Advisory Committee Notes to try to answer this riddle: "The subdivision does not extend to cases in which the appropriate final relief relates exclusively or predominantly to money damages." The following two decisions attempt to make sense of this caution from the Advisory Committee. Ask yourself whether the Supreme Court's approach to this issue in the more recent decision in the *Wal-Mart* case is inconsistent with the Fifth Circuit's approach in *In re Monumental* below.

Rule 23(b)(2)

(2) the party opposing the class has acted or refused to act on grounds that apply generally to the class, so that final injunctive relief or corresponding declaratory relief is appropriate respecting the class as a whole;

In re Monumental Life Ins. Co.

365 F.3d 408 (5th Cir. 2004)

SMITH, J.,

In what may be the ultimate negative value class action lawsuit,[1] plaintiffs challenge defendants' alleged practice of paying lower benefits and charging higher premiums to blacks in the sale of low-value life insurance. The district court denied plaintiffs' motion to certify a class pursuant to Fed. R. Civ. P. 23(b)(2), finding, *inter alia*, that the majority of class members would not benefit from injunctive relief. Based primarily on *Allison v. Citgo Petroleum Co.*, 151 F.3d 402 (5th Cir. 1998), we reverse and remand.

I.

This is a consolidation of civil rights actions against three life insurance companies: Monumental Life Insurance Company ("Monumental"), American National Insurance Company ("ANICO"), and Western and Southern Insurance Company ("Western and Southern"). Plaintiff policy owners, all of whom are black, allege that, for decades, defendants discriminated against them in the sale and administration of low-value life insurance policies, known as industrial life policies, that have face amounts of $2000 or less and require small weekly or monthly premiums. Defendants comprise over 280 companies that issued industrial life policies over a fifty- to sixty-five-year period. [Over the years, defendants acquired other insurance companies and assumed blocks of in-force policies issued by them. Monumental administers policies originally issued by over 200 companies, for example.]

Plaintiffs allege two overtly discriminatory practices. First, they accuse defendants of placing blacks in industrial policies offering the same benefits as do policies sold to whites, but at a higher premium (dual rates). Second, defendants allegedly placed blacks in specially-designed substandard industrial policies providing fewer or lower benefits than do comparable plans sold to whites (dual plans). These practices are memorialized in the insurer's rate books and records, which explicitly distinguish dual rate and dual plan policies by race. Although, before filing their motion for class certification, plaintiffs challenged the insurers' alleged practice of charging blacks substandard premiums because of non-racial underwriting factors, such as mental condition, occupation, socioeconomic status, educational level, living conditions, and personal habits, plaintiffs no longer complain of such pretextual underwriting procedures.

Defendants state that they issued "hundreds, perhaps thousands, of different industrial life insurance products" encompassing a countless variety of underwriting standards. It is undisputed that all companies that sold dual rate or dual plan policies have not done so since the early 1970's. Also, as early as 1988, some insurers voluntarily adjusted premiums and/or death benefits to equalize the amount of coverage per premium dollar. Still, plaintiffs estimate that over 4.5 million of the 5.6 million industrial policies issued by defendants remain in-force; many other policies have been terminated, surrendered, or paid-up without remediation. Defendants' expert estimates that the ratio of terminated policies to outstanding policies is approximately five to one, meaning that slightly more than one million policies remain in-force.

---

1. A "negative value" suit is one in which class members' claims "would be uneconomical to litigate individually." *Phillips Petroleum v. Shutts*, 472 U.S. 797, 809, 86 L. Ed. 2d 628, 105 S. Ct. 2965 (1985); see also *Castano v. Am. Tobacco Co.*, 84 F.3d 734, 748 (5th Cir. 1996).

What ps
seek

Plaintiffs sued for violations of 42 U.S.C. §§ 1981 and 1982, seeking (1) an injunction prohibiting the collection of discriminatory premiums, (2) reformation of policies to equalize benefits, and (3) restitution of past premium overcharges or benefit underpayments. Pursuant to 28 U.S.C. § 1407, the Judicial Panel for Multidistrict Litigation ("MDL") consolidated the actions against Monumental and transferred them to the Eastern District of Louisiana for pretrial proceedings. Later, the MDL Panel took the same action with the cases against ANICO and Western and Southern.

DC denied
cert., held
indv. hearings
needed

Plaintiffs moved for certification of a class pursuant to rule 23(b)(2), requesting that class members be provided notice and opt-out rights. The district court denied certification, finding that plaintiffs' claims for monetary relief predominate over their claims for injunctive relief, making rule 23(b)(2) certification inappropriate. The court also found that, given the large number of companies and policies involved, individualized hearings were necessary to determine damages and whether claims were barred by the statute of limitations.

II.

All classes must satisfy the four baseline requirements of rule 23(a): numerosity, commonality, typicality, and adequacy of representation. Fed. R. Civ. P. 23(a). Assuming these requirements are satisfied, a rule 23(b)(2) class may be certified if "the party opposing the class has acted or refused to act on grounds generally applicable to the class, thereby making appropriate final injunctive relief or corresponding declaratory relief with respect to the class as a whole." Fed. R. Civ. P. 23(b)(2). Plaintiffs premise rule 23(b)(2) certification on their request for an injunction prohibiting the further collection of discriminatory premiums.

A.

The court observed that "many" proposed class members—those whose policies have lapsed, those whose policies have already been voluntarily adjusted by defendants, and those whose death benefits already have been paid—would not benefit from injunctive relief. The court concluded that "this is a case in which individuality overrides any blandgroup-think, and money becomes the prime goal ... not injunctive relief." Rule 23(b)(2) certification is improper, the court held, where the class's request for injunctive relief merely serves as a bootstrap for a claim of monetary damages.

In *Allison*, we carefully explained the statement in the advisory committee notes that rule 23(b)(2) certification "does not extend to cases in which the appropriate final relief relates exclusively or *predominantly* to money damages." Fed. R. Civ. P. 23 advisory committee notes (emphasis added). *Allison* did not hold, as the district court believed, that monetary relief predominates where it is the "prime goal" or a mere bootstrap to injunctive relief. Instead, "determining whether one form of relief actually predominates in some quantifiable sense is a wasteful and impossible task that should be avoided." *Allison*, 151 F.3d at 412 (citing 7A Charles A. Wright et al., Federal Practice and Procedure § 1775, at 470 (2d ed. 1986)). In other words, certification does not hinge on the subjective intentions of the class representatives and their counsel in bringing suit.[10]

---

10. But see *Molski v. Gleich*, 318 F.3d 937, 950 (9th Cir. 2003) (expressly rejecting *Allison* and instead "focusing on the language of Rule 23(b)(2) and the intent of the plaintiffs in bringing the suit"); *Robinson v. Metro-North Commuter R.R.*, 267 F.3d 147, 163–64 (2d Cir. 2001) (stating that rule 23(b)(2) certification is appropriate only where "reasonable plaintiffs would bring the suit to obtain the injunctive or declaratory relief sought" and "the injunctive or declaratory relief sought would be both reasonably necessary and appropriate were the plaintiffs to succeed on the merits").

Instead, *Allison* looked to the nature of the rule 23(b)(2) device in defining when monetary relief predominates. That rule's focus on injunctive and declaratory relief presumes a class best described as a "homogenous and cohesive group with few conflicting interests among its members." *Id.* at 413. Class certification centers on the defendants' alleged unlawful conduct, not on individual injury. Once monetary damages enter the picture, however, class cohesiveness is generally lost, because "monetary remedies are more often related directly to the disparate merits of individual claims." *Id.* (citations omitted). Where the need to address the merits of individual claims requires separate hearings, the efficiency gained by class litigation is lost.

In *Allison*, therefore, we held, *id.* at 415, that monetary relief, to be viable in a rule 23(b)(2) class, must "flow directly from liability to the class *as a whole* on the claims forming the basis of the injunctive or declaratory relief." Monetary relief must be incidental, meaning that it is "capable of computation by means of objective standards and not dependent in any significant way on the intangible, subjective differences of each class member's circumstances."[11] *Id.* Additional hearings to resolve "the disparate merits of each individual's case" should be unnecessary.

Of course, certification under rule 23(b)(2) is appropriate only if members of the proposed class would benefit from the injunctive relief they request. The question whether the proposed class members are properly seeking such relief is antecedent to the question whether that relief would predominate over money damages.

In *Bolin v. Sears Roebuck & Co.*, 231 F.3d 970 (5th Cir. 2000), we considered a proposed rule 23(b)(2) class of one million consumers who claimed to seek injunctive relief, alleging that defendant had employed various unlawful practices to coerce payment of otherwise-discharged pre-bankruptcy debt. Before applying the *Allison* predominance test, however, we observed that "most of the class consists of individuals who do not face further harm from Sear's [*sic*] actions." *Id.* at 978. Because only a negligible proportion of proposed class members were properly seeking injunctive relief, we held that rule 23(b)(2) certification was inappropriate. Here, by contrast, defendants' and plaintiffs' experts estimate that between one million and 4.5 million of 5.6 million issued policies remain in-force. Although the exact number of class members continuing to pay discriminatory premiums is unknown, the proportion is sufficient, absent contrary evidence from defendants, that the class as a whole is deemed properly to be seeking injunctive relief.

B.

Bolin reflects a concern that plaintiffs may attempt to "shoehorn damages actions into the Rule 23(b)(2) framework, depriving classmembers of notice and opt-out protections." Indeed, we suggested in *Allison*, 151 F.3d at 413, that monetary relief may predominate "when its presence in the litigation suggests that the procedural safeguards of notice and opt-out are necessary." Defendants seize on this point, arguing that plaintiffs' request for notice and opt-out is a tacit admission that rule 23(b)(2) certification is inappropriate. This ignores the discretion given a district court to order notice and opt-out rights when certifying a rule 23(b)(2) class. *See* Fed. R. Civ. P. 23(d)(2).

As "fundamental requisites of the constitutional guarantees of procedural due process," *Eisen v. Carlisle & Jacquelin*, 417 U.S. 156, 174, 40 L. Ed. 2d 732, 94 S. Ct. 2140 (1974),

---

11. The predomination requirement serves two basic purposes, namely the interests of class members who may wish to pursue monetary claims individually, and interests of judicial economy. *Allison*, 151 F.3d at 415.

notice and opt-out are mandatory for damage classes certified under rule 23(b)(3). Though rule 23 does not explicitly extend these safeguards to rule 23(b)(2) classes, due process requires the provision of notice where a rule 23(b)(2) class seeks monetary damages.

On the other hand, there is no absolute right of opt-out in a rule 23(b)(2) class, "even where monetary relief is sought and made available." *Penson*, 634 F.2d at 994; *Kincade v. Gen. Tire & Rubber Co.*, 635 F.2d 501, 505–07 (5th Cir. Jan. 1981). Under our precedent, should the class be certified on remand, class members must be provided adequate notice, and the district court should consider the possibility of opt-out rights.

Allison's statement that monetary relief may predominate where notice and opt-out are necessary reflects only the inescapable fact that such safeguards are most appropriate where individual issues diminish class cohesiveness. Then, conflicts among class members and issues of adequate representation are most likely to surface. Rule 23(b)(3) is the default vehicle for certification, but only because notice and opt-out rights are mandatory components. A district court is empowered by rule 23(d)(2) to provide notice and opt-out for any class action, so rule 23(b)(2) certification should not be denied on the mistaken assumption that a rule 23(b)(3) class is the only means by which to protect class members.

All of this further demonstrates the futility of the district court's and dissent's inquiry as to whether the "prime goal" of the class is injunctive or monetary relief. The rule 23(b)(2) predominance requirement, by focusing on uniform relief flowing from defendants' liability, "serves essentially the same functions as the procedural safeguards and efficiency and manageability standards mandated in (b)(3) class actions." *Allison*, 151 F.3d at 414–15. Therefore, to deny certification on the basis that the damage claims would be better brought as a rule 23(b)(3) class serves no function other than to elevate form over substance. Indeed, interests of judicial economy are best served by resolving plaintiffs' claims for injunctive and monetary relief together.

III.

Applying *Allison*'s predominance test, the district court determined that the requested monetary relief does not flow from liability to the class as a whole. The court stated that "many and a variety of hearings would be required to determined personalized harm to each individual plaintiff because of the mass of policies involved, differing underwriting practices among some 280 companies, differing built-in benefits, account dividends, and age at policy issuance."

A.

Plaintiffs contend they seek equitable restitution in the form of a constructive trust for class members who no longer have in-force policies. By characterizing this relief as equitable, plaintiffs hope to demonstrate that that relief is inherently compatible with rule 23(b)(2) certification, thereby avoiding Allison's monetary predominance inquiry. Defendants argue that plaintiffs, who never used the term "constructive trust" in the district court, are trying to "re-package" their straightforward request for damages.

Equitable monetary relief is compatible with a rule 23(b)(2) class. Importantly, this pronouncement has been limited to the context of title VII backpay, a remedy designated by statute as "equitable." 42 U.S.C. § 2000e-5(g)(1); *Great-West Life & Annuity Ins. Co. v. Knudson*, 534 U.S. 204, 218 n.4, 151 L. Ed. 2d 635, 122 S. Ct. 708 (2002). Backpay is therefore unique in that it is "an integral component of Title VII's 'make whole' remedial scheme." *Allison*, 151 F.3d at 415; *see also Johnson v. Ga. Highway Express, Inc.*, 417 F.2d

1122, 1125 (5th Cir. 1969). Not coincidentally, as compared to compensatory damages, "calculation of back pay generally involves less complicated factual determinations and fewer individual issues." *Coleman v. GMAC*, 296 F.3d 443, 449 (6th Cir. 2002). In *Allison*, 151 F.3d at 415, we recognized that, for this reason, backpay generally does not predominate over injunctive or declaratory relief.

It would be mistaken to presume that because backpay—a remedy readily calculable on a classwide basis—is compatible with a rule 23(b)(2) class, any other remedy designated as equitable may automatically piggyback a claim for injunctive relief. To be sure, equitable monetary remedies are less likely to predominate over a class's claim for injunctive relief, but this has more to do with the uniform character of the relief rather than with its label. Therefore, rather than decide whether plaintiffs' claim for restitution is legal or equitable in nature, we apply *Allison* and examine whether the claim predominates over the request for injunctive relief.

B.

This is not a case in which class members are entitled to a one-size-fits-all refund; assuming liability is established, individual damages will depend on the idiosyncrasies of the particular dual rate or dual plan policy. For example, the age at which a class member purchased a dual rate policy will have an impact on how long the insured paid premiums and consequently on the amount of damages. Some policies contain built-in benefits covering occurrences outside of death, such as loss of limb; others pay periodic dividends. As we have observed, some defendants, beginning in 1988, voluntarily adjusted premiums and benefits for some policies sold on a race-distinct basis.

Plaintiffs propose using standardized formulas or restitution grids to calculate individual class members' damages. Defendants counter that "thousands" of grids must be constructed to account for the myriad of policy variations. That may be so, but the monetary predominance test does not contain a sweat-of-the-brow exception. Rather, we are guided by its command that damage calculation "should neither introduce new and substantial legal or factual issues, nor entail complex individualized determinations." *Allison*, 151 F.3d at 415.

In the list of [insurance] policy variables cited by defendants and the district court, none requires the gathering of subjective evidence. This is not, for example, like *Allison*, a title VII case in which class members' claims for compensatory and punitive damages necessarily "implicate[] the subjective differences of each plaintiff's circumstances." *Id.* at 417. Rather, assuming that unlawful discrimination is found, class members automatically will be entitled to the difference between what a black and a white paid for the same policy. Not coincidentally, such damages flow from liability in much the same manner that an award of backpay results from a finding of employment discrimination.

We are well aware that, as *Allison* qualifies, the calculation of monetary damages should not "entail complex individualized determinations." Although it is arguable that the construction of thousands of restitution grids, though based on objective data, involves the sort of complex data manipulations forbidden by *Allison*, we read *Allison* to the contrary. The policy variables are identifiable on a classwide basis and, when sorted, are capable of determining damages for individual policyowners; none of these variables is unique to particular plaintiffs. The prevalence of variables common to the class makes damage computation "virtually a mechanical task."

Finally, defendants' records contain the information necessary to determine disparities between, on the one hand, dual rate and dual plan policies, and on the other hand, plans sold to whites. Damage calculations do not require the manipulation of data kept outside defendants' normal course of business. Defendants' complaints to the contrary are belied by the fact that, since 1988, many policies have been adjusted to account for racial disparity.

The order denying class certification is REVERSED, and this matter is REMANDED for further proceedings consistent with this opinion. We express no view on the district court's ultimate decision whether to certify in light of today's opinion, nor do we opine on the ultimate merits of the substantive claims.

Wal-Mart Stores, Inc. v. Dukes (Part B)
564 U.S. 338 (2011)

We also conclude that respondents' claims for backpay were improperly certified under Federal Rule of Civil Procedure 23(b)(2). Our opinion in *Ticor Title Ins. Co.* v. *Brown*, 511 U.S. 117, 121 (1994) (per curiam) expressed serious doubt about whether claims for monetary relief may be certified under that provision. We now hold that they may not, at least where (as here) the monetary relief is not incidental to the injunctive or declaratory relief.

A

Rule 23(b)(2) allows class treatment when "the party opposing the class has acted or refused to act on grounds that apply generally to the class, so that final injunctive relief or corresponding declaratory relief is appropriate respecting the class as a whole." One possible reading of this provision is that it applies only to requests for such injunctive or declaratory relief and does not authorize the class certification of monetary claims at all. We need not reach that broader question in this case, because we think that, at a minimum, claims for individualized relief (like the backpay at issue here) do not satisfy the Rule. The key to the (b)(2) class is "the indivisible nature of the injunctive or declaratory remedy warranted—the notion that the conduct is such that it can be enjoined or declared unlawful only as to all of the class members or as to none of them." Nagareda, 84 N.Y.U. L. Rev., at 132. In other words, Rule 23(b)(2) applies only when a single injunction or declaratory judgment would provide relief to each member of the class. It does not authorize class certification when each individual class member would be entitled to a different injunction or declaratory judgment against the defendant. Similarly, it does not authorize class certification when each class member would be entitled to an individualized award of monetary damages.

That interpretation accords with the history of the Rule. Because Rule 23 "stems from equity practice" that predated its codification, *Amchem Products, Inc.* v. *Windsor*, 521 U.S. 591, 613, 117 S. Ct. 2231, 138 L. Ed. 2d 689 (1997), in determining its meaning we have previously looked to the historical models on which the Rule was based, *Ortiz* v. *Fibreboard Corp.*, 527 U.S. 815, 841–845, 119 S. Ct. 2295, 144 L. Ed. 2d 715 (1999). As we observed in *Amchem*, "[c]ivil rights cases against parties charged with unlawful, class-based discrimination are prime examples" of what (b)(2) is meant to capture. 521 U.S., at 614, 117 S. Ct. 2231, 138 L. Ed. 2d 689. In particular, the Rule reflects a series of decisions involving challenges to racial segregation—conduct that was remedied by a single classwide order. In none of the cases cited by the Advisory Committee as examples of (b)(2)'s antecedents did the plaintiffs combine any claim for individualized relief with their classwide injunction. See Advisory Committee's Note, 39 F.R.D. 69, 102 (1966) (citing cases); e.g., *Potts* v. *Flax*, 313 F.2d 284, 289, n. 5 (CA5 1963); *Brunson* v. *Board of Trustees of Univ. of School Dist. No. 1, Clarendon Cty.*, 311 F.2d 107, 109 (CA4 1962) (per curiam); *Frasier* v.

Board of Trustees of N.C., 134 F. Supp. 589, 593 (NC 1955) (three-judge court), aff'd, 350 U.S. 979, 76 S. Ct. 467, 100 L. Ed. 848 (1956).

Permitting the combination of individualized and classwide relief in a (b)(2) class is also inconsistent with the structure of Rule 23(b). Classes certified under (b)(1) and *(b)(2)* share the most traditional justifications for class treatment—that individual adjudications would be impossible or unworkable, as in a (b)(1) class, or that the relief sought must perforce affect the entire class at once, as in a (b)(2) class. For that reason these are also mandatory classes: The Rule provides no opportunity for (b)(1) or (b)(2) class members to opt out, and does not even oblige the District Court to afford them notice of the action. Rule 23(b)(3), by contrast, is an "adventuresome innovation" of the 1966 amendments, *Amchem*, 521 U.S., at 614, 117 S. Ct. 2231, 138 L. Ed. 2d 689 (internal quotation marks omitted), framed for situations "in which 'class-action treatment is not as clearly called for,'" *id.*, at 615, 117 S. Ct. 2231, 138 L. Ed. 2d 689 (quoting Advisory Committee's Notes, 28 U.S.C. App., p. 697 (1994 ed.)). It allows class certification in a much wider set of circumstances but with greater procedural protections. Its only prerequisites are that "the questions of law or fact common to class members predominate over any questions affecting only individual members, and that a class action is superior to other available methods for fairly and efficiently adjudicating the controversy." Rule 23(b)(3). And unlike (b)(1) and (b)(2) classes, the (b)(3) class is not mandatory; class members are entitled to receive "the best notice that is practicable under the circumstances" and to withdraw from the class at their option. See Rule 23(c)(2)(B).

Given that structure, we think it clear that individualized monetary claims belong in Rule 23(b)(3). The procedural protections attending the (b)(3) class—predominance, superiority, mandatory notice, and the right to opt out—are missing from (b)(2) not because the Rule considers them unnecessary, but because it considers them unnecessary to a (b)(2) class. When a class seeks an indivisible injunction benefitting all its members at once, there is no reason to undertake a case-specific inquiry into whether class issues predominate or whether class action is a superior method of adjudicating the dispute. Predominance and superiority are self-evident. But with respect to each class member's individualized claim for money, that is not so—which is precisely why (b)(3) requires the judge to make findings about predominance and superiority before allowing the class. Similarly, (b)(2) does not require that class members be given notice and opt-out rights, presumably because it is thought (rightly or wrongly) that notice has no purpose when the class is mandatory, and that depriving people of their right to sue in this manner complies with the Due Process Clause. In the context of a class action predominantly for money damages we have held that absence of notice and opt-out violates due process. See *Phillips Petroleum Co.* v. *Shutts*, 472 U.S. 797, 812, 105 S. Ct. 2965, 86 L. Ed. 2d 628 (1985). While we have never held that to be so where the monetary claims do not predominate, the serious possibility that it may be so provides an additional reason not to read Rule 23(b)(2) to include the monetary claims here.

B

Against that conclusion, respondents argue that their claims for backpay were appropriately certified as part of a class under Rule 23(b)(2) because those claims do not "predominate" over their requests for injunctive and declaratory relief. They rely upon the Advisory Committee's statement that Rule 23(b)(2) "does not extend to cases in which the appropriate final relief relates *exclusively or predominantly* to money damages." 39 F.R.D., at 102 (emphasis added). The negative implication, they argue, is that it does extend to cases in which the appropriate final relief relates only partially and nonpredominantly to money damages. Of course it is the Rule itself, not the Advisory

Committee's description of it, that governs. And a mere negative inference does not in our view suffice to establish a disposition that has no basis in the Rule's text, and that does obvious violence to the Rule's structural features. The mere "predominance" of a proper (b)(2) injunctive claim does nothing to justify elimination of Rule 23(b)(3)'s procedural protections: It neither establishes the superiority of class adjudication over individual adjudication nor cures the notice and opt-out problems. We fail to see why the Rule should be read to nullify these protections whenever a plaintiff class, at its option, combines its monetary claims with a request—even a "predominating request"—for an injunction.

Respondents' predominance test, moreover, creates perverse incentives for class representatives to place at risk potentially valid claims for monetary relief. In this case, for example, the named plaintiffs declined to include employees' claims for compensatory damages in their complaint. That strategy of including only backpay claims made it more likely that monetary relief would not "predominate." But it also created the possibility (if the predominance test were correct) that individual class members' compensatory-damages claims would be precluded by litigation they had no power to hold themselves apart from. If it were determined, for example, that a particular class member is not entitled to backpay because her denial of increased pay or a promotion was not the product of discrimination, that employee might be collaterally estopped from independently seeking compensatory damages based on that same denial. That possibility underscores the need for plaintiffs with individual monetary claims to decide for themselves whether to tie their fates to the class representatives' or go it alone—a choice Rule 23(b)(2) does not ensure that they have.

The predominance test would also require the District Court to reevaluate the roster of class members continually. The Ninth Circuit recognized the necessity for this when it concluded that those plaintiffs no longer employed by Wal-Mart lack standing to seek injunctive or declaratory relief against its employment practices. The Court of Appeals' response to that difficulty, however, was not to eliminate all former employees from the certified class, but to eliminate only those who had left the company's employ by the date the complaint was filed. That solution has no logical connection to the problem, since those who have left their Wal-Mart jobs since the complaint was filed have no more need for prospective relief than those who left beforehand. As a consequence, even though the validity of a (b)(2) class depends on whether "final injunctive relief or corresponding declaratory relief is appropriate respecting the class *as a whole*," Rule 23(b)(2) (emphasis added), about half the members of the class approved by the Ninth Circuit have no claim for injunctive or declaratory relief at all. Of course, the alternative (and logical) solution of excising plaintiffs from the class as they leave their employment may have struck the Court of Appeals as wasteful of the District Court's time. Which indeed it is, since if a backpay action were properly certified for class treatment under (b)(3), the ability to litigate a plaintiff's backpay claim as part of the class would not turn on the irrelevant question whether she is still employed at Wal-Mart. What follows from this, however, is not that some arbitrary limitation on class membership should be imposed but that the backpay claims should not be certified under Rule 23(b)(2) at all.

Finally, respondents argue that their backpay claims are appropriate for a (b)(2) class action because a backpay award is equitable in nature. The latter may be true, but it is irrelevant. The Rule does not speak of "equitable" remedies generally but of injunctions and declaratory judgments. As Title VII itself makes pellucidly clear, backpay is neither. See 42 U.S.C. § 2000e-5(g)(2)(B)(i) and (ii) (distinguishing between declaratory and injunctive relief and the payment of "backpay," see § 2000e-5(g)(2)(A)).

C

In *Allison* v. *Citgo Petroleum Corp.*, 151 F.3d 402, 415 (CA5 1998), the Fifth Circuit held that a (b)(2) class would permit the certification of monetary relief that is "incidental to requested injunctive or declaratory relief," which it defined as "damages that flow directly from liability to the class as a whole on the claims forming the basis of the injunctive or declaratory relief." In that court's view, such "incidental damage should not require additional hearings to resolve the disparate merits of each individual's case; it should neither introduce new substantial legal or factual issues, nor entail complex individualized determinations." *Ibid.* We need not decide in this case whether there are any forms of "incidental" monetary relief that are consistent with the interpretation of Rule 23(b)(2) we have announced and that comply with the Due Process Clause. Respondents do not argue that they can satisfy this standard, and in any event they cannot.

Contrary to the Ninth Circuit's view, Wal-Mart is entitled to individualized determinations of each employee's eligibility for backpay. Title VII includes a detailed remedial scheme. If a plaintiff prevails in showing that an employer has discriminated against him in violation of the statute, the court "may enjoin the respondent from engaging in such unlawful employment practice, and order such affirmative action as may be appropriate, [including] reinstatement or hiring of employees, with or without backpay ... or any other equitable relief as the court deems appropriate." § 2000e-5(g)(1). But if the employer can show that it took an adverse employment action against an employee for any reason other than discrimination, the court cannot order the "hiring, reinstatement, or promotion of an individual as an employee, or the payment to him of any backpay." § 2000e-5(g)(2)(A).

We have established a procedure for trying pattern-or-practice cases that gives effect to these statutory requirements. When the plaintiff seeks individual relief such as reinstatement or backpay after establishing a pattern or practice of discrimination, "a district court must usually conduct additional proceedings ... to determine the scope of individual relief." *Teamsters*, 431 U.S., at 361, 97 S. Ct. 1843, 52 L. Ed. 2d 396. At this phase, the burden of proof will shift to the company, but it will have the right to raise any individual affirmative defenses it may have, and to "demonstrate that the individual applicant was denied an employment opportunity for lawful reasons." *Id.*, at 362, 97 S. Ct. 1843, 52 L. Ed. 2d 396.

The Court of Appeals believed that it was possible to replace such proceedings with Trial by Formula. A sample set of the class members would be selected, as to whom liability for sex discrimination and the backpay owing as a result would be determined in depositions supervised by a master. The percentage of claims determined to be valid would then be applied to the entire remaining class, and the number of (presumptively) valid claims thus derived would be multiplied by the average backpay award in the sample set to arrive at the entire class recovery—without further individualized proceedings. 603 F.3d, at 625–627. We disapprove that novel project. Because the Rules Enabling Act forbids interpreting Rule 23 to "abridge, enlarge or modify any substantive right," 28 U.S.C. § 2072(b); see *Ortiz*, 527 U.S., at 845, 119 S. Ct. 2295, 144 L. Ed. 2d 715, a class cannot be certified on the premise that Wal-Mart will not be entitled to litigate its statutory defenses to individual claims. And because the necessity of that litigation will prevent backpay from being "incidental" to the classwide injunction, respondents' class could not be certified even assuming, arguendo, that "incidental" monetary relief can be awarded to a 23(b)(2) class.

The judgment of the Court of Appeals is reversed.

Notes and Problems

1. In *In re Monumental*, the Fifth Circuit rejected tests for "predominance"—comparing the equitable claims and the damage claims—two other circuits had come up with which inquired into the motivations for filing suit. In other words, absent a damages claim, would the class representative have bothered to seek injunctive relief? The Fifth Circuit, considering the functional differences between a mandatory Rule 23(b)(2) class and a Rule 23(b)(3) damages class, inquired instead into the extent to which injection of a damages remedy into the class action destroyed the "cohesiveness" of the class. In that case, the Fifth Circuit found that the damages sought (e.g., for overpayment of discriminatory premiums) flowed incidentally from the injunctive relief claims because they would not require individual hearings and testimony from impacted class members to compute the damages. While perhaps complex, the damages would merely be mathematical calculations that could potentially be done by a computer. In this sense, the Fifth Circuit believed that there was no need for opt-out rights as would be required in a Rule 23(b)(3) damages class action.

2. In *Wal-Mart*, the U.S. Supreme Court, at a minimum, overruled the prior *Allison* case from the Fifth Circuit (discussed in both of the foregoing cases) that had held backpay claims in employment discrimination class actions did not predominate over injunctive relief claims. The Supreme Court explained why in a case involving claims for employee backpay, the defendant could raise non-discriminatory grounds for its treatment of a singular employee that would make backpay improper. This individual inquiry would require individual hearings and would destroy the cohesiveness of the class adjudication under Rule 23(b)(2). But the Supreme Court also made several shots across the bow of any hybrid class action under Rule 23(b)(2)—suggesting the potential impropriety of any Rule 23(b)(2) class including claims for monetary damages. What language in the opinion suggests this alternative reading of *Wal-Mart*? Which interpretation is more accurate of the opinion—the limited holding that implicitly agrees with *In re Monumental* or the blanket prohibition of hybrid Rule 23(b)(2) class actions?

3. *Chapter Problem.* In the Merri Chance putative class action against TMG, she has requested injunctive relief to prohibit TMG's "continued sales of contaminated corn products" as well as "actual damages (economic losses as well as for personal injuries for any class member who became ill) and punitive damages." After reading the two foregoing opinions regarding Rule 23(b)(2), would this be a proper case to certify under that rule? If not, what could class counsel for Merri Chance modify in the complaint to increase the odds of a Rule 23(b)(2) certification?

3. Rule 23(b)(3) Damage Classes

Unlike Rules 23(b)(1) and (2) which were mostly retrospective in terms of their goals, having pre-1966 precedents for such class actions, Rule 23(b)(3) was more visionary. And of the three subdivisions, Rule 23(b)(3) engendered the most heated debates, sparking a "holy war over the rule's creation of opt-out classes" with "polarized opinions, with class action proponents seeing the rule as a panacea for a myriad of social ills and opponents seeing the rule as a form of legalized blackmail or a Frankenstein monster."[1] After 1966, Rule 23(b)(3) would eventually become the most frequent type of certified class action.

---

1. Thomas E. Wilging, *Empirical Study of Class Actions in Four Federal District Courts: Final Report to the Advisory Committee on Civil Rules* 1 (Federal Judicial Center 1996).

We will begin by seeing its application to a consumer, negative-value class action for economic losses—the scenario the 1966 drafters had most in mind for the damage class action and, therefore, the least controversial. Consider in the context of *Smilow* why class treatment of such claims might work better than the alternatives of the traditional litigation model. Also pay close attention to the requirements for Rule 23(b)(3) certification. Unlike (b)(1) and (b)(2) contexts where fundamental concerns for fairness mandate class treatment (and, hence, no opt-out rights), the cornerstone behind Rule 23(b)(3) certification is efficiency. Because of this, a class claimant will have to convince the court not just that there are common issues that arise among the class claims but that these common issues *predominate* over individual issues and, further, that class treatment is the *superior* method for adjudication of the class claims.

Rule 23(b)(3)

(3) the court finds that the questions of law or fact common to the class members predominate over any questions affecting only individual class members, and that a class action is superior to other available methods for fairly and efficiently adjudicating the controversy. The matters pertinent to these finds include:

   (A) the class members' interests in individually controlling the prosecution or defense of separate actions;

   (B) the extent and nature of any litigation concerning the controversy already begun by or against class members;

   (C) the desirability of undesirability of concentrating the litigation of the claims in the particular forum; and

   (D) the likely difficulties in managing a class action.

---

a. Economic Loss Classes

Smilow v. Southwestern Bell Mobile Systems
323 F.3d 32 (7th Cir. 2003)

Lynch, J.,

This is an appeal from a decision decertifying a class action brought by and on behalf of wireless phone customers of Cellular One, the doing-business name of Southwestern Bell Mobile Systems, Inc. The putative class members are Massachusetts and New Hampshire residents who were charged for incoming calls despite having signed a standard form contract, used mainly between August 1994 and February 1996, purportedly guaranteeing free incoming call service.

Class representative Jill Ann Smilow brought suit in 1997 for breach of contract and violations of Massachusetts General Laws chapter §§ 93A, 2(a), 9, 11 (West 1997), and the Telecommunications Act (TCA) of 1996, 47 U.S.C. § 201(b) (2000). The district court first certified and then decertified the contract, ch. 93A, and TCA classes. We reverse.

I.

Smilow and proposed class representative Margaret L. Bibeau each signed a standard form contract for cellular telephone services with Cellular One in 1995. The form contract says, "Chargeable time for calls originated by a Mobile Subscriber Unit starts when the Mobile Subscriber Unit signals call initiation to C1's facilities and ends when the Mobile Subscriber Unit signals call disconnect to C1's facilities and the call disconnect signal has been confirmed." The parties contest the meaning of "originated." Smilow alleges that this language precludes Cellular One from charging for incoming calls. It is undisputed that a large group of Cellular One customers signed the same contract and were subject to charges for incoming calls. The contract contains an integration clause providing that changes must be in writing and signed by both parties.

Smilow and Bibeau purport to represent a class of Massachusetts and New Hampshire residents who subscribed for Cellular One services under this contract. The potential class members all signed the standard form contract, which was in broad use from August 1994 to February 1996. They did have a variety of rate plans and usage patterns. Some Cellular One customers paid a flat fee for a fixed number of minutes each month and an additional per-minute charge if they exceeded this fixed amount of air time (for example, $40/month for the first 300 minutes/month and 10 cents/minute thereafter). Many Cellular One customers paid different rates for day-and night-time calls.

Cellular One charged Smilow, Bibeau and the potential class members for incoming as well as outgoing calls. Smilow received just one incoming call; Bibeau received many incoming calls. Cellular One invoices clearly indicate that customers are charged for incoming calls. The user guide mailed to new Cellular One customers also states that the company charges for both incoming and outgoing calls. Bibeau paid her invoices knowing she was being charged for incoming calls.

II.

On February 11, 1997, Smilow, as a purported class representative, filed suit in federal district court against Cellular One for breach of contract and violations of ch. 93A and the TCA. The district court had jurisdiction over the federal claims under 28 U.S.C. § 1331 (2000) and over the state law claims under 28 U.S.C. § 1367. The district court originally certified the ch. 93A, breach of contract, and TCA classes on October 9, 1998 [under Rule 23(b)(3)]. [Plaintiff later moved to substitute Bibeau as a new class representative. Defendant opposed this motion, arguing that nobody could adequately represent the class. The trial court denied the motion to substitute and decertified the class. The trial court believed that class members (estimated at nearly 275,000) paid for incoming calls still failed to show any harm because they received phone services in exchange for those sums paid. The trial court was also concerned that damages could not be proven from resort to Defendant's phone records and that the case lacked a predominance of common issues.]

II. The Predominance Requirement

The district court's decertification of the classes for the contract, ch. 93A, and TCA claims, as well as its denial of the motion to substitute a new class representative, all rested on fundamental errors of law and fact. Once these errors are corrected, it becomes clear that common issues as to both liability and damages predominate on the elements of the breach of contract and ch. 93A claims. We first consider the contract claim.

a. *Breach of Contract Claim*

The first error was initially contained in the following statement from the district court's opinion decertifying the class: "Proof of charges and payments is not evidence of harm or an amount of harm on the basis of which damages could be awarded in the face

Reasons for class decert.

of (i) a strong likelihood that services were received in return for billed payments and (ii) lack of admissible evidence to rebut that strong likelihood."

From this statement we understand the district court to have believed that the defendant would be entitled to payment for incoming calls on a theory of *quantum meruit* even if plaintiffs were to prevail on their breach of contract claim. Under the doctrine of quantum meruit, one who renders goods or services in the absence of an enforceable contract may be entitled to payment for those services to the extent the recipient benefitted from them. *See, e.g., Meng v. Trs. of Boston Univ.*, 44 Mass. App. Ct. 650, 693 N.E.2d 183, 187 n.4 (Mass. App. Ct. 1998). "If the plaintiff is entitled to recover on a contract, he cannot recover in quantum meruit." *Marshall v. Stratus Pharms., Inc.*, 51 Mass. App. Ct. 667, 749 N.E.2d 698, 703 n.6 (Mass. App. Ct. 2001). Though we do not decide the question here, it would similarly seem that where a defendant is clearly not due payment under the terms of an enforceable contract, such defendant cannot claim a right to payment under quantum meruit. "Where ... there is an enforceable express or implied in fact contract that regulates the relations of the parties or that part of their relations about which issues have arisen, there is no room for quasi contract." A.L. Corbin, *Corbin on Contracts* § 1.20 (J.M. Perillo ed., rev'd ed. 1993).

The district court's reliance on the doctrine of quantum meruit led it to overlook questions of law and fact common to all class members. As plaintiffs' brief says, "The plaintiffs' claims are based entirely on a standard form contract which the defendant used with every member of the class." The common factual basis is found in the terms of the contract, which are identical for all class members. The common question of law is whether those terms precluded defendant from charging for incoming calls.

Cellular One's waiver defense is also common to the class. "Affirmative defenses should be considered in making class certification decisions." *Mowbray*, 208 F.3d at 295. Again, both the factual basis for and the legal defense of waiver present common issues for all class members.[7] All class members received a user guide and monthly invoices showing that defendant charged the class members for the incoming calls.

Even in the unlikely event that individual waiver determinations prove necessary, the proposed class may still satisfy the predominance requirement. *See id.* at 296. Courts traditionally have been reluctant to deny class action status under Rule 23(b)(3) simply because affirmative defenses may be available against individual members. *See, e.g., Hoxworth v. Blinder, Robinson & Co.*, 980 F.2d 912, 924 (3d Cir. 1992) ("Given a sufficient nucleus of common questions, the presence of the individual issue of compliance with the statute of limitations has not prevented certification of class actions in securities cases.") (internal quotation omitted); *Cameron v. E.M. Adams & Co.*, 547 F.2d 473, 478 (9th Cir. 1976) (same). *See generally Mowbray*, 208 F.3d at 295 (identifying statute of limitations as an affirmative defense).

Instead, where common issues otherwise predominated, courts have usually certified Rule 23(b)(3) classes even though individual issues were present in one or more affirmative defenses. *See, e.g., Wal-Mart Stores, Inc. v. Visa USA Inc. (In re Visa Check/Mastermoney Antitrust Litig.)*, 280 F.3d 124, 138–40 (2d Cir. 2001); *Hoxworth*, 980 F.2d at 924; *Cameron*, 547 F.2d at 477–78. After all, Rule 23(b)(3) requires merely that common issues predominate, not that all issues be common to the class. *Krell v. Prudential Ins. Co. of Am.*

(handwritten margin note: common questions of law or fact)

(handwritten margin note: predom. requirement)

---

7. At oral argument defendant first advanced and then wisely withdrew the argument that oral representations made by sales representatives to potential customers would vary the contract terms by customer and so defeat commonality. The contract contains an integration clause.

(In re Prudential Ins. Co. Am. Sales Practice Litig. Agent Actions), 148 F.3d 283, 315 (3rd Cir. 1998); *see* 5 J.W. Moore, *Moore's Federal Practice* § 23.46[.1], at 23-206 to 23-207 (3d ed. 1997 & Supp. 2002). If, moreover, evidence later shows that an affirmative defense is likely to bar claims against at least some class members, then a court has available adequate procedural mechanisms. *In re Visa Check/MasterMoney Antitrust Litig.*, 280 F.3d at 141 (describing procedural options and collecting authorities); 1 H. Newberg & A. Conte, *Newberg on Class Actions* § 4.26, at 4-91 to 4-97 (3d ed. 1992) (same). For example, it can place class members with potentially barred claims in a separate subclass, 29A Fed. Proc., L. Ed. 70:411 & n.69, *Predominance of Common Issues* (2002) (citing cases); *see* Fed. R. Civ. P. 23(c)(4)(B), or exclude them from the class altogether, *In re Visa Check/ MasterMoney Antitrust Litig.*, 280 F.3d at 141; 6A Fed. Proc., *supra*, § 12:248 & n.6 (citing cases).

Cellular One argues that even if there are common questions of law and fact, the district court did not abuse its discretion by decertifying the class because individual issues predominate on damages. This is largely an issue of whether plaintiffs could use a computer program to extract from Cellular One's computer records information about individual damages. The district court viewed this question as mostly beside the point and its decertification orders rested mainly on other grounds.

The individuation of damages in consumer class actions is rarely determinative under Rule 23(b)(3). Where, as here, common questions predominate regarding liability, then courts generally find the predominance requirement to be satisfied even if individual damages issues remain. *In re Visa Check/MasterMoney Antitrust Litig.*, 280 F.3d at 139; *Bogosian v. Gulf Oil Corp.*, 561 F.2d 434, 456 (3d Cir. 1977); *Gold Strike Stamp Co. v. Christensen*, 436 F.2d 791, 798 (10th Cir. 1970); 5 Moore, *supra*, § 23.46[2][a], at 23-208 & n.11 (collecting additional cases); 4 Newberg & Conte, *supra*, § 18.27, at 18–89; *see Blackie v. Barrack*, 524 F.2d 891, 905 (9th Cir. 1975) ("The amount of damages is invariably an individual question and does not defeat class action treatment.").[8]

There is even less reason to decertify a class where the possible existence of individual damages issues is a matter of conjecture. *See Mowbray*, 208 F.3d at 298–99. Common issues predominate where individual factual determinations can be accomplished using computer records, clerical assistance, and objective criteria — thus rendering unnecessary an evidentiary hearing on each claim. See *Roper v. Consurve, Inc.*, 578 F.2d 1106, 1112 (5th Cir. 1978), *aff'd on other grounds sub nom.*, *Deposit Guar. Nat'l Bank v. Roper*, 445 U.S. 326, 63 L. Ed. 2d 427, 100 S. Ct. 1166 (1980); 5 Moore, *supra*, § 23.46[3], at 23-210 & n.18 (collecting cases holding that class certification is appropriate where damages are calculable by mathematical formula).

Still, the parties here dispute whether it will be possible to establish breach, causation, and damages using a mechanical process. Cellular One argues that Smilow has not shown that she could use defendant's computer records either to distinguish the subset of incoming call recipients who exceeded their monthly allotment of "free" minutes or to calculate how much extra each class member was charged as a result of receiving incoming calls.

The plaintiffs' expert, Erik Buchakian, says he could fashion a computer program that would extract from Cellular One's records (1) a list of customers who received incoming calls during the class period; (2) a list of customers who paid extra during the class period

---

8. Courts have denied class certification where these individual damages issues are especially complex or burdensome. *See* 5 Moore, *supra*, § 23.46[2][b], at 23-209 & n.17. That does not appear to be the case here.

because they were billed for incoming calls; and (3) actual damages for each class member during the class period. Buchakian had access to more than adequate materials—including a sample computer tape and the deposition of defendant's expert—and has more than adequate expertise—degrees in business and computer science and thirteen years of relevant work experience. The affidavits of defendant's expert, Susan Quintiliani, are consistent with Buchakian's conclusions.

If later evidence disproves Buchakian's proposition, the district court can at that stage modify or decertify the class, *see Gen. Tel. Co.*, 457 U.S. at 160 ("Even after a certification order is entered, the judge remains free to modify it in light of subsequent developments in the litigation."), or use a variety of management devices, *In re Visa Check/MasterMoney Antitrust Litig.*, 280 F.3d at 141; 1 Newberg & Conte, *supra*, §4.26, at 4-91 to 4-97. Indeed, even if individualized determinations were necessary to calculate damages, Rule (23)(c)(4)(A) would still allow the court to maintain the class action with respect to other issues. *See, e.g., In re Visa Check/MasterMoney Antitrust Litig.*, 280 F.3d at 141; *Sterling v. Velsicol Chem. Corp.*, 855 F.2d 1188, 1197 (6th Cir. 1988); *Jenkins v. Raymark Indus., Inc.*, 782 F.2d 468, 470–71 (5th Cir. 1986).

Consideration of the policy goals underlying Rule 23(b)(3) also supports class certification. The class certification prerequisites should be construed in light of the underlying objectives of class actions. S.S. Partridge & K.J. Miller, *Some Practical Considerations for Defending and Settling Products Liability and Consumer Class Actions*, 74 Tul. L. Rev. 2125, 2129 (2000); *see Mace v. Van Ru Credit Corp.*, 109 F.3d 338, 344 (7th Cir. 1997); *see also* Fed. R. Civ. Pro. 23(b)(3) advisory committee's note (construing predominance as a prerequisite for obtaining economies of scale). *Rule* 23(b)(3) is intended to be a less stringent requirement than Rule 23(b)(1) or (b)(2). *See Amchem Prods., Inc.*, 521 U.S. at 615 ("Framed for situations in which class-action treatment is not as clearly called for as it is in Rule 23(b)(1) and (b)(2) situations, Rule 23(b)(3) permits certification where class suit may nevertheless be convenient and desirable.") (internal quotations omitted). The core purpose of Rule 23(b)(3) is to vindicate the claims of consumers and other groups of people whose individual claims would be too small to warrant litigation. *See id.* at 617 ("While the text of Rule 23(b)(3) does not exclude from certification cases in which individual damages run high, the Advisory Committee had dominantly in mind vindication of the rights of groups of people who individually would be without effective strength to bring their opponents into court at all.").

In this case, the claims of most if not all class members are too small to vindicate individually. Smilow, for example, received just a single incoming call and so can obtain only minimal contract damages.

Overall, we find that common issues of law and fact predominate here. The case turns on interpretation of the form contract, executed by all class members and defendant. *See* W.D. Henderson, *Reconciling the Juridical Links Doctrine with the Federal Rules of Civil Procedure and Article III*, 67 U. Chi. L. Rev. 1347, 1373–74 (2000) (the fact that prospective class members signed nearly identical consumer contracts might, in itself, satisfy the predominance requirement).

b. *The Ch. 93A Class*

The decertification of the ch. 93A class is similarly flawed: it also rests on the premise that individual inquiries would be required because "services were received" for the charges on incoming calls.

As plaintiffs' brief says, "the Ch. 93A claim is not an oral misrepresentation claim, but [is] based on the same standard form contract which was signed by all class members."

See generally Anthony's Pier Four, Inc. v. HBC Assoc., 411 Mass. 451, 583 N.E.2d 806, 821 (Mass. 1991) ("Conduct in disregard of known contractual arrangements and intended to secure benefits for the breaching party constitutes an unfair act or practice for ch. 93A purposes."). Cellular One points to law to the effect that a mere breach of contract is not a ch. 93A violation. *See Whitinsville Plaza, Inc. v. Kotseas*, 378 Mass. 85, 390 N.E.2d 243, 251 (Mass. 1979). That defense, though, argues for, not against, the commonality of liability issues. Plaintiffs disclaim any intent to rely on oral misrepresentations, and must adhere to that position or risk losing class status.[10]

Our prior discussion is adequate to dispose of any argument that decertification would be required because of a need for individual damages determinations. Since Smilow can compute actual damages using a computer program, we need not address plaintiffs' argument that common issues would predominate only on a claim for statutory damages, and not on a claim for individual damages. As to statutory damages, the Supreme Judicial Court has held that plaintiffs who cannot show actual damages under ch. 93A may nonetheless obtain statutory damages if liability is established. *Leardi v. Brown*, 394 Mass. 151, 474 N.E.2d 1094, 1101–02 (Mass. 1985) (awarding statutory damages under ch. 93A §9(3)). This too supports class certification.

We are left with the district court's concern that any ch. 93A class would be composed of two groups: a statutory damages group and an actual damages group. But plaintiffs' position is that should any conflict develop between the two groups, the action would seek only statutory damages, class members would be given notice to that effect, and those who wish to pursue individual claims for actual damages could opt-out. We agree this is an option and, in this context, the hypothetical conflict provides no basis for decertification.

III.

We *reverse* the orders decertifying the class under the contract and ch. 93A theories. On remand, there should be reconsideration of the denial of class representative status to Bibeau. To the extent the denial rested on the decertification of the class, this opinion disposes of that ground. Costs are awarded to plaintiffs. *So ordered.*

Notes and Problems

1. Why did the class counsel make a motion to substitute a different class representative for the original claimant? After all, it was only when class counsel filed this motion that the court reconsidered the original certification decision.

2. *Smilow* is illustrative of a classic negative value case where, on its own, no sane claimant would ever bother to pursue the claim. Because of the small damages incurred by each consumer, some would not notice they had been wronged and others might simply shrug it off. But without the class device, the defendant such as the cell phone provider in the foregoing case, would be left undeterred from profiting through wrongdoing. In this sense, the class representative and counsel, by pursuing the litigation on behalf of the class, serve as a private attorney general to try to remove the profit incentive from

---

10. We doubt that defendants will rely on oral representations. If its sales representatives, familiar with the terms of the contract, represented that there would be a charge for incoming calls without notifying the consumers that the contract language could be read differently, that could be viewed as evidence in plaintiffs' favor of an unfair or deceptive act. If the sales representatives represented that there would be no charge for incoming calls and the customer was charged, then that is also evidence in plaintiffs' favor.

wrongdoing. Of course, the fact that the class counsel seeks to earn a sizable fee and that the class representative might also reap a bonus (see Chapter 6 on incentive awards) might provide less high-minded incentives to pursue such a claim.

3. The court believed in *Smilow* that it was useful to consider some of the underlying purposes behind the class device in applying Rule 23(b)(3)'s standards to the case. In what way did that support class certification in this case? If a case like *Smilow* cannot be certified, what is the alternative for adjudicating the claims of the individual class members? Is that realistic? How do these concerns impact the *superiority* analysis required by Rule 23(b)(3)?

4. The court in *Smilow* stated that in consumer class actions the individual nature of the damage inquiry should rarely defeat certification but, in a footnote, observed that this might not be the case in situations where damages were more "complex." Can you think of a type of damage case where the calculation of damages would be more difficult (and individual) than the arithmetic necessary to calculate overcharges to the cell phone customers?

5. *Chapter Problem.* Are there any features of the Merri Chance case that remind you of the circumstances of *Smilow*? If Merri Chance decided only to pursue claims for economic losses arising from the class members' being fraudulently induced to purchase tainted corn products, could the court certify the case under Rule 23(b)(3)? Are there any distinguishing circumstances that might still portend a problem?

b. Mass Tort Classes

When Rule 23(b)(3) was adopted in 1966, there was considerable debate about its application to mass tort scenarios with advocates for both sides. One opponent, John Frank, was vehement in his opposition, arguing that in tort cases, the individual's interest in litigating her own claim was always paramount. With the final adoption of the current version of this rule, the Advisory Committee seemed to acquiesce generally to the idea that mass tort claims should not often be subject to certification under Rule 23(b)(3), offering this cautionary note: "A mass accident resulting in injuries to numerous persons is ordinarily not appropriate for a class action because of the likelihood that significant questions, not only of damages but also of liability and defenses to liability, would be present, affecting the individuals in different ways. In these circumstances, an action conducted nominally as a class action would degenerate in practice into multiple lawsuits separately tried." For some time, courts seemed very cautious about certifying such mass tort claims. Signaling a possible watershed moment in the opposite direction, the *Jenkins v. Raymark Industries* asbestos case opined that times demanded a new attitude. Ten years later, the same court seemed to retrench on this attitude in the tobacco case of *Castano v. American Tobacco Co.* Read these two opinions and consider under what circumstances it would still be appropriate to certify a mass tort case today.

Jenkins v. Raymark Industries, Inc.
782 F.2d 468 (5th Cir. 1986)

REAVLEY, J.,

In this interlocutory appeal, the thirteen defendants challenge the decision of District Judge Robert M. Parker to certify a class of plaintiffs with asbestos-related claims. We affirm.

I. Background to Judge Parker's Plan

Experts estimate that at least 21 million American workers have been exposed to "significant" amounts of asbestos at the workplace since 1940; other millions have been exposed through environmental contact or contact with relatives who have worked with the products. Because of its injurious propensities, such exposure, in human terms, has meant that literally tens of thousands of people fall ill or die from asbestos-related diseases every year. In legal terms, it has translated into thousands of lawsuits, over 20,000 as of 1983, centered mainly in industrialized areas along the country's coasts.

Courts, including those in our own circuit, have been ill-equipped to handle this "avalanche of litigation." Our numerous opinions in asbestos-related cases have repeatedly recognized the dilemma confronting our trial courts, and expressed concern about the mounting backlog of cases and inevitable, lengthy trial delays.

About 5,000 asbestos-related cases are pending in this circuit. Much, though by no means all, of the litigation has centered in the Eastern District of Texas. Nearly nine hundred asbestos-related personal injury cases, involving over one thousand plaintiffs, were pending there in December of 1984. Despite innovative streamlined pretrial procedures and large-scale consolidated trials of multiple plaintiffs, the dockets of that district's courts remained alarmingly backlogged. Plaintiffs had waited years for trial, some since 1979 — and new cases were (and still are) being filed every day. It is predicted that, because asbestos-related diseases will continue to manifest themselves for the next 15 years, filings will continue at a steady rate until the year 2000.

In early 1985, ten of these plaintiffs responded by moving to certify a class of all plaintiffs with asbestos-related personal injury actions pending in the Eastern District on December 31, 1984. These plaintiffs hoped to determine in the class action one overarching issue — the viability of the "state of the art" defense. Because the trial of that issue consistently consumed substantial resources in every asbestos trial, and the evidence in each case was either identical or virtually so, they argued, a class determination would accelerate their cases.

II. The Plan

Following copious briefing and several hearings, the district court granted the motion. In his order of October 16, 1985, Judge Parker carefully considered the request under Rule 23(a), (b)(1) and (b)(3) of the Federal Rules of Civil Procedure. Finding a "limited fund" theory too speculative, he refused to certify the class under Rule 23(b)(1); by contrast, he found all of the elements for a 23(b)(3) action present. Drawing on his past experience, the judge concluded that evidence concerning the "state of the art" defense would vary little as to individual plaintiffs while consuming a major part of the time required for their trials. Considerable savings, both for the litigants and for the court, could thus be gained by resolving this and other defense and defense-related questions, including product identification, product defectiveness, gross negligence and punitive damages, in one class trial. The court further found that the named representatives had "typical" claims, and that they and their attorneys would adequately represent the other class members. Accordingly, it certified the class as to the common questions, ordering them resolved for the class by a class action jury. The class jury would also decide all the individual issues in the class representatives' underlying suits; individual issues of the unnamed members would be resolved later in "mini-trials" of seven to ten plaintiffs. Although the class action jury would evaluate the culpability of defendants' conduct for a possible punitive damage award, any such damages would be awarded only after class members had won or settled their individual cases. The court subsequently appointed a special master to survey the class and prepare a report, detailing the class members and their claims, to apprise the jury of the gravity and extent of the absent members' claims and the typicality of the representatives' claims.

Defendants moved for reconsideration or, in the alternative, certification of the decision for interlocutory appeal. The court granted defendants' alternate motion.

On appeal, defendants challenge the court's decision on three grounds: (1) the class fails to meet the requirements of Rule 23; (2) Texas law proscribes a bifurcated determination of punitive damages and actual damages; and (3) the contemplated class format is unconstitutional.

III. Discussion

The purpose of class actions is to conserve "the resources of both the courts and the parties by permitting an issue potentially affecting every [class member] to be litigated in an economical fashion." *General Telephone Co. of Southwest v. Falcon*, 457 U.S. 147, 155, 102 S. Ct. 2364, 2369, 72 L. Ed. 2d 740 (1982) (quoting *Califano v. Yamasaki*, 442 U.S. 682, 701, 99 S. Ct. 2545, 2557, 61 L. Ed. 2d 176 (1979)). To ensure that this purpose is served, Rule 23 demands that all class actions certified under Rule 23(b)(3) meet the requirements of both 23(a): numerosity, commonality, typicality, and adequacy of representation; and 23(b)(3): predominance and superiority. The district court has wide discretion in deciding whether or not to certify a proposed class. Assuming the court considers the Rule 23 criteria, we may reverse its decision only for abuse of discretion. *Horton v. Goose Creek Independent School District*, 690 F.2d 470, 483 (5th Cir. 1982), cert. denied, 463 U.S. 1207, 77 L. Ed. 2d 1387, 103 S. Ct. 3536 (1983); *Boggs v. Alto Trailer Sales, Inc.*, 511 F.2d 114, 117 (5th Cir. 1975).

Defendants argue that this class meets none of the Rule 23 requirements, except "numerosity." There is no merit to this argument.

The threshold of "commonality" is not high. Aimed in part at "determining whether there is a need for combined treatment and a benefit to be derived therefrom," the rule requires only that resolution of the common questions affect all or a substantial number of the class members. Defendants do not claim that they intend to raise a "state of the art" defense in only a few cases; the related issues are common to all class members.

The "typicality" requirement focuses less on the relative strengths of the named and unnamed plaintiffs' cases than on the similarity of the legal and remedial theories behind their claims. Defendants do not contend that the named plaintiffs' claims rest on theories different from those of the other class members.

The "adequacy" requirement looks at both the class representatives and their counsel. Defendants have not shown that the representatives are "inadequate" due to an insufficient stake in the outcome or interests antagonistic to the unnamed members. Neither do they give us reason to question the district court's finding that class counsel is "adequate" in light of counsel's past experience in asbestos cases, including trials involving multiple plaintiffs.

We similarly find no abuse in the court's determination that the certified questions "predominate," under Rule 23(b)(3). In order to "predominate," common issues must constitute a significant part of the individual cases. See *In re Asbestos School Litigation*, 104 F.R.D. at 431–32; *In re Tetracycline Cases*, 107 F.R.D. 719, 727 (W.D.Mo. 1985); see also *In re Asbestos School Litigation*, 107 F.R.D. 215, 218–20 (E.D.Pa. 1985). It is difficult to imagine that class jury findings on the class questions will not significantly advance the resolution of the underlying hundreds of cases.

Defendants also argue that a class action is not "superior"; they say that better mechanisms, such as the Wellington Facility [an ADR mechanism] and "reverse bifurcation," [whereby plaintiff in a first trial proves only that exposure to asbestos has caused their damages with remaining issues, such as product identification and liability reserved for later trials] exist for resolving these claims. Again, however, they have failed to show that the district court abused its discretion by reaching the contrary conclusion. We cannot find that the Wellington Facility, whose merits we do not question, is so superior that it must be used to the exclusion of other forums. Similarly, even if we were prepared to weigh the merits of other procedural mechanisms, we see no basis to conclude that this class action plan is an abuse of discretion.

Courts have usually avoided class actions in the mass accident or tort setting. Because of differences between individual plaintiffs on issues of liability and defenses of liability, as well as damages, it has been feared that separate trials would overshadow the common disposition for the class. See Advisory Committee Notes to 1966 Amendment to Fed. R. Civ. P. 23(b)(3). The courts are now being forced to rethink the alternatives and priorities by the current volume of litigation and more frequent mass disasters. See McGovern, Management of Multiparty Toxic Tort Litigation: Case Law and Trends Affecting Case Management, 19 Forum 1 (1983). If Congress leaves us to our own devices, we may be forced to abandon repetitive hearings and arguments for each claimant's attorney to the extent enjoyed by the profession in the past. Be that as time will tell, the decision at hand is driven in one direction by all the circumstances. Judge Parker's plan is clearly superior to the alternative of repeating, hundreds of times over, the litigation of the state of the art issues with, as that experienced judge says, "days of the same witnesses, exhibits and issues from trial to trial."

This assumes plaintiffs win on the critical issues of the class trial. To the extent defendants win, the elimination of issues and docket will mean a far greater saving of judicial resources. Furthermore, attorneys' fees for all parties will be greatly reduced under this plan, not only because of the elimination of so much trial time but also because the fees collected from all members of the plaintiff class will be controlled by the judge. From our view it seems that the defendants enjoy all of the advantages, and the plaintiffs incur the disadvantages, of the class action—with one exception: the cases are to be brought to trial. That counsel for plaintiffs would urge the class action under these circumstances is significant support for the district judge's decision.

Necessity moves us to change and invent. Both the Agent Orange and the Asbestos School courts found that specific issues could be decided in a class "mass tort" action— even on a nationwide basis. We approve of the district court's decision in finding that this "mass tort" class could be certified.

Other Contentions

Defendants' remaining arguments challenge the bifurcate trials under Texas law and the United States Constitution. Defendants contend that, under Texas law, punitive damages cannot be determined separately from actual damages because the culpability of their conduct must be evaluated relative to each plaintiff. We disagree.

The purpose of punitive damages is not to compensate the victim but to create a deterrence to the defendant, *Maxey v. Freightliner Corp.*, 665 F.2d 1367, 1378 (5th Cir. 1982), and to protect the public interest, *Bank of North America v. Bell*, 493 S.W.2d 633, 636 (Tex. Civ. App.—Houston 1973, no writ) (also noting that "we perceive it to be our duty to examine this record to determine whether the exemplary award is excessive standing alone and without reference to the finding on actual damages"). The focus is on the defendant's conduct, rather than on the plaintiff's. While no plaintiff may receive an award of punitive damages without proving that he suffered actual damages, e.g., *Doubleday & Co., Inc. v. Rogers*, 674 S.W.2d 751, 753–54 (Tex. 1984); *City Products Corp. v. Berman*, 610 S.W.2d 446, 450 (Tex. 1980) (jury finding of no actual damages precludes award of punitive damages), the allocation need not be made concurrently with an evaluation of the defendant's conduct. The relative timing of these assessments is not critical.

The critical issue in Texas punitive damages law is excessiveness or "reasonable proportionality." Whether a given award is excessive is a question of fact. See *Tatum v. Preston Carter Co.*, 702 S.W.2d 186, 29 Tex. Sup. Ct. J. 151, 152 (1986); *Alamo National Bank v. Kraus*, 616 S.W.2d 908, 910 (Tex. 1981). "The reasonable proportion rule does not, standing alone, serve to fix a particular ratio," *Tatum*, 29 Tex. S. Ct. J. at 152; that ratio will vary according to the facts of the case, *id.* at 151. In determining whether an award is excessive the court must consider: (1) the nature of the wrong; (2) the character of the conduct involved; (3) the degree of culpability of the wrongdoer; (4) the situation and sensibilities of the parties concerned; and (5) the extent to which such conduct offends a public sense of justice and propriety. *Id.* at 151–52; *Alamo National Bank*, 616 S.W.2d at 910.

The format in this case allows for the district court's review of the reasonableness of each plaintiff's punitive damage award and for our review of the standards which the court has applied. Texas law does not require more.

Defendants' constitutional challenges to bifurcation are equally unavailing. Like their other claims, these arguments only recast in constitutional terms their concern that, because the representatives' cases are "better" than the unnamed plaintiffs', the jury's view of the class claims will be skewed.

Although it fails to raise an issue of constitutional magnitude, this concern is nevertheless legitimate. Care must, of course, be taken to ensure fairness. Whatever the jury is told about the claims of the unnamed plaintiffs, it must be made aware that none of those claims have been proved; even after the class trial, they will still be mere allegations. The jury must not assume that all class members have equivalent claims: whatever injuries the unnamed plaintiffs have suffered may differ from the class representatives' as well as from one another's. Should the jury be allowed to award in the aggregate any punitive damages it finds appropriate, it must be instructed to factor in the possibility that none of the unnamed plaintiffs may have suffered any damages. Alternatively, the jury could be allowed to award an amount of money that each class member should receive for each dollar of actual damages awarded. Either way, the jury should understand that it must differentiate between proven and still-unproved claims, and that all class members, who recover actual damages from a defendant held liable for punitive damages, will share in the punitive award.

Furthermore, fairness as well as necessity dictates that both the parties and the court ensure that all of the necessary findings can be and are made in the class action trial. Sufficient evidence must be adduced for every one of each defendant's products to which a class member claims exposure so that the class jury can make the requisite findings as to each product and each defendant for such questions as periods of manufacture; areas and dates of distribution; "state of the art" knowledge for each relevant kind of product, use and user; when, if ever, conduct was grossly negligent; and dates and types of warnings if marketing defect is alleged.

The task will not be easy. Nevertheless, particularly in light of the magnitude of the problem and the need for innovative approaches, we find no abuse of discretion in this court's decision to try these cases by means of a Rule 23(b)(3) class suit.

AFFIRMED.

Castano v. American Tobacco Co.

84 F.3d 734 (5th Cir. 1996)

SMITH, J.,

In what may be the largest class action ever attempted in federal court, the district court in this case embarked "on a road certainly less traveled, if ever taken at all," and entered a class certification order. The court defined the class as:

(a) All nicotine-dependent persons in the United States ... who have purchased and smoked cigarettes manufactured by the defendants;

(b) the estates, representatives, and administrators of these nicotine-dependent cigarette smokers; and

(c) the spouses, children, relatives and "significant others" of these nicotine-dependent cigarette smokers as their heirs or survivors.

Id. at 560–61. The plaintiffs limit the claims to years since 1943.[1]

This matter comes before us on interlocutory appeal, under 28 U.S.C. § 1292(b), of the class certification order. Concluding that the district court abused its discretion in certifying the class, we reverse.

I.

A. The Class Complaint

The plaintiffs filed this class complaint against the defendant tobacco companies and the Tobacco Institute, Inc., seeking compensation solely for the injury of nicotine addiction. The gravamen of their complaint is the novel and wholly untested theory that the defendants fraudulently failed to inform consumers that nicotine is addictive and manipulated the level of nicotine in cigarettes to sustain their addictive nature. The class complaint alleges nine causes of action: fraud and deceit, negligent misrepresentation, intentional infliction of emotional distress, negligence and negligent infliction of emotional distress, violation of state consumer protection statutes, breach of express warranty, breach of implied warranty, strict product liability, and redhibition pursuant to the Louisiana Civil Code.

The plaintiffs seek compensatory and punitive damages and attorneys' fees. In addition, the plaintiffs seek equitable relief for fraud and deceit, negligent misrepresentation, violation of consumer protection statutes, and breach of express and implied warranty. The equitable remedies include a declaration that defendants are financially responsible for notifying all class members of nicotine's addictive nature, a declaration that the defendants manipulated nicotine levels with the intent to sustain the addiction of plaintiffs and the class members, an order that the defendants disgorge any profits made from the sale of cigarettes, restitution for sums paid for cigarettes, and the establishment of a medical monitoring fund.

---

1. The court defined "nicotine-dependent" as:
   (a) All cigarette smokers who have been diagnosed by a medical practitioner as nicotine-dependent; and/or
   (b) All regular cigarette smokers who were or have been advised by a medical practitioner that smoking has had or will have adverse health consequences who thereafter do not or have not quit smoking.
   Id. at 561. The definition is based upon the criteria for "dependence" set forth in American Psychiatric Association, *Diagnostic and Statistical Manual of Mental Disorders* (4th ed.).

The plaintiffs initially defined the class as "all nicotine dependent persons in the United States," including current, former and deceased smokers since 1943. Plaintiffs conceded that addiction would have to be proven by each class member; the defendants argued that proving class membership will require individual mini-trials to determine whether addiction actually exists.

In response to the district court's inquiry, the plaintiffs proposed a four-phase trial plan. In phase 1, a jury would determine common issues of "core liability." Phase 1 issues would include (1) issues of law and fact relating to defendants' course of conduct, fraud, and negligence liability (including duty, standard of care, misrepresentation and concealment, knowledge, intent); (2) issues of law and fact relating to defendants' alleged conspiracy and concert of action; (3) issues of fact relating to the addictive nature/dependency creating characteristics and properties of nicotine; (4) issues of fact relating to nicotine cigarettes as defective products; (5) issues of fact relating to whether defendants' wrongful conduct was intentional, reckless or negligent; (6) identifying which defendants specifically targeted their advertising and promotional efforts to particular groups (e.g. youths, minorities, etc.); (7) availability of a presumption of reliance; (8) whether defendants' misrepresentations/suppression of fact and/or of addictive properties of nicotine preclude availability of a "personal choice" defense; (9) defendants' liability for actual damages, and the categories of such damages; (10) defendants' liability for emotional distress damages; and (11) defendants' liability for punitive damages.

Phase 1 would be followed by notice of the trial verdict and claim forms to class members. In phase 2, the jury would determine compensatory damages in sample plaintiff cases. The jury then would establish a ratio of punitive damages to compensatory damages, which ratio thereafter would apply to each class member. Phase 3 would entail a complicated procedure to determine compensatory damages for individual class members. The trial plan envisions determination of absent class members' compensatory economic and emotional distress damages on the basis of claim forms, "subject to verification techniques and assertion of defendants' affirmative defenses under grouping, sampling, or representative procedures to be determined by the Court."

The trial plan left open how jury trials on class members' personal injury/wrongful death claims would be handled, but the trial plan discussed the possibility of bifurcation. In phase 4, the court would apply the punitive damage ratio based on individual damage awards and would conduct a review of the reasonableness of the award.

B. The Class Certification Order

Following extensive briefing, the district court granted, in part, plaintiffs' motion for class certification, concluding that the prerequisites of Fed. R. Civ. P. 23(a) had been met. The court rejected certification, under Fed. R. Civ. P. 23(b)(2), of the plaintiffs' claim for equitable relief, including the claim for medical monitoring. 160 F.R.D. at 552. Appellees have not cross-appealed that portion of the order.

The court did grant the plaintiffs' motion to certify the class under Fed. R. Civ. P. 23(b)(3), organizing the class action issues into four categories: (1) core liability; (2) injury-in-fact, proximate cause, reliance and affirmative defenses; (3) compensatory damages; and (4) punitive damages. Id. at 553–58. It then analyzed each category to determine whether it met the predominance and superiority requirements of rule 23(b)(3). Using its power to sever issues for certification under Fed. R. Civ. P. 23(c)(4), the court certified the class on core liability and punitive damages, and certified the class conditionally pursuant to Fed. R. Civ. P. 23(c)(1). [The court found that a class action was appropriate for "core liability" issues such as fraud, breach of warranty, and strict liability as well as for punitive damages. It did not certify a class on the injury-in-fact, proximate cause, reliance, affirmative defenses or compensatory damages.]

II.

A district court must conduct a rigorous analysis of the rule 23 prerequisites before certifying a class.

The district court erred in its analysis in two distinct ways. First, it failed to consider how variations in state law affect predominance and superiority. Second, its predominance inquiry did not include consideration of how a trial on the merits would be conducted.

Each of these defects mandates reversal. Moreover, at this time, while the tort is immature, the class complaint must be dismissed, as class certification cannot be found to be a superior method of adjudication.

A. Variations in State Law

In a multi-state class action, variations in state law may swamp any common issues and defeat predominance. *See Georgine v. Amchem Prods.*, 83 F.3d 610, 1996 U.S. App. LEXIS 11191, 1996 WL 242442, at *2 (3d Cir. 1996) (decertifying class because legal and factual differences in the plaintiffs' claims "when exponentially magnified by choice of law considerations, eclipse any common issues in this case."); *American Medical Sys.*, 75 F.3d at 1085 (granting mandamus in a multi-state products liability action, in part because "the district court ... failed to consider how the law of negligence differs from jurisdiction to jurisdiction").

Accordingly, a district court must consider how variations in state law affect predominance and superiority.

A district court's duty to determine whether the plaintiff has borne its burden on class certification requires that a court consider variations in state law when a class action involves multiple jurisdictions. "In order to make the findings required to certify a class action under Rule 23(b)(3) ... one must initially identify the substantive law issues which will control the outcome of the litigation." *Alabama v. Blue Bird Body Co.*, 573 F.2d 309, 316 (5th Cir. 1978).

A requirement that a court know which law will apply before making a predominance determination is especially important when there may be differences in state law. Given the plaintiffs' burden, a court cannot rely on assurances of counsel that any problems with predominance or superiority can be overcome. *Windham v. American Brands, Inc.*, 565 F.2d 59, 70 (4th Cir. 1977), *cert. denied*, 435 U.S. 968, 56 L. Ed. 2d 58, 98 S. Ct. 1605 (1978).

A thorough review of the record demonstrates that, in this case, the district court did not properly consider how variations in state law affect predominance. The court acknowledged as much in its order granting class certification, for, in declining to make a choice of law determination, it noted that "the parties have only briefly addressed the conflict of laws issue in this matter." 160 F.R.D. at 554. Similarly, the court stated that "there has been no showing that the consumer protection statutes differ so much as to make individual issues predominate."

The district court's review of state law variances can hardly be considered extensive; it conducted a cursory review of state law variations and gave short shrift to the defendants' arguments concerning variations. In response to the defendants' extensive analysis of how state law varied on fraud, products liability, affirmative defenses, negligent infliction of emotional distress, consumer protection statutes, and punitive damages,[15] the court examined a sample phase 1 jury interrogatory and verdict form, a survey of medical monitoring decisions, a survey of consumer fraud class actions, and a survey of punitive damages law in the defendants' home states. The court also relied on two district court opinions granting certification in multi-state class actions. The district court's consideration of state law variations was inadequate. The surveys provided by the plaintiffs failed to discuss, in any meaningful way, how the court could deal with variations in state law. The consumer fraud survey simply quoted a few state courts that had certified state class actions. The survey of punitive damages was limited to the defendants' home states. Moreover, the two district court opinions on which the court relied did not support the proposition that variations in state law could be ignored. Nothing in the record demonstrates that the court critically analyzed how variations in state law would affect predominance.

The court also failed to perform its duty to determine whether the class action would be manageable in light of state law variations. The court's only discussion of manageability is a citation to *Jenkins* and the claim that "while manageability of the liability issues in this case may well prove to be difficult, the Court finds that any such difficulties pale in comparison to the specter of thousands, if not millions, of similar trials of liability proceeding in thousands of courtrooms around the nation." *Id.* at 555–56.

The problem with this approach is that it substitutes case-specific analysis with a generalized reference to *Jenkins*. The *Jenkins* court, however, was not faced with managing a novel claim involving eight causes of action, multiple jurisdictions, millions of plaintiffs, eight defendants, and over fifty years of alleged wrongful conduct. Instead, *Jenkins* involved only 893 personal injury asbestos cases, the law of only one state, and the prospect of trial occurring in only one district. Accordingly, for purposes of the instant case, *Jenkins* is largely inapposite.

In summary, whether the specter of millions of cases outweighs any manageability problems in this class is uncertain when the scope of any manageability problems is unknown. Absent considered judgment on the manageability of the class, a comparison to millions of individual trials is meaningless.

B. Predominance

The district court's second error was that it failed to consider how the plaintiffs' addiction claims would be tried, individually or on a class basis. *See* 160 F.R.D. at 554. The district

---

15. The *Castano* class suffers from difficulties. The class members were exposed to nicotine through different products, for different amounts of time, and over different time periods. Each class member's knowledge about the effects of smoking differs, and each plaintiff began smoking for different reasons. Each of these factual differences impacts the application of legal rules such as causation, reliance, comparative fault, and other affirmative defenses.

Variations in state law magnify the differences. In a fraud claim, some states require justifiable reliance on a misrepresentation, while others require reasonable reliance. States impose varying standards to determine when there is a duty to disclose facts.

Products liability law also differs among states. Some states do not recognize strict liability. Some have adopted Restatement (Second) of Torts § 402A. Among the states that have adopted the Restatement, there are variations.

Differences in affirmative defenses also exist. Assumption of risk is a complete defense to a products claim in some states. In others, it is a part of comparative fault analysis. Some states utilize "pure" comparative fault, others follow a "greater fault bar," e.g., Conn. Gen. Stat. Ann. §52-572h (West 1988); and still others use an "equal fault bar," e.g., Ark. Code Ann. §16-64-122 (Michie 1991).

Negligent infliction of emotional distress also involves wide variations. Some states do not recognize the cause of action at all. Some require a physical impact. Despite these overwhelming individual issues, common issues might predominate. We are, however, left to speculate. The point of detailing the alleged differences is to demonstrate the inquiry the district court failed to make.

court, based on *Eisen v. Carlisle & Jacquelin*, 417 U.S. 156, 177–78, 40 L. Ed. 2d 732, 94 S. Ct. 2140 (1974), and *Miller v. Mackey Int'l*, 452 F.2d 424 (5th Cir. 1971), believed that it could not go past the pleadings for the certification decision. The result was an incomplete and inadequate predominance inquiry.

A district court certainly may look past the pleadings to determine whether the requirements of rule 23 have been met. Going beyond the pleadings is necessary, as a court must understand the claims, defenses, relevant facts, and applicable substantive law in order to make a meaningful determination of the certification issues. See Manual for Complex Litigation § 30.11 (3d ed. 1995).

The district court's predominance inquiry demonstrates why such an understanding is necessary. The premise of the court's opinion is a citation to *Jenkins* and a conclusion that class treatment of common issues would significantly advance the individual trials. Absent knowledge of how addiction-as-injury cases would actually be tried, however, it was impossible for the court to know whether the common issues would be a "significant" portion of the individual trials. The court just assumed that because the common issues would play a part in every trial, they must be significant.[18] The court's synthesis of *Jenkins* and *Eisen* would write the predominance requirement out of the rule, and any common issue would predominate if it were common to all the individual trials.

The court's treatment of the fraud claim also demonstrates the error inherent in its approach.[19] According to both the advisory committee's notes to Rule 23(b)(3) and this

---

18. The district court's approach to predominance stands in stark contrast to the methodology the district court used in *Jenkins*. There, the district judge had a vast amount of experience with asbestos cases. He certified the state of the art defense because it was the most significant contested issue in each case. *Jenkins*, 109 F.R.D. 269 at 279. To the contrary, however, the district court in the instant case did not, and could not, have determined that the common issues would be a significant part of each case. Unlike the judge in *Jenkins*, the district judge *a quo* had no experience with this type of case and did not even inquire into how a case would be tried to determine whether the defendants' conduct would be a significant portion of each case.

19. An incorrect predominance finding also implicates the court's superiority analysis: The greater the number of individual issues, the less likely superiority can be established. *American Medical Sys.*, 75 F.3d at 1084–85 (distinguishing a single disaster mass tort from a more complex mass tort). The relationship between predominance and superiority in mass torts was recognized in the Advisory Committee's note to rule 23(b)(3), which states:

> A "mass accident" resulting in injuries to numerous persons is ordinarily not appropriate for a class action because of the likelihood that significant questions, not only of damages but of liability and defenses to liability, would be present, affecting the individuals in different ways. In these circumstances an action conducted nominally as a class action would degenerate in practice into multiple lawsuits separately tried.

Fed. R. Civ. P. 23(b)(3) advisory committee's note (citation omitted), reprinted in 39 F.R.D. 69, 103 (1966). *See also Georgine*, 83 F.3d 610, 1996 U.S. App. LEXIS 11191, 1996 WL 242442, at *12–*13 (relying on the Advisory Committee's note); *American Medical Sys.*, 75 F.3d at 1084–85.

The plaintiffs assert that Professor Charles Allen Wright, a member of the Advisory Committee, has now repudiated this passage in the notes. *See* H. Newberg, 3 Newberg on Class Actions § 17.06 (3d ed. 1992). Professor Wright's recent statements, made as an advocate in *School Asbestos*, must be viewed with some caution. As Professor Wright has stated:

> I certainly did not intend by that statement to say that a class should be certified in all mass tort cases. I merely wanted to take the sting out of the statement in the Advisory Committee Note, and even that said only that a class action is "ordinarily not appropriate" in mass-tort cases. The class action is a complex device that must be used with discernment. I think for example that Judge Jones in Louisiana would be creating a Frankenstein's monster if he should allow certification of what purports to be a class action on behalf of everyone who has ever been addicted to nicotine.

Letter of Dec. 22, 1994, to N. Reid Neureiter, Williams & Connolly, Washington, D.C.

court's decision in *Simon v. Merrill Lynch, Pierce, Fenner & Smith, Inc.*, 482 F.2d 880 (5th Cir. 1973), a fraud class action cannot be certified when individual reliance will be an issue. The district court avoided the reach of this court's decision in *Simon* by an erroneous reading of *Eisen*; the court refused to consider whether reliance would be an issue in individual trials.

The problem with the district court's approach is that after the class trial, it might have decided that reliance must be proven in individual trials. The court then would have been faced with the difficult choice of decertifying the class after phase 1 and wasting judicial resources, or continuing with a class action that would have failed the predominance requirement of rule 23(b)(3).[21]

III.

In addition to the reasons given above, regarding the district court's procedural errors, this class must be decertified because it independently fails the superiority requirement of rule 23(b)(3). In the context of mass tort class actions, certification dramatically affects the stakes for defendants. Class certification magnifies and strengthens the number of unmeritorious claims. *Agent Orange*, 818 F.2d at 165–66. Aggregation of claims also makes it more likely that a defendant will be found liable and results in significantly higher damage awards. Manual for Complex Litigation § 33.26 n.1056; Kenneth S. Bordens and Irwin A. Horowitz, *Mass Tort Civil Litigation: The Impact of Procedural Changes on Jury Decisions*, 73 JUDICATURE 22 (1989).

In addition to skewing trial outcomes, class certification creates insurmountable pressure on defendants to settle, whereas individual trials would not. *See* Peter H. Schuck, *Mass Torts: An Institutional Evolutionist Perspective*, 80 Cornell L. Rev. 941, 958 (1995). The risk of facing an all-or-nothing verdict presents too high a risk, even when the probability of an adverse judgment is low. *Rhone-Poulenc*, 51 F.3d at 1298. These settlements have been referred to as judicial blackmail.

It is no surprise then, that historically, certification of mass tort litigation classes has been disfavored.[23] The traditional concern over the rights of defendants in mass tort class actions is magnified in the instant case. Our specific concern is that a mass tort cannot be properly certified without a prior track record of trials from which the district court

---

21. Severing the defendants' conduct from reliance under rule 23(c)(4) does not save the class action. A district court cannot manufacture predominance through the nimble use of subdivision (c)(4). The proper interpretation of the interaction between subdivisions (b)(3) and (c)(4) is that a cause of action, as a whole, must satisfy the predominance requirement of (b)(3) and that (c)(4) is a housekeeping rule that allows courts to sever the common issues for a class trial. *See In re N.D. Cal. Dalkon Shield IUD Prods. Liability Litig.*, 693 F.2d 847, 856 (9th Cir. 1982) (balancing severed issues against the remaining individual issues), *cert. denied*, 459 U.S. 1171, 103 S. Ct. 817, 74 L. Ed. 2d 1015 (1983); *see also Jenkins*, 109 F.R.D. at 278 (comparing state of the art defense to individual questions of exposure and degree of injury in a class action certified only on the common issue of the state of the art defense). Reading rule 23(c)(4) as allowing a court to sever issues until the remaining common issue predominates over the remaining individual issues would eviscerate the predominance requirement of rule 23(b)(3); the result would be automatic certification in every case where there is a common issue, a result that could not have been intended.

23. At the time rule 23 was drafted, mass tort litigation as we now know it did not exist. Schuck, *supra*, at 945. The term had been applied to single-event accidents. *Id.* Even in those cases, the advisory committee cautioned against certification. *See supra* note 19. As modern mass tort litigation has evolved, courts have been willing to certify simple single disaster mass torts, *see Sterling v. Velsicol Chem. Corp.*, 855 F.2d 1188, 1197 (6th Cir. 1988), but have been hesitant to certify more complex mass torts.

can draw the information necessary to make the predominance and superiority requirements required by rule 23. This is because certification of an immature tort results in a higher than normal risk that the class action may not be superior to individual adjudication.

We first address the district court's superiority analysis. The court acknowledged the extensive manageability problems with this class. Such problems include difficult choice of law determinations, subclassing of eight claims with variations in state law, *Erie* guesses, notice to millions of class members, further subclassing to take account of transient plaintiffs, and the difficult procedure for determining who is nicotine-dependent. Cases with far fewer manageability problems have given courts pause.

The district court's rationale for certification in spite of such problems i.e., that a class trial would preserve judicial resources in the millions of inevitable individual trials is based on pure speculation. Not every mass tort is asbestos, and not every mass tort will result in the same judicial crises. The judicial crisis to which the district court referred is only theoretical.

What the district court failed to consider, and what no court can determine at this time, is the very real possibility that the judicial crisis may fail to materialize. The plaintiffs' claims are based on a new theory of liability and the existence of new evidence. Until plaintiffs decide to file individual claims, a court cannot, from the existence of injury, presume that all or even any plaintiffs will pursue legal remedies. Nor can a court make a superiority determination based on such speculation.

Severe manageability problems and the lack of a judicial crisis are not the only reasons why superiority is lacking. The most compelling rationale for finding superiority in a class action—the existence of a negative value suit—is missing in this case. *Accord Phillips Petroleum Co. v. Shutts*, 472 U.S. 797, 809, 86 L. Ed. 2d 628, 105 S. Ct. 2965 (1985); *Rhone-Poulenc*, 51 F.3d at 1299.

As he stated in the record, plaintiffs' counsel in this case has promised to inundate the courts with individual claims if class certification is denied. Independently of the reliability of this self-serving promise, there is reason to believe that individual suits are feasible. First, individual damage claims are high, and punitive damages are available in most states. The expense of litigation does not necessarily turn this case into a negative value suit, in part because the prevailing party may recover attorneys' fees under many consumer protection statutes.

In a case such as this one, where each plaintiff may receive a large award, and fee shifting often is available, we find Chief Judge Posner's analysis of superiority to be persuasive:

> For this consensus or maturing of judgment the district judge proposes to substitute a single trial before a single jury.... One jury ... will hold the fate of an industry in the palm of its hand.... That kind of thing can happen in our system of civil justice.... But it need not be tolerated when the alternative exists of submitting an issue to multiple juries constituting in the aggregate a much larger and more diverse sample of decision-makers. That would not be a feasible option if the stakes to each class member were too slight to repay the cost of suit.... But this is not the case.... Each plaintiff if successful is apt to receive a judgment in the millions. With the aggregate stakes in the tens or hundreds of millions of dollars, or even in the billions, it is not a waste of judicial resources to conduct more than one trial, before more than six jurors, to determine whether a major segment of the international pharmaceutical industry is to follow the asbestos manufacturers into Chapter 11.

Rhone-Poulenc, 51 F.3d at 1300. So too here, we cannot say that it would be a waste to allow individual trials to proceed, before a district court engages in the complicated pre-dominance and superiority analysis necessary to certify a class. Fairness may demand that mass torts with few prior verdicts or judgments be litigated first in smaller units even single-plaintiff, single-defendant trials until general causation, typical injuries, and levels of damages become established. Thus, "mature" mass torts like asbestos or Dalkon Shield may call for procedures that are not appropriate for incipient mass tort cases, such as those involving injuries arising from new products, chemical substances, or pharmaceuticals. Manual for Complex Litigation § 33.26.

Principles

"[N]otwithstanding the advent of nonclass aggregate litigation, Rule 23 class litigation remains a vital feature of the litigation landscape. However, class litigation in the twenty-first century has moved a very long way from the golden age of class litigation during the 1960s. Instead, class litigation is now dominated by Rule 23(b)(3) damage class actions, rather than the injunctive classes of the Civil Rights Era. This tectonic shift to damage class actions, in turn, has exposed troubling fault lines in the pursuit of and implementation of class action relief. [C]lass actions are not dead but ... they are just badly done, indicating a compelling need for rethinking the class action rule."

Linda S. Mullenix, *Ending Class Actions as We Know Them: Rethinking the American Class Action*, 64 Emory L.J. 399, 404 (2014).

The remaining rationale for superiority judicial efficiency is also lacking. In the context of an immature tort, any savings in judicial resources is speculative, and any imagined savings would be overwhelmed by the procedural problems that certification of a *sui generis* cause of action brings with it.

Even assuming *arguendo* that the tort system will see many more addiction-as-injury claims, a conclusion that certification will save judicial resources is premature at this stage of the litigation. Take for example the district court's plan to divide core liability from other issues such as comparative negligence and reliance. The assumption is that after a class verdict, the common issues will not be a part of follow-up trials. The court has no basis for that assumption.

It may be that comparative negligence will be raised in the individual trials, and the evidence presented at the class trial will have to be repeated. The same may be true for reliance. The net result may be a waste, not a savings, in judicial resources. Only after the courts have more experience with this type of case can a court certify issues in a way that preserves judicial resources. *See Jenkins*, 782 F.2d 468 (certifying state of the art defense because experience had demonstrated that judicial resources could be saved by certification).

Even assuming that certification at this time would result in judicial efficiencies in individual trials, certification of an immature tort brings with it unique problems that may consume more judicial resources than certification will save. These problems are not speculative; the district court faced, and ignored, many of the problems that immature torts can cause.

The primary procedural difficulty created by immature torts is the inherent difficulty a district court will have in determining whether the requirements of rule 23 have been met. We have already identified a number of defects with the district court's predominance and manageability inquires, defects that will continue to exist on remand because of the unique nature of the plaintiffs' claim.

The district court's predominance inquiry, or lack of it, squarely presents the problems associated with certification of immature torts. Determining whether the common issues are a "significant" part of each individual case has an abstract quality to it when no court in this country has ever tried an injury-as-addiction claim. As the plaintiffs admitted to the district court, "we don't have the learning curb [sic] that is necessary to say to Your Honor 'this is precisely how this case can be tried and that will not run afoul of the teachings of the 5th Circuit.'"

Yet, an accurate finding on predominance is necessary before the court can certify a class. It may turn out that the defendant's conduct, while common, is a minor part of each trial. Premature certification deprives the defendant of the opportunity to present that argument to any court and risks decertification after considerable resources have been expended.

The court's analysis of reliance also demonstrates the potential judicial inefficiencies in immature tort class actions. Individual trials will determine whether individual reliance will be an issue. Rather than guess that reliance may be inferred, a district court should base its determination that individual reliance does not predominate on the wisdom of such individual trials. The risk that a district court will make the wrong guess, that the parties will engage in years of litigation, and that the class ultimately will be decertified (because reliance predominates over common issues) prevents this class action from being a superior method of adjudication.

The complexity of the choice of law inquiry also makes individual adjudication superior to class treatment. The plaintiffs have asserted eight theories of liability from every state. Prior to certification, the district court must determine whether variations in state law defeat predominance. While the task *may not* be impossible, its complexity certainly makes individual trials a more attractive alternative and, *ipso facto*, renders class treatment not superior.

In Practice

"The trend [after *Castano*] appears to be that cases involving significant personal injuries should not be certified for trial [under Rule 23(b)(3)], particularly on a nationwide or multistate basis, because individual issues of causation and individual damages often predominate and state law often varies.

"Some courts have addressed these difficulties by certifying some, but not all, issues for class treatment, and by structuring subclasses under Rule 23(c)(4) to reflect state law differences."

Manual for Complex Litigation, Fourth, § 22.70.

Through individual adjudication, the plaintiffs can winnow their claims to the strongest causes of action. The result will be an easier choice of law inquiry and a less complicated predominance inquiry. State courts can address the more novel of the plaintiffs' claims, making the federal court's *Erie* guesses less complicated. It is far more desirable to allow state courts to apply and develop their own law than to have a federal court apply "a kind of Esperanto [jury] instruction." *Rhone-Poulenc*, 51 F.3d at 1300; Manual for Complex Litigation § 33.26 (discussing the full cycle of litigation necessary for a tort to mature).

Another factor weighing heavily in favor of individual trials is the risk that in order to make this class action manageable, the court will be forced to bifurcate issues in violation of the Seventh Amendment. This class action is permeated with individual issues, such as proximate causation, comparative negligence, reliance, and compensatory damages. In order to manage so many individual issues, the district court proposed to empanel a class jury to adjudicate common issues. A second jury, or a number of "second" juries, will pass on the individual issues, either on a case-by-case basis or through group trials of individual plaintiffs.

The Seventh Amendment entitles parties to have fact issues decided by one jury, and prohibits a second jury from reexamining those facts and issues.

The Seventh Circuit recently addressed Seventh Amendment limitations to bifurcation. In *Rhone-Poulenc*, 51 F.3d at 1302–03, Chief Judge Posner described the constitutional limitation as one requiring a court to "carve at the joint" in such a way so that the same issue is not reexamined by different juries. "The right to a jury trial ... is a right to have juriable issues determined by the first jury impaneled to hear them (provided there are no errors warranting a new trial), and not reexamined by another finder of fact." *Id.* at 1303. Severing a defendant's conduct from comparative negligence results in the type of risk that our court forbade in *Blue Bird*. Comparative negligence, by definition, requires a comparison between the defendant's and the plaintiff's conduct. At a bare minimum, a second jury will rehear evidence of the defendant's conduct. There is a risk that in apportioning fault, the second jury could reevaluate the defendant's fault, determine that the defendant was not at fault, and apportion 100% of the fault to the plaintiff. In such a situation, the second jury would be impermissibly reconsidering the findings of a first jury. The risk of such reevaluation is so great that class treatment can hardly be said to be superior to individual adjudication.

The plaintiffs' final retort is that individual trials are inadequate because time is running out for many of the plaintiffs. They point out that prior litigation against the tobacco companies has taken up to ten years to wind through the legal system. While a compelling rhetorical argument, it is ultimately inconsistent with the plaintiffs' own arguments and ignores the realities of the legal system. First, the plaintiffs' reliance on prior personal injury cases is unpersuasive, as they admit that they have new evidence and are pursuing a claim entirely different from that of past plaintiffs.

Second, the plaintiffs' claim that time is running out ignores the reality of the class action device. In a complicated case involving multiple jurisdictions, the conflict of law question itself could take decades to work its way through the courts. Once that issue has been resolved, discovery, subclassing, and ultimately the class trial would take place. Next would come the appellate process. After the class trial, the individual trials and appeals on comparative negligence and damages would have to take place. The net result could be that the class action device would lengthen, not shorten, the time it takes for the plaintiffs to reach final judgment.

IV.

The district court abused its discretion by ignoring variations in state law and how a trial on the alleged causes of action would be tried. Those errors cannot be corrected on remand because of the novelty of the plaintiffs' claims. Accordingly, class treatment is not superior to individual adjudication.

We have once before stated that "traditional ways of proceeding reflect far more than habit. They reflect the very culture of the jury trial...." *In re Fibreboard Corp.*, 893 F.2d 706, 711 (5th Cir. 1990). The collective wisdom of individual juries is necessary before this court commits the fate of an entire industry or, indeed, the fate of a class of millions, to a single jury. For the forgoing reasons, we REVERSE and REMAND with instructions that the district court dismiss the class complaint.

Notes and Problems

1. In *Jenkins*, how did the court find that the complex issues raised by the assertion of personal injury damage claims did not predominate over the common core liability issues in that case? Were you persuaded by the court's relatively brief discussion of the Rule 23(b)(3) certification standards? Why was the court so motivated to certify the class? Are these proper considerations under the Rule 23(b)(3) *superiority* factors?

2. Rightly or wrongly, *Jenkins* signaled to other federal courts a more lenient attitude toward applying Rule 23(b)(3)'s standards to mass tort claims involving personal injuries, notwithstanding the 1966 caution from the Advisory Committee over such application. Was the court correct that changing times call for changing attitudes and interpretations of the Federal Rules of Civil Procedure?

3. In *Castano*, the court rejected the certification of the proposed mass tort Rule 23(b)(3) class for a number of reasons. In part, the court distinguished the case from its prior opinion in the *Jenkins* case on a number of grounds. Can you identify all the ways in which the two cases are materially distinguishable? On the other hand, the court in *Castano* included some language that suggested a different philosophical perspective on the advisability of certifying any mass tort claim under Rule 23(b)(3). What language in the opinion casts the deepest shadows over the potential for certifying any personal injury cases under Rule 23(b)(3)? In the immediate wake of *Castano*, some prophesized that it amounted to the possible "death knell for the mass tort class action." *See e.g.*, Mary J. Davis, *Toward the Proper Role for Mass Tort Class Actions*, 77 Or. L. Rev. 157, 158 (1998) (reporting on what others believed to be the implications for *Castano* but also opining for the appropriateness of certifying "mass tort class actions [as not only] appropriate, but desirable, when evaluated against the backdrop of substantive tort law policies.").

4. Notice what the court in *Castano* says about the "nimble use" of Rule 23(c)(4). That subsection permits a certifying court to allow a class action to be brought "as a class action with respect to particular issues" rather than certifying the entire case for classwide adjudication. If taken to its logical extreme, a court could say that all of the common issues in a proposed Rule 23(b)(3) class action were being certified but none of the individual issues and, therefore, the common issues predominated as that would comprise the entirety of the class action. Different lower federal courts have had different reactions to such a practice but in *Castano* (at footnote 21), the court rejects such a shoe-horned approach to Rule 23(c)(4), instead saying that the entire case must meet the Rule 23(b)(3) requirement of predominance of common issues prior to a court utilizing Rule 23(c)(4).

5. *Castano* has been highly influential and has doubtlessly caused many other lower federal courts to exercise caution before certifying a mass tort under Rule 23(b)(3). Yet nowhere in its opinion does it offer a per se rule against the certification of a mass tort. As we will see in the *Treasure Chest Casino* case next, even the Fifth Circuit a few years after *Castano* has continued to certify, under appropriate circumstances, a mass tort case.

Other circuits have likewise generally passed at the chance to declare categorically that Rule 23(b)(3) cannot tolerate the certification of a mass tort. *See, e.g., Valentino v. Carter-Wallace*, 97 F.3d 1227 (9th Cir. 1996) (refusing invitation to reject class treatment of all personal injury claims, in context of pharmaceutical mass tort). Also, in the next chapter, we will see another example of a federal court certifying a mass tort claim in the *Klein v. O'Neal* case.

As the following case reveals, certification under Rule 23(b)(3) of a mass tort personal injury case—while more difficult after the decision in *Castano*—is far from dead. As you read the following case (out of the same circuit that decided *Castano*), consider whether the problems we saw in the above care are missing in *Treasure Chest Casino*.

Mullen v. Treasure Chest Casino

186 F.3d 620 (5th Cir. 1999)

BENAVIDES, CIRCUIT JUDGE:

Treasure Chest Casino, LLC ("Treasure Chest") appeals from an interlocutory order of the district court certifying under Federal Rule of Civil Procedure 23(b)(3) a plaintiff class consisting of injured Treasure Chest employees. We affirm the district court's class certification

I. BACKGROUND

The appellees, Dennis Mullen, Sheila Bachemin, and Margaret Phipps (collectively, the "Named Plaintiffs"), are former employees of the M/V Treasure Chest Casino (the "Casino"), a floating casino owned and operated out of Kenner, Louisiana by appellant Treasure Chest. Mullen was an assistant pit boss, Bachemin was a dealer, and Phipps was employed as a slot-floor person and dealer.

Each Named Plaintiff has suffered respiratory illness allegedly caused by the Casino's defective and/or improperly maintained air-conditioning and ventilating system. Each was diagnosed with asthma and bronchitis while employed aboard the Casino. Mullen and Bachemin, while aboard the Casino, suffered respiratory attacks requiring hospitalization. Kathleen McNamara, the Named Plaintiffs' physician, testified in a deposition that as many as half of the 300 Casino employees that she had treated suffered from similar respiratory problems. She attributed the Named Plaintiffs' and other crew members' maladies to extremely smoky conditions in the Casino.

In January 1996, the Named Plaintiffs filed suit against Treasure Chest, making Jones Act, unseaworthiness, and maintenance and cure claims. They sought Rule 23 certification of a class consisting of:

> All members of the crew of the M/V Treasure Chest Casino who have been stricken with occupational respiratory illness caused by or exacerbated by the defective ventilation system in place aboard the vessel.

The parties conducted pre-certification discovery that included deposing the Named Plaintiffs, Dr. McNamara, and two other physicians. The parties then briefed the district court, which heard arguments in July 1997.

On August 29, 1997, the district court certified the proposed class under Rule 23(b)(3). Under the court's plan, the liability issues common to all class members will be tried together in an initial trial phase. Those common issues include whether the employees of the Casino are seamen within the meaning of the Jones Act, whether the Casino is a vessel within the meaning of the Jones Act, whether the Casino was rendered unseaworthy by the air quality aboard, and whether Treasure Chest was negligent in relation to the Casino's ventilation system. If the class prevails on the common liability issues in phase one, the issues affecting only individual class members will be tried in a second phase in waves of approximately five class members at a time. These limited issues include causation, damages, and comparative negligence.

Treasure Chest sought to appeal the class certification order, and the district court certified the issue for interlocutory appeal under 28 U.S.C. § 1292(b). We granted Treasure Chest permission to appeal.

II. DISCUSSION

A class may be certified under Rule 23(b)(3) only if it meets the four prerequisites found in Rule 23(a) and the two additional requirements found in Rule 23(b)(3). The two 23(b) requirements are "predominance" and "superiority":

> Common questions must "predominate over any questions affecting only individual members"; and class resolution must be "superior to other available methods for the fair and efficient adjudication of the controversy."

117 S. Ct. at 2246 (quoting Fed. R. Civ. P. 23(b)(3)).

Treasure Chest argues on appeal that the district court erred in finding any of the Rule 23 requirements satisfied.[2] Before evaluating the six requirements seriatim, we note that the district court maintains great discretion in certifying and managing a class action. We will reverse a district court's decision to certify a class only upon a showing that the court abused its discretion, *see Jenkins v. Raymark Industries*, 782 F.2d 468, 471–72 (5th Cir. 1986).

A. Numerosity

The court found that "the class is so numerous that joinder of all members is impracticable," Fed. R. Civ. P. 23(a)(1), referring to three factors. First, the class would likely consist of between 100 and 150 members. Second, owing to the transient nature of employment in the gambling business, it was likely that some of the putative class members were geographically dispersed and unavailable for joinder. Third, putative class members still employed by the Casino might be reluctant to file individually for fear of workplace retaliation. Treasure Chest challenges only the second of the district court's

---

2. Treasure Chest also argues on appeal that implicit in Rule 23 is an additional requirement that any class must be capable of objective identification before it can be certified. It contends that because being a member of the class in this case is contingent upon ultimate issues of causation, i.e., whether the class member's illness was "caused or exacerbated by the defective ventilation system," Treasure Chest is prejudiced by being forced to defend against claimants who may not end up being members of the class. This same argument was already rejected by this Court in *Forbush v. J.C. Penney Co.*, 994 F.2d 1101 (5th Cir. 1993). There, we considered a defendant's contention that a class of pension beneficiaries was "hopelessly 'circular'" because membership in the class was defined by the improper reduction of the class members' benefits, which was also the ultimate issue in the case. *Id.* at 1105. We found that the defendant's argument was "meritless and, if accepted, would preclude certification of just about any class of persons alleging injury from a particular action. These persons are linked by this common complaint, and the possibility that some may fail to prevail on their individual claims will not defeat class membership." *Id.*

three reasons. It asserts that the district court's claim that class members would be geographically dispersed was unsupported by evidence. They reference the court's own comment that the "plaintiff has not introduced any specific evidence that there are potential class members that have moved out of the area."

We find no abuse of discretion in the district court's finding of numerosity. Although the number of members in a proposed class is not determinative of whether joinder is impracticable, *see Zeidman v. J. Ray McDermott & Co.*, 651 F.2d 1030, 1038 (5th Cir. 1981), the size of the class in this case—100 to 150 members—is within the range that generally satisfies the numerosity requirement. *See* 1 Newberg on Class Actions § 3.05, at 3-25 (3d ed. 1992) (suggesting that any class consisting of more than forty members "should raise a presumption that joinder is impracticable"); *cf. Boykin v. Georgia-Pacific Corp.*, 706 F.2d 1384, 1386 (5th Cir. 1983) (finding that numerosity requirement would not be met by a class with 20 members but was met by a class with 317 members).

Furthermore, the additional factors mentioned by the district court support its finding of numerosity. *See Zeidman*, 651 F.2d at 1038 (discussing relevant factors including, for example, "the geographical dispersion of the class, the ease with which class members may be identified, the nature of the action, and the size of each plaintiff's claim"). Notwithstanding the lack of any direct evidence, the district court reasonably inferred from the nature of the putative class members' employment that some of them would be geographically dispersed. It also reasonably presumed that those potential class members still employed by Treasure Chest might be unwilling to sue individually or join a suit for fear of retaliation at their jobs. Based upon those considerations, it was within the district court's discretion to find that joinder of all 100 to 150 class members would be impracticable.

B. Commonality

The district court found that "there are questions of law or fact common to the class," Fed. R. Civ. P. 23(a)(2), on the basis of the class members' identical theories of liability, their common claims under the Jones Act, and their uniform allegations of suffering injury from second-hand smoke. Treasure Chest challenges the district court's assertion that all plaintiffs' claims relate to second-hand smoke.

The district court did not abuse its discretion in finding commonality. The test for commonality is not demanding and is met "where there is at least one issue, the resolution of which will affect all or a significant number of the putative class members." *Lightbourn v. County of El Paso*, 118 F.3d 421, 426 (5th Cir. 1997). In this case, the putative class members will assert claims for negligence under the Jones Act and for operating an unseaworthy vessel. The common issues pertaining to these theories of liability—i.e., the class members' status as Jones Act seamen, the negligence of Treasure Chest, and the unseaworthiness of the Casino—are independently sufficient to establish commonality. It is therefore irrelevant whether the class members uniformly allege damages from second-hand smoke.

C. Typicality

The district found the "the claims or defenses of the parties are typical of the claims or defenses of the class," Fed. R. Civ. P. 23(a)(3), because the Named Plaintiffs and the class members, by definition, all allege to have suffered occupation-related respiratory illness. Treasure Chest contends that the Named Plaintiffs' claims are not typical of the class because a wide array of claims could fall under the "respiratory illness" category.

We find no abuse in the district court's finding of typicality. Like commonality, the test for typicality is not demanding. It "focuses on the similarity between the named plaintiffs' legal and remedial theories and the theories of those whom they purport to represent." *Lightbourn*, 118 F.3d at 426. In this case, the Named Plaintiffs' and the proposed class members' legal and remedial theories appear to be exactly the same. The class complaint indicates that they will all premise liability for the Casino's defective air ventilation system under the Jones Act and the doctrine of seaworthiness. Any variety in the illnesses the Named Plaintiffs and the class members suffered will not affect their legal or remedial theories, and thus does not defeat typicality.

D. Adequacy of Representation

The district court stated that "the representative parties will fairly and adequately protect the interests of the class," Fed. R. Civ. P. 23(a)(4), because the Named Plaintiffs' interests are identical to the interests of the proposed class and their attorneys have extensive experience litigating class actions and Jones Act cases. Treasure Chest argues on the appeal that the district court's finding was erroneous because the Named Plaintiffs and the class members have suffered from varied illnesses and have varying susceptibilities to respiratory ailments.

We find no abuse of discretion in the district court's finding. Differences between named plaintiffs and class members render the named plaintiffs inadequate representatives only if those differences create conflicts between the named plaintiffs' interests and the class members' interests. *See Jenkins v. Raymark Industries, Inc.*, 782 F.2d 468, 472 (5th Cir. 1986) (considering whether named plaintiffs have "an insufficient stake in the outcome or interests antagonistic to the unnamed members" in evaluating adequate representation requirement). The differences described by Treasure Chest may create variances in the ways that the Named Plaintiffs and class members will prove causation and damages. A class member who has never smoked, for example, may have less difficulty in proving that the conditions inside the Casino caused her asthma than will Bachemin, who has a history of smoking and whose claim may be subject to a defense of contributory negligence. Such a difference, however, does not affect the alignment of their interests. Nothing indicates that the class members will be inadequately represented by the Named Plaintiffs and their counsel.

E. Predominance

We see no abuse in the district court's finding that "the questions of law or fact common to the members of the class predominate over any questions affecting only individual members." Fed. R. Civ. P. 23(b)(3). "In order to 'predominate,' common issues must constitute a significant part of the individual cases." *Jenkins*, 782 F.2d at 472. The district court held that the issues to be tried commonly—seamen status, vessel status, negligence, and seaworthiness—were significant in relation to the individual issues of causation, damages, and contributory negligence. Treasure Chest argues on appeal that the district court abused its discretion by failing to weigh the common against the individual issues and by improperly finding causation to be a common issue.

Treasure Chest's arguments are without merit. First, although the court's predominance inquiry was not lengthy, there is no indication that the court limited its inquiry to counting issues instead of weighing them. Second, explicit in the district court's decision is a finding that causation is a unique issue that will be resolved in the trial plan's second-phase individual trials.

Even examining the district court's predominance analysis more closely, we find no abuse. The common issues in this case, especially negligence and seaworthiness, are not only significant but also pivotal. They will undoubtedly require the parties to produce extensive evidence regarding the Casino's air ventilation system, as well as testimony concerning Treasure Chest's knowledge of, and response to, the Casino employees' respiratory problems and complaints. The phase-one jury will have the difficult task of determining whether the air quality aboard the Casino resulted from a negligent breach of Treasure Chest's duty to its employees or rendered the Casino unseaworthy. If Treasure Chest prevails on those two issues alone, they will prevail in the case.

Moreover, this case does not involve the type of individuated issues that have in the past led courts to find predominance lacking. For example, in *Amchem Products, Inc. v. Windsor*, 521 U.S. 591 (1997), the Supreme Court found that common issues did not predominate where the members of the plaintiff class were exposed to asbestos-containing products from different sources over different time periods, some of the class members were asymptomatic while others had developed illnesses, and the class members were from a variety of states requiring the application of a multitude of different legal standards. Similarly, in *Castano v. American Tobacco Co.*, 84 F.3d 734 (5th Cir. 1996), this Court found that a putative class of addicted smokers did not meet the predominance requirement because there were complex choice-of-law issues and the case involved novel addiction-as-injury claims with no track record from which a court could determine which issues were "significant." Here, by contrast, the putative class members are all symptomatic by definition and claim injury from the same defective ventilation system over the same general period of time. Because all of the claims are under federal law, there are no individual choice-of-law issues. And, because negligence and doctrine-of-seaworthiness claims are time-tested bases for liability, the district court could reasonably evaluate the significance of the common issues without first establishing a track record.

F. Superiority

We also find no abuse of discretion in the district court's finding that "a class action is superior to other available methods for the fair and efficient adjudication of the controversy." Fed. R. Civ. P. 23(b)(3). The district court based its superiority finding on the fact that the class litigation in this case would not present the degree of managerial complexities that prompted this Court to decertify the putative class in *Castano*. Specifically, the district court mentioned the lack of any complex choice-of-law or *Erie* problems, and that the class would consist of only hundreds, instead of millions, of members. The bifurcated-trial plan, the court found, would "promote judicial economy and avoid the wasteful, duplicative litigation which would inevitably result if these cases were tried individually." Treasure Chest argues that the district court abused its discretion by failing adequately to consider how a trial on the merits would be conducted. It contends that because the Named Plaintiffs describe somewhat different causes for their ailments, a phase-one judgment of negligence or unseaworthiness related solely to tobacco smoke would be inadequate insofar as it would preclude plaintiffs from recovering for ailments that were caused by sources other than tobacco smoke in the phase-two trials.

We find no merit in Treasure Chest's argument. First, Treasure Chest overstates the importance of the Named Plaintiffs' conjecture regarding their own illnesses. It is true that, in addition to making second-hand smoke complaints, Dennis Mullen has complained about the temperature aboard the Casino, Sheila Bachemin has described one incident where paint fumes on the Casino "kicked in" her asthma, and Margaret Phipps has stated that her asthma might have been caused by dust on the air vents or germs on the radios used by multiple casino employees. As lay witnesses, however, the Named Plaintiffs' opinions about the possible causes of their own respiratory conditions are of negligible evidentiary weight and probably would not be admissible at trial. The medical experts already deposed in this case have unwaveringly cited excessive second-hand smoke as the most likely Casino-related factor to have exacerbated or caused the putative class members' respiratory problems. It is thus likely that the trial will focus on excessive second-hand smoke as both the effect of the defective ventilation system and the cause of the putative class members' respiratory problems.

Furthermore, even if the class does claim at trial that the Casino's ventilation system was defective in relation to more than tobacco smoke, we are confident that the district court can ably manage this case as a class action. Our precedent limits a negligent party's liability to injuries that are caused by the same condition that rendered the party negligent. *See Gavagan v. United States*, 955 F.2d 1016, 1020–21 (5th Cir. 1992). The court can easily abide by this precedent by instructing the jury to answer special verdicts finding whether the Treasure Chest was negligent, or the Casino was unseaworthy, as to each alleged causal agent, i.e., tobacco smoke, dust mites, fungi, paint fumes, et cetera. The court can then properly limit the injuries for which the phase-two juries could find Treasure Chest liable. Thus, if the phase-one jury were to find that Treasure Chest was negligent as to tobacco smoke but not as to paint fumes, any class member whose injuries were found by a phase-two jury to be caused by paint fumes would be unable to recover. Even though rendering multiple special verdicts would complicate the task for the phase-one jury and the court, we would see no abuse in the district court's finding such a process superior to conducting duplicative individual trials.

We also agree with the district court that none of the superiority concerns raised by our decision in *Castano* requires a different result. There, many of the manageability problems stemmed from the million-person class membership, the complex choice-of-law issues, the novel addiction-as-injury cause of action, and the extensive subclassing requirements. As already discussed, none of those problems exist in this case. In fact, unlike the "Frankenstein's monster" feared in *Castano*, 84 F.3d at 745 n.19, this class is akin to other bifurcated class actions this Court has approved. *See Watson v. Shell Oil Co.*, 979 F.2d 1014 (5th Cir. 1992) (finding no abuse in the district court's certification of a bifurcated class action arising from an oil refinery explosion where liability and punitive damages would be resolved commonly and injury, causation, and actual damages would be resolved individually); *Jenkins*, 782 F.2d 468 (finding no abuse of discretion in district court's certification of a bifurcated class action where asbestos producers' "state of the art defense" as well as product identification, product defectiveness, negligence, and punitive damages would be resolved commonly and causation, actual damages, and comparative fault would tried individually); *Hernandez v. Motor Vessel Skyward*, 61 F.R.D. 558 (S.D. Fla. 1973), *aff'd*, 507 F.2d 1278, 1279 (5th Cir. 1975) (unpublished) (certifying bifurcated class action on behalf of 350 passengers who were fed contaminated food aboard cruise ship where negligence would be tried commonly and causation and damages would be tried individually).

In *Castano*, this Court expressed a concern that having one jury consider the defendant's conduct and another consider the plaintiffs' comparative negligence could create Seventh Amendment problems. *See Castano*, 84 F.3d at 750–51 (citing *In re Rhone-Poulenc Rorer Inc.*, 51 F.3d 1293, 1303 (7th Cir. 1995)). This does not change our view of the district court's superiority finding. Treasure Chest did not raise this issue to the district court nor has it been argued on appeal. We are reluctant to find that the district abused its discretion by failing to consider an issue that was not raised by the parties.

In any case, we would not find the risk of infringing upon the parties' Seventh Amendment rights significant in this case. The Seventh Amendment does not prohibit bifurcation of trials as long as the "'the judge [does] not divide issues between separate trials in such a way that the same issue is reexamined by different juries.'" *Cimino v. Raymark Industries, Inc.*, 151 F.3d 297, 320 n.50, (5th Cir. 1998) (quoting *Rhone-Poulenc*, 51 F.3d at 1303); *see Alabama v. Blue Bird Body Co., Inc.*, 573 F.2d 309, 318 (5th Cir. 1978). In *Castano*, we were concerned that allowing a second jury to consider the plaintiffs' comparative negligence would invite that jury to reconsider the first jury's findings concerning the defendants' conduct. We believe that such a risk has been avoided here by leaving all issues of causation for the phase-two jury. When a jury considers the comparative negligence of a plaintiff, "the focus is upon causation. It is inevitable that a comparison of the conduct of plaintiffs and defendants ultimately be in terms of causation." *Lewis v. Timco, Inc.*, 716 F.2d 1425, 1431 (5th Cir. 1983) (en banc); *see id.* (permitting the use of comparative negligence in strict liability claims). Thus, in considering comparative negligence, the phase-two jury would not be reconsidering the first jury's findings of whether Treasure Chest's conduct was negligent or the Casino unseaworthy, but only the degree to which those conditions were the sole or contributing cause of the class member's injury. Because the first jury will not be considering any issues of causation, no Seventh Amendment implications affect our review of the district court's superiority finding.

III. CONCLUSION

For the foregoing reasons, we find that the district court did not abuse its discretion in certifying under Rule 23(b)(3) a class of all Casino employees stricken with occupation-related respiratory illnesses. AFFIRMED.

Notes and Problems

1. Notice the way the class was defined in the *Treasure Chest Casino* case—"all members … who have been stricken with … illness … caused by … the defective ventilation system in place on board the vessel." If the jury were to reject the allegation that the ventilation system was defective, is there an argument that the defense verdict should not be binding on any class member? Or what if a group of class members alleged that they had emphysema and the jury returned a verdict finding that the ventilation system, while perhaps causing other lung problems, did not cause emphysema. Would this verdict be binding on those particular class members? How does the court get around this *fail safe* definition problem? (Pay close attention to footnote 2.) Do you find that satisfying?

2. In fairly easily affirming the trial court's certification of the *Treasure Chest Casino* case as a Rule 23(b)(3) class, the appellate court spends considerable time distinguishing this case from the prior *Castano* opinion issued a few years earlier by the same appellate court. What are the most significant distinctions between the two cases, thereby permitting the court to certify a personal injury mass tort case as a proper Rule 23(b)(3) damage class? With these distinctions in mind, what rules of thumb might be appropriate to consider if counsel is contemplating fashioning a new class lawsuit involving personal injury tort claims? What strategies should be suggested to increase the odds of obtaining certification?

3. *Chapter Problem.* In light of the *Jenkins, Castano,* and *Treasure Chest Casino* cases, re-examine the likelihood of a case like that filed by Merri Chance against TMG being certified under Rule 23(b)(3). What attributes of the case remind you of the *Jenkins* or *Treasure Chest Casino* cases? What attributes, if any, remind you of the *Castano* case?

F. Appointment of Class Counsel

Prior to 2003, when Rule 23 was last amended, assessment and appointment of class counsel was handled as part of the Rule 23(a)(4) "adequacy of representation" analysis. In 2003, Rule 23 was amended to add the current Rule 23(g) which governs the appointment of counsel and the authorization for payment of attorney's fees in class actions. For a long time, courts have played a prominent role in complex litigation in the appointment of lead counsel. For example, when courts use their consolidation powers bestowed by Rule 42(a), they will often name one of the lawyers as the lead counsel to coordinate with the court and speak for one side of litigants. Further, in cases transferred under the Multi-District Litigation Statute, 28 U.S.C. § 1407, the MDL judge will typically name lead counsel or a group of liaison counsel to speak for the various plaintiffs' lawyers, conduct discovery, and handle contested hearings. In these scenarios, the appointment of lead counsel is done for practical convenience and to ease communications and speed up decisionmaking. But in the context of a class action, it has long been understood that appointment of class counsel is necessitated as part of the mandatory provision of adequate representation of the absent class members lacking their own chosen counsel.

Rule 23(c)(1)(B)

"An order that certifies a class action must define the class and the class claims, issues, or defenses, and must appoint class counsel under Rule 23(g)."

You might assume that the plaintiff's counsel who filed a putative class action automatically became the class counsel upon certification. This does happen. But with increasing frequency, courts have understood the special role they play in ensuring that the absent class members receive the best representation possible. This sometimes means that the court might appoint as class counsel someone other than the original plaintiff's lawyer. Or when multiple related putative class actions have been filed, the court certifying a class action has a number of plaintiffs' counsel from which to choose. This has led to the practice of courts sometimes taking competitive bids from different lawyers each seeking the prized and lucrative appointment as lead class counsel. With the 2003 revisions to Rule 23, subpart (g) now expressly invites this practice: "If more than one adequate applicant seeks appointment [as class counsel], the court must appoint the applicant best able to represent the interests of the class." The case below shows an example of a court deciding to use competitive bidding from a large number of aspiring lawyers for the designation as lead class counsel.

Rule 23(g)

(g)(1) Unless a statute provides otherwise, a court that certifies a class must appoint class counsel. In appointing class counsel, the court:

(A) must consider:

(i) the work counsel has done in identifying or investigating potential claims in the action;

    (ii) counsel's experience in handling class actions, other complex litigation, and the types of claims asserted in the action;

    (iii) counsel's knowledge of the applicable law; and

    (iv) the resources that counsel will commit to representing the class;

 (B) may consider any other matter pertinent to counsel's ability to fairly and adequately represent the interests of the class;

In re Auction Houses Antitrust Litig.

197 F.R.D. 71 (S.D.N.Y. 2000)

KAPLAN, J.,

Class action lawsuits protect plaintiffs' rights and promote accountability by permitting dispersed, disorganized plaintiffs who may have suffered only small injuries to find redress by acting as a group where they would lack sufficient incentive to do so individually. At the same time, however, the relationship between a plaintiff class and its attorney may suffer from a structural flaw, a divergence of economic interests of the class and its counsel. The class action mechanism can redound more to the benefit of the attorney than to that of the class, as counsel has an incentive to act in its own best interest, rather than that of the class. Thus, the class action mechanism on occasion has proved to be Janus-faced.

> The phrase "Janus-faced" makes reference to the two-faced god "Janus" and refers to one who is hypocritical or deceitful.

This case has presented an occasion to seek to ease this tension and improve the class action as an instrument of justice. The Court, over the objection of some of plaintiffs' counsel, employed an auction in selecting lead counsel. This opinion sets forth the basis for the Court's decision to conduct an auction and the reasoning behind the manner in which it was conducted.

I

Background

Defendants Sotheby's Holding, Inc. and its subsidiary Sotheby's Inc. (collectively "Sotheby's") and Christie's International PLC and its subsidiary Christie's, Inc. (collectively "Christie's") are in the business of providing auction services of fine and applied arts, furniture, antiques, automobiles, collectibles and other items. The primary sources of revenues of the defendant auction houses are so-called buyers' premiums and sellers' commissions. A buyer's premium is, typically, a percentage of the price at which the buyer successfully bids on an item at auction that is added to the auction sales price and retained by the auction house. The seller's commission is a percentage of the auction sales price deducted from the sale proceeds paid to the seller and retained by the auction house.

On December 24, 1999, Christie's International's former chief executive officer, Christopher Davidge, resigned abruptly. Subsequently, Christie's reportedly provided evidence of price fixing with Sotheby's to the Department of Justice and is said to have received conditional amnesty from criminal prosecution in exchange for providing evidence.

In late January and February 2000, following press reports of these events, a large number of individual and class action complaints were filed in this District against Christie's and Sotheby's. All were referred to the undersigned as related cases. The complaints allege that the auction house defendants, beginning at least as early as January 1, 1993, conspired to manipulate the prices at which they provided non-Internet auction services. The conspiracy allegedly began in 1993 with an agreement to employ a common rate schedule for the premiums charged to buyers. It allegedly was expanded in 1995, when they allegedly agreed to use substantially similar rates for sellers' commissions. Further, plaintiffs maintain that the auction houses agreed in 1995 to terminate the previous practice of negotiating the amounts of sellers' commissions with some of their customers.

The first status conference in this case was held on February 23, 2000. Dozens of plaintiffs' attorneys attended, and a consortium of five law firms immediately proposed themselves as plaintiffs' executive committee or co-lead counsel in the case. The group of five represented that it had been selected in an earlier meeting attended by all of the plaintiffs' lawyers, that all possessed the highest credentials, and that the selection was unopposed. Nevertheless, a sixth firm then suggested to the Court that it be permitted to join the committee of five. And yet another objected to the proposed executive committee as too large and instead proposed an alternative executive committee consisting of itself and two other firms. The Court advised counsel that it had not decided how to select lead counsel for the class, if one were certified, but appointed interim lead counsel pending a decision on the class motion.

On April 20, 2000, the Court certified the plaintiff class. In a separate order, the Court announced that it was considering the use of an auction to select lead counsel. The order set forth a tentative set of procedures governing the auction and solicited bids from interested counsel. The Court solicited also *amicus* briefs from a number of well-respected academic authorities in the field and invited counsel to submit briefs commenting on the merits of the proposed auction procedure.

Proposed Fee Structure

[The Court initially proposed a fee structure with two figures, X and Y. Below the dollar value of X, the class would receive 100% of the judgment. Between X and Y the lead counsel would receive 100% of the judgment. After Y, lead counsel would receive 25% of the judgment.]

In Practice

"Few decisions by the court in complex litigation are as difficult and sensitive as the appointment of designated counsel. There is often intense competition for appointment by the court as designated counsel, an appointment that may implicitly promise large fees and a prominent role in the litigation."

Manual for Complex Litigation, Fourth, § 10.224.

After considering the comments of the *amici* and bidders, the Court issued a second order revising the fee structure and soliciting a new round of bids. This second proposed fee structure included only one variable, X, rather than two. One hundred percent of any gross recovery up to and including X was to go to the class. And twenty-five percent of any recovery in excess of X would be paid to counsel, with the remainder going to the class. Each bid was to state the value of X pursuant to which the bidder was prepared to serve as lead counsel. As before, bidders were required to submit explanatory memoranda and sworn certifications. As with the previous round of bidding, the Court stated that it would select lead counsel based on its judgment as to which bidder was likely best to serve the interests of the class, taking into account the economic terms of the bids as well as the bidder's qualifications.

All additional terms contained in the first proposed fee structure were included in the Court's second proposal as well, including the provision that the attorney's fee would be inclusive of all costs, disbursements and other charges incurred in connection with the litigation. The Court noted further that it did not intend to disclose any of the bids prior to the earlier of (a) final adjudication of the action, or (b) notice to the class of a proposed settlement, and it ordered that lead counsel thus selected not disclose the terms of its bid to defendants or anyone else without approval of the Court.

Selection of Lead Counsel for the Class

By May 25, 2000, the final day for submission of the bids, the Court had received twenty-one sealed bids for the position of lead counsel, of which seventeen complied with the Court's proposed fee structure. After careful review, the Court selected David Boies and Richard B. Drubel of Boies, Schiller & Flexner, LLP as lead counsel in the case.

II

Problems of Choosing and Compensating Counsel

The modern class action device undoubtedly has proved an important innovation for plaintiffs' rights. It provides a means of redress to dispersed and disorganized plaintiffs who may have suffered only small injuries and who, in its absence, likely would lack sufficient incentives to bring their own claims. By serving as a vehicle for these claims, the class action plays an important part in enforcement policy in many areas, including securities regulation and antitrust. Nonetheless, the class action mechanism is not free of problems, foremost among them for purposes of this case difficulties in obtaining counsel who will manage the case efficiently and effectively on behalf of the class and the mismatch of economic incentives between the plaintiff class and its attorney.

When, as here, multiple related claims are filed by different plaintiffs' attorneys, a case may threaten quickly to become unmanageable, as coordination and strategy problems arise. To remedy the problem of unmanageability, courts traditionally select lead counsel from among the attorneys representing the individual plaintiffs. Lead counsel typically is responsible for working with other counsel to develop positions on substantive and procedural issues in the case, presenting arguments to the court, initiating discovery requests and responses, employing expert witnesses, conducting depositions and insuring that schedules are met. By placing these responsibilities in the hands of one or a small group of counsel, the selection of lead counsel is meant to permit large numbers of cases in which common questions predominate to be prosecuted simultaneously as consolidated or class actions, thereby avoiding duplicated efforts, wasted resources and inconsistent or preclusive judgments. Nevertheless, problems of coordination and duplication of effort may exist.

Lead counsel generally litigates a class action case on behalf of dozens, hundreds or thousands of individual plaintiffs, all of whom seek to recover from defendants. Given the potential for massive plaintiffs' recoveries in such cases, the lead counsel position may involve a potentially large attorney's fee. The role therefore has become a coveted prize to be fought over or bargained for among competing plaintiff's attorneys. This process typically occurs in one of two ways, neither of which necessarily leads to an optimal outcome. Often, interested counsel jockey for the lead counsel position, leaving the court to choose one of the contenders, sometimes with little guidance. Counsel thus selected is not necessarily the most qualified or that who will best protect the interests of the class. Alternatively, the plaintiffs' lawyers negotiate among themselves to select lead counsel or a team of lead counsel, and the choice is presented as a *fait accompli* for the court summarily to endorse. Here again, the choice is not necessarily in the plaintiffs' best interests. These two scenarios threatened to replay themselves almost exactly in this case.

Compensation — Drawbacks of Commonly Utilized Fee Structures

Plaintiffs' attorney is, of course, duty bound to act in the best interests of the class. However, because of the manner in which attorney's fees in class actions frequently are calculated, the optimal recovery for the class often does not yield the highest attorney's fee. Likewise, the result yielding the highest attorney's fee is not necessarily in the class' best interests. This tension can lead counsel to neglect the class' interests in pursuit of a higher fee. These mismatched incentives predominate when the fee is determined by using either of the two most common fee structures used in common fund cases, the lodestar method and the percentage-of-recovery method. [The lodestar method essentially takes the reasonable hourly rate and multiplies it by the reasonable hours incurred in pursuing the claims subject to various discretionary multipliers that might serve to increase or decrease the basic subtotal. The percentage-of-recovery is easier to implement and just assigns a reasonable percentage of the total award obtained for the class as attorney's fees. Each system is subject to various pro and con arguments. One problem with the lodestar is that it discourages early settlement and encourages unnecessary attorney time on the case. A problem with the percentage-of-recovery is that it can result in enormous fees for counsel even if the case settles early on with little effort expended. In fact, it might incentivize counsel to a prematurely early settlement before significant costs and time are incurred by counsel. This debate will be discussed more in Chapter 6 Attorney's Fees.]

Collective Action Dilemma in Class Actions

These problems of mismatched incentives are present not only in class actions, but also in traditional attorney-client relationships where both the hourly rate fee structure and the contingency fee can motivate the attorney to pursue his or her own economic interest at the expense of the client. However, they often can be far more severe in the class action context, primarily because classes tend to be large, dispersed and disorganized and therefore suffer from a collective action dilemma not faced by individual litigants. This collective action dilemma leads to significantly less monitoring of the attorney by the class and consequential higher agency costs. The danger of a suboptimal result for plaintiffs, therefore, is far more severe in the class action context than in traditional litigation.

Procedural Disadvantages for Class Action Plaintiffs

Plaintiffs are prohibited from exerting the same supervisory control over the litigation as exists in the non-class action context.[31] They usually lack control even over the selection of counsel, giving rise to a situation in which a poorly qualified lawyer may be chosen to represent the class when few individuals in the class would have selected that lawyer in an open market. [Further, unlike with traditional litigation, the class does not negotiate

---

31. For instance, class members lack veto power over any proposed settlement, and they have no right to be kept informed of developments in the case. *See* Alexander, *Do the Merits Matter?*, 43 Stan. L. Rev. at 535.

a fee arrangement with counsel that will determine the method of fee computation.] These problems further contribute to suboptimal outcomes in the class action context.

In consequence of these drawbacks, the class action mechanism cannot work wholly in the interests of the litigants. Under either of the most common fee structures, attorney/client agency costs are extraordinarily high. In some cases, they allow the class action device to serve the interests of the lawyers more than those of their clients. A few courts recently have begun to experiment with reform.

Use of Auctions to Select Lead Counsel

Judge Vaughan Walker in the Northern District of California was the first to experiment with an auction to select and compensate lead counsel in a class action. In *In re Oracle Securities Litigation*, [131 F.R.D. 688 (N.D. Cal. 1990), he insisted that the various counsel competing for lead counsel status submit independent and sealed bids from which the court would select lead counsel. After counsel was selected, the case eventually settled. Based upon the bid, lead counsel received attorney's fees of $4.8 million or roughly 19% of the settlement recovery.]

Since Judge Walker first experimented with a lead counsel auction, several other courts have followed suit. A number have embraced fee structures with built-in incentives similar to those endorsed in *Oracle*, including the declining percentage-of-recovery fee and the expense cap. Others have endorsed a cap on attorney's fees, presumably in order to prevent windfall recovery by plaintiffs' counsel. Still other courts have asked bidders to submit their evaluations of the case, including the probability of success, in order better to compare the competing proposals. Finally, some courts have given a right of first refusal to counsel for the lead plaintiff, allowing counsel to match the terms of the winning bid if it so chooses. This undoubtedly reflects a presumption, *ceteris paribus*, in favor of counsel for the lead plaintiff.

Possible Drawbacks of Lead Counsel Auctions

The use of auctions to select lead counsel in class actions has been the subject of much criticism. It has been argued that a simple auction that awards the lead counsel position to the bidder proposing the lowest fee carries substantial risks. Although this approach may keep attorney's fees at a minimum, it limits the potential upside gain for counsel of a substantial award to plaintiff and consequently can encourage quick and cheap settlements. Further, use of price as the sole criterion for selection does nothing to ensure that plaintiffs receive quality representation.

The lead counsel auction unwittingly may undermine also the efficacy of the class action device. Courts in certain cases have been known to award the lead counsel position to the attorney that files the first complaint in the case or to a group of which that attorney is a part. The rationale behind this first-to-file rule is that it creates an incentive for attorneys to ferret out wrongs that may be difficult or impossible for individual plaintiffs ever to identify. By rewarding attorneys that incur these search costs, the award of the lead counsel position to the first attorney to file arguably makes the class action mechanism a more vital means of redress for injured plaintiffs. This, in turn, benefits society by creating a deterrent to wrongful behavior by others.

The routine selection of lead counsel by auction, in contrast, may discourage attorneys from searching out and identifying illegal activity, as the attorney who takes this initiative is not necessarily compensated for his or her effort. This casts doubt on the desirability of holding any auction at all, at least in cases in which attorney initiative played an important role in uncovering the alleged wrong.

Granting counsel to the lead plaintiff a right of first refusal conceivably might address this concern by promising the attorney that incurred the search costs, if willing to offer his or her services at a competitive price, a reward for this action. However, a right of first refusal takes control over the selection of lead counsel out of the court's hands and thereby undermines the court's ability to ensure that the class receives the highest quality representation.

Mindful of these considerations, the Court in this case undertook to establish a method of counsel selection and a fee structure that, in the context of this case, would begin to address some of these concerns and seek to align counsel's and plaintiffs' interests more fully.

III

The Court was mindful of these considerations when considering the possibility of an auction for the position of lead counsel. It concluded that this case is singularly appropriate for the use of an auction for several reasons.

Unlike many class actions, no attorney initiative was required here to ferret out the alleged wrong committed by defendants. Rather, the alleged wrong came to light only after it was announced that the Department of Justice had begun to investigate defendants and that Christie's had sought conditional amnesty from criminal prosecution. The attorney who filed the first complaint in this case therefore is not necessarily any more deserving of the lead counsel position than is any other attorney involved, and selection as lead counsel of someone other than the first-to-file did not deprive an investigating attorney of his or her just reward or dissuade attorneys in other cases from searching out a wrong.

This case is well suited for a lead counsel auction also because several factors are present that permit an auction nearly to approximate an efficient market. First, this case has received extensive media attention and consequently attracted large numbers of able plaintiffs' attorneys. Indeed, whereas most previous experiments with lead counsel auctions have involved bids from very few attorneys, the Court in this case received bids from upward of twenty firms in each of two rounds of bidding. As larger markets lead to more competition, and as competition leads to more efficient results, the number of prospective qualified bidders in this case undoubtedly contributed to the submission of many high quality bids from which to choose.

Second, the form of relief sought in this case is monetary damages, rather than equitable relief. This makes the case easier to evaluate, simplifies the bidding process and permits the Court more easily to compare the bids.

The circumstances in this case allowed the lead counsel auction to approach an efficient market for legal services for a third reason as well — the bidding attorneys had far more information with which to evaluate the case, both as to liability and damages, than typically is available. With respect to liability, this case differs from those in which plaintiffs simply make a claim that defendants deny, or even cases in which the government is undertaking a criminal investigation of defendants. Rather, Christie's reportedly had sought to take advantage of the government's amnesty program and allegedly has received conditional amnesty from prosecution. Although this alone certainly does not establish liability or speak to the scope or temporal duration of the alleged conspiracy, it appears to give plaintiffs a better prospect for success on the merits than is often the case.

With respect to damages, too, there are fewer unknowns here than often is the case. The essence of plaintiffs' claim is that Christie's and Sotheby's acted as duopolists to rig prices in what is principally a two firm market. Significant information is available regarding the market shares of the two companies, and Sotheby's is a publicly held company, the financial statements of which are available and informative. This information alone provided bidders with a strong base of information from which to calculate potential damages. Further, as the case developed, it became clear that there had been at least preliminary settlement negotiations in which defendants furnished financial information to Interim Lead Counsel, and they had ordered expert analysis of this information. The Court ordered that the expert analysis be made available to all bidders prior to the time the bids were due in order to equalize the information base and create the most competitive process possible. In consequence, there was an unusually substantial base of information from which bidders intelligently could evaluate the case.

Reasoning Behind the Court's First Proposed Fee Structure

[The Court believed its fee structure, where all of the first fruits up to the X variable went to the class, would avoid an incentive to prematurely settle the case, but that counsel would be encouraged to obtain as large of relief as possible for the class by earning a 25% fee on all sums gained above the X amount.] The use of a single variable, X, rather than two, as in the first proposal, was meant to eliminate the potential conflict of interest created by the first proposal.

The Court's prohibition in the second proposal of disclosure of the terms of the successful bid was designed also to reduce perverse incentives that may have been created under the first proposal. Were defendants apprised of the amount of the bid, they might be inclined to formulate settlement offers in order best to take advantage of any perverse attorney incentives created by the fee structure.

Selection of Lead Counsel

After careful review of the bids, the Court selected David Boies and Richard B. Drubel of Boies, Schiller & Flexner, LLP as lead counsel in the case. This choice does not reflect adversely on the capability or integrity of other bidders, many of whom are known to and respected by the Court. It merely reflects the Court's judgment as to which bidder, in all the circumstances, likely would best serve the interests of the plaintiff class. In short, the Court sought to act as a fiduciary to the class in selecting counsel. In light of the pendency of the litigation, the Court is not prepared at this time to disclose the terms of the winning bid.

IV

The benefits of any auction for lead counsel are difficult to assess. It is simple to compare *post facto* the fee awarded to counsel selected by auction to that which would have been awarded using a traditional percentage-of-recovery method. Likewise, ready comparison can be made with the fees that would have been awarded to other bidders, had their bids been selected. However, the relative value of the attorney's fee does not adequately measure the success of the auction. Instead, the true value of the auction lies in its effect, if any, on the net recovery obtained by plaintiffs. In this respect, the jury on the lead counsel auction in this case is still out, but it is anticipated that the fee structure and the auction process will function as they were intended—to align attorney-client interests more closely, reduce agency costs, and help ensure that the class action mechanism acts as an effective mechanism of justice.

SO ORDERED.

Notes and Problems

1. The court in the foregoing case articulates its rationale as to why it felt the process used to obtain bids from various lawyers would be the best way to decide the Rule 23(g) appointment of counsel issue. Were you impressed with this process or did you find

potential objections to this method of appointing class counsel? Does it strike you as odd that a class member will have the court appoint counsel in this manner?

2. The court spends some time discussing the issue of attorney's fees and possibly different methods for calculating the fee. What were some of the criticisms of each method? Did the court strike the right balance in this case? The issue of attorney's fees in complex litigation will be explored further in Chapter 6 Attorney's Fees.

3. Why did the court believe it was necessary to receive secret bids from the various lawyers seeking the appointment? How could the defendants have used this information, were it available, to their advantage in settlement discussions?

Pulling It All Together Exercise

Julia is a third-year attorney at her own solo practice—Julia Thomas & Associates, L.L.C. A client came to her wondering if they had been cheated by their credit card company by charging a different interest amount than what she had agreed to pay and what her monthly statements indicated was being used. Julia engaged, out of her own pocket, a local accountant to review all of the client's bills for the last three years and discovered that the client's suspicions were correct. Julia thereafter did substantial legal research into the available causes of action and spent time drafting a complaint and strategizing over the best venue. After the putative class action was filed (on behalf of the client and all other credit card customers of this bank during the prior three-year period), the bank appeared and filed a motion to dismiss due to a mandatory arbitration clause. Julia spent extensive time researching the law on the enforceability of such clauses, drafting a brief in opposition to the bank's motion, and finally prevailed in having the court overrule the motion. Afterwards, Julia spent six months exchanging discovery with the bank concerning issues of class certification. The trial court finally agreed to certify the class under Rule 23(b)(3). At this point, another law firm emerged on the scene (as counsel for another class member), Reavus & Pogue, L.L.P., and filed a motion asking that it be chosen as lead class counsel instead of Julia. Reavus & Pogue is a national firm based in this jurisdiction, with partners who have decades of experience working on class actions (both pursuing and defending), has been class counsel on several prior cases before the same judge (all were highly successful in the outcome), has a partner at the firm who has published a textbook on consumer fraud claims, and the managing partner of the entire firm is the recently elected president of the state bar association. Julia, of course, also seeks appointment for herself as class counsel pursuant to Rule 23(g).

You are the law clerk for the district judge presiding over this case. What are the best arguments respectively of Julia and Reavus & Pogue as to why they should be appointed class counsel pursuant to Rule 23(g) and its standards? Who will you recommend to the judge be appointed, and why? As the court's law clerk, spend 30 minutes reducing to writing your assessment of these issues for the judge's benefit.

Chapter Problem Revisited

Now that we have covered each of the different types of class actions under the modern Rule 23(b), analyze which subsection offers the best opportunity for

Merri Chance to obtain certification of her putative class action. Are multiple pathways to certification available given the circumstances and allegations of her case? If more information would be needed to analyze these issues, make a list of the discovery that would be appropriate for the counsel for TMG to undertake in responding to a motion for certification.

Upon Further Review

Whether to certify a putative class is perhaps the most crucial decision a trial court will have to make in the class action context. Much hinges on this decision. A claim without certification might be a nuisance lawsuit subject to either voluntary dismissal or settlement for a trifling sum. But upon receipt of a favorable certification order from the trial court, that same case might become a "bet the company" piece of complex litigation with dizzying varieties of legal issues and lengthy disputed hearings and settlement discussions. Many lawyers, both plaintiff and defendant, have built remarkably lucrative practices specializing in handling class actions. While the number of reported decisions involving class certification issues are legion, the basic analysis of such decisions is something that you should be in a position at this point to undertake. It is essentially a two-step analysis: (1) are the implicit and explicit prerequisites of Rule 23(a) satisfied in a manner that offers the promise to the court of an efficient means of resolving multiple potential cases at once while ensuring fair representation for the interests of class members? And, (2) does the case fit into one of the categories that Rule 23(b) contemplates for appropriate class treatment — either because fairness to an existing party or to the absent members renders class adjudication essential (so that a mandatory class is required) or due to the incredible levels of efficiency in instances when the presence of significant common questions of fact or law dominate over any individual issues and class treatment is deemed superior to any other alternative of traditional litigation?

Going Deeper

Additional recommended readings to enhance your understanding of some of the topics in this Chapter include:

- Manual for Complex Litigation, 4th, §§ 21–22.

- Newberg on Class Actions Vol. 1, Chapters 3–4 (5th ed. West).

- Allen Kamp, *The History Behind Hansberry v. Lee*, 20 U.C. Davis L. Rev. 481 (1987) (providing rich historical context for the dynamics and factual background behind this historic due process case).

- Jonathan R. Macey & Geoffrey P. Miller, *The Plaintiffs' Attorney's Role in Class Action and Derivative Litigation: Economic Analysis and Recommendations for Reform*, 58 U. Chi. L. Rev. 1 (1991).

Chapter 5

Managing Class Actions

Chapter Goals

- Learn how the normal limitations for personal jurisdiction and federal subject matter jurisdiction have been enlarged in the class action context.

- Grasp the consequences of the choice of law rule that a forum state cannot arbitrarily choose to apply its own substantive law in a national class action.

- Learn the difference in the due process and Rule 23(c) rules governing notice owed to class members upon certification.

- Recognize the range of options class members have regarding opt-out rights, intervention, and objecting to class action proceedings.

- Know the special tolling rules for statutes of limitations for class members.

- Appreciate the special role of the court in the class settlement process.

- Realize some exceptions to normal application of res judicata and collateral estoppel in the class context.

A. Overview

As stated in the last chapter, the issue of whether to certify a case as a class action is typically the most important decision in the life of a class action; but other issues beyond certification have important impact on the viability of class actions, strategy regarding their filing, how they are conducted, and their final disposition. In this chapter, we will first consider application of some foundational civil procedure topics to a class action — personal jurisdiction, choice of law, and subject matter jurisdiction. As you will see, many traditional rules on those subjects are altered when you shift from traditional litigation to the class action context. We will then consider the Rule 23(c) issues regarding when and how a class must receive notice of the certification decision and what rights class members have to attempt to either extricate themselves from a class or to intervene as an additional named party. We will also pause briefly to consider how the class action model of adjudication applies to traditional procedural topics such as statutes of limitations and res judicata and collateral estoppel. Finally, we will endeavor to consider the typical resolution of a class action — issues pertaining to court approval of class settlement and consideration of alternative remedies available in certain class action scenarios. But we will first consider a possible context for these issues with the following Chapter Problem.

B. Chapter 5 Problem

Huey News
@huey_news

Farmer/Proud American
Mena, Arkansas

7,498 Following   **16** Followers

Huey News @huey_news
So excited to announce I have filed (with help of my lawyer) a national class action in Little Rock today against TicketNinja fer their fraudulent, un-American and illegal credit surcharges! Tweet back your own horror stories about this auful company, tryin to profit frum honest, God-fearin Americans.

Huey News @huey_news
Having a helluva time in Potter Junction with the old woman at Country Nights Music Festival.

Huey News @huey_news
Got my tickets, got my guns! Who's redy for some Country Nights next week?!

Underwood & Associates, P.A.
Internal Memo

To: Associate
From: Jim Underwood, Sr. Partner
Re: Class Action Defense

Got a good new case I'm gonna need your help with. Drop everything else for awhile and get familiar with this new file. Tomorrow at 8:00 a.m. we will be meeting with Roger Sterling, CEO of TicketNinja.Com who is flying into Little Rock from Los Angeles to help us plan our defense of this new case.

You being a concert lover, I'm sure you've done business before with TicketNinja.Com (Ninja). Ninja sells tickets for concerts, sporting events, and other special events nationwide. They sell most of their tickets over the internet but also have special kiosks set up around the country mostly inside StarCafe locations and, in more rural areas, at other random small retailers. Most of their profits come from their "service charge" that is added to the face value of the tickets they sell. Increasingly, most of their transactions are handled via credit card. (Obviously this is the only way to sell online. Cash transactions occur at the kiosk locations which handle both cash and credit cards.) As I assume you're also aware, retailers have to pay a certain percentage of their total sales on credit cards to the credit card issuing banks. Ninja passes along these credit card charges only to their credit card customers, offering their cash purchasers a "cash discount" when they use cash to buy their tickets at the kiosk locations.

This cash discount program has never received a single complaint before until a new national class action was just filed against Ninja in Arkansas state court in Little Rock by some individual who'd just recently made a single credit card purchase (the only one ever for him as near as we can tell) in Mena, Arkansas to an upcoming "Country Nights" musical festival event in Potter Junction, Arkansas.

Ninja is incorporated in Delaware with its headquarters in Los Angeles, California. It uses StarCafe kiosks in 49 states (everywhere except Alaska). In rural areas not serviced by a StarCafe, Ninja also has relationships with random other small retailers. In this case, the actual ticket was purchased by the plaintiff (Huey News) at a kiosk in Mena called "Simply Beautiful," a bakery owned by sole proprietor Shauna Beautiful. Mr. News has named as defendants both Ninja and Ms. Beautiful. News has filed a suit seeking a declaration that the cash discount program is, in economic reality if not name, an unlawful credit surcharge that amounts to common law fraud, violates Arkansas' consumer deceptive trade practices statute, and also sues on a third-party beneficiary breach of contract claim saying that Ninja's credit card agreements with the various banks issuing credit cards prohibit credit surcharges. Mr. News' individual damages? 25 lousy cents. (On the other hand, Ninja earned $200 million last year in service charges.) Plaintiff also asks for disgorgement of all illegal credit surcharge profits and an injunction to stop the two-tiered pricing.

I need you to consider our answer and other preliminary motions. But first figure out if we can remove this case to federal court, if the court can exercise personal jurisdiction over this entire class (in Arkansas), whether Arkansas law can be applied to all the claims, and begin to think about contesting certification. In other words, and as always, … please do the necessary.

See you tomorrow morning when we meet Mr. Sterling.

C. Personal Jurisdiction and Choice of Law

Prior to the Supreme Court's decision in *Phillips Petroleum Co. v. Shutts,* apparently nobody thought about the concept of applying the *International Shoe* rules of minimum contacts to a *plaintiff* class in a putative class action. Every personal jurisdiction case you covered in your first-year Civil Procedure class involved a non-resident defendant challenging another court's assertion of personal jurisdiction over that defendant. In the following case, the defendant makes a powerful argument on behalf of the missing plaintiff class members—that the court's attempt to adjudicate the causes of action of these non-residents violated their due process rights. (This is another odd instance where the defendant is speaking up for the rights of the class members—in an effort to win on a technicality.) Consider the ramifications for multi-state class action practice if the Supreme Court had fully accepted defendant's arguments. After finding that the Kansas courts could exercise jurisdiction over non-resident class members, however, the Court held that Kansas could not arbitrarily apply Kansas law to all of those claims. Thus, *Shutts* is the seminal class action case still today on the issues of both personal jurisdiction and choice of law in a class action.

Principles

"From the perspective of the common law tradition of individual justice, class actions are a necessary evil, but an evil nonetheless."

David Rosenberg, *Class Actions for Mass Torts: Doing Individual Justice by Collective Means*, 62 Ind. L.J. 561, 561 (1987).

Phillips Petroleum Co. v. Shutts
472 U.S. 797 (1985)

REHNQUIST, J.,

Petitioner is a Delaware corporation which has its principal place of business in Oklahoma. During the 1970's it produced or purchased natural gas from leased land located in 11 different States, and sold most of the gas in interstate commerce. Respondents are some 28,000 of the royalty owners possessing rights to the leases from which petitioner produced the gas; they reside in all 50 States, the District of Columbia, and several foreign countries. Respondents brought a class action against petitioner in the Kansas state court, seeking to recover interest on royalty payments which had been delayed by petitioner. They recovered judgment in the trial court, and the Supreme Court of Kansas affirmed the judgment over petitioner's contentions that the Due Process Clause of the Fourteenth Amendment prevented Kansas from adjudicating the claims of all the respondents, and that the Due Process Clause and the Full Faith and Credit Clause of Article IV of the Constitution prohibited the application of Kansas law to all of the transactions between petitioner and respondents. We granted certiorari to consider these claims. We reject petitioner's jurisdictional claim, but sustain its claim regarding the choice of law.

Because petitioner sold the gas to its customers in interstate commerce, it was required to secure approval for price increases from what was then the Federal Power Commission, and is now the Federal Energy Regulatory Commission. Under its regulations the Federal Power Commission permitted petitioner to propose and collect tentative higher gas prices, subject to final approval by the Commission. If the Commission eventually denied petitioner's proposed price increase or reduced the proposed increase, petitioner would have to refund to its customers the difference between the approved price and the higher price charged, plus interest at a rate set by statute.

Although petitioner received higher gas prices pending review by the Commission, petitioner suspended any increase in royalties paid to the royalty owners because the higher price could be subject to recoupment by petitioner's customers. Petitioner agreed to pay the higher royalty only if the royalty owners would provide petitioner with a bond or indemnity for the increase, plus interest, in case the price increase was not ultimately approved and a refund was due to the customers. Petitioner set the interest rate on the indemnity agreements at the same interest rate the Commission would have required petitioner to refund to its customers. A small percentage of the royalty owners provided this indemnity and received royalties immediately from the interim price increases; these royalty owners are unimportant to this case.

The remaining royalty owners received no royalty on the unapproved portion of the prices until the Federal Power Commission approval of those prices became final. Royalties on the unapproved portion of the gas price were suspended three times by petitioner, corresponding to its three proposed price increases in the mid-1970's. In three written opinions the Commission approved all of petitioner's tentative price increases, so petitioner paid to its royalty owners the suspended royalties of $3.7 million in 1976, $4.7 million in 1977, and $2.9 million in 1978. Petitioner paid no interest to the royalty owners although it had the use of the suspended royalty money for a number of years.

Respondents Irl Shutts, Robert Anderson, and Betty Anderson filed suit against petitioner in Kansas state court, seeking interest payments on their suspended royalties which petitioner had possessed pending the Commission's approval of the price increases. Shutts is a resident of Kansas, and the Andersons live in Oklahoma. Shutts and the Andersons own gas leases in Oklahoma and Texas. Over petitioner's objection the Kansas trial court granted respondents' motion to certify the suit as a class action under Kansas law. The class as certified was comprised of 33,000 royalty owners who had royalties suspended by petitioner. The average claim of each royalty owner for interest on the suspended royalties was $100.

After the class was certified respondents provided each class member with notice through first-class mail. The notice described the action and informed each class member that he could appear in person or by counsel; otherwise each member would be represented by Shutts and the Andersons, the named plaintiffs. The notices also stated that class members would be included in the class and bound by the judgment unless they "opted out" of the lawsuit by executing and returning a "request for exclusion" that was included with the notice. The final class as certified contained 28,100 members; 3,400 had "opted out" of the class by returning the request for exclusion, and notice could not be delivered to another 1,500 members, who were also excluded. Less than 1,000 of the class members resided in Kansas. Only a minuscule amount, approximately one quarter of one percent, of the gas leases involved in the lawsuit were on Kansas land.

After petitioner's mandamus petition to decertify the class was denied, the case was tried to the court. The court found petitioner liable under Kansas law for interest on the suspended royalties to all class members. The trial court relied heavily on an earlier, unrelated class action involving the same nominal plaintiff and the same defendant. The Kansas Supreme Court had held in [that case,] *Shutts, Executor* that a gas company owed interest to royalty owners for royalties suspended pending final Commission approval of a price increase. No federal statutes touched on the liability for suspended royalties, and the court in *Shutts, Executor* held as a matter of Kansas equity law that the applicable interest rates for computation of interest on suspended royalties were the interest rates at which the gas company would have had to reimburse its customers had its interim price increase been rejected by the Commission. The court in *Shutts, Executor* viewed these as the fairest interest rates because they were also the rates that petitioner required the royalty owners to meet in their indemnity agreements in order to avoid suspended royalties.

The trial court in the present case applied the rule from *Shutts, Executor,* and held petitioner liable for prejudgment and postjudgment interest on the suspended royalties, computed at the Commission rates governing petitioner's three price increases. The applicable interest rates were: 7% for royalties retained until October 1974; 9% for royalties retained between October 1974 and September 1979; and thereafter at the average prime rate. The trial court did not determine whether any difference existed between the laws of Kansas and other States, or whether another State's laws should be applied to non-Kansas plaintiffs or to royalties from leases in States other than Kansas.

Petitioner raised two principal claims in its appeal to the Supreme Court of Kansas. It first asserted that the Kansas trial court did not possess personal jurisdiction over absent plaintiff class members as required by *International Shoe* and similar cases. Related to this first claim was petitioner's contention that the "opt-out" notice to absent class members, which forced them to return the request for exclusion in order to avoid the suit, was insufficient to bind class members who were not residents of Kansas or who did not possess "minimum contacts" with Kansas. Second, petitioner claimed that Kansas courts could not apply Kansas law to every claim in the dispute. The trial court should have looked to the laws of each State where the leases were located to determine, on the basis of conflict of laws principles, whether interest on the suspended royalties was recoverable, and at what rate.

The Supreme Court of Kansas held that the entire cause of action was maintainable under the Kansas class-action statute, and the court rejected both of petitioner's claims. First, it held that the absent class members were plaintiffs, not defendants, and thus the traditional minimum contacts test of *International Shoe* did not apply. The court held that nonresident class-action plaintiffs were only entitled to adequate notice, an opportunity to be heard, an opportunity to opt out of the case, and adequate representation by the named plaintiffs. If these procedural due process minima were met, according to the court, Kansas could assert jurisdiction over the plaintiff class and bind each class member with a judgment on his claim. The court surveyed the course of the litigation and concluded that all of these minima had been met.

The court also rejected petitioner's contention that Kansas law could not be applied to plaintiffs and royalty arrangements having no connection with Kansas. The court stated that generally the law of the forum controlled all claims unless "compelling reasons" existed to apply a different law. The court found no compelling reasons, and noted that "[the] plaintiff class members have indicated their desire to have this action determined under the laws of Kansas." The court affirmed as a matter of Kansas equity law the award of interest on the suspended royalties, at the rates imposed by the trial court. The court set the postjudgment interest rate on all claims at the Kansas statutory rate of 15%.

I

As a threshold matter we must determine whether petitioner has standing to assert the claim that Kansas did not possess proper jurisdiction over the many plaintiffs in the class who were not Kansas residents and had no connection to Kansas. Respondents claim that a party generally may assert only his own rights, and that petitioner has no standing to assert the rights of its adversary, the plaintiff class, in order to defeat the judgment in favor of the class. [The Court rejected this no-standing argument by Respondents. The Court reasoned that, "[a]s a class-action defendant, petitioner is in a unique predicament. If Kansas does not possess personal jurisdiction over this plaintiff class, petitioner will be bound to 28,100 judgment holders scattered across the globe, but none of these will be bound by the Kansas decree." Therefore, Petitioners were permitted to assert as ground for appeal the trial court's lack of personal jurisdiction over the absent plaintiff class members.]

II

Reduced to its essentials, petitioner's argument is that unless out-of-state plaintiffs affirmatively consent, the Kansas courts may not exert jurisdiction over their claims.

Petitioner claims that failure to execute and return the "request for exclusion" provided with the class notice cannot constitute consent of the out-of-state plaintiffs; thus Kansas courts may exercise jurisdiction over these plaintiffs only if the plaintiffs possess the sufficient "minimum contacts" with Kansas as that term is used in cases involving personal jurisdiction over out-of-state defendants. *E.g., International Shoe Co. v. Washington,* 326 U.S. 310 (1945); *Shaffer v. Heitner,* 433 U.S. 186 (1977); *World-Wide Volkswagen Corp. v. Woodson,* 444 U.S. 286 (1980). Since Kansas had no prelitigation contact with many of the plaintiffs and leases involved, petitioner claims that Kansas has exceeded its jurisdictional reach and thereby violated the due process rights of the absent plaintiffs.

In *International Shoe* we were faced with an out-of-state corporation which sought to avoid the exercise of personal jurisdiction over it as a defendant by a Washington state court. We held that the extent of the defendant's due process protection would depend "upon the quality and nature of the activity in relation to the fair and orderly administration of the laws...." 326 U.S., at 319. We noted that the Due Process Clause did not permit a State to make a binding judgment against a person with whom the State had no contacts, ties, or relations.

The purpose of this test, of course, is to protect a defendant from the travail of defending in a distant forum, unless the defendant's contacts with the forum make it just to force him to defend there. In *Insurance Corp. of Ireland v. Compagnie des Bauxites de Guinee,* 456 U.S. 694, 702–703, and n. 10 (1982), we explained that the requirement that a court have personal jurisdiction comes from the Due Process Clause's protection of the defendant's personal liberty interest, and said that the requirement "represents a restriction on judicial power not as a matter of sovereignty, but as a matter of individual liberty."

Although the cases like *Shaffer* and *Woodson* which petitioner relies on for a minimum contacts requirement all dealt with out-of-state defendants or parties in the procedural posture of a defendant, petitioner claims that the same analysis must apply to absent class-action plaintiffs. In this regard petitioner correctly points out that a chose in action is a constitutionally recognized property interest possessed by each of the plaintiffs. An adverse judgment by Kansas courts in this case may extinguish the chose in action forever through res judicata. Such an adverse judgment, petitioner claims, would be every bit as onerous to an absent plaintiff as an adverse judgment on the merits would be to a defendant. Thus, the same due process protections should apply to absent plaintiffs: Kansas should not be able to exert jurisdiction over the plaintiffs' claims unless the plaintiffs have sufficient minimum contacts with Kansas.

We think petitioner's premise is in error. The burdens placed by a State upon an absent class-action plaintiff are not of the same order or magnitude as those it places upon an absent defendant. An out-of-state defendant summoned by a plaintiff is faced with the full powers of the forum State to render judgment *against* it. The defendant must generally hire counsel and travel to the forum to defend itself from the plaintiff's claim, or suffer a default judgment. The defendant may be forced to participate in extended and often costly discovery, and will be forced to respond in damages or to comply with some other form of remedy imposed by the court should it lose the suit. The defendant may also face liability for court costs and attorney's fees. These burdens are substantial, and the minimum contacts requirement of the Due Process Clause prevents the forum State from unfairly imposing them upon the defendant.

A class-action plaintiff, however, is in quite a different posture. The Court noted this difference in *Hansberry v. Lee,* 311 U.S. 32, 40–41 (1940), which explained that a "class" or "representative" suit was an exception to the rule that one could not be bound by judgment *in personam* unless one was made fully a party in the traditional sense. As the Court pointed out in *Hansberry*, the class action was an invention of equity to enable it to proceed to a decree in suits where the number of those interested in the litigation was too great to permit joinder. The absent parties would be bound by the decree so long as the named parties adequately represented the absent class and the prosecution of the litigation was within the common interest. [In *Hansberry*, we found no adequate representation due to the inherent conflicts of interest. In this case there is no question on appeal about the adequacy of representation by the class representative.]

Modern plaintiff class actions follow the same goals, permitting litigation of a suit involving common questions when there are too many plaintiffs for proper joinder. Class actions also may permit the plaintiffs to pool claims which would be uneconomical to litigate individually. For example, this lawsuit involves claims averaging about $100 per plaintiff; most of the plaintiffs would have no realistic day in court if a class action were not available.

In sharp contrast to the predicament of a defendant haled into an out-of-state forum, the plaintiffs in this suit were not haled anywhere to defend themselves upon pain of a default judgment. As commentators have noted, from the plaintiffs' point of view a class action resembles a "quasi-administrative proceeding, conducted by the judge."

A plaintiff class in Kansas and numerous other jurisdictions cannot first be certified unless the judge, with the aid of the named plaintiffs and defendant, conducts an inquiry into the common nature of the named plaintiffs' and the absent plaintiffs' claims, the adequacy of representation, the jurisdiction possessed over the class, and any other matters that will bear upon proper representation of the absent plaintiffs' interest. The court and named plaintiffs protect his interests. Indeed, the class-action defendant itself has a great interest in ensuring that the absent plaintiffs' claims are properly before the forum. In this case, for example, the defendant sought to avoid class certification by alleging that the absent plaintiffs would not be adequately represented and were not amenable to jurisdiction.

The concern of the typical class-action rules for the absent plaintiffs is manifested in other ways. Most jurisdictions, including Kansas, require that a class action, once certified, may not be dismissed or compromised without the approval of the court. In many jurisdictions such as Kansas the court may amend the pleadings to ensure that all sections of the class are represented adequately.

Besides this continuing solicitude for their rights, absent plaintiff class members are not subject to other burdens imposed upon defendants. They need not hire counsel or appear. They are almost never subject to counterclaims or cross-claims, or liability for fees or costs.[2] Absent plaintiff class members are not subject to coercive or punitive remedies. Nor will an adverse judgment typically bind an absent plaintiff for any damages, although a valid adverse judgment may extinguish any of the plaintiff's claims which were litigated.

Unlike a defendant in a normal civil suit, an absent class-action plaintiff is not required to do anything. He may sit back and allow the litigation to run its course, content in

---

2. Petitioner places emphasis on the fact that absent class members might be subject to discovery, counterclaims, cross-claims, or court costs. Petitioner cites no cases involving any such imposition upon plaintiffs, however. We are convinced that such burdens are rarely imposed upon plaintiff class members, and that the disposition of these issues is best left to a case which presents them in a more concrete way.

knowing that there are safeguards provided for his protection. In most class actions an absent plaintiff is provided at least with an opportunity to "opt out" of the class, and if he takes advantage of that opportunity he is removed from the litigation entirely. This was true of the Kansas proceedings in this case. The Kansas procedure provided for the mailing of a notice to each class member by first-class mail. The notice, as we have previously indicated, described the action and informed the class member that he could appear in person or by counsel, in default of which he would be represented by the named plaintiffs and their attorneys. The notice further stated that class members would be included in the class and bound by the judgment unless they "opted out" by executing and returning a "request for exclusion" that was included in the notice.

Petitioner contends, however, that the "opt out" procedure provided by Kansas is not good enough, and that an "opt in" procedure is required to satisfy the Due Process Clause of the Fourteenth Amendment. Insofar as plaintiffs who have no minimum contacts with the forum State are concerned, an "opt in" provision would require that each class member affirmatively consent to his inclusion within the class.

Because States place fewer burdens upon absent class plaintiffs than they do upon absent defendants in nonclass suits, the Due Process Clause need not and does not afford the former as much protection from state-court jurisdiction as it does the latter. The Fourteenth Amendment does protect "persons," not "defendants," however, so absent plaintiffs as well as absent defendants are entitled to some protection from the jurisdiction of a forum State which seeks to adjudicate their claims. In this case we hold that a forum State may exercise jurisdiction over the claim of an absent class-action plaintiff, even though that plaintiff may not possess the minimum contacts with the forum which would support personal jurisdiction over a defendant. If the forum State wishes to bind an absent plaintiff concerning a claim for money damages or similar relief at law,[3] it must provide minimal procedural due process protection. The plaintiff must receive notice plus an opportunity to be heard and participate in the litigation, whether in person or through counsel. The notice must be the best practicable, "reasonably calculated, under all the circumstances, to apprise interested parties of the pendency of the action and afford them an opportunity to present their objections." *Mullane,* 339 U.S., at 314–315; cf. *Eisen v. Carlisle & Jacquelin,* 417 U.S. 156, 174–175 (1974). The notice should describe the action and the plaintiffs' rights in it. Additionally, we hold that due process requires at a minimum that an absent plaintiff be provided with an opportunity to remove himself from the class by executing and returning an "opt out" or "request for exclusion" form to the court. Finally, the Due Process Clause of course requires that the named plaintiff at all times adequately represent the interests of the absent class members.

We reject petitioner's contention that the Due Process Clause of the Fourteenth Amendment requires that absent plaintiffs affirmatively "opt in" to the class, rather than be deemed members of the class if they do not "opt out." We think that such a contention is supported by little, if any precedent, and that it ignores the differences between class-action plaintiffs, on the one hand, and defendants in nonclass civil suits on the other. Any plaintiff may consent to jurisdiction. The essential question, then, is how stringent the requirement for a showing of consent will be.

---

3. Our holding today is limited to those class actions which seek to bind known plaintiffs concerning claims wholly or predominately for money judgments. We intimate no view concerning other types of class actions, such as those seeking equitable relief. Nor, of course, does our discussion of personal jurisdiction address class actions where the jurisdiction is asserted against a *defendant* class.

We think that the procedure followed by Kansas, where a fully descriptive notice is sent first-class mail to each class member, with an explanation of the right to "opt out," satisfies due process. Requiring a plaintiff to affirmatively request inclusion would probably impede the prosecution of those class actions involving an aggregation of small individual claims, where a large number of claims are required to make it economical to bring suit. The plaintiff's claim may be so small, or the plaintiff so unfamiliar with the law, that he would not file suit individually, nor would he affirmatively request inclusion in the class if such a request were required by the Constitution.[4] If, on the other hand, the plaintiff's claim is sufficiently large or important that he wishes to litigate it on his own, he will likely have retained an attorney or have thought about filing suit, and should be fully capable of exercising his right to "opt out."

In this case over 3,400 members of the potential class did "opt out," which belies the contention that "opt out" procedures result in guaranteed jurisdiction by inertia. Another 1,500 were excluded because the notice and "opt out" form was undeliverable. We think that such results show that the "opt out" procedure provided by Kansas is by no means *pro forma*, and that the Constitution does not require more to protect what must be the somewhat rare species of class member who is unwilling to execute an "opt out" form, but whose claim is nonetheless so important that he cannot be presumed to consent to being a member of the class by his failure to do so. Petitioner's "opt in" requirement would require the invalidation of scores of state statutes and of the class-action provision of the Federal Rules of Civil Procedure, and for the reasons stated we do not think that the Constitution requires the State to sacrifice the obvious advantages in judicial efficiency resulting from the "opt out" approach for the protection of the *rara avis* portrayed by petitioner.

We therefore hold that the protection afforded the plaintiff class members by the Kansas statute satisfies the Due Process Clause.

III

The Kansas courts applied Kansas contract and Kansas equity law to every claim in this case, notwithstanding that over 99% of the gas leases and some 97% of the plaintiffs in the case had no apparent connection to the State of Kansas except for this lawsuit. [For example, as to the leases impacted by one of the Commission's opinions, more than 5,600 leases in question were from Oklahoma and Texas yet only 3 were located in the State of Kansas.] Out of those same leases, Petitioner protested that the Kansas courts should apply the laws of the States where the leases were located, or at least apply Texas and Oklahoma law because so many of the leases came from those States. The Kansas courts disregarded this contention and found petitioner liable for interest on the suspended royalties as a matter of Kansas law, and set the interest rates under Kansas equity principles.

Petitioner contends that total application of Kansas substantive law violated the constitutional limitations on choice of law mandated by the Due Process Clause of the Fourteenth Amendment and the Full Faith and Credit Clause of Article IV, § 1. We must first determine whether Kansas law conflicts in any material way with any other law which

---

4. [T]he Reporter for the 1966 amendments stated:

> "[Requiring] the individuals affirmatively to request inclusion in the lawsuit would result in freezing out the claims of people — especially small claims held by small people — who for one reason or another, ignorance, timidity, unfamiliarity with business or legal matters, will simply not take the affirmative step."

Kaplan, *Continuing Work of the Civil Committee: 1966 Amendments of the Federal Rules of Civil Procedure (I)*, 81 Harv. L. Rev. 356, 397–398 (1967).

could apply. There can be no injury in applying Kansas law if it is not in conflict with that of any other jurisdiction connected to this suit. [The Court found that possible material differences in the substantive laws did exist between Kansas, on the one hand, and Oklahoma and Texas. Oklahoma had no published case law imposing liability for interest on suspended royalties. Further, even if Oklahoma law did require liability for interest, it appears Oklahoma would apply at most a 6% interest rate, lower than Kansas law. Further, Oklahoma law might raise a waiver defense in cases where the creditor accepts partial payment. Texas law does not recognize any possible liability for interest in excess of 6%. Further, at least some Texas caselaw suggests that once the gas company offers to take an indemnity from the royalty owner and pay him the suspended royalty, it excuses liability for any interest. "The conflicts on the applicable interest rates, alone — which we do not think can be labeled 'false conflicts' — certainly amounted to millions of dollars in liability."]

Four Terms ago we addressed a similar situation in *Allstate Ins. Co. v. Hague*, 449 U.S. 302 (1981). In that case we were confronted with two conflicting rules of state insurance law. Minnesota permitted the "stacking" of separate uninsured motorist policies while Wisconsin did not. Although the decedent lived in Wisconsin, took out insurance policies and was killed there, he was employed in Minnesota, and after his death his widow moved to Minnesota for reasons unrelated to the litigation, and was appointed personal representative of his estate. She filed suit in Minnesota courts, which applied the Minnesota stacking rule.

The plurality in *Allstate* noted that a particular set of facts giving rise to litigation could justify, constitutionally, the application of more than one jurisdiction's laws. The plurality recognized, however, that the Due Process Clause and the Full Faith and Credit Clause provided modest restrictions on the application of forum law. These restrictions required "that for a State's substantive law to be selected in a constitutionally permissible manner, that State must have a significant contact or significant aggregation of contacts, creating state interests, such that choice of its law is neither arbitrary nor fundamentally unfair."

The plurality in *Allstate* affirmed the application of Minnesota law because of the forum's significant contacts to the litigation which supported the State's interest in applying its law. Kansas' contacts to this litigation, as explained by the Kansas Supreme Court, can be gleaned from the opinion below.

Petitioner owns property and conducts substantial business in the State, so Kansas certainly has an interest in regulating petitioner's conduct in Kansas. Moreover, oil and gas extraction is an important business to Kansas, and although only a few leases in issue are located in Kansas, hundreds of Kansas plaintiffs were affected by petitioner's suspension of royalties; thus the court held that the State has a real interest in protecting "the rights of these royalty owners both as individual residents of [Kansas] and as members of this particular class of plaintiffs." The Kansas Supreme Court pointed out that Kansas courts are quite familiar with this type of lawsuit, and "[the] plaintiff class members have indicated their desire to have this action determined under the laws of Kansas." Finally, the Kansas court buttressed its use of Kansas law by stating that this lawsuit was analogous to a suit against a "common fund" located in Kansas.

We do not lightly discount this description of Kansas' contacts with this litigation and its interest in applying its law. There is, however, no "common fund" located in Kansas that would require or support the application of only Kansas law to all these claims. As the Kansas court noted, petitioner commingled the suspended royalties with its general corporate accounts. There is no specific identifiable res in Kansas, nor is there any limited amount which may be depleted before every plaintiff is compensated. Only by somehow aggregating all the separate claims in this case could a "common fund" in any sense be created, and the term becomes all but meaningless when used in such an expansive sense.

We also give little credence to the idea that Kansas law should apply to all claims because the plaintiffs, by failing to opt out, evinced their desire to be bound by Kansas law. Even if one could say that the plaintiffs "consented" to the application of Kansas law by not opting out, plaintiff's desire for forum law is rarely, if ever controlling. In most cases the plaintiff shows his obvious wish for forum law by filing there. "If a plaintiff could choose the substantive rules to be applied to an action ... the invitation to forum shopping would be irresistible." *Allstate, supra,* at 337. Even if a plaintiff evidences his desire for forum law by moving to the forum, we have generally accorded such a move little or no significance. Thus the plaintiffs' desire for Kansas law, manifested by their participation in this Kansas lawsuit, bears little relevance.

The Supreme Court of Kansas in its opinion in this case expressed the view that by reason of the fact that it was adjudicating a nationwide class action, it had much greater latitude in applying its own law to the transactions in question than might otherwise be the case.

We think that this is something of a "bootstrap" argument. The Kansas class-action statute, like those of most other jurisdictions, requires that there be "common issues of law or fact." But while a State may, for the reasons we have previously stated, assume jurisdiction over the claims of plaintiffs whose principal contacts are with other States, it may not use this assumption of jurisdiction as an added weight in the scale when considering the permissible constitutional limits on choice of substantive law. It may not take a transaction with little or no relationship to the forum and apply the law of the forum in order to satisfy the procedural requirement that there be a "common question of law." The issue of personal jurisdiction over plaintiffs in a class action is entirely distinct from the question of the constitutional limitations on choice of law; the latter calculus is not altered by the fact that it may be more difficult or more burdensome to comply with the constitutional limitations because of the large number of transactions which the State proposes to adjudicate and which have little connection with the forum.

Kansas must have a "significant contact or significant aggregation of contacts" to the claims asserted by each member of the plaintiff class, contacts "creating state interests," in order to ensure that the choice of Kansas law is not arbitrary or unfair. Given Kansas' lack of "interest" in claims unrelated to that State, and the substantive conflict with jurisdictions such as Texas, we conclude that application of Kansas law to every claim in this case is sufficiently arbitrary and unfair as to exceed constitutional limits.

When considering fairness in this context, an important element is the expectation of the parties. There is no indication that when the leases involving land and royalty owners outside of Kansas were executed, the parties had any idea that Kansas law would control. Kansas "may not abrogate the rights of parties beyond its borders having no relation to anything done or to be done within them." *Home Ins. Co. v. Dick, supra,* at 410.

Here the Supreme Court of Kansas took the view that in a nationwide class action where procedural due process guarantees of notice and adequate representation were met, "the law of the forum should be applied unless compelling reasons exist for applying a different law." Whatever practical reasons may have commended this rule to the Supreme Court of Kansas, for the reasons already stated we do not believe that it is consistent with the decisions of this Court. We make no effort to determine for ourselves which law must apply to the various transactions involved in this lawsuit, and we reaffirm our observation in *Allstate* that in many situations a state court may be free to apply one of several choices of law. But the constitutional limitations laid down in cases such as *Allstate* must be respected even in a nationwide class action.

We therefore affirm the judgment of the Supreme Court of Kansas insofar as it upheld the jurisdiction of the Kansas courts over the plaintiff class members in this case, and reverse its judgment insofar as it held that Kansas law was applicable to all of the transactions which it sought to adjudicate. We remand the case to that court for further proceedings not inconsistent with this opinion.

It is so ordered.

Notes and Problems

1. In the case of traditional litigation, how is it that when a non-resident plaintiff files her lawsuit in the forum, the court can exercise personal jurisdiction over the plaintiff? Why is this same analysis not applicable to assertions of personal jurisdiction over unnamed plaintiff class members? Given this distinction, how does the Supreme Court justify the Kansas courts in *Shutts* adjudicating the claims of the non-resident plaintiff class members? Do you find the argument compelling or questionable?

2. What if a plaintiff brought a defendant class action — suing a resident defendant individually and on behalf of a class of other defendants (like the plaintiff attempted to do in *Kline* in the case at the beginning of Chapter 4 Class Actions: Certification)? Would the court's analysis from *Shutts* still lead to the same conclusion? *See Thillens, Inc. v. Community Currency Exchange Associates of Ill.,* 97 F.R.D. 668 (N.D. Ill. 1983) (noting practical differences between being a plaintiff class member and a defendant class member).

3. Why was the defendant in *Shutts* permitted to raise the due process arguments on behalf of the opposing parties (the plaintiff class)? If the *Shutts* court had ruled in favor defendant on the issue of personal jurisdiction — finding that express consent was necessary — how would that have caused Rule 23(b)(3) practice to revert to pre-1966 requirements? Notice, by the way, that the Supreme Court opines that due process standards are flexible and vary according to the context. Is this just being result-oriented or is such flexibility a good thing?

4. In terms of the choice of law aspect of the *Shutts* opinion, what are the ramifications for certification of subsequent nationwide Rule 23(b)(3) class actions given the requirement that a forum state cannot just arbitrarily apply its own substantive laws to the claims of non-residents? How does this impact the certification decision? (Recall the *Castano* tobacco litigation case from the previous chapter.) Why can the court not apply the same implied consent argument that it used to justify personal jurisdiction over non-residents in order to similarly justify applying the forum state's substantive law?

5. *Chapter Problem.* In the putative class action asserted by the ticket purchasers of defendant, because it would likely be true that most of the class members would be residents of states outside the Arkansas forum, what would plaintiff Huey News have to do in order to secure the court's personal jurisdiction over those non-residents? Also, while it is unclear under what portion of Rule 23 Mr. News will seek certification, because his state court complaint references both equitable relief (declaratory judgment and injunctive relief) as well as damages (under an unjust enrichment theory), if this case is being pursued under a Rule 23(b)(2) hybrid theory, how does this impact the personal jurisdiction analysis under *Shutts*? Consider footnote 3 in the opinion.

D. Subject Matter Jurisdiction

1. Jurisdiction under §§ 1331, 1332(a) & 1367

As we saw in Chapter 3 Forum Battles, litigants and their counsel care passionately about the venue of their case. In particular, the issue of whether federal courts can exercise subject matter jurisdiction over particular class actions has been of profound importance to both class counsel and defense counsel for a long time. Lawyers have been known to engage in incredible machinations to create and destroy federal jurisdiction. You may recall in Chapter 3 Forum Battles we covered the *In re Diet Drugs* case on the topic of the "in aid of federal court jurisdiction" exception to the Anti-Injunction Act. Plaintiff's class counsel in the Texas state court case attempted to manipulate the pleadings to both destroy diversity jurisdiction (naming a local defendant) and intentionally omitting any claim for attorney's fees in order to keep the amount in controversy below the minimum needed to trigger federal court jurisdiction. Nevertheless, defendant attempted two times to remove the case to federal court; and for good reason, as the state court was most eager to assist the plaintiff's counsel in that case with a quick certification and attempted opt-out order. That case was just one example of the tactics that attorneys will employ to maneuver in or out of a federal court in the class context.

---

28 U.S.C. § 1331 Federal Question

The district courts shall have original jurisdiction of all civil actions arising under the Constitution, laws, or treaties of the United States.

In terms of providing an overview of how subject matter jurisdiction rules apply in the class context, the easiest to explain concerns federal question jurisdiction under 28 U.S.C. § 1331 — "arising under" jurisdiction. As you may recall from your first year studies, the "well pleaded complaint" rule from *Louisville & Nashville Railroad v. Mottley,* 211 U.S. 149 (1908), insists that federal courts look to the nature of the cause of action pled by the plaintiff in their complaint to determine if the case arises under federal law rather than just containing some reference to or a mere "federal ingredient" which are considered insufficient to bestow federal jurisdiction. The good news is that everything you learned about "arising under" § 1331 jurisdiction applies with equal force to a putative class action. In this one instance, there are no new rules for you to learn.

---

28 U.S.C. § 1332(a) Diversity of Citizenship

The district courts shall have original jurisdiction of all civil actions where the matter in controversy exceeds the sum or value of $75,000, exclusive of interest and costs, and is between—

(1) citizens of different States;

(2) citizens of a State and citizens or subjects of a foreign state;

(3) citizens of different States and in which citizens or subjects of a foreign state are additional parties; and

(4) a foreign state, as defined in section 1603(a) of this title, as plaintiff and citizens of a State or of different States.

Turning to federal diversity jurisdiction, you may recall that §1332(a) has two components that must be met to demonstrate federal jurisdiction over claims that only arise under state law. First, the litigants on each side of the case must be completely diverse from one another under the Supreme Court's famous, restrictive reading of §1332(a) in *Strawbridge v. Curtiss,* 7 U.S. 267 (1806). This means in a multi-party case, that if even one plaintiff shares the same state citizenship (domicile) with any single named defendant, this overlapping citizenship destroys complete diversity and the case cannot be filed in or removed to a federal court. As you might imagine, strict adherence to this concept in a national class action would pose problems for any federal court to ever hear the case on diversity grounds. In such a case, at least one class member would almost certainly share state citizenship with at least one defendant (unless the defendant was a foreign citizen). If you believe federal courts should play a role in adjudicating important nationwide class disputes, you will be relieved to discover that in *Supreme Tribe of Ben-Hur v. Cauble,* 255 U.S. 356 (1921), the U.S. Supreme Court ruled that in the context of class actions, the only parties whose citizenship counts in determining whether complete diversity exists are the named litigants and *not any unnamed class members.* This means that in a putative nationwide class action, if the only named plaintiff class representative is from Idaho, complete diversity will exist so long as none of the defendants are Idaho citizens. This rule prevails regardless of how many unnamed plaintiff class members might also be citizens of Idaho—their citizenship is simply disregarded perhaps under the theory that they are not true litigants in the traditional sense. In any event, *Ben-Hur* has been viewed as a very practical interpretation of the diversity statute to class actions.

"The practical effect of the *Zahn* decision was to eliminate small-claim state-law class actions from federal court."

Lloyd C. Anderson, *The American Law Institute Proposal to Bring Small-Claim State-Law Class Actions Within Federal Jurisdiction: An Affront to Federalism That Should Be Rejected,* 35 Creighton L. Rev. 325, 331–332 (2002).

The second requirement of federal diversity jurisdiction under §1332(a) is the amount-in-controversy requirement (not found in Article III). How to apply this statutory requirement—designed to ensure only "big" diversity cases would end up in federal courts—has been more troublesome. In *Snyder v. Harris,* 394 U.S. 332 (1969), none of the plaintiff class representative had an individual claim in excess of the minimum jurisdictional amount at the time. However, the aggregate of the class claims were significantly higher than the threshold amount needed to trigger §1332(a) jurisdiction. However, the Supreme Court ruled in that Rule 23(b)(3) case that the class claims could not be aggregated to meet the minimum amount. This can be viewed as somewhat consistent with federal courts' application of the amount-in-controversy requirement to more traditional forms of joinder, such as Rule 20 where courts have required each named plaintiff joined together to possess their own large enough claim. But the Supreme Court took this concept further in *Zahn v. International Paper Co.,* 414 US. 291 (1973). In that case, the named plaintiffs' claims were each independently greater than the statutory requirement but other unnamed class members' claims were too small on their own. One might think that, in line with the *Ben-Hur* decision, federal courts would simply ignore the size of the unnamed class members' claims. But the Supreme Court ruled otherwise, holding that each and every class member (named or not) had to possess their own independent claim in an amount greater than the minimum found in § 1332(a) in order for the case to be granted federal diversity jurisdiction.

The *Zahn* decision troubled many observers because, at a conceptual level, the holding seemed antagonistic with the rule from *Ben-Hur* permitting courts to simply ignore the citizenship of the class members. Further, the holding in *Zahn* was troubling at a practical level because it made it virtually impossible in a negative-value, consumer class action based upon state law to get the case inside a federal courthouse. Imagine, for example, a class with one million members, each having a per capita claim of about $10. Under *Zahn*, this case would be considered too small for federal court attention despite having an aggregate amount in controversy of $10 million. Many considered this an unnecessary impediment to federal court adjudication of national negative-value, state-law class actions. *See, e.g.,* James M. Underwood, *Rationality, Multiplicity & Legitimacy: Federalization of the Interstate Class Action,* 46 S. Tex. L. Rev. 391, 433–34 (2004) (discussing why a legislative overruling of *Zahn* would reflect sound public policy); Brian Mattis & James S. Mitchell, *The Trouble with Zahn: Progeny of Snyder v. Harris Further Cripples Class Actions,* 53 Neb. L. Rev. 137, 194 (1974). Like it or not, such was the state of the law until 1990.

In 1989 troubling language appeared in Justice Scalia's opinion for the Supreme Court in *Finley v. United States,* 490 U.S. 545 (1989), suggesting that there might be no congressional authorization for the imminently practical and important federal jurisdictional doctrines of pendent and ancillary jurisdiction. (The case involved a claim against the FAA under the Federal Tort Claims Act along with a pendent claim under state law against another party arising out of the same airplane crash.) Fearful of the implications for this language in the opinion, Congress reacted swiftly by almost immediately passing 28 U.S.C. § 1367—the Supplemental Jurisdiction Statute.

---

28 U.S.C. § 1367(a)–(b)

(a) Except as provided in subsections (b) and (c) or as expressly provided otherwise by Federal statute, in any civil action of which the district courts have original jurisdiction, the district courts shall have supplemental jurisdiction over all other claims that are so related to claims in the action within such original jurisdiction that they form part of the same case or controversy under Article III of the United States Constitution. Such supplemental jurisdiction shall include claims that involve the joinder or intervention of additional parties.

(b) In any civil action of which the district courts have original jurisdiction founded solely on section 1332 of this title, the district courts shall not have supplemental jurisdiction under subsection (a) over claims by plaintiffs against persons made parties under Rule 14, 19, 20, or 24 of the Federal Rules of Civil Procedure, or over claims by persons proposed to be joined as plaintiffs under Rule 19 of such rules, or seeking to intervene as plaintiffs under Rule 24 of such rules, when exercising supplemental jurisdiction over such claims would be inconsistent with the jurisdictional requirements of section 1332.

According to the legislative history, it was essentially an attempt to codify the doctrines of pendant and ancillary jurisdiction as they had always been recognized prior to *Finley*. Aided by the hand of a law professor in drafting the statute, however, it appears that a scrivener's error omitted certain key language. An argument was raised that the new statute had, perhaps inadvertently, overruled the Supreme Court's prior decisions in *Zahn* involving class actions as well as other precedents in the Rule 20 joinder context (*e.g., Clark v. Paul Gray, Inc.*, 306 U.S. 583 (1939)). The intermediate courts of appeals were deeply divided over whether to interpret § 1367 as literally written and opening the federal courthouse doors to such small-claim cases or to peek at the legislative history and interpret the statute as some courts believe it was actually intended to be written. In the *Exxon Mobil* case below, the Supreme Court finally granted cert to resolve the circuit split in a very pro-federal court jurisdictional manner. Pay close attention to the following case because it impacts not only class actions but offers expanded federal court jurisdiction to certain other multiple-party joinder scenarios.

Exxon Mobil Corp. v. Allapattah Services, Inc.
545 U.S. 546 (2005)

Kennedy, J.,

These consolidated cases present the question whether a federal court in a diversity action may exercise supplemental jurisdiction over additional plaintiffs whose claims do not satisfy the minimum amount-in-controversy requirement, provided the claims are part of the same case or controversy as the claims of plaintiffs who do allege a sufficient amount in controversy. Our decision turns on the correct interpretation of 28 U.S.C. § 1367. The question has divided the Courts of Appeals, and we granted certiorari to resolve the conflict.

We hold that, where the other elements of jurisdiction are present and at least one named plaintiff in the action satisfies the amount-in-controversy requirement, § 1367 does authorize supplemental jurisdiction over the claims of other plaintiffs in the same Article III case or controversy, even if those claims are for less than the jurisdictional amount specified in the statute setting forth the requirements for diversity jurisdiction. We affirm the judgment of the Court of Appeals for the Eleventh Circuit, and we reverse the judgment of the Court of Appeals for the First Circuit.

I

In 1991, about 10,000 Exxon dealers filed a class-action suit against the Exxon Corporation in the United States District Court for the Northern District of Florida. The dealers alleged an intentional and systematic scheme by Exxon under which they were overcharged for fuel purchased from Exxon. The plaintiffs invoked the District Court's § 1332(a) diversity jurisdiction. After a unanimous jury verdict in favor of the plaintiffs, the District Court certified the case for interlocutory review, asking whether it had properly exercised § 1367 supplemental jurisdiction over the claims of class members who did not meet the jurisdictional minimum amount in controversy.

The Court of Appeals for the Eleventh Circuit upheld the District Court's extension of supplemental jurisdiction to these class members. "We find," the court held, "that § 1367 clearly and unambiguously provides district courts with the authority in diversity class actions to exercise supplemental jurisdiction over the claims of class members who do not meet the minimum amount in controversy as long as the district court has original jurisdiction over the claims of at least one of the class representatives." This decision accords with the views of the Courts of Appeals for the Fourth, Sixth, and Seventh Circuits. See *Rosmer v. Pfizer, Inc.*, 263 F.3d 110 (CA4 2001); *Olden v. LaFarge Corp.*, 383 F.3d 495 (CA6 2004); *Stromberg Metal Works, Inc. v. Press Mechanical, Inc.*, 77 F.3d 928 (CA7 1996); *In re Brand Name Prescription Drugs Antitrust Litigation*, 123 F.3d 599 (CA7 1997). The Courts of Appeals for the Fifth and Ninth Circuits, adopting a similar analysis of the statute, have held that in a diversity class action the unnamed class members need not meet the amount-in-controversy requirement, provided the named class members do. These decisions, however, are unclear on whether all the named plaintiffs must satisfy this requirement.

In the other case now before us the Court of Appeals for the First Circuit took a different position on the meaning of § 1367(a). In that case, a 9-year-old girl sued Star-Kist in a diversity action in the United States District Court for the District of Puerto Rico, seeking damages for unusually severe injuries she received when she sliced her finger on a tuna can. Her family joined in the suit, seeking damages for emotional distress and certain medical expenses. The District Court granted summary judgment to Star-Kist, finding that none of the plaintiffs met the minimum amount-in-controversy requirement. The Court of Appeals for the First Circuit, however, ruled that the injured girl, but not her family members, had made allegations of damages in the requisite amount.

The Court of Appeals then addressed whether, in light of the fact that one plaintiff met the requirements for original jurisdiction, supplemental jurisdiction over the remaining plaintiffs' claims was proper under § 1367. The court held that § 1367 authorizes supplemental jurisdiction only when the district court has original jurisdiction over the action, and that in a diversity case original jurisdiction is lacking if one plaintiff fails to satisfy the amount-in-controversy requirement. Although the Court of Appeals claimed to "express no view" on whether the result would be the same in a class action, its analysis is inconsistent with that of the Court of Appeals for the Eleventh Circuit. The Court of Appeals for the First Circuit's view of § 1367 is, however, shared by the Courts of Appeal for the Third, Eighth, and Tenth Circuits, and the latter two Courts of Appeals have expressly applied this rule to class actions. See *Meritcare, Inc. v. St. Paul Mercury Ins. Co.*, 166 F.3d 214 (CA3 1999); *Trimble v. Asarco, Inc.*, 232 F.3d 946 (CA8 2000); *Leonhardt v. Western Sugar Co.*, 160 F.3d 631 (CA10 1998).

II

A

The district courts of the United States, as we have said many times, are "courts of limited jurisdiction. They possess only that power authorized by Constitution and statute." ... Although the district courts may not exercise jurisdiction absent a statutory basis, it is well established—in certain classes of cases—that, once a court has original jurisdiction over some claims in the action, it may exercise supplemental jurisdiction over additional claims that are part of the same case or controversy. The leading modern case for this principle is *Mine Workers v. Gibbs*, 383 U.S. 715, 16 L. Ed. 2d 218, 86 S. Ct. 1130 (1966).... As we later noted, the decision allowing jurisdiction over pendent state claims in *Gibbs* did not mention, let alone come to grips with, the text of the jurisdictional statutes and the bedrock principle that federal courts have no jurisdiction without statutory authorization. *Finley v. United States*, 490 U.S. 545, 548, 104 L. Ed. 2d 593, 109 S. Ct. 2003 (1989).

We have not, however, applied *Gibbs'* expansive interpretive approach to other aspects of the jurisdictional statutes. For instance, we have consistently interpreted § 1332 as requiring complete diversity: In a case with multiple plaintiffs and multiple defendants, the presence in the action of a single plaintiff from the same State as a single defendant deprives the district court of original diversity jurisdiction over the entire action. *Strawbridge v. Curtiss,* 7 U.S. 267, 3 Cranch 267, 2 L. Ed. 435 (1806). The complete diversity requirement is not mandated by the Constitution, or by the plain text of § 1332(a). The Court, nonetheless, has adhered to the complete diversity rule in light of the purpose of the diversity requirement, which is to provide a federal forum for important disputes where state courts might favor, or be perceived as favoring, home-state litigants. The presence of parties from the same State on both sides of a case dispels this concern, eliminating a principal reason for conferring § 1332 jurisdiction over any of the claims in the action. The specific purpose of the complete diversity rule explains both why we have not adopted *Gibbs'* expansive interpretive approach to this aspect of the jurisdictional statute and why *Gibbs* does not undermine the complete diversity rule. In order for a federal court to invoke supplemental jurisdiction under *Gibbs,* it must first have original jurisdiction over at least one claim in the action. Incomplete diversity destroys original jurisdiction with respect to all claims, so there is nothing to which supplemental jurisdiction can adhere.

In contrast to the diversity requirement, most of the other statutory prerequisites for federal jurisdiction, including the federal-question and amount-in-controversy requirements, can be analyzed claim by claim.... Thus, with respect to plaintiff-specific jurisdictional requirements, the Court held in *Clark v. Paul Gray, Inc.,* 306 U.S. 583 (1939), that every plaintiff must separately satisfy the amount-in-controversy requirement. The Court reaffirmed this rule, in the context of a class action brought invoking § 1332(a) diversity jurisdiction, in *Zahn v. International Paper Co.,* 414 U.S. 291 (1973). It follows "inescapably" from *Clark,* the Court held in *Zahn,* that "any plaintiff without the jurisdictional amount must be dismissed from the case, even though others allege jurisdictionally sufficient claims." 414 U.S., at 300.

B

In *Finley* we emphasized that "whatever we say regarding the scope of jurisdiction conferred by a particular statute can of course be changed by Congress." 490 U.S., at 556. In 1990, Congress accepted the invitation. It passed the Judicial Improvements Act, 104 Stat. 5089, which enacted § 1367, the provision which controls these cases.

All parties to this litigation and all courts to consider the question agree that § 1367 overturned the result in *Finley.* There is no warrant, however, for assuming that § 1367 did no more than to overrule *Finley* and otherwise to codify the existing state of the law of supplemental jurisdiction. We must not give jurisdictional statutes a more expansive interpretation than their text warrants; but it is just as important not to adopt an artificial construction that is narrower than what the text provides. No sound canon of interpretation requires Congress to speak with extraordinary clarity in order to modify the rules of federal jurisdiction within appropriate constitutional bounds. Ordinary principles of statutory construction apply. In order to determine the scope of supplemental jurisdiction authorized by § 1367, then, we must examine the statute's text in light of context, structure, and related statutory provisions.

Section 1367(a) is a broad grant of supplemental jurisdiction over other claims within the same case or controversy, as long as the action is one in which the district courts would have original jurisdiction. The last sentence of § 1367(a) makes it clear that the grant of supplemental jurisdiction extends to claims involving joinder or intervention of additional parties. The single question before us, therefore, is whether a diversity case in which the claims of some plaintiffs satisfy the amount-in-controversy requirement, but the claims of others plaintiffs do not, presents a "civil action of which the district courts have original jurisdiction." If the answer is yes, § 1367(a) confers supplemental jurisdiction over all claims, including those that do not independently satisfy the amount-in-controversy requirement, if the claims are part of the same Article III case or controversy. If the answer is no, § 1367(a) is inapplicable and, in light of our holdings in *Clark* and *Zahn*, the district court has no statutory basis for exercising supplemental jurisdiction over the additional claims.

We now conclude the answer must be yes. When the well-pleaded complaint contains at least one claim that satisfies the amount-in-controversy requirement, and there are no other relevant jurisdictional defects, the district court, beyond all question, has original jurisdiction over that claim. The presence of other claims in the complaint, over which the district court may lack original jurisdiction, is of no moment. If the court has original jurisdiction over a single claim in the complaint, it has original jurisdiction over a "civil action" within the meaning of § 1367(a), even if the civil action over which it has jurisdiction comprises fewer claims than were included in the complaint. Once the court determines it has original jurisdiction over the civil action, it can turn to the question whether it has a constitutional and statutory basis for exercising supplemental jurisdiction over the other claims in the action.

Section 1367(a) commences with the direction that §§ 1367(b) and (c), or other relevant statutes, may provide specific exceptions, but otherwise § 1367(a) is a broad jurisdictional grant, with no distinction drawn between pendent-claim and pendent-party cases. In fact, the last sentence of § 1367(a) makes clear that the provision grants supplemental jurisdiction over claims involving joinder or intervention of additional parties.

If § 1367(a) were the sum total of the relevant statutory language, our holding would rest on that language alone. The statute, of course, instructs us to examine § 1367(b) to determine if any of its exceptions apply, so we proceed to that section. While § 1367(b) qualifies the broad rule of § 1367(a), it does not withdraw supplemental jurisdiction over the claims of the additional parties at issue here. The specific exceptions to § 1367(a) contained in § 1367(b), moreover, provide additional support for our conclusion that § 1367(a) confers supplemental jurisdiction over these claims. Section 1367(b), which applies only to diversity cases, withholds supplemental jurisdiction over the claims of plaintiffs proposed to be joined as indispensable parties under Federal Rule of Civil Procedure 19, or who seek to intervene pursuant to Rule 24. Nothing in the text of § 1367(b), however, withholds supplemental jurisdiction over the claims of plaintiffs permissively joined under Rule 20 (like the additional plaintiffs in No. 04-79) or certified as class-action members pursuant to Rule 23 (like the additional plaintiffs in No. 04-70). The natural, indeed the necessary, inference is that § 1367 confers supplemental jurisdiction over claims by Rule 20 and Rule 23 plaintiffs. This inference, at least with respect to Rule 20 plaintiffs, is strengthened by the fact that § 1367(b) explicitly excludes supplemental jurisdiction over claims against defendants joined under Rule 20.

We cannot accept the view, urged by some of the parties, commentators, and Courts of Appeals, that a district court lacks original jurisdiction over a civil action unless the court has original jurisdiction over every claim in the complaint. As we understand this position, it requires assuming either that all claims in the complaint must stand or fall as a single, indivisible "civil action" as a matter of definitional necessity — what we will refer to as the "indivisibility theory" — or else that the inclusion of a claim or party falling outside the district court's original jurisdiction somehow contaminates every other claim

in the complaint, depriving the court of original jurisdiction over any of these claims—
what we will refer to as the "contamination theory."

The indivisibility theory is easily dismissed, as it is inconsistent with the whole notion
of supplemental jurisdiction. If a district court must have original jurisdiction over every
claim in the complaint in order to have "original jurisdiction" over a "civil action," then in
Gibbs there was no civil action of which the district court could assume original jurisdiction
under § 1331, and so no basis for exercising supplemental jurisdiction over any of the claims.

The contamination theory, as we have noted, can make some sense in the special context
of the complete diversity requirement because the presence of nondiverse parties on both
sides of a lawsuit eliminates the justification for providing a federal forum. The theory,
however, makes little sense with respect to the amount-in-controversy requirement, which
is meant to ensure that a dispute is sufficiently important to warrant federal-court attention.
The presence of a single nondiverse party may eliminate the fear of bias with respect to all
claims, but the presence of a claim that falls short of the minimum amount in controversy
does nothing to reduce the importance of the claims that do meet this requirement.

It is fallacious to suppose, simply from the proposition that § 1332 imposes both the
diversity requirement and the amount-in-controversy requirement, that the
contamination theory germane to the former is also relevant to the latter. There is no
inherent logical connection between the amount-in-controversy requirement and § 1332
diversity jurisdiction.

Finally, it is suggested that our interpretation of § 1367(a) creates an anomaly regarding
the exceptions listed in § 1367(b). It is not immediately obvious why Congress would
withhold supplemental jurisdiction over plaintiffs joined as parties "needed for just adjudication" under Rule 19 but would allow supplemental jurisdiction over plaintiffs permissively joined under Rule 20. The omission of Rule 20 plaintiffs from the list of exceptions
in § 1367(b) may have been an "unintentional drafting gap," *Meritcare,* 166 F.3d at 221
and n. 6. If that is the case, it is up to Congress rather than the courts to fix it. The
omission may seem odd, but it is not absurd.

And so we circle back to the original question. When the well-pleaded complaint in
district court includes multiple claims, all part of the same case or controversy, and some,
but not all, of the claims are within the court's original jurisdiction, does the court have
before it "any civil action of which the district courts have original jurisdiction"? It does.
Under § 1367, the court has original jurisdiction over the civil action comprising the claims
for which there is no jurisdictional defect. No other reading of § 1367 is plausible in light
of the text and structure of the jurisdictional statute. Though the special nature and
purpose of the diversity requirement means that a single nondiverse party can contaminate
every other claim in the lawsuit, the contamination does not occur with respect to
jurisdictional defects that go only to the substantive importance of individual claims.

It follows from this conclusion that the threshold requirement of § 1367(a) is satisfied
in cases, like those now before us, where some, but not all, of the plaintiffs in a diversity
action allege a sufficient amount in controversy. We hold that § 1367 by its plain text
overruled *Clark* and *Zahn* and authorized supplemental jurisdiction over all claims by
diverse parties arising out of the same Article III case or controversy, subject only to enumerated exceptions not applicable in the cases now before us.

C

The proponents of the alternative view of § 1367 insist that the statute is at least
ambiguous and that we should look to other interpretive tools, including the legislative

history of § 1367, which supposedly demonstrate Congress did not intend § 1367 to overrule *Zahn*. We can reject this argument at the very outset simply because § 1367 is not ambiguous. For the reasons elaborated above, interpreting § 1367 to foreclose supplemental jurisdiction over plaintiffs in diversity cases who do not meet the minimum amount in controversy is inconsistent with the text, read in light of other statutory provisions and our established jurisprudence.

[The majority went on to discuss the fact that, even if they did look at the legislative history behind the statute, the history is itself ambiguous as to whether Congress intended to expand the doctrines of pendent/ancillary jurisdiction rather than to generally codify it.]

D

Finally, we note that the Class Action Fairness Act (CAFA), Pub. L. 109-2, 119 Stat. 4, enacted this year, has no bearing on our analysis of these cases. Subject to certain limitations, the CAFA confers federal diversity jurisdiction over class actions where the aggregate amount in controversy exceeds $5 million. It abrogates the rule against aggregating claims, a rule this Court recognized in *Ben-Hur* and reaffirmed in *Zahn*. The CAFA, however, is not retroactive, and the views of the 2005 Congress are not relevant to our interpretation of a text enacted by Congress in 1990. The CAFA, moreover, does not moot the significance of our interpretation of § 1367, as many proposed exercises of supplemental jurisdiction, even in the class-action context, might not fall within the CAFA's ambit. The CAFA, then, has no impact, one way or the other, on our interpretation of § 1367.

The judgment of the Court of Appeals for the Eleventh Circuit is affirmed. The judgment of the Court of Appeals for the First Circuit is reversed, and the case is remanded for proceedings consistent with this opinion.

It is so ordered.

Notes and Problems

1. The eagerly awaited opinion from the Court in *Exxon* resolved that the courts are to interpret § 1367 literally even if that makes it easier for some class actions to find their way into federal court. Notice that under the court's opinion, all named plaintiff class representatives and all named defendants need to be diverse from one another. And at least one of the plaintiffs must have a claim exceeding the current jurisdictional amount of $75,000. Many scholars had been highly critical of a literal interpretation of the statute and assumed the Supreme Court would fix the congressional drafting error. *See, e.g.,* Thomas C. Arthur & Richard D. Freer, *Close Enough for Government Work: What Happens When Congress Doesn't Do Its Job?*, 40 Emory L.J. 1007 (1991). At least a few were no doubt relieved by the Supreme Court's decision to be faithful to the statute's text and to the fact that more nationwide class actions might make their way into federal courts for resolution. *See, e.g.,* James M. Underwood, *Supplemental Serendipity: Congress' Accidental Improvement of Supplemental Jurisdiction,* 36 Akron L. Rev. 653 (2004) ("[T]he Supplemental Jurisdiction Statute is neither broke nor in need of major overhaul or abandonment.").

2. Why does the Supreme Court in *Exxon* say that to have an anchor claim over which federal jurisdiction exists, the named parties must have complete diversity but that not all of the parties need to be able to satisfy the amount in controversy requirements? Does this make sense? What are the implications for the *Exxon* holding in class actions and other multi-party joinder scenarios?

3. Does *Exxon* hold that § 1367 overrules *Zahn*? Does it also overrule *Snyder*?

4. At the end of the opinion, the Court mentions the recent passage of the Class Action Fairness Act (CAFA). This is discussed in the next subsection. The court explains that while some claims can now find a jurisdictional basis in CAFA, there may be other claims that would not satisfy CAFA but could still find their way into federal court utilizing the combination of grants contained in § 1332(a) and § 1367 — just like the class action in *Exxon*.

5. *Problems.* Would federal diversity jurisdiction exist in the following multi-party scenarios?

a. Juanita is a citizen of Oklahoma and files a class action against Xenon Mortgage, Inc., a company with its principal place of business in Utah and incorporated in Delaware. She claims they misrepresented the terms of a mortgage loan she entered into with them and alleges her damages are $100,000. She seeks to represent a nationwide class of other customers of Xenon, some of whom have claims as large as Juanita's but many of whom have claims no more than a few thousand dollars.

b. Jacqueline is a citizen of New York and is suing FunToys, Inc., claiming the walkie talkie radio sets they sold simply do not work. FunToys is both incorporated and has its principal place of business in California. On behalf of herself and the nationwide class, she seeks a court order mandating that FunToys, Inc. reimburse each and every class member for the total cost of their radio set (retail value $19.99). According to reports, FunToys sold approximately 250,000 units of the walkie talkies.

c. Travis, a Delaware citizen, is suing Picks & Strings, Inc. a nationwide guitar retailer alleging the company committed fraud in selling a knock-off original edition Fender "Stratocaster" guitars supposedly used by Stevie Ray Vaughan in a concert and autographed by the famous musician. The guitars sold for $50,000 each. Picks & Strings is based in Florida and incorporated in Delaware. Travis seeks actual damages of the total purchase price of the guitar and punitive damages in at least an equal amount. He is also suing on behalf of all similarly situated consumers who were duped into buying the same false merchandise.

d. Diego, an 18-year-old boy, was hurt when a car came speeding down the street in front of his house and ran over him, crushing one of his feet and causing extensive bruising. His mother watched as this happened and was disturbed by the awful scene, seeking several weeks of counseling. Diego has sued the driver asking for damages of $250,000. His mother has joined in his lawsuit pursuant to Rule 20 and asks for $50,000 in emotional distress damages. Diego and his mother are both citizens of New Jersey. The driver was there on vacation and is a citizen of New Hampshire.

6. *Chapter Problem.* Would federal diversity jurisdiction possibly exist that would permit removal by TicketNinja under the combination of § 1332(a) and § 1367?

2. Jurisdiction under the Class Action Fairness Act

In 2005, after several decades of debate, Congress finally passed the Class Action Fairness Act with strong bipartisan support (it passed in the Senate by a vote of 72–26). The act did several things, but undoubtedly its most sweeping change to class action practice was in thrusting wide open the doors to federal courthouses to hear nationwide state-law based class actions. It did this by adding to the general diversity statute, § 1332, a new sub-part (d) which applies only to putative class actions. This subsection provides an additional pathway for class actions to be filed in or removed to federal courts. Subsection (d) offers federal jurisdiction when there is "minimal" diversity—rather than complete diversity—and the class actions claims add up to at least $5 million. In other words, rather than looking only to the named parties and demanding complete diversity, the statute now asks the court to consider the citizenship of everyone—including each unnamed class member—in order to see if a single class member is diverse from a single defendant. As you might imagine, this analysis almost always results in a finding that minimal diversity exists, at least it any nationwide class. Further, turning *Snyder* and *Zahn* completely on their heads, this subsection allows a court to use the aggregate size of the amount in controversy in the class action. Again, many decent-sized class actions can easily add up to $5 million even with the per capita damages being quite modest. As a result of this addition to the subject matter jurisdiction orchard, an attorney planning a class action and desiring federal court can get there in one of three ways: (a) suing on at least one federal cause of action (§ 1331), (b) only using a named class representative who is diverse from the defendants and has an individual claim worth at least $75,000 (§§ 1332(a) & 1367), or (c) using CAFA's terms and suing for a class with claims in the aggregate of more than $5 million and with at least one diverse party.

---

28 U.S.C. § 1332(d)(2) & (6)

(2) The district courts shall have original jurisdiction of any civil action in which the matter in controversy exceeds the sum or value of $5,000,000, exclusive of interest and costs, and is a class action in which—

   (A) any member of a class of plaintiffs is a citizen of a State different from any defendant ...

(6) In any class action, the claims of the individual class members shall be aggregated to determine whether the matter in controversy exceeds the sum or value of $5,000,000, exclusive of interest and costs.

The rationale behind this Congressional expansion of subject matter jurisdiction over state-law class actions is worthwhile to consider. Consider these comments from the Senate Report on CAFA:

> As set forth in Article III of the Constitution, the Framers established diversity jurisdiction to ensure fairness for all parties in litigation involving persons from multiple jurisdictions, particularly cases in which defendants from one state are sued in the local courts of another state. Interstate class actions—which often involve millions of parties from numerous states—present the precise concerns that diversity jurisdiction was designed to prevent: frequently in such cases, there appears to be state court provincialism against out-of-state defendants or a judicial failure to recognize the interests of other states in the litigation. Yet, because of a technical glitch in the diversity jurisdiction statute (28 U.S.C. § 1332), such cases are usually excluded from federal court. This glitch is not surprising given that class actions as we now know them did not exist when the statute's concept was crafted in the late 1700s.
>
> The current rules governing federal jurisdiction have the unintended consequence of keeping most class actions out of federal court, even though most class actions

are precisely the type of case for which diversity jurisdiction was created. In addition, current law enables plaintiffs' lawyers who prefer to litigate in state courts to easily "game the system" and avoid removal of large interstate class actions to federal court.

The ability of plaintiffs' lawyers to evade federal diversity jurisdiction has helped spur a dramatic increase in the number of class actions litigated in state courts — an increase that is stretching the resources of the state court systems.

Notably, many of these cases are being filed in improbable jurisdictions. A study conducted in three venues with reputations as hotbeds for class action activity found exponential increases in the numbers of class actions filed in recent years. For example, in the Circuit Court of Madison County, Illinois, a mostly rural county that covers 725 square miles and is home to less than one percent of the US population, the number of class actions filed annually grew from 2 in 1998 to 39 in 2000 — an increase of 3,650 percent. The same studies found that most of the class actions brought in Madison County and other magnet courts had little — if anything — to do with the venues where they were brought.

The effect of class action abuses in state courts is being exacerbated by the trend toward "nationwide" class actions, which invite one state court to dictate to 49 others what their laws should be on a particular issue, thereby undermining basic federalism principles. Clearly a system that allows state court judges to dictate national policy on these and numerous other issues from the local courthouse steps is contrary to the intent of the Framers when they crafted our system of federalism.

Senate Report No. 109-14 (109th Cong. 2005).

CAFA has certainly made it easier for plaintiffs to file class actions in federal court, or more likely, for defendants in putative class actions to remove them to federal court. Indeed, CAFA also modified some normal removal rules in the case of putative class actions: (a) no longer requiring all defendants to join or consent to the removal; (b) permitting removal even when the case is filed in a state that is home to one of the defendants; and (c) removing the one-year limit on diversity removals. *See* 28 U.S.C. § 1453. CAFA also contains a few other important limitations. First, by its own terms it does not apply to classes of less than 100 people. Second, § 1332(d)(3) and (d)(4) contain, respectively, exceptions that either permit or mandate that a federal district court "decline to exercise jurisdiction" in the case of certain statutorily-defined *local controversy* scenarios. The following case discusses this local controversy exception.

28 U.S.C. § 1332(d)(4)

(4) A district court shall decline to exercise jurisdiction under paragraph (2) —

    (A)(i) over a class action in which —

        (I) great than two-thirds of the members of all proposed plaintiff classes in the aggregate are citizens of the State in which the action was originally filed;

        (II) at least 1 defendant is a defendant —

            (aa) from whom significant relief is sought by members of the plaintiff class;

   (bb) whose alleged conduct forms a significant basis for the claims asserted by the proposed plaintiff class; and

   (cc) who is a citizen of the State in which the action was originally filed; and

   (III) principal injuries resulting from the alleged conduct or any related conduct of each defendant were incurred in the State in which the action was originally filed; and

   (ii) during the 3-year period preceding the filing of that class action, no other class action has been filed asserting the same or similar factual allegations against any of the defendants on behalf of the same or other persons.

Evans v. Walter Indus.

449 F.3d 1159 (11th Cir. 2006)

ANDERSON, J.,

Appellants United Defense LP, MeadWestvaco Corporation, Scientific-Atlanta, Inc., and Huron Valley Steel Corporation challenge the district court's decision to remand this case to the Alabama state court. Appellants argue that this case belongs in federal court under the recently-enacted Class Action Fairness Act ("CAFA"), Pub. L. No. 109-2, 119 Stat. 4 (2005) (codified in scattered sections of 28 U.S.C.), and because the plaintiffs fraudulently joined non-diverse defendants in order to evade federal jurisdiction. We hold that the federal district court has jurisdiction over this case under CAFA. We need not reach the issue of fraudulent misjoinder.

BACKGROUND

On April 8, 2005, plaintiffs filed this case in the Circuit Court of Calhoun County, Alabama, on behalf of a class of people who were allegedly injured by the actions of 18 named defendants and a number of fictitious defendants. The plaintiffs allege that the defendants operated manufacturing facilities in the Anniston, Alabama area. Plaintiffs allege both property damage and personal injury that they attribute to defendants' release of various waste substances over an approximately 85-year period. Four of the defendants removed this case to federal court under CAFA, which expanded federal jurisdiction for class actions. Defendants' Notice of Removal also contained a footnote that stated that defendants believed that plaintiffs may have improperly joined non-diverse defendants.

Plaintiffs filed a motion to remand the case to state court. Plaintiffs' sole argument for remand is that the case fell within CAFA's "local controversy" exception to federal jurisdiction. Plaintiffs argued that their case was a local controversy because more than two-thirds of the plaintiff class were Alabama citizens and at least one Alabama defendant, U.S. Pipe, was a "significant" defendant within the meaning of CAFA. Plaintiffs proffered the affidavits of two of their attorneys to support their claim. The district court agreed that this case fell within CAFA's local controversy exception, and remanded the case to state court.[1] The four removing defendants appeal the district court's ruling.

---

1. The district court also held that the defendants had waived their claim of fraudulent misjoinder by failing to raise the claim clearly in the defendants' Notice of Removal. As noted, we need not reach issues related to fraudulent misjoinder.

ANALYSIS

CAFA and the Local Controversy Exception

1. Legal Background

Congress enacted CAFA on February 18, 2005. Under CAFA, federal courts now have original jurisdiction over class actions in which the amount in controversy exceeds $5,000,000 and there is minimal diversity (at least one plaintiff and one defendant are from different states). 28 U.S.C. § 1332(d)(2). CAFA, however, does have an exception to federal jurisdiction for cases that are truly local in nature. 28 U.S.C. § 1332(d)(4)(A).

In this case, the parties do not dispute that the controversy exceeds $5,000,000 and that there is minimal diversity. The issue before us is whether this case falls within CAFA's local controversy exception to federal jurisdiction. CAFA's local controversy exception provides:

(4) A district court shall decline to exercise jurisdiction under paragraph (2)—

(A)(i) over a class action in which—

(I) greater than two-thirds of the members of all proposed plaintiff classes in the aggregate are citizens of the State in which the action was originally filed;

(II) at least 1 defendant is a defendant—

(aa) from whom significant relief is sought by members of the plaintiff class;

(bb) whose alleged conduct forms a significant basis for the claims asserted by the proposed plaintiff class; and

(cc) who is a citizen of the State in which the action was originally filed; and

(III) principal injuries resulting from the alleged conduct or any related conduct of each defendant were incurred in the State in which the action was originally filed; and

(ii) during the 3-year period preceding the filing of that class action, no other class action has been filed asserting the same or similar factual allegations against any of the defendants on behalf of the same or other persons;

28 U.S.C. § 1332(d).[2] CAFA's language favors federal jurisdiction over class actions and CAFA's legislative history suggests that Congress intended the local controversy exception to be a narrow one, with all doubts resolved "in favor of exercising jurisdiction over the case." S. Rep. No. 109-14 at 42. The Senate Report on CAFA further states that the local controversy exception:

is a narrow exception that was carefully drafted to ensure that it does not become a jurisdictional loophole. Thus, the Committee wishes to stress that in assessing whether each of these criteria is satisfied by a particular case, a federal court should bear in mind that the purpose of each of these criteria is to identify a truly local controversy—a controversy that uniquely affects a particular locality to the exclusion of all others.

S. Rep. 109-14, at 39. The language and structure of CAFA itself indicates that Congress contemplated broad federal court jurisdiction, *see e.g.,* Pub. L. No. 109-2, § 2(b)(2), 119 Stat. 4 ("providing for Federal court consideration of interstate cases of national importance

---

2. The "local controversy" exception can be satisfied in either of two ways, as provided for respectively in 28 U.S.C. § 1332(d)(4)(A) or (B). The instant case involves only § 1332(d)(4)(A).

under diversity jurisdiction"), with only narrow exceptions. These notions are fully confirmed in the legislative history.

2. The Burden of Proof

The district court correctly determined that the plaintiffs bear the burden of establishing that they fall within CAFA's local controversy exception. CAFA allows for removal of class actions that meet certain minimal requirements. CAFA does not change the traditional rule that the party seeking to remove the case to federal court bears the burden of establishing federal jurisdiction. *See Brill v. Countrywide Home Loans, Inc.,* 427 F.3d 446 (7th Cir. 2005). The parties do not dispute that the defendants have carried this burden and established that this action meets CAFA's basic requirements for removal to federal court—i.e., the controversy exceeds $5,000,000 and at least one plaintiff and one defendant are from different states (the minimal diversity requirement). However, when a party seeks to avail itself of an express statutory exception to federal jurisdiction granted under CAFA, as in this case, we hold that the party seeking remand bears the burden of proof with regard to that exception. *Cf. Breuer v. Jim's Concrete of Brevard, Inc.,* 538 U.S. 691, 697–98, 123 S. Ct. 1882, 1886, 155 L. Ed. 2d 923 (2003) (when a defendant removes a case under 28 U.S.C. § 1441(a), the burden is on a plaintiff to find an express exception to removal).[3]

In addition to *Breuer,* we find support for our decision in *Castleberry v. Goldome Credit Corp.,* 408 F.3d 773 (11th Cir. 2005) and *Lazuka v. FDIC,* 931 F.2d 1530 (11th Cir. 1991). Both cases addressed the removal of actions involving the Federal Deposit Insurance Corporation (FDIC). The courts held that once the FDIC has established the prerequisites for removal under 12 U.S.C. § 1819(b)(2)(B) (i.e., the action was filed against the FDIC, and the FDIC removed the action within 90 days), then the burden of establishing the "state action" exception to federal jurisdiction shifts to the party objecting to removal. *Castleberry,* 408 F.3d at 785; *Lazuka,* 93 F.2d at 1538. As in our situation, the removing party bears the initial burden of establishing federal jurisdiction, but the objecting party bears the burden of proving an express statutory exception once federal jurisdiction has been established under the main provisions of the statute. The instant case is very similar, and the instant statute is very similar. Here 28 U.S.C. § 1332(d)(2) provides that federal courts shall have original jurisdiction of any civil action that is a class action satisfying the $5,000,000 amount in controversy and the minimal diversity requirements. Then § 1332(d)(4) sets out a very specific exception, the local controversy exception, to the jurisdiction otherwise provided in § 1332(d)(2). We conclude that the statutory framework at issue here is very similar to that involved in *Castleberry* and *Lazuka.* We hold that the plaintiffs here—the parties objecting to removal after the prerequisites for removal jurisdiction have been met—have the burden of proving the local controversy exception.

No other Circuit appears to have addressed the specific question of which party should bear the burden of proof on CAFA's local controversy exception. Two other Circuits have determined that CAFA does not upset the traditional rule that the removing party bears

---

3. Moreover, placing the burden of proof on the plaintiff in this situation is not only consistent with the statutory design, we believe it places the burden on the party most capable of bearing it. The local controversy exception will require evidence about the composition of the plaintiff class. The plaintiffs have defined the class and have better access to information about the scope and composition of that class. With respect to the "significant defendant" prong, both plaintiffs and defendants have access to relevant information. Defendants have better access to information about conduct by the defendants, but plaintiffs have better access to information about which plaintiffs are injured and their relationship to various defendants.

the burden of proof with regard to establishing federal court jurisdiction. *Abrego Abrego v. Dow Chemical Co.*, 443 F.3d 676 (9th Cir. 2006); *Brill*, 427 F.3d 446. We agree with these courts that CAFA does not change the well-established rule that the removing party bears that burden of proof. However, neither case involved a removing defendant who did satisfy its burden of proving the jurisdictional prerequisites, as the defendants here did when they proved that the amount in controversy exceeded $5,000,000 and that there was the necessary minimal diversity.[4] Neither case involved the local controversy exception.

Thus, we address as a question of first impression the issue of who bears the burden of proving the local controversy exception, once the removing defendants have proved the amount in controversy and the minimal diversity requirement, and thus have established federal court jurisdiction under § 1332(d)(2). For the reasons set out above, and by analogy to *Breuer*, 123 S. Ct. at 1886, *Castleberry*, 408 F.3d at 784–85, and *Lazuka*, 91 F.3d at 1538, we hold that the plaintiffs bear the burden of proving the local controversy exception to the jurisdiction otherwise established.

We turn next to the merits of the local controversy exception as applied to this case. The parties dispute only two prongs of the local controversy exception: (1) whether more than two-thirds of the plaintiff class members are Alabama citizens; and (2) whether U.S. Pipe is a defendant from whom "significant relief" is sought and whose conduct forms a "significant basis" for the claims asserted by the plaintiffs. We conclude that plaintiffs have failed to prove either prong.

3. Citizenship of Plaintiff Class

To avail themselves of the local controversy exception, the plaintiffs must prove that greater than two-thirds of the proposed class members are Alabama citizens. In this case, the class includes:

> All property owners, lessees, licensees of properties on which the class defendants' [sic] deposited waste substances ... and/or engaged in conduct or practices that allowed such substances and materials to migrate to and/or become located on the plaintiffs' property [and]

> All individuals who have come in contact ... with any of the class defendants' deposited waste substances ... who as a result of which has suffered personal injury or damages to their health, safety and welfare.

The complaint alleges harms from 18 defendants extending over a period of at least 85 years. The district court held that plaintiffs had adduced sufficient evidence that more than two-thirds of the plaintiff class are Alabama citizens. We disagree.

Plaintiffs have offered little proof that Alabama citizens comprise at least two-thirds of the plaintiff class. In order to prove that two-thirds of the plaintiff class are Alabama citizens, the plaintiffs submitted an affidavit by attorney Jennifer Smith.[5] Smith avers that she reviewed or interviewed 10,118 potential plaintiffs. Of these, Smith determined that 5200 are members of the class. Of the 5200 class members, 4876 (93.8%) are Alabama

---

4. *Brill* involved the determination of the $5,000,000 amount in controversy. 427 F.3d 446. *Abrego Abrego* involved whether the removing defendant could prove that it fell under the definition of a "mass action" to enable it to be deemed a class action for purposes of the CAFA removal provisions. 443 F.3d at 685–86.

5. In light of our resolution of this case, we need not reach issues relating to the admissibility of the evidence contained in the affidavits of the several attorneys participating in this case. The court's concerns in this regard were sufficiently expressed at oral argument.

residents. The plaintiffs argue that if 93.8% of the known plaintiffs are Alabama residents, then surely two-thirds of the entire plaintiff class are Alabama citizens.

We are not persuaded by plaintiffs' argument. Smith's affidavit tells us nothing about how she selected the 10,118 people who were considered "potential plaintiffs." We do not know if these 10,118 people represent both the property damage and personal injury classes. We do not know if Smith's method favored people currently living in Anniston over people who have left the area.[6] In short, we know nothing about the percentage of the total class represented by the 10,118 people on which plaintiffs' evidence depends. Moreover, the class, as defined in the complaint, is extremely broad, extending over an 85-year period. We do not know if Smith made any effort to estimate the number of people with claims who no longer live in Alabama.

In sum, plaintiffs have not carried their burden of demonstrating that more than two-thirds of the plaintiff class are Alabama citizens. We understand that evidence of class citizenship might be difficult to produce in this case. That difficulty, however, is to a considerable degree a function of the composition of the class designed by plaintiffs. The local controversy exception is designed to ensure that state courts hear cases of a truly local nature. We have no way of knowing what percentage of the plaintiff class are Alabama citizens. We conclude that the evidence adduced by the plaintiffs wholly fails to present a credible estimate of the percentage of the plaintiff class who are citizens of Alabama. Accordingly, we hold that Plaintiffs have failed to prove that more than two-thirds of the plaintiff class are Alabama citizens.

4. Significant Defendant Test

We also hold that plaintiffs have failed to prove the "significant defendant" prong of the local controversy exception. In order to avail itself of the local controversy exception, pursuant to § 1332(d)(4)(A), the plaintiffs must prove that:

> (II) at least 1 defendant is a defendant
>
> > (aa) from whom significant relief is sought by members of the plaintiff class;
> >
> > (bb) whose alleged conduct forms a significant basis for the claims asserted by the proposed plaintiff class; and
> >
> > (cc) who is a citizen of the State in which the action was originally filed.

28 U.S.C. § 1332(d)(4)(A)(i)(II). The district court held that U.S. Pipe, an Alabama corporation, was a significant defendant. We disagree and hold that plaintiffs have failed to prove that U.S. Pipe was a significant defendant as defined by CAFA.

Only a few courts have interpreted the local controversy exception to federal jurisdiction. At least two courts have held that a class seeks "significant relief" against a defendant when the relief sought against that defendant is a significant portion of the entire relief sought by the class. See Robinson v. Cheetah Transp., 2006 U.S. Dist. LEXIS 10129, 2006 WL 468820 (W.D. La. Feb. 27, 2006); Kearns v. Ford Motor Company, 2005 U.S. Dist. LEXIS 41614, 2005 WL 3967998 (C.D. Cal. Nov. 21, 2005). As the Robinson court stated:

---

6. At oral argument, plaintiffs' counsel suggested that most of the potential plaintiffs had contacted the attorneys after hearing about the case through "word of mouth." It seems likely that people in Anniston are most likely to have heard about the case and contacted the attorneys. Potential plaintiffs outside of Anniston would seem to be under-represented in such a pool.

whether a putative class seeks significant relief from an in-state defendant includes not only an assessment of how many members of the class were harmed by the defendant's actions, but also a comparison of the relief sought between all defendants and each defendant's ability to pay a potential judgment.

Robinson, 2006 U.S. Dist. LEXIS 10129, 2006 WL 468820, at *3.

U.S. Pipe operated two metal casting facilities in Anniston during the relevant time period: a foundry located at 2101 W. 10th Street and another foundry at 1831 Front Street. The district court held that the plaintiffs sought significant relief from U.S. Pipe because: (1) the complaint accused all the defendants of contamination in the Anniston area; and (2) U.S. Pipe owned and operated two foundry facilities during a substantial portion of the relevant time period.

Plaintiffs rely on their complaint and an attorney affidavit to establish that U.S. Pipe is a significant defendant. These documents, however, do not provide any enlightenment at all with respect to the significance of the relief that is sought against U.S. Pipe, or its comparative significance relative to the relief sought from the other 17 named co-defendants. In short, there is simply no evidence that U.S. Pipe was "significant" with respect to liability.

With respect to whether the conduct of U.S. Pipe "forms a significant basis" for the plaintiffs' claims, plaintiffs' evidence offers no insight into whether U.S. Pipe played a significant role in the alleged contamination, as opposed to a lesser role, or even a minimal role. The evidence does not indicate that a significant number or percentage of putative class members may have claims against U.S. Pipe, or indeed that any plaintiff has such a claim.[7]

Moreover, the limited facts before this court give rise to an inference that U.S. Pipe is not a significant defendant. The plaintiffs charge that U.S. Pipe has operated two facilities in Anniston: one on West 10th Street and the property at 1831 Front Street. The evidence shows that U.S. Pipe sold the 10th Street location in 1951 and believes that operations ceased considerably before 1951. The number of plaintiffs injured by pre-1951 foundry operations is very unlikely to be significant when compared to the class as a whole. U.S. Pipe did operate the Front Street location from 1961–2003. However, that site appears to be somewhat south of the area occupied by most of the class members identified by plaintiffs. Numerous other defendants have operations much nearer the largest concentration of identified class members, suggesting that U.S. Pipe's liability might not be significant compared to other defendants, and that the conduct of U.S. Pipe might not form a significant basis for the claims of the class. Plaintiffs do allege in their complaint that the defendants gave out foundry sand as fill dirt to local residents but, again, we have no evidence about whether U.S. Pipe has significant liability for distributing fill dirt, or that its conduct in this regard forms a significant basis for the claims of the class.

---

7. The parties dispute whether the complaint can fairly be read to allege joint and several liability on the part of the defendants. We need not resolve that dispute. Even if the complaint does, and even if that satisfied the plaintiffs' burden with respect to the significant relief prong, § 1332(d)(4)(A)(i)(II)(aa), plaintiffs nevertheless have failed to satisfy § 1332(d)(4)(a)(i)(II)(bb) which requires that the "alleged conduct [of a significant defendant] form[] a significant basis for the claims asserted by the proposed class." In other words, the mere fact that relief might be sought against U.S. Pipe for the conduct of others (via joint liability) does not convert the conduct of others into conduct of U.S. Pipe so as to also satisfy the "significant basis" requirement.

CONCLUSION

For all the foregoing reasons, we hold that plaintiffs have failed to prove that their case belongs in state court under the local controversy exception to CAFA.[8] Because of our holding on this issue, we need not reach defendants' claim that the plaintiffs fraudulently misjoined defendants in their complaint.

REVERSED and REMANDED.

Notes and Problems

1. How did the facts in *Evans* show that the general requirements for jurisdiction under § 1332(d) were satisfied, as an initial matter?

2. In *Evans* the court had to analyze some of the interpretational difficulties behind the intense verbiage in the statutory *local controversy* exception to § 1332(d)'s otherwise very generous grant of minimal diversity jurisdiction to class actions. The idea behind this exception was to keep predominantly local matters in state courts while keeping truly national-oriented class actions in federal courts. But the statute offers its own definition of what constitutes a truly local action and those terms are subject to some debate. Given the facts in *Evans*, why did the court determine that the case was not local? If that case is not considered local — despite being a toxic tort where residents of one small town were exposed to chemical through local plant operations — how broad can this local controversy exception be?

3. For practice, and using the facts from *Evans*, analyze whether federal removal jurisdiction would have existed under either § 1331 (federal question), § 1332(a) (the general diversity grant) and/or § 1367(a) (supplemental jurisdiction).

4. Do you agree with the *Evans* court's conclusion that the plaintiff bore the burden of demonstrating that the case fell within the local controversy exception? Is it not more typical for a defendant attempting to remove a case to establish that federal court subject matter jurisdiction exists? *See, e.g., Hart v. Fed Ex Ground Package System, Inc.,* 457 F.3d 675 (7th Cir. 2006) (agreeing that placing the burden on the party seeking remand to show that an exception to jurisdiction applies is consistent with the policies behind CAFA).

5. *Chapter Problem.* As counsel for TicketNinja, which path to potential federal removal jurisdiction offers you the most hope? Be prepared to explain your answer. Does it matter if Ms. Beautiful (the local defendant who was added by the plaintiff to the case as a co-defendant) is unwilling to join in your removal?

Pulling It All Together Exercise

Using the facts from the *Phillips Petroleum v. Shutts* case, analyze whether that case could have been filed today using either § 1331, § 1332(a) & § 1367, or § 1332(d).

Spend 15 minutes writing out your analysis of federal subject matter jurisdiction and giving your conclusion.

---

8. Because plaintiffs have adduced little or no evidence in this case to satisfy two requirements for the local controversy exception, we need not address the kind or quantity of evidence that should be required.

Upon Further Review

As applied to class actions, the history of federal subject matter jurisdiction has been fascinating. Beginning with the *Ben-Hur* decision, the Supreme Court recognized that the typical analysis might be different for traditional litigation than for class actions. The conceptually different status of class members from normal litigants facilitated the Supreme Court's very practical decision to exclude unnamed class members from the normal complete diversity analysis. The subsequent seemingly inconsistent decision to yet require those unnamed class members to each independently meet the statute's minimum jurisdictional amount left many defendants and scholars frustrated and baffled. The first "fix" to this problem was accidental — the drafting error in the Supplemental Jurisdiction Statute that resulted in the inadvertent overruling of both *Zahn* (Rule 23) and *Clark* (Rule 20) and permitted the small claimants to piggyback on the large-enough claim of another plaintiff. Yet even § 1367 could not rescue a true negative-value class action where none of the class members could independently satisfy the current $75,000 amount in controversy requirement. This was true even though the class might be national in scope with tens of thousands of class members and multiple millions of dollars (in the aggregate) at stake. Such a case was deemed not important enough for a federal court's attention while a traditional breach of contract case brought by one Oklahoman against a Colorado defendant for $76,001 would find a federal forum. The 2005 passage of the Class Action Fairness Act has dramatically widened the doors to the federal courthouse for state-law based class actions requiring only "minimal diversity" and shifting the amount in controversy requirement to an aggregate figure of $5 million. While not all class actions can satisfy these new requirements, many can. As a result, many more national class actions are finding their home among the federal courts. Depending upon class counsel's preferred forum, many strategic decisions must be made in framing the scope of the case; defendant's counsel must be sharp as well in analyzing possible removal grounds.

E. Notice

As alluded to in Chapter 4 Class Actions: Certification, Rule 23(b)(1)–(2) classes are treated fundamentally differently from Rule 23(b)(3) classes in terms of notice and whether opt-out rights exist. The mandatory class action obviously does not generally involve opt-out rights and Rule 23(c)(1) further, does not require a court to even give notice to class members of the decision to grant certification. Rule 23(c)(1) does permit a court to order some method of notice in such cases, but the court is under no compulsion to do so. On the other hand, notice of some sort is mandatory in every Rule 23(b)(3) class action. An important early decision regarding the notice requirements for such a class under both the Due Process Clause and Rule 23(c) came in *Eisen*. As you read this opinion, ask yourself why the rules are so different regarding notice for the different categories of class actions. If notice, even individual notice, is demanded for Rule 23(b)(3) classes, why not for mandatory classes? And why aren't the notice requirements in a Rule 23(b)(3) class a bit more flexible? Is the cost of notice really worthwhile when most class members will just ignore it?

Rule 23(c)(2)

(A) For any class certified under Rule 23(b)(1) or (b)(2), the court may direct appropriate notice to the class.

(B) For any class certified under Rule 23(b)(3), the court must direct to class members the best notice practicable under the circumstances, including individual notice to all members who can be identified through reasonable effort. The notice must clearly and concisely state in plain, easily understood language:

    (i)   the nature of the action;

    (ii) the definition of the class certified;

    (iii) the class claims, issues, or defenses;

    (iv) that a class member may enter an appearance through an attorney if the member so desires;

    (v) that the court will exclude from the class any member who requests exclusion;

    (vi) the time and manner for requesting exclusion; and

    (vii) the binding effect of a class judgment on members under Rule 23(b)(3).

Eisen v. Carlisle & Jacquelin
417 U.S. 156 (1974)

POWELL, J.,

Petitioner brought this class action in the United States District Court for the Southern District of New York. [Petitioner] sued on behalf of all who traded in odd lots [on the New York Stock Exchange] during the period from May 1, 1962, through June 30, 1966. Throughout this period odd-lot trading was not part of the Exchange's regular auction market but was handled exclusively by special odd-lot dealers, who bought and sold for their own accounts as principals. [Odd lot trading involves shares of less than 100 shares or, at least, not in multiples of 100. Plaintiff alleged that defendants conspired to fix the commissions charged on such trades in violation of the federal antitrust and securities laws. The class had an estimated 6 million members. The district court, in certifying a Rule 23(b)(3) class action, found that 2,250,000 of the members could be identified with reasonable effort. The cost of mailing notice to this group would be $225,000. The class representative's individual claim was only $70. Instead of imposing these costs of notice on the Plaintiff, the district court authorized a different notice procedure costing only $22,000. This plan involved individual mailed notice to all identifiable class members with ten or more odd-lot trades during the relevant time period as well as to 5,000 other identifiable class members selected randomly. Further, the court required notice by publication in the Wall Street Journal and New York Times as well as other national papers. The trial court made the preliminary determination that plaintiff was likely to win and, therefore, directed that defendants pay 90% of the costs of notice up front. Defendants appealed this order.]

Turning to the merits of the case, we find that the District Court's resolution of the notice problems was erroneous in two respects. First, it failed to comply with the notice requirements of Rule 23 (c)(2), and second, it imposed part of the cost of notice on respondents.

A

Rule 23 (c)(2) provides that, in any class action maintained under subdivision (b)(3), each class member shall be advised that he has the right to exclude himself from the action on request or to enter an appearance through counsel, and further that the judgment, whether favorable or not, will bind all class members not requesting exclusion. To this end, the court is required to direct to class members "the best notice practicable under the circumstances, *including individual notice to all members who can be identified through reasonable effort.*" We think the import of this language is unmistakable. Individual notice must be sent to all class members whose names and addresses may be ascertained through reasonable effort.

The Advisory Committee's Note to Rule 23 reinforces this conclusion. See 28 U. S. C. App., p. 7765. The Advisory Committee described subdivision (c)(2) as "not merely discretionary" and added that the "mandatory notice pursuant to subdivision (c)(2) ... is designed to fulfill requirements of due process to which the class action procedure is of course subject." *Id.*, at 7768. The Committee explicated its incorporation of due process standards by citation to *Mullane v. Central Hanover Bank & Trust Co.*, 339 U.S. 306 (1950), and like cases.

In *Mullane* the Court addressed the constitutional sufficiency of publication notice rather than mailed individual notice to known beneficiaries of a common trust fund as part of a judicial settlement of accounts. The Court observed that notice and an opportunity to be heard were fundamental requisites of the constitutional guarantee of procedural due process. It further stated that notice must be "reasonably calculated, under all the circumstances, to apprise interested parties of the pendency of the action and afford them an opportunity to present their objections." The Court continued:

> But when notice is a person's due, process which is a mere gesture is not due process. The means employed must be such as one desirous of actually informing the absentee might reasonably adopt to accomplish it. The reasonableness and hence the constitutional validity of any chosen method may be defended on the ground that it is in itself reasonably certain to inform those affected.

The Court then held that publication notice could not satisfy due process where the names and addresses of the beneficiaries were known. In such cases, "the reasons disappear for resort to means less likely than the mails to apprise them of [an action's] pendency."

Viewed in this context, the express language and intent of Rule 23 (c)(2) leave no doubt that individual notice must be provided to those class members who are identifiable through reasonable effort. In the present case, the names and addresses of 2,250,000 class members are easily ascertainable, and there is nothing to show that individual notice cannot be mailed to each. For these class members, individual notice is clearly the "best notice practicable" within the meaning of Rule 23(c)(2) and our prior decisions.

Petitioner contends, however, that we should dispense with the requirement of individual notice in this case, and he advances two reasons for our doing so. First, the prohibitively high cost of providing individual notice to 2,250,000 class members would end this suit as a class action and effectively frustrate petitioner's attempt to vindicate the policies underlying the antitrust and securities laws. Second, petitioner contends that individual notice is unnecessary in this case, because no prospective class member has a large enough stake in the matter to justify separate litigation of his individual claim. Hence, class members lack any incentive to opt out of the class action even if notified.

The short answer to these arguments is that individual notice to identifiable class members is not a discretionary consideration to be waived in a particular case. It is, rather, an unambiguous requirement of Rule 23. As the Advisory Committee's Note explained, the Rule was intended to insure that the judgment, whether favorable or not, would bind all class members who did not request exclusion from the suit. Accordingly, each class member who can be identified through reasonable effort must be notified that he may request exclusion from the action and thereby preserve his opportunity to press his claim separately or that he may remain in the class and perhaps participate in the management of the action. There is nothing in Rule 23 to suggest that the notice requirements can be tailored to fit the pocketbooks of particular plaintiffs.[13]

Petitioner further contends that adequate representation, rather than notice, is the touchstone of due process in a class action and therefore satisfies Rule 23. We think this view has little to commend it. To begin with, Rule 23 speaks to notice as well as to adequacy of representation and requires that both be provided. Moreover, petitioner's argument proves too much, for it quickly leads to the conclusion that no notice at all, published or otherwise, would be required in the present case. This cannot be so, for quite apart from what due process may require, the command of Rule 23 *is* clearly to the contrary. We therefore conclude that Rule 23 (c)(2) requires that individual notice be sent to all class members who can be identified with reasonable effort.[14]

B

We also agree with the Court of Appeals that petitioner must bear the cost of notice to the members of his class. The District Court reached the contrary conclusion and imposed 90% of the notice cost on respondents. This decision was predicated on the court's finding, made after a preliminary hearing on the merits of the case, that petitioner was "more than likely" to prevail on his claims. Apparently, that court interpreted Rule 23 to authorize such a hearing as part of the determination whether a suit may be maintained as a class action. We disagree.

In the absence of any support under Rule 23, petitioner's effort to impose the cost of notice on respondents must fail. The usual rule is that a plaintiff must initially bear the cost of notice to the class. The exceptions cited by the District Court related to situations where a fiduciary duty pre-existed between the plaintiff and defendant, as in a shareholder derivative suit. Where, as here, the relationship between the parties is truly adversary, the plaintiff must pay for the cost of notice as part of the ordinary burden of financing his own suit.

---

13. Petitioner also argues that class members will not opt out because the statute of limitations has long since run out on the claims of all class members other than petitioner. This contention is disposed of by our recent decision in *American Pipe & Construction Co. v. Utah*, 414 U.S. 538 (1974), which established that commencement of a class action tolls the applicable statute of limitations as to all members of the class.

14. We are concerned here only with the notice requirements of subdivision (c)(2), which are applicable to class actions maintained under subdivision (b)(3). By its terms subdivision (c)(2) is inapplicable to class actions for injunctive or declaratory relief maintained under subdivision (b)(2). Petitioner's effort to qualify his suit as a class action under subdivisions (b)(1) and (b)(2) was rejected by the Court of Appeals.

Petitioner has consistently maintained, however, that he will not bear the cost of notice under subdivision (c)(2) to members of the class as defined in his original complaint. We therefore remand the cause with instructions to dismiss the class action as so defined.

The judgment of the Court of Appeals is vacated and the cause remanded for proceedings consistent with this opinion.

It is so ordered.

Notes and Problems

1. With regard to the issue of how to provide notice to the class members whose identities and whereabouts could be ascertained with reasonable effort, is the Supreme Court's decision in *Eisen* merely an interpretation of Rule 23(c) (and thus subject to change) or is the holding compelled by constitutional notions of due process? If the latter, what about the argument (from *Shutts* earlier in this chapter) that the Due Process Clause is flexible and reasonable? Is it reasonable to require an expenditure of such a large sum by the plaintiff class representative (possessing only a small claim) to provide notice that most class members will disregard? What will most of the class members do upon receiving notice in a case like *Eisen*?

2. What notice are class members who cannot be ascertained with reasonable efforts entitled to receive—under Rule 23 and the Due Process Clause? Did the Court in *Eisen* have any problems with that aspect of the trial court's order? In terms of alternatives to individual notice, courts have considered mechanisms like websites, publication of notice in newspapers and magazines that would be of interest to the class, radio or television advertisements, or some other combination of methods. In terms of the timing, typically certification notice is given promptly after the decision and with a deadline for class members to opt out through some affirmative act set forth in the notice. As we will see later in this chapter, a second notice may also be forthcoming later in the case if the court is considering approving a tentative settlement agreement, in accordance with Rule 23(e). This settlement notice is arguably more flexible than the individual notice standard explicitly required by Rule 23(c)(2) if only because Rule 23(e) only states that notice must be directed in a "reasonable" manner. Of course, if the certification decision happens concurrently with the court's tentative approval of a settlement, then one notice is issued covering both the certification (and giving opt-out rights) and notice of the settlement (providing methods by which class members can object to the settlement).

3. Given the cultural shifts in our society since *Eisen*, is there a good argument that individual notice by email rather than "snail mail" would be acceptable? Which are you more likely to disregard and trash?

4. Notice in footnote 14 that the Court expressly limits its holding to Rule 23(b)(3) class actions, where individual notice is typically required by the express terms of Rule 23(c)(2). On the other hand, recall that in *In re Monumental* (in Chapter 4 Class Actions: Certification), that court required in a Rule 23(b)(2) hybrid (injunctive relief and some ancillary monetary relief) notice of some variety to the class members. Setting aside the hybrid type of case, most have felt that the cohesion of a properly certified class under Rule 23(b)(1)–(2) argues against the due process need for notice to class members:

> I think this conclusion is reinforced by the nature of (b)(1) and (b)(2) classes. They tend to be cohesive groups because the rule requires that the members have similar interests in the subject matter of the litigation or be seeking relief applicable to all of them (an injunction or declaratory judgment). Thus, members of a Rule 23(b)(1) or a Rule 23(b)(2) class usually are related in interest in the sense that

they are seeking the same remedy or asserting the same claims or defenses. Therefore, it is not imperative that each of them receive individual notice to insure the full presentation of the merits of the litigation. This cohesiveness, of course, does not exist in the Rule 23(b)(3) case; in these actions the class members are bound together only by the fact that they are asserting one or more common questions of law or fact.

Arthur R. Miller, *Problems in Giving Notice in Class Actions,* 58 F.R.D. 313, 315 (1972).

5. With regard to the second portion of the *Eisen* opinion, prohibiting the trial court from requiring the defendant to front the costs of providing notice, one has to take this holding with a grain of salt. At the conclusion of the litigation, *if* the plaintiff is successful, the costs of providing notice to the class can be considered taxable court costs properly assessed against the defendant. Further, some lower courts as a matter of practice have taxed notice costs to the defendant in cases where at the time of certification the court had already ruled on a partial summary judgment (on a liability issue) against the defendant. Because the plaintiff is already assured some form of victory at that point, it is considered safe to tax costs at the early date. *See, e.g., Barahona-Gomez v. Reno,* 167 F.3d 1228, 1236 (9th Cir. 1999) (after granting plaintiff's motion for preliminary injunction). Also, if the district court orders discretionary notice to be issued in a Rule 23(b)(1) or (b)(2) case (as Rule 23(c)(1) mentions), in practice courts have been willing in some cases to require defendant to share all or a portion of those costs of notice. *See, e.g., S. Ute Indian Tribe v. Amoco Prod. Co.,* 2 F.3d 1023, 1030 (10th Cir. 1993). In situations involving a consumer class action where the defendant still has a business relationship with the class members (e.g., customers of a utility company), some courts have required the defendant to include the individual notice in a routine mailing (e.g., a monthly billing statement) sent to the class members. *See, e.g., Oppenheimer Fund, Inc. v. Sanders,* 437 U.S. 340, 356 n. 22 (1978) (observing the practice of some lower courts to do this in order to save money and despite objections from defendants).

6. Part of the much ballyhooed 2003 amendments to Rule 23 included the addition of language in Rule 23(c)(2) that, in a Rule 23(b)(3) case, the notice must state the required information "clearly and concisely [and] in plain, easily understood language." Such a sweeping pronouncement sounds grand—who, after all, could argue in favor of notice that is "opaque and makes no sense"?—but inexorably raises a tension between precision and the use of plain, easily understood language. Members of the bar serving on pattern jury instruction committees run into the same problem—how do you correctly articulate a legal proposition while making it easily understood by non-lawyers? Something has to give. In that regard, some rather humorous anecdotes have been reported by Professor Arthur R. Miller highlighting certain class member responses to a class notice issued in a case in North Carolina concerning a particular antibiotic. As you read some of his few examples below, ask yourself how well ordinary class members will comprehend their legal rights after reading a class action notice:

a. "Dear Mr. Clerk: I have your notice that I owe for $300 for selling drugs. I have never sold any drugs, especially those you have listed; but I have sold a little whiskey once in awhile."

b. "Dear Sir: I received your pamphlet on drugs, which I think will be of great value to me in the future. I am unable to attend your class, however."

c. "Dear Sir: I received this paper from you. I guess I really don't understand it, but if I have been given one of those drugs, nobody told me why. If it means what I think it does, I have not been with a man in nine years."

Arthur R. Miller, *Problems in Giving Notice in Class Actions,* 58 F.R.D. 313, 322 (1972) (also opining that the "sad truth is that notices issued by courts … typically are much too larded with legal jargon to be understood by the average citizen.").

7. *Chapter Problem.* If the proposed class is certified against TicketNinja, what form of notice would likely be required for the class members? How easy will it be to determine the identities and whereabouts of the class? In terms of the substance, can you practice the "plain, easily understood language" mandate by drafting a sentence describing the litigation so that a layperson can understand it?

F. Res Judicata and Rule 23

We have already looked at the basics of res judicata and collateral estoppel in Chapter 2. But these concepts have a slightly different application under some circumstances when the prior adjudication of a claim or issue was in the context of a class action. This is particularly true when the prior case was a Rule 23(b)(1) or (2) injunctive relief only class action where the class representative was not even attempting to seek recovery of actual damages for the class members. If and when a class member seeks their own individual damages in a later suit, does the doctrine of res judicata bar that attempt? Would that be fair, particularly, when the class member received no notice of the prior certification?

In re Jackson Lockdown/MCO Cases
568 F. Supp. 869 (E.D. Mich. 1983)

COHN, J.,

OPINION AND ORDER ON MOTION FOR SUMMARY JUDGMENT

"Principles of *res judicata* are not ironclad."
Bogard v. Cook, 586 F.2d 399, 408 (5th Cir. 1978)

Twenty-two prisoner civil rights cases, arising out of the May 1981 riots at the State Prison of Southern Michigan (SPSM) have been assigned to my docket for pre-trial purposes. The complaint in each case is essentially the same. The prisoners allege that the Michigan Corrections Organization (MCO), the labor union for the prison guards, instigated the riots by taking over SPSM on the morning of May 22 with the intent of confining its prisoners to their cells indefinitely (a "lockdown") and otherwise violating their constitutional rights. The plaintiffs seek declaratory relief and money damages.

Now before me is a motion for summary judgment by defendants Michigan Corrections Organization and Gerald Fryt, its president (referred to collectively as MCO). The only issue is whether these actions are entirely barred by the judgment in *Walker v. Johnson,* 544 F. Supp. 345 (E.D. Mich. 1982), since the plaintiff class in *Walker,* of which these plaintiffs were members, failed to bring claims for damages.

II.

Walker was a class action challenging the constitutionality of a wide variety of conditions of confinement at three Michigan prisons; only state prison authorities were named as defendants in *Walker*.[3] The common link between *Walker* and these cases is that the conditions challenged in Walker were imposed by the prison authorities following the May riots for the professed reason of restoring and maintaining order. In a detailed opinion and order entered after a seven-week trial, Judge Stewart Newblatt of this district found a number of the post-riot conditions constitutionally flawed and also found that a number of these conditions passed constitutional muster. The only relief sought in *Walker* was declaratory and injunctive. *Walker* is currently on appeal to the Court of Appeals for the Sixth Circuit.

Paragraph 21 of the amended complaint in *Walker* stated:

> "Damage actions for individual injuries suffered in violation of constitutional rights will be brought in individual actions by plaintiffs and members of plaintiff class."

Shortly after the filing of the amended complaint defendants in *Walker* filed a motion to strike Paragraph 21 as "irrelevant and immaterial," because the only relief sought under the amended complaint was declaratory and injunctive. (Apparently an initial complaint filed by the named plaintiff sought money damages). On August 20, 1981, the parties stipulated to strike Paragraph 21.

On October 21, Judge Newblatt entered the following class certification order:

> "IT IS HEREBY ORDERED, that this action shall proceed on a class action basis pursuant to Federal Rules of Civil Procedure 23(b)(2). The class shall be defined as all prisoners who are, or will be, confined at Marquette Branch Prison, Michigan Reformatory, and/or State Prison at Southern Michigan, North, Central and South complexes.

> This being an action for declaratory and prospective relief, notice to the class is not ordered, subject to further order of the Court."

There is no dispute that plaintiffs in these cases are members of the class certified in *Walker*.

III.

MCO contends that to permit plaintiffs to now assert individual claims for damages would violate the principle against splitting a single cause of action into separate pieces of litigation. Although MCO cites a multitude of cases, only a single district court decision supports their position.[4] The court in *International Prisoners' Union v. Rizzo*, 356 F. Supp.

---

3. "Plaintiffs have named four defendants in this action: One defendant is the Michigan Department of Corrections. The other three defendants, sued individually and in their official capacities, are: Perry Johnson, Director of the Michigan Department of Corrections; Barry Mintzes, Warden of Southern Michigan Reformatory at Ionia; Theodore Koehler, Warden of Marquette Prison." 544 F. Supp. at 347, note 3.

4. Two court of appeals cases cited by MCO do not support its argument. In *Goff v. Menke*, 672 F.2d 702 (8th Cir. 1982), the court held that an individual prisoner action should be dismissed without prejudice and the prisoner directed to seek his relief through a concurrently pending class action. The court in *Goff* indicated that equitable relief directed at the same prison conditions should be rendered in a single class action if possible, while noting that individual claims for money damages could be handled on an individual basis. *Id.* at 704. The plaintiff in *Smallwood v. Missouri Board of Probation and Parole*, 587 F.2d 369 (8th Cir. 1978), was barred from relitigating the constitutionality of certain parole procedures previously upheld in a class action in which he was a member of the class; however, two issues not raised in the prior class action were considered on their merits. Moreover, the court noted that the plaintiff, appearing *pro se*, had not even challenged the district court's ruling that he was bound by the prior class action. *Id.* at 371. A third decision from the Eighth Circuit cited by MCO, although not directly pertinent, appears to support plaintiffs' position in *dicta, Cotton v. Hutto*, 577 F.2d 453, 454, note 4 (8th Cir. 1978).

806 (E.D. Pa. 1973) held that individual claims for damages based on allegations of unconstitutional prison conditions were barred by the failure of a previous plaintiff class to raise a claim for damages in an action for injunctive relief directed at the same or similar prison conditions. However, in that previous class action notice was sent to the entire class, a factor missing in *Walker*.

In contrast, every federal court of appeals that has considered the question has held that a class action seeking only declaratory and injunctive relief does not bar subsequent individual suits for damages based on the same or similar conditions. *See Crowder v. Lash*, 687 F.2d 996, 1007–9 (7th Cir. 1982); *Herron v. Beck*, 693 F.2d 125 (11th Cir. 1982); *Bogard v. Cook*, 586 F.2d 399, 406–9 (5th Cir. 1978); *Jones-Bey v. Caso*, 535 F.2d 1360 (2nd Cir. 1976). The reasoning of *Bogard* for not giving the prior class action, *Gates v. Collier*, 349 F. Supp. 881 (N.D. Miss. 1972), *aff'd*, 501 F.2d 1291 (5th Cir. 1974), preclusive effect is equally applicable here:

> Nor is it by any means certain that the *Gates* class action would have remained manageable if it had been expanded to include claims for damages by individual prisoners. The real defendant in *Gates* was the Parchman Prison itself; all of the District Court's energy and attention were (and still are) necessarily focused on the broad expanse of constitutional violations exposed and the proper dimension of judicial intervention required to correct them. The abuses at the heart of *Gates* ... were broad-based and affected the prisoners as a community.

> Claims for individual damage relief, by contrast, would have required separate mini-trials for each prisoner. Because damage relief could only have been sought against officials in their individual capacity, the problem of qualified immunity would have been injected into the suit.... Significantly, the district court only certified *Gates* as a Rule 23(b)(1) and (2) class action, and not a (b)(3) action, which would have been the proper classification if joinder of all individual damage claims had been sought. Given the lack of common questions of fact as to many of those claims, and the unmanageability of the suit had they been included, we cannot believe that the district court would have allowed the claims as part of that action if they had been recognized as potentially possible.

586 F.2d at 409.

The controlling Sixth Circuit precedent cited by MCO is simply not relevant. The Sixth Circuit, in *Laskey v. International Union, United Auto., etc.*, 638 F.2d 954 (6th Cir. 1981), affirmed the finding of the district court that representation of the class in a previous case had been adequate and held that dissident class members were bound by the approved settlement and could not relitigate identical claims in a subsequent action. *Lasky* did not involve the issues presented here, whether the failure to raise damage claims in a prior class action seeking declaratory and injunctive relief bars subsequent individual actions for damages. *Alexander v. Aero Lodge No. 735*, 565 F.2d 1364 (6th Cir. 1977), is authority for the proposition that under some circumstances notice need not be given to member of a Fed. R. Civ. P. 23(b)(2) class action prior to entry of judgment; however, in *Alexander* all claims, including those for damages, were raised in the class action and there was no issue raised of barring subsequent individual actions. *Stewart v. Butz*, 491 F.2d 165 (6th Cir. 1974), merely held that the defendant Secretary of Agriculture was bound by prior adjudications as to liability in other class actions in the instant class action where identical issues were presented in all three class actions. None of these cases were prisoner civil rights actions. Neither did they address the problems which would face a district court attempting to adjudicate thousands of damage claims in the context of a sweeping class action for prospective injunctive relief aimed at pervasive prison conditions. *Lasky* and *Alexander* merely carve out very narrow exceptions to the general rule that Fed R. Civ. P. 23(b)(2) is an inappropriate device for handling claims for money damages, and in both cases the monetary relief was essentially equitable in nature and ancillary to the primary injunctive relief.[5]

MCO's argument is further flawed in its assumption that the plaintiff class in *Walker* could have litigated a damage claim by each individually injured prisoner. Judge Newblatt carefully limited class cetification to claims for declaratory and prospective relief only, thus dispensing with the need to give notice to the class. The careful limitation of the scope of the *Walker* litigation so as not to encompass or preclude individual damage actions is consistent with good class action practice:

> It may be appropriate to reduce the complexity of class litigation by imposing special limits on the basic transactional approach to defining a claim or cause of action. A sophisticated transactional approach, indeed, includes trial convenience in its calculus.... Such limitations on claim preclusion, indeed, are often built into the determination that identifies the scope of the class action.... Pursuant to the same general principle that claim preclusion does not apply to matters that could not be advanced in a prior action, individual actions remain available to pursue any other questions that were expressly excluded from the class action.

18 Wright & Miller, *Federal Practice & Procedure*, ¶ 4455 at 475 (1981).

Accordingly, MCO's motion for summary judgment is DENIED.[7]

SO ORDERED.

Notes and Problems

1. If the doctrine of res judicata was designed, at least in part, to preclude claimants from splitting their cause of action into multiple lawsuits, for reasons of both efficiency and fairness, why does the court permit the claims for damages in *In re Jackson Lockdown* to be asserted in a later action? What principles override in this scenario?

2. If courts held that Rule 23(b)(2) class members in injunctive-only relief classes would be barred from suing for their individual damages in later actions, what would such a class member have to do to avoid, in effect, having their individual damage claim waived? One option might be to engage in a collateral attack of the Rule 23(b)(2) judgment, asserting an inadequacy of representation by the class representative having foregone the pursuit of damages for the aggrieved class members. The recent *Wal-Mart v. Dukes* case we read (twice) in the previous chapter has language suggesting such a possibility. Another option would be to attempt to intervene in the lawsuit under Rule 24(a). We will see one example of such an attempt in the next section in *Woolen & Wharton v. Surtran Taxicabs.*

---

5. In *Lasky* the damages sought were reimbursement of back insurance premiums in an action to enjoin termination of insurance benefits; in *Alexander,* back pay in a Title VII action.

7. MCO filed a twenty-five page brief in support of its motion citing forty-five cases; most of these cases are only authority for general *res judicata* principles and are not pertinent to the specific argument raised by the motion. MCO's reply brief of twenty pages suffers from the same deficiency. A focused discussion of the directly pertinent cases such as *Bogard* and *Crowder* would have conserved both my energy and that of the parties, and certainly reduced the legal costs undoubtedly associated with the motion.

3. You may recall we covered the concept of *non-mutual offensive collateral estoppel* in Chapter 2: Joinder of Claims & Parties. In a fairly ironclad rule that makes abundant sense, courts have not permitted a former class member who "opted out" of a Rule 23(b)(3) class action—and thus avoided being bound by the results—from invoking any class victories against the class defendant in subsequent litigation relying upon collateral estoppel. You may recall the Supreme Court in *Parklane Hosiery* declaring that non-mutual offensive collateral estoppel has to be evaluated on a case-by-case basis to be sure that its invocation is fair. Courts have adopted a per se rule against opt-out class members relying upon collateral estoppel because (a) they should not get to benefit from a case they chose to exclude themselves from and (b) holding otherwise would encourage more class members to opt out which defeats some of the efficiency goals of a Rule 23(b)(3) class action. *See, e.g., Premier Electrical Construction Co. v. National Electric Contractors Association*, 814 F.2d 358 (7th Cir. 1987).

4. *Chapter Problem.* If Mr. News and his counsel decided to simply pursue certification of their class as a pure declaratory and injunctive relief class (because the consumer deception statute in the case provides for recovery of statutory attorney's fees regardless of whether actual damages are sought or recovered), would class members later be permitted to pursue individual damage claims?

G. Opt-Out and Intervention Rights of Class Members

When you recall the impetus for class treatment in a Rule 23(b)(1) or (b)(2) scenario, it is easy to understand why these are considered *mandatory* class actions by necessity. Recall the *limited fund* Rule 23(b)(1) class—if we permitted individual class members to opt out of the class action and pursue their own relief separately, we would still have the "feast before the famine" phenomenon. Individual class members could dissipate the limited fund in their own lawsuits and cause other class members to be left with no fund from which to recover. The problem can only be addressed by forcing all the claimants into the same suit so that equal treatment can be afforded. Also, with the Rule 23(b)(1)(A) or (b)(2) class action for injunctive relief, not only does class treatment make more sense from an efficiency perspective, but it would be potentially unfair to the defendant to allow it to have multiple different courts consider affirmative equitable relief against it. Such a defendant might be in the untenable position of having to serve two masters with different ideas for the defendant's prospective behavior. In this instance, the only way to avoid this problem is through a mandatory class action that does not tolerate any opt-out rights. So, typically any effort to opt out by such a class member will be unavailing.

This can leave a Rule 23(b)(2) class member who has their own ideas with few options for having input into the litigation conducted on their behalf. Of course, they might file objections (to possible settlement proposals), but much can happen during the life of the litigation that does not offer opportunities for such input. One can also engage in a collateral attack of the final judgment by arguing that there was no adequate representation, but that might be an uphill battle, and comes after the litigation has already been conducted. Another option would be to attempt to intervene in the lawsuit using Rule 24(a) which we discussed in Chapter 2: Joinder of Parties and Claims. It can be easy to imagine such a class member arguing effectively that they have an interest in the litigation that might be impaired or impeded in their absence. But, after a court has already ruled in favor of class certification—and necessarily finding "adequate representation" under Rule 23(a)(4)—would this not make it impossible to show under Rule 24(a) that the proposed class member/intervenor is not already "adequately represented"? In the following case that illustrates some very hostile differing groups of class members, the court holds that "adequacy of representation" under Rule 23 does not necessarily mean the same thing under Rule 24.

Woolen & Whorton v. Surtran Taxicabs, Inc.
684 F.2d 324 (5th Cir. 1982)

BROWN, J.,

This case presents us with both unique facts and issues within the context of an antitrust class action challenging the Dallas/Fort Worth airport's restriction of solicitation of taxicab passengers to limited holders of permits. The controversy surrounding the antitrust claim which forms the merits of this case pales in comparison to this donnybrook between two factions of plaintiffs, the Woolen/Campisi (Campisi) group and the Whorton group. The loser in the first round, the Whorton plaintiffs, sought exclusion from the class suit filed by the Campisi plaintiffs, or intervention in that suit, alleging inadequate representation and imposition of a class attorney antagonistic to their interests. The District Court denied intervention, certified the class as a F.R.Civ.P. 23(b)(2) suit, and thus in practical effect denied exclusion. Unfortunately, although too frequently true, a ruling in the District Court made to avoid delay has itself engendered more delay. At the outset we face the threshold question of whether we have jurisdiction to address the Whorton's interlocutory appeal and the intertwined issue of whether a member of a class may intervene as of right. We find that the denial of intervention of right is an appealable order and that a class member may theoretically intervene in a class action. Because the District Court's findings on the issue of intervention are not adequate, we reverse and remand.[1]

This Court has considered the right to opt out of a class under Rule 23(b)(2) and the right to notice generally within the context of settlements or consent decrees in Title VII cases. In *Johnson v. General Motors Corp.,* 598 F.2d 432 (5th Cir. 1979), we found that where monetary relief was sought in a Title VII case certified under Rule 23(b)(2), notice was required before an absent class member could be barred from pursuing an individual damage claim. In *Penson v. Terminal Transport Co.,* 634 F.2d 989, 992–95 (5th Cir. 1981), after surveying prior Circuit law, we held that a member of a class certified under Rule 23(b)(2) had no absolute right to opt out of the class, although a District Court has the power to require an opt out right under Rule 23(d)(2). *See* 3B Moore's Federal Practice para. 23.55 (2d ed. 1982). Thus, this Court has addressed the opt out requirement in retrospect in the context of the res judicata effect of a prior action and the due process re-

---

1. Although the Whorton plaintiffs filed a request for exclusion from the Campisi suit, at least through the time of oral argument in this case, the District Court had not ruled on the motion. The District Judge certified the class action in this case as a (b)(2) action. Although there is some debate whether in certain circumstances notice must be given to the members of the class with the attendant right to opt out in a (b)(2) action, F.R.Civ.P. 23 requires notice and the opportunity to be excluded specifically only in a (b)(3) action. Thus, at least at this point, the practical effect of certification under (b)(2) is to deny the motion for exclusion. However, since the District Court has not ruled on this motion for exclusion, we need not reach the issue of whether the Whorton plaintiffs have a right to opt out of the class action.

quirements necessary for a prior action to be binding on absent members of a class. The inquiry then generally becomes one of adequacy of representation under the standard of *Hansberry v. Lee*, 311 U.S. 32, 61 S. Ct. 115, 85 L. Ed. 22 (1940). For instance, in this case should the Campisi class action continue as a (b)(2) action without the intervention of the Whorton plaintiffs or the consolidation of these two cases, and should the Campisi plaintiffs either lose on the merits or settle with the defendants, the Whorton plaintiffs could argue in this case or in a separate action the flip-side of the opt out argument, that of adequacy of representation. Although there may be no right to opt out in a (b)(2) action, the judgment is always subject to attack on the premise that those absent members were inadequately represented and thus are not bound. For this reason it is essential that representation of absent class members be adequate from the start.

A Touch of Class

The underlying litigation in which the Whorton plaintiffs seek to intervene or from which they seek to be excluded is an antitrust action stemming from the establishment by the cities of Dallas and Fort Worth of the D/FW Surtran System to provide ground transportation for the D/FW airport. Surtran apparently accepted competitive bids for the privilege of picking up passengers at the airport. The winning bid was submitted by Yellow Cab of Dallas, Inc. and Fort Worth Cab and Baggage Company who together formed Surtran Taxicabs, Inc., which contracted with Surtran System to pick up taxicab passengers at the airport for transportation to points in the ten counties surrounding the airport. The contract between Surtran System and Surtran Taxicabs set the rates to be charged, and provided that Surtran System would be paid seventy-five cents per trip plus fifty percent of all profits above a five percent operating profit. Both Dallas and Fort Worth adopted ordinances providing that only holders of permits issued by the airport board may provide ground transportation from the airport. The effect of these ordinances was that only Surtran Taxicabs, as the sole holder of a permit, could pick up taxi passengers at the airport.

On May 22, 1978, plaintiffs John Woolen, Jack Stephens, and John D. Campisi, individually and on behalf of a class of taxi drivers filed suit against Surtran Taxicabs, the City of Dallas, City of Fort Worth, and three surrounding cities. [Woolen is no longer a party.] The Campisi class action suit alleged that the arrangement between the cities and Surtran Taxicabs violated the Sherman Act by both restraining trade and creating a monopoly, in violation of Sections 1 and 2 of the Act, 15 U.S.C. §§ 1, 2. The initial complaint sought both injunctive relief and treble damages on behalf of taxicab drivers who held permits to operate cabs within the ten-county region surrounding the airport. Two weeks later, on June 6, 1978, the Campisi plaintiffs amended their complaint to add Yellow Cab as a defendant and to add approximately 50 additional named representatives as class members, including the Dallas Taxicab Association. On that same day, the Whorton plaintiffs filed over 200 requests for exclusion from the Campisi suit, alleging that they would not be represented adequately and that the suit would not be prosecuted vigorously since at least two of the three named members of the Woolen class suit were members of the Dallas Taxicab Association, a nonprofit association of taxicab drivers operating in Dallas and formed by Yellow Cab Co., itself a defendant in this lawsuit. Ten days later, the Whorton plaintiffs filed a separate suit naming over 200 individual plaintiffs, but not in the form of a class action, seeking to recover treble damages for the antitrust violations.

On June 29, 1978, the Campisi plaintiffs filed a motion to consolidate their action with the Whorton plaintiffs and to designate the Campisi's attorney, Tom Thomas, as lead counsel. In November 1978, the defendants' subsequent motion to dismiss was denied by the District Court. In December 1978, the Campisi plaintiffs moved for class certification to represent a class of all licensed taxicab drivers in the ten county area, a class estimated to be between 2000 and 2500 persons. The class included Woolen and 50 other named plaintiffs as well as the Dallas Taxicab Association. The motion requested certification under Rule 23(b)(2) and (b)(3). In February 1979, the Campisi and Whorton cases were consolidated for purposes of discovery and a hearing to determine class certification was set for late April and subsequently rescheduled for May 1979. In May 1979 the case was reassigned to another District Judge.

Trying to Get to the Head of the Class

In August 1979, four of the Whorton plaintiffs filed a motion to intervene in the Campisi case under Rule 24(a)(2), alleging that they had an interest in the transaction, were so situated that the disposition of the action might impair or impede their ability to protect that interest, and were not adequately represented by existing parties.

In October 1979, the four Whorton plaintiffs seeking to intervene filed "Requested Findings of Fact and Conclusions of Law in Opposition to Class Certification", alleging that the Campisi case should not be certified as a class action. The filing of this opposition is one of the more graphic examples of the antagonism and conflict between the Campisi and Whorton groups. The relations between the Campisi and Whorton plaintiffs continued to deteriorate for the next year as the attorneys for both groups were less than cooperative in discovery attempts.

On December 31, 1980, the District Judge filed an order certifying the Campisi suit as a 23(b)(2) class action and finding the Campisi plaintiffs adequate representatives for purposes of the class action. The class was defined as all taxicab operators who held permits to operate taxicabs issued by the municipalities located within the ten county area. Campisi's attorney, Tom Thomas, was appointed lead class action counsel. In addition, the District Judge denied the motion of the four Whorton plaintiffs to intervene. Although the District Judge did not rule on the motion for exclusion from the class suit, filed by the Whorton plaintiffs, the practical effect of certification under (b)(2) was to deny the right to opt out to these class members. From this December 31, 1980 order the Whorton plaintiffs appeal.

United We Fall, Divided We Stand

Why, one might wonder, would two groups of taxicab drivers whom one would expect to be aligned against one common set of defendants, instead attempt to keep the other from active participation in the lawsuit? Each set of plaintiffs has tried to inhibit discovery by the other set. The Campisi group has worked to keep the Whorton group from intervening while the Whorton group has been busy trying to defeat the certification of the Campisi group. What we have in the final analysis is two factions of plaintiffs, each seeking to be represented by the attorney of their choice, and each seeking to get through the courtroom door first. While the underlying claim is the same, the Campisi plaintiffs seek injunctive relief as evident from their initial motion for certification. The Whorton group, on the other hand, is concerned primarily with damages.

Tax(i)ation Without Representation

In this appeal, the Whorton plaintiffs basically argue that the District Judge's order of December 31, 1980 results in their being locked into a class action in which they are not adequately represented, in which their interests are antagonistic to other members of the class, and in which they have no desire to participate unless they are allowed representation by the attorney of their choice. They assert that the class action device has been abused to preempt their claim through a sham class action filed by the Campisi group and that the District Judge's orders have conclusively determined their rights in such a way that review on appeal from a final judgment will be ineffective. Through certification under Rule 23(b)(2), they fear that their claims for damages may eventually be lost should the Campisi class action fail on the merits or settle. To support these claims, the Whorton plaintiffs allege a pattern of delays, less than diligent prosecution by Campisi and the class attorney, antagonism between the two groups of plaintiffs, and conflicts of interest, both within the class and between Campisi and the defendants. For instance, they allege that the Dallas Taxicab Association, certified to represent the drivers, has members from only one of the ten counties, and was originally formed by Yellow Cab, one of the defendants, for the purpose of helping Yellow Cab drivers. Thus, the Whorton plaintiffs contend that the representation is inadequate. In addition, they allege that three of the four named Campisi plaintiffs are members of the Dallas Taxicab Association. Not only are there connections between the class representatives and defendant Yellow Cab, but, according to the Whorton group, there are connections between Campisi's lawyer and Yellow Cab. The Whorton plaintiffs charge that Campisi's attorney chose certification as a (b)(2) class action and included the denial of the request for intervention, without any specific request by the court, an assertion substantiated in a letter to the District Judge from the attorney for the defendants. Through a series of statements and examples, the Whorton plaintiffs attempt to demonstrate inadequate representation by class members and their counsel and to create the implication that the Campisi representatives are likely to compromise the Whorton claims for damages because of the connections between the Campisi plaintiffs and the defendants. While several examples are given of the inadequacy of representation, both by the named class representatives and their attorney, we find it unnecessary to provide more than the bare outline so far sketched.

In this appeal, the Whorton plaintiffs raise several issues. First they contend that they have an absolute right to intervene under F.R.Civ.P. 24(a)(2) because their interest is not adequately represented. Second, they maintain that the District Judge's order of December 31, 1980 was an abuse of discretion by eliminating the representation of the Whorton plaintiffs, including those 200 who originally requested exclusion from the Campisi suit. This abuse is demonstrated by certifying a class action with no opportunity to opt out or without any subclasses, denying exclusion to the 200 drivers, denying intervention to the representatives of these 200 drivers, staying the individual damage actions of these drivers, and imposing antagonistic class representation and counsel on these drivers through mandatory inclusion in the class action.

[The] notion of adequacy of representation sufficient to satisfy the prerequisites for a class action under Rule 23(a)(4) is not necessarily equivalent to the adequacy of representation contemplated by Rule 24 within the context of intervention of right. In the Advisory Committee's note to the 1966 amendment to Rule 24(a), the Committee indicated that the rule, as amended, no longer contained the prior requirement that as a condition of intervention an applicant be bound. Rather, "[a] class member who claims that his 'representative' does not adequately represent him, and is able to establish that proposition with sufficient probability, should not be put to the risk of having a judgment entered in the action which by its terms extends to him, and be obliged to test the validity of the judgment as applied to his interest by a later collateral attack. Rather he should, as a general rule, be entitled to intervene in the action."

From this statement it is clear that the Committee contemplated that one who was already a class member could intervene in a lawsuit. It is also apparent that the notion of adequacy for purposes of Rule 23(a)(4) is one having more concern with the res judicata effects of a judgment on absent members of a class. Without adequate representation a judgment cannot bind those absent class members. Rule 24(a), as amended, specifically drops the requirement that a party is or may be bound by a judgment, substituting instead a practical test, requiring only that the disposition of the action "*may as a practical* matter impair or impede his ability to protect that interest, ..." (emphasis added). As revised, the Rule clearly leaves room for a situation where one's interest may be impaired by inadequate representation without necessarily requiring a res judicata effect. One therefore could intervene, claiming inadequacy of representation without necessarily claiming that he will be precluded by the other action. This would appear to establish a lower threshold or showing of inadequacy for purposes of intervention as opposed to class action certification. The adequacy of representation in Rule 23(a)(4) is that essential to due process under *Hansberry v. Lee* before absent class members can be bound. The problem of intervention within a class action would appear to arise most likely in a class certified under 23(b)(1) or (b)(2), rather than under a class certified under 23(b)(3). A class member who does not consider that he is being represented adequately has the option in a (b)(3) action to opt out under 23(c)(2) or to enter an appearance through counsel of his choosing. Should he choose to opt out of the lawsuit, the plaintiff would not be bound. The concept of intervention within a class certified under 23(b)(2) balances the more likely impairment of the individual's interest since he is unable to opt out of this class. Also by allowing intervention, subsequent collateral attacks on the due process preclusive effect of a judgment are avoided.

Rule 24(a)(2) establishes three conditions which must be met for intervention of right. The applicant must (1) claim "an interest relating to the property or transaction which is the subject of the action"; (2) be "so situated that the disposition of the action may as a practical matter impair or impede his ability to protect that interest"; *and* (3) his interest is not adequately represented by existing parties. In this case the Whorton plaintiffs have claimed an interest in the transaction which is the subject of the action, that is in the alleged antitrust violations. However, the interest is not identical to that of the Campisi plaintiffs who have clearly indicated that at this point their interest is in injunctive relief, while that of the Whorton plaintiffs is in damages. The Whorton plaintiffs have alleged that the disposition of the Campisi class action *may* as a *practical matter* impair their ability to protect their interest. Should the Campisi plaintiffs fail on the liability issue in the class action, at least as a practical matter, the Whorton plaintiffs' ability to recover may be impaired. It is possible that any judgment on the issue of liability in the Campisi (b)(2) class action may be binding on the Whorton plaintiffs in a separate action unless they can demonstrate in a subsequent or collateral attack that they were inadequately represented and thus denied due process. Finally, the Whorton plaintiffs have alleged that their interest is not adequately represented by the existing parties. They contend that neither the class representatives nor their attorney adequately presents their position and have failed to protect their interest. On the basis of the pleadings and motions before the District Court, it is clear that the Whorton plaintiffs are "without a friend in this litigation." *Atlantis Development Corp. v. United States,* 379 F.2d 818, 825 (5th Cir. 1967). The Whorton plaintiffs have alleged that the Campisi plaintiffs have attempted to hamper their discovery, have encouraged burdensome damage interrogatories against the Whorton plaintiffs, and have abandoned any interest in the damage claims. From proceedings in this Court, it is clear that the Campisi plaintiffs, through opposing the motion of intervention and subsequent appeal, are not aligned with the Whorton plaintiffs.

The District Court held a hearing on the question of class certification at which the intervenors were allowed to participate. In its order of December 31, 1980, the District Court denied intervention. This order, entitled "Order Certifying Class Action," while containing findings of fact and conclusions of law, made no specific findings or conclusions as to the issue of intervention. This Court, in reviewing motions to intervene in school desegregation suits, has required the District Court to conduct an evidentiary hearing and to enter findings based upon an adequate record. *See Adams v. Baldwin County Board of Education,* 628 F.2d at 897; *Jones v. Caddo Parish School Board,* 499 F.2d 914 (5th Cir. 1974). In this case the District Court has provided no indication of why it denied intervention of right and we are thus unable to tell whether the action was based on the proper considerations or perhaps based on some incorrect assumptions such as that class members may not intervene in a class suit. In the order certifying the Campisi class, the District Judge made findings of fact that the class representatives would fairly and adequately protect the interest of the class. The first of the subfindings is that "there is no significant antagonism or conflict between the class action representatives and the class." This finding is perhaps the only relevant one to the issue of intervention and it is not clear whether at the time the District Court was considering the intervenors as members of the class. If so, this finding is clearly erroneous since the antagonism between the Whorton plaintiffs who, at least as defined by the District Court, are members of the class, and the class action representatives is too blatant to be ignored. For example, the Whorton plaintiffs had earlier attempted to defeat certification. Based on the filings in this case and the hearing, the District Court could not possibly find no antagonism. However, we think that given the lack of findings of fact specifically relating to the issue of intervention, in this case where the credibility of the parties, both the Campisi representatives and the Whorton plaintiffs, is so essential, this action should be remanded to the District Court to consider again the right to intervene under Rule 24(a)(2) so that this Court is provided with an adequate record on the merits of intervention of right, should this Court need to consider again the right to intervene.

Keeping the Meter Running

From our disposition of this case, we are in no way intimating our opinion on the merits of the claim of intervention of right, other than to indicate that the Whorton plaintiffs have alleged a colorable claim which needs further exploration, perhaps evidentiary detail and findings by the District Court before we could pass on the merits. Nor are we indicating that we consider intervention the best route through this Serbonian Bog. Were this case before us in a different posture we would be free to indicate that consolidation of the Whorton and Campisi cases would offer the most, and perhaps *only*, manageable solution. Under consolidation, the issue of liability could be tried *once* and *only once*, while allowing the parties to be represented by counsel of their choice. With representation satisfactory to each of the two groups, the court could likely avoid a subsequent attack on the adequacy of representation under the guise of res judicata effects should the defendants succeed on the issue of liability or should the Campisi plaintiffs settle with the defendants. Nor need consolidation hinder the Campisi plaintiffs' efforts to proceed. The District Court may stay discovery on the issue of damages until the issue of liability is resolved since the District Court need not, indeed should not, assume that the defendants will be held liable. Discovery exploration of possible potential damages at this early state in the detail sought is obviously inefficient and wasteful of services of counsel. Consolidation also avoids the question of which lawsuit proceeds first. Obviously consolidation will succeed only if the attorneys for both the Whorton and Campisi plaintiffs mend their differences and unite in their efforts to defeat what one assumes is their common enemy, the defendants. Certainly consolidation would benefit the class members, who after all are, or should be, the true focus of these lawsuits.

Obviously the problems in this case would not have arisen had the District Court certified the action as a (b)(3) action, in which case the Whorton plaintiffs would have had the opportunity to opt out. Certification as a (b)(3) action would also have protected their damage claim. Generally antitrust actions are certified under 23(b)(3) since the usual focus is on treble damages and the Advisory Committee note makes clear that certification under (b)(2) is not appropriate where the primary relief sought is not injunctive.

Notes and Problems

1. The court in *Woolen* declares that intervention is possible by a Rule 23(b)(2) class member. How does the court explain this possibility given the class has already been found to have "adequate representation" under Rule 23(a)(4)? Does this make sense? Can you think of any other examples we have covered in the Federal Rules of Civil Procedure (perhaps under the various joinder rules) where we have seen courts arguably construe the same phrase from different provisions in the rules differently?

2. Why in *Woolen* could the two factions not get along? Was it a strategic difference of opinion, with the class claims seeking only injunctive relief and the individual action seeking primarily monetary relief? Or did the discord go deeper? Can you imagine why the two sets of lawyers might have been so antagonistic toward one another? What were some of the court's examples of antagonism it found might suggest inadequacy of representation, at least for Rule 24(a) intervention purposes?

3. At the end of the opinion, the Fifth Circuit in *Woolen* suggests there might be better alternatives rather than the district court granting intervention upon remand. Can you explain and evaluate those alternatives?

4. *Chapter Problem.* Assume Mr. News and his counsel decide to only seek injunctive relief against TicketNinja and the court certifies a Rule 23(b)(2) class action. Imagine that a class member—"TicketsRUs"—comes to you for legal advice interested in pursuing its own damage claim. This class member is a corporate ticket broker so it has purchased a multitude of tickets from TicketNinja using a corporate credit card. By its best estimates, TicketsRUs has been charged nearly $250,000 in so-called credit surcharges during the last four years. It is not content to let some other negative-value class member (Huey News) make all of its litigation decisions for it, much less to possibly have its sizable damage claim precluded as a result of the class action (in the event the class action is lost). Should it seek to intervene? Is a mere difference in size of claims enough to argue for inadequate representation and permit intervention or subsequent collateral attack? Should it merely do nothing and, depending upon the results of the case, subsequently file its own claim for damages?

Pulling It All Together Exercise

After studying the relative rights of Rule 23(b)(2) injunctive relief class members, and having previously examined Rule 42(a) consolidation and Rule 24(a) intervention, consider the relative degrees of autonomy in each context on the part of the involved litigant.

Take 20 minutes to compare and contrast the relative autonomy of an unnamed Rule 23(b)(2) class member, a litigant in a case being consolidated for trial of a common liability issue with another case under Rule 42(a), and an absent litigant seeking to intervene in another's lawsuit pursuant to Rule 24(a). Explain which one has the most and least degrees of autonomy; that is, which one is most the master of their own lawsuit? Which one is least in control?

H. Settlement and Remedies

In traditional litigation, one does not ordinarily need the court's blessing or permission to settle the case. Settlement is mostly a private contract matter between the parties (assuming they are all adults capable of entering into binding contractual relationships). But this is not true of class actions. Because the class members are not necessarily present, have not been conducting the litigation, have been excluded from any settlement discussions, and have not agreed to settle their claims, the court needs to act as protector of the class. Notice that once settlement discussions are underway, class counsel has an inherent conflict of interest with the class members, at least theoretically. A class counsel, standing to be rewarded richly with court-approved legal fees (more on this in the next chapter), might be inclined to agree to a settlement despite leaving money on the settlement table. Because the class members are not present in the litigation to approve the deal for themselves (and, even if they were, with a large class it would be virtually impossible to get all class members to agree on anything), the court plays a very important role in approving or rejecting a class settlement. Rule 23(e) compels the court to issue notice, schedule an evidentiary hearing, listen to objections asserted by class members, and then to weigh the merits of the proposed settlement on behalf of the entire class. The following case does an exhaustive job of walking through the traditional factors courts have invoked to consider whether a proposed class settlement is, in the words of Rule 23(e)(2), "fair, reasonable, and adequate."

Rule 23(e)

(e) The claims, issues, or defenses or a certified class may be settled, voluntarily dismissed, or compromised only with the court's approval. The following procedures apply to a proposed settlement, voluntary dismissal, or compromise:

(1) The court must direct notice in a reasonable manner to all class members who would be bound by the proposal.

(2) If the proposal would bind class members, the court may approve it only after a hearing and on finding that it is fair, reasonable, and adequate.

(3) The parties seeking approval must file a statement identifying any agreement made in connection with the proposal.

(4) If the class action was previously certified under Rule 23(b)(3), the court may refuse to approve a settlement unless it affords a new opportunity to request exclusion to individual class members who had an earlier opportunity to request exclusion but did not do so.

(5) Any class member may object to the proposal if it requires approval under this subdivision (e); the objection may be withdrawn only with the court's approval.

1. Court Approval of Settlements

Klein v. O'Neal, Inc.

705 F. Supp. 2d 632 (N.D. Tex. 2010)

FITZWATER, J.,

MEMORANDUM OPINION AND ORDER

The court must decide whether the proposed $110 million settlement of this class action alleging personal injury and death claims arising from the manufacture, marketing, and distribution of E-Ferol Aqueous Solution ("E-Ferol") is fair, reasonable, and adequate, as Fed. R. Civ. P. 23(e)(2) requires, and not the product of collusion between the parties. Following a two-day fairness hearing and consideration of the parties' extensive submissions, and for the reasons that follow, the court approves the settlement and the request of the class plaintiffs' attorneys for a fee award of 30% of the settlement amount, reimbursement of reasonable and necessary expenses associated with the litigation, $300,000 from the settlement amount to pay for costs of administration and distribution of the settlement proceeds, and $75,000 each as compensation for the two class representatives.

I

A

This mass tort class action arises from defendants' manufacture, marketing, and distribution in 1983 and 1984 of E-Ferol, a vitamin E supplement administered primarily to premature infants to aid in preventing a vision impairment known as retrolental fibroplasia, believed to be caused by a vitamin E deficiency. Defendants marketed E-Ferol as a vitamin supplement rather than as a drug. The class plaintiffs allege that defendants made this marketing decision so that they could bypass testing requirements mandated by the U.S. Food and Drug Administration ("FDA") for the sale of a "drug"; there were no similar requirements for new "supplements." The class plaintiffs also assert that defendants specifically marketed E-Ferol as a means of reducing or preventing retrolental fibroplasia, and that physicians and hospitals began using E-Ferol under the mistaken impression that it had FDA approval. E-Ferol's appeal was its suitability for intravenous administration, a delivery method that was considered superior to the previously available oral or intramuscular applications of vitamin E for premature infants. To allow for intravenous use, E-Ferol contained an emulsifying agent known as Polysorbate 80, which made the vitamin E water soluble.

Several months after the initial release of E-Ferol, medical providers, the FDA, and the Centers for Disease Control and Prevention ("CDC") became aware of a pattern of harmful symptoms in premature infants to whom the drug had been given. These symptoms—which generally involved failure of the kidneys and liver—in many cases led to brain injury, blindness, and/or death, and came to be known as "E-Ferol syndrome." The FDA and CDC ordered defendants to conduct a full recall of the product and began investigating possible causes of the symptoms that neonatologists were reporting. Research determined that the ingredient Polysorbate 80 in E-Ferol caused the symptoms associated with E-Ferol syndrome. The investigation into E-Ferol eventually led to criminal convictions for the defendant corporations as well as some of their individual officers. *See United States v. Hiland,* 909 F.2d 1114 (8th Cir. 1990).

B

This lawsuit was filed as a putative class action on behalf of all persons who were administered E-Ferol during the months that it was in use, the representatives or heirs of persons whose deaths were caused by E-Ferol, and family members, guardians, and legal representatives of persons who died from or were injured by E-Ferol. Plaintiffs alleged claims for negligence, strict liability, and negligent misrepresentation, and they sought actual and punitive damages for the deaths and injuries that E-Ferol allegedly caused. Judge Buchmeyer, to whom the case was initially assigned, certified the following plaintiffs class under Rule 23(b)(3):

> All persons in the United States, including any estate representatives or heirs of deceased persons, who, during the period from November 1, 1983, until April 30, 1984, were administered E-Ferol. Included in the class are parents, spouses, children, guardians, and legal representatives of such persons with direct or derivative claims.

Klein v. O'Neal, Inc., 222 F.R.D. 564, 566 (N.D. Tex.) (Buchmeyer, J.) (*"Klein I"*), *pet. for leave to appeal denied,* No. 04-00028 (5th Cir. June 21, 2004) (per curiam) (order). [The Fifth Circuit denied defendants' petition for leave to obtain discretionary interlocutory appeal of the class certification decision.]

Counsel for the class undertook a lengthy process of identifying and contacting potential class members. They began by obtaining a list from the FDA of all hospitals nationwide that had administered E-Ferol, and then contacting these hospitals to request the names of the individual recipients. Eventually, 89 locations nationwide were identified as having administered E-Ferol. Some hospitals were willing to share information with class counsel. Others did not produce information until they were subpoenaed and/or were unsuccessful in moving to quash efforts to obtain patient names. Once potential class members were identified, class counsel contacted them and requested that they complete a medical questionnaire and an authorization to release hospital records.

Notification to the class was given in July 2006 by direct mail (for those whose names and addresses were known) and through simultaneous publication in numerous daily newspapers throughout the United States, including *USA Today,* in an attempt to notify unidentified class members whose hospital records were still unknown. Class counsel also created a website at "www.eferol.com." The website contained information about E-Ferol's distribution and effects, an explanation of this lawsuit, links to the parties' filings and the court's opinions, a list of relevant deadlines, and contact information for any person who believed he should be included in the class. The court set September 11, 2006 as the opt out date for class members. [Four members of the class opted out.]

Class counsel eventually identified 328 recipients of E-Ferol. The class is currently comprised of 369 members, including the families and representatives of deceased recipients. Of the 328 identified cases of E-Ferol administration, 34 are infants who allegedly died from the effects of E-Ferol, 22 are infants who allegedly suffered brain or neurological injuries (i.e., cerebral palsy) from E-Ferol exposure, and 239 are class members who either received E-Ferol without apparent injury, but require ongoing medical monitoring, or are the parents of children who died after being administered E-Ferol but whose deaths are not believed to have been caused by E-Ferol.

After the court decided *Klein II,* it stayed the case so that the parties could pursue settlement. The parties participated in mediation, including a two-day meeting, in 2009. A retired United States District Judge, John S. Martin, Jr. ("Judge Martin"), served as mediator. Although the parties were initially unsuccessful, subsequent negotiations over several months led to the Settlement Agreement and Release ("Settlement Agreement"). As discussed more fully below, in exchange for the release of all claims brought by the class plaintiffs, the Settlement Agreement provides a lump sum payment to the class for distribution among its members. [Attorney's fees for class counsel will come from this lump sum.] The allocation to each member varies according to the category to which the member's claim is assigned. Medical experts retained by class counsel determined each class member's initial category, with stronger claims resulting in higher-paying categorization. The parties presented the Settlement Agreement to the court for a preliminary fairness review in October 2009.

Following initial approval, the class plaintiffs sent notices to each class member informing the member of the details of the Settlement Agreement, the member's category assignment, and the scheduled fairness hearing on February 16 and 17, 2010. The notices also included instructions for how class members could object to court approval of the Settlement Agreement, make requests for a change in category, and/or submit documents supporting such requests. The notices were sent in October 2009, and the deadline for filing objections and making requests for category changes was December 30, 2009. Class counsel also published a new notice in *USA Today* containing information about the proposed settlement.

C

The Settlement Agreement comprehensively resolves all claims between the class plaintiffs and defendants. The negotiations between the parties and the drafting of the Settlement Agreement included the input and eventual consent of various insurers of defendants, who bear all responsibility for paying the settlement proceeds. The Settlement Agreement calls for a maximum payment of $110 million to the entire class.

Under the terms of the Settlement Agreement, each class member is assigned to one of five categories. Category 1 consists of death claims in which E-Ferol was a substantial cause of the death. Category 2 represents death claims for which E-Ferol was only a contributing cause of death. Category 3 is composed of claims that E-Ferol was a substantial contributing cause of cerebral palsy or another neuroglial impairment, with subcategories defined for impairments that are (a) severe, (b) moderate, or (c) mild. Category 4 contains claims alleging injury that do not qualify for Categories 1 through 3, including claims for ongoing medical monitoring costs due to the potential effects of E-Ferol. Category 5 consists of class members whose claims the court has previously dismissed on various grounds, and it is divided into subcategories based on the primary category under which the dismissed claim otherwise would fall. The initial assignment of a class member into a category and subcategory was made by medical experts, and the assignment was based on the strength of the medical records and other evidence relevant to each class member's claim.

The total settlement proceeds are allocated by percentages among the five categories. Class members each take an equal per capita share of the payout amount allocated to their particular category or subcategory. The allocations are: (1) 40% for Category 1 (approximately $2,001,594.20 per claim); (2) 17.78% for Category 2 (approximately $1,000,797.14 per claim); (3) 31.11% for Category 3 (approximately $1,501,195.62, $1,250,996.34, or $1,000,789.68 per claim, based on subcategory); (4) 9.29% for Category 4 (approximately

$35,027.19 per claim); and (5) 1.82% for Category 5 (approximately $236,647.45, $118,323.27, or $4,141.50 per claim, based on subcategory). The attorney's fees and expenses that the court awards class plaintiffs' counsel, and the awards to the class representatives, are to be deducted from each class member's recovery on a pro rata basis.

There is no provision in the Settlement Agreement that allows a class member to opt out. Under Rule 23(e)(4), however, the court "may refuse to approve a settlement unless it affords a new opportunity to request exclusion to individual class members who had an earlier opportunity to request exclusion but did not do so." The Settlement Agreement provides that, if the court does allow class members to opt out, each defendant or insurer can withdraw from the settlement. Alternatively, defendants can choose to ratify the Agreement notwithstanding an allowance for opt outs. In the latter case, any class member who opted out would still be counted for purposes of assigning category awards under the settlement payout, but the funds that would otherwise be paid to the excluded class member would be retained by defendants and not included in the overall payment to the class.

D

Following notice of the proposed settlement, 97.3% of the class members — 359 of 369 — responded to class counsel with affirmative requests that the court approve the proposed settlement. The 97.3% who approve include all but one class member in Category 1, and all members in Categories 2 and 3. [Only one class member has maintained objections through the date of the final fairness hearing — Lawrence V. Long.]

Long is a member of the class by reason of the death of his daughter, CL. CL died in 1984 after receiving E-Ferol while in the care of the neonatal intensive care unit at Miami Valley Hospital ("Miami Valley") in Dayton, Ohio. Because the E-Ferol recipient list from Miami Valley was still unknown when notice was mailed to class members in 2006, class counsel published notices of this class action in two local newspapers: the *Dayton Daily News* (Dayton, Ohio) and *The Blade* (Toledo, Ohio). In October 2007 class counsel obtained the recipient list from Miami Valley, and they mailed notice of the class action to Long. It was at this point, according to Long, that he and his late wife first became aware of the possibility that E-Ferol played a part in CL's death. Long then obtained independent legal representation (i.e., apart from class counsel) and filed a motion seeking leave to opt out of the class. He filed the motion on January 9, 2009, although the deadline for doing so had expired on September 11, 2006. The court denied Long's motion. *Klein v. O'Neal, Inc.,* 2009 U.S. Dist. LEXIS 36395, 2009 WL 1174638, at *5 (N.D. Tex. Apr. 29, 2009) (Fitzwater, C.J.) ("*Klein III*") (holding, *inter alia,* that due process was satisfied because it was undisputed that Long received constructive notice of the suit through publication in July 2006, and failed to request opt out by the court-ordered September 2006 deadline). Long has renewed the request to opt out in a motion filed on September 23, 2009.

Essentially, Long seeks to opt out so that he can pursue an independent lawsuit against the defendants and against Miami Valley and the physicians who treated CL (the "Miami Valley Providers"). Long maintains that he can obtain a larger award through an independent lawsuit than he will receive under the proposed settlement. He also objects to the provision of the Settlement Agreement requiring that he release third-party medical providers, such as the Miami Valley Providers, as a condition of receiving his share of the settlement proceeds. In addition to objecting on various grounds to the Settlement Agreement, Long also moves for decertification of the class, for leave to intervene, and to opt out of the class.

E

The court conducted a two-day fairness hearing on February 16 and 17, 2010. During the hearing, the parties, Long, and Jenkins (until she withdrew her objection) presented evidence and arguments regarding whether the Settlement Agreement is fair, reasonable, and adequate, as Rule 23(e)(2) requires, and not the product of collusion between the parties. They also presented evidence through witnesses and exhibits. Counsel also cross-examined witnesses and presented argument.

[The class plaintiffs called several medical experts to testify about the causes and effects of E-Ferol syndrome. They testified to the causal link between the drug and the deaths of many of the infants. They also admitted that, with respect to those who survived with brain injuries, the causal connection was weaker medically though still probable.]

After the two class representatives testified, lead class counsel, Art Brender, Esquire ("Brender"), testified in support of the settlement and the motion for attorney's fees, costs, and expenses. Brender was cross-examined by lawyers for Long, who challenged his assertions about the fairness of the settlement and class counsels' request for attorney's fees. Plaintiffs then called Professor Jim Underwood ("Prof. Underwood"), an Associate Professor of Law at Baylor Law School, who testified that the settlement is fair, reasonable, and adequate and that the requested award of attorney's fees, costs, and expenses is not only reasonable, but is less than expected in a case of this scale. Drawing on his experience as a class-action litigator and professor of torts and complex litigation (the thrust of which is federal class action law), Prof. Underwood opined that class counsel had provided exceptional representation to the class by identifying and contacting as many potential members as could be found. He testified that the motion practice in the case indicated hard-fought litigation that placed an unusually high burden on the attorneys and resulted in a favorable settlement for the class. Prof. Underwood praised the arrangement of the settlement categories and the process by which class members could appeal their category placement. He concluded that "[t]his [settlement] would be a poster child for a class action that works for the benefit of the class."

The class plaintiffs concluded by making a video presentation consisting of several class members who could not attend the hearing and of the decedents of some members. Several class members attended some or all of the hearing and were introduced after the parties' opening statements. All of these class members support the proposed settlement.

Defendants first presented Barry Chasnoff, Esquire ("Chasnoff"), their lead counsel, who testified, among other things, about the defenses to liability that his clients intended to raise if the case were to proceed to trial. He stated that defendants intended to challenge the class plaintiffs' overall expert evidence, especially the causation evidence related to the Category 3 neurological injury claims. Defendants then called a legal expert, Professor Charles Silver ("Prof. Silver"), a professor at The University of Texas School of Law, who specializes in class action research and has served as class counsel in numerous cases. Prof. Silver, like Prof. Underwood, opined that the settlement is fair and reasonable overall. He especially noted the lengths to which class counsel had gone to identify and contact as many individual members of the class as possible. He found it significant that 97.3% of class members had affirmatively approved the Settlement Agreement, and, of those who had not, only one had raised formal objections. Prof. Silver stated that such overwhelming affirmative support for a class action settlement, as opposed to mere acquiescence by class members, was extremely rare, and this reinforced his conclusion that the proposed settlement is fair and should be approved.

After the class plaintiffs and defendants completed their presentations, Long testified in support of his objections to the Settlement Agreement. He primarily testified about CL's medical treatment, and he stated that no physician had informed him or his wife of the possibility that E-Ferol could have caused CL's death. Long averred that he first became aware of the possibility that E-Ferol may have caused CL's death when class plaintiffs' counsel mailed him notice after obtaining his identity from Miami Valley. Long testified that he should be excluded from the settlement, on two principal grounds: (1) the settlement amount was too low and undervalued his claim, and (2) the release of third-party medical providers infringed on his right to sue the Miami Valley Providers. Long stressed that his right to his day in court would be improperly extinguished if the proposed settlement is approved.

II

The court determines first whether the Settlement Agreement is fair, reasonable, and adequate to the class plaintiffs as a whole and not the product of collusion between the parties. A proposed settlement in a class action must undergo rigorous testing by the court to ensure that the interests of absent class members are represented. "The gravamen of an approvable proposed settlement is that it be fair, adequate, and reasonable and is not the product of collusion between the parties." *Newby v. Enron Corp.*, 394 F.3d 296, 301 (5th Cir. 2004) (internal quotation marks omitted); *see also Cotton v. Hinton*, 559 F.2d 1326, 1330 (5th Cir. 1977). In exercising its discretion to approve a settlement, the court must "ensure that the settlement is in the interests of the class, does not unfairly impinge on the rights and interests of dissenters, and does not merely mantle oppression." *Pettway v. Am. Cast Iron Pipe Co.*, 576 F.2d 1157, 1214 (5th Cir. 1978); *see also Reed v. Gen. Motors Corp.*, 703 F.2d 170, 172 (5th Cir. 1983).

In evaluating a proposed settlement, "a trial judge is dependent upon a match of adversary talent because he cannot obtain the ultimate answers without trying the case. Indeed, that uncertainty is a catalyst of settlement." *Id.* at 175. Courts assess the efficacy of representation in large part by the barometer of the relief that counsel have obtained for the class. The adequacy of the representation is linked to the question whether the settlement is fair and reasonable. *See Reed*, 703 F.2d at 175; *Parker v. Anderson*, 667 F.2d 1204, 1211 (5th Cir. Unit A 1982). Where the court finds that counsel have adequately represented the interests of the class, "the trial judge, absent fraud, collusion, or the like, should be hesitant to substitute its own judgment for that of counsel." *Cotton*, 559 F.2d at 1330. The Fifth Circuit has repeatedly stated that the opinion of class counsel should be accorded great weight.

The court must apply a six-part test to determine whether the proposed settlement is fair, reasonable, and adequate under Rule 23(e). *See Newby*, 394 F.3d at 301; *Reed*, 703 F.2d at 172. The six *Reed* factors are:

> (1) the existence of fraud or collusion behind the settlement; (2) the complexity, expense, and likely duration of the litigation; (3) the stage of the proceedings and the amount of discovery completed; (4) the probability of plaintiffs' success on the merits; (5) the range of possible recovery; and (6) the opinions of the class counsel, class representatives, and absent class members.

Reed, 703 F.2d at 172 (citing *Parker*, 667 F.2d at 1209). In balancing the six factors, "absent fraud or collusion, the most important factor is the probability of the plaintiffs' success on the merits." *Parker*, 667 F.2d at 1209.

"When considering [the *Reed*] factors, the court should keep in mind the strong presumption in favor of finding a settlement fair." *Purdie v. Ace Cash Express, Inc.*, 2003 U.S.

Dist. LEXIS 22547, 2003 WL 22976611, at *4 (N.D. Tex. Dec. 11, 2003) (Lindsay, J.). "Particularly in class action suits, there is an overriding public interest in favor of settlement." *Cotton*, 559 F.2d at 1331. Moreover, the public interest in settlement is best served when a settlement binds all parties without allowing for individual opt outs.

That one class member of 369 has objected to the proposed settlement does not preclude the court from approving it. "[A] settlement can be approved despite opposition from class members, including named plaintiffs." *Ayers v. Thompson,* 358 F.3d 356, 373 (5th Cir. 2004) (citing *Reed, Parker,* and *Cotton*). "[I]n assessing the fairness of a proposed compromise, the number of objectors is a factor to be considered, but a settlement can be fair notwithstanding a large number of class members who oppose it." *Pettway*, 576 F.2d at 1215 (citing *Cotton*, 559 F.2d at 1331); *see also Reed,* 703 F.2d at 174 (holding that while total number of objectors is not dispositive, it is one factor that courts should consider in conducting a fairness evaluation).

III

The court now turns to the *Reed* factors.

A

The court first looks for the existence of fraud or collusion behind the settlement. "The Court may presume that no fraud or collusion occurred between counsel, in the absence of any evidence to the contrary." *Liger v. New Orleans Hornets NBA Ltd. P'ship.,* 2009 U.S. Dist. LEXIS 85733, 2009 WL 2856246, at *3 (E.D. La. Aug. 28, 2009). Here, no allegations of fraud or collusion have been raised, and none is apparent. Judge Martin, the mediator, avers that "[t]he settlement was reached only after a period of hard fought negotiations," Ps. Ex. 41 at 1, and "was the result of arms length bargaining among the plaintiffs' counsel, the defendants and their insurers," *id.* at 2. This opinion is confirmed by the fairness-hearing testimony of counsel for the class plaintiffs and defendants, and by the legal experts who carefully evaluated the proposed settlement. *See, e.g.,* Tr. 1:238 (testimony of Prof. Underwood) ("This case was hard fought from the beginning."); Ds. Ex. 2 at 7 (statement of Prof. Silver) ("[T]he relationship between Class Counsel and Defendants was genuinely adversarial.").

The court finds that the proposed settlement is not the product of fraud or collusion.

B

Under the second *Reed* factor, the court considers the complexity, expense, and likely duration of the litigation.

When the prospect of ongoing litigation threatens to impose high costs of time and money on the parties, the reasonableness of approving a mutually-agreeable settlement is strengthened. This factor weighs strongly in favor of approving the proposed settlement. Although much has been done since 2004 (when the class was certified), considerable work will be required before the suit can proceed to trial. The testimony of counsel for both sides supports the finding that, despite substantial efforts already invested in this case, a great deal more time and resources will be required to prosecute it to a verdict. Brender states in his pre-hearing declaration that "[this] litigation has been extremely expensive and will prove to be even more so in the event this settlement is not approved."

The medical experts called by both sides offered evidence regarding the nature of the scientific disputes, concerning both the appropriate methodology and the substance of the claims that would be at issue. They especially noted the complex causation issues related to the Category 3 brain injury claims. Each of the class plaintiffs' medical witnesses opined that the brain injuries could be tied to E-Ferol, but each admitted that there was no published study that conclusively proves this link. Likewise, in his pre-hearing statement, Prof. Underwood opines that "class members would face significant issues of both general and specific causation and there is every reason to believe that Defendants would mount formidable challenges on these elements of the claims."

Defendants intend to challenge vigorously the causation evidence that the class plaintiffs offer to support their claims, particularly for the Category 3 brain injury allegations and for the claims for costs of ongoing medical monitoring for Category 4 class members who have suffered no apparent injuries.

Finally, defendants intend to appeal the court's decision in *Klein II* denying in part their motion for partial summary judgment asserting the affirmative defense of limitations. If such an appeal were successful, class members' claims could be barred altogether. The issues recounted above make clear that prolonging the case would lead to an increase in the already-sizeable investments of time and resources by the parties over the seven years since the case was filed. The fact that it has taken this long for the litigation to proceed to the point of a possible settlement speaks to the nature and scope of the issues in dispute.

Approval of the Settlement Agreement provides relief while simultaneously freeing class members and defendants alike from the burdens and uncertainty inherent in additional litigation. The court finds that the complexity, expense, and likely duration of the case supports approving the proposed settlement.

C

Under the third *Reed* factor, the court considers the stage of the proceedings and the amount of discovery completed. It evaluates whether "the parties and the district court possess ample information with which to evaluate the merits of the competing positions." *Ayers*, 358 F.3d at 369. A settlement can be approved under this factor even if the parties have not conducted much formal discovery. *See, e.g., Cotton*, 559 F.2d at 1332. Furthermore, "[t]he scope of the discovery to be conducted in each case rests with the sound discretion of the trial judge." *Id.* at 1333.

The testimony of lead counsel for the class plaintiffs and defendants, the legal expert witnesses, and the court's familiarity with the discovery in this case confirm that the merits of the claims are well known to both sides. Settlement negotiations took place over a period of 14 months and did not begin until five years after suit was filed. Moreover, the parties benefited from the large number (estimated at over 130) of individual lawsuits alleging E-Ferol claims that preceded this case, as well as the prior criminal prosecution. The foundation laid by these cases aided in the development of the facts in this action and provided a means for counsel to measure the approximate value of the claims of class members.

The court finds that the litigation is at an appropriate stage for settlement. Accordingly, this factor supports approving the proposed settlement.

D

The fourth *Reed* factor examines the probability of plaintiffs' success on the merits of their claims. Evaluating the likelihood of success "contains an internal tension." *Reed*, 703 F.2d at 172.

> A district court faced with a proposed settlement must compare its terms with the likely rewards the class would have received following a successful trial of the case. The court, however, must not try the case in the settlement hearings because the very purpose of the compromise is to avoid the delay and expense of such a trial.

Id. (citation and internal quotation marks omitted). Despite this tension, absent fraud or collusion, the most important *Reed* factor is the probability of plaintiffs' success on the merits. *Parker,* 667 F.2d at 1209.

The court finds that the evidence regarding the class plaintiffs' probability of success on the merits favors approving the proposed settlement. On the one hand, the class plaintiffs have asserted strong claims that are similar to others that have obtained favorable settlements in prior E-Ferol lawsuits. There is little dispute about the underlying liability of defendants for manufacturing a defective product; the inherent dangers of E-Ferol are not contested; and the conduct at issue resulted in criminal convictions. The claims of the class plaintiffs are compelling, and jurors could be persuaded of their merit.

On the other hand, the possibility of defendants' successfully appealing the court's summary judgment decision presents a risk of no recovery for many class members. Likewise, the difficulty of proving causation, especially for the Category 3 claims, is real. The medical evidence overall is based on a limited pool of available information and would be subject to challenges both in its inherent reliability and in its application to each claim. Moreover, a jury might be reluctant to award damages for acts that took place far in the past, particularly when considering claims for emotional injury and the like. Finally, the Settlement Agreement provides for sizeable awards to claims in Category 5 that, apart from the settlement, would have no chance of recovery absent the prosecution of a successful appeal, necessitating additional expense and perhaps substantial delay.

Accordingly, the fourth *Reed* factor favors approval of the settlement.

E

The fifth *Reed* factor requires that the court consider the range of possible recovery by the class. This factor compares the recovery for the class under the proposed agreement with the likely estimated value of the claims if they went to trial. Under this factor, a court should consider the views of objecting class members when their "objections to the settlement agreement center on their view that the relief it provides is inadequate." *Ayers,* 358 F.3d at 370.

"Parties give and take to achieve settlements. Typically neither Plaintiffs nor Defendants end up with exactly the remedy they would have asked the Court to enter absent the settlement."

The Settlement Agreement divides the class members into five categories (and some sub-categories). Class members are classified according to the type of injury claimed and the strength of available proof. Settlement funds are allocated among these categories by prescribed percentages, and each class member is entitled to a pro rata share of the percentage allocated to the member's category. The payments to each of the classes are reduced by the court's award of attorney's fees and expenses to class counsel and of compensation to the class representatives.

At the fairness hearing and in their written submissions defendants have presented evidence that the proposed settlement amounts are within the range of reasonableness for E-Ferol litigation as compared with settlements in prior suits.

The data presented by defense counsel, the accuracy of which is unchallenged, reveal that the anticipated payments under the Settlement Agreement compare favorably with the median recoveries obtained in prior settlements of similarly-classified injuries.

Prof. Underwood testified that the division of the settlement funds among the various categories of the settlement were fair and appropriate. He noted that the allocation of funds was atypical, in that the neurological injury cases under Category 3 receive lower payments than the death claims under Categories 1 and 2. Prof. Underwood explained this anomaly by pointing to the causation evidence. Whereas the causation arguments in the death cases are fairly well established (although still disputed), the medical evidence establishing causation in the brain injury cases is much thinner and is vulnerable to challenge. Thus it is reasonable to reduce the value of Category 3 claims to account for problems proving causation that would likely occur if the case were tried. He also opines in his pre-hearing declaration that "[t]he scarcity of class members who have voiced any problems with the category into which they have been placed is indicative of a fair and impartial process." His analysis concludes that the overall recovery by the class, and the divisions among categories, are adequate, fair, and reasonable.

The court finds that the evidence comparing the recoveries in this case to those in other E-Ferol settlements supports approval of the proposed settlement. Furthermore, the recoveries under the proposed settlement are significantly higher than the typical recoveries for class actions involving infant death and injury claims in medical malpractice cases. The Settlement Agreement does not contain any provisions for essentially valueless or so-called "coupon" payments. Even the class members who have no apparent injury will receive relief. According to Prof. Underwood, the proposed settlement is a "poster child" for settlements that are fair and beneficial to the class. He opined that "most of these class members probably would be getting zero dollars because they probably wouldn't even know that they had a claim, much less had an advocate to push those claims, but for what counsel has done here and the court's decision to certify it."

The uncontroverted evidence presented by defendants demonstrates that the settlement payments to class members are within the range of reasonably expected damages for cases of this type.

The court concludes that the fifth *Reed* factor supports approving the Settlement Agreement. The evidence demonstrates that the recoveries allowed under the Settlement Agreement bear a reasonable relationship to those in other E-Ferol litigation settlements and compare favorably with settlements in similar class actions overall. Especially when the expected recovery in this case is discounted for the obstacles to the class's succeeding on the merits, combined with the age of the class plaintiffs' claims, the settlement is fair, reasonable, and adequate. Accordingly, this factor favors approval.

F

The sixth *Reed* factor examines the opinions of the class counsel, class representatives, and absent class members.

"Counsel are the Court's 'main source of information about the settlement,' *Manual for Complex Litigation* § 21.641, and therefore the Court will give weight to class counsel's opinion regarding the fairness of settlement." *Turner*, 472 F.Supp.2d at 852 (citing *Cotton*, 559 F.2d at 1330 ("[T]he trial court is entitled to rely upon the judgment of experienced counsel for the parties.")). The *Reed* panel held:

> in reviewing proposed class settlements, a trial judge is dependent upon a match of adversary talent because he cannot obtain the ultimate answers without trying

the case. Indeed, that uncertainty is a catalyst of settlement. Because the trial judge must predict, the value of the assessment of able counsel negotiating at arm's length cannot be gainsaid. Lawyers know their strengths and they know where the bones are buried.

Reed, 703 F.2d at 175. Because the court is to give significant weight to the opinion of class counsel, it is not routine for a court to overrule a decision that settlement is in the best interest of the class. "[T]he trial judge, absent fraud, collusion, or the like, should be hesitant to substitute its own judgment for that of counsel." *Cotton,* 559 F.2d at 1330. The opinions of class counsel and class representatives clearly favor approving the Settlement Agreement. In his declaration, Brender opines that "it is the overwhelming opinion and request of class counsel, class representatives, and class members that the court approve the settlement."

As for the class members, the support for approval is overwhelming. Of 369 class members, 569 (97.3%) affirmatively request that the court approve the settlement. One person (Long), representing .27% of the class, opposes the settlement. Moreover, support for approval of the settlement is broad throughout the five categories. Dozens of class members attended the fairness hearing in person, and others appeared through a video presentation. All requested approval of the Settlement Agreement.

It is notable that thorough judicial review of class action settlements is required, at least in part, because in the typical case, a court cannot know the opinion of the class that will be bound by the proposed agreement. In this class action, however, the court has the benefit of declarations from virtually all class members evincing support for the settlement and requesting that the court approve it. Prof. Underwood considered the proposed settlement to be unique in that virtually the entire class has requested approval by affirmative statement. He stated that he was unaware of any precedent for a court's failing to approve a proposed settlement as fair when it was explicitly supported by 97.3% of the class. Prof. Underwood testified that "to the extent the court can divine what the general class reaction is to settlement, that ought to be very persuasive to a court as to whether or not this is fair, adequate, and reasonable, because those are all opinions." As even Long notes in his objections, "[p]resumably, all class members who have not objected have no interest in or desire to opt-out and are satisfied with the settlement."

"[A] settlement can be approved despite opposition from class members, including named plaintiffs." *Ayers,* 358 F.3d at 373. The presence of objectors does not necessarily defeat a settlement, and approval can be given even if a significant portion of the class objects.

Accordingly, the court finds that the opinions of class counsel, class representatives, and class members support approval of the settlement.

G

In sum, the court finds as follows: (1) there is no evidence of fraud or collusion in the conduct of the litigation or the negotiation of the Settlement Agreement; (2) the case, if allowed to proceed to trial, would present highly complex issues of fact and law, would entail considerable expense, and would likely remain unresolved for a number of years; (3) the litigation is more than adequately mature for the parties to know the merits of their claims and defenses, especially considering the extensive research done by class counsel and the wealth of information available from prior E-Ferol lawsuits; (4) although the class plaintiffs present strong liability arguments, for the class plaintiffs to prevail on their claims there are significant issues related to limitations and causation (particularly for the Category 3 brain injury claims) that must still be overcome and that leave the ultimate result in question; (5) the payments made under the Settlement Agreement are within the range of reasonable expectations for recoveries if the case were tried; and (6) approval is overwhelmingly supported by class counsel, class representatives, and all but one class member. Accordingly, the court finds and concludes from its analysis of the *Reed* factors that the proposed settlement should be approved.

Notes and Problems

1. Notice in *Klein* that the court certified a Rule 23(b)(3) nationwide class action under the laws of multiple states (where each child was injured). Compare the *Klein* case with *Castano* (Chapter 4 Class Actions: Certification) and analyze what might have been so different between the two cases to justify certification in *Klein* but not *Castano*. Or do you disagree with the certification of this class? Fairness hearings can be lengthy ordeals with many witnesses called before the judge to testify as to the settlement criteria. The length of the *Klein* opinion going through these factors is hardly unusual.

2. Was *Klein* truly a "poster child" for a good Rule 23(b)(3) mass tort class action that actually benefited the class members? In the absence of a certified class, what would have become of most of the individual damage claims? How persuasive was it that such a higher percentage of the class took the affirmative step of mailing letters to the court asking the court to approve the settlement? If the entire class evidenced such an attitude, should a court even possess the power to refuse to approve it?

3. As mentioned in the prior section about class notices, a notice to the class of a proposed settlement is required under Rule 23(e). Some courts have said that the form of this notice is less rigid than under Rule 23(c)(2) (for Rule 23(b)(3) classes) and that the trial court has "virtually complete discretion" as to the manner of notice. *Franks v. Kroger Co.*, 649 F.2d 1216, 1222 (6th Cir. 1981). However, when individual notice has previously been required at the time of certification and when the settlement will require class members to file claims to obtain their funds, it would seem that something more than a mere token form of notice would be essential.

4. Notice the breakdown in *Klein* for how the settlement funds would be disbursed—according to category of damages and other criteria (e.g. whether a claim had previously been dismissed on statute of limitations grounds). Was the settlement equally fair for each category of class member? One class member was vehement in asserting objections to the settlement—how much weight should a court afford a class member's objections to a settlement? Is the court's job to make every class member satisfied or just to approve a settlement that is, in general, in the best interests of the class in the aggregate?

5. As you read *Klein*, and taking the relevant six *Reed* factors into account, what aspects of the case and settlement struck you as most clearly justifying approval of the proposed settlement? Or did you believe that the objections to the settlement were well founded and should have been sustained? The law is now clear that objections properly lodged by a class member can be the basis for an appeal by that class member even without that class member having first intervened to be a named litigant to the case. *See Devlin v. Scardelletti*, 536 U.S. 1 (2002) (non-intervening class member who had asserted objections to the settlement at the fairness hearing was permitted to appeal the district court's approval despite never being a named party to the case).

6. Consider the dynamics of the fairness hearing when a proposed settlement is pending before the court. Is either the plaintiff or defendant, or their respective counsel,

arguing against the settlement? For the class counsel, getting the court to approve the settlement in a sense requires counsel to point out all of the inherent weaknesses in the plaintiffs' case in order to show what a terrific deal the settlement is for the class. It is an odd bit of litigation where the normal adversarial nature of the proceedings is suddenly lost — except to the extent any class members have appeared on the scene to file objections. In this way, do you see how objecting class members can actually help the court to fulfill its paternal obligations to oversee the settlement approval process? Some courts have referred to their role in the settlement approval as being akin to a "fiduciary" role:

> The principal issue ... is whether the district judge discharged the judicial duty to protect the members of the class in class action litigation from lawyers for the class who may, in derogation of their professional and fiduciary obligations, place their pecuniary self-interest ahead of the class. This problem, repeatedly remarked by judges and scholars, requires district judges to exercise the highest degree of vigilance in scrutinizing proposed settlements of class actions. We and other courts have gone so far as to term the district judge in the settlement phase of a class action suit a fiduciary of the class, who is subject therefore to the high duty of care that the law requires of fiduciaries.

Reynolds v. Beneficial National Bank, 288 F.3d 277, 279 (7th Cir. 2002) (reversing district judge's approval of a questionable settlement based upon different view of the value of the settlement to the class).

7. One relatively new feature of Rule 23(e) is that which gives a court the discretion, in a Rule 23(b)(3) case, to require a second opt-out period for class members as a condition of approving the settlement. When this is provided, a class member is equipped with much more precise information to guide their decision as to whether they would like to be included in the settlement or proceed with their own litigation. Often both class counsel and defense counsel argue against such a second opt-out window because it can unsettle the delicate balance of a settlement and its hope to achieve a lasting peaceful resolution of all controversy. Indeed, sometimes class settlements include a provision allowing defendant to unilaterally cancel the settlement if too many class members opt out of the case.

8. Earlier in this chapter we introduced some of the primary provisions of the Class Action Fairness Act impacting subject matter jurisdiction. Another provision of that statute concerned judicial scrutiny over "coupon settlements." These are settlements where the class members literally get a coupon from the defendant in lieu of any cash payments. It might bestow an economic benefit on the class member but only to the extent the class member desires to continue doing business with the defendant. Attacks on class actions in the past few decades have often resorted to anecdotal stories of such coupon settlements, where the class members got a worthless piece of paper and class counsel received paper that was legal tender (i.e., cash). 28 U.S.C. § 1712 was added with the Class Action Fairness Act and, among other features, includes the following language inviting scrutiny by federal courts before approving a coupon settlement:

> § 1712(e) Judicial Scrutiny of Coupon Settlements — In a proposed settlement under which class members would be awarded coupons, the court may approve the proposed settlement only after a hearing to determine whether, and making a written finding that, the settlement is fair, reasonable, and adequate for class members. The court, in its discretion, may also require that a proposed settlement agreement provide for the distribution of a portion of the value of unclaimed coupons to 1 or more charitable or governmental organizations, as agreed to by

the parties. The distribution and redemption of any proceeds under this subsection shall not be used to calculate attorney's fees under this section.

Compare the language of § 1712(e) with the general language of Rule 23(e). What exactly did this statute add?

9. In traditional litigation with the normal attorney-client relationships, one cannot conceive of a settlement happening without the approval of the plaintiff (absent some ethical problems). But oddly enough, when a court is asked to approve a class settlement it has to bear in mind what is in the best interests of the entire class, even over the objections of the plaintiffs' class representative who initiated the lawsuit and hired the class counsel (originally). Courts have sustained approvals of settlements even where most of the class representatives asserted vigorous objections to the settlement. *See, e.g., Parker v. Anderson,* 667 F.2d 1204 (5th Cir. 1982) (court approved settlement despite fact that ten of the eleven class representatives objected to the final settlement). Courts recognize that "the duty owed by class counsel is to the entire class and is not dependent on the special desires of the named plaintiffs." *Id.*

Pulling It All Together Exercise

In the *Klein* decision, the court enumerates the so-called six *Reed* factors utilized in that circuit to determine whether a proposed class settlement was "fair, reasonable, and adequate" under Rule 23(e).

Consider each of the six Reed factors; identify those factors that would seem to be relevant settlement criteria for counsel on any traditional piece of litigation. Are any of the six factors unique to class actions? If so, which ones and how should they be utilized to evaluate the fairness of a proposed settlement in the class context?

---

2. Cy Pres and Fluid Recovery Settlements

Despite the fact that a class action complaint may seek damages for class members initially, the reality may be that due to the actual circumstances unrelated to the case merits, this is not feasible. What if class members cannot be located or identified? What if the cost mechanisms of transferring funds to class members is greater than the amount to be distributed? These circumstances are often true in certain consumer-oriented negative-value class actions. What if, for example, a taxi company has been overcharging its customers for the last few years. At least back when almost all such customers paid in cash, would there be any feasible way for a court to determine the identity and whereabouts of all of those customers? And even if theoretically it were possible to do so, if the average transaction overcharge was 25 cents, do you understand why it would not even be worthwhile to make the effort? In such instances, should the court de-certify the class action (or refuse initially to certify it) and dismiss the class action? Where would that leave the wrongdoing defendant? Courts frequently have to ask if imperfect, rough justice is better than no justice at all—this question usually arises in the context of a proposed settlement The answer to the question is not always clear. Consider these issues as you read the following two cases. *Simer* demonstrates a court deciding that no legitimate purpose would be served by permitting any *cy pres* or fluid recovery. The *Kellogg* case that follows shows a scenario where some *cy pres* relief might be warranted but not the *cy pres* relief the parties were proposing to the court.

Cy pres is French for "as near as possible."

Simer v. Rios (Part II)
661 F.2d 655 (7th Cir. 1981)

[We have previously read the portion of this opinion articulating one major problem with the certification of this proposed class—the identification of a class based upon "state of mind" criteria. The proposed class would have included all those who were either refused assistance under the government's Crisis Intervention Program or were *discouraged* from applying because of the wrongful requirement that applicants produce a "turn-off" notice from the utility company in order to receive benefits. The following portion of the opinion explains why a possible fluid recovery—in lieu of cash payments to class members—is not available to help fix the earlier identification hurdle.

CSA had indicated that any settlement that would put funds back into the hands of those the program was designed to help would be an "administrative nightmare"—this would be particularly true regarding those who were "frustrated" and never applied. Therefore, included in the terms of the proposed settlement were an allocation of settlement funds that would be used to offer "long range solutions to the energy problems for the elderly," the inclusion of funds for a "hypothermia program," money to purchase "energy conservation kits," and money to monitor these educational programs.]

Another possible procedural alternative, and one which actually is reflected in the settlement decree, is the use of a fluid recovery. The fluid recovery is used where the individuals injured are not likely to come forward and prove their claims or cannot be given notice of the case. In a fluid recovery the money is either distributed through a market system in the way of reduced charges or is used to fund a project which will likely benefit the members of the class.

Plaintiffs similarly contend that in the instant case the fluid recovery remedy will provide redress for the general class of individuals harmed by defendants' conduct. In raising this contention plaintiffs rely on *Bebchick v. Public Utilities Commission*, 115 U.S. App. D.C. 216, 318 F.2d 187 (D.C.Cir.) (en banc), cert. denied, 373 U.S. 913, 83 S. Ct. 1304, 10 L. Ed. 2d 414 (1963).

Bebchick concerned a challenge to a rate increase by the Washington, D.C. transit system. The court of appeals invalidated the rate increase and in a supplemental opinion addressed the issue of how to structure a judgment to carry out the opinion of the court since the illegal rate had been in effect for a time prior to invalidation. The court acknowledged that it was not possible to order refunds to individuals who had paid the increased fare. Nevertheless, the court ordered that the Transit should utilize the money for the benefit of the users of the system.

The analogy of *Bebchick* to the present case is not unfounded. Yet, we believe that an analysis of the fluid recovery mechanism must take a more critical tack. Plaintiffs apparently contend that the harmed individuals cannot be identified and therefore a fluid recovery should be utilized. Strictly speaking, plaintiffs' contention proves too much. It sets forth no criteria for determining when class certification is unnecessary and when the requirements of class certification may be restructured. Indeed, to accept plaintiffs' position would be to ignore the requirements of Rule 23, such as whether an identifiable class exists and whether notice to the class can be executed. Therefore, we reject any approach which would automatically utilize a fluid recovery mechanism as a procedural alternative to class action disposition.

At the other extreme is the position that a fluid recovery mechanism is unconstitutional. The argument raised is that it violates defendant's right to trial by jury. See, e.g., *Dickinson v. Burnham*, 197 F.2d 973, 980–81 (2d Cir.), cert. denied, 344 U.S. 875, 73 S. Ct. 169, 97 L. Ed. 678 (1952); *Developments*, supra, at 1524–25. In *Windham v. American Brands, Inc.*, 565 F.2d 59, 72 (4th Cir. 1977) the Fourth Circuit Court of Appeals apparently rejected the use of a fluid recovery. The court stated:

> Nor ... can the difficulties inherent in proving individual damages be avoided by use of a form of "fluid recovery." Such a method of computing damages in a class action has been branded as "illegal, inadmissible as a solution of the manageability problems of class actions and wholly improper."

Id. at 72.

We need not adopt either of the two extreme positions that is, whether a fluid recovery always can be used to surmount problems in the going forward of a class action or whether a fluid recovery is per se unconstitutional. Rather, we believe that a careful case-by-case analysis of use of the fluid recovery mechanism is the better approach. In this approach we focus on the various substantive policies that use of a fluid recovery would serve in the particular case. The general inquiry is whether the use of such a mechanism is consistent with the policy or policies reflected by the statute violated. This matter can be more particularized into an assessment of to what extent the statute embodies policies of deterrence, disgorgement, and compensation.

First, we focus on whether a fluid recovery is needed to deter the defendant from illegal conduct. We think not. CSA has been charged with administering a large and complex program and it is inevitable that problems arise. While in no way do we applaud or encourage the passage of invalid regulations, there is no indication that CSA's actions have been in bad faith or with the specific intent of disobeying its statutory obligation. This is not a case where the defendant has intentionally violated a statute which was intended to regulate socially opprobrious conduct such as that reflected in the antitrust or securities laws. Thus, the deterrence factor weighs against the use of a fluid recovery.

The second factor, that of disgorging illegally obtained profits, also counsels against use of a fluid recovery. Those cases where a corporate defendant engages in unlawful conduct and illegally profits is most appropriate for a fluid recovery. In this manner, the *Bebchick* decision also involved the disgorging of profits illegally obtained. The transit system of Washington relied on private investment and profits were returned to investors. The court of appeals properly ordered that the Transit not retain the illegally obtained profits. In the present case neither CSA, nor any shareholders, benefited financially from its allegedly illegal conduct. Rather, if anything, CSA would have been able to disburse more funds had the regulation not been in effect. The money CSA refused to spend merely reverted to the Treasury. In sum, this is not a case where the defendant would retain illegally obtained profits once the termination date of the program passed CSA no longer had the money to spend and did not benefit from its unlawful conduct.

The final factor, whether the statute has a compensatory purpose, does weigh in favor of fluid recovery. The Act authorizing CSA to administer assistance programs had as its

380 5 · MANAGING CLASS ACTIONS

chief aim assisting low income individuals in dealing with the high cost of energy. Indeed, the purpose of the statute is purely compensatory.

However, we believe that even this factor does not clearly require fluid recovery. For fiscal year 1980 Congress funded a much larger energy assistance program and therefore absence of fluid recovery will not deprive plaintiffs of relief. The plaintiffs in this action challenged CSA's administration of the 1979 CIP. For 1980 CSA administered an energy assistance program of approximately 1.6 billion dollars. The program was referred to as the "Energy Crisis Assistance Program" (ECAP). 44 Fed.Reg. 58876 (1979). App. at 127. (Letter of Dockterman to Moran). This funding was part of a congressional appropriation made in 1979. Pub.L.No.96-126, 93 Stat. 954 (1979). Therefore, the amount of money at issue in the instant case which offered assistance to the poor and the elderly, while hardly trivial, is quite a bit less than the funding provided for CSA in fiscal year 1980.

In light of these three factors we believe that the use of a fluid recovery mechanism is not necessary to further the substantive policies at issue. The policies of deterrence and disgorgement are inapplicable and therefore weigh heavily against fluid recovery. To be sure, the compensatory policy is seriously implicated by the withholding of this relief. Yet, as we note above, the needy individuals continued to receive assistance through appropriations for 1980. Thus, even the compensatory policy does not definitively lead one to conclude that fluid recovery is needed. In sum, the relevant policies weigh against fluid recovery.

Dennis v. Kellogg Co.
697 F.3d 858 (9th Cir. 2012)

TROTT, J.,

Most cases in our judicial system never make it to trial. Litigants often find it advantageous to secure a resolution more quickly by settling the case and negotiating a result the parties can tolerate, even though neither side can call it a total win. Normally, that is the end of the story, and the parties walk away—not entirely happy, but not entirely unhappy either.

In a class action, however, any settlement must be approved by the court to ensure that class counsel and the named plaintiffs do not place their own interests above those of the absent class members. In this false advertising case, we confront a class action settlement, negotiated prior to class certification, that includes *cy pres* distributions of money and food to unidentified charities. It also includes $2 million in attorneys' fees while offering class members a sum of (at most) $15.

After carefully reviewing the class settlement, we conclude that it must be set aside. The district court did not apply the correct legal standards governing *cy pres* distributions and thus abused its discretion in approving the settlement. The settlement neither identifies the ultimate recipients of the product and cash *cy pres* awards nor sets forth any limiting restriction on those recipients, other than characterizing them as charities that feed the indigent. To the extent that we can meaningfully review such distributions where the parties fail to identify the recipients, we hold that both *cy pres* portions of the settlement are not sufficiently related to the plaintiff class or to the class's underlying false advertising claims. Moreover, the $5.5 million valuation the parties attach to the product *cy pres* distribution is, at best, questionable. We therefore reverse the district court's approval of the settlement, vacate the judgment and the award of attorneys' fees, and remand for further proceedings consistent with this opinion.

BACKGROUND

In January 2008, Kellogg Co., the maker of Frosted Mini-Wheats cereal, began a marketing campaign that claimed the cereal was scientifically proven to improve children's cognitive functions for several hours after breakfast. Obviously aimed at parents of school-age children, Kellogg's advertisements allegedly included the following statements:

- "Does your child need to pay more attention in school? ... A recent clinical study showed that a whole grain and fiber-filled breakfast of Frosted Mini-Wheats® helps improve children's attentiveness by nearly 20%."

- "Kellogg recently commissioned research to measure the effect on kids of eating a breakfast of Frosted Mini-Wheats® cereal. An independent research group conducted a series of standardized, cognitive tests on children ages 8 to 12 who ate either a breakfast of Frosted Mini-Wheats® cereal or water. The result? The children who ate a breakfast of Frosted Mini-Wheats® cereal had a nearly 20% improvement in attentiveness."

- "Based upon independent clinical research, kids who ate Kellogg's® Frosted Mini-Wheats® cereal for breakfast had up to 18% better attentiveness three hours after breakfast than kids who ate no breakfast."

[This lawsuit involved the collaboration of two plaintiffs and their respective counsel who joined forced to pursue a class action alleging violation of state consumer protection laws and unfair competition statutes as well as a claim for unjust enrichment. Eventually, after a mediation, a proposed settlement was reached.]

Ultimately, the [parties] agreed to settle the case on the following terms:

- Kellogg agreed to establish a $2.75 million settlement fund for distribution to class members on a claims-made basis. Class members submitting claims would receive $5 per box of cereal purchased, up to a maximum of $15. Any remaining funds would not revert to Kellogg, but would instead be donated to unidentified "charities chosen by the parties and approved by the Court pursuant to the *cy pres* doctrine. If the total amount of eligible claims exceeds the Settlement Fund, then each claim's award shall be proportionately reduced."

- Kellogg agreed to distribute, also pursuant to the *cy pres* doctrine, $5.5 million "worth" of specific Kellogg food items to charities that feed the indigent. The settlement does not specify the recipient charities, nor does it indicate how this $5.5 million in food will be valued—at cost, wholesale, retail, or by some other measure.

- Kellogg agreed that for three years, it would "refrain from using in its advertising and on its labeling for the Product any assertion to the effect that 'eating a bowl of Kellogg's® Frosted Mini-Wheats cereal for breakfast is clinically shown to improve attentiveness by nearly 20%.'" Kellogg would still be allowed to claim that "[c]linical studies have shown that kids who eat a filling breakfast like Frosted Mini-Wheats have an 11% better attentiveness in school than kids who skip breakfast."

- Kellogg agreed to pay class counsel's attorneys' fees and costs "not to exceed a total of $2 million." Class counsel eventually requested the full $2 million in fees and costs.

- The Plaintiffs agreed to release all claims arising out of the challenged advertising.

Together with notice and administrative costs approximated at $391,500, the parties value the settlement, or the constructive common fund, at $10,641,500.

The claims period has now closed. Although there is nothing in the record to indicate how many class members submitted claims, class counsel represented at oral argument that the claims submitted total approximately $800,000.

On the Plaintiffs' motion, the district court certified the class—defined as "[a]ll persons or entities in the United States who purchased the Product" during the settlement class period—granted preliminary approval of the settlement, and approved the proposed class notice. Because Kellogg sells its products to wholesalers, not directly to consumers, there was no way to identify each member of the class. Therefore, the class notice was published in *Parents* magazine and other "targeted sources based on market research about consumers who purchased the products," including 375 websites.

Two class members objected to the settlement: Stephanie Berg and Omar Rivero (Objectors). As relevant to this appeal, the Objectors argued that the settlement's use of *cy pres* relief was improper because "the only relationship between this lawsuit and feeding the indigent is that they both involve food in some way." They argued also that the *cy pres* distributions would benefit class counsel and Kellogg, but not the class members, because class members "have no idea how their funds might be used or in whose hands their monies will end up." Finally, the Objectors argued that the attorneys' fees—which represented approximately 19% of a common fund allegedly worth over $10.64 million— were excessive. The district court approved the class settlement and dismissed the case with prejudice. In doing so, however, the court did not address the Objectors' argument that the *cy pres* distributions were too remote from the class members and were not sufficiently related to their UCL and CLRA claims. The court also approved the requested attorneys' fees.

The Objectors timely appealed.

STANDARD OF REVIEW

The settlement of a class action must be fair, adequate, and reasonable. Fed. R. Civ. P. 23(e)(2). "We review a district court's approval of a proposed class action settlement, including a proposed *cy pres* settlement distribution, for abuse of discretion. A court abuses its discretion when it fails to apply the correct legal standard or bases its decision on unreasonable findings of fact." *Nachshin v. AOL, LLC,* 663 F.3d 1034, 1038 (9th Cir. 2011) (internal citations omitted).

Appellate review of a settlement agreement is generally "extremely limited." *Hanlon v. Chrysler Corp.,* 150 F.3d 1011, 1026 (9th Cir. 1998). But where, as here, class counsel negotiates a settlement agreement before the class is even certified, courts "must be particularly vigilant not only for explicit collusion, but also for more subtle signs that class counsel have allowed pursuit of their own self-interests and that of certain class members to infect the negotiations." *In re Bluetooth Headset Prods. Liab. Litig.,* 654 F.3d 935, 947 (9th Cir. 2011). In such a case, settlement approval "requires a higher standard of fairness" and "a more probing inquiry than may normally be required under Rule 23(e)." *Hanlon,* 150 F.3d at 1026. "To survive appellate review, the district court must show it has explored comprehensively all factors," *id.,* and must give "a reasoned response" to all non-frivolous objections, *Officers for Justice v. Civil Serv. Comm'n,* 688 F.2d 615, 624 (9th Cir. 1982).

DISCUSSION

The Cy Pres Distributions of Food and Unclaimed Funds

Cy pres is shorthand for the old equitable doctrine *"cy prés comme possible"* — French for "as near as possible." Although the doctrine originated in the area of wills as a way to effectuate the testator's intent in making charitable gifts, federal courts now frequently apply it in the settlement of class actions " 'where the proof of individual claims would be burdensome or distribution of damages costly.' " *Nachshin,* 663 F.3d at 1038 (quoting *Six Mexican Workers v. Ariz. Citrus Growers,* 904 F.2d 1301, 1305 (9th Cir. 1990)). Used in lieu of direct distribution of damages to silent class members, this alternative allows for "aggregate calculation of damages, the use of summary claim procedures, and distribution of unclaimed funds to indirectly benefit the entire class." *Six Mexican Workers,* 904 F.2d at 1305. To ensure that the settlement retains some connection to the plaintiff class and the underlying claims, however, a *cy pres* award must qualify as "the next best distribution" to giving the funds directly to class members. *Id.* at 1308 (internal quotation marks omitted).

Not just any worthy recipient can qualify as an appropriate *cy pres* beneficiary. To avoid the "many nascent dangers to the fairness of the distribution process," we require that there be "a driving nexus between the plaintiff class and the *cy pres* beneficiaries." *Nachshin,* 663 F.3d at 1038. A *cy pres* award must be "guided by (1) the objectives of the underlying statute(s) and (2) the interests of the silent class members," *id.* at 1039, and must not benefit a group "too remote from the plaintiff class," *Six Mexican Workers,* 904 F.2d at 1308. Thus, in addition to asking "whether the *class settlement,* taken as a whole, is fair, reasonable, and adequate to all concerned," we must also determine "whether the *distribution* of the approved class settlement complies with our standards governing *cy pres* awards." *Nachshin,* 663 F.3d at 1040 (internal quotation marks omitted).

A review of our relevant precedent reveals that the settlement here fails to satisfy those standards. In *Six Mexican Workers v. Arizona Citrus Growers,* a class of undocumented Mexican farm workers sued various companies for violations of the Farm Labor Contractor Registration Act. After a bench trial, the district court found the defendants liable for over $1.8 million, which we later reduced to $850,000, in statutory damages. The district court identified the Inter-American Fund, which provided humanitarian aid in Mexico, as the *cy pres* recipient of any unclaimed funds.

We held that the *cy pres* distribution was an abuse of discretion because there was "no reasonable certainty" that any class member would benefit from it, even though the money would go "to areas where the class members may live." *Id.* at 1308. The choice of charity and its relation to the class members and class claims — or lack thereof — figured heavily in our analysis. The purpose of the statute was to compensate victims of unscrupulous employers and to deter future violations, but the Inter-American Fund was "not an organization with a substantial record of service nor [was] it limited in its choice of projects," and any distribution would therefore have required court supervision "to ensure that the funds [were] distributed in accordance with the goals of the remedy." *Id.* at 1308. Because "the district court's application [of the *cy pres* doctrine] was inadequate to serve the goals of the statute and protect the interests of the silent class members," we reversed the *cy pres* distribution.

We recently came to a similar conclusion in *Nachshin v. AOL, LLC.* In that case, AOL was accused of violating a number of statutes, including the UCL and the CLRA, by wrongfully inserting commercial footers into the plaintiffs' outgoing emails. Because damages would be small and distribution to the class prohibitively expensive, AOL agreed, as part of a class settlement, to make substantial donations to three charities: the Legal Aid Foundation of Los Angeles, the Federal Judicial Center Foundation, and the Los Angeles and Santa Monica chapters of the Boys and Girls Club of America.

We held that the *cy pres* distribution "fail[ed] to target the plaintiff class, because it d[id] not account for the broad geographic distribution of the class." *Id.* at 1040. The class included over 66 million AOL users across the country, but two-thirds of the donations were slated for Los Angeles charities. Further, although the donation to the Federal Judicial Center Foundation "at least conceivably benefit[ed] a national organization," the Foundation "ha[d] no apparent relation to the objectives of the underlying statutes, and it [wa]s not clear how this organization would benefit the plaintiff class." *Id.* We noted, however, that it would not be difficult for the parties to come up with an appropriate charity if they wished to do so:

> It is clear that all members of the class share two things in common: (1) they use the internet, and (2) their claims against AOL arise from a purportedly unlawful advertising campaign that exploited users' outgoing e-mail messages. The parties should not have trouble selecting beneficiaries from any number of non-profit organizations that work to protect internet users from fraud, predation, and other forms of online malfeasance.

Id. at 1041. In approving the *cy pres* distribution to charities that had no relation to the class or to the underlying claims, the district court "applied the incorrect legal standard" and abused its discretion.

The *cy pres* awards in the settlement here are likewise divorced from the concerns embodied in consumer protection laws such as the UCL and the CLRA. As California courts have stated, "[t]he UCL is designed to preserve fair competition among business competitors and protect the public from nefarious and unscrupulous business practices," *Wells v. One2One Learning Found.,* 116 Cal. App. 4th 515, 10 Cal. Rptr. 3d 456, 463–64 (Ct. App. 2004), rev'd in part on other grounds, 39 Cal. 4th 1164, 48 Cal. Rptr. 3d 108, 141 P.3d 225 (Cal. 2006), and the purpose of the CLRA is similarly "to protect consumers against unfair and deceptive business practices," Cal. Civ. Code § 1760. Although there is no way to identify either the product or the cash *cy pres* beneficiaries from this record, we do know that according to the settlement, any charity to receive a portion of the *cy pres* distributions will be one that feeds the indigent. This noble goal, however, has "little or nothing to do with the purposes of the underlying lawsuit or the class of plaintiffs involved." *Nachshin,* 663 F.3d at 1039.

At oral argument, Kellogg's counsel frequently asserted that donating food to charities who feed the indigent relates to the underlying class claims because this case is about "the nutritional value of food." With respect, that is simply not true, and saying it repeatedly does not make it so. The complaint nowhere alleged that the cereal was unhealthy or lacked nutritional value. And no law allows a consumer to sue a company for selling cereal that does not improve attentiveness. The gravamen of this lawsuit is that Kellogg *advertised* that its cereal *did* improve attentiveness. Those alleged misrepresentations are what provided the Plaintiffs with a cause of action under the UCL and the CLRA, not the nutritional value of Frosted Mini-Wheats. Thus, appropriate *cy pres* recipients are not charities that feed the needy, but organizations dedicated to protecting consumers from, or redressing injuries caused by, false advertising. On the face of the settlement's language, "charities that provide food for the indigent" may not serve a single person within the plaintiff class of purchasers of Frosted Mini-Wheats.

Our concerns are not placated by the settlement provision that the charities will be identified at a later date and approved by the court—a decision from which the Objectors might again appeal. Our standards of review governing pre-certification settlement agreements require that we carefully review the entire settlement, paying special attention to "terms of the agreement contain[ing] convincing indications that the incentives favoring pursuit of self-interest rather than the class's interests in fact influenced the outcome of the negotiations." *Staton v. Boeing Co.*, 327 F.3d 938, 960 (9th Cir. 2003). *Cy pres* distributions present a particular danger in this regard. "When selection of *cy pres* beneficiaries is not tethered to the nature of the lawsuit and the interests of the silent class members, the selection process may answer to the whims and self interests of the parties, their counsel, or the court." *Nachshin*, 663 F.3d at 1039. This record leaves open the distinct possibility that the asserted $5.5 million value of the product *cy pres* award and the remaining cash *cy pres* award will only be of serendipitous value to the class purportedly protected by the settlement. The difficulty here is that, by failing to identify the *cy pres* recipients, the parties have restricted our ability to undertake the searching inquiry that our precedent requires. The *cy pres* problem presented in this case is of the parties' own making, and encouraging multiple costly appeals by punting down the line our review of the settlement agreement is no solution.

On remand, the parties are free to negotiate a new settlement or proceed with litigation. If they again decide to settle, they must correct the additional serious deficiencies we find in this settlement agreement. Not only does the settlement fail to identify the *cy pres* recipients of the unclaimed money and food, but it is unacceptably vague and possibly misleading in other areas as well.

The settlement states only that Kellogg will donate "$5.5 million *worth*" of food. (emphasis added). But the settlement document gives no hint as to how that $5.5 million will be valued. Is it valued at Kellogg's cost? At wholesale value? At retail? The exact answer to this question has important ramifications relating to the accurate valuation of the constructive common fund and thereby the reasonableness of attorneys' fees. Kellogg stated at oral argument and in its briefs to the district court that it will value the food donation at wholesale, but the only legally-enforceable document—the settlement—says nothing of the sort. Additionally, the settlement fails to include any restrictions on how Kellogg accounts for the *cy pres* distributions. Can Kellogg use the value of the distributions as tax deductions because they will go to charity? And given that Kellogg already donates both food and money to charities every year—which is unquestionably an admirable act—will the *cy pres* distributions be in addition to that which Kellogg has already obligated itself to donate, or can Kellogg use previously budgeted funds or surplus production to offset its settlement obligations? Again, the settlement is silent, and we have only Kellogg's statements as to its future intentions. All of this vagueness detracts from our ability to determine the true value of the constructive common fund.

Moreover, Plaintiffs' counsel tells us that settlements like this serve the purposes of "restitutionary disgorgement and deterrence." If the product *cy pres* distribution is form over substance and not worth nearly as much to Kellogg as the settlement claims, then these goals are not served. To the contrary, the settlement is a paper tiger.

This deficiency raises in turn serious issues about the alleged dollar value of the product *cy pres* award, an important number used to measure the appropriateness of attorneys' fees. For example, if the alleged $5.5 million value of the product *cy pres* distribution turns out on close examination to be an illusion and is subtracted from the alleged $10.64 million value of the common fund, the dollar value of the settlement fund plummets to

$5.14 million, and the $2 million attorneys' fees award becomes 38.9% of the total, which is clearly excessive under our guidelines. This possibility gives us an additional reason to be vigilant regarding the particulars of this class action settlement: is it all that it appears to be? Are the assigned numbers real, or not? This issue is particularly critical with a *cy pres* product settlement that has a tenuous relationship to the class allegedly damaged by the conduct in question. The issue of the valuation of this aspect of a settlement must be examined with great care to eliminate the possibility that it serves only the "self-interests" of the attorneys and the parties, and not the class, by assigning a dollar number to the fund that is fictitious. Neither class counsel nor Kellogg offers any credible reason for the mysteries in the current settlement. To approve this settlement despite its opacity would be to abdicate our responsibility to be "particularly vigilant" of pre-certification class action settlements.

For the foregoing reasons, we conclude that the district court did not apply the correct legal standards for *cy pres* distributions as set forth in *Six Mexican Workers* and *Nachshin*. Therefore, the approval of the settlement was an abuse of discretion.

We do not have the authority to strike down only the *cy pres* portions of the settlement. "It is the settlement taken as a whole, rather than the individual component parts, that must be examined for overall fairness," and we cannot "delete, modify or substitute certain provisions. The settlement must stand or fall in its entirety." *Hanlon,* 150 F.3d at 1026 (internal quotation marks omitted). *See also Jeff D. v. Andrus,* 899 F.2d 753, 758 (9th Cir. 1989) ("[C]ourts are not permitted to modify settlement terms or in any manner to rewrite agreements reached by parties."). Thus, we reverse the district court's order approving the settlement and dismissing the case, vacate the judgment and award of attorneys' fees, and remand for further proceedings.

CONCLUSION

Class counsel and Kellogg ask us for the impossible—a verdict before the trial. They essentially say, "Just trust us. Uphold the settlement now, and we'll tell you what it is later." But that is not how appellate review works. The settlement provides no assurance that the charities to whom the money and food will be distributed will bear any nexus to the plaintiff class or to their false advertising claims and therefore violates our well-established standards governing *cy pres* awards. Moreover, the true value of the product *cy pres* initiative has yet to be determined, making it impossible to assess, and thus evaluate, the true value of the common fund.

REVERSED, JUDGMENT VACATED, and CASE REMANDED.

Notes and Problems

1. In *Simer*, the court refuses to allow the use of a proposed *cy pres* remedy that involved an expenditure of settlement funds to provide certain educational resources to people that might include class members. As you will recall when we first encountered that case in Chapter 4 Class Certification, the court in an earlier portion of the opinion found the class was too ill-defined to permit certification. The class definition included those who were eligible for benefits but discouraged from applying for them because of the defendant's unlawful requirement that the applicants show a shut-off notice from their utility company. To try to ameliorate the court's inability to figure out who would be class members and eligible to receive any monetary benefits from the case, the parties agreed to the alternative remedy of this *cy pres* distribution of settlement funds through the educational benefits. This would have worked to fix the problem with the definition—because the proposed

cy pres remedy would not require the court to send funds to specific individuals in the class—but the court found the *cy pres* approach improper. Using the court's three-pronged inquiry, what was essentially wrong with using a form of *cy pres* relief under the circumstances of that case? Would this same reasoning apply often to other cases?

2. In *Kellogg*, the court did not opine that *cy pres* relief was improper. Rather, it found that the proposed *cy pres* relief agreed to by the parties was not adequately tied to the class members or to the nature of the wrong the case was designed to remediate. If you were class counsel reading the court's opinion, how might you try to fix the settlement to satisfy the court's concerns? Would your proposed alternative provide significant relief to class members?

3. Both courts acknowledge the fact that *cy pres* relief is not perfect. It is by its very nature almost always over-inclusive and under-inclusive. Given this reality, have courts' embrace of *cy pres* remedies under some circumstances gone too far astray of the traditional function of courts in adjudicating disputes and provide compensatory damages to victims? Some have been critical of the practice of courts approving *cy pres* relief in order to benefit particular charities or causes sympathetic to the judge and view *cy pres* relief as something that should be a last resort. *See* American Law Institute, *Principles of the Law: Aggregate Litigation* § 3.07(a) (2010) ("[I]f individual class members can be identified through reasonable effort, and the distributions are sufficiently large to make individual distributions economically viable, settlement proceeds should be distributed directly to individual class members."). Would it be better when circumstances prevent the bestowal of a remedy upon the actual class members to refuse to certify the class and dismiss the putative class action?

4. *Problems.* Consider whether a court should approve *cy pres* relief in the following scenarios:

   a. Class includes all current and former students of a school district sued for violating civil rights of students by forcing them to participate in unlawful prayer during the morning of each school day. Class sought injunction and damages for emotional distress suffered by any such student. Settlement proposal includes entry of consent decree whereby school promises to discontinue the practice and school district expenditure of $100,000 over the course of the next ten years to bring speakers to the school on Law Day each year to discuss the First Amendment's implications.

   b. Class includes all purchasers of a certain model pickup truck manufactured by the defendant during the previous six years that had alleged braking problems. Proposed settlement is for a coupon to be issued by the defendant to any prior purchaser for $1,000 off the purchase of a new pickup made by the same manufacturer. Distribution would be in the form of every dealer asking any purchasing customer if they were a prior owner of the particular model pickup involved in the suit. If the customer answers "yes," then a discount would be given on the new purchase.

   c. Class includes all citizens of Ohio who have been exposed to secondary smoke and suffered respiratory problems. Defendant is a tobacco company that explicitly marketed its products by falsely claiming that they were safe for smoking around others. The proposed settlement involves the company paying $5 million to take out advertisements within Ohio during the next year warning about the dangers of second-hand smoke.

5. *Chapter Problem.* Thinking creatively, imagine that you are the defendant's counsel in the class action outlined at the beginning of this chapter. You would like to make a set-

tlement offer that does not necessarily require a direct outlay of significant funds from your client but would arguably bestow a benefit on the class members (more or less). Can you come up with any possible *cy pres* form of settlement offer? Would a court likely approve it?

I. Statutes of Limitations and Class Actions

Earlier in this chapter, we saw the plaintiff in *Eisen* raise an argument against having to provide individual notice to Rule 23(b)(3) class members based upon the idea that none of them would want to opt out of the case because it would be too late for them to file an individual lawsuit due to the running of the statute of limitations. This argument, of course, raises the issue of whether the filing of a putative class action in any way tolls the applicable statute of limitations on individual class members' claims. So long as the class action was timely filed, is ultimately certified, and the class member does not opt out of it, the question might be a moot point. If all of that occurred and the case proceeded to final judgment, there would be no limitations issue. But if the case is not certified or the class member opts out, would the subsequent filing of an individual case (or attempted intervention by the class member in the original action) still be timely? Below is the seminal case on whether the filing of a putative class action tolls limitations for all who fit the class definition. As you read the decision, ask yourself why it might be fair to the defendant to allow what would otherwise be an untimely lawsuit in this context.

American Pipe & Constr. Co. v. Utah
414 U.S. 538 (1974)

[Defendant was sued in a putative class action for an alleged bid-rigging scheme brought in Utah federal court by the State of Utah, which was timely filed under federal law. The Judicial Panel on Six thereafter transferred the case to federal court in California because of the pendency of other related cases. Approximately six months after the case's filing, the district court denied the class certification motion finding that numerosity was lacking under Rule 23(a)(1). Eight days thereafter, Respondents filed a motion to intervene in that prior case to assert their own individual claims—identical to the putative class claims. Respondents consist of more than 60 towns, municipalities, and water districts in the State of Utah, all of which had been claimed as members of the original class. They sought intervention as of right, under Rule 24(a)(2) or, in the alternative, by permission under Rule 24(b)(2), The district court refused intervention solely on the grounds that Respondents' claims were barred by limitations; the court ruled that the filing of the putative class action did not toll the period of limitations which would have been necessary for their claims to be timely. The Ninth Circuit Court of Appeals reversed, holding that Respondents should have been granted intervention under Rule 24(b)(2). Finding that "as to members of the class Utah purported to represent, and whose claims it tendered to the court, suit was actually commenced by Utah's filing," the appellate court concluded that "if the order [denying class action status], through legal fiction, is to project itself backward in time it must fictionally carry backward with it the class members to whom it was directed, and the rights they presently possessed. It cannot leave them temporarily stranded in the present." The U.S. Supreme Court "granted certiorari to consider a seemingly important question affecting the administration of justice in the federal courts."]

STEWART, J.,

This case involves an aspect of the relationship between a statute of limitations and the provisions of Fed. Rule Civ. Proc. 23 regulating class actions in the federal courts.

Under Rule 23 as it stood prior to its extensive amendment in 1966, a so-called "spurious" class action could be maintained when "the character of the right sought to be enforced for or against the class is … several, and there is a common question of law or fact affecting the several rights and a common relief is sought." The Rule, however, contained no mechanism for determining at any point in advance of final judgment which of those potential members of the class claimed in the complaint were actual members and would be bound by the judgment. Rather, "when a suit was brought by or against such a class, it was merely an invitation to joinder—an invitation to become a fellow traveler in the litigation, which might or might not be accepted." 3B J. Moore, Federal Practice para. 23.10 [1], p. 23-2603 (2d ed.). Cf. *Snyder v. Harris,* 394 U.S. 332, 335; *Zahn v. International Paper Co., ante,* at 296 and n. 6. A recurrent source of abuse under the former Rule lay in the potential that members of the claimed class could in some situations await developments in the trial or even final judgment on the merits in order to determine whether participation would be favorable to their interests. If the evidence at the trial made their prospective position as actual class members appear weak, or if a judgment precluded the possibility of a favorable determination, such putative members of the class who chose not to intervene or join as parties would not be bound by the judgment. This situation—the potential for so-called "one-way intervention"—aroused considerable criticism upon the ground that it was unfair to allow members of a class to benefit from a favorable judgment without subjecting themselves to the binding effect of an unfavorable one. The 1966 amendments were designed, in part, specifically to mend this perceived defect in the former Rule and to assure that members of the class would be identified before trial on the merits and would be bound by all subsequent orders and judgments.

Under the present Rule, a determination whether an action shall be maintained as a class action is made by the court "as soon as practicable after the commencement of an action brought as a class action…." Rule 23 (c)(1). Once it is determined that the action may be maintained as a class action under subdivision (b)(3), the court is mandated to direct to members of the class "the best notice practicable under the circumstances" advising them that they may be excluded from the class if they so request, that they will be bound by the judgment, whether favorable or not if they do not request exclusion, and that a member who does not request exclusion may enter an appearance in the case. Rule 23(c)(2). Finally, the present Rule provides that in Rule 23(b)(3) actions the judgment shall include all those found to be members of the class who have received notice and who have not requested exclusion. Rule 23(c)(3). Thus, potential class members retain the option to participate in or withdraw from the class action only until a point in the litigation "as soon as practicable after the commencement" of the action when the suit is allowed to continue as a class action and they are sent notice of their inclusion within the confines of the class. Thereafter they are either nonparties to the suit and ineligible to participate in a recovery or to be bound by a judgment, or else they are full members who must abide by the final judgment, whether favorable or adverse.

Under former Rule 23, there existed some difference of opinion among the federal courts of appeals and district courts as to whether parties should be allowed to join or intervene as members of a "spurious" class after the termination of a limitation period, when the initial class action complaint had been filed before the applicable statute of limitations period had run. A majority of the courts ruling on the question, emphasizing the representative nature of a class suit, concluded that such intervention was proper. Other courts concluded that since a "spurious" class action was essentially a device to permit individual joinder or intervention, each individual so participating would have to satisfy the timeliness requirement. This conflict in the implementation of the former Rule was never resolved by this Court.

Under present Rule 23, however, the difficulties and potential for unfairness which, in part, convinced some courts to require individualized satisfaction of the statute of limitations by each member of the class, have been eliminated, and there remain no conceptual or practical obstacles in the path of holding that the filing of a timely class action complaint commences the action for all members of the class as subsequently determined.[20] Whatever the merit in the conclusion that one seeking to join a class after the running of the statutory period asserts a "separate cause of action" which must individually meet the timeliness requirements, such a concept is simply inconsistent with Rule 23 as presently drafted. A federal class action is no longer "an invitation to joinder" but a truly representative suit designed to avoid, rather than encourage, unnecessary filing of repetitious papers and motions. Under the circumstances of this case, where the District Court found that the named plaintiffs asserted claims that were "typical of the claims or defenses of the class" and would "fairly and adequately protect the interests of the class," Rule 23(a)(3), (4), the claimed members of the class stood as parties to the suit until and unless they received notice thereof and chose not to continue. Thus, the commencement of the action satisfied the purpose of the limitation provision as to all those who might subsequently participate in the suit as well as for the named plaintiffs. To hold to the contrary would frustrate the principal function of a class suit, because then the sole means by which members of the class could assure their participation in the judgment if notice of the class suit did not reach them until after the running of the limitation period would be to file earlier individual motions to join or intervene as parties—precisely the multiplicity of activity which Rule 23 was designed to avoid in those cases where a class action is found "superior to other available methods for the fair and efficient adjudication of the controversy." Rule 23(b)(3).

We think no different a standard should apply to those members of the class who did not rely upon the commencement of the class action (or who were even unaware that such a suit existed) and thus cannot claim that they refrained from bringing timely motions for individual intervention or joinder because of a belief that their interests would be represented in the class suit. Rule 23 is not designed to afford class action representation only to those who are active participants in or even aware of the proceedings in the suit prior to the order that the suit shall or shall not proceed as a class action. During the pendency of the District Court's determination in this regard, which is to be made "as soon as practicable after the commencement of an action," potential class members are mere passive beneficiaries of the action brought in their behalf. Not until the existence and limits of the class have been established and notice of membership has been sent does a class member have any duty to take note of the suit or to exercise any responsibility with respect to it in order to profit from the eventual outcome of the case. It follows that even as to asserted class members who were unaware of the proceedings brought in their interest or who demonstrably did not rely on the institution of those proceedings, the later running of the applicable statute of limitations does not bar participation in the class action and in its ultimate judgment.

---

20. The courts that have dealt with this problem under present Rule 23 have reached this conclusion. *Esplin* v. *Hirschi*, 402 F.2d 94 (CA10 1968); *Philadelphia Elec. Co.* v. *Anaconda Am. Brass Co.*, 43 F.R.D. 452 (ED Pa. 1968).

II

In the present case the District Court ordered that the suit could *not* continue as a class action, and the participation denied to the respondents because of the running of the limitation period was not membership in the class, but rather the privilege of intervening in an individual suit pursuant to Rule 24(b)(2). We hold that in this posture, at least where class action status has been denied solely because of failure to demonstrate that "the class is so numerous that joinder of all members is impracticable," the commencement of the original class suit tolls the running of the statute for all purported members of the class who make timely motions to intervene after the court has found the suit inappropriate for class action status. As the Court of Appeals was careful to note in the present case, "maintenance of the class action was denied not for failure of the complaint to state a claim on behalf of the members of the class (the court recognized the probability of common issues of law and fact respecting the underlying conspiracy)[,] not for lack of standing of the representative, or for reasons of bad faith or frivolity."

A contrary rule allowing participation only by those potential members of the class who had earlier filed motions to intervene in the suit would deprive Rule 23 class actions of the efficiency and economy of litigation which is a principal purpose of the procedure. Potential class members would be induced to file protective motions to intervene or to join in the event that a class was later found unsuitable. In cases such as this one, where the determination to disallow the class action was made upon considerations that may vary with such subtle factors as experience with prior similar litigation or the current status of a court's docket, a rule requiring successful anticipation of the determination of the viability of the class would breed needless duplication of motions. We are convinced that the rule most consistent with federal class action procedure must be that the commencement of a class action suspends the applicable statute of limitations as to all asserted members of the class who would have been parties had the suit been permitted to continue as a class action.

This rule is in no way inconsistent with the functional operation of a statute of limitations. As the Court stated in *Order of Railroad Telegraphers v. Railway Express Agency*, 321 U.S. 342, statutory limitation periods are "designed to promote justice by preventing surprises through the revival of claims that have been allowed to slumber until evidence has been lost, memories have faded, and witnesses have disappeared. The theory is that even if one has a just claim it is unjust not to put the adversary on notice to defend within the period of limitation and that the right to be free of stale claims in time comes to prevail over the right to prosecute them." The policies of ensuring essential fairness to defendants and of barring a plaintiff who "has slept on his rights," *Burnett v. New York Central R. Co.*, 380 U.S. 424, 428, are satisfied when, as here, a named plaintiff who is found to be representative of a class commences a suit and thereby notifies the defendants not only of the substantive claims being brought against them, but also of the number and generic identities of the potential plaintiffs who may participate in the judgment. Within the period set by the statute of limitations, the defendants have the essential information necessary to determine both the subject matter and size of the prospective litigation, whether the actual trial is conducted in the form of a class action, as a joint suit, or as a principal suit with additional intervenors.

Principles

"Too often, the gravitational pull of the venerable *Erie* doctrine draws state courts into filling state law lacuna with doctrines 'promulgated' by federal courts. [Yet]

Erie does not require state courts to embrace the rulings of their federal counterparts, although state courts may choose to do so. [T]he federal class action tolling doctrine is not state law simply because of its provenance. If it does anything, *Erie* prohibits federal courts from meddling in substantive state law and ... an automatic extension of *American Pipe* to state law claims constitutes exactly that kind of meddling."

Mitchell A. Lowenthal & Norman Menachem Feder, *The Impropriety of Class Action Tolling for Mass Tort Statutes of Limitations*, 64 Geo. Wash. L. Rev. 532, 532 (1996).

Since the imposition of a time bar would not in this circumstance promote the purposes of the statute of limitations, the tolling rule we establish here is consistent both with the procedures of Rule 23 and with the proper function of the limitations statute. While criticisms of Rule 23 and its impact on the federal courts have been both numerous and trenchant, see, *e.g.*, American College of Trial Lawyers, Report and Recommendations of the Special Committee on Rule 23 of the Federal Rules of Civil Procedure (1972); H. Friendly, Federal Jurisdiction: A General View 118–120 (1973); Handler, The Shift from Substantive to Procedural Innovations in Antitrust Suits—The Twenty-Third Annual Antitrust Review, 71 Col. L. Rev. 1, 5–12 (1971); Handler, Twenty-Fourth Annual Antitrust Review, 72 Col. L. Rev. 1, 34–42 (1972), this interpretation of the Rule is nonetheless necessary to insure effectuation of the purposes of litigative efficiency and economy that the Rule in its present form was designed to serve.

III.

Finally, the petitioners urge that the Court of Appeals' reversal of the District Court for failure to permit intervention under Rule 24(b)(2) was nonetheless improper because the District Court in denying such permission was doing no more than exercising a legal discretion which the Court of Appeals did not find to be abused. They point out that Rule 24(b) explicitly refers to a district judge's permission to intervene as an exercise of discretion, and that this Court has held that "the exercise of discretion in a matter of this sort is not reviewable by an appellate court unless clear abuse is shown...." *Allen Calculators, Inc. v. National Cash Register Co.*, 322 U.S. 137, 142.

In denying permission to intervene in this case, however, Judge Pence did not purport to weigh the competing considerations in favor of and against intervention, but simply found that the prospective intervenors were absolutely barred by the statute of limitations. This determination was not an exercise of discretion, but rather a conclusion of law which the Court of Appeals correctly found to be erroneous. The judgment of the Court of Appeals reversing the District Court's order directed that the case be remanded "for further proceedings upon the motions [to intervene]." Rather than reviewing an exercise of discretion, the Court of Appeals merely directed that discretion be exercised.

IV.

It remains to determine the precise effect the commencement of the class action had on the relevant limitation period. Section 5(b) of the Clayton Act provides that the running of the statutes of limitations be "suspended" by the institution of a Government antitrust suit based on the same subject matter. The same concept leads to the conclusion that the commencement of the class action in this case suspended the running of the limitation period only during the pendency of the motion to strip the suit of its class action character. The class suit brought by Utah was filed with 11 days yet to run in the period as tolled by

§ 5(b), and the intervenors thus had 11 days after the entry of the order denying them participation in the suit as class members in which to move for permission to intervene. Since their motions were filed only eight days after the entry of Judge Pence's order, it follows that the motions were timely.

The judgment of the Court of Appeals for the Ninth Circuit is therefore Affirmed.

Notes and Problems

1. What are the primary purposes behind a statute of limitations? In the context of the *American Pipe* case, were those purposes fulfilled notwithstanding the fact that the proposed intervenors' claims would normally have been time-barred?

2. Another way to consider the foundation for the *American Pipe* rule is to consider the alternative. If no tolling occurred by the filing of a putative class action, what risks would a class member be taking by failing to file their own lawsuit or seeking intervention? Would encouraging the filing of those individual lawsuits or mass interventions be helpful in any way? How does the *American Pipe* rule eliminate such incentives? Does this case elevate efficiency concerns over fairness for the rights of defendants?

3. *Problem.* A potential new client, Amy, comes to see you concerning an accident in her Chevy Malibu three years ago due to the brakes' failure. In your state, the applicable statute of limitations on personal injury products liability suits is two years from the date of the injury. Should you simply dismiss her from your office with the bad news that it is already too late to sue the manufacturer? What advice should you give?

Chapter Problem Revisited

Assume the class counsel and defendant's counsel, after engaging in six months' worth of discovery and motion practice, have reached a tentative settlement. They have agreed to file a joint motion for class certification under Rule 23(b)(3), to provide notice to the entire class by publication (arguing that the whereabouts of class members today is difficult to ascertain given the passage of time and the fact that defendant did not keep records of residential addresses of ticket purchasers— their address information being the possession of their credit card issuing banks), and to the following relief: (a) plaintiff and defendant have agreed that defendant will alter its business practices by using larger signage at its ticket kiosks (and larger, more conspicuous print online) advising purchasers that they will pay a higher "service charge" for using a credit card; (b) that the court will enter a declaration stating that this altered business practice is lawful and does not constitute an impermissible "credit surcharge"; (c) that because the class members' identities are so difficult to ascertain and their current addresses are not in the possession of the parties, there will be a *cy pres* award of $5 million worth of tickets that defendant will provide to concerts during the next two years through local boy scout and girl scout groups; (d) that defendant will not oppose any request by class counsel for attorney's fees in an amount to be determined by the court up to $3 million; and (e) plaintiff's class representative will receive an incentive award of $25,000 for her time spent assisting class counsel in this matter (visiting with counsel, attending depositions, giving her own deposition, etc).

You are the law clerk for the district court overseeing this class action and this tentative settlement is put before you for tentative, preliminary approval. Using the appropriate factors under Rule 23(e), should you recommend to your judge that she approve the settlement? Do you see any red flags about which the court should inquire further? Spend 30 minutes writing out your advice to the court in memorandum form.

Upon Further Review

Even beyond the ultimate class action issue — certification — there are a host of other legal issues that impact where a class action can be filed (geographically), whether a federal forum will be available (subject matter jurisdiction), which states' laws will need to be applied if a diversity class action, who is entitled to notice of certification (and in what form) and what rights are bestowed upon individual unnamed class members. Beyond this, perhaps the next most important decision a trial court must make in most class actions is whether to approve a settlement. Because of the court's unique role as a near fiduciary of the absent class members, the court must hear testimony and reach a decision binding upon the entire class as to whether to approve a settlement and bind the class members to its terms. Trial courts have a very active role to play in class action management and this chapter has presented a sampling of those but far from a comprehensive examination of all of the day to day oversight trial judges are called upon to undertake for proper adjudication and resolution of a class action.

Going Deeper

Additional recommended readings to enhance your understanding of some of the topics in this Chapter include:

- Manual for Complex Litigation, 4th, §§ 21–22.

- Newberg on Class Actions Vol. 1, Chapters 3–4 (5th ed. West).

- On the issue of whether CAFA is pro-plaintiff class or pro-defendant, compare *Class Action Fairness Act: A Panel of Experts Discuss Whether the New Law Governing Class Actions Is a Needed Fix or a Bad Idea*, 27 National L.J. 18 (2005) (arguing CAFA is decidedly pro-defendant), with Andrew McGuinness & Richard Gottlieb, *New Class Action Law Contains Pitfalls for Defendants*, 28 Chicago Lawyer 60 (2005).

- William B. Rubenstein, *The Fairness Hearing: Adverserial and Regulatory Approaches*, 53 U.C.L.A. L. Rev. 1435 (2006).

Chapter 6

Attorney's Fees

Chapter Goals

- Understand the different ways attorneys might bill for their services and the benefits and criticisms of each approach.

- Grasp the two scenarios where courts are called upon to decide the manner of computation and to assess attorney's fees when there is no governing contract to control the answers to those questions.

- Learn the differences between fee-shifting and common fund scenarios in terms of the source of the attorney's fee payments and the preferences of courts for using either the lodestar or the percentage method to calculate reasonable fees.

- Recognize the various ways a common fund might be created through a lawyer's efforts.

- Appreciate the unique role and power of a trial judge on the paramount issue of attorney's fees in complex litigation.

A. Overview

The final stop on our study involves the all-important subject of attorney's fees. Complex litigation typically involves intensive efforts by legal counsel and is sometimes fueled by the specter of a sizable award of attorney's fees at the conclusion of the litigation. In fact, some class action lawsuits seem to be solely motivated by the potential recovery of attorney's fees, such as some negative-value class actions where the typical class member might have a claim worth pennies but counsel might recover millions in fees. It is worth pausing to consider directly the role of attorney's fees in complex litigation and some of the legal issues involved with a court's assessment of attorney's fees. Below, consider the context where this issue will frequently arise—after the resolution of a class action when the class counsel comes to the court with a fee request pursuant to Rule 23(h).

B. Chapter 6 Problem

The following problem is a continuation of the problem from Chapter 5 Management of Class Actions. As you will recall, Huey News filed a class action against TicketNinja.Com and a local authorized seller of its tickets, Simply Beautiful, in Little Rock, Arkansas, federal court. Consider the following additional materials showing the resolution of that lawsuit and class counsel's request for fees.

Arkansas Democrat Gazette

Little Rock—A Little Rock federal judge held a so-called "fairness hearing" today on the national class action brought by a Mena resident against mega-ticket seller TicketNinja.Com and others. The case alleged an unlawful business practice to assess an illegal credit surcharge on ticket-buying customers using credit cards in lieu of cash. Today the court was full of lawyers from across the nation presenting arguments for and against the settlement. The settlement involves a change of business practices by Ninja to add transparency to its dual-line charging system, a declaration of the legality of that new practice, a promise by Ninja to contribute $10 million annually for the next three years in free tickets to charitable organizations (primarily boy scouts and girl scouts troops across the country), a one-time donation of $5 million to the University of Arkansas-Little Rock Law School to fund a new advocacy center for consumer rights, and an agreement to pay the attorney's fees of class counsel in an amount to be determined by the court. During the hearing, counsel for Ninja (Jackie Chiles) argued passionately that the original claims were "weak, unjustified, unfounded, unprecedented, and unconscionable!" Oddly enough, counsel for the class (D. Bumpers) admitted that while the claims were brought in a good faith effort to lessen the costs of doing business with Ninja through the use of credit cards, he was not aware of any prior court holding that a cash discount was unlawful. He said that given this lack of precedent, he did the best he could to at least force a settlement that would make the business practices more "above board and fair to future customers of Ninja" and to "do some good for boys and girls in Arkansas and throughout the nation." Mr. Bumpers also stated that starting the advocacy center for consumers at the University of Arkansas Law School (where both he and the trial judge graduated) would be something that would "benefit all consumers in Arkansas and the nation for a long time in the future." After a full day hearing, the court said that "given the questionable nature of the claims and the difficulty in getting cash back into the pockets of class members, this was the best deal" he could imagine for the class and approved it. Next up on the agenda is determining legal fees for Mr. Bumpers and his firm. In the settlement, defendant Ninja agreed it would not oppose an order imposing fees on it of up to $5 million as part of the settlement.

United States District Court
Eastern District of Arkansas
Little Rock Division

Huey News	§	
	§	
vs.	§	Civil Action
	§	No. 17-6185
TicketNinja.Com	§	

Order Approving Settlement

Before the court is the Joint Motion for Final Approval of the Proposed Settlement Agreement pursuant to Rule 23(e).

The Court has previously provided preliminary approval of the settlement and ordered a Fairness Hearing. That hearing was held on this date and the court heard testimony from proponents of the settlement and testimony from one objecting class member. The essence of the objection was the failure to provide monetary relief directly to the pockets of any class members. The court agrees with plaintiff and defendant that doing so would be virtually impossible due to the circumstances of this case. Further, the court concludes that the proposed settlement is the best deal that could be obtained for the class given the nature of the claims. Accordingly, it is hereby ORDERED as follows:

1. The settlement is found to be fair, reasonable, and adequate and in the best interests of the class members previously certified in this matter.

2. The court also accepts the new "Business Practices" of defendant TicketNinja and declares these practices to be lawful and proper.

3. The court determines that the notice of settlement previously authorized by publication was undertaken appropriately and that the class has received the notice that it was due.

4. All Rule 23(a)–(b) prerequisites for maintenance of this class action were satisfied.

5. The parties' settlement is hereby APPROVED.

6. All claims in this case are hereby DISMISSED and defendants RELEASED from further liability. The class claims are hereby DISMISSED WITH PREJUDICE.

7. This Court will maintain jurisdiction over this matter to determine the appropriate attorney's fees under Rule 23(h) and to monitor the defendants' compliance with the terms of the settlement agreement.

8. Plaintiff Huey News is awarded a $25,000 payment from TicketNinja as an incentive award.

9. Class counsel is directed to file its motion for attorney's fees within 10 days from the date of entry of this order.

Honorable Judge of Said Court

United States District Court
Eastern District of Arkansas
Little Rock Division

Huey News	§		
	§		
vs.	§	Civil Action	
	§	No. 17-6185	
TicketNinja.Com	§		

Rule 23(h) Motion for Attorney's Fees

Now comes class counsel, D. Bumpers, Esq., and moves this court for approval of the following requested fees and expenses:

1. Class counsel asks this court to determine the "reasonable attorney's fees" due him pursuant to this Court's inherent authority and Rule 23(h). As counsel for this class, appointed by this Court, the undersigned has faithfully pursued the class claims for nearly two years devoting the majority of his time to this case. Counsel has not been paid any fees from his original client, Mr. News, nor will counsel be sharing in any of the benefits bestowed on the class by virtue of this lawsuit and the settlement now approved by this Court.

2. Counsel's efforts bestowed a significant benefit on the class of at least $15 million. The actual value may increase due to the anticipated efforts of the new University of Arkansas Law School Advocacy Center for Consumer Reports being funded by the settlement. Counsel has also managed to cause Defendant TicketNinja to alter its business practices going forward to avoid further consumer confusion and harm.

3. A reasonable fee for consumer cases such as this would be set as a percentage of the total recovery. In this case 30% is appropriate for a fee of $5 million. Counsel also seeks recovery of $150,000 in out of pocket expenses incurred for discovery, filing fees, and retention of expert witnesses. Mr. News did not fund any of the costs of this action.

4. Counsel would also show the court via the affidavits being filed simultaneously herewith that he and the two associates working under his guidance on this case have together spent nearly 5,000 hours on this case during the last two years. At a reasonable hourly aggregate rate (the normal rates charged by similarly experienced counsel in large metropolitan areas) of $500 per hour, this amounts to $2.5 million in time. Given the contingency nature of the representation, counsel asks for a multiplier of 2 for a total request of $5 million plus expenses.

5. Finally, defendant TicketNinja has indicated per the settlement agreement a willingness to pay up to $5 million in fees in addition to funding the remaining settlement obligations.

Respectfully submitted.

C. Historical Perspective on Attorney Fee Calculation

Many instances of attorney representation involve no significant role for the court to play in fee assessment. The United States' general policy is, of course, referred to as the "American Rule"—that each party to litigation absorbs the cost of its own counsel. And because clients normally retain counsel pursuant to agreements which spell out the terms of representation, including how compensation will be determined, courts have virtually no role to play in determining the amount of attorney's fees in such instances. If Peter hires Mary to represent him in suing General Motors, they will enter into a fee agreement that will set forth the scope of representation and the method by which Mary's legal fees will be determined. Unless there is a dispute between the two over the proper amount of fees (or an ethical grievance is filed against Mary involving a claim that her fees were excessive), the courts will not be involved.

"A contingency fee arrangement is 'the poor man's key to the courthouse.'"

Nicole Luguori Micklich, *Providing Keys to the Courthouse Without Giving Up Full Recovery*, 2 Construct! 15 (Winter 2006, American Bar Association).

The private methods of determining the amount of attorney's fees have shifted over time. At one point, it was standard for a lawyer to assess a fixed (or "flat") fee for a particular type of legal representation. You may recall the fictional character Atticus Finch from "To Kill a Mockingbird" charging his client "Mr. Cunningham" a bag of hickory nuts in exchange for some legal work. This was a fairly simple and straightforward mechanism for determining the fee where both lawyer and client knew up front about the costs of the legal representation. During the 1960s and 1970s, it seems that many law firms began instead shifting to an hourly fee approach, perhaps in response to litigation becoming increasingly time-intensive as both new causes of action were created, liberalized joinder (and class action) rules resulted in multi-party cases, and enhanced discovery methods were resulting in lawyers having to expend more time handling litigation. Or perhaps the shift resulted from lawyers recognizing that they could "churn" their files and make more money at the expense of their clients—if you tend toward the cynical world-view. Of course, not all clients could afford to hire counsel at their normal hourly rates. For many aggrieved victims, paying a lawyer by the hour was writing a blank check that their pocketbooks could not afford. For such clients, a contingency fee arrangement was the only way that they could afford to retain the services of a lawyer. And until recently, this had become the way legal fees were calculated—the rich would pay lawyers by the hour and the poor would sell a piece of their cause of action (a percentage of the ultimate recovery) in exchange for the lawyer taking the case.

"Alternative fee arrangements are like teenage sex. There's a lot more people talking about it than doing it—and those that are doing it don't really know what they're doing."

Loomis, *GCs Say the Pressure's On to Get Rid of the Billable Hour*, S.F. Recorder (August 21, 2009 at 2).

Particularly with the economic recessions of the early 1980s and, more recently, the near collapse of the world's economy in 2008, clients began pressing law firms for more options than the hourly fee. So-called *alternative fee arrangements* have been on the rise. An alternative fee arrangement is simply referring to some attorney's fees method that involves something other than normal hourly fees. A contingency fee is one example; while these are not new, their application to corporate interests that can afford to pay by the hour is relatively novel. Another alternative has been a slight trend back toward a fixed fee method. Perhaps you've seen a billboard by the highway advertising legal services for a "Simple Uncontested Divorce" or "Simple Bankruptcy" or the writing of a will for a flat, advertised amount by the lawyer. Experimentation with a return back to this model for certain transactional legal work has become more familiar. There are also hybrid models, such as a mixed hourly-fee and contingent fee arrangement whereby the firm receives an hourly fee during the litigation at a reduced amount (perhaps 50% of the standard hourly fee) as well as a small contingency fee interest in the case (perhaps at 10%). In litigation, there have also been instances of a "reverse contingency fee." At least one personal instance where this author has witnessed this type of fee is when another law professor agreed to handle the appeal on a sizable judgment for the defendant. The professor would receive no compensation unless he obtained a reversal of the judgment on appeal. If successful, the professor would be paid a fee of $1 million. (The professor did win the appeal.) Some firms have more recently experimented with taking an equity interest in a client's business in exchange for legal work, such as organizational work done on behalf of a small internet start-up company.

"If I had only one wish for our profession from the proverbial genie, I would want us to move toward something better than dollars times hours. We have created a zero-sum game in which we are selling our lives, not just our time."

Scott Turrow, *The Billable Hour* (ABA Journal, August 2007).

As for the merits of the various methods used to assess fees, one can fairly say that each approach has some merit. An hourly fee assessment for attorney's fees helps to prevent a windfall of a lawyer receiving compensation far out of proportion to their efforts, is typically paid on a regular basis while litigation drags on, and provides a regular source of cash flow for a lawyer to run their practice. Also, because litigation is often so unpredictable, hourly-assessed fees seem far better than a lawyer's guess at the inception of litigation as to the amount of work that will be necessary to bring the case to a conclusion. A flat fee has the benefit of making it easy for the client to budget for the expense of representation but is awfully hard to set in a fair and precise manner for anything beyond the most routine and simple representation. A flat fee also encourages counsel to work as efficiently as possible, unlike the hourly fee, because the lawyer will not get paid any extra fees no matter how much extra time they expend. A contingency fee has the enormous benefit of permitting someone of modest means to still be able to afford legal representation. It also comes closest to aligning the interests of client and lawyer because they are both interested in maximizing the greatest possible recovery. With a contingency fee, lawyer and client are almost partners in the endeavor of obtaining a recovery for their common distribution. Contingency fee representation also removes any incentive for a lawyer to pad their hours or churn the file. It encourages maximum efficiency in representation by the lawyer who will get paid the same fee regardless of how many hours are expended. On the other hand, if a client with a great case comes to a lawyer and has signed a contingency fee contract, the lawyer may recover handsomely regardless of the quality or inferiority of their work.

But thus far we have focused upon the varieties of methods available to lawyer and client when they choose to form a relationship and pursue a litigation objective together. Which method is best is up to them to decide. What about instances when there is no opportunity to set forth by contract the manner and methods of assessing attorney's fees?

D. Courts' Involvement in Assessing Attorney's Fees

1. Exceptions to the American Rule

You may wonder why courts ever would need to be involved in the assessment of attorney's fees. Isn't it just a matter of private contract between client and counsel, where courts only need to intervene if ethics rules have been violated by attempted imposition of a particularly excessive demand? While this is typically true, there are a few important instances where courts need to assess the amount of fees themselves without any governing contractual guidance.

Principles

"Under most fee-shifting statutes, attorney's fees are only awarded to a 'prevailing' plaintiff. A prevailing litigant is one 'who has succeeded on any significant claim affording it some of the relief sought' and does not require victory on every issue or every claim." *See, e.g., Texas Teachers Ass'n v. Garland School District*, 489 U.S. 782, 791 (1989).

There are two primary occasions when the court needs to set the attorney's fee: (1) when a fee-shifting statute (or perhaps a contract between the litigants) provides for the recovery of attorney's fees by a prevailing party—in this instance the losing party pays the fees as an additional item of damages, in effect; and (2) in "common fund" scenarios where the court determines that, despite the absence of any enforceable attorney's fee agreement, because the attorney's efforts have bestowed a benefit on the "client," the lawyer should be entitled to a reasonable fee—these fees come out of the common fund and serve to decrease the recovery by the clients. In either instance, because there is no contract setting forth the terms of compensation and method of computation, the court presiding over the case must make that decision.

Complex litigation often involves statutory claims for which the prevailing plaintiff might be authorized to receive from the litigation loser attorney's fees. As to common funds, the two most recurring common fund scenarios arise in MDL litigation conducted pursuant to § 1407 and Rule 23 class actions. Another has framed the dynamics of this inquiry as follows:

> The amount of fees and expenses paid to class counsel must ultimately be de-termined by the court. With respect to fee-shifting statutes ... the fees will be

paid by the defendant ... [who doesn't] have the ability to control the reasonableness of class counsel's fee requests. In the case of fees from a common fund, counsel's request for compensation creates a direct conflict of interest with the class. Because class members are dispersed, disorganized, and typically have a relatively small stake in the outcome of the litigation, the class cannot protect itself against an unreasonable fee request. Again, court protection is required to prevent counsel from enriching themselves at the expense of the class.[1]

When the court is required to set the fee because the party paying the fees has not already agreed to a method of calculating attorney's fees pursuant to a contract (whether that is the defendant or the represented class) there are two prevailing methods available—the lodestar calculation and the percentage method. Which method to employ has been the subject of many published decisions from the courts and ongoing scholarly debate. We turn to that issue next.

2. How to Calculate the Fee

When a court is called upon the set the fee, either in the fee-shifting statute scenario or the common fund scenario, most courts have considered between the two options of the so-called *lodestar method* and the *percentage fee* recovery models. The lodestar method essentially involves finding, for the circumstances of that particular case, what the reasonable hourly rate should be and then multiplying that by the number of hours reasonably expended by counsel (and their legal assistants) in achieving the litigation victory. Under this model, courts will then consider whether some "multiplier" should be used to enhance the sum of the lodestar perhaps due to exceptional circumstances such as the improbability of achieving success in the first place, particular barriers to recovery that were overcome, the emergency nature of the litigation that required counsel to drop other matters during the pendency of the case, and any other number of circumstances that compel courts to conclude that the hourly approach might undercompensate counsel.

In Practice

Some examples of federal fee-shifting statutes include claims of prevailing parties under the following:

- Fair Labor Standard Act, 29 U.S.C. § 8
- Age Discrimination Act, 29 U.S.C. § 621
- American with Disabilities Act, 42 U.S.C. § 1211
- Civil Rights Act, 42 U.S.C. § 1983
- Equal Access to Justice Act, 42 U.S.C. § 2412
- Clayton Antitrust Act, 15 U.S.C. § 12
- Copyright Act, 17 U.S.C. § 505
- RICO Act, 18 U.S.C. § 1964

---

1. Theodore Eisenberg & Geoffrey P. Miller, *Attorney Fees in Class Actions: An Empirical Study*, 1 Journal of Empirical Legal Studies 27, 30 (2004).

- Fair Debt Collection Act, 15 U.S.C. § 1692

- Patent Infringement, 35 U.S.C. § 385 (only in certain cases involving in-equitable conduct).

- Freedom of Information Act, 5 U.S.C. § 552

A few examples under some states' laws where fee-shifting statutes depart from the American rule:

- Breach of contract actions

- Deceptive trade practices claims

- Lemon laws

The alternative method is for the court to simply find what an appropriate percentage would be to apply toward the total monetary amount obtained through the lawyer's efforts on the case and to give the counsel this resulting sum. *In re Activision Sec. Litig.* illustrates a court trying to determine as between these two methods which one to choose. As you read the opinion, consider three possible perspectives on the issue as you contemplate which method is best: (a) the perspective of the plaintiff's counsel who presumably desires the fee to be as great as possible, (b) the perspective of the person from whom the fees will be paid (either the "clients" in the case of class action representation or the defendant in a fee-shifting scenario) who presumably would desire for the fee to be as small as possible, and (c) the perspective of the court that has to do the dirty work of determining the fee.

In re Activision Sec. Litigation

723 F. Supp. 1373 (N.D. Cal. 1989)

PATEL, J.,

This case has followed the all too familiar path of large securities cases. It was filed as a class action by a number of well-recognized lawyers who specialize in plaintiffs' securities litigation. The complaint named the usual cast of defendants—the corporation issuing the shares, in this case when the corporation went public; the officers and directors; the underwriters; the corporation's accountants; and a variety of venture capital defendants who sold their shares at or near the time the corporation went public. Various defendants moved to dismiss and the case moved lugubriously through the pleadings phase. Discovery assumed its usual massive proportions, and finally, as the case wound down toward trial, settlement negotiations became serious and were aggressively pursued. On the eve of trial, after the parties had expended significant attorneys' time and, hence, accumulated the routinely anticipated hours and fees, the case was settled.

Then began the process which all too often consumes a disproportionate share of the court's time, the application for attorneys' fees. It is at this point in these and other common fund cases that the court is abandoned by the adversary system and left to the plaintiff's unilateral application and the judge's own good conscience. Rarely do the settling defendants, who have created the pool of money from which the attorneys' fees are awarded, offer any counterpoint; rarely do members of the class come forward with any response or opposition to the fees sought. There are no amici curiae who volunteer their advice.

For its guidance during this solitary inquiry, the court is confronted with a mountain of computerized billing records and, of course, the obligatory *Lindy* or *Kerr* factors. See

Lindy Bros. Builders, Inc. of Philadelphia v. Am. Radiator & Standard Sanitary Corp., ("*Lindy I*"), 487 F.2d 161 (3d Cir. 1973), aff'd in part and vacated in part, 540 F.2d 102 (3d Cir. 1976) ("*Lindy II*"); *Kerr v. Screen Extras Guild, Inc.,* 526 F.2d 67, 48 L. Ed. 2d 195, 96 S. Ct. 1726 (9th Cir. 1975), cert. denied sub nom., *Perkins v. Screen Extras Guild, Inc.,* 425 U.S. 951, 48 L. Ed. 2d 195, 96 S. Ct. 1726 (1976). *Lindy* established the "lodestar" system for calculation of fees. Under this system the court determines the hours reasonably expended and a reasonable hourly rate. The product of these two factors is the "lodestar" to which a multiplier may be applied in appropriate circumstances. Keri is this circuit's adoption of the Fifth Circuit formulation in *Johnson v. Georgia Highway Express, Inc.,* 488 F.2d 714 (5th Cir. 1974). Under *Johnson* and *Kerr*, a twelve-factor analysis is applied. The *Lindy* and *Kerr-Johnson* approaches are not dissimilar. However, the latter method is the more cumbersome and includes factors that are often inapplicable to a particular case.

Courts have pursued a number of alternatives at the fee application stage. Some, by themselves or with the assistance of a magistrate, have waded through the computer printouts, which often represent years of work by several firms, their partners, associates, and paralegals. Others have appointed special masters familiar with the field and with attorney billing to perform the details of the task and to make a recommendation. The special master is then paid from the common fund. This court has used both of these alternatives. Undoubtedly, there are more creative ones that other courts have found. What is curious is that whatever method is used and no matter what billing records are submitted to the *Lindy* or *Kerr-Johnson* regimen, the result is an award that almost always hovers around 30% of the fund created by the settlement.

The question this court is compelled to ask is, "Is this process necessary?" Under a cost-benefit analysis, the answer would be a resounding, "No!" Not only do the *Lindy* and *Kerr-Johnson* analyses consume an undue amount of court time with little resulting advantage to anyone, but, in fact, it may be to the detriment of the class members. They are forced to wait until the court has done a thorough, conscientious analysis of the attorneys' fee petition. Or, class members may suffer a further diminution of their fund when a special master is retained and paid from the fund. Most important, however, is the effect the process has on the litigation and the timing of settlement. Where attorneys must depend on a lodestar approach there is little incentive to arrive at an early settlement. The history of these cases demonstrates this as noted below in the discussion of typical percentage awards.

In Practice

"Over 150 statutes, covering actions ranging from antitrust and civil rights to little known types of claims, authorize courts to depart from the American Rule and award attorney's fees to a prevailing party."

Manual for Complex Litigation, Fourth, § 14.11 (2004).

Adoption of a policy of awarding approximately 30% of the fund as attorneys' fees in the ordinary case is well-justified in light of the lengthy line of cases which find such an award appropriate and reasonable before or after superimposing the *Lindy* or *Kerr* factors. Several years of this practice and the body of case law across the circuits validate this approach. The Supreme Court has accepted it. In *Blum v. Stenson*, 465 U.S. 886, 900 n. 16 (1984), the Court noted approvingly the use of a percentage of the common fund to set attorneys' fees in common fund cases. In fact, the language of the note appears to assume that the percentage approach is routine. Distinguishing attorneys' fee determinations under fee shifting statutes such as 42 U.S.C. § 1988, the Court observed:

> Unlike the calculation of attorney's fees under the "common fund doctrine," where a reasonable fee is based on a percentage of the fund bestowed on the class, a reasonable fee under § 1988 reflects the amount of attorney time reasonably expended on the litigation.

Id.

The Third Circuit, home of the *Lindy* formulation, recently criticized its application in common fund cases and recommended a return to a percentage of the fund approach. In the *Report of the Third Circuit Task Force, Court Awarded Attorney Fees*, 108 F.R.D. 237 (1985), the Task Force concluded that the *Lindy* method was a "cumbersome, enervating, and often surrealistic process of preparing and evaluating fee petitions that now plagues the Bench and Bar...." *Id.* at 258. According to the Task Force, the percentage scheme with appropriate judicial supervision would ordinarily be adequate to protect the integrity of the fee award process. It recommended that early in the litigation the court set or "negotiate" a percentage-based fee and offered a number of suggestions for fashioning a mechanism for fee setting. *Id.* at 255–58. This court agrees with the Task Force's conclusion that a number of salutary effects can be achieved by this procedure, including removing the inducement to unnecessarily increase hours, prompting early settlement, reducing burdensome paperwork for counsel and the court and providing a degree of predictability to fee awards.

[Many commentators] criticize the use of *Lindy* or *Kerr-Johnson* in common fund cases and recommend a percentage approach. It has been wisely stated by Professor Coffee that:

> If one wishes to economize on the judicial time that is today invested in monitoring class and derivative litigation, the highest priority should be given to those reforms that restrict collusion and are essentially self-policing. The percentage of the recovery award formula is such a "deregulatory" reform because it relies on incentives rather than costly monitoring. Ultimately, this "deregulatory" approach is the only alternative to converting the courts into the equivalent of public utility commissions that oversee the plaintiff's attorney and elaborately fix the attorney's "fair" return.

Coffee, *Understanding the Plaintiffs' Attorney: The Implications of Economic Theory for Private Enforcement of Law Through Class and Derivative Actions*, 86 Colum. L. Rev. 669, 724–25 (1986).

One circuit has explicitly approved the percentage approach in holding that the "'common fund' doctrine recognizes percentage awards and is not restricted purely to the lodestar method." *Bebchick v. Wash. Metro. Area Transit Comm'n*, 805 F.2d 396, 407 (D.C.Cir. 1986). In *Bebchick*, the court determined the lodestar and the multiplier with a thorough consideration of each of these components. The court still ended up with an attorneys' fee award that was approximately 25% of the common fund and justified that amount as equitable.

In another recent decision, the Seventh Circuit described the difference between the common fund and statutory fee-shifting bases for attorneys' fees. *Skelton v. Gen. Motors Corp.*, 860 F.2d 250 (7th Cir. 1988), cert. denied, 493 U.S. 810 (1989). *Skelton* involved class action consumer claims under the Magnuson-Moss Warranty-Federal Trade Commission Improvement Act ("Magnuson-Moss Act"), 15 U.S.C. §§ 2301–2312. That

Act contains a fee-shifting provision. The parties ultimately settled the action and as a part of the settlement established a fund of $17 million. The district court had awarded a fee representing approximately 11% of the fund, but had denied the attorneys' request for a multiplier of 75%.

The court of appeals noted that there is greater reluctance to award multipliers in fee-shifting or "statutory" cases than in common fund or "equitable" cases. Despite the differences, the court found that a risk multiplier was not precluded under the Magnuson-Moss Act and instructed the district court to reconsider whether a 75% or less enhancement was appropriate. It is interesting that after its lengthy discussion of the doctrinal differences between the two methods, the court still indicated the same approach for both types of cases — calculation of the lodestar and, where justified, determination of the multiplier.

Judge Peckham of this court has observed that the Ninth Circuit, while adhering to the *Kerr-Johnson* factors, "has not, however, disapproved the use of the percentage of recovery approach in an appropriate case." *Kirkorian v. Borelli*, 695 F. Supp. 446, 455 (N.D.Cal. 1988). Nevertheless, after faithfully applying the *Kerr-Johnson* methodology to a class action securities settlement where a fund of $4 million was created, the court still awarded attorneys' fees of approximately 25% of the fund.

This week this circuit for the first time acknowledged that the percentage method may be a better approach in some cases, referring to *Paul, Johnson, Alston & Hunt v. Graulty*, 886 F.2d 268 (9th Cir. 1989). Citing only to *Mashburn*, the court noted the acceptance of 25% as the benchmark from which the award may be adjusted upward or downward. The court concluded that "25 percent has been a proper benchmark figure, ..." and any adjustment should be "accompanied by a reasonable explanation of why the benchmark is unreasonable under the circumstances." The Ninth Circuit's opinion does not appear to foreclose, upon appropriate findings, the setting of a different benchmark, since it left "to the district court the task of determining what this reasonable percentage should be." *Id*. The 25% was given for guidance and the court indicated it would approve use of that figure.

This court's review of recent reported cases discloses that nearly all common fund awards range around 30% even after thorough application of either the lodestar or twelve-factor method. Most of these cases achieve this result after lengthy motion practice, volumes of discovery, and hence, the accumulation of extensive attorney time on behalf of all parties.

A review of the cases and this court's own analysis of other recent cases shows that the benchmark is at approximately 30% of the fund. See, e.g., *Golden v. Shulman*, [1988–89 Decisions Transfer Binder] Fed.Sec.L.Rep. (CCH) P 94,060 (E.D.N.Y. 1988) (calculating lodestar, applying multiplier and finding that 30% is within range and justified; action pending for three years, class had been certified and significant amount of discovery completed); *In re AIA Indus., Inc. Sec. Litig.*, No. 84-2276 (E.D. Pa. March 31, 1988) (1988 WL 33883 (E.D. Pa.) (33% awarded after substantial discovery done and lengthy settlement negotiations; case pending approximately 4 years); *Sherin v. Smith*, [1987–88 Decisions Transfer Binder] Fed.Sec.L.Rep. (CCH) P 93,582 (E.D. Pa. 1987) (award including multiplier 27.9%; court commented on the efficiency with which the case was resolved and took that into consideration in setting fee); *In re Fiddler's Woods Bondholders Litig.*, [1987–88 Decisions Transfer Binder] Fed.Sec.L.Rep. (CCH) P 93,537 (E.D.Pa.1987) (award of 32.7% in settlement entered into mid-trial); *Greene v. Emersons Ltd.*, [1987 Decisions Transfer Binder] Fed.Sec.L.Rep. (CCH) P 93,263 (S.D.N.Y. 1987) (fees and costs were 46.2% in this protracted case taking over ten years to resolve); *Spencer v. Comserv Corp.*, [1987 Decisions Transfer

Binder] Fed.Sec.L.Rep. (CCH) P 93,124 (D. Minn. 1986) (25% award in action involving substantial motion practice, discovery and hard fought class certification); *Basile v. Merrill Lynch, Pierce, Fenner, & Smith, Inc.*, 640 F. Supp. 697 (S.D.Ohio 1986) (25% awarded where case tenaciously litigated over four year period, tens of thousands of documents produced, many depositions taken); *Fickinger v. C.I.* Planning Corp., 646 F. Supp. 622 (E.D. Pa. 1986) (33% given in case pending for five years, plaintiffs had survived summary judgment and a number of other motions, and done significant amount of discovery); *Friedlander v. Barnes*, [1986–87 Decisions Transfer Binder] Fed.Sec.L.Rep. (CCH) P 92,754 (S.D.N.Y. 1986) (approximately 30% in case pending for two years where class certified, motion for summary judgment successfully opposed, substantial discovery and trial preparation completed); *Eltman v. Grandma Lee's, Inc.*, [1986–87 Decisions Transfer Binder] Fed.Sec.L.Rep. (CCH) P 92,798 (E.D.N.Y. 1986) (33% granted after four years of extensive discovery, motions and settlement negotiations).

Reviewing this history, the court is compelled to conclude that the accepted practice of applying the lodestar or *Kerr-Johnson* regime to common fund cases does not achieve the stated purposes of proportionality, predictability and protection of the class. It encourages abuses such as unjustified work and protracting the litigation. It adds to the work load of already overworked district courts. In short, it does not encourage efficiency, but rather, it adds inefficiency to the process.

Therefore, this court concludes that in class action common fund cases the better practice is to set a percentage fee and that, absent extraordinary circumstances that suggest reasons to lower or increase the percentage, the rate should be set at 30%. This will encourage plaintiffs' attorneys to move for early settlement, provide predictability for the attorneys and the class members, and reduce the time consumed by counsel and court in dealing with voluminous fee petitions.

In this case, the Special Master, Jerome I. Braun, has done a skillful job of thoroughly analyzing the attorney billing records, declarations, and documentation in light of *Lindy* and the *Kerr-Johnson* factors. The court adopts and approves the Special Master's Report and awards fees accordingly [recommending a 32.8% fee].

In the future, however, the court will opt for the percentage approach in common fund cases. This case demonstrates the reasons as discussed above. After three years of litigation, substantial discovery and motion practice, and on the eve of trial, a settlement was reached from which the attorneys will receive 32.8%. A similar result could have been achieved much earlier in the litigation. With early disposition there are fewer expenses to be deducted from the settlement fund, thereby creating an incentive of receiving a greater percentage of the fund in attorneys' fees. The integrity of the attorneys' fee application process would be enhanced and the class members would receive at least the same benefits and receive them earlier.

IT IS SO ORDERED.

Notes and Problems

1. Rule 23(h) now governs a court award of attorney's fees, at least in a procedural sense. Among other things, it states that "[i]n a certified class action, the court may award reasonable attorney's fees and nontaxable costs that are authorized by law or by the parties' agreement." Other than when a fee-shifting statute is involved, and thus statutory authority for an award of fees by the defendant to class counsel exists, the common law has authorized payment of fees out of the class reward (either from judgment after trial or from settlement)

based upon the common fund doctrine. As the U.S. Supreme Court has summarized this doctrine:

> Since the decisions in *Trustees v. Greenough*, 105 U.S. 527 (1882), this Court has recognized consistently that a litigant or a lawyer who recovers a common fund for the benefit of persons other than himself or his client is entitled to a reasonable attorney's fee from the fund as a whole. The common-fund doctrine reflects the traditional practice in courts of equity ... The doctrine rests on the perception that persons who obtain the benefit of a lawsuit without contributing to its cost are unjustly enriched at the successful litigant's expense. Jurisdiction over the fund involved in the litigation allows a court to prevent this inequity by assessing attorney's fees against the entire fund, thus spreading fees proportionately among those benefited by the suit.

Boeing Co. v. Van Gemert, 444 U.S. 472 (1980) (applying common fund to pay additional attorney's fees out of unclaimed portion of settlement funds created by a judgment). Thus, the common fund doctrine rests upon restitutionary principles. *See* Charles Silver, *A Restitutionary Theory of Attorney's Fees in Class Actions*, 76 Cornell L. Rev. 656 (1991). By contrast, under fee-shifting statutes, no such theory is necessary to justify the fee. The payment of the fees by the wrongdoer is more akin to an additional element of damages it must pay as a price for its wrongdoing.

2. What did the court consider to be the relative strengths of the lodestar method and the percentage method? Why did the court indicate that, moving forward, it would simply find the reasonable percentage and use that mechanism as its sole analysis for setting attorney's fees, even in common fund cases? Another court has suggested that courts (at least in common fund scenarios) use both methods—first considering the lodestar and then considering a reasonable percentage—before settling on its conclusion as to the total reasonable fee to assess in a case. *Matter of Superior Beverages/Glass Container Consolidated Pretrial*, 133 F.R.D. 119 (N.D. Ill. 1990) (addressing pros and cons of each technique and settling on a hybrid mechanism whereby court looks at both types of analysis before choosing the reasonable fee, the court referring stating that "fee determinations call for the exercise of informed discretion."). The Manual for Complex Litigation finds that in a common fund scenario, "the vast majority of courts of appeals now permit or direct district courts to use the percentage method." Manual for Complex Litigation, Fourth, § 14.121 (2004). The Manual for Complex Litigation also articulates some of the following critiques of the two methods:

- "In practice, the lodestar method is difficult to apply, time-consuming to administer, inconsistent in results, and capable of manipulation. In addition, the lodestar creates inherent incentive to prolong litigation until sufficient hours have been expended."

- "The percentage method also has been criticized as arbitrary, especially 'when applied by courts in an automatic fashion.' [A] single rate ... cannot capture variations in class actions' characteristics. A fixed benchmark will often yield fee awards that are excessive for certified class actions in which the risk of non-recovery is relatively small. Accordingly, in 'mega-cases' in which large settlements are awards serve as the basis for calculating a percentage, courts have often found considerably lower percentages of recovery to be appropriate."

Id.

3. As the court above indicated, the U.S. Supreme Court has expressed a preference (if not outright requirement) for use of the lodestar method in fee-shifting cases. *Hensley*

v. Eckerhart, 461 US 424, 428 (1983). On the other hand, *Hensley* at least implicitly approves of the use of the percentage method in common fund cases. Why would these two different contexts result in different preferences for the method of fee determination?

3. Fee Requests from Objectors' Counsel

Consistent with the common fund rationale undergirding courts' power to extract class counsel fees from the recovery obtained by class counsel for the class, courts have also recognized that sometimes a fee has been earned by counsel for class members who have objected to settlements (or class counsel fee requests) when their efforts have improved the net benefits obtained by the class. In the context of a fee request in the common fund scenario (where counsel fees come from the fruits of the litigation rather than an additional payment by defendant), courts are often left without any true adversarial process to help them sort through the issues and determine with assistance of counsel the appropriate fee. Class counsel is obviously interested in the issue and defendant may have no dog in the hunt. Because class members are often unaware or disinterested, the fee request may come with no healthy opposition. In this context, opposition from class members represented by their own separate counsel can be both desirable by, and useful to, the court. Courts have accordingly long recognized that objectors' counsel should be rewarded for producing positive fruit by transforming the settlement process into more of an adversarial process and improving the ultimate award received by the class members. In this way, objectors' efforts can increase the size of the net common fund, out of which objectors' counsel may be awarded a reasonable fee. But such entitlement to a fee is proper only when the objector's efforts have actually produced a better result for the class. From the first sentence of the following district court opinion, the court's view of the lack of such entitlement could not be more clear.

In re UnitedHealth Group PSLRA Litig.

643 F. Supp. 2d 1107 (D. Minn. 2009)

ROSENBAUM, J.,

The remoras are loose again. The Court has received a motion from attorneys Edward Siegel, Edward Cochran, Stuart Yoes, and Scott Browne (styling themselves "Objectors' Counsel"), seeking an award of fees. Their motion is emphatically denied.

I. *Background*

On December 22, 2008, the Court preliminarily approved a proposed settlement in this matter. The class received notice and was advised objections were due February 17, 2009. On that date, Objectors' Counsel, representing UnitedHealth shareholders Ernest J. Browne and Bruce Botchik, filed a single page document, later identified as an exhibit to their objections, purportedly documenting Mr. Botchik's UnitedHealth stock holdings.

"The single most important action that judges can take to support the public goals of class action litigation is to reward class action attorneys only for lawsuits that actually accomplish something of value to class members and society."

RAND, *Executive Summary, Class Action Dilemmas* 33 (1999).

Objectors' remaining submissions were untimely. On February 18, 2009, they filed a single-paragraph Notice identifying their prior filing as Exhibit A to their objections. No actual objections were filed until two weeks later, on March 4, 2009. Their late submission objected to class counsel's request for $110 million in attorney's fees and to reimbursement of class counsel's expenses—which class counsel were not seeking.

On August 11, 2009, this Court approved the class action settlement, and awarded class counsel nearly $64.8 million in attorney's fees.

II. *Analysis*

Rule 23 allows a court to award "reasonable attorney's fees." Fed. R. Civ. P. 23(h). Such an award is committed to the court's sound discretion. Those objecting to a class action settlement are not entitled to a fee award unless they confer a benefit on the class. See *In re Cardinal Health, Inc. Sec. Litig.*, 550 F. Supp. 2d 751, 753 (S.D. Ohio 2008). Objectors may add value to the process by:

> (1) transforming the fairness hearing into a truly adversarial proceeding; (2) supplying the Court with both precedent and argument to gauge the reasonableness of the settlement and lead counsel's fee request; and (3) preventing collusion between lead plaintiff and defendants.

These objectors have contributed nothing. Instead, in a pleading which may charitably be described as disingenuous, Objectors' Counsel argue they assisted the Court in finding class counsel's fee request unreasonable. They claim their efforts convinced the Court to reduce class counsel's fee from $110 million to $64.8 million. They have the temerity to suggest they are the ones who saved the class $45 million in attorney fees, entitling them to a six-figure fee of their own.[1]

Their suggestion is laughable. If the Court may be permitted an egregious paraphrase of Winston S. Churchill: Seldom in the field of securities litigation was so little owed by so many to so few. Objectors' Counsel make "outlandish fee requests in return for doing virtually nothing." *In re Cardinal Health,* 550 F. Supp. 2d at 753. And nothing is the quantity of assistance they have provided to the Court and the class. Their goal was, and is, to hijack as many dollars for themselves as they can wrest from a negotiated settlement. Objectors' eight-page-long, two-week-late pleading presented no facts, offered no law, and raised no argument upon which the Court relied in its deliberation or ruling concerning class counsel's motion for fees. Indeed, the Court expressly rejected the lion's share of objectors' arguments directed to the use of paralegals and contract attorneys.

Objectors' request and their motion ill-befit attorneys admitted to the bar. Accordingly, the Court holds, as a matter of fact and law, objectors have conferred no benefit whatsoever on the class or on the Court. Objectors' Counsel are entitled to an award equal to their contribution … nothing.

III. *Conclusion*

IT IS ORDERED that the motion is denied.

---

1. Objectors' Counsel maintain their "lodestar" is "approximately $74,500," and request a multiplier of 2.5. The Court considers it preposterous that any legitimate lawyer would charge $74,500 to prepare an eight-page submission, and submit it tardy to boot.

Notes and Problems

1. While courts may sometimes appreciate the efforts of objector's counsel, as you might imagine class counsel is never thrilled to see such characters arise on the scene. They are seen as at best disruptive and, at worst, as thieves trying to steal fees from class counsel for themselves. Or when the objector is pointing out flaws in the overall proposed settlement (rather than just critiquing the class counsel fee request), their objections might cause the court, under Rule 23(e), to refuse to approve the deal. Sometimes this can mean the case will have to be tried. More often, a court's refusal to approve a class settlement causes the parties to go back to the negotiating table to see if the deal can be re-worked to obtain court approval. Whether they are seen as good or evil, therefore, objectors and their counsel sometimes provide a useful service and sometimes do not. Some attorneys have become specialists at spotting possible objections with publicized pending class settlements and finding class members on whose behalf they file objections. When done properly, the rewards for such objector's counsel can be sizable, assuming their efforts are seen as valuable by the court rather than just an attempted grab at a piece of the pie.

2. In the foregoing case, where did objector's counsel go wrong? You can tell by the very opening line of the opinion that the court is upset with someone.

3. Another provision enacted as part of the Class Action Fairness Act deals with the computation of attorney's fees when a class action settlement results in coupon payments to the class:

> If a proposed settlement in a class action provides for a recovery of coupons to a class member, the portion of any attorney's fees award to class counsel that is attributable to the award of coupons shall be based on the value to class members of the coupons that are redeemed.

28 U.S.C. § 1712(a). Unlike another subsection of § 1712 we saw earlier — demanding that settlements involving coupons only be approved by courts if found to be "fair, reasonable, and adequate" for class members — the provision limiting attorney's fees to a ratio of the value of coupons actually redeemed by class members adds some real teeth to the perceived problem of junk coupon settlements. Some prior coupon settlements involved coupons of very questionable value to the class, most of which would probably never be utilized by class members. But if class counsel will only earn a fee based upon coupons actually utilized by class members, then counsel has extra incentive to only negotiate settlement involving coupons of real value and that are designed to truly benefit class members.

4. Can you articulate conceptually how a lawyer representing an objecting class member can earn a fee under the common fund doctrine?

5. *Chapter Problem.* Imagine that the Huey News case is certified as a Rule 23(b)(3) class action and the parties have agreed to a settlement, now approved by the court. At the fairness hearing, class counsel has requested a 30% share of the fees as attorney's fees using the common fund doctrine. A lawyer for an objecting class member succeeds in convincing the court to reduce that class counsel fee to 15% of the total recovery. If this reduction in fees serves to increase the total net settlement fund available to the class by an additional $5 million, should objecting counsel be able to obtain a fee from this additional $5 million in effect added back to the class fund? If so, how much in fees should the court award? Does it matter if the objecting counsel only spent 10 hours of time drafting the objections and attending the fairness hearing?

4. Fees in Non-Class Complex Litigation for Lead and Liaison Counsel

In some instances outside of class actions, complex litigation requires a court to deal with multiple lawyers representing multiple different clients on related cases that frequently involve common questions of law or fact. One example might involve a court's use of Rule 42(a) consolidation powers. Or when an MDL judge has received the transfer of a great number of related cases from the Judicial Panel on Multi-District Litigation under 28 U.S.C. § 1407. The traditional model of representation—where each lawyer gets to make their own decisions and communicate their client's positions directly to the court—is practically unworkable in some of these scenarios just due to the number of involved counsel. Affiliated or at least commonly-aligned parties need to stake out a certain position and communicate that to the court so that the court can make some pretrial ruling to keep the case moving forward. And the court needs a small group of counsel to take depositions, not hundreds of lawyers engaging in redundant examination of the same witness. A court trying to hear from every counsel would be inefficient, cause confusion, and generally be the source of a major headache for the court. Instead, the court can designate one or more counsel (from the assembled group) to speak for the larger group. Such counsel are sometimes referred to as *liason* or *lead* counsel. *See, e.g., In re San Juan Dupont Plaza Hotel Fire Litig.*, MDL No. 721, 1989 WL 168401 at *19–20 (D.P.R. 1988) (discussing role of "liaison persons" for both plaintiff and defendant groups of counsel). Of course, it would be unfair for such a lead counsel to require that counsel's own specific client to pay for all of the attorney's time spent pursuing the litigation aims of the larger group. Accordingly, utilizing the "common fund" idea, courts appointing such counsel have required the larger group to reimburse the lead counsel for their time in coordinating, directing, and conducting the litigation on behalf of the larger group.

According to the Manual for Complex Litigation, once a court has appointed lead or liaison counsel, "the court should define designated counsel's functions, determine the method of compensation, specify the records to be kept, and establish the arrangements for their compensation, including setting up a fund to which designated parties should contribute in specific proportions. Guidelines should cover staffing, hourly rates, and estimated charges for services and expenses." Manual for Complex Litigation, Fourth, § 14.215 (2004).

The following case provides a terrific example of an MDL court playing that role in overseeing an extremely large MDL case (through settlement) and then having to decide at the very end of the litigation how to compensate the lead counsel it had previously appointed. The very process by which this court undertakes its task is fascinating to anyone who has only been exposed to traditional one-on-one litigation. Consider as you read this opinion how well this process works and the fairness of taking portions of the recovery and giving it to select counsel. Also, are you convinced by the court's articulation of its power to divide up the pie? Is there any better alternative?

In re Vioxx Prods. Liabl. Litig.

802 F. Supp. 2d 740 (E.D. La. 2011)

FALLON, J.,

The Court has previously determined the value of the common benefit work in the Vioxx MDL and associated state litigations which produced the global settlement of

November 9, 2007. The value was fixed at 6.5% of the $4.85 billion settlement amount for a total of Three Hundred and Fifteen Million, Two Hundred and Fifty Thousand Dollars ($315,250,000.00). Now, the Court must allocate those common benefit attorneys' fees among the attorneys who did the work which produced this settlement. This allocation is in addition to common benefit costs, which have already been distributed.

Factual Background

To put this matter in perspective, a brief review of this litigation is appropriate.

This multidistrict products liability litigation involves the prescription drug Vioxx, known generically as Rofecoxib. Merck, a New Jersey corporation, researched, designed, manufactured, marketed, and distributed Vioxx to relieve pain and inflammation resulting from osteoarthritis, rheumatoid arthritis, menstrual pain, and migraine headaches. On May 20, 1999, the Food and Drug Administration approved Vioxx for sale in the United States. Vioxx remained publicly available until September 20, 2004, when Merck withdrew it from the market after data from a clinical trial known as APPROVe indicated that the use of Vioxx increased the risk of cardiovascular thrombotic events such as myocardial infarction (heart attack) and ischemic stroke. Thereafter, thousands of individual lawsuits and numerous class actions were filed against Merck in state and federal courts throughout the country alleging various products liability, tort, fraud, and warranty claims. It is estimated that 105 million prescriptions for Vioxx were written in the United States between May 20, 1999 and September 30, 2004. Based on this estimate, it is thought that approximately 20 million patients have taken Vioxx in the United States.

California was the first state to institute a consolidated state court proceeding on October 30, 2002. New Jersey and Texas soon followed suit, on May 20, 2003 and September 6, 2005, respectively. On February 16, 2005, the Judicial Panel on Multidistrict Litigation ("MDL") conferred MDL status on Vioxx lawsuits filed in various federal courts throughout the country and transferred all such cases to this Court to coordinate discovery and to consolidate pretrial matters pursuant to 28 U.S.C. § 1407. *See In re Vioxx Prods. Liab. Litig.*, 360 F. Supp. 2d 1352 (J.P.M.L. 2005). Even after the creation of this federal MDL, many cases remained pending in the various state courts, particularly the courts in California, New Jersey, and Texas. It is estimated that the census of the litigation totaled over 50,000 claims.

On March 18, 2005, this Court held the first status conference in the Vioxx MDL to discuss procedures for moving this matter forward. Shortly thereafter, the Court appointed steering committees of counsel to represent the parties. In addition, the Court announced at monthly meetings that any attorney who was not appointed but who wished to do common benefit work on behalf of Vioxx claimants could do so by joining a subcommittee. The Plaintiffs' Steering Committee ("PSC") was encouraged to establish subcommittees and include non-PSC members on these subcommittees.

Discovery rapidly commenced. The common benefit attorneys were responsible for all aspects of pre-trial preparation, including document discovery, the taking of depositions, preparation of experts, motions practice, and to some extent, coordination of federal and state court proceedings. Over nine million documents were discovered and collated. Thousands of depositions were taken and at least 1,000 discovery motions were argued to the Court. After a reasonable period for discovery, the Court assisted the parties in selecting and preparing certain test cases for bellwether trials. Additionally, a number of similar trials were scheduled in state courts.

[After six of the bellwether trials and further extensive discovery, serious settlement negotiations began.] Negotiating Plaintiffs' Counsel ("the NPC") were appointed to explore and engage in settlement discussions with Merck. Counsel for Merck and the NPC met together more than fifty times and held several hundred telephone conferences. Although the parties met and negotiated independently, they kept this Court and the coordinate state courts of Texas, New Jersey, and California informed of their progress in settlement discussions.

On November 9, 2007, Merck and the NPC formally announced that they had reached a Settlement Agreement [that included an agreement for defendant to pay $4.85 billion to the plaintiffs through a voluntary opt-in program for any current or other claimants.]

Procedures for Performing and Documenting Common Benefit Work

As previously mentioned, from the very beginning of this MDL, and before the Settlement Agreement was contemplated or announced, steps were taken to create a fair and open environment for all interested attorneys to perform work for the common benefit of the Vioxx plaintiffs and to create a transparent factual record for an eventual application for common benefit fees.

Thirteen members, including Plaintiffs' Liaison Counsel ("PLC"), were appointed to the PSC. Appointment of a supervising Plaintiffs' Steering Committee is necessary to create centralized leadership and control of litigation of this magnitude. But the Court, the plaintiffs, and the justice system in general also have an interest in broadening the range of attorney participation in MDL cases, lest the work be confined to a specialized bar of MDL attorneys which would result in exclusivity, unfairness, and discrimination, and inure to the disadvantage of litigants and their attorneys. Therefore, as mentioned above, the Court authorized and encouraged the PSC to "organiz[e] subcommittees comprised of plaintiffs' attorneys not on the PSC and assign[] them tasks consistent with the duties of the PSC." All interested attorneys, including those in the state court litigations, were encouraged to coordinate with the PSC and to do work for the common benefit. Over one hundred firms or attorneys availed themselves of the opportunity to perform common benefit work.

To receive and vet records of the time spent and expenses incurred by attorneys performing common benefit work, the Court appointed a CPA, Phillip Garrett. *Id.* Those doing common benefit work and incurring common benefit expenses were ordered to report their hours and expenses contemporaneously to the Court-appointed CPA for review and reporting to the Court.

Early in the litigation, the Court entered Pretrial Order No. 19, which established a Plaintiffs' Litigation Expense Fund to compensate and reimburse attorneys for services performed and expenses incurred for the common benefit. Pursuant to this Order, any case that was settled, compromised, dismissed, or otherwise reduced to judgment for monetary relief, with or without trial, was subject to an assessment. In order to avail themselves of the benefit of the initial work of the common benefit attorneys, individual plaintiffs' counsel could, for a limited time, enter into a contract that was to dictate the assessment amount. The "Full Participation Option," which was one such option, established an assessment of 2% of the recovery for fees and 1% of the recovery for costs. Counsel were able to select the "Full Participation Option" within 90 days of the entry of Pretrial Order 19. Following that period, counsel could accept a "Traditional Assessment Option" providing for 6% assessment of recoveries in MDL cases and 4% assessment of recoveries in state court cases.

As mentioned above, the case then proceeded through a period of extensive discovery, pretrial motions, *Daubert* hearings, six MDL bellwether trials, and over a dozen trials in state court. After several years, the settlement occurred.

When consummated, the Settlement Agreement modified the landscape regarding common benefit attorneys' fees for those interested in participating in the settlement. The Settlement Agreement provides for a common benefit fee assessment to create a common benefit fund, to "be administered by the Honorable Eldon E. Fallon," and to be awarded "upon due consideration by him in consultation with the Honorable Victoria G. Chaney, the Honorable Carol E. Higbee, and the Honorable Randy Wilson, and in accordance with established Fifth Circuit precedent." *Id.* § 9.2.3. Additionally, the Settlement Agreement states that this contractual common benefit fee assessment supersedes the assessments provided for in Pretrial Order No. 19.

LAW & ANALYSIS
Court's Authority and Jurisdiction to Award Common Benefit Fees

First, it is worth reiterating the source of the Court's authority to award and allocate the common benefit fund. Since the nineteenth century, the Supreme Court has recognized an equitable exception to the general rule that a prevailing litigant is not entitled to collect attorneys' fees from the loser. This exception has become known as the common fund or common benefit doctrine and permits the creation of a common fund in order to pay reasonable attorneys' fees for legal services beneficial to persons other than a particular client, thus spreading the cost of the litigation to all beneficiaries. *See In re Zyprexa Prods. Liab. Litig.*, 594 F.3d 113, 128 (2d Cir. 2010) (Kaplan, J., concurring). This equitable common fund doctrine was originally, and perhaps still is, most commonly applied to awards of attorneys' fees in class actions. *E.g.*, 4 Alba Conte & Herbert B. Newberg, *Newberg on Class Actions* § 13:76 (4th ed. 2002) (discussing common fund doctrine in context of class actions); Fed. R. Civ. P. 23(h).

But the common fund doctrine is not limited solely to class actions. *See Sprague v. Ticonic National Bank*, 307 U.S. 161 (1939) (employing common benefit doctrine to award fees and costs to litigant whose success benefitted unrelated parties by establishing their legal rights); Alan Hirsh & Diane Sheeley, Fed. Judicial Ctr., *Awarding Attorneys' Fees and Managing Fee Litigation* 51 (2nd ed. 2005) ("Although many common fund cases are class actions ... the common fund doctrine is not limited to class actions."); Manual for Complex Litigation (Fourth) § 14.121 (2004). As class actions morph into multidistrict litigation, as is the modern trend, the common benefit concept has migrated into the latter area. The theoretical bases for the application of this concept to MDLs are the same as for class actions, namely equity and her blood brother, quantum meruit. However, there is a difference. In class actions the beneficiary of the common benefit is the claimant; in MDLs the beneficiary is the primary attorney.[12]

MDL courts have consistently cited the common fund doctrine as a basis for assessing common benefit fees in favor of attorneys who render legal services beneficial to all MDL plaintiffs. *E.g.*, *In re Genetically Modified Rice Litig.*, MDL No. 06-1811, 2010 U.S. Dist. LEXIS 19168, 2010 WL 716190, at *4 (E.D. Mo. Feb. 24, 2010) (relying on common fund doctrine as an alternate basis to inherent managerial authority and concluding that "[b]oth sources of authority provide the same result"); *In re Guidant Corp. Implantable Defibrillators Prods. Liab. Litig.*, MDL No. 05-1708, 2008 U.S. Dist. LEXIS 17535, 2008 WL 682174, at *4 (D. Minn. Mar. 7, 2008); *accord In re Zyprexa*, 594 F.3d at 128–30 (Kaplan, J., concurring).

---

12. The designation of "primary attorney" as used in this opinion refers to the attorney who has the contract with the litigant.

In addition to judicial precedent the Court also finds authority to assess common benefit attorneys' fees in its inherent managerial authority, particularly in light of the complex nature of this MDL. The Fifth Circuit has long recognized that a court's power to consolidate and manage litigation necessarily implies a corollary authority to appoint lead or liaison counsel and to compensate them for their work. *See In re Air Crash Disaster at Fl. Everglades on Dec. 29, 1972*, 549 F.2d 1006 (1977) ("*Everglades*"). In *Everglades*, the JPML transferred all federal cases arising out of a passenger plane crash near Miami to the Southern District of Florida. *Id.* at 1008. The transferee court appointed a Plaintiffs' Committee to coordinate discovery and pretrial matters, and then to conduct bellwether trials. *Id.* The court compensated the Committee through an assessment on the contingent fees of attorneys who represented MDL plaintiffs but were not on the Committee. *Id.* The non-Committee attorneys appealed and the Fifth Circuit upheld the district court's authority to make that assessment. The Fifth Circuit explained that a district court has inherent authority "to bring management power to bear upon massive and complex litigation to prevent it from monopolizing the services of the court to the exclusion of other litigants." *Id.* at 1012. Therefore, an MDL court "may designate one attorney or set of attorneys to handle pre-trial activity on aspects of the case where the interests of all co-parties coincide." *Id.* at 1014. Naturally, this authority would be "illusory if it is dependent upon lead counsel's performing the duties desired of them for no additional compensation." *Id.* at 1016. Assessment of those fees against other retained lawyers who benefitted from the work done was permissible and appropriate. *See id.* at 1019–20.[13]

Other courts have applied this inherent authority to compensate common benefit counsel in complex litigation. *E.g., In re Diet Drugs*, 582 F.3d 524, 546–47 (3rd Cir. 2009); *In re Genetically Modified Rice Litig.*, 2010 U.S. Dist. LEXIS 19168, 2010 WL 716190, at *4 ("An MDL court's authority to establish a trust and to order compensations to compensate leadership counsel derives from its 'managerial' power over the consolidated litigation, and, to some extent, from its inherent equitable power."); *In re Guidant*, 2008 U.S. Dist. LEXIS 17535, 2008 WL 682174, at *5; *In re Zyprexa Prods. Liab. Litig.*, 467 F. Supp. 2d 256, 265–66 (E.D.N.Y. 2006); *In re Linerboard Antitrust Litig.*, 292 F. Supp. 2d 644, 653–56 (E.D. Pa. 2003); *see also* Manual for Complex Litigation (Fourth) § 22.62 (2004); Restatement (Third) of Restitution § 30 Reporter's Note b (Tentative Draft No. 3, 1994) ("In contrast to the standard view of class-action fees, which explains them as restitutionary, the leading accounts of fees to court-appointed counsel in consolidated litigation properly emphasize factors independent of restitution to justify the imposition of a liability by court order.") (citing *Everglades*).

In addition to equity, quantum meruit, and inherent managerial authority, the Court derives express authority in this case from the very terms of the Settlement Agreement entered into by the parties and consented to by their primary attorneys. Section 9.2 of the Settlement Agreement governs common benefit fees and expressly authorizes this Court to determine common benefit attorneys' fees, as explained in greater detail above.

Thus, all parties to the MSA expressly agreed to the creation of a common benefit fund to be administered by the Court.

---

13. The Fifth Circuit also found support in "the body of law concerning the inherent equitable power of a trial court to allow counsel fees and litigation expenses out of the proceeds of a fund that has been created … by successful litigation," which the Court discussed above.

Some Final Thoughts About the Process for Allocating
Common Benefit Fees

Before determining the proper fee allocation in this case some general comments are in order.

First, the Court capped the total amount of attorneys' fees for primary counsel at 32% of the $4.85 billion settlement which means that the primary counsel's attorneys' fees in this case are one billion, five hundred and fifty-two million dollars ($1,552,000,000). Out of that 32%, the Court has created a fund for common benefit counsel of 6.5% of the total settlement amount, or Three Hundred and Fifteen Million, Two Hundred and Fifty Thousand Dollars ($315,250,000.00). This amount has been escrowed and the remainder has been paid to primary counsel. Thus, primary counsel for individual claimants have already received over one billion dollars pursuant to contingent fee agreements. Many if not all of the common benefit fee applicants are also primary counsel in at least some if not many cases and thus have already received substantial compensation pursuant to contingent fee agreements with their own clients. For this reason, it is disconcerting and disappointing to receive such vexatious, vitriolic, and acerbic briefs from some of the attorneys who seek common benefit fees.

Second, there has been much discussion regarding the process by which this Court, or any court, should allocate attorneys' fees. The Fifth Circuit's opinion in *In re High Sulfur* is instructive in this respect. In *High Sulfur*, the Fifth Circuit reviewed an allocation of attorneys' fees in a class action case. The takeaway from *High Sulfur* is that in allocating a fund of attorneys' fees, the Court must conform to "traditional judicial standards of transparency, impartiality, procedural fairness, and ultimate judicial oversight." 517 F.3d at 234. That requires creating a sufficient record, making sufficient factual findings, considering the time worked and the *Johnson* factors, providing an opportunity to be heard to all the applicants, and exercising independent judgment in allocating those fees rather than simply rubber-stamping a committee recommendation. The Court has been guided by these principles throughout this process.

Third, there has been much ink spilt in this case discussing the methodology by which common benefit attorneys' fees should be calculated. As explained in the Court's Order and Reasons of October 19, 2010, there is a growing trend in this country to use a blended approach to determine the appropriate common benefit fee in an MDL. Such an approach seeks an appropriate percentage through an analysis of similar cases, then modifies it upward or downward by a review of the *Johnson* factors and tests it through a lodestar cross-check. In this case, the Court applied this blended approach. The lodestar process played an important part in the analysis but the lodestar cross-check did not generate the common benefit award in the first instance; rather, it verified that the percentage fixed by the Court did not represent a windfall relative to the total hours worked.

It is not inconsistent, as some have suggested, to rely on lodestar as a cross-check but to reject it as the sole basis for allocation. The reason it is not inconsistent is because the objective is different. The objective of the lodestar method is to cross-check the accuracy of the percentage method to determine whether the totality of the hours spent and an amount assigned to it under the lodestar has a realistic relevance to the amount assigned as a common benefit fee. But when the focus is on the allocation of that fee the lodestar analysis is incomplete because it is necessary to drill down on the hours and prioritize them, consistent with the facts of each MDL. For those MDLs that are resolved without trials the priority may be different from this case. In this case there were nearly twenty trials: six in the MDL and the remainder in the various state courts. Those trials and the preparation involved therein played a substantial role in creating an environment in which settlement could be spawned, birthed, and nurtured. Therefore, in this case the attorneys who took up the cudgels and participated in those trials deserve an appropriate recognition for their efforts. To simply total the hours spent, apply an appropriate lodestar factor, and allocate the fee on that basis alone would not be appropriate in this case.

However, to uniformly recognize each trial counsel with the same common benefit fee would also be improper. The goal or objective of the proper allocation of the common benefit fee is not to pay counsel for his or her work at the trial stage of a particular case. That is the purpose of the contingent fee in that case. The purpose of the common benefit fee is to materially recognize counsel for the work which inured to the common benefit of the litigation as a whole. Thus, in allocating common benefit fees to trial counsel it is important to determine when the trial occurred, whether the work was shared with other counsel, whether the work was helpful in other cases or just in that one case. In this latter event, it does not mean that such counsel would not be entitled to some common benefit fee because there is a salutary rippling effect which a win or "hard fought case" has on other cases. But it also does not mean that such counsel may be entitled to the same common benefit fee as a colleague whose work was shared with other counsel and had a meaningful effect on subsequent trials.

Fourth, some comments on the role of a fee-allocating committee are also warranted. It is beyond dispute that a court may "appoint a committee of plaintiffs' counsel to recommend how to divide up an aggregate fee award." *In re High Sulfur I*, 517 F.3d at 227. The Court has previously used this mechanism with the hope that the committee could "achieve a unanimous agreement as to how the Common Benefit Fund should be allocated among counsel. *Murphy Oil*, 582 F. Supp. 2d at 801. If all counsel had an opportunity for informed arms-length discussion with an allocating committee, and the committee could recommend an allocation of a fixed pot of common benefit fees acceptable to all interested counsel, the Court would give weight to that mutual agreement. Unfortunately, unanimity is hard to achieve. Hence, the Court maintains the "responsibility to closely scrutinize the attorneys' fee allocation, especially when the attorneys recommending the allocation have a financial interest in the resulting awards." *High Sulfur I*, 517 F.3d at 227. To deal with this potential conflict a Special Master was appointed who had no financial interest in the awards. The Special Master was charged with conducting discovery and making his own recommendation.

In this case, the lengthy fee allocation procedure has provided an opportunity for common benefit fee applicants to review the FAC's recommendation and the Special Master's recommendation as they pertain to all applicants, and to comment on those recommendations. In some circumstances this dialogue between the FAC, the Special Master, and the applicants has resolved objections and produced consensus. Some might criticize any negotiation between the FAC or the Special Master and the applicants as "horse-trading" or "side deals." The Court interprets this ongoing development of the FAC's and the Special Master's recommended allocations as an indication that the allocation process was working properly. The effectiveness of this process in this case is supported by the fact that only 4 out of the 108 common benefit fee applicants continue to maintain their objections.

Fifth, there is some criticism expressed that allocation of common benefit fees contains an element of subjectivity. It is this Court's view that some subjectivity is unavoidable in allotting common benefit fees. In the fictional and perfect "best of all possible worlds" of Voltaire's *Candide*, an appropriate allocation might be achieved by applying purely objective criteria such as the billing-rate-times-hours method described above. But in the real and imperfect world of litigation it is an accepted fact that not all work hours are entitled to the same compensation rate. The nature of the work, the skill and experience of the party doing the work, and the result achieved all factor into the appropriate allocation. How these factors are weighed injects an unavoidable amount of subjectivity in the analysis. The best that can be done to assure the validity of the analysis is to base the subjectivity quotient on sufficient facts and experience, and to invite input from those affected. This Court has attempted to do this through a tedious and long drawn-out process.

Finally, after reviewing the documents and transcripts compiled by the Fee Allocation Committee, the detailed report and recommendations of the Special Master, as well as the exhibits cited therein, consulting with the Honorable Victoria G. Chaney, the Honorable Carol E. Higbee, and the Honorable Randy Wilson, and drawing upon this Court's experience in this case accumulated during the course of over five years in which there were six bellwether trials, hundreds of meetings, dozens of hearings, and nearly 1000 Court rulings, and consistent with applicable law, this Court makes the following allocation of common benefit fees.

[The court went through details regarding the time each counsel applying for a common fund fee — over 100 separate applications were involved — spent on the case and discussing the importance of that work to bringing about the settlement. For each applicant, the court either awarded no common fund fees or awarded a specific dollar amount.]

Notes and Problems

1. Notice that the lawyers applying for an additional portion of attorney's fees under the common fund doctrine in the foregoing case had already received attorney's fees from their individual clients under their various contingency fee agreements. Given this reality, is the receipt of additional sums a windfall for these lawyers? How would the above court respond to such an accusation?

2. In the *Vioxx* case, the amount of *additional* fees, if any, bestowed upon the various lead or liaison counsel varied from $0 to $36 million. The firm that received the $36 million was found to have dedicated a large number of senior partners "almost exclusively" to working on this case for a number of years, taking key leadership over the conduct of the case and making "significant contributions" according to the court. Given the upside of being one of the lead counsel, do you see why plaintiffs' lawyers might sometimes have a bit of a power struggle in coordinated litigation, like an MDL case, for designation as a lead counsel? How did the *Vioxx* court try to avoid such power struggles at the inception of the case?

3. The court mentioned that MDLs are emerging as one of the preferred methods for adjudicating mass tort claims rather than through class certification. Given the level of involvement by the court and the degree of coordination, is it easy as you read the *Vioxx* opinion to become confused and think that this was a class action? Given that reality, would it be better for courts to take a more flexible attitude toward applying Rule 23(b)(3)'s guidelines to mass torts and simply certifying them rather than engaging in the MDL process to get the cases (perhaps temporarily) in front of one court?

4. *Problem.* Imagine that you have been hired by a client to pursue a personal injury claim arising out of your client having suffered side effects from taking a product, like Vioxx. The next thing you know, your case has been removed to federal court and then immediately transferred across the country (perhaps to Louisiana) for coordinated pretrial

adjudication in front of an MDL judge due to a prior decision by the Judicial Panel on Multidistrict Litigation. Your case is a tag-along case having been filed after the MDL was already created. By the time of your involvement, lead counsel have already been appointed by the court, a discovery schedule entered, motions for summary judgment have been argued, and there is nothing you can do even if you wanted to try to become more involved in managing your client's case. Then you begin to receive quarterly "assessments" of attorney's fee that you (or your client) are required to make toward paying attorney's fees for the lead counsel doing all of the work. At the end of the pre-trial activities (imagine there is no settlement), you are given your case back along with several "trial notebooks" filled with depositions, documents deemed relevant to your client's case, and proposed trial examination outlines. You find these materials to be worthless. If you win the trial on behalf of your client, the court may order you to pay a portion of the recovery to the lead MDL counsel who did the pretrial discovery. How do you feel about all of this? Is there anything you can do?

Upon Further Review

The subject of attorney's fees is near and dear to you, or it will be as soon as you complete your studies, pass the bar exam, and begin your newfound life as a young lawyer. Every day you will likely be dividing up your time into tenths of an hour to fill out time sheets. Every month you will be involved in finalizing billing records and invoices to clients. You will also have to call clients sometimes when they are late paying your bills. Further, when and how lawyers handling complex litigation can have courts award them attorney's fees is a very important subject and not just at the end of a lawsuit. It is the very prospect of being awarded such fees that often provides the motivation for a lawyer to bring a putative class action or to become heavily involved in MDL litigation. Before taking this class, you had already heard stories of class action lawyers being awarded enormous fees. Perhaps you had not stopped to consider by what authority such fees were handed out, given that most class members have not agreed to legal representation much less to pay any attorney's fees to anyone. As we have seen, there are two sources for such fees: (a) either a statute has authorized attorney's fees to be paid by defendant in addition to any other items of damage they are forced to pay the class as a result of their liability; or (b) the common fund doctrine has recognized that, as a matter of equity, lawyers who have achieved success on behalf of another (e.g., a class) deserve to be paid something out of that fund. Whether and how much to award in fees is left in both cases to the discretion of the trial courts.

Chapter Problem Revisited

You are the law clerk to the presiding federal district court judge overseeing the Huey News v. TicketNinja litigation. Your judge has asked you to write a brief memorandum recommending the methodology to be used and the amount to be awarded for compensation of the class counsel in the case, pursuant to Rule 23(h). Go back and review the class counsel motion for assessment of fees and consider all of the circumstances of the case and its resolution.

Spent 20 minutes writing your memo to the district court judge explaining your recommendations for the attorney's fees to be awarded to class counsel. Be sure to include your rationale and authorities as the judge will use your memo, in part, to write the court's order.

Going Deeper

Additional recommended readings to enhance your understanding of some of the topics in this Chapter include:

- Kevin Miller, *Lawyers as Venture Capitalists: An Economic Analysis of Law Firms That Invest in Their Clients*, 13 Harv. J. Law & Tech. 435 (2000) (providing overview of alternative fee arrangements with particular emphasis on lawyers taking an equity stake in their clients in both transactional and litigation representation).

- Manual for Complex Litigation, 4th, §§ 21–22.

- Newberg on Class Actions Vol. 1, Chapters 3–4 (5th ed. West).

- Theodore Eisenberg & Geoffrey P. Miller, 1 *Journal of Empirical Legal Studies*, 7 (2004) (empirical studies of class counsel fees in class actions).

Appendix 1

Selected Rules and Statutes

Rule 1.— Scope and Purpose

These rules govern the procedure in all civil actions and proceedings in the United States district courts, except as stated in Rule 81. They should be construed and administered to secure the just, speedy, and inexpensive determination of every action and proceeding.

Rule 13. Counterclaim and Crossclaim

(a) Compulsory Counterclaim.

(1) In General.

A pleading must state as a counterclaim any claim that—at the time of its service—the pleader has against an opposing party if the claim:

    (A) arises out of the transaction or occurrence that is the subject matter of the opposing party's claim; and

    (B) does not require adding another party over whom the court cannot acquire jurisdiction.

(2) Exceptions.

The pleader need not state the claim if:

    (A) when the action was commenced, the claim was the subject of another pending action; or

    (B) the opposing party sued on its claim by attachment or other process that did not establish personal jurisdiction over the pleader on that claim, and the pleader does not assert any counterclaim under this rule.

(b) Permissive Counterclaims.

A pleading may state as a counterclaim against an opposing party any claim that is not compulsory.

(c) Relief Sought in a Counterclaim.

A counterclaim need not diminish or defeat the recovery sought by the opposing party. It may request relief that exceeds in amount or differs in kind from the relief sought by the opposing party.

(e) Counterclaim Maturing or Acquired After Pleading.

The court may permit a party to file a supplemental pleading asserting a counterclaim that matured or was acquired by the party after serving an earlier pleading.

(f) Omitted Counterclaim.

The court may permit a party to amend a pleading to add a counterclaim if it was omitted through oversight, inadvertence, or excusable neglect or if justice so requires.

(g) Crossclaim Against a Coparty.

A pleading may state as a crossclaim any claim by one party against a coparty if the claim arises out of the transaction or occurrence that is the subject matter of the original action or of a counterclaim, or if the claim relates to any property that is the subject matter of the original action. The crossclaim may include a claim that the coparty is or may be liable to the crossclaimant for all or part of a claim asserted in the action against the crossclaimant.

(h) Joining Additional Parties.

Rules 19 and 20 govern the addition of a person as a party to a counterclaim or crossclaim.

Rule 14. Third-Party Practice

(a) When a Defending Party May Bring in a Third Party.

(1) Timing of the Summons and Complaint.

A defending party may, as third-party plaintiff, serve a summons and complaint on a nonparty who is or may be liable to it for all or part of the claim against it. But the third-party plaintiff must, by motion, obtain the court's leave if it files the third-party complaint more than 10 days after serving its original answer.

(2) Third-Party Defendant's Claims and Defenses.

The person served with the summons and third-party complaint — the "third-party defendant":

>   (A) must assert any defense against the third-party plaintiff's claim under Rule 12;

>   (B) must assert any counterclaim against the third-party plaintiff under Rule 13(a), and may assert any counterclaim against the third-party plaintiff under Rule 13(b) or any crossclaim against another third-party defendant under Rule 13(g);

>   (C) may assert against the plaintiff any defense that the third-party plaintiff has to the plaintiff's claim; and

>   (D) may also assert against the plaintiff any claim arising out of the transaction or occurrence that is the subject matter of the plaintiff's claim against the third-party plaintiff.

(3) Plaintiff's Claims Against a Third-Party Defendant.

The plaintiff may assert against the third-party defendant any claim arising out of the transaction or occurrence that is the subject matter of the plaintiff's claim against the third-party plaintiff. The third-party defendant must then assert any defense under Rule 12 and any counterclaim under Rule 13(a), and may assert any counterclaim under Rule 13(b) or any crossclaim under Rule 13(g).

(5) Third-Party Defendant's Claim Against a Nonparty.

A third-party defendant may proceed under this rule against a nonparty who is or may be liable to the third-party defendant for all or part of any claim against it.

(b) When a Plaintiff May Bring in a Third Party.

When a claim is asserted against a plaintiff, the plaintiff may bring in a third party if this rule would allow a defendant to do so.

Rule 18. Joinder of Claims

(a) A party asserting a claim, counterclaim, crossclaim, or third-party claim may join, as independent or alternative claims, as many claims as it has against an opposing party.

Rule 19. Required Joinder of Parties

(a) Persons Required to Be Joined if Feasible.

(1) Required Party.

A person who is subject to service of process and whose joinder will not deprive the court of subject-matter jurisdiction must be joined as a party if:

> (A) in that person's absence, the court cannot accord complete relief among existing parties; or

> (B) that person claims an interest relating to the subject of the action and is so situated that disposing of the action in the person's absence may:

(i) as a practical matter impair or impede the person's ability to protect the interest; or

(ii) leave an existing party subject to a substantial risk of incurring double, multiple, or otherwise inconsistent obligations because of the interest.

(2) Joinder by Court Order.

If a person has not been joined as required, the court must order that the person be made a party. A person who refuses to join as a plaintiff may be made either a defendant or, in a proper case, an involuntary plaintiff.

(3) Venue.

If a joined party objects to venue and the joinder would make venue improper, the court must dismiss that party.

(b) When Joinder Is Not Feasible.

If a person who is required to be joined if feasible cannot be joined, the court must determine whether, in equity and good conscience, the action should proceed among the existing parties or should be dismissed. The factors for the court to consider include:

> (1) the extent to which a judgment rendered in the person's absence might prejudice that person or the existing parties;

> (2) the extent to which any prejudice could be lessened or avoided by:

>> (A) protective provisions in the judgment;

>> (B) shaping the relief; or

>> (C) other measures;

> (3) whether a judgment rendered in the person's absence would be adequate; and

> (4) whether the plaintiff would have an adequate remedy if the action were dismissed for nonjoinder.

Rule 20. Permissive Joinder of Parties

(a) Persons Who May Join or Be Joined.

(1) Plaintiffs.

Persons may join in one action as plaintiffs if:

> (A) they assert any right to relief jointly, severally, or in the alternative with respect to or arising out of the same transaction, occurrence, or series of transactions or occurrences; and

> (B) any question of law or fact common to all plaintiffs will arise in the action.

(2) Defendants.

Persons — as well as a vessel, cargo, or other property subject to admiralty process in rem — may be joined in one action as defendants if:

(A) any right to relief is asserted against them jointly, severally, or in the alternative with respect to or arising out of the same transaction, occurrence, or series of transactions or occurrences; and

(B) any question of law or fact common to all defendants will arise in the action.

(3) Extent of Relief.

Neither a plaintiff nor a defendant need be interested in obtaining or defending against all the relief demanded. The court may grant judgment to one or more plaintiffs according to their rights, and against one or more defendants according to their liabilities.

(b) Protective Measures.

The court may issue orders — including an order for separate trials — to protect a party against embarrassment, delay, expense, or other prejudice that arises from including a person against whom the party asserts no claim and who asserts no claim against the party.

Rule 21. Misjoinder and Non-Joinder of Parties

Misjoinder of parties is not a ground for dismissing an action. On motion or on its own, the court may at any time, on just terms, add or drop a party. The court may also sever any claim against a party.

Rule 23. Class Actions

(a) Prerequisites.

One or more members of a class may sue or be sued as representative parties on behalf of all members only if:

(1) the class is so numerous that joinder of all members is impracticable,

(2) there are questions of law or fact common to the class,

(3) the claims or defenses of the representative parties are typical of the claims or defenses of the class; and

(4) the representative parties will fairly and adequately protect the interests of the class.

(b) Types of Class Actions.

A class action may be maintained if Rule 23(a) is satisfied and if:

(1) prosecuting separate actions by or against individual class members would create a risk of:

(A) inconsistent or varying adjudications with respect to individual class members that would establish incompatible standards of conduct for the party opposing the class; or

(B) adjudications with respect to individual class members that, as a practical matter, would be dispositive of the interests of the other members not parties to the individual adjudications or would substantially impair or impede their ability to protect their interests;

(2) the party opposing the class has acted or refused to act on grounds that apply generally to the class, so that final injunctive relief or corresponding declaratory relief is appropriate respecting the class as a whole; or

(3) the court finds that the questions of law or fact common to class members predominate over any questions affecting only individual members, and that a class action is superior to other available methods for fairly and efficiently adjudicating the controversy. The matters pertinent to these findings include:

(A) the class members' interests in individually controlling the prosecution or defense of separate actions;

(B) the extent and nature of any litigation concerning the controversy already begun by or against class members;

(C) the desirability or undesirability of concentrating the litigation of the claims in the particular forum; and

(D) the likely difficulties in managing a class action.

(c) Certification Order; Notice to Class Members; Judgment; Issues Classes; Subclasses.

(1) Certification Order.

(A) *Time to Issue.* At an early practicable time after a person sues or is sued as a class representative, the court must determine by order whether to certify the action as a class action.

(B) *Defining the Class; Appointing Class Counsel.* An order that certifies a class action must define the class and the class claims, issues, or defenses, and must appoint class counsel under Rule 23(g).

(C) *Altering or Amending the Order.* An order that grants or denies class certification may be altered or amended before final judgment.

(2) Notice.

(A) *For (b)(1) or (b)(2) Classes.* For any class certified under Rule 23(b)(1) or (b)(2), the court may direct appropriate notice to the class.

(B) *For (b)(3) Classes.* For any class certified under Rule 23(b)(3), the court must direct to class members the best notice that is practicable under the circumstances, including individual notice to all members who can be identified through reasonable effort. The notice must clearly and concisely state in plain, easily understood language:

(i) the nature of the action;

(ii) the definition of the class certified;

(iii) the class claims, issues, or defenses;

(iv) that a class member may enter an appearance through an attorney if the member so desires;

(v) that the court will exclude from the class any member who requests exclusion;

(vi) the time and manner for requesting exclusion; and

(vii) the binding effect of a class judgment on members under Rule 23(c)(3).

(3) Judgment.

Whether or not favorable to the class, the judgment in a class action must:

(A) for any class certified under Rule 23(b)(1) or (b)(2), include and describe those whom the court finds to be class members; and

(B) for any class certified under Rule 23(b)(3), include and specify or describe those to whom the Rule 23(c)(2) notice was directed, who have not requested exclusion, and whom the court finds to be class members.

(4) Particular Issues.

When appropriate, an action may be brought or maintained as a class action with respect to particular issues.

(5) Subclasses.

When appropriate, a class may be divided into subclasses that are each treated as a class under this rule.

(d) Conducting the Action.

(1) In General.

In conducting an action under this rule, the court may issue orders that:

(A) determine the course of proceedings or prescribe measures to prevent undue repetition or complication in presenting evidence or argument;

(B) require — to protect class members and fairly conduct the action — giving appropriate notice to some or all class members of:

(i) any step in the action;

(ii) the proposed extent of the judgment; or

(iii) the members' opportunity to signify whether they consider the representation fair and adequate, to intervene and present claims or defenses, or to otherwise come into the action;

(C) impose conditions on the representative parties or on intervenors;

(D) require that the pleadings be amended to eliminate allegations about representation of absent persons and that the action proceed accordingly; or

(E) deal with similar procedural matters.

(e) Settlement, Voluntary Dismissal, or Compromise.

The claims, issues, or defenses of a certified class may be settled, voluntarily dismissed, or compromised only with the court's approval. The following procedures apply to a proposed settlement, voluntary dismissal, or compromise:

(1) The court must direct notice in a reasonable manner to all class members who would be bound by the proposal.

(2) If the proposal would bind class members, the court may approve it only after a hearing and on finding that it is fair, reasonable, and adequate.

(3) The parties seeking approval must file a statement identifying any agreement made in connection with the proposal.

(4) If the class action was previously certified under Rule 23(b)(3), the court may refuse to approve a settlement unless it affords a new opportunity to request exclusion to individual class members who had an earlier opportunity to request exclusion but did not do so.

(5) Any class member may object to the proposal if it requires court approval under this subdivision (e); the objection may be withdrawn only with the court's approval.

(f) Appeals.

A court of appeals may permit an appeal from an order granting or denying class-action certification under this rule if a petition for permission to appeal is filed with the circuit clerk within 10 days after the order is entered. An appeal does not stay proceedings in the district court unless the district judge or the court of appeals so orders.

(g) Class Counsel.

(1) Appointing Class Counsel.

Unless a statute provides otherwise, a court that certifies a class must appoint class counsel. In appointing class counsel, the court:

    (A) must consider:

        (i) the work counsel has done in identifying or investigating potential claims in the action;

        (ii) counsel's experience in handling class actions, other complex litigation, and the types of claims asserted in the action;

        (iii) counsel's knowledge of the applicable law; and

        (iv) the resources that counsel will commit to representing the class;

    (B) may consider any other matter pertinent to counsel's ability to fairly and adequately represent the interests of the class;

    (C) may order potential class counsel to provide information on any subject pertinent to the appointment and to propose terms for attorney's fees and nontaxable costs;

    (D) may include in the appointing order provisions about the award of attorney's fees or nontaxable costs under Rule 23(h); and

    (E) may make further orders in connection with the appointment.

(2) Standard for Appointing Class Counsel.

When one applicant seeks appointment as class counsel, the court may appoint that applicant only if the applicant is adequate under Rule 23(g)(1) and (4). If more than one adequate applicant seeks appointment, the court must appoint the applicant best able to represent the interests of the class.

(3) Interim Counsel.

The court may designate interim counsel to act on behalf of a putative class before determining whether to certify the action as a class action.

(4) Duty of Class Counsel.

Class counsel must fairly and adequately represent the interests of the class.

(h) Attorney's Fees and Nontaxable Costs.

In a certified class action, the court may award reasonable attorney's fees and nontaxable costs that are authorized by law or by the parties' agreement. The following procedures apply:

    (1) A claim for an award must be made by motion under Rule 54(d)(2), subject to the provisions of this subdivision (h), at a time the court sets. Notice of the motion must be served on all parties and, for motions by class counsel, directed to class members in a reasonable manner.

    (2) A class member, or a party from whom payment is sought, may object to the motion.

(3) The court may hold a hearing and must find the facts and state its legal conclusions under Rule 52(a).

(4) The court may refer issues related to the amount of the award to a special master or a magistrate judge, as provided in Rule 54(d)(2)(D).

Rule 24. Intervention

(a) Intervention of Right.

On timely motion, the court must permit anyone to intervene who:

(1) is given an unconditional right to intervene by a federal statute; or

(2) claims an interest relating to the property or transaction that is the subject of the action, and is so situated that disposing of the action may as a practical matter impair or impede the movant's ability to protect its interest, unless existing parties adequately represent that interest.

(b) Permissive Intervention.

(1) In General.

On timely motion, the court may permit anyone to intervene who:

(A) is given a conditional right to intervene by a federal statute; or

(B) has a claim or defense that shares with the main action a common question of law or fact.

(3) Delay or Prejudice.

In exercising its discretion, the court must consider whether the intervention will unduly delay or prejudice the adjudication of the original parties' rights.

(c) Notice and Pleading Required.

A motion to intervene must be served on the parties as provided in Rule 5. The motion must state the grounds for intervention and be accompanied by a pleading that sets out the claim or defense for which intervention is sought.

Rule 42. Consolidation; Separate Trials

(a) Consolidation.

If actions before the court involve a common question of law or fact, the court may:

(1) join for hearing or trial any or all matters at issue in the actions;

(2) consolidate the actions; or

(3) issue any other orders to avoid unnecessary cost or delay.

(b) Separate Trials.

For convenience, to avoid prejudice, or to expedite and economize, the court may order a separate trial of one or more separate issues, claims, crossclaims, counterclaims, or thirdparty claims. When ordering a separate trial, the court must preserve any federal right to a jury trial.

§ 1331. Federal question

The district courts shall have original jurisdiction of all civil actions arising under the Constitution, laws, or treaties of the United States.

§ 1332. Diversity of citizenship; amount in controversy; costs

(a) The district courts shall have original jurisdiction of all civil actions where the matter in controversy exceeds the sum or value of $75,000, exclusive of interest and costs, and is between —

    (1) citizens of different States;

    (2) citizens of a State and citizens or subjects of a foreign state;

    (3) citizens of different States and in which citizens or subjects of a foreign state are additional parties; and

    (4) a foreign state, defined in section 1603 (a) of this title, as plaintiff and citizens of a State or of different States.

For the purposes of this section, section 1335, and section 1441, an alien admitted to the United States for permanent residence shall be deemed a citizen of the State in which such alien is domiciled.

(b) Except when express provision therefor is otherwise made in a statute of the United States, where the plaintiff who files the case originally in the Federal courts is finally adjudged to be entitled to recover less than the sum or value of $75,000, computed without regard to any setoff or counterclaim to which the defendant may be adjudged to be entitled, and exclusive of interest and costs, the district court may deny costs to the plaintiff and, in addition, may impose costs on the plaintiff.

(c) For the purposes of this section and section 1441 of this title —

    (1) a corporation shall be deemed to be a citizen of any State by which it has been incorporated and of the State where it has its principal place of business, except that in any direct action against the insurer of a policy or contract of liability insurance, whether incorporated or unincorporated, to which action the insured is not joined as a party-defendant, such insurer shall be deemed a citizen of the State of which the insured is a citizen, as well as of any State by which the insurer has been incorporated and of the State where it has its principal place of business; and

    (2) the legal representative of the estate of a decedent shall be deemed to be a citizen only of the same State as the decedent, and the legal representative of an infant or incompetent shall be deemed to be a citizen only of the same State as the infant or incompetent.

(d)

    (1) In this subsection —

        (A) the term "class" means all of the class members in a class action;

        (B) the term "class action" means any civil action filed under rule 23 of the Federal Rules of Civil Procedure or similar State statute or rule of judicial procedure authorizing an action to be brought by 1 or more representative persons as a class action;

        (C) the term "class certification order" means an order issued by a court approving the treatment of some or all aspects of a civil action as a class action; and

        (D) the term "class members" means the persons (named or unnamed) who fall within the definition of the proposed or certified class in a class action.

    (2) The district courts shall have original jurisdiction of any civil action in which the matter in controversy exceeds the sum or value of $5,000,000, exclusive of interest and costs, and is a class action in which —

(A) any member of a class of plaintiffs is a citizen of a State different from any defendant;

(B) any member of a class of plaintiffs is a foreign state or a citizen or subject of a foreign state and any defendant is a citizen of a State; or

(C) any member of a class of plaintiffs is a citizen of a State and any defendant is a foreign state or a citizen or subject of a foreign state.

(3) A district court may, in the interests of justice and looking at the totality of the circumstances, decline to exercise jurisdiction under paragraph (2) over a class action in which greater than one-third but less than two-thirds of the members of all proposed plaintiff classes in the aggregate and the primary defendants are citizens of the State in which the action was originally filed based on consideration of—

(A) whether the claims asserted involve matters of national or interstate interest;

(B) whether the claims asserted will be governed by laws of the State in which the action was originally filed or by the laws of other States;

(C) whether the class action has been pleaded in a manner that seeks to avoid Federal jurisdiction;

(D) whether the action was brought in a forum with a distinct nexus with the class members, the alleged harm, or the defendants;

(E) whether the number of citizens of the State in which the action was originally filed in all proposed plaintiff classes in the aggregate is substantially larger than the number of citizens from any other State, and the citizenship of the other members of the proposed class is dispersed among a substantial number of States; and

(F) whether, during the 3-year period preceding the filing of that class action, 1 or more other class actions asserting the same or similar claims on behalf of the same or other persons have been filed.

(4) A district court shall decline to exercise jurisdiction under paragraph (2)—

(A)

(i) over a class action in which—

(I) greater than two-thirds of the members of all proposed plaintiff classes in the aggregate are citizens of the State in which the action was originally filed;

(II) at least 1 defendant is a defendant—

(aa) from whom significant relief is sought by members of the plaintiff class;

(bb) whose alleged conduct forms a significant basis for the claims asserted by the proposed plaintiff class; and

(cc) who is a citizen of the State in which the action was originally filed; and

(III) principal injuries resulting from the alleged conduct or any related conduct of each defendant were incurred in the State in which the action was originally filed; and

(ii) during the 3-year period preceding the filing of that class action, no other class action has been filed asserting the same or similar factual allegations against any of the defendants on behalf of the same or other persons; or

(B) two-thirds or more of the members of all proposed plaintiff classes in the aggregate, and the primary defendants, are citizens of the State in which the action was originally filed.

(5) Paragraphs (2) through (4) shall not apply to any class action in which—

(A) the primary defendants are States, State officials, or other governmental entities against whom the district court may be foreclosed from ordering relief; or

(B) the number of members of all proposed plaintiff classes in the aggregate is less than 100.

(6) In any class action, the claims of the individual class members shall be aggregated to determine whether the matter in controversy exceeds the sum or value of $5,000,000, exclusive of interest and costs.

(7) Citizenship of the members of the proposed plaintiff classes shall be determined for purposes of paragraphs (2) through (6) as of the date of filing of the complaint or amended complaint, or, if the case stated by the initial pleading is not subject to Federal jurisdiction, as of the date of service by plaintiffs of an amended pleading, motion, or other paper, indicating the existence of Federal jurisdiction.

(8) This subsection shall apply to any class action before or after the entry of a class certification order by the court with respect to that action.

(9) Paragraph (2) shall not apply to any class action that solely involves a claim—

(A) concerning a covered security as defined under 16(f)(3) [1] of the Securities Act of 1933 (15 U.S.C. 78p (f)(3) [2]) and section 28(f)(5)(E) of the Securities Exchange Act of 1934 (15 U.S.C. 78bb (f)(5)(E));

(B) that relates to the internal affairs or governance of a corporation or other form of business enterprise and that arises under or by virtue of the laws of the State in which such corporation or business enterprise is incorporated or organized; or

(C) that relates to the rights, duties (including fiduciary duties), and obligations relating to or created by or pursuant to any security (as defined under section 2(a)(1) of the Securities Act of 1933 (15 U.S.C. 77b (a)(1)) and the regulations issued thereunder).

(10) For purposes of this subsection and section 1453, an unincorporated association shall be deemed to be a citizen of the State where it has its principal place of business and the State under whose laws it is organized.

(11)

(A) For purposes of this subsection and section 1453, a mass action shall be deemed to be a class action removable under paragraphs (2) through (10) if it otherwise meets the provisions of those paragraphs.

(B)

(i) As used in subparagraph (A), the term "mass action" means any civil action (except a civil action within the scope of section 1711 (2)) in which monetary relief claims of 100 or more persons are proposed to be tried jointly on the ground that the plaintiffs' claims involve common questions of law or fact, except that jurisdiction shall exist only over those plaintiffs whose claims in a mass action satisfy the jurisdictional amount requirements under subsection (a).

(ii) As used in subparagraph (A), the term "mass action" shall not include any civil action in which—

(I) all of the claims in the action arise from an event or occurrence in the State in which the action was filed, and that allegedly resulted in injuries in that State or in States contiguous to that State;

(II) the claims are joined upon motion of a defendant;

(III) all of the claims in the action are asserted on behalf of the general public (and not on behalf of individual claimants or members of a purported class) pursuant to a State statute specifically authorizing such action; or

(IV) the claims have been consolidated or coordinated solely for pretrial proceedings.

(C)

(i) Any action(s) removed to Federal court pursuant to this subsection shall not thereafter be transferred to any other court pursuant to section 1407, or the rules promulgated thereunder, unless a majority of the plaintiffs in the action request transfer pursuant to section 1407.

(ii) This subparagraph will not apply—

(I) to cases certified pursuant to rule 23 of the Federal Rules of Civil Procedure; or

(II) if plaintiffs propose that the action proceed as a class action pursuant to rule 23 of the Federal Rules of Civil Procedure.

(D) The limitations periods on any claims asserted in a mass action that is removed to Federal court pursuant to this subsection shall be deemed tolled during the period that the action is pending in Federal court.

(e) The word "States", as used in this section, includes the Territories, the District of Columbia, and the Commonwealth of Puerto Rico.

§ 1367. Supplemental jurisdiction

(a) Except as provided in subsections (b) and (c) or as expressly provided otherwise by Federal statute, in any civil action of which the district courts have original jurisdiction, the district courts shall have supplemental jurisdiction over all other claims that are so related to claims in the action within such original jurisdiction that they form part of the same case or controversy under Article III of the United States Constitution. Such supplemental jurisdiction shall include claims that involve the joinder or intervention of additional parties.

(b) In any civil action of which the district courts have original jurisdiction founded solely on section 1332 of this title, the district courts shall not have supplemental jurisdiction under subsection (a) over claims by plaintiffs against persons made parties under Rule 14, 19, 20, or 24 of the Federal Rules of Civil Procedure, or over claims by persons proposed to be joined as plaintiffs under Rule 19 of such rules, or seeking to intervene as plaintiffs under Rule 24 of such rules, when exercising supplemental jurisdiction over such claims would be inconsistent with the jurisdictional requirements of section 1332.

(c) The district courts may decline to exercise supplemental jurisdiction over a claim under subsection (a) if—

(1) the claim raises a novel or complex issue of State law,

(2) the claim substantially predominates over the claim or claims over which the district court has original jurisdiction,

(3) the district court has dismissed all claims over which it has original jurisdiction, or

(4) in exceptional circumstances, there are other compelling reasons for declining jurisdiction.

(d) The period of limitations for any claim asserted under subsection (a), and for any other claim in the same action that is voluntarily dismissed at the same time as or after the dismissal of the claim under subsection (a), shall be tolled while the claim is pending and for a period of 30 days after it is dismissed unless State law provides for a longer tolling period.

§ 1391. Venue generally

(a) A civil action wherein jurisdiction is founded only on diversity of citizenship may, except as otherwise provided by law, be brought only in

(1) a judicial district where any defendant resides, if all defendants reside in the same State,

(2) a judicial district in which a substantial part of the events or omissions giving rise to the claim occurred, or a substantial part of property that is the subject of the action is situated, or

(3) a judicial district in which any defendant is subject to personal jurisdiction at the time the action is commenced, if there is no district in which the action may otherwise be brought.

(b) A civil action wherein jurisdiction is not founded solely on diversity of citizenship may, except as otherwise provided by law, be brought only in

(1) a judicial district where any defendant resides, if all defendants reside in the same State,

(2) a judicial district in which a substantial part of the events or omissions giving rise to the claim occurred, or a substantial part of property that is the subject of the action is situated, or

(3) a judicial district in which any defendant may be found, if there is no district in which the action may otherwise be brought.

(c) For purposes of venue under this chapter, a defendant that is a corporation shall be deemed to reside in any judicial district in which it is subject to personal jurisdiction at the time the action is commenced. In a State which has more than one judicial district and in which a defendant that is a corporation is subject to personal jurisdiction at the time an action is commenced, such corporation shall be deemed to reside in any district in that State within which its contacts would be sufficient to subject it to personal jurisdiction if that district were a separate State, and, if there is no such district, the corporation shall be deemed to reside in the district within which it has the most significant contacts.

§ 1404. Change of venue

(a) For the convenience of parties and witnesses, in the interest of justice, a district court may transfer any civil action to any other district or division where it might have been brought.

(b) Upon motion, consent or stipulation of all parties, any action, suit or proceeding of a civil nature or any motion or hearing thereof, may be transferred, in the discretion of the court, from the division in which pending to any other division in the same district. Transfer of proceedings in rem brought by or on behalf of the United States may be transferred under this section without the consent of the United States where all other parties request transfer.

(c) A district court may order any civil action to be tried at any place within the division in which it is pending.

(d) As used in this section, the term "district court" includes the District Court of Guam, the District Court for the Northern Mariana Islands, and the District Court of the Virgin Islands, and the term "district" includes the territorial jurisdiction of each such court.

§ 1406. Cure or waiver of defects

(a) The district court of a district in which is filed a case laying venue in the wrong division or district shall dismiss, or if it be in the interest of justice, transfer such case to any district or division in which it could have been brought.

(b) Nothing in this chapter shall impair the jurisdiction of a district court of any matter involving a party who does not interpose timely and sufficient objection to the venue.

(c) As used in this section, the term "district court" includes the District Court of Guam, the District Court for the Northern Mariana Islands, and the District Court of the Virgin Islands, and the term "district" includes the territorial jurisdiction of each such court.

§ 1407. Multidistrict litigation

(a) When civil actions involving one or more common questions of fact are pending in different districts, such actions may be transferred to any district for coordinated or consolidated pretrial proceedings. Such transfers shall be made by the judicial panel on multidistrict litigation authorized by this section upon its determination that transfers for such proceedings will be for the convenience of parties and witnesses and will promote the just and efficient conduct of such actions. Each action so transferred shall be remanded by the panel at or before the conclusion of such pretrial proceedings to the district from which it was transferred unless it shall have been previously terminated: Provided, however, That the panel may separate any claim, cross-claim, counter-claim, or third-party claim and remand any of such claims before the remainder of the action is remanded.

(b) Such coordinated or consolidated pretrial proceedings shall be conducted by a judge or judges to whom such actions are assigned by the judicial panel on multidistrict litigation. For this purpose, upon request of the panel, a circuit judge or a district judge may be designated and assigned temporarily for service in the transferee district by the Chief Justice of the United States or the chief judge of the circuit, as may be required, in accordance with the provisions of chapter 13 of this title. With the consent of the transferee district court, such actions may be assigned by the panel to a judge or judges of such district. The judge or judges to whom such actions are assigned, the members of the judicial panel on multidistrict litigation, and other circuit and district judges designated when needed by the panel may exercise the powers of a district judge in any district for the purpose of conducting pretrial depositions in such coordinated or consolidated pretrial proceedings.

(c) Proceedings for the transfer of an action under this section may be initiated by—

(i) the judicial panel on multidistrict litigation upon its own initiative, or

(ii) motion filed with the panel by a party in any action in which transfer for co-ordinated or consolidated pretrial proceedings under this section may be appropriate. A copy of such motion shall be filed in the district court in which the moving party's action is pending.

The panel shall give notice to the parties in all actions in which transfers for coordinated or consolidated pretrial proceedings are contemplated, and such notice shall specify the time and place of any hearing to determine whether such transfer shall be made. Orders of the panel to set a hearing and other orders of the panel issued prior to the order either directing or denying transfer shall be filed in the office of the clerk of the district court in which a transfer hearing is to be or has been held. The panel's order of transfer shall be based upon a record of such hearing at which material evidence may be offered by any party to an action pending in any district that would be affected by the proceedings under this section, and shall be supported by findings of fact and conclusions of law based upon such record. Orders of transfer and such other orders as the panel may make thereafter shall be filed in the office of the clerk of the district court of the transferee district and shall be effective when thus filed. The clerk of the transferee district court shall forthwith transmit a certified copy of the panel's order to transfer to the clerk of the district court from which the action is being transferred. An order denying transfer shall be filed in each district wherein there is a case pending in which the motion for transfer has been made.

(d) The judicial panel on multidistrict litigation shall consist of seven circuit and district judges designated from time to time by the Chief Justice of the United States, no two of whom shall be from the same circuit. The concurrence of four members shall be necessary to any action by the panel.

(e) No proceedings for review of any order of the panel may be permitted except by ex-traordinary writ pursuant to the provisions of title 28, section 1651, United States Code. Petitions for an extraordinary writ to review an order of the panel to set a transfer hearing and other orders of the panel issued prior to the order either directing or denying transfer shall be filed only in the court of appeals having jurisdiction over the district in which a hearing is to be or has been held. Petitions for an extraordinary writ to review an order to transfer or orders subsequent to transfer shall be filed only in the court of appeals having jurisdiction over the transferee district. There shall be no appeal or review of an order of the panel denying a motion to transfer for consolidated or coordinated proceedings.

(f) The panel may prescribe rules for the conduct of its business not inconsistent with Acts of Congress and the Federal Rules of Civil Procedure.

(g) Nothing in this section shall apply to any action in which the United States is a complainant arising under the antitrust laws. "Antitrust laws" as used herein include those acts referred to in the Act of October 15, 1914, as amended (38 Stat. 730; 15 U.S.C. 12), and also include the Act of June 19, 1936 (49 Stat. 1526; 15 U.S.C. 13, 13a, and 13b) and the Act of September 26, 1914, as added March 21, 1938 (52 Stat. 116, 117; 15 U.S.C. 56); but shall not include section 4A of the Act of October 15, 1914, as added July 7, 1955 (69 Stat. 282; 15 U.S.C. 15a).

(h) Notwithstanding the provisions of section 1404 or subsection (f) of this section, the judicial panel on multidistrict litigation may consolidate and transfer with or without the consent of the parties, for both pretrial purposes and for trial, any action brought under section 4C of the Clayton Act

§ 1441. Actions removable generally

(a) Except as otherwise expressly provided by Act of Congress, any civil action brought in a State court of which the district courts of the United States have original jurisdiction, may be removed by the defendant or the defendants, to the district court of the United States for the district and division embracing the place where such action is pending. For purposes of removal under this chapter, the citizenship of defendants sued under fictitious names shall be disregarded.

(b) Any civil action of which the district courts have original jurisdiction founded on a claim or right arising under the Constitution, treaties or laws of the United States shall be removable without regard to the citizenship or residence of the parties. Any other such action shall be removable only if none of the parties in interest properly joined and served as defendants is a citizen of the State in which such action is brought.

§ 1446. Procedure for removal

(a) A defendant or defendants desiring to remove any civil action or criminal prosecution from a State court shall file in the district court of the United States for the district and division within which such action is pending a notice of removal signed pursuant to Rule 11 of the Federal Rules of Civil Procedure and containing a short and plain statement of the grounds for removal, together with a copy of all process, pleadings, and orders served upon such defendant or defendants in such action.

(b) The notice of removal of a civil action or proceeding shall be filed within thirty days after the receipt by the defendant, through service or otherwise, of a copy of the initial pleading setting forth the claim for relief upon which such action or proceeding is based, or within thirty days after the service of summons upon the defendant if such initial pleading has then been filed in court and is not required to be served on the defendant, whichever period is shorter.

If the case stated by the initial pleading is not removable, a notice of removal may be filed within thirty days after receipt by the defendant, through service or otherwise, of a copy of an amended pleading, motion, order or other paper from which it may first be ascertained that the case is one which is or has become removable, except that a case may not be removed on the basis of jurisdiction conferred by section 1332 of this title more than 1 year after commencement of the action.

§ 1453. Removal of class actions

(a) **Definitions.** — In this section, the terms "class", "class action", "class certification order", and "class member" shall have the meanings given such terms under section 1332 (d)(1).

(b) **In General.** — A class action may be removed to a district court of the United States in accordance with section 1446 (except that the 1-year limitation under section 1446 (b) shall not apply), without regard to whether any defendant is a citizen of the State in which the action is brought, except that such action may be removed by any defendant without the consent of all defendants.

(c) **Review of Remand Orders.** —

　　　(1) **In general.** — Section 1447 shall apply to any removal of a case under this section, except that notwithstanding section 1447 (d), a court of appeals may accept an appeal from an order of a district court granting or denying a motion to remand a class action to the State court from which it was removed if application is made to the court of appeals not less than 7 days after entry of the order.

(2) **Time period for judgment.**—If the court of appeals accepts an appeal under paragraph (1), the court shall complete all action on such appeal, including rendering judgment, not later than 60 days after the date on which such appeal was filed, unless an extension is granted under paragraph (3).

(3) **Extension of time period.**—The court of appeals may grant an extension of the 60-day period described in paragraph (2) if—

(A) all parties to the proceeding agree to such extension, for any period of time; or

(B) such extension is for good cause shown and in the interests of justice, for a period not to exceed 10 days.

(4) **Denial of appeal.**—If a final judgment on the appeal under paragraph (1) is not issued before the end of the period described in paragraph (2), including any extension under paragraph (3), the appeal shall be denied.

(d) **Exception.**—This section shall not apply to any class action that solely involves—

(1) a claim concerning a covered security as defined under section 16(f)(3) of the Securities Act of 1933 (15 U.S.C. 78p (f)(3) [1]) and section 28(f)(5)(E) of the Securities Exchange Act of 1934 (15 U.S.C. 78bb (f)(5)(E));

(2) a claim that relates to the internal affairs or governance of a corporation or other form of business enterprise and arises under or by virtue of the laws of the State in which such corporation or business enterprise is incorporated or organized; or

(3) a claim that relates to the rights, duties (including fiduciary duties), and obligations relating to or created by or pursuant to any security (as defined under section 2(a)(1) of the Securities Act of 1933 (15 U.S.C. 77b (a)(1)) and the regulations issued thereunder).

§ 1711. Definitions

In this chapter:

(1) **Class.**—The term "class" means all of the class members in a class action.

(2) **Class action.**—The term "class action" means any civil action filed in a district court of the United States under rule 23 of the Federal Rules of Civil Procedure or any civil action that is removed to a district court of the United States that was originally filed under a State statute or rule of judicial procedure authorizing an action to be brought by 1 or more representatives as a class action.

(3) **Class counsel.**—The term "class counsel" means the persons who serve as the attorneys for the class members in a proposed or certified class action.

(4) **Class members.**—The term "class members" means the persons (named or unnamed) who fall within the definition of the proposed or certified class in a class action.

(5) **Plaintiff class action.**—The term "plaintiff class action" means a class action in which class members are plaintiffs.

(6) **Proposed settlement.**—The term "proposed settlement" means an agreement regarding a class action that is subject to court approval and that, if approved, would be binding on some or all class members.

§ 1712. Coupon settlements

(a) **Contingent Fees in Coupon Settlements.**—If a proposed settlement in a class action provides for a recovery of coupons to a class member, the portion of any attorney's fee award to class counsel that is attributable to the award of the coupons shall be based on the value to class members of the coupons that are redeemed.

(b) Other Attorney's Fee Awards in Coupon Settlements. —

    (1) In general. — If a proposed settlement in a class action provides for a recovery of coupons to class members, and a portion of the recovery of the coupons is not used to determine the attorney's fee to be paid to class counsel, any attorney's fee award shall be based upon the amount of time class counsel reasonably expended working on the action.

    (2) Court approval. — Any attorney's fee under this subsection shall be subject to approval by the court and shall include an appropriate attorney's fee, if any, for obtaining equitable relief, including an injunction, if applicable. Nothing in this subsection shall be construed to prohibit application of a lodestar with a multiplier method of determining attorney's fees.

(c) Attorney's Fee Awards Calculated on a Mixed Basis in Coupon Settlements. — If a proposed settlement in a class action provides for an award of coupons to class members and also provides for equitable relief, including injunctive relief—

    (1) that portion of the attorney's fee to be paid to class counsel that is based upon a portion of the recovery of the coupons shall be calculated in accordance with subsection (a); and

    (2) that portion of the attorney's fee to be paid to class counsel that is not based upon a portion of the recovery of the coupons shall be calculated in accordance with subsection (b).

(d) Settlement Valuation Expertise. — In a class action involving the awarding of coupons, the court may, in its discretion upon the motion of a party, receive expert testimony from a witness qualified to provide information on the actual value to the class members of the coupons that are redeemed.

(e) Judicial Scrutiny of Coupon Settlements. — In a proposed settlement under which class members would be awarded coupons, the court may approve the proposed settlement only after a hearing to determine whether, and making a written finding that, the settlement is fair, reasonable, and adequate for class members. The court, in its discretion, may also require that a proposed settlement agreement provide for the distribution of a portion of the value of unclaimed coupons to 1 or more charitable or governmental organizations, as agreed to by the parties. The distribution and redemption of any proceeds under this subsection shall not be used to calculate attorneys' fees under this section.

§ 1713. Protection against loss by class members

The court may approve a proposed settlement under which any class member is obligated to pay sums to class counsel that would result in a net loss to the class member only if the court makes a written finding that nonmonetary benefits to the class member substantially outweigh the monetary loss.

§ 1714. Protection against discrimination based on geographic location

The court may not approve a proposed settlement that provides for the payment of greater sums to some class members than to others solely on the basis that the class members to whom the greater sums are to be paid are located in closer geographic proximity to the court.

§ 2283. Stay of State court proceedings

A court of the United States may not grant an injunction to stay proceedings in a State court except as expressly authorized by Act of Congress, or where necessary in aid of its jurisdiction, or to protect or effectuate its judgments.

Appendix 2

Checking Yourself

Checking Yourself

Test your comprehensive knowledge of various materials covered in this book by taking the following practice test. It is divided into three sections—"short answer," "essay," and "multiple choice." The short essay section is designed to be taken in approximately 75 minutes (each question demonstrating the number of points available on that question). The short essay is worth 75 points in the aggregate. The essay is a one half hour question that is worth 30 points. The multiple choice section is designed to also be taken in 90 minutes. Each question on it would be worth 3 points for a total aggregate of 90 points available on the multiple choice section. The total exam time, if taken in one sitting, is 3 hours and 15 minutes.

Short Answer (1.25 Hours; 75 Points)

1. Would it make sense for federal courts to permit the application of offensive non-mutual collateral estoppel by a plaintiff who was previously part of a putative class action but chose to opt out after it was certified under Rule 23(b)(3)? Explain your answer. (**5 points**)

2. Identify the two most prevailing analytical models federal courts use to analyze an allegation of fraudulent joinder and, with respect to each, articulate the most significant criticism of that approach. (**8 points**)

3. In terms of litigant autonomy, briefly compare and contrast the practical differences among (a) being an unnamed class member of a Rule 23(b)(2) injunctive relief class action, (b) being a Rule 24 intervenor in a lawsuit, and (c) being a litigant whose case is consolidated with another case under Rule 42(a) for the limited purpose of having one common question decided. (**7 points**)

4. Which single rule, statute, or doctrine covered in this book in your opinion best illustrates the delicate balancing of all of the course themes (i.e., autonomy, efficiency, and fairness)? Please explain. (**7 points**)

5. Your client is about to present a pre-suit demand letter to an out-of-state defendant manufacturer of the product that hurt your client. Give your client some advice about the possible ramifications for giving such notice and explain briefly how to best position the client to maintain her own ultimate forum choice in the event of litigation. (**7 points**)

6. Give an example of a statute, rule (or interpretation of a rule), or doctrine we have covered that is available in federal court and that might provide an important

motivation for a defendant to attempt to remove a case from state to federal court. Explain why the statute/rule/doctrine might be important enough to a defendant to impact their decision whether to attempt removal. (**7 points**)

7. In terms of their specific language and concerns, Rules 19(a), 23(b)(1)(B), and 24(a) appear to have some overlap. What is this apparent overlap in coverage and, given the purposes behind each of these provisions and the consequences of their application in a case, should the similar language be construed consistently or differently? Please discuss. (**6 points**)

8. Given the way federal courts have applied the doctrine of *forum non conveniens*, what two circumstances present the most likely scenario for a court to grant a motion to dismiss based upon this doctrine? Why do these two circumstances point so strongly in favor of dismissal? (**6 points**)

9. In the context of a proposed nationwide Rule 23(b)(3) class action, what is the primary significance of the Supreme Court's choice-of-law holding in *Phillips Petroleum v. Shutts*? (**3 points**)

10. In light of what can be accomplished through Rule 42(a)–(b), what is the practical significance of Rule 20? (**4 points**)

11. A potential new client comes to your law office interested in suing Chevrolet. The client had been in a serious accident when the brakes on her 2010 Chevy Suburban truck failed and caused her to hit a tree in a one-vehicle accident. Unfortunately the accident occurred more than two years ago and the local, applicable statute of limitations is only two years accruing on the date of the accident. Before you send away the potential new client with bad news, is there anything else you should consider checking? Briefly explain. (**5 points**)

12. The relatively recent Supreme Court decision in *Wal-Mart v. Dukes* invalidated a nationwide Rule 23(b)(2) class action involving sex discrimination. There is a narrow interpretation of that decision that suggests that the 5th Circuit's prior decision in *In re Monumental* is still valid. There is also a broader interpretation of *Wal-Mart* that argues that it implicitly overrules the *In re Monumental* decision. Please explain the basis for each such interpretation. (**6 points**)

Essay (30 Minutes; 30 Points)

Paula (who lives in Utah) regularly buys software for her sole proprietorship business from David who lives and works from his home office in California. David's business is incorporated in Nevada with its principal place of business in California. Paula bundles this software with other computer supplies and resells them for profit at a mortar and bricks software store in her town. Paula and David have a contract governing their regular business transactions which states that California law will govern any disputes between them arising out of the sales of software (but there is no forum selection clause in the contract). Paula typically pays for the software upon receipt. On February 1, Paula received a new supply of software for which she made immediate payment. However, numerous customers later began complaining that it had many glitches. Paula complained to David but ordered a fresh supply of the software, having received assurances from David that the glitch was fixed. Paula did not make immediate payment for this second supply, which was delivered on March 15. Paula didn't pay because she wanted to be sure this shipment was better quality and to potentially offset her losses from the February 1 shipment. Because David had never refunded the price paid for the February 1 shipment, Paula fairly quickly filed suit against David's company for contract breach seeking recoupment of the full price and lost profits for damage to her business' reputation. This was filed in federal court in *fed ct. Utah* Utah under diversity jurisdiction. While that suit was pending, David became infuriated with Paula and filed his own suit against her for non-payment of the price for the March 15th shipment and for business disparagement. David filed his company's suit in federal *fed ct. Nevada* court in Nevada (where his attorney brother-in-law lives; the same one who incorporated his business for him). Paula now believes both supplies of software suffer from the same glitch and is wondering what to do about the second lawsuit.

You are Paula's counsel in Utah. What is her best option in this scenario? In response to this, how should the court(s) rule? Please explain

Multiple Choice (1.5 Hours; 90 Points)   *A*

1. In comparing pretrial consolidation under § 1407 and transfer for convenience under § 1404, which of the following statements is most accurate?

   a. Because of the deference usually given to the plaintiff's forum choice in § 1404, it may be easier for a transfer to occur under § 1407 where no such deference applies.

   b. Unlike a § 1404 motion, which can only impact the movement of a federal case to another federal court, with § 1407, the Judicial Panel on Multidistrict Litigation can move both state court and federal court cases to a single district for final adjudication.

   c. The grant of either motion can upset the plaintiff's original forum choice but this is less disruptive of the plaintiff's autonomy under § 1404 than it is under § 1407 with respect to the forum choice.

   d. The standard for whether to grant either motion is essentially the same.

   e. None of the above statements is accurate.

2. In comparing pretrial consolidation under § 1407 with Rule 42(a) consolidation, *B* which of the following statements is most accurate?

   a. Section 1407 consolidation is more limited because it can only be invoked when the multiple cases all arise out of the same transaction or occurrence.

   b. Rule 42 consolidation is more limited in its potential breadth of application because cases cannot be consolidated from different parts of the country under it.

   c. Rule 42 consolidation is more limited because it only permits consolidation of two cases arising out of the same transaction or occurrence.

   d. Section 1407 and Rule 42 consolidation are essentially equivalent in terms of the scope of their application.

   e. None of the above statements is accurate.

3. In terms of litigant autonomy, which of the following statements is most accurate? *E*

   a. Rule 42 consolidation may force two independent plaintiffs to try a portion of their lawsuits together or to have a common hearing on some common question of law raised in both cases.

   b. Rule 24 intervention maximizes an original plaintiff's autonomy, because it never permits a stranger to the suit to force its way into the plaintiff's existing lawsuit.

   c.   Rule 24 fundamentally limits the original plaintiff's autonomy by forcing the plaintiff to litigate with (or against) a party the plaintiff has not chosen to include in the case.

   d.   From the perspective of the unnamed 23(b)(2) class member, certification of the class typically precludes any meaningful input into the actual litigation of the class claims.

   e.   A, C, and D are all accurate statements.

4.   The Due Process Clause

   a.   Demands that a litigant who has failed to assert a compulsory counterclaim in one case be barred from attempting to assert the claim in a subsequent case.

   b.   Compels the same requirements already contained within Rules 23(a)(4) and 23(c)(2), at least in instances where the plaintiff class members do not otherwise have sufficient minimum contacts with the forum state in a damages class action.

   c.   Permits a defendant who has prevailed on an issue of fact in one case to apply that finding defensively against a new plaintiff making the same allegation against it in a subsequent case.

   d.   Is unwavering and inflexible in that it applies equally without regard to the circumstances of its application.

   e.   All of the above statements are accurate.

5.   With respect to federal courts' subject matter jurisdiction over a class action, which of the following statements is most accurate?

   a.   § 1367 overruled *Zahn* but not *Snyder*.

   b.   CAFA made it easier to find a class action "arises under" federal law.

   c.   CAFA permits aggregation of the class members' claims in order to meet the modified amount in controversy requirement.

   d.   CAFA's grant of minimal diversity jurisdiction is likely in violation of Article III of the US Constitution.

   e.   Both A and C are accurate statements.

6.   With respect to a court's exercise of personal jurisdiction over the claims of unnamed plaintiff class members, which of the following statements is most accurate?

   a.   They are deemed to have implicitly consented to the court's jurisdiction when each of the requirements of Rule 23 has been met.

   b.   A court may exercise personal jurisdiction over their claims only if each class member has sufficient minimum contacts with the forum state.

   c.   The Due Process Clause is unconcerned with a court's exercise of personal jurisdiction over plaintiff class members.

   d.   So long as there is adequate representation and the named class representative has minimum contacts with the forum state, there is no due process violation.

   e.   None of the above answers is accurate.

7.   With respect to the doctrine of *forum non conveniens*, which of the following statements is most accurate?

   a.   When the substantive law of the proposed alternate forum is less favorable to the plaintiff, the court should deny the motion to dismiss.

b. A court is very likely to grant the motion when a foreign plaintiff is suing on a claim that arose outside the forum.

c. The plaintiff's original forum choice should always receive great deference.

d. The doctrine is an effective tool when a case is pending in a federal district in one state to move the case to a federal district in another state.

e. Both A and C are accurate statements.

8. With respect to the Supreme Court's holding in *Phillips Petroleum v. Shutts*, which of the following statements is most accurate?

   a. It implicitly overrules the 5th Circuit's decision in *Castano v. American Tobacco*.

   b. It makes it extremely difficult to certify a 23(b)(2) hybrid class action involving both injunctive relief and monetary damages.

   c. It makes it virtually impossible to have a nationwide plaintiff class action unless every member of the class has sufficient minimum contacts with the forum state.

   d. It makes nationwide 23(b)(3) class actions arising under state law potentially more difficult to certify.

   e. All of the above answers are accurate.

9. With respect to the interplay between Rules 42 and 20, which of the following statements is most accurate?

   a. Given their mutually exclusive tests, there should be no parties joined together under Rule 20 that would be appropriately severed for trial under Rule 42.

   b. Given their mutually exclusive tests, there should be no scenario where parties incapable of being joined together under Rule 20 should have their cases consolidated for trial under Rule 42.

   c. When Rule 20's standards are satisfied, this creates a strong presumption that the parties joined by the plaintiff should have the claims by/against them tried together.

   d. Once a court determines whether a joinder of parties is appropriate under Rule 20, it should have no reason to consider any subsequent Rule 42 motion.

   e. Both A and B are accurate statements.

Facts for Questions 10 through 18

Intending to broadcast on Sunday evening the classic movie "Mary Poppins," Waco television station KWTU mistakenly broadcasts an excerpt from a pornographic movie — at least 15 minutes of it before a viewer finally called to complain. Mrs. Walton, a concerned local mother of three young boys, has come to your law office upset about the bizarre dreams her boys have experienced during the last four nights after seeing the fifteen minutes of the pornographic movie. She has heard about a tort claim for reckless infliction of emotional distress related to outrageous conduct and she is interested in having you pursue the case to seek compensation for the damage to her boys' fragile emotional condition, to make an example of this television station and to ensure that nothing like this ever happens again. She desires to sue for at least one million dollars in actual damages on behalf of her boys. KWTU is owned and operated by Good Shows, Inc. (GSI), a corporation incorporated in Delaware with its principal place of business in New York. You plan to file the case as a class action in Waco federal court.

10. If you file your tort claims for Mrs. Walton and her sons against GSI in Waco federal court relying upon the court's diversity jurisdiction, which of the following statements is most accurate?

    a. Any possible counterclaim (whether or not related) by GSI against your clients would be within the court's supplemental jurisdiction.

    b. If GSI filed a counterclaim against Mrs. Walton alleging that she failed to fulfill a pledge she made to the station the prior year during a fundraiser, GSI would have to demonstrate that this pledge was for more than $75,000 in order for the court to exercise jurisdiction over this breach of contract claim.

    c. No counterclaims by GSI would be within the court's supplemental jurisdiction.

    d. Any counterclaim raising a common question of law or fact with the original claim by Mrs. Walton would be within the court's supplemental jurisdiction.

    e. Both B and C are accurate.

11. If you desire to pursue a class action with Mrs. Walton as the class representative, which of the following statements is most accurate?

    a. Mrs. Walton cannot be an adequate representative unless she demonstrates that she has more knowledge of the underlying facts than any other possible member of the class.

    b. The best class definition would be "any person who saw the KWTU pornographic broadcast and was offended by it."

    c. The best class definition would be "any person who is entitled to recover emotional distress damages due to the defendant's intentional and wrongful misconduct."

    d. The best class definition would be "any child who saw the KWTU pornographic broadcast."

    e. The type of relief requested in a class action has no impact on how specific and objective the class definition must be.

12. If you desire to pursue a class action with Mrs. Walton as the class representative, which of the following statements is most accurate?

    a. If she were to sue on behalf of all residents of Waco seeking an injunction to prevent any future broadcasts of pornography, she would likely be adequate to represent the interests of the entire class.

    b. In any case in which the proposed class consists of at least forty persons, Rule 23(a)(1) is necessarily satisfied.

    c. To satisfy 23(a)(3), you would have to show that the amount of actual damages Mrs. Walton's children sustained was the same as all of the other class members.

    d. Both B and C are accurate.

    e. None of the above answers are accurate.

13. If you desire to seek certification of a class action for Mrs. Walton under Rule 23(b)(1), which of the following statements is most accurate?

    a. A class certified under Rule 23(b)(1)(A) must be given notice and a right to opt out of the litigation.

    b. If the court certifies the case, it will have to direct that individual mailed notice go to every member of the class who can be identified through reasonable effort.

c. You might be able to obtain certification by offering evidence that GSI is in bankruptcy with no liability insurance and that several thousand young children were likely viewers of the pornographic broadcast.   limited class

d. The Supreme Court has invalidated the "limited fund" theory of certification under Rule 23(b)(1)(B).

e. None of the above answers are correct.

14. If you desire to seek certification of a class action for Mrs. Walton under Rule 23(b)(2), which of the following statements is most accurate?

a. Permitting the combination of individualized and classwide relief in a (b)(2) class is generally consistent with the structure of Rule 23(b).

b. Classes properly certified under either 23(b)(1) or (b)(2) share the most traditional justification for class treatment—that individual adjudications would be unworkable or impossible.

c. Certification under 23(b)(2) is no longer possible after *Wal-Mart v. Dukes* in any scenario in which any type of damages are sought in addition to injunctive or declaratory relief.

d. If the court can characterize the actual damages for the emotional distress sought by the class as "equitable," seeking such damages would not predominate over any request for an injunction against continued broadcasting of pornography.

e. Both A and D are accurate statements.

15. If certification is sought for Mrs. Walton under Rule 23(b)(3), which of the following statements is most accurate?

a. The fact that all claims arose out of the same, singular event makes certification more likely. ✓

b. The fact that Texas law will likely apply to all of the class members' claims makes certification more likely. ✓

c. The fact that the amount of actual damages incurred by each class member is likely relatively small makes certification more likely. ✓

d. Both A and B are accurate statements.

e. A, B and C are all accurate statements.

16. If the district court certifies a class action under Rule 23(b)(3), which of the following statements is most accurate?

a. Because the district court has already found that Mrs. Walton is an adequate class representative, this finding will bind all class members precluding any subsequent collateral attack on a final judgment in this case.

b. The court will have to decertify the class action if class counsel promised Mrs. Walton that he might ask the court to consider an incentive award for her if they won the case, depending upon the results.

c. So long as the court has given appropriate notice of certification to the class members, it need not give additional notice of a subsequent proposed settlement of the case.

d. Though class members will have already been given one opportunity to opt out of the case, in the event of a settlement, the district court may consider conditioning approval of the settlement on affording the same class members a second opportunity to opt out.

e.   None of the above statements are accurate.

17. As you are preparing your pleadings to file the class action on behalf of Mrs. Walton and the class members, you become aware that a similar putative class action has already been filed in Waco federal court. Which of the following statements is the most accurate?

a.   If Mrs. Walton opts out of the other class action she will necessarily have to prove the liability facts against GSI in her own suit regardless of the outcome of the prior case.

b.   You should go ahead and file Mrs. Walton's putative class action and then move the Waco federal court to stay the other case.

c.   If the court in the prior case has already certified a class action, this order will preclude any possibility of Mrs. Walton intervening in that case pursuant to Rule 24.

d.   You should file a motion to dismiss the prior class action under Rule 19 due to the failure to name Mrs. Walton as a party plaintiff.

e.   None of the above statements are accurate.

18. If the court certifies Mrs. Walton's case as a Rule 23(b)(3) class action, which of the following statements is most accurate?

a.   A final judgment in the case will be binding upon all of the class members only if most of the class members have sufficient minimum contacts with the State of Texas to satisfy the Due Process Clause.

b.   The district court will only have to rule upon the issue of attorney's fees for class counsel if there is an applicable fee-shifting statute.

c.   A final judgment in the case will be binding upon all of the class members due to their implied consent so long as each of the requirements of Rules 23(a)(4) and 23(c) are satisfied.

d.   Class counsel can be awarded attorney's fees in the event of a favorable judgment only if the class members have expressly agreed to pay such sums.

e.   A *cy pres* form of relief for the class members would not be appropriate in any Rule 23(b)(3) class action.

19. With respect to a motion to stay a proceeding in deference to another related lawsuit, which of the following statements is most accurate?

a.   Whether the two cases are both pending in state courts, or both in federal courts, or in some combination of the two does not significantly change the analysis or likely outcome of the motion.

b.   When the two cases are in state and federal court, litigants can generally either obtain a stay from the state court or obtain an injunction from the federal court to enjoin prosecution of the duplicative state court proceeding, in order to prevent waste.

c.   When presented to most state courts, or when a federal court is asked to stay in deference to another federal court, the general rule is that the earlier-filed case has priority.

d.   Where there is evidence that a litigant has chosen one forum to obtain a strategic advantage, courts always refuse to give any priority to an earlier-filed case.

e.   All of the above statements are accurate.

20. In a class action on behalf of all current employees of Ford Motor Company, seeking solely to prevent the company from implementing a plan to close many of its manufacturing facilities and to lay off 50% of its employees, on the ground that the layoffs are designed to disproportionately impact older workers, which of the following is most accurate?

a.   Because the interests of the workers in stopping the threatened actions of Ford are so homogeneous, it will not be necessary to advise the employees of the court's decision to permit one of their co-workers to litigate the claims on their behalf.

b.   Certification under 23(b)(1) would be required because there is likely some limit to the company's assets, and if too many older workers sued, decided to seek money damages in individual lawsuits and won big awards, future claimants at some point might find the company judgment-proof.

c.   In all cases, the trial court will need to determine whether the employees practically impacted by any final judgment have expressly consented to being represented by the class representative.

d.   Including in the prayer for relief a request for attorney's fees for prosecuting the class action would undermine the court's ability to certify this case under Rule 23(b)(2).

e.   Both B and C are accurate statements.

21. In response to a threatened swine flu epidemic, Global Vaccines, Inc. obtains fast-track approval by the U.S. FDA for a vaccine, and this vaccine is administered to all public school children in the United States. The following year, many of these children start to lose their fingernails and experience dizziness. The Surgeon General of the United States empanels a committee to investigate these complaints. The day after the committee releases its report finding that the symptoms experienced by the children were linked to the vaccine and that their condition is permanent (an illness called "Dizzy Pig Syndrome"), thousands of individual tort lawsuits are filed across the United States against the company. Which of the following statements is most accurate?

a.   The first federal court to certify one of the cases as a nationwide class action can enjoin immediately the prosecution of any other competing putative class action, in state or federal court, in order to avoid wasting its time working on various pretrial matters.

b.   If the company wins the first case to go to trial (e.g., a finding of no product defect), it will likely be protected from having that same issue relitigated against it by other claimants using defensive collateral estoppel.

c.   If one of the cases is certified as a Rule 23(b)(3) class action, and you are a member of that class, you should consider opting out of the class and waiting to see if the class action succeeds in establishing the company's negligence, and using that finding in your own individual lawsuit as offensive non-mutual collateral estoppel against the company.

d.   In seeking nationwide class certification of one of the cases for monetary damages, it would be important to study the differences in the various states' tort laws and to come up with a plan for having possible sub-classes (based upon these substantive legal differences) and to formulate a trial plan.

e. Both C and D are accurate statements.

22. The Texas Legislature has just passed the State Abortion Law eliminating a woman's right to have an abortion and making any doctor or healthcare giver who performs or assists an abortion for any reason guilty of a felony criminal offense. The Texas Attorney General has issued an opinion letter stating her belief that the law is constitutional and that it should be enforced against any physician who disobeys its prohibitions. Dr. Jack Frost is an abortion provider and has filed a lawsuit against the Texas Attorney General in federal court seeking a declaration that this law is unconstitutional and violates a woman's federally protected right of privacy. Which of the following statements is most accurate?

   a. If a pro-life group, such as Texas Citizens United for Life, files a motion to intervene in the above lawsuit under Rule 24(a), the district court should deny it.

   b. If Texas Citizens United for Life files a motion under Rule 24(a) seeking to intervene, the district court should grant it in order to ensure that the group's important constitutional views are given a full airing.

   c. When a party seeking to intervene in a lawsuit shares the same ultimate objectives as an existing party to the suit, there arises an irrefutable presumption that the representation is inadequate.

   d. If the requirements of Rule 24(a) are otherwise satisfied, a motion to intervene made at any time prior to a final adjudication must be granted.

   e. Both B and D are accurate statements.

23. Shortly after the passage of the Texas Abortion Law (mentioned in the above question), Dr. Jekyll performs an abortion on Emma in violation of the statute. Dr. Jekyll was assisted during the abortion by Nurse Poole. Several weeks later, Emma (an Oklahoma citizen) regrets her decision and sues Dr. Jekyll (a Texas citizen) in federal district court in Waco (where the abortion was performed) for $1 million dollars for battery—arguing that she could not effectively consent to his procedure since it involved felony misconduct. Dr. Jekyll maintains that the statute is unconstitutional and that he had Emma's express consent to perform the procedure. Emma does not sue Nurse Poole. Which of the following statements is most accurate?

   a. It would have been procedurally improper for Emma to name Nurse Poole as a co-defendant in her Original Complaint.

   b. Upon a motion by Dr. Jekyll, or at its own initiative, the trial court should dismiss the lawsuit for failure to join Nurse Poole unless Emma amends her pleading to name Poole as a co-defendant with Dr. Jekyll.

   c. If Emma has failed to pay her $1,500 bill to Dr. Jekyll for the abortion, the federal district court cannot exercise supplemental jurisdiction over a counterclaim by Dr. Jekyll for this nonpayment of debt, because it would only be a permissive counterclaim as it raises no common questions of law/fact with the original claim.

   d. The trial court must grant a motion to intervene by a non-profit pro-choice group, Texans United for Choice, seeking to advocate on behalf of Dr. Jekyll against the statute.

    e.   Each of the above statements is incorrect.

24. An unnamed member of a certified class action

    a.   Never has a right to intervene in the case because, by definition, there is already an adequate representative for them in the case.

    b.   If dissatisfied with the judgment in that class action, can file their own lawsuit and avoid res judicata if they can demonstrate a lack of adequate representation.

    c.   Is precluded from engaging in any collateral attack on the class action judgment because that might result in an inefficient relitigation of certain issues.

    d.   Is generally held liable for any taxable court costs in the event the class loses the case.

    e.   May not object to either certification or settlement of the case but is simply bound by the final judgment.

25. The Texas Lottery Commission has announced that there is only one winning ticket in its recent $100 million Super Lotto Jackpot. The Lottery Commission has already disbursed the other revenues from the lottery to various school districts (as required by state law), withholding only the $100 million jackpot promised to the winner. However, Peter, Paul and Mary have each separately announced that they hold the true one winning lottery ticket. In Paul's lawsuit against the Texas Lottery Commission, filed in federal district court in Austin pursuant to the court's diversity jurisdiction, to recover the $100 million cash award

    a.   With Paul's permission, Peter and Mary could also join as co-plaintiffs.

    b.   The defendant Texas Lottery Commission could appropriately ask the court to order that Peter and Mary be joined as additional parties even over the possible objection of Paul.

    c.   Mary and Peter could each insist, together or separately, that they be made additional parties to the lawsuit even without Paul's permission.

    d.   If Peter, Paul and Mary each filed their own lawsuits against the Texas Lottery Commission in federal court in Austin, the court could order a common trial to determine which one held the true winning ticket.

    e.   All of the above statements are accurate.

26. Using the same lottery scenario from the previous question, which of the following statements is most accurate?

    a.   In a class action against the Texas Lottery Commission, Peter would be an adequate class representative suing on behalf of all others similarly situated.

    b.   If Peter, Paul and Mary each filed lawsuits against the Texas Lottery Commission in different federal district courts, it would be appropriate for any of the courts to consider granting a motion to transfer under § 1404 to one of the other districts where the same claims were already pending.

    c.   Class certification would be granted in a lawsuit against the lottery, because all Rule 23(a) prerequisites would be satisfied and because the $100 million jackpot is a true limited fund subject to more than one — in this instance three — competing claims.

    d.   Class certification would be inappropriate in a case filed by Peter against the Texas Lottery Commission only because there are no common questions of law or fact with the claims of Paul and Mary (since they each rely upon a different alleged winning ticket).

e. Both B and C are accurate statements.

27. An Oceanic Airlines jet with 100 passengers takes off from Sydney, Australia headed toward Los Angeles, California. Midway across the Pacific Ocean, the jet crashes and many of the passengers die. Twenty survivors are eventually rescued and file separate lawsuits against Oceanic Airlines (a British company) in various state and federal courts in the United States seeking compensation for their injuries. Which of the following statements is most accurate?

a. The Multi-District Litigation Panel can order the consolidation of all these related cases because there are common questions of fact in each of the cases and it would be in the interests of justice to have these cases coordinated.

b. If all of the cases were in various federal courts, either through original federal filings or removals from state to federal court, it would be appropriate to consolidate the cases under Rule 42(a) for a common trial.

c. Because of the risk of inconsistent adjudications of liability against Oceanic Airlines, certification of one of the lawsuits in federal court as a class action under Rule 23(b)(1) would be appropriate.

d. Oceanic Airlines' motion to dismiss one of the cases filed in Miami, FL state court for *forum non conveniens* in deference to an Australian court would fail if Australian law does not permit punitive damages to be assessed.

e. None of the above statements are accurate.

28. Former University President Violet Lilly, in the waning days of her failed administration, decided that she would like to have a glorious aerial photograph made of her perched atop the pinnacle of Old Main Hall. She hired a local aviator to fly the plane and to take the photo. On a bright summer morning, President Lilly carefully climbed on the outside of Old Main to the very top, strapped herself to the tower, and began waving and smiling to the plane as it approached. Concerned that the photo might not capture an adequate image of her face — as it was partially obscured by the brim of her big white sombrero — she kept waving to the pilot to get closer. To the horror of hundreds of University's students watching this debacle, the pilot got too close on one pass, clipped Old Main with a wing of the plane, and crashed into a nearby Live Oak tree. President Lilly was killed in the process. A local enterprising lawyer is contacted by one of the students who was on the ground nearby during the crash and they have discussed filing a class action against Lilly's estate on behalf of all students who witnessed the horror and who were in fear. Which of the following statements is most accurate?

a. In a class action for damages, the court must provide individual notice of certification unless reasonable efforts fail to disclose the identity and location of the class members.

b. A *cy pres* form of recovery would certainly be permitted here because of the need to provide compensation, deter wrongdoing and disgorge profits.

c. During the pendency of the putative class action, if the defendant chooses to seek summary judgment on the merits in its favor (i.e., arguing that no bystander recovery is recognized under applicable law here) prior to the court's ruling on class certification and the trial court grants the motion and immediately enters final judgment, this order will preclude any putative class member from filing his/her own lawsuit at a later date.

    d.   Courts uniformly take the position that fluid recovery mechanisms violate the defendant's right to a trial by jury.

    e.   A, B and D are accurate statements.

29. With respect to a comparison of their treatment of the "common question of law or fact" requirement in Rules 20 and 23 in *Mosley v. General Motors* and in *Wal-Mart v. Dukes*, which of the following statements is most accurate?

    a.   Courts never make such comparisons because the "common question" component of the two rules serves no parallel function.

    b.   A possible distinction exists between them because in *Mosley*, unlike *Dukes*, the plaintiff alleged one overarching policy of discrimination by the company.

    c.   A possible distinction exists between them because the ramifications for finding the "common question" test satisfied in *Dukes* were potentially far more significant than in the context of *Mosley*.

    d.   *Mosley*'s broad application of this standard overrules the holding in *Dukes*.

    e.   Both B and C are accurate statements.

30. Tommy Texan (Texas citizen) has a bad reaction to a drug manufactured by Yankee Corporation (NY corporation). Tommy sues Yankee in Texas state court alleging a state law tort claim. Tommy adds to this suit a claim against Dixie Doc (another Texas citizen) for medical malpractice for prescribing the defective medicine. Yankee files a notice of removal on diversity grounds. With of the following statements is most accurate?

    a.   The Supreme Court has determined that fraudulent joinder requires proof of bad faith motives on the part of the plaintiff.

    b.   To demonstrate that fraudulent joinder is inapplicable, Tommy will bear the burden of proving the elements of his malpractice claim in order to have a motion to remand granted.

    c.   Yankee will bear the burden of showing that no possible claim exists by Tommy against Dixie Doc.

    d.   All circuit courts have held that fraudulent joinder is analyzed solely by reference to the allegations of the plaintiff's pleadings.

    e.   All of the above statements are accurate.

Index

Res J. - P18 → Only brought by Δ?] trying to bar a case or

Collateral Estop - P18 & P26 | Virtual Rep - P28] issue

Rule 13 - Compulsory Counter Claim - P37

· elements - P38 · Logical relationship test - P43

Rule 20 - Permissive Joinder - P49

Rule 42 - Consolidation/Severance - PG 56 & 30

Product Liability Joinder - Same Core Allegation P59

Rule 19 - Compulsory Joinder - P 71 & 72 | Requires 2 separate inquiries. 2 categories

Rule 14 - Impleader - Pg 79 & 80 - exception | of person should be joined.

Rule 24 - Intervention - P84 & 86, work(s) on Δ + Π

Bringing
in
a suit

First to File should have priority

" absent the showing of balance of convience
in favor of the second suit" P100

Exceptions - P99

· Forum Shopping - Filing 2 cases and picking the favorable JDX

· Patent - Case w/ direct infringer takes precedent over indirect infringer

· Second suit just makes WAY more sense.

· Anticipatory exception - P 114 / factors P115

· Second filed suit can provide Π complete relief

Filing Race + Avoidne
of first to file
Rule

· Concurrent Fed + State case

· Fed court decline JDX w/ Doctrine of Abstention / Factors P117

· Does Fed court want to hear the case? weigh factors of

- Colorado River Doctrine P120

    · Should Fed court stay a declaratory judgment pending parallel
    state proceedings?

    - Use Brillhart: Court's discretion

- Piecemeal litigation: Circumstances in which more than one court
  is adjudicating the same issue w possibility of conflicting judgments

- Fed court staying an action of declaratory judgment to wait
  pending state court action.

· Transfer of venue: 1404A - P131

- weigh public v Private interest factors - P135

· Forum non convience - P142

- Must be an alternate forum

- Balance Private + Public

Party's ability to relate control or just win race to more convient forum

MDL - P148

Pro's → Efficient

Cos - Black hole, losing control, Delay

· Upon pretrial activities judge MUST remand

· MDL judge abilities - P161 & 163 [*3]

· No opt out

Discovery + promoting efficiency if no class

Anti-injunction Act - P163

- bars a federal court from enjoining
a state claim

Exceptions - P163

- Necessary in aid exception - P174 - where a state action
interferes w Federal court's own path to judgment
- Prompting State - not necessary, but helpful - P177

Fradulent Joinder P179

Fed Court Enjoining
State Claim

- 1206 - P182

Exception to
Diversity

- District court can't look on merits of the case, only the state can
make the decision on the merits P184

- District court can't pierce proceedings to investigate fradulent joinder.

- SmJ Fradulent Joinder - P186

- Reasonable basis test - Can pierce proceedings

- Differences between the two options - P187

Class action - 23a   Fail safe class - class cannot be defined until the case
is resolved on its merits.
Negative value - P263 - class members' claims would be uneconomical to litigate
individually.
Class action definition - P206

1. Numerosity - P212 · impracticable standard
- geographic location of π's to see if joinder is impractical
2. Commonality - P214 & 217
"Questions of law and fact common to the class"
3. Typicality - P225
- Probe behind the pleadings to see if met
4. Adequacy - P227 & 237 - Rep have no antagonistic interest
- Counsel has the requisite expertise to prosecute the action

PJDX class action- 322 & 323

· 23bA: "inconsistent or varying adjudication class" P243
- Requires injunction or declatory relief
- No monetary damages
- No opt out: Mandatory
- Often used when separate suits in different courts could result
  in inconsistent judgments

· 23bB: "limited fund" P245, 261
- Limited fund rationale
- Requires evidence
- Must be able to compute claims- P265
- No opt out: Mandatory

· 23b2
- Civil Rights
- Injunctive or declatory relief, but must apply to each member-P2
- Can have monetary damages, but if so, must provide opt-out notice
- Predominate standard - P265
Does not apply when the appropriate final relief relates
exclusively or predominately to money damages